Private Helicopter Pilot Studies

EASA Edition

Phil Croucher

"Never allow your ego, self-confidence, love of flying, pressure from a customer, boss or co-pilot, or economic need to interfere with your good judgement during any stage of a flight. There is no amount of pride, no thrill, pleasure, schedule or job that is worth your licence or your life and the lives of your passengers. Complacency kills, and so does being a cowboy." John Bulmer

ISBN 978-0-9780269-4-3

TABLE OF CONTENTS

CAPT

European Union
United Kingdom Civil Aviation Authority

APPROVED TRAINING ORGANISATION CERTIFICATE

GBR.ATO.0129

Pursuant to Commission Regulation (EU) No 1178/2011 and subject to the conditions specified below, the UK Civil Aviation Authority hereby certifies

CALEDONIAN ADVANCED PILOT TRAINING LIMITED

Wycombe Air Centre Building
Wycombe Air Park
SL7 3DP

C/O Helicentre Aviation
Leicester Airport
Gartree Road
Leicester
LE2 2FG

as an Approved Training Organisation with the privilege to provide Part-FCL training courses, including the use of FSTDs, as listed in the attached course approval.

CONDITIONS:

1. This certificate is limited to the privileges and the scope of providing the training courses, including the use of FSTDs, as listed in the attached training course approval.

2. This certificate is valid whilst the approved organisation remains in compliance with Part-ORA, Part-FCL and other applicable regulations.

3. Subject to compliance with the foregoing conditions, this certificate shall remain valid unless the certificate has been surrendered, superseded, limited, suspended or revoked.

Date of issue: 15 February 2013

Signed

For the UK Civil Aviation Authority

EASA FORM 143 Issue 1 – page 1/2

INTRODUCTION

0

W elcome to the world of flying! Many of you will be studying this material because you eventually want to fly for a living - others will only be interested in a rewarding hobby. Either way, you must start somewhere, and this is it!

This is the only text for private pilots based on an approved JAA/EASA professional training course - full details if you want to investigate flying for a living can be found at **www.captonline.com**.

Note: The Private Pilot's Licence deserves the most attention, especially for people intending to further their careers as commercial pilots - if you are going to occupy some of the airspace taken up by professionals, it's only fair that you should have a fair amount of their knowledge. This book has been specially written for such people, and for those who want to acquire more knowledge than the basics. It covers the whole 100 hour syllabus required by EASA, and more!

As with anything new, a lot is very strange at first, but you will soon get used to the odd noises and begin to settle down. Once that happens, you will find that flying demands a good deal of concentration - it is not something to be approached lightly, although there's no reason why it can't be fun. There are risks involved with almost everything we do, it's part of the price of living on a planet but, with aviation, you can't fix things once you are up in the air, which is why there is a lot of preparation before you get airborne, to ensure that as little as possible goes wrong or, if it does, you are better able to cope with it. It's safe to say that at least as much work on the ground should go into every flight hour.

The Private Pilot's Licence has pretty much the same syllabus throughout the world, so much so that, between countries, they are (mostly) immediately exchangeable after taking a local aviation law exam. This is because most countries adopt the standards from the *International Civil Aviation Organisation* (ICAO), although the EASA version can get a bit more technical.

The subject matter is not demanding, but there is a lot of it, and it all needs to be learnt at the same time, as opposed to doing each subject by itself. It can also require a lot of memory work, especially law, but even that has been simplified in this book as much as possible, and translated into Plain English.

Note: Although most of what you need is included, a basic knowledge of maths and physics is assumed.

To save space, information such as map symbols that are readily found in common (and free!) CAA publications has been left out, for more useful stuff. Words in italics are *keywords*, to be remembered for exams.

Look for a document called CAP 673 which is downloadable from the CAA website and contains details of marshalling signals, lighting and airfield signs.

There is a companion book to this one called PPL Q & A. It ontains hundreds of PPL-type questions, available from **www.electrocution.com/aviation**.

DIFFERENCES

Coming To Europe

First of all, although there are areas where you don't need to speak to anyone on the radio, they are very few and far between, and at low level, as almost all airspace is controlled in some way or another. The transition level is also very low, at 3,000 feet (the transition level can loosely be called the point at which professional pilots start flying on instruments, or without looking through the window, so there are strict rules to follow).

Next, another barometer setting is typically used for takeoffs, landings and operations within the circuit, called QFE, which is simply one that gives you a reading of zero feet when on the ground. It isn't used in North America because many aerodromes are at high elevations and the readings would be off the scale. The setting you are used to, the nearest aerodrome setting against mean sea level, is QNH (QFE is *always* used in the circuit).

And what about all those Q codes? They are a hangover from the old wireless telegraphy days, and are not officially supposed to be used, although everyone does (the idea was to use short codes instead of commonly used expressions to reduce transmission times. QSY, for example, is "changing frequency").

You should also join the circuit overhead and there is no UNICOM.

UNITED KINGDOM CIVIL AVIATION AUTHORITY

CERTIFICATE OF REGISTRATION

This certificate is issued to:

CALEDONIAN ADVANCED PILOT TRAINING LIMITED

Number: OCP2310

Registered with the UK CAA to conduct the course(s) listed below in accordance with JAR-FCL and the Air Navigation Order 2009:

Private Pilot Licence (Aeroplane) Theoretical Knowledge
Private Pilot Licence (Helicopter) Theoretical Knowledge

Validity

This certificate remains valid until

- the EASA Rules for the conduct of PPL training take effect for existing training providers

or

- the Authority is informed by the operator that PPL training is to cease or the Authority establishes that training is not being carried out safely and/or in compliance with JAR-FCL. In both of these situations the registration of the facility will be revoked.

Conditions

Any changes to the information entered on the registration form shall be communicated to the Authority.

Date of issue: 21 August 2012

S E James
For the Civil Aviation Authority

If this page is a photocopy, it is not authorised!

Everyone is responsible for flight safety!

HUMAN PERFORMANCE & LIMITATIONS

1

Aircraft are getting more reliable so accidents should happen less often. Unfortunately, this is not the case, so we need to look somewhere else for the causes. Believe it or not, accidents are very carefully planned - it's just that the results are very different from those expected, based on the idea that the folks who had them were doing things that made sense to them at the time (*Dekker*, 2006).

The essential problem is that our bodies are not constructed to live under the conditions imposed by aviation. In the air, physical and psychological stresses occur on top of the normal stuff of everyday life that should be taken note of in order to fly properly. Minor illnesses, stress, fatigue, alcohol and even caffeine can all affect your performance as a pilot, and there are even regulations to cover their use, all discussed later in this section. To this end, you must be medically fit and be certified as such by a physician at regular intervals.

You may not act as flight crew if you know or suspect that your physical or mental condition renders you unfit to do so. In other words, you may not exercise licence privileges once you are aware of a decrease in your medical fitness that makes you unable to exercise them safely. **Medicals are only valid if you meet the initial issuing requirements.** A Board of Inquiry or insurance company may interpret the words "medically fit" a little differently than you think if you fly with a cold or under the influence of alcohol or drugs. In any case, you should talk to a medical examiner as soon as possible in case of:

- admission to a hospital or clinic for over 12 hours
- surgery or other invasive procedures
- regular use of medication
- regular use of correcting lenses

In addition, you should inform the authorities in writing of significant personal injuries involving your capacity to act as a member of a flight crew, or illness that lasts for more than 21 days, or pregnancy.

"The least experienced press on, while the more experienced turn back to join the most experienced who never left the ground in the first place."

ACCIDENTS

A *reportable* accident occurs when:

- anyone is killed or injured from contact with the aircraft (or any bits falling off), including jet blast or rotor downwash
- the aircraft sustains damage or structural failure
- The aircraft is missing or inaccessible

between the time any person boards it *with the intention of flight*, and all persons have disembarked. This does not include injuries from natural causes, which are self-inflicted or inflicted by other people, or any to stowaways hiding in places not normally accessible to passengers and crew. *Significant* or *Substantial Damage* in this context essentially means anything that may involve an insurance claim, but officially is damage or failure affecting structure or performance, normally needing major repairs.

An **incident** is any happening other than an accident which hazards or, if not corrected, would hazard any aircraft, its occupants or anyone else, not resulting in substantial damage to the aircraft or third parties, crew or passengers. In other words, a dangerous event, but without any serious consequences.

An accident is the end product of a chain of events, so, in theory, if you can recognise the sequence it should be possible to nip any problems in the bud. A common saying is that "the well oiled nut behind the wheel is the most dangerous part of any car". Not necessarily true for aviation, perhaps, but, in looking for causes other than the hardware when it comes to accidents, it's hard not to focus on the pilot (or other people - e.g. the human factor) as the weak link in the chain - around 75% of accidents can be attributed to this, although it's also true to say that the *situations* some aircraft (and people) are put into make them liable to misfortune, particularly with helicopters - if you continually land on slippery logs, something untoward is bound to happen sometime!

The current teaching is that the human factor is the weak link at the root of most accidents (remove the bad apple and the problem goes away), but it isn't the whole story.

If this page is a photocopy, it is not authorised!

Circumstances can also be involved, and even experienced pilots can get caught out. Take, for example, one who is tasked to do two flights in an afternoon, the first one with a light load of two people and the second with four. It would seem logical to fill the helicopter up with enough fuel to cover both flights, since the loads allow it and the schedule is tight between the flights, so you can save some time by not refuelling. But what happens if the first passengers are late, or don't even turn up at all? You are then faced with doing the second trip with more fuel than you would normally plan for to allow for safety margins, even though you might be within the machine's weight limits. Of course, you could defuel, but that can be a major inconvenience when you are the only one there and the passengers are waiting in the usual car-park-as-a-passenger-lounge! Thus, it is not necessarily a person's character, but their circumstances that can be at the root of an accident, as has been proven by many psychological studies involving prison guards. The above pilot would not be doing anything "wrong" or illegal by taking off heavier than would be prudent - it just wouldn't be sensible.

And if you are thinking that safety might be expensive, review the consequences of an accident:

- Fatalities and/or injuries

- You need another aircraft.......

- ....while still making payments on the one you just crashed

- The insurance is increased

- You end up with unwanted attention from the media and the authorities

THE HUMAN FACTOR

The emphasis on the human element in relation to accidents was recognised in '79 and '80, where over 500 incidents relating to shipping were analysed, and 55% were found to be related to human factors. Did you think that was *1979* & 80? It was actually in *1879* and 80! In fact, as well as the iceberg, the *Titanic* had to dodge the *Deutschland*, which was floating around the shipping lanes, having run out of coal (it also nearly collided with the *New York* on its way out of Southampton). Since then, through the *1980*s and 90s, aviation accidents in the USA were analysed in depth, and it was found that *crew interaction* was a major factor in them since, nearly 75% of the time, it was the first time they had flown together, and nearly half were on the first leg, in situations where there was pressure from the schedule (over 50%) and late on in the duty cycle, so fatigue was significant (doesn't everything happen late on Friday afternoon?)

The Captain was also flying 80% of the time. The problem is, that it's not much different now - 70% of aircraft accidents in the USA in 2000 were pilot-related, based on mistakes that could easily be avoided with a little forethought, and it was more or less the same figure way back in 1940. Now, the figure worldwide is around 80%. The accident rate is highest in the takeoff and landing phases, but as a percentage of flight time, it is highest in the cruise, usually because the machine hits something in the way - one of the highest causes of accidents is *Controlled Flight Into Terrain*, or CFIT, where a perfectly serviceable aircraft under the positive control of the crew hits an obstacle.

For helicopters, a study of 147 accidents in the USA found that human error was the primary cause in 68% (many of those based on human error involved inadequate pre-flight planning and decision making, or inadequate evaluation of the weather).

If air traffic continues to grow at the present rate, we will be losing 1 airliner per week by 2010, and even more GA aircraft - the Australian authorities are looking at 1 helicopter per week, which is why Human Factors training is now an ICAO requirement, with the syllabus drawn from many sources, including Psychology, Engineering, Physiology, Medicine, Sociology, Biology and others.

Modern life is stressful enough - we are all hostages to other peoples' expectations and attitudes, and it often seems that, within an hour of waking up, we have an attitude all of our own, by the time the toast has been dropped and everyone's had their bite. It is very important not to let what happens outside it into the cockpit - one function that checklists perform is to help keep your mind on the job and exclude outside influences.

It has also (finally) been realised that traditional methods of flight instruction have been missing something - the assumption has always been that, just because you have a licence, you know what you are doing, or that good, technically qualified pilots (or doctors, for example) make good decisions as a matter of course (I know many stupid doctors!) Naturally, everybody on the shop floor has always known that this is not necessarily so, and a lot of experienced pilots make mistakes, so experience is not the answer, either. In fact, experience can be a harsh teacher, assuming you heed its lessons anyway, so ways have had to be found to use training instead, hence the ICAO requirements for Human Performance training, which is meant to *increase the safety and efficiency of flight operations* and *maintain the well-being of the people involved*. This means that manipulating the flying controls is less than half of the training required to be a competent pilot.

Currently, aeronautical decision making is seen as a function that comes under standard psychological theory and practice (*Brecke*, 1982; *Stokes and Kite*, 1994). In fact,

CAPT

HUMAN PERFORMANCE & LIMITATIONS
The Human Factor

*The terms CRM, PDM, ADM and Human Factors are used interchangeably in this section

research into the human factors related to aircraft accidents and incidents has highlighted decision making as a crucial element (*Jensen*, 1982; *O'Hare, Wiggins, Batt, and Morrison*, 1994). The irony is that people who are aware that such training is a Good Thing do not need the courses - the sort that should most benefit are like the Enstrom owner who mentioned to his shocked engineer that he didn't like the look of two bolts in the tail rotor assembly, so he turned them round and shortened one of them, since it was longer than the other. After patiently explaining during wall-to-wall counselling that the reason why one bolt was longer was for balance purposes, and that they were inserted a particular way round for a reason, the engineer suggested the owner-pilot took his custom elsewhere.

As with most other things, aviation is more of a mental process than a physical one. For example, it takes much longer to become a captain than it does to become a pilot, and CRM/PDM/Human Factors* training aims to shorten the gap by substituting training for experience. Almost the first thing you have to take on board is that feedback is missing if you are flying by yourself, which is useful for making decisions.

As single crew, of course, there is only you in your cockpit, but you still have to talk to others. In this context, the word "crew" includes anybody else who can help you deliver the end product, which is:

. . Safe Arrival!

The only real replacement for this is reviewing your flights and discussing them with others, which is more difficult for helicopter pilots, because of the lack of meeting places (but licensed premises are good). Single pilot operations need more planning and rehearsal.

The aim of this sort of training is to increase flight safety by showing you how to make the best use of any resources available to you, which include your own body (physical and psychological factors), information, equipment and other people (including passengers and ATC), whether in flight or on the ground, even engine handling or using the humble map. Using a GPS for navigation, and ignoring the other navigation aids or the map, is bad CRM.

Previously, you might have been introduced to the concept of *Airmanship*, which involved many things, such as looking out for fellow pilots, doing a professional job, not flying directly over aircraft, always doing pre-flight inspections, doing a clearing turn before taking off, etc. In other words, actions relating to being the "gentleman aviator", or exhibiting professional behaviour as an airman, which involves discipline, skill, knowledge (of yourself and the aircraft), risk management, etc., but the

new term is *Captaincy*, as flying is a lot more complex now than when the original term was more appropriate.

Note: *Airmanship* is still a valid concept, and is to be treated with as much respect as the regulations!

You should be able to make better decisions after being introduced to the concepts, principles and practices of CRM, or Decision Making, with the intention of reducing the accident rate even further. That is to say, we know all about the hardware, now it's time to take a look at ourselves. An *accident-prone person*, officially, is *somebody to whom things happen at a higher rate than could be statistically expected by chance alone*. Taking calculated risks is completely different from taking chances. Know your capabilities, and your limits. Things that can help, particularly with single-pilot operations, are:

- *Knowledge* - know the flight manual, and its limitations*

- *Preparation* - do as much as you can before the flight - Is that runway *really* large enough to stop in if one engine fails? Has all the servicing been done? Is the paperwork correct? Visualise the route from the map - and fold it as best you can for the route. Got enough batteries for the GPS? Do you know the MSA if you get caught in cloud? And who to call?

It has been noticed that pilots who receive decision-making training outperform others in flight tests and make 10-15% fewer bad decisions, and the results improve with the comprehensiveness of the training. Remember that your training cannot cater for everything. Instead, as with licences everywhere, you are given enough training to be able to make decisions for yourself, hence the importance of decision making training.

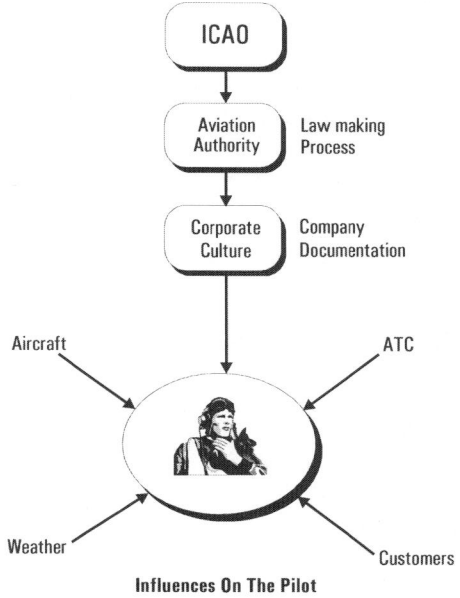

Influences On The Pilot

"I used to be
indecisive, but now
I'm not so sure!"

Single Pilot Operations

Single pilot operations demand much higher standards, because they typically take place in unstabilised machines with the least accurate instruments in the worst weather. To achieve the higher standards of competency and discipline that single pilot operations demand, you must:

- Maintain a positive attitude

- Maintain medical fitness

- Be less willing to accept unserviceabilities

- Spend more time on planning & preparation, so you have a yardstick by which your flight can be compared when you do an after flight review - be prepared for eventualities before they happen!

- Maintain situational awareness

- Resist pressure from other people

- Be more willing to ask for help, especially with clearances or directions to a reporting point

- Make more use of checklists and SOPs. If you have to design them as well, make them easier to read

- Workload Management, especially at critical moments. Make sure you have the right equipment in the first place, you know its capabilities, and that you use it properly:

  - Manage time - use relatively slack periods in the cruise to prepare for busy ones during the arrival. Prioritise!

  - Manage the cockpit - get the maps in the right order! Make sure they are folded properly! Ensure you have a map holder, writing instrument, stopwatch, etc. Don't throw the departure plates away too soon, in case you have to return to the field after takeoff

  - Use the autopilot if you have one

  - Make more effective use of the GPS. Instead of just putting in waypoints, and therefore pushing more buttons in flight, put them all into a route so that the screen changes automatically as you go around

  - Tune and use normal navaids as well as GPS

  - Before you operate a switch or press a button, make sure it is the right one

  - Cross check the readings for logic!

Be critical of your performance so you can improve the next flight

"Most people are woefully inadequate
processors of information, who stumble along
ill-chosen paths to reach bad conclusions"

DECISIONS, DECISIONS
• •

The best way out of trouble is not to get into it. You, the pilot, are the decision-maker - in fact, under the Chicago Convention, your word is law when in flight, but the other side of the coin is that you are liable for what goes on.

Aviation is noticeable for its almost constant decision-making. As you fly along, particularly in a helicopter, you're probably updating your next engine-off landing point every five seconds or so. Or maybe you're keeping an eye on your fuel and continually calculating your endurance. It all adds to the many tasks you're meant to keep up to date with, because the situation is always changing. In fact, a decision *not* to make a decision (or await developments) is also a decision, always being aware that we don't want indecision. To drive a car 1 mile, you must process 12,000 pieces of information - that's 200 per second at 60 mph! It has to be worse with flying, and possibly over our limits - our capability of processing information is actually quite marginal, and is vulnerable to fatigue and stress - the most demands are at the beginning and end of a flight, but the latter is when you are most tired (your heart rate is most just after landing).

Information Processing

The way we interpret information on which we base decisions can be quite complex. With eyes and ears, *the processing is done in the brain*, which uses past experience to interpret what it senses - it therefore has expectations, and can pre-judge a situation. In fact, as accident reports routinely show, in high stress conditions, the brain may even blank out information not directly concerned with the task in hand. Certainly, the processing of information before it is brought to our conscious attention is done in such a way as to protect our self-esteem and confidence. In other words, when people act contrary to their self-identity, anything that doesn't pass through that filter is either rejected or made to fit.

Information processing usually means the interpretation of signals from the sensory organs by the brain, which can be selective. It is the process of receiving information through the senses, analysing it and making it meaningful. This is represented by the diagram below.

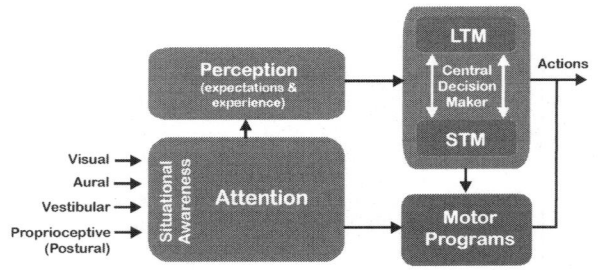

© Phil Croucher, 2013

If this page is a photocopy, it is not authorised!

CAPT

In the process, physical stimuli, such as sound and sight, are perceived, given attention and received into sensory memory for final interpretation by the brain, where it can be worked on by *Short Term* (STM) or *Long Term* Memory (LTM). Some processes can bypass all that completely, such as motor programs, which operate subconsciously, discussed later.

The system works also in reverse, in that feedback on the results of any actions can be used to improve knowledge and future judgement.

Perception at this point means converting that information into something meaningful, or realising that it's relevant to what you're doing. What comes out depends on past experience of those events, your expectations, and whether you're able to cope with the information at that time (or are even paying attention to the situation). Good examples are radio transmissions from ATC, which you can understand, even if you can't hear them properly, because you expect certain items to be included, and you know from experience that they're bad anyway. The danger is that you may hear what you want to hear and not what is actually sent! (see *Communication*, later).

It is important to realise at this stage that the brain is only a single channel computer, meaning that processing is done one item at a time. This can be a limitation under certain circumstances, and switching between tasks effectively needs proper training and practice.

Memory

Memory is a feature in human information processing. We need it to learn new things - without it, we could not capture information, or draw on past experience to apply it in new situations (i.e. remembering). Thus, there are three processes involved in using memory, *input* (or *encoding*), *storage* and *retrieval*, any one of which can fail and make you think you're losing your memory, though this can depend on whether the items are placed in *short term* or *long term* memory (see below). However, to encode something in the first place, it must be given *attention*, which ultimately depends on whether it can be *perceived* against all the other stuff going on (discussed elsewhere). This means that much of what we are exposed to never even enters short term memory, and thus is not available for recall. As a result, what are often called memory problems are really lapses in attention.

In 1951, Dr Wilder Penfield began a series of scientific experiments in which he proved that, by touching the temporal cortex with a weak electrical probe, the brain could be caused to play back some past experiences, and the feelings associated with them, despite the patients not normally being able to recall them. He came to the following widely accepted conclusions:

- The brain acts like a tape recorder, and whilst we may forget some experiences, they are recorded somewhere

- The brain also records the feelings associated with the experiences, and they stay locked together

- A person can exist in two states simultaneously (patients replaying hidden events and feelings could talk about them objectively at the same time)

- Hidden experiences when replayed are vivid, and affect how we feel at the time of replaying

- There is a connection between mind and body, or a link between the biological and the psychological

Anyhow, most psychologists (by no means all!) agree there are 3 (possibly 4*) types of memory:

INSTINCT

What Jung called "race memory", gives an immediate (gut reaction) response to a stimulus, like being hard-wired. Some psychologists call this *sensory memory*, as it provides a raw reaction to sensory input (like a knee jerk). That is, it can retain information long enough to allow you to decide whether a stimulus is important or not, or whether it is for the eyes or ears. Information that is not lost from sensory memory is passed on to..........

SHORT TERM MEMORY

Otherwise known as *Working*, Memory, this is for data that is used and forgotten almost instantly (actually, nothing is ever forgotten, as any psychologist will tell you, but the point is that Short Term Memory is for "on the spot" work, such as fuel calculations or ATC clearances, and figures greatly with situational awareness, which can follow short term memory's limitations). It can only handle somewhere between 5-9 items at a time (that is, 7 ± 2), for about 15 seconds, unless some tricks are used, such as grouping or association (*chunking*), meaning that what can be held in short term memory depends on the rules used for its organisation, which are in long-term memory. Mnemonics are also good, since STM appears to like words, albeit taking things rather literally - words will be recalled exactly, and in the order they were processed, unlike in long term memory, which will recall their *meaning* instead. Data in short term memory typically lasts about 10-20 seconds, and is affected by *distraction*, and is probably what Einstein was referring to when he thought that as soon as one fact was absorbed, one was discarded (there are only 27 lines to the Xanadu poem, because Coleridge was disturbed by the milkman).

Note: Don't expect to remember short term information - *always write clearances down!*

Because the capacity of short-term memory is so limited, items must clamour for attention, which may be based on *emotion*, *personal interest*, or the *unusual*. As mentioned, you can extend working memory's capabilities, either by *rehearsal* (mental repetition), or *chunking* (associating it with something meaningful), or breaking up the information into sequences, as you might with a telephone number. The sequence of letters ZNEBSEDECREM becomes a lot easier to remember once you realise it is MERCEDES BENZ backwards, and suddenly your short term memory has 5 or so spaces for more information.

Ultra short term memory lasts for about 2 seconds, and acts like a buffer, in that it stores information until we are ready to deal with it, although there are suggestions that this is actually handled by control processes such as rehearsal, or repetition.

Unfortunately, you cannot do any chunking or association without ....

LONG TERM MEMORY

This is where all our basic knowledge (e.g. memories of childhood, training, etc.) is kept - you might liken it to the unconscious, with more capacity and ability to retain information than short-term memory - its storage capacity is regarded as unlimited. LTM works better with information that has special relevance or meaning, whereas short-term memory is more meaning-free. Where training is concerned, many processes can be carried out automatically in LTM, with little thinking. Repetition (or *rehearsing*) is used to get information into it, combined with organising it, placing it into some sort of context or associating it with an emotion (when studying, concentrate on the *meaning* rather than the subject matter).

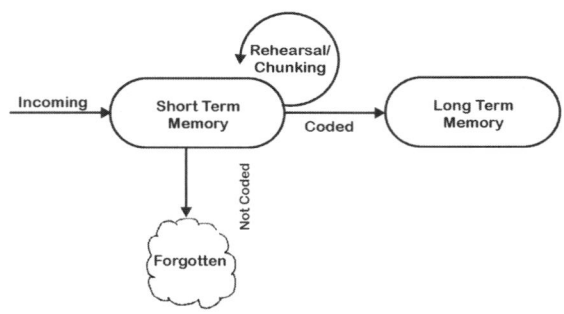

The reason why you need long term memory for association purposes is because it contains rules that give the items meaning. Chess players can have extraordinary short term memory for positioning on the board, *if the rules, which are in long-term memory, are obeyed*. Upon random positioning, short term recall reverts to normality. People with brain damage (after accidents, etc.) can often remember only one type of information, which supports the idea that the above types of memory are quite distinct, and that data can go directly into long term memory.

Perception

This is the process of giving meaning to what is sensed, or *interpreting*, *organising* and *elaborating* on the input, discarding anything non-relevant (which implies that knowledge and experience is required). After *visual* or *oral* perception comes *cognitive* perception, or understanding, leading to *expectations* or *mind set* (*Set* is a tendency to respond in a certain way, in line with expectations based on past experience - *perceptual set* relates this to the perception process). Variations on this theme could come from:

- The **stimulus** itself. For example, the moon at the horizon appears larger than when overhead, even though the image on the retina will be the same, because many of the visual cues for greater distance occur when it is viewed near land

- The **situation**, or the context in which an image is viewed. The figures 1 and 3 could be seen as the letter B if they were included together in a list of letters (like on number plates)

- The **state of the perceiver** with regard to motivation or emotion, or memories and expectations. If you are hungry, pictures of food can appear to be brighter, and the colour of a drink can affects the taste of the contents

Perception therefore happens in the brain, after a *stimulus* has been detected by the sense organs. The process by which sensory information gets to the brain (that is, transforming input into electrochemical energy) is called *transduction*. The brain distinguishes between stimuli by paying attention to the part of it that is activated.

However, the world is full of information that can be picked up by our senses - what makes us pay attention to some in particular? The answer is that there is a minimum level of stimulation that must occur before anything is noticed, so we are bound by our sense organs. These are samples for most humans in ideal conditions:

- *Sight* - A candle flame seen from 17 miles away

- *Touch* - a bee's wing falling on your cheek from 1 cm away

- *Taste* - 1 teaspoon of sugar in 2 gallons of distilled water

- *Smell* - 1 drop of perfume in a three-roomed house (1:500,000)

- *Hearing* - Ticking of a watch in a room 20 feet away

A shark, on the other hand, can sense one drop of blood in thousands of gallons of water!

Sensory stimulation is the first stage in the information process, and the basis of perception is the intensity of the stimulus. The *absolute threshold* is the minimum level (for a sensor) at which a stimulus is noticed, for 50% of the time.

CAPT

Attention

All the stimulation in the world is no good if you ignore it! Attention is a limited resource that can be affected by *distraction*, *selectivity* or *motivation*, which is where habit takes over. You can omit essential actions after interruptions in your work, because you are not paying attention. You can also include actions that are associated with the interruption in the original sequence of actions. A *premature exit* (relevant for engineers) is the termination of a job before everything is complete.

As mentioned above, the human body is not a good multi-tasker, and to keep the various balls in the air over a typical flight, we must learn to *prioritise* and switch rapidly between tasks, which depends on how much attention the primary task is demanding. This can be reduced by using standard procedures - the less thought secondary tasks require, the less attention they take up, especially when an external event happens to upset those well-made plans and flood the system.

What Is A Decision?

A decision is supposed to be the end result of a chain of events involving judgment, after which you choose between alternatives. The process involves not only our eyes and ears which gather data, but our attention, which should not be preoccupied all the time. The human body is not a multi-tasker, and to keep track of what's going on it's necessary to split your attention for a short period between everything, typically a split second at a time, having prioritised all the tasks that need to be completed.

Risk assessment, discussed at the end of this section, is part of the process, as is timing, as a good decision that is made too late is useless, although this does not mean that you should become impulsive.

Things often seem to happen all at once, so it's important not to get fixated on one thing at the expense of another, which is typically what happens when flying under stress. Gather all the information you can in the time available or, better still, get in the habit of updating information you're likely to need in an emergency as the flight progresses, especially when single-pilot, because then you will have much of the information you need in place.

When evaluating a situation, you should stay as cool as possible and not let emotions cloud your decision - that is, do not let false hopes affect your thinking, as they might if your engine fails over trees - you first have to get over the idea that you will hit something! Once you have all the information, of course, there is no point in delaying the making of the decision, which must be followed by action! Time should always be taken to explain the reasons for a decision, even if it is after landing.

A poor decision is often attributed to faulty reasoning. For example, from the fact that cats and dogs both have four legs, you might conclude that a cat is a dog. Alternatively, if a pilot comes from a broken home, and you know that people who come from broken homes are social misfits, you might also conclude that the pilot concerned is a social misfit. In this case, your faulty conclusion arises from a *false premise*, because not all people from broken homes are social misfits. In addition to misinterpreting a premise, you might rely on cherished beliefs rather than logical analysis, where you know that a certain part of an engine is prone to give problems, but, when troubleshooting, you automatically assume that the part is causing the problem, and don't look anywhere else for the cause (*stereotyping*).

The point about decision-making, as distinct from problem solving, is that the possible solutions are already known - you are faced with various alternatives, from which you have to make a choice. Problem solving involves reconciling a present position with a goal, with no obvious way of getting there - it is an attempt to achieve the goal through a series of logical stages, which might include defining the problem, generating possible solutions and evaluating them, which leads to the decision-making process - the last two options above.

The above decision making steps are not rigid, but may be merged or even repeated in a situation. For example, when adverse weather is ahead, you might get the updated weather, then vary the route or land to wait it out. Then you might get airborne and find you have to do it all over again, but this time land for refuelling, before getting airborne once more. The whole thing can be a continuously evolving process, which can be made quicker if some experience has already been gained, hence the value of training, which can allow you to make short cuts.

Training can reduce the need for making decisions - after all, the reaction to engine failure is pretty much cut and dried. However, there are many decisions that can be made before that point to reduce the after effects, such as choosing a good position if something happens. Falling engine oil pressure is one example - do you cut the engine and autorotate, or keep it running if you need its help?

The trouble is that our brains were designed for a more simple life, with decision making taken completely out of the loop (if you came across a dinosaur, you ran - simple!) With the vast amount of choices available to us these days (just try ordering a sandwich in Subway) we have to think as well - either rationalise our decisions or risk making bad ones. The result is that we choose not to choose, or rationalise a decision afterwards, based on our prejudices and expectations. Another problem is that many decisions are beyond our awareness.

Analysing decision-making steps in detail is inappropriate in the midst of an emergency. Sometimes we have to make rapid-fire decisions under high pressure and with little information, but you may be surprised to hear that you might not actually need that much information, especially with proper training, rules and rehearsal.

For example, many instructors are able to size up a student in less than a minute when it comes to deciding whether they will get their pilot's licence or not, and policemen have their hunches.

It should also be noted that the kind of decisions that can have far-reaching effects are actually quite small. Say you have just landed in twilight, and it is reported that your port and starboard navigation lights are not working. These, of course, are required equipment when flying at night. Do you shut down and wait for an engineer to fix them, or stay overnight and try again in the morning?

Or do you take off in what is still officially daylight and pretend to yourself that they stopped working while you were in flight, relying on ATC radar to tell you about other traffic, and *vice versa*, and put the landing light on, figuring that if it were on under normal circumstances, people wouldn't see the navigation lights anyway?

Anyhow, the normal process is to recognise a change, assess alternative actions, make a decision and monitor the results. This can be enhanced with *awareness of undesirable attitudes*, learning to *find relevant information*, and *motivation* to act in a timely fashion.

Each decision you make eliminates the choice of another so, once you make a poor one, a chain of them usually follows. In fact, a decision-making chain can often be traced back up to and over fifty years, depending on whether the original cause was a design flaw (the F-15 and F-16, for example, are functionally identical to fly, except that the speed bands go the opposite way in each aircraft). Another factor is the data itself; if it's incomplete, or altered through some emotional process, you can't base a proper decision on it. So:

- Don't make a decision unless you have to (which does not mean waiting until the last minute, but using the time you need *within the time available*)

- Keep it under review once you've made it

- No decision can be a decision (but watch for indecision)

Most important, though, is to be prepared to *change* a decision! Of course, by definition, the nature of most incidents means there's no time for proper evaluation, and you have to use instinct, experience or training. In this respect, there are two decision-making processes that affect us, both of which really speak for themselves - *ample-time* and *time-critical*.

Ample-Time Decision Making

You start with the awareness of a situation, which means having some idea of the big picture (similar to the continual updating mentioned above). The situation is developing slowly and you have time to start thinking up alternative courses of action. A good example is flying towards bad weather - once you know that it is close, you have to start thinking of returning to base or risk having to wait it out if you get caught. You might change your route to go towards it initially, so in the latter parts of the journey you are flying towards the clearer weather.

SITUATIONAL AWARENESS

Situational awareness refers to your knowledge of all relevant information, past or present, conscious or subconscious, which includes your cultural background. Of course, you have to know how things *should* be to recognise what's wrong! The main constituent is *vigilance*, or monitoring a situation without lapses in attention, which both uses up energy and processing power. In short, what the layman would call being alert.

For a good example of situational awareness, imagine yourself overtaking two trucks, one behind the other, in your car. The one behind is going faster than the one in front, and you know that there is a lot of momentum involved in driving a truck, so you figure it isn't going to slow down, but is more likely to want to overtake instead. You therefore expect the rear truck to want to occupy the lane you are in, so you either slow down, speed up or move over to the next lane to give it room (advanced drivers call this *reading the road*). In aviation terms, it can be likened to keeping a mental picture of what aircraft are around you, and what they are doing, by listening to ATC transmissions. SA involves knowledge of the past, present and future, and requires anticipation, so you need *vigilance* and *continual alertness*, with regard to what *may* happen on top of what *is* happening, which is difficult at the end of a long day. Being a pilot, most of the information you will base a decision on comes from your instruments and navigation equipment, but this can be affected by your physical state, discussed below.

Time-Critical Decision Making

Where decisions have to be made quickly, based on past experience or training, there is often no time to be creative or think up new solutions. In other words, time dictates your decision, and this is where checklists can help, because they will be based on other peoples' experience (training should make your actions as near to reflex as possible, to make way for creative thought).

Where time is critical, it pays to have a plan ready in case something goes wrong, which is where your training, plus a preflight briefing comes in (run it through your head by yourself if there's nobody else there).

THREAT & ERROR MANAGEMENT

The assumption is that, because you have a qualification, you know what you are doing. The truth is, we are surrounded by incompetence and people make mistakes all the time. Even the simplest jobs can be rampant with them, and they are not performed by idiots, but normal, otherwise intelligent people. Take the exam questions - surely it's not hard to produce an accurate database?

If these jobs are so simple, it's not hard to figure out that a fair proportion of the people involved in aviation will also make mistakes, especially when they are forced to work under the typical pressures involved.

Threat and Error Management (TEM) is a new framework (largely sponsored by the University of Texas) for what used to be called Airmanship, or simply common sense. Although this could also be a definition of CRM, TEM is more concerned with particular flights than aviation in general. It is a way of flying that either minimizes risk or maximizes safety margins, allowing pilots to recognize and counter everyday problems that may result in accidents or incidents with non-technical skills (NOTECHS), based on the analysis of aeronautical incidents and accidents in high capacity airlines.

Defensive flying, if you like.

Threats are events or hazards that are:

- outside the control of pilots, for which good situational awareness is a good antidote

- increase the operational complexity of the flight

- need crew attention and management, which takes up resources, especially when they are already busy

Examples include the weather, other traffic, etc. Most can be anticipated, especially with experience, but how a threat is perceived is the basis of any stress experienced.

The difference is that threats come *at* pilots, whereas errors come *from* pilots. Resisting threats is managing the future and resisting errors, the past.

The accepted progression is that unmanaged *threats* can lead to *errors*, and to *undesirable aircraft states*, the severity of which can depend on whether the pilot is experienced or under training, as the same error can have different consequences. Undesired aircraft states are deviations from flight paths or configurations that reduce safety margins, which are considered to be the last stages before an accident or incident occurs.

Examples include:

- being off altitude, off airspeed or off course

- being late

- being short of fuel

In short, threats, errors and undesired aircraft states are everyday events that must be managed to maintain safety. Crews that do this successfully are assumed to increase their potential for maintaining adequate safety margins. As such, it offers a flexible approach to risk management.

The importance lies not in the fact that threats and errors exist, but how they are managed (they are assumed to be handled sequentially). Threats and errors are considered to be an inevitable part of modern operations, so they are usually immediately dangerous.

Threat Management

A threat is a situation or event that may have a negative impact on the safety of a flight, or any influence that provides an opportunity for pilot error, such as:

- **Environmental threats**, that could include bad weather, aerodrome conditions, terrain, other traffic, ATC requirements, etc.

- **Organisational or operational threats, that** could include pressure from management, aircraft malfunctions, maintenance errors, etc.

- **Other errors**, such as stress, fatigue or distractions

Threats can also be expected (anticipated) or unexpected (unanticipated). Expected threats can be pre-handled, but unexpected ones require use of your skill and knowledge.

Error Management

Errors need management in order not to affect safety. They are cumulative!

Officially, errors are actions or inactions that:

- lead to deviations from intentions or expectations

- reduce safety margins

- increase the probability of adverse operational events on the ground and during flight

One working definition of human error is *"where planned sequences of mental or physical activity fail to achieve intended outcomes, not attributable to chance."* Another is *"the mismatch between the intention and the result of an action."*

The ICAO definition is: *An action or inaction by a flight crew that leads to deviations from organisational or flight crew intentions or expectations.*

Error Management could be regarded as *a counter-measure against bad decisions.* New pilots naturally make mistakes - experienced pilots tend to have monitoring errors, and are more likely to think they are flying an older type. There are three lines of defence against errors:

- **Avoiding** them in the first place (that is, not getting into a position that requires your superior skills to get out of). This requires a great deal of situational awareness and, by implication, active monitoring of the situation. Designers of systems and trainers can do their bit, too

- If they happen, **detecting** and trapping errors before they are significant

- Sorting out the mess afterwards (error **recovery**)

Error management accepts that mistakes happen, and adopts a non-punitive approach to minimise the effects (which does not mean that you should break the rules on purpose!) Evidence of this can be seen in anonymous reporting procedures, such as CHIRP in the UK and the *Aviation Safety Action Program* (ASAP) in the US.

There have also been attempts to remove the human from the system altogether (although someone still has to program the computer!) However, "they" have finally combined reducing the causes of errors, with reducing their *consequences*. That is, sh*t happens, and it is impossible to eliminate mistakes, so clearing up the mess is important. For more details, read Professor James Reason's book, *Human Error*, in which he points out that the barriers against accidents (or the sequence of human events) can be likened to several slices of Swiss cheese, with the holes as weaknesses in them.

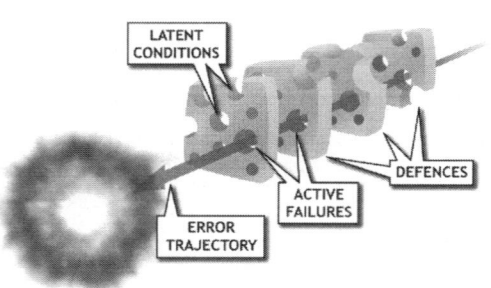

Although the slices represent layers between management decision making and the incident concerned, it does not mean that all accidents stem from management!

On the day the holes line up, something will happen, so if you can recognise the sequence, you should, in theory, be able to pull some of the holes out of line, and prevent an accident. One Australian fire fighting pilot went to transmit, pushed the wrong button and dropped his water bucket instead. He landed, picked it up and went home for a couple of days, figuring that he must be tired and was better off out of it. Unfortunately, the chain can sometimes not be broken in time.

Recognising an *Error Chain* will not necessarily mean that an accident will actually occur, but detecting the holes in the cheese slices lining up should be cause for concern and spark off an investigation. However, the events in a chain may not happen one after the other, and may not even depend on each other. There could be months between incidents.

The 4-7 links in the average chain means you have up to seven opportunities to stop an accident.

SITUATIONAL AWARENESS

Being aware of what's going on is your biggest weapon against errors.

PROCEDURAL ERRORS

These include:

- A **slip**, or a failure that occurs when carrying out required actions (a pilot dropping fuel drums might write down the wrong GPS coordinates). That is, there is a substitution or insertion of an inappropriate action into a sequence that was otherwise good. *Slips do not satisfy the operator's intent.*

- A **lapse** is an *omission* of one or more steps of a sequence. As mentioned previously, it is possible to miss out entire checklists.

In the above, the intentions may be correct, but the execution may be flawed.

Latent errors, like unnoticed waypoint errors in a GPS database, have consequences that lie dormant, and are difficult to recognise (or foresee) because of the time lag between their generation and occurrence. They may also only be found in certain circumstances, so they can lull pilots into a false sense of security. Their consequences could be serious. Latent errors are hard to prevent, but should be made visible by a Safety Management System.

Active errors, on the other hand, are committed *at the human/system interface*, and have immediate consequences, which is how they can be detected. They can also be corrected relatively quickly, with fewer consequences.

MISTAKES & VIOLATIONS

The majority of fatal crashes are not down to errors in execution (35%) or perception (23%), but in the original decision-making process (43%), because decision errors are not typically slips or lapses, but *mistakes*. Mistakes arise where the *planned actions* are incorrect. This may be the result of incorrect knowledge or diagnosis. For example, shutting down the wrong engine after incorrectly identifying the failed one. Whereas slips are mostly found in skill-based mode, mistakes happen more often in rule- or knowledge based modes.

Violations are more deliberate acts, usually done for speed or convenience, however well-meaning. Technically, they are *deliberate deviations from rules, procedures or regulations,* although unintentional ones can occur when the person is unaware of a rule or procedure.

Whether violations occur is down to the attitudes, beliefs, norms and company culture. Aside from ignoring safety rules on a particular task, they put the rest of the system in jeopardy because it is assumed that rules will be followed.

The SHEL Model

This is one factor of decision making that was originally presented by a psychologist called Edwards. It is a framework that describes the components and interfaces between the various subsystems to do with aviation Its proper application can help prevent errors, and is a particular factor in the design of flight decks.

The letters of the word *SHEL* stand for *Software, Hardware, Environment* and *Liveware,* which represent influences on the typical pilot. *Hardware,* naturally enough, is the mechanical environment, *Environment* covers such things as hypoxia, temperature, etc., whilst *Software* covers checklists, etc. *Liveware* copes with interactions between the pilot and other people, including the pilot himself - the centre of the model is Liveware, and the other components must be carefully matched in the following areas to avoid stress and lower performance:

- **Physical parameters** - size and shape of the body, based on the middle 90% of the population.

- **Fuel** - Food, water and oxygen.

- **Information gathering** - sight, sound, touch, and other senses.

- **Information processing** - short and long term memory, decision making capabilities, etc.

- **Output characteristics** - how the controls are moved, speech, etc.

- **Environment** - acceptable ranges of humidity, temperature, noise, pressure, time of day and light and darkness, to mention but a few

Of course, humans can vary considerably in terms of the above. They can, however, be controlled in terms of pilot selection (not too tall, or short), and standardisation - the *Design Eye Reference Point* is one example, mentioned under *Eyes* in *The Body.*

LIVEWARE-HARDWARE

This is the first area that needs attention. Adjustable seats and controls are a good start (*ergonomics,* mentioned overleaf), but displays are important as well. As an example, the 3-needle altimeter was a classic example of poor design that led to accidents, where people confused the hundred- and thousand-foot needles (see right). EFIS/ECAS displays are also not entirely satisfactory because, although they present a lot of information in a small space, they fail to show patterns and trends, and it is harder to read digits than it is to read analogue dials, where you get used to a picture of needle positions, and any misplaced are easily noticed. When you have to read numbers, it takes a second or two to interpret the information. *Analogue presentation is most suitable for qualitative or comparative information.*

LIVEWARE-SOFTWARE

Liveware-software problems occur when documentation is poorly written and presented. Below is an example of the sort of checklist that comes from a typical Chief Pilot's office. It would appear to do the job quite well, but closer inspection reveals that it could do with a little tweaking here and there.

For example, it is not obvious what are headings and what are not.

FIRE

<u>Immediate Actions</u>

ON GROUND:	
Respective EMER OFF sw[1]	Open switch guard, press and release
Fuel Prime Pumps	Both OFF
Engines	OFF
Rotor Brake	ON
Battery	OFF
Passengers	Evacuate
IN FLIGHT:	
OEI flight condition	Establish
Respective EMER OFF sw[1]	Open switch guard, press and release
Affected engine	Identify, then OFF
Passengers	Alert
Check for signs of fire	
Warning light off	LAND AS SOON AS POSSIBLE
Warning light on	LAND IMMEDIATELY

<u>Considerations</u>

1.   Respective engine will be automatically cut off. ACTIVE will illuminate on the EMER OFF sw panel and F VALVE CL will illuminate on the CAD.

Here is the same checklist, suitably tweaked:

FIRE

Immediate Actions

On Ground

1. Switch guard	Open, press and release
2. Fuel Prime Pumps	Both OFF
3. Engines	OFF
4. Rotor Brake	ON
5. Battery	OFF
6. Passengers	Evacuate

In Flight

1. OEI flight condition	Establish
2. Switch guard	Open, press and release
3. Affected engine	Identify, then OFF
4. Passengers	Alert
5. Fire	Check for signs
6. LAND AS SOON AS POSSIBLE	

Considerations

1. Respective engine will be automatically cut off. ACTIVE will illuminate on the EMER OFF sw panel and F VALVE CL will illuminate on the CAD.

It didn't take much effort to improve things, with a little spacing and layout. This is very much in keeping with the SHEL model.

Contrast this with this example from the airline world, which violates almost every rule of technical writing:

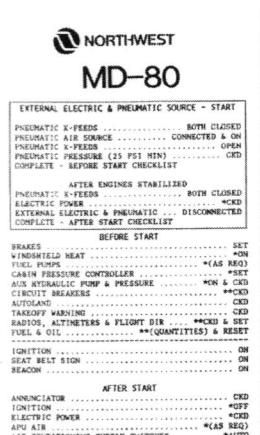

LIVEWARE-ENVIRONMENT

In the early days of aviation, the human was matched to the environment, with special suits, etc. Now, technology allows the environment to be better matched to the human to provide the optimum working environment. Noise, vibration, temperature, air quality and heat all need to be carefully controlled, as do work patterns and shifts that fail to take account of sleep disturbance and jet lag.

Prolonged amounts of noise, vibration or turbulence is fatiguing and annoying - noise is particularly prevalent in helicopters, especially with the doors off. Vibration at the right frequency (8-12 Hz) causes back pain.

Flicker occurs when light is interrupted by rotor blades or propellers (see *Disorientation*, below). It can cause anything from mild discomfort to fatigue, and even convulsions or unconsciousness. Flicker certainly modifies certain neuro-physiological processes; 3-30 a second appears to be a critical range, while 6-8 will diminish your depth perception (the Germans set their searchlights to flicker, during World War II, to get up the nose of bomber pilots). Hangovers make you particularly susceptible.

LIVEWARE-LIVEWARE

Poor relationships or communication between crew members, outside workers and even management have led to disasters, so group dynamics are becoming important in getting people to work together properly in teams. See also *Communication*.

Automation

The brain's limitations, in terms of speed of computation and the ability to multi-task (i.e. none!) began to be recognised as early as 1959, with the Boeing 707. This was when it was realised that pilots could soon begin to exceed their design capabilities, and that the help of various black boxes was needed. A lot of work can be done for you by computers, which are just electronic machines - the man-machine system is meant to *relieve pilot workload and increase time for supervision*.

But how much control should be given to black boxes? If they have too much, the cockpit becomes boring and errors can go unnoticed amongst the monotony (hypovigilance). Although automation can conserve resources and attention, it can result in routine errors, or *slips,* such as when programming waypoints into the system (it can also reduce your flying competence). Machines can wait for infrequent information without getting bored, and can perform long-term control and set values, again, without getting bored, but people can exercise judgment, make better decisions and detect unusual conditions (smells, noises, etc.), whilst getting bored very easily. On the one hand, automation is good, because it can take much routine work away from you. For example, a FADEC (fuel control thingy) has a lot of monitoring functions. As well, the chances for human error are reduced and reliability is better.

On the other hand, automation can induce a feeling of *automation complacency* (too much reliance on the machine) and lead you not to check things as often as you should (*reduced vigilance*), or push the envelope, as when using a GPS in bad weather - with much of the navigation task taken away from you, it is tempting to fly in worse weather than you can really cope with (flying in bad weather is like sex - the further you get into it, the harder it is to stop). As your visual clues decrease, your mental processes focus more on trying to see where you're going and less on

If this page is a photocopy, it is not authorised!

CAPT

flying until you lose control, when flying on instruments is no help because you are not mentally prepared for it.

However, one major benefit is the integration of many sources of information and its presentation in a clear and concise manner (sometimes!), as with the glass cockpit, and providing a major contribution towards situational awareness, as long as you keep a mental plot going, as the information presented can be highly filtered. Put more in exam language, *the use of modern technology in glass cockpits facilitates feedback from the machine via more concise data for communication on the flight deck.* So there. What it doesn't help with is the fact that one knob used to have one function in older systems - now several functions may be hidden at different levels, for which there is no substitute for knowledge of the menu system.

ERGONOMICS

Here's an illustration of how bad design can be the start of an *event chain*:

A relatively inexperienced RAF Phantom (F4) pilot had a complete electrics failure, as if being over the North Sea at night in winter wasn't stressful enough. For whatever reason, he needed to operate the Ram Air Turbine, but he deployed the flaps instead, as the levers were close together.

Of course, doing that at 420 knots made the flaps fall off the back, and the hydraulic fluid followed. Mucking around with the generators got the lights back on, and he headed for RAF Coningsby, with no brakes. Unfortunately, on landing, the hook bounced over the top of the arrester wire, so he used full afterburner to go around in a strong crosswind, but headed towards the grass instead. The pilot and navigator both ejected, leaving the machine to accelerate through 200 knots, across the airfield at ground level.

Meanwhile, the Station Commander was giving a dinner party for the local mayor in the Mess, and the guests had just come out on the steps (near the runway), in time to watch the Phantom come past on the afterburner, with two ejections. The mayor's wife was just thanking him for the firework display as it went through a ditch, lost its undercarriage and fell to bits in a field.

The Fire Section had by this time sent three (brand new) appliances after it without any hope of catching up, but they tried anyway. The first one wrote itself off in a ditch because it was going too fast, the driver of the second suddenly put the brakes on because he realised there had been an ejection and that he might run over a pilot on the runway, at which point the number three appliance smashed into the back of him.

We are in a similar situation - how many times have you jumped into the cockpit of a different machine, to find the switches you need in a totally different place? This doesn't help you if you rely on previous experience to find what you need (in emergencies you tend to fall back to previous training), so the trick is to know what you need at all times, and take the time to find out where it is (*read the switches*).

THE BODY

The human body is wonderful, but only up to a point. It has limitations that affect your ability to fly efficiently, as your senses don't always tell you the truth, which is why you need extensive training to fly on instruments - you have to unlearn so much. The classic example is the "leans", where you think you're performing a particular manoeuvre, but your instruments tell you otherwise. However, although the sensors in the eyes and ears are actually quite sensitive, the brain isn't, and does not always notice their signals. Sometimes it even fills in bits by itself, according to various rules, which include your expectations and past experience. Thus, at each stage in the perception process, there is the possibility of error, because we are not necessarily sensing reality. For example, the reason why there is a *white balance* setting on a digital camera is because the brain interprets what is white in its own way and compensates all by itself - indoor bulbs actually glow quite red, and an overcast sky might have some blue in it, despite what you think you see. If the camera doesn't compensate, your pictures will be tinted the wrong way. The diagram on the right shows how limited the range of visible light is against the spectrum of electromagnetic waves available. If the full spectrum were 2 yards long, visible light would occupy 1/32 of an inch.

But why do you need to learn about the body? Well, parts of it are used to get the information you need to make decisions with, and, of course, if it isn't working properly, you can't process the information or implement any action based on it. In the single-pilot case, it needs to be efficient because there is nobody else to take over if you get incapacitated. Also, presumably, you want to pass your next medical!

G Tolerance

If you pull back on the controls, your body (after Newton) wants to carry on in a straight line, but is forced upward by the seat, which feels the same as if you were being pushed into it. This extra pressure is called G, and it affects the whole body, including the blood, so the heart must change its action to keep the system running.

The body can only cope with certain amounts of G-force, which comes from the effects of *acceleration*, that increase your weight artificially. When there is no acceleration, you are subject to 1G. We are often subject to acceleration forces beyond our design limits, hence some illusions when the mind misinterprets the proper clues.

- *Linear or Transverse acceleration* (Gx) concerns forward and backward movement, with speed only. Under forward linear acceleration, you might think you are climbing. The body can tolerate 45G horizontally. If you don't wear shoulder straps, tolerance to forward deceleration reduces to below

25G, and you will jack-knife over your lapstrap with your head hitting whatever is in front of it at 12 times the speed of it coming the other way.

- *Lateral acceleration* (Gy) has effects from left to right. It typically occurs when your direction changes, with alteration in speed. It is also known as *transverse acceleration*

- *Vertical acceleration* (Gz) occurs while moving up or down. The body can tolerate 25G vertically

Negative G acts upwards and can *increase the blood flow to the head*, leading to *red out*, facial pain and slowing down of the heart (your lower eyelids will close at -3G). Positive G is more normal, but will *drain* the blood, with the obvious consequences, including loss of vision, called *grey out*, at +3.5 G. This could end up as *black out* (where you are fully conscious but cannot see) at +6 G and unconsciousness between +7 and +8 G.

Both are affected by hyperventilation, hypoxia, heat, hypoglycaemia, smoking and alcohol, discussed later. This is because they all affect the action of the heart.

Central Nervous System

Whatever your body gets up to, the processes involved must be coordinated and integrated. This is done by the central nervous system, with a little help from the endocrine system. Although making an approach to land might seem to be automatic, the control responses that occur as a result of input from your eyes and ears, and experience, plus the feedback required from your limbs so that you don't over control, are all transmitted over complex nerve cells (*neurons*) for processing inside the CNS, which consists of the brain and spinal cord, though, for exam purposes, it also includes the visual and aural systems (eyes and ears), proprioceptive system (the so-called "seat-of-the-pants" sense) and other senses.

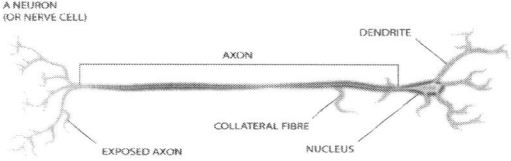

Cells communicate with a combination of electrical and chemical signals. Chemical ones either diffuse between cells (*neurotransmitters*) or are disseminated in the blood (*hormones*) to act on more distant parts of the body.

Neurons don't touch each other directly - if a message needs to be transmitted, a neurotransmitter (of which there are over 50 types) carries it across the small gap between them, after triggering by an electrical signal.

PERIPHERAL NERVOUS SYSTEM

This connects the Central Nervous System with the sense organs, muscles and glands, and therefore with the outside world. The PNS is divided into:

- the *somatic* nervous system, which contains the peripheral pathways for communicating with the environment and control of skeletal muscles, and

- the *autonomic* nervous system, which regulates vital functions over which you have no conscious control, like heartbeat and breathing (unless you're a high grade Tibetan monk, of course), or anything that is not to do with skeletal muscle. The ANS in turn consists of the:

  - *sympathetic*

  - *parasympathetic*

nervous systems. The former prepares you for fight-or-flight (see *Stress*, below) and tends to act on *several organs at once*, while the latter calms you down again, *acting on one organ at a time*. Being under the influence of fight-or-flight is like being in a powerful car in permanent high gear, which you can't do all the time - you need rest & relaxation to allow time for the parasympathetic system to kick in, such as meditation, or a snooze. Being in such a high state of readiness all the time produces steroids, and can lead to depression.

The Brain

The brain is a switchboard, which is constantly in touch with the 639 muscles inside the body. It can also store vast amounts of information - the Hungarian physicist and mathematician John van Neumann calculated that the brain stored around 2.8×10^{20} bits of information over the course of the average lifetime! Although the brain is only 2% of the body mass, it takes up to 20% of the volume of each heartbeat - its blood supply needs to be continuous, as it cannot store oxygen.

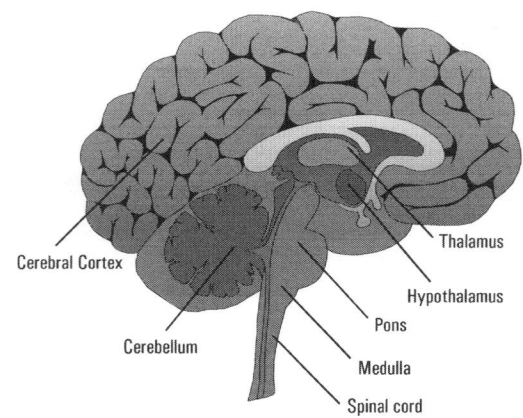

Many of the brain's departments merge into each other, and work closely together, but it still has three distinct areas, namely the *central core*, the *limbic system* and the *cerebral hemispheres*.

The brain itself doesn't register pain (but the scalp and skull should be deadened with a local anaesthetic if you want to go poking around!)

Cerebral Hemispheres consist of the "grey matter" you see when looking at a picture of the brain. Each half is basically symmetrical, but the left and right hemispheres are interconnected (through the corpus callosum), with women having more connections between them than men, which accounts for their ability to think of several things at once, often contradictory. Each hemisphere has four *lobes*. The hemispheres work in different ways, leading to two types of thinking:

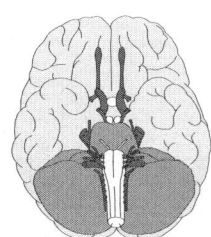

- *Left Brain*, or logical - governs language, skilled in mathematics

- *Right Brain* - conceptual. The artist type

Note that, although the two hemispheres work differently, they still work very much together.

Vision

LIGHT

In the electromagnetic spectrum, as radio waves get higher in frequency, they approach the lower reaches of visible light, which is what is detected by your eyes. This indicates that radio and light waves are of the same nature (just running at different speeds), so the eye can be viewed as a specialised radio receiver, or at least a frequency analyser, so the work of converting light into an electrical impulse that can be sent to the brain suddenly does not seem quite so hard. Sub-ranges within the range of visible light are detected as colour, with the lowest frequency being red and the highest violet, in this order: R O Y G B I V. Their combination creates white light, and black is the absence of any radiation, so black and white do not exist as "colours" at all.

The diagram on the right shows how limited the range of visible light is against the spectrum of

Cosmic Rays	
Gamma Rays	
X Rays	
UV	Light Waves
Visible Light	
IR	
Radar	
FM	Radio Waves
TV	
AM	

electromagnetic waves available. If the full spectrum were 2 yards long, visible light would occupy 1/32 of an inch.

Vision is your primary (and most dependable) source of information - 70% of data enters the visual channel. It gets harder with age to distinguish moving objects; between 40 - 65, this ability diminishes by up to 50%, but this is only one limitation, and we need to examine the eye in detail to see how you overcome them all.

THE EYE

The eye is a dual sensor, in terms of central and peripheral vision. The latter is imprecise, but it covers a large area. Central vision is more exact, and narrowly focussed. You can only read instruments with central vision.

The eye is nearly round, and its rotation in its socket (and focussing) is controlled by external muscles. It has three coatings, or layers of membrane:

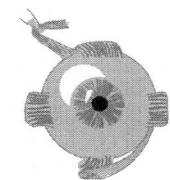

- the *sclerotic*, which is transparent at the front

- the *choroid*, which lines the sclerotic and contains tiny blood vessels

- the *retina*, which is the light sensitive bit that detects electromagnetic waves of the frequency of light, and converts them to electrical signals that are interpreted by the brain, and which is sensitive to hypoxia

The transparent part of the sclerotic is the *cornea*, behind which is the *lens*, whose purpose is to bend light rays inwards, to focus on the retina. The lens, iris and cornea control the amount of light entering the eye through the *pupil*, which is the black bit inside the coloured iris. Generally, vision is better with more light, but too much will produce glare (older people need twice as much light to see well than younger people do). The iris appears black because any light that does not get absorbed by the retina is usually absorbed by a layer behind it called the *retinal pigment epithelium*, as if you didn't know already. If it wasn't, your vision would be blurred by randomly scattered light. Redeye occurs when not all the light can be absorbed and some is reflected back.

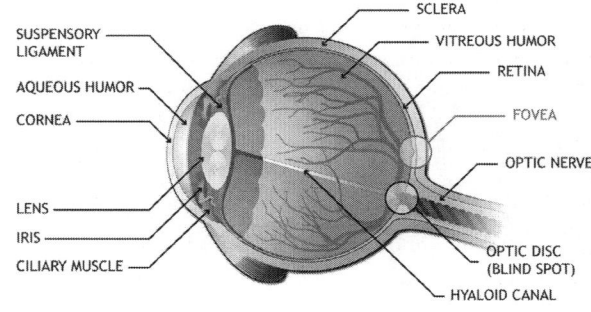

CAPT

70% of light is refracted by the cornea, and 30% by the lens. The more your iris is open, the less *depth of field* you have, so in darkness it is hard to see beyond or before the point of focus, and you may require glasses to help (the depth of field in photography is an area either side of the focus point in which everything is sharp. The wider the aperture, or iris, the shorter this distance is, and *vice versa*).

The retina is composed of ten very thin layers, with nerve endings that act as light sensors (actually, *neurons*) which are called *rods* and *cones*, in the ninth. Their names arise from the way they are shaped. Each is more efficient than the other in different kinds of light. Cones are sensitive to day or high-intensity light and rods are used at night or in low-intensity light. As the periphery of the retina consists mainly of rods, peripheral vision is less precise because they only see shades of grey and vague shapes (you see colours because the vibrations they give out are strong enough to wake the cones up, and the brain mixes the colours received by them. The most common colour blindness is red/green). The rods contain *visual purple*, also known as *rhodopsin*, which builds up over a period of 30-45 minutes as light decreases until the approximate level of moonlight, which is when the rods take over from the cones. As rods are sensitive to shorter wavelengths of light, in very low light, blue objects are more likely to be seen than red (neither will be in colour), which is why cockpit lighting is sometimes red because it affects the rods used for night vision less than white light.

Light waves from objects in the *right* visual field fall on the *left* half of each retina, for transmission to the *left* cerebral hemisphere, and *vice versa*. This is so that each side of the brain has input from both eyes at once.

The *optic nerve* carries signals from the eye to the brain. The point where it joins the retina is mostly populated with cones, which work best in daylight and become less effective at night, or where oxygen levels are reduced (which is significant for smokers, whose blood has less oxygen carrying capacity), so you get a blind spot in the direct field of vision, which is why you see things more clearly at night if you look slightly to the side of what you need to see. You don't normally notice the blind spot because the brain superimposes the images from each eye.

Once light falls on the retina, the visual pigment is bleached, which creates the electrical current. However, once bleached, the pigment must be reactivated by a further chemical reaction, which is called *nystagmus*, caused by the eye jerking to a new position, there to remain steady. The movement period is edited out by the brain, and the multiple images are merged, so continuous vision is actually an illusion, as an *after image* is produced when light falls on the retina - that is, the image of what you are looking at remains there for a short period, as light has a momentum (try it by closing your eyes and looking at the picture that remains). As the eye does not need to be

seeing constantly (and can therefore be regarded as a detector of *movement*), it can spend the spare time in repair and replacement of tissue. 30-40 images per second are taken in the average person, and an image takes about 1/50th of a second to register. It has also been discovered that, when we blink, the visual cortex in the brain (the bit that interprets what the eye sees) closes down for that period. As it happens, if 90% of a rat's visual cortex is removed, it can still perform quite complex tasks that require visual skills. Similarly, a cat can have up to 98% of its optic nerves severed without much effect.

All this means you *see with the brain*, giving a difference between *seeing* and *perceiving*. It also means that vision problems can arise from the brain's processing ability and not the eyes themselves. This is because the eye's optical quality is actually very poor (you would get better results from a pinhole camera), hence the need for the brain, which can actually modify what you see, based on experience, and so is reliant on expectations. If the brain fills in the gaps wrongly, you get visual illusions. **Less than 50% of what you see is actually based on information entering your eyes!** The remainder is pieced together out of your expectations of what you should be seeing.

For example, your mind can get so accustomed to seeing a given set of words that your unconscious can edit out what is really there and make you see what you expect to see, as experienced by writers who can miss a prominent typographical error for ages. Pilots used to seeing a certain instrument picture can miss any changes in the same way.

An aircraft heading towards you can disappear from sight under the same circumstances. A high speed aircraft approaching head-on will grow the most in size very rapidly in the last moments, so it's possible for it to be hidden by a bug on the windscreen for a high proportion of its approach time (you might only see it in the last few seconds). Lack of relative movement makes an object harder to detect.

You should be able to see another aircraft directly at 7 miles, or 2.5 miles if it was 45° off - at 60° it's down to half a mile! The reason why you must scan is because the eye needs to latch on to something, which is difficult with a clear blue sky, or on a hazy day. With an empty field of vision, your eyes will actually focus at relatively short distances, anywhere from between 56 cm ahead (*Aviation Week*) to 3-10 metres ahead, and miss objects further away (*empty field myopia*). In other words, you effectively become short-sighted (myopic). The ratio of looking in- and outside should be 5:15 seconds.

Close your left eye and stare at the dot in the middle of the grid at the top of the next page with your right eye. As you move the page back and forth along your line of vision (about 10-15 inches away), the right one will vanish

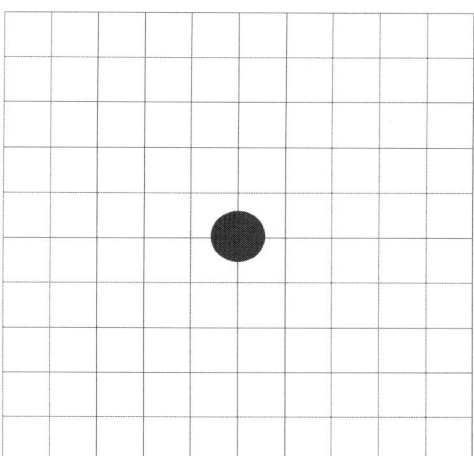

because it is falling inside your blind spot. Now close your right eye and stare at the dot on the right. The one on the left will vanish as well, but all the lines on the grid will remain intact. This is because your brain is filling in with what it thinks should be there. Thus, there are gaping holes in what we think we see - if we are only seeing about half of what is out there, what are we missing? How many readings on our instruments do we not see at all?

The eye/brain combination is therefore not trustworthy, as it can tinker with its world view before you become conscious of it. In fact, visual information entering the brain is modified by the temporal lobes before being passed on to the visual cortices (*Pribram*).

The only part of the eye that sees perfectly clearly is in the centre of the retina, an area not much larger than a pinhead, called the *fovea centralis*, where the first eight layers of the retina are missing, so the rods and cones are directly exposed to light (that is, the light doesn't have to battle through the first layers) for clearer vision at that point. It is the area of best day vision, and no night vision at all. The area of sharp vision is therefore very small, at 4 feet, the size of a small coin. 5° away from the foveal axis, it reduces by a quarter, and one-twentieth at 20° away. Outside of that area, vision is quite blurred - if you look at the top part of this page, for example, you will not be able to see the rest clearly without shifting your vision. The illusion of seeing large areas clearly (that is, more than two words at a time) comes from the rapidity of shifting - attempting to do this otherwise means seeing without focussing, and results in eyestrain. Sometimes your eye and brain can get out of the habit of looking at one point together. Vibrations can also cause blurred vision.

NIGHT VISION

The rods contain a chemical called visual purple, also known as rhodopsin, which builds up over 30-45 minutes* as light decreases until the approximate level of moonlight, which is when the rods take over from the cones. As rods

are sensitive to shorter wavelengths of light, in very low light, blue objects are more likely to be seen than red (neither will be in colour), which is why cockpit lighting is sometimes red because it affects the rods used for night vision less than white light does.

The eye is slow to adapt from light to dark because it takes time to create visual purple, a process requiring Vitamin A, of which the retina contains enormous amounts - having too little Vitamin A could result in night blindness.

*The changeover from light to dark takes about 20-30 minutes and should always be allowed for when night flying (some say 30-45 minutes - actually, the cones take 7 minutes, and the retina can take up to 45).

Night vision is most sensitive to lack of oxygen and can be significantly reduced (by more than 25%) at 15 000 feet if you are affected by hypoxia. As hypoxia affects you more if you are a smoker, use of tobacco will also affect night vision, as will the presence of carbon monoxide and anything else that affects the blood's ability to carry oxygen, such as drugs or alcohol.

You must normally look directly at an object to see it best. Unfortunately, the eyes are not well designed to see straight ahead in the dark, or in poorly lit environments. At night, you should look slightly to one side, as the rods that are sensitive to lower levels of light are outside the fovea, at the peripheral of the retina (scan slowly as well).

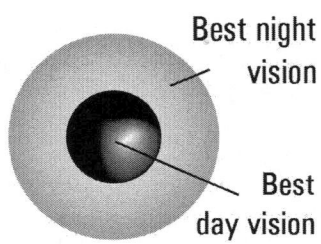
Best night vision

Best day vision

CAPT

Picture: Operation of the Eye

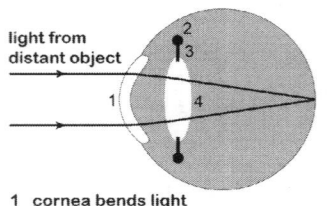

pupil dilated

1 cornea bends light
2 circular ciliary muscle relaxed
3 suspensory ligament taught
4 lens pulled thin

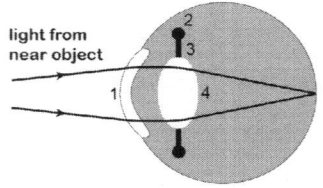

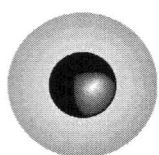

pupil contracted

1 cornea bends light
2 circular ciliary muscle contracted
3 suspensory ligament slack
4 lens more circular

DEFECTIVE VISION

HYPERMETROPIA

Short Eyeball   **Convex Lens**

MYOPIA

Long Eyeball   **Concave Lens**

The major causes of defective vision are:

- *Hypermetropia** - where the eyeball is too short, and images focus behind the retina (farsightedness). Requires a convex lens

- *Myopia** - where the eyeball is too long, and images focus in front of the retina (short sight). Needs a concave lens

- *Presbyopia* - the lens hardens, leading to *hypermetropia* and difficulty in focussing, lack of accommodation (comes with old age)

- *Cataracts* - the lens becomes opaque

- *Glaucoma* - increase in pressure of liquid in the eyeball interferes with accommodation for the progressive narrowing of the visual field

- *Astigmatism* - unequal curvature of cornea or lens

*Both conditions cause blurred vision, which is correctable by glasses, that vary the refraction of the light waves until they focus in the proper place.

Illusions exist when what you sense does not match reality. They occur because our senses are limited, especially when it comes to the demands of flight - the missing bits tend to get filled in by the brain, sometimes wrongly. Looking directly at an object under water is difficult, because light rays bend due to refraction as they pass the surface and the object appears to be displaced:

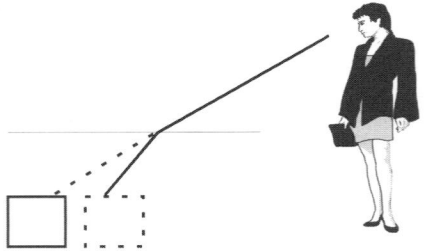

This has obvious parallels with looking at a runway through a wet windshield. *Distortion* occurs when viewing objects through a windshield covered with rain, where water is thicker near the bottom (nearer to the windshield), causing a *prismatic effect* - like looking through a base-down prism, which tends to make objects look higher or closer. Raindrops on a windscreen can double the apparent size of lights outside and make you think you are closer.

In the image on the right (a Ponzo illusion), the two horizontal lines are the same length, but they look different because your perspective cues are not correct.

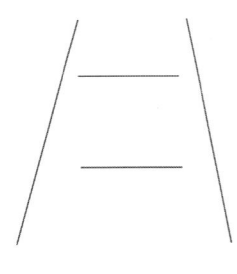

On the radar screen in the picture below, the two aircraft tracks look to be safely separate, but they are not.

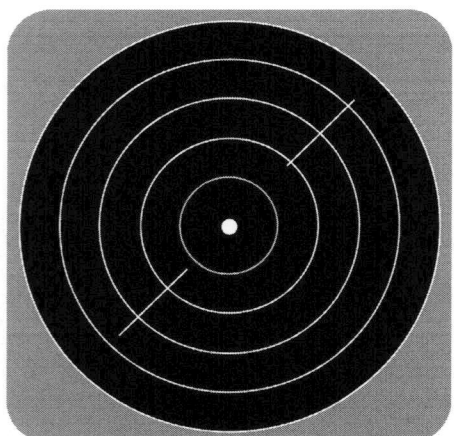

CAPT

One classic illusion for pilots is *whiteout*, which is defined by the American Meteorological Society as:

"An atmospheric optical phenomenon of the polar regions in which the observer appears to be engulfed in a uniformly white glow".

That is, you can only see dark nearby objects - no shadows, horizon or clouds, and you lose depth perception. It occurs over unbroken snow cover beneath a uniformly overcast sky, when the light from both is about the same. Blowing snow doesn't help, and it's particularly a problem if the ground is rising. *Flat light* is a similar phenomenon, but comes from different causes, where light is diffused through water droplets suspended in the air, particularly when clouds are low. *Objects seen through fog or haze will seem to be further away.*

A good example of an optical illusion is a wider runway tending to make you think the ground is nearer:

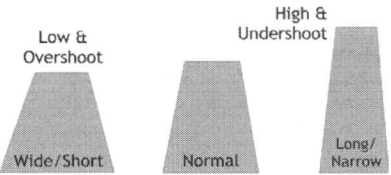

A narrow runway delays your reactions, possibly leading to a late flare and early touchdown. In the diagram above, all three landing strips are the same distance and angle away from the aircraft, but the one on the left is wider and shorter (looks nearer, and low on the glideslope, so you might carry out a higher approach) and the one on the right is longer and thinner (looks further away and high on the glideslope, so you might go lower and land short while you try to keep the same sight picture). A pilot used to a runway 27 m wide, who lands on one 42 m wide, will think he is nearer than usual and fly a lower and flatter approach with a tendency to undershoot and a high roundout.

The illusions you might get with sloping ground include:

Problem	Illusion	Risk
Downslope	Too low	High approach/overshoot
Upslope	Too high	Low approach/undershoot
Rain	Closer	Low approach
Narrow	Too high	Low approach
Wide	Too low	High approach & flare
Bright lights	Too low	High approach

An approach to a downsloping runway should be started higher, with a steeper angle, because the perceived glide path angle is smaller than that of the actual glide path. However, the slope away from the aircraft presents a smaller image to your eyes, and you see less of the runway, so you try to see more by flying too high to correct the apparent undershooting. An approach to an upsloping runway should be started lower, at a shallower angle - good reasons why you should use VASIS when provided.

Helicopters A and C in the picture below both see an approach path of 5 degrees. Boeing researchers found that a big black hole effect at night could cause a curved approach, so the trick is to avoid long approach paths.

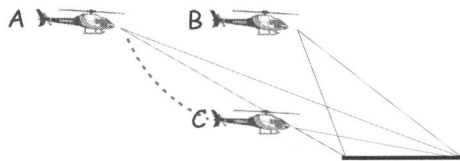

Another symptom is of nothing moving, and you get the impression of being too high, hence the bent approach.

If an object is brighter than its surroundings (a well-lit runway), you will think you are closer to it, so on an approach, you might start early and be lower than you should. In haze, objects appear to be further away because of their lack of brightness.

Even going to the cinema is an optical illusion; still frames are shown so quickly it looks as if movement is taking place - the switching is done in the brain, in alliance with the eye's *persistence of vision*, which is the ability to retain an impression of the shape, colour and brightness of an image for a fraction of a second after light from the image stops being received. *Vectional illusions* are caused by movement, as when sitting in a railway carriage and wondering whether it's the train next to you or the one you're in that is moving (this is also called the *illusion of relative movement*) - helicopter pilots can experience something similar when hovering close to moving water - the *waterfall effect* happens when hovering or in slow flight at low altitudes. The downwash causes the air to pick up water and to displace it upward at the edge of the blades and downward directly under them, so you might see drops of water going downward in your field of vision to give you a climbing sensation. A corrective manoeuvre to descend will put the helicopter in the water.

When mountain flying, it's often difficult to fly straight and level because the sloping ground around affects your judgment. Similarly, you can't judge your height when landing on a peak.

One of the optical illusions you might come across at night is the apparent motion of a stationary object (*autokinesis*) which isn't helped by rain on the windscreen. Apart from reducing visibility, it's a particular threat when fixing your position by a single light source. When little or no light is on the surface and a prominent one comes into view, it may seem that the light is above the horizon, which could lead you to pitch into a steep attitude in keeping with the resulting false horizon. The light source may also appear to change colour. Autokinesis gives the illusion that an object is moving, when it is actually your eye, typically encountered when staring at a single light in the dark. It could make you think that a star is an aircraft.

Sometimes the effect is not much more than an uncomfortable climbing sensation even when you're straight and level, but an obscured windscreen could make objects appear lower than they really are. This will be more apparent with high intensity runway lighting, which may also give you the same effect that actors have on stage, where they can't see the audience through the bright lighting. The lack of normal contrast will also upset your altitude perception, making you feel further away and higher than you are. *Distortion* occurs when viewing objects through a windshield covered with rain, where water is thicker near the bottom (nearer to the windshield), causing a *prismatic effect* - like looking through a base-down prism, which tends to make objects look higher or closer. Raindrops on a windscreen can double the apparent size of lights outside and make you think you are closer.

The solution is to use every piece of sensory information you can, including landing lights and instruments (if you keep two lights in view, and the lower one goes out of sight, your view of it has been obstructed, so go up until you see them both again).

NIGHT MYOPIA AND NIGHT PRESBYOPIA

Night myopia (nearsightedness), also known as *twilight myopia*, causes some people who are slightly myopic in daylight to become more so after dark.

Presbyopia is a condition in which the crystalline lens of your eye loses its flexibility, which makes it difficult to focus on close objects. Also known as *red light presbyopia*, night presbyopia occurs in presbyopic individuals who are subjected to red light, which is found in some cockpits during night operations. Red light has the longest wavelength, so when you try to read instruments or charts in red light, the demand for accommodation is more than if you were using white light, making it difficult to read small print. In effect, your depth of field is reduced.

Vitamin A deficiency can cause night blindness because it is needed for the regeneration of visual purple. Night vision can be reduced above 8,000 ft.

SPACE MYOPIA

Also known as *Empty Field Myopia*, this describes myopia experienced when there is nothing to look at outside the cockpit. For example, when flying VFR on top, clouds prevent you from seeing the ground, and the light they reflect reduces your visual cues. Your eyes will tend to lock-in on the instruments and remain fixated for that distance, so when you look outside, *the resulting myopia could stop you seeing other aircraft.* Look at the wingtips from time to time to allow relaxation of the *ciliary muscles* (the ones that control the shape of the lens for near and far vision).

DESIGN EYE REFERENCE POINT

The DERP allows crews to obtain the best visibility outside and inside. The pilot compartment should be designed for a clear, undistorted, and adequate external field of vision, so seats need to be adjusted to position your eyes as close to the DERP as possible for the best views while manipulating the controls. You should be aware of the hazards and compromises associated with seating positions away from the DERP. It should be set up before flight.

SUNNIES

Pilots are exposed to higher light levels, if only because light is reflected back from cloud tops. In addition, light at altitude contains more of the damaging blue and ultra-violet wavelengths. When flying towards the Sun, the eyes cannot adjust quickly to the instrument panel that is in the relative shade, which causes eyestrain and can be tiring. All are good reasons for using sunglasses.

The requirement for good sunglasses is to absorb enough visible light to eliminate glare without decreasing visual acuity, absorb UV and IR radiation and absorb all colours equally. A neutral-grey lens with 15% transmission (following British Standard 2724) would appear to be the most suitable, as it virtually eliminates invisible electromagnetic radiation. It is also recommended that sunglasses be made from scratch-resistant hard-coated polycarbonate with thin metal frames. Photochromic lenses are generally not advised because they take too long to change over (up to 30 minutes for bleaching time), but even when fully bleached, they still absorb slightly more light than untinted lenses. Their operation also depends on UV light which is screened by the windscreen. Polaroids should be avoided in digital cockpits.

The Ears (Vestibular System)

The ears allow you to hear and assist you to maintain balance. They are important because an auditory stimulus is the one most often attended to. How many times do you answer the phone when you're busy, even though you've ignored everything else for hours?

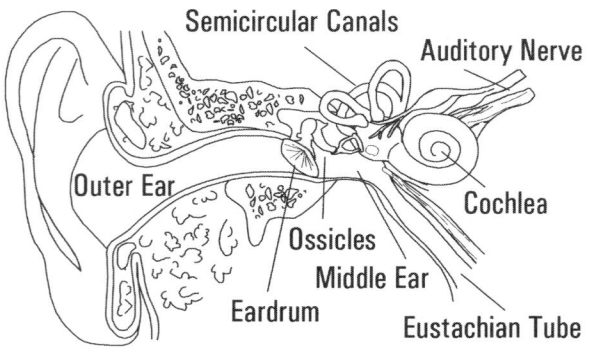

The eardrum is the boundary between the outer ear and the inner ear. Sound waves make the eardrum vibrate, and the vibrations are transmitted by a chain of linked bones in the middle ear known as the *hammer, anvil* and *stirrup* (collectively, the *ossicles*) to the *cochlea* in the inner ear (via the *oval window*), which is full of fluid. As you climb and outside air pressure reduces, the eardrum will bulge outwards, and *vice versa*. Such pressures can affect the balance mechanism. The difference in pressures is equalised by air leaking out through the *Eustachian Tubes,* which are canals that connect the throat with the middle ear; and their purpose is to equalise air pressure. When you swallow, the tubes open, allowing air to enter, which is why swallowing helps to clear the ears when changing altitude. Blocked Eustachian tubes can be responsible for split eardrums, due to the inability to equalise pressure. Since the eardrum takes around 6 weeks to heal, the best solution is not to go flying with a cold, but commercial pressures don't always allow that. If you have to, make sure you use a decongestant with no side effects.

The cochlea is the coiled bit in the right hand side of the diagram above - it is a tube which narrows progressively. There are thousands of fibres (*cupula*) of different lengths inside it which vibrate in sympathy at various frequencies.

The fibres are linked to the brain and, as with sight, it is now, when the signal reaches the brain, that we "hear". Ear defenders reduce noise levels by up to 40 dbA and ear plugs by only about 20 - of course, wearing either doesn't help with communication!

As some of the fibres get damaged (through too severe vibration), the ability to hear the frequency they cover goes (they do not regenerate). You can recover from some deafness, such as that caused by illness, but not that caused by damage to the fibres in the fluid. See *Deafness.*

The *semicircular canals* are what we use to keep balanced *on the ground*, because they monitor angular accelerations. However, orientation in the air depends largely on vision, discussed under *Disorientation*, below. The canals are arranged at right angles to each other and use the fluid in the *inner ear*, which acts against sensory hairs with chalky deposits on the end to send electrical signals to the brain so you can tell which way is up. The semicircular canals sense angular acceleration, while the *otolith organs* on the top of the cochlea in the inner ear pick up changes in linear movement. The otolith organs consist of the *utricle*, for horizontal movement, and the *saccule*, for vertical.

The inertia of otoliths (which are small particles made up of a gelatinous matrix and calcium carbonate in the viscous fluid of the saccule and utricle) causes them to stimulate hair cells when the head moves. The hair cells send signals down sensory nerve fibres which are interpreted by the brain as motion. The problem is that, because our bodies are designed to operate on the ground,

the vestibular system is more suited to stop-go motion and cannot register sustained motion very well.

Additional sources of positional information include *somatosensory receptors* inside the skin, joints and muscles. As they respond to pressure and stretching signals, they can be an important source of information about your equilibrium. They are called the "seat of the pants" sense because it was thought that you could tell which way was up by the seat of your pants sensing the most pressure. *The seat of the pants sense is completely unreliable as an attitude indicator when your body is moving in the aerial environment.*

The audible range of the human ear is 20 Hz to 20 KHz, with the most sensitive range between 750-3000 Hz.

DEAFNESS

Hearing actually depends on the proper working of the *eighth cranial nerve*, which carries signals from the inner ear to the brain. Obviously, if this gets damaged, deafness results. The nerve doesn't have to be severed, though; deterioration will occur if you don't get enough Vitamin B-Complex (deafness is a symptom of beriberi or pellagra, for example, which comes from Vitamin B deficiency).

There are three types of hearing loss:

- **Sensori-neural**, where the ability to process sound is lost. In aviation, high-tone deafness from sustained exposure to jet engines is very common. *Noise Induced Hearing Loss,* or NIHL, occurs through prolonged exposure to loud noise, usually 90 db and above.

- **Conductive Hearing Loss** is caused by interference with the transmission of sound waves from the outer to the inner ear. In other words, it is damage to the physical hearing mechanism (middle ear bones), which can include hardened ear wax!

- **Presbycusis**. Age-related hearing loss, where the high tones go first.

DISORIENTATION

A feeling of turning detected by the inner ear, but not confirmed by the eyes, frequently produces nausea.

Disorientation refers to a loss of your bearings in relation to position or movement, and it is more likely to happen when you are subject to colds, in IMC, and frequently changing between inside and outside visual references. The "leans" is the classic case, which occur because your semicircular canals get used to a particular sustained motion in a very short time. If you start a turn and keep it going, your canals will think this is normal, because they lag, or are slow to respond. When you straighten up, they will try to tell you you're turning, where you're actually flying straight and level, to create a *vestibular illusion*. Your natural inclination is to obey your senses, but your

instruments are there as a cross-reference. In fact, the whole point of instrument training is to overcome your dependence on your senses. Particularly dangerous is recovering from a spin of 2-3 turns, where, without visual reference, you think you are actually turning the opposite way and enter another spin when you try to correct it. Eventually an extreme nose-up condition results, which turns into an extreme nose-down attitude and a tight graveyard spiral before entering Terrain Impact Mode. To combat the leans, close your eyes and shake your head vigorously from side to side for a couple of seconds, which will topple the semi-circular canals (the official answer is *to rely on your instruments*).

When flying, you are always subject to illusions, especially when carrying out extreme manoeuvres and/or at night. The input from your senses is interpreted (rightly or wrongly) by both your conscious and subconscious minds. The former handles the visual aspects, and the latter all the rest, through the peripheral nervous system, part of which, if you remember, runs your body automatically. When the subconscious becomes confused about your position in space (it assumes you are on the ground), the only link between you and reality is the visual system linked to the conscious mind, which is a lot slower and less capable in its processing ability. This is why you must rely on your instruments when you get disorientated.

During linear acceleration, you can get the impression of pitching up or climbing (*somatogravic illusion*), making you want to push the nose down. This is because the fluid in the inner ear flows backwards. The eyes help to overcome this, but at night, with no visual clues, say on takeoff, this can be mistaken for a steep climb in which you put the nose down and could hit the ground. You get a pitch-down illusion from deceleration. The danger here is that lowering the gear or flaps causes the machine to slow down, which makes you think you are pitching down and want to bring the nose up, which could cause a stall at the wrong moment on approach.

In fact the brain gets its information from the eyes, the inner ear (otoliths), and positioning of the skeleton and muscles (proprioceptive clues)

The *coriolis illusion* with relation to vertigo is easily demonstrated with a revolving chair - sit in one, and get someone to spin it while you have your chin on your breast. When you raise your head sharply, you will find yourself on the floor inside two seconds. This has obvious parallels with flying, so make all your head movements as gently as possible, especially when making turns in IMC, or picking up a pen from the cockpit floor (mention of fluid, above, implies that if you are dehydrated, you may also get spatial disorientation - if you feel thirsty, you are probably already 5% there).

The Respiratory System

The respiratory system consists of two lungs, an oronasal passage, pharynx, larynx, trachea, bronchi, bronchioles and alveoli.

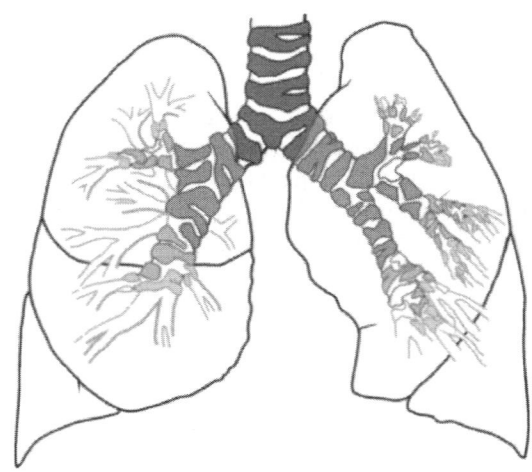

The two lungs are separated by the heart, airways and the major blood vessels in the centre of the chest, all of which are enclosed by the chest wall, which is a combination of ribs, cartilage and muscle. Each lung is covered by a thin, moist tissue called the *pleura*, which also lines the chest wall. The lungs and chest wall are elastic, but as you breathe in and out, the lungs recoil inward while your chest wall expands outward. These two opposing forces create a negative pressure in the pleural space between the rib cage and lung. If air enters that space, from in- or outside the lungs, the pressure can cause all or part of the affected lung to collapse.

The whole system performs various functions, including:

- acting as a blood filter or reservoir

- acting as an air filter, warmer and humidifier

- contributing to heat loss through ventilation

Internal Respiration exists when the chest cavity is expanded or contracted by the actions of the intercostal muscles and the diaphragm so that air rushes into the lungs to fill the empty space (or rushes out), due to the pressure gradients created between the mouth or nose and the alveoli, from where oxygen is diffused (actually, pushed, under pressure) into the *haemoglobin* in the blood (haemoglobin is a protein molecule). This takes place 12-15 times a minute at rest (some say 18), exchanging about ½ ltr on average. This *tidal volume* (also known as V_T) is the volume of an individual breath (in and out).

CAPT

*The alveoli are the final branchings of the respiratory tree that act as the primary gas exchange units in the lung. The oxygen in the lung has to get across a thin membrane to reach the blood in the alveoli. The gas-blood barrier between the alveolar space and the pulmonary capillaries is extremely thin, to allow for a rapid exchange. To reach the blood, oxygen must diffuse through the *alveolar epithelium*, a thin interstitial space, and the *capillary endothelium*. The waste product, CO_2, is carried by the blood mainly as sodium bicarbonate, and broken down by enzymes. When CO_2 is released, it is diffused into the alveoli and breathed out.

Breathing is controlled by the autonomic nervous system, but it can change according to your activity. Breathe with your stomach and chest - not only does this fill the lungs better, but it also stimulates blood flow in the liver.

The oxygen thus absorbed is carried to the tissues of the body, especially the brain, which is the most sensitive organ to its lack. The blood is then pumped around the body by the heart. Waste products in the form of carbon dioxide go the other way, via plasma to the lungs, or *from the blood to the alveoli* - it is the carbon dioxide (and acidity) level in the blood that regulates respiration, which is monitored by several chemical receptors in the brain that are very sensitive to CO_2.

The air inspired per minute is *respiratory minute volume*.

The maximum amount of gas you can hold in your lungs after breathing in is predictably called the *total lung capacity*, which is typically 6½ litres for a healthy adult. Normal breathing involves volumes of half that, or 3-3½ ltrs.

It consists of four volumes:

• Tidal Volume

• Inspiratory Reserve Volume

• Expiratory Reserve Volume

• Residual Volume

The diffusion of oxygen into the blood depends on *partial pressure* (that is, its pressure in proportion to its presence in the mix - it follows *Henry's Law* and, presumably, *Dalton's*) so, as this falls, oxygen assimilation is impaired. Although the air gets thinner, the ratio of gases remains the same, so there is still 21% oxygen at 35 000. However, even if you increase the proportion of oxygen to 100% as you climb, there is an altitude (around 33 700 feet) where the pressure is so low that the partial pressure is actually less than that at sea level, so just having oxygen is not enough, because, as altitude increases, the partial pressure of water vapour and carbon dioxide in the lungs also remains the same, reducing the partial pressure of oxygen in the lungs still further (the partial pressure of CO_2 in the alveoli is *lower*

than it is in the blood). Also, at altitude, other gases dissolved in the blood, such as nitrogen, may bubble out and cause the bends or similar effects.

From 0-10 000 ft you can survive on normal air; above this, you need more oxygen, up to 33 700 feet, when you need pure oxygen to survive (breathing 100% oxygen at that height is the same as breathing at sea level. At 40 000' it is the equivalent of breathing air at 10 000 feet). Above 40 000 the oxygen needs pressure, meaning that you must exhale by force (also, exposure to 0_3 becomes significant).

Having said all that, your learning ability can be compromised as low as 6 000 feet (*Source*: RAF).

Breathing	First Signs	Death
Air'	10,000 ft	22,000 ft
100% Oxygen'	38,000 ft	43,000 ft
Pressure Oxygen	45,000 ft	50,000 ft

THE ATMOSPHERE

Life exists in the biosphere, of which the *atmosphere* is one component. The other two are the *lithosphere* (the solid part of the Earth) and the *hydrosphere* (all the water, including water vapour). The biosphere is within, and influenced by, the atmosphere, which is an ocean of gases that surrounds the Earth. 21% of it, luckily for us, is oxygen, but 78% is nitrogen (N_2), with 1% of odds and ends, like argon (0.9%) and CO_2 (0.03%), and others, that need not concern us here, plus bits of dust and the odd pollutant, and water in various forms in suspension (the nitrogen, as an inert gas, keeps the proportion of oxygen down, since it is actually quite corrosive).

Normally, because of the constant mixing, these proportions remain constant (in dry air) up to about 80 km, but there are exceptions:

• **Water**. 2% of the Earth's total water supply can be found suspended in the atmosphere as:

    • a gas (water vapour)

    • a liquid (clouds or rain)

    • a solid (ice)

Because it weighs five-eighths of an equivalent amount of dry air, water vapour will also reduce the density of the air and your engine's punch, but that's the subject of the *Performance* chapter. The water vapour content on average is around 1%, but can get as high as 4%. *The troposphere (the lower part of the atmosphere) contains more than 90% of all water vapour*. The presence of water is expressed as *relative humidity*, and its importance lies in the energy that is released and consumed as it changes from gas to liquid to ice and back.

- **Ozone**. 0.001%. This is toxic, and the main gaseous constituent of airborne pollution

- **Carbon Dioxide** (CO_2). 0.05%. This absorbs infrared radiation and allegedly contributes to the greenhouse effect, described later

If the air wasn't continually being stirred up, the heavier gases would simply sink to the lower levels.

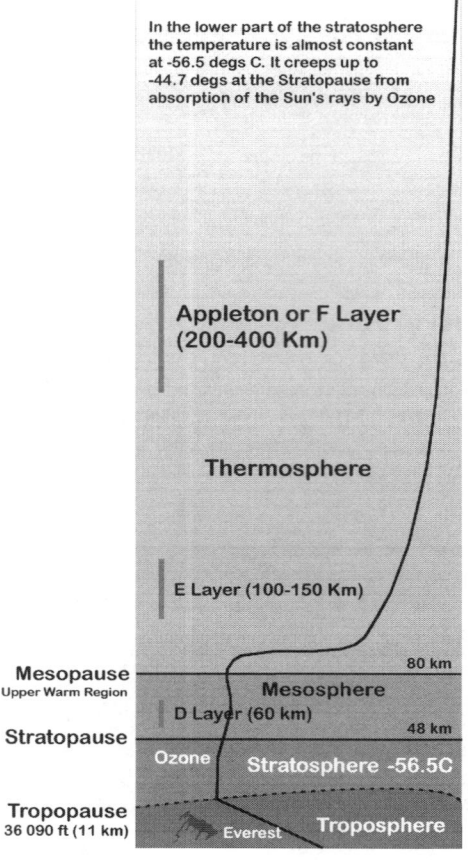

In the lower part of the stratosphere the temperature is almost constant at -56.5 degs C. It creeps up to -44.7 degs at the Stratopause from absorption of the Sun's rays by Ozone

Appleton or F Layer (200-400 Km)

Thermosphere

E Layer (100-150 Km)

80 km

Mesopause
Upper Warm Region

Mesosphere

D Layer (60 km)

48 km

Stratopause

Ozone

Stratosphere -56.5C

Tropopause
36 090 ft (11 km)

Everest

Troposphere

Thus, the atmosphere provides oxygen for us to breathe, and filters out harmful cosmic rays, aside from helping to regulate the Earth's temperature. It is split into four concentric(ish) gaseous areas, according to the mean variation of temperature with height. Starting from the bottom, these are the *troposphere*, *stratosphere*, *mesosphere* and *thermosphere*, although the last two are not of much concern to the average pilot. The first two are, however, and the boundary (or transition zone) between them is the *tropopause*, where any clouds are made of ice crystals.

In the lower levels of the stratosphere, the temperature is mostly constant with height, but you can detect a gradual increase above 20 km because there is a layer of ozone that absorbs ultra violet radiation from the Sun. When you're up that high, the ozone levels are above toxic limits, so the air needs to be filtered (and monitored) before it comes into the cabin (most UV radiation is absorbed by ozone in the stratosphere, whilst water vapour in the lower atmosphere absorbs much of the near Infra Red).

HUMIDITY

To function properly, the human body requires a certain amount of humidity, which concerns the amount of invisible water (vapour) contained in a parcel of air. The *absolute humidity* is the actual mass, expressed in grams per cubic metre (i.e. as a volume). For a particular temperature, the *relative humidity* is a measure of how much moisture an air parcel is holding against the maximum possible at that temperature (and pressure) or, in other words, the *percentage saturation*, which will *decrease* if the air gets warmer, as when subsiding in a high pressure area, because temperature is raised by compression, and it can absorb more moisture. Thus, the amount of water vapour that air can hold is determined by the temperature.

THE GENERAL GAS LAWS

A gas has three variables - *pressure, density** and *temperature*, which are all intimately related. For example, if a gas were restrained in a rigid container (so the volume doesn't change), increasing the temperature increases the pressure inside it, and *vice versa*. If the container were not rigid, the volume could change instead, and affect the gas's density. Air density affects aircraft performance.

*Density, which is the mass of air occupying a given volume, depends on pressure, temperature and humidity. Density and pressure are directly related, and density and temperature are inversely related. Density and humidity are also inversely related as water has less mass than air.

An ideal gas is one that obeys the gas laws, although no gas is really ideal, but they are considered to be so in low subsonic flow, which is about 40% of the speed of sound.

The *kinetic theory of gases* (from Maxwell, after Bernoulli's ideas) states that gases are comprised of molecules that are in constant motion, and their properties depend on this motion. The *volume* of a gas is the space through which molecules are free to move.

The average kinetic energy increases with temperature, and *vice versa* (this also applies to liquids and solids). Contributions to the kinetic theory of gases include:

- **Charles'** Law, from a frenchman, Jacques Charles, which states that, if the *pressure* remains constant, there is a proportionate change in temperature with volume, meaning that, the hotter a gas gets, the more space it takes up, or the more you compress it into a smaller space, the hotter it gets, and *vice versa*. If you double the temperature of a gas, you double its volume. This law helped Charles make the first meteorological flight in a balloon, taking a barometer with which to work out his height.

CAPT

If this page is a photocopy, it is not authorised!

- **Boyle**, an Irish physicist, discovered that, for a perfect gas, if *temperature* remains constant, the volume of a gas varies inversely with its pressure, so if you double the pressure of a gas, you halve its volume. Thus, density is directly proportional to pressure, so if density doubles, so does pressure

- **Dalton** says that the total pressure of a mixture of gases is the same as the sum of the *partial pressures* exerted by each of the gases in the mixture, assuming they don't react chemically with each other, which is relevant when it comes to dealing with oxygen. In other words, each gas's pressure contributes a part of the total according to its constituent proportion, or exerts the same pressure that it would do on its own, and the total pressure of the mixture is equal to their sum. This allows meteorologists to figure out how much water vapour there is in a given parcel of air

Boyle's and Charles' laws are only accurate within small temperature ranges - otherwise it's 3 or 5%, which is close enough, but pressure, volume and temperature very rarely stay still. When they all change at once, you must use a combination of Boyle's and Charles' laws, in that order.

OXYGEN

Pure oxygen is a colourless, tasteless, odourless and *non-combustible* gas that takes up about 21% of the air we breathe (it is actually quite corrosive - it belongs to the same chemical family as chlorine and fluorine, so too much is toxic). Although it doesn't burn itself, it does support combustion, which is why we need it, because the body turns food into heat, in the process producing water and waste as by-products of burning fats. As we can't store oxygen, we survive from breath to breath.

How much you use depends on your physical activity and/or mental stress - for example, you need 4 times more for walking than sitting quietly. The proportion of oxygen to air (21%) actually remains constant up to about 9 km, but its *partial pressure decreases* because the barometric pressure does. However, water vapour and CO_2 have a constant partial pressure, so you can see that, at some point, they will restrict the partial pressure of oxygen. The percentage fraction of air in alveolar air is 15%.

At about 15 240 m (49 707 feet), the combined pressure of water vapour and CO_2 in the lungs is more or less equal to barometric pressure and gas exchange is not possible. At 19 202 m (62 630 feet), when the water vapour pressure of body fluids equals the barometric pressure, bubbles form in just about every part of the body that contains a liquid (ebullism). In short, the liquids in your body start to boil!

Normally, air pressure forces oxygen into the blood, so the higher you go, the less effective this will be. The net result is that you must use oxygen when the cabin pressure is lower than 10 000 feet. No extra oxygen is needed below 5 000 feet, as 95% of what you would find on the ground is there. However, at over 8 000 feet, you may find measurable changes in blood pressure and respiration, although healthy people should perform OK.

Lack of oxygen leads to.......

HYPOXIA

This is a condition where the oxygen concentration in the blood is below normal, or where oxygen cannot be used by the body, but anaemia can produce the same effect, as can alcohol. There are several types of hypoxia:

- *Hypoxic Hypoxia* arises from insufficient partial pressure, and is what people normally mean when they refer to the subject in general

- *Anaemic Hypoxia* is a reduction in the blood's carrying capacity

- *Stagnant (Ischaemic) Hypoxia* - poor blood circulation

- *Histotoxic Hypoxia* exists where the body cannot utilise oxygen, possibly due to toxics, like cyanide

So, there may really be too little oxygen, or you don't have enough blood (haemoglobin) to carry what oxygen you need around the body - you may have donated some, or have an ulcer. You might also be a smoker, with your haemoglobin affected by carbon monoxide (*anaemic hypoxia*). A blockage of 5-8%, typical for a heavy smoker, gives an equivalent altitude of 5-7000 feet before you get airborne! Short-term memory impairment starts at 12 000 feet. In short, hypoxia is a *reduced partial pressure* in the lungs. To help compensate for it, *descend below 10,000 feet*, *breathe 100% oxygen* and *reduce your activity*.

The effects of hypoxia are similar to those of alcohol, but classic signs are:

- *Personality changes*. You get jolly, aggressive and less inhibited

- *Judgement changes*. Your abilities are impaired; you think you can do anything with less self-criticism

- *Muscle movement*. Becomes sluggish, not in tune with your mind

- *Short-term memory loss*, leading to reliance on training, or long-term memory

- *Sensory loss*. Blindness occurs (colour first), then touch, orientation and hearing

- *Loss of consciousness*. You get confused first, then semi-conscious, then unconscious

- *Blueness*

In summary, you can expect *fast & heavy breathing*, *impairment of vision, muscles* and *judgement*.

The above are *subjective* signs, so they need to be recognised by the person actually suffering from hypoxia, who is in the wrong state to recognise anything. External observers may notice some of them, but especially lips and fingertips turning blue and possible hyperventilation (see later) as the victim tries to get more oxygen. However, the normal reaction to lack of oxygen, such as panting, does not appear, because there is no excess CO_2. As with carbon monoxide poisoning, the onset of hypoxia is insidious and can be recognised only by being very aware of the symptoms, which are aggravated by:

- *Altitude*. Less oxygen, less pressure
- *Time*. The more exposure, the greater the effect
- *Exercise*. Increases energy and oxygen usage
- *Cold*. Increases energy and oxygen usage
- *Illness*. Increases energy and oxygen usage
- *Fatigue*. Symptoms arise earlier
- *Drugs* or *alcohol*. Reduced tolerance
- *Smoking*. Haemoglobin has an affinity for CO (carbon monoxide) 210-250 times that of oxygen

PRESSURE CHANGES (BAROTRAUMA)

Aside from oxygen, the body contains gases of varying descriptions in many places; some occur naturally, and some are created by the body's normal working processes. The problem is that these gases expand and contract as the aircraft climbs and descends. Some need a way out, and some need a way back as well.

- Gas in the ears normally vents via the Eustachian tubes. If these are blocked (say with a cold), the pressure on either side of the eardrum is not balanced, which could lead (at the very least) to considerable pain, and (at worst) a ruptured eardrum. It is called *aerotitis*.

- Sinus* cavities are also vulnerable to imbalances of pressure, and are affected in the same way as eardrums are. A *aerosinusitis* is caused by differences in pressure between the sinus cavity and the ambient air.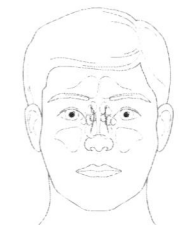

- Gas in the gut can be vented from both ends

- Teeth may have small pockets of air in them, if filled, together with the gums.

*Although associated with the nose, the *sinuses* are hollow spaces or cavities inside the head surrounding the base of the nose and the eye sockets. Amongst other things, they act as sound boxes for the voice. Being hollow, they provide structural strength whilst keeping the head light;

there are normally between 15-20 of them. Blockages arise from fluid that can't escape through the narrow passages - pain results from fluid pressure. Blocked sinuses can give you severe headaches, and you will get them from a bad cold. Changes are similar to those of the middle ear, but they are affected equally by ascents or descents.

MOTION SICKNESS

Vertigo is the result of *Coriolis Effect* from a mismatch between the information sent to the brain by the eyes and ears. Accelerating from straight and level flight may give the impression of pitching up (climbing), because the sensors in the inner ear perceive the body's weight as going rearwards and downwards. As the most dependable source of sensory information is your eyes, believe your instruments. *Pilot's Vertigo* is dizziness and a tumbling sensation from making head movements in a tight turn, or a sensation of rotation coming from multiple irritation of several semicircular canals. Airsickness can also be caused by vibration, when the body (i.e. the skull), is vibrated at frequencies less than 0.5Hz, common in turbulence. Keeping the head still and closing the eyes helps.

Medications and alcohol can have similar effects. It's well known that lying down when drunk causes the ceiling to revolve, and this can lead to stationary objects appearing to move when standing upright. This is because the brain detects the movement of fluid in the inner ear and tries to rationalise things through the eyes. In other words, eye movements are used to compensate for head movement - the difference between the specific gravities of alcohol and inner fluid is enough to cause the sensors to move and be wrongly interpreted as a head movement. Since your head is not really moving, it looks as if the rest of the world is.

DECOMPRESSION SICKNESS

Where pressures are low, nitrogen in the blood comes out of solution, just like when you open a fizzy drink. Bubbles can form, and are especially painful in the joints, as you find with the *bends*. Other symptoms include the *creeps* (skin), *chokes* (lungs) and the *staggers* (brain). All this derives from *Henry's Law*. Unfortunately, the bubbles do not redissolve on descent, so if you are affected you may need to go into a decompression chamber. At the very least, you should *descend as low as you can and land as soon as possible*.

Diving before flight should be avoided, as extra nitrogen is absorbed while breathing pressurised gas, which dissolves out as you surface again. If you go flying too soon, this is accentuated, and the symptoms can appear as low as 8,000 feet. A diver 30 feet under water is under twice the normal sea level pressure. Don't fly for 12 hours if the depth is less than 30 feet, or 24 hours if it is over 30 feet.

Factors that *decrease* resistance to DCS include *SCUBA diving*, *obesity* and *old age*. If you get pains in the joints *within a few hours of landing*, see a doctor as soon as possible.

CAPT

TIME OF USEFUL CONSCIOUSNESS

Note: It is dangerous to fly above 10,000 feet without using additional oxygen or being in a pressurised cabin.

When you climb, oxygen levels fall, but the CO_2 levels in your blood do not, and the brain does not know it has to compensate. Also known as *Effective Performance Time*, the times of useful consciousness (from interruption of the oxygen supply to when you are exposed to hypoxia) are quite short, being the amount of time you can perform flying duties efficiently with inadequate oxygen supply, or the time from the interruption of the supply or exposure to an oxygen-poor environment, to the time when useful function is lost (it is *not* the time to total unconsciousness). Officially, it is: *The time during which you can act with physical and mental efficiency and alertness from when you are exposed to hypoxia,* or *when you lose the available oxygen supply.*

HYPERVENTILATION

The balance of O_2 against CO_2 in the body affects the alkaline/acidic properties of the blood, which in turn affects the rate of breathing - their ratio is detected by a part of the brain which regulates breathing.

Hyperventilation is simply overbreathing, caused by exhaling more than you are inhaling. The excess oxygen causes CO_2 to be washed out of the bloodstream, so that the plasma gets too alkaline, and the arteries reduce in size, meaning that less blood gets to the brain.

The usual cause is worry, fright or sudden shock, but hypoxia can be a factor - in fact, the symptoms are similar to hypoxia and include:

- Dizziness
- Pins and needles, tingling
- Blurred sight
- Hot/Cold feelings
- Anxiety
- Impaired performance
- Loss of consciousness

The last one is actually one of the best cures, since the body's automatic systems take over to restore normality. Whenever you are unsure of whether you are suffering from hyperventilation or hypoxia, treat for hypoxia, since this will almost always be the root cause - reach for the oxygen mask. You can treat hyperventilation by talking aloud through the procedure to calm the emotions and reduce the rate of breathing.

The Cardiovascular System

This is actually a double system which is joined at the heart. There is one circulation to the lungs (pulmonary) and one to the rest of the body (systemic). It consists of the heart, arteries, arterioles, capillaries, veins (over many miles!) and blood, and provides a transport system that links the external environment to the tissues and distributes essential substances, such as hormones, oxygen and nutrients around the body. It also removes carbon dioxide and other waste products from the tissues and delivers them to the lungs, kidneys and liver.

The system can anticipate physiological and metabolic demands by increasing heart action before it is required.

THE HEART

This item is pear-shaped, and found lying slightly to the left inside the thoracic cavity. It is surrounded by a protective membrane which contains a fluid filled cavity called the *pericardium*, which prevents friction between the heart and the surrounding tissues.

The heart has 2 pumps, side by side, each with an *atrium* (at the top) and a *ventricle* (underneath), and separated by the *septum*. There is normally no direct transfer of blood between them. The "pacemaker" is in the right atrium.

Oxygen-rich haemoglobin in the red blood cells passes from the alveolar capillaries into the pulmonary vein and enters the left atrium at low pressure. It is pumped into the left ventricle and than at high pressure into the systemic circulation via the aorta, which is the body's main artery, so the left ventricle has the thickest muscle walls. The weight of blood above the height of the heart returns the deoxygenated blood through gravity to the right atrium, then the right ventricle to the lungs. The rest comes up through a combination of non-return valves and muscular action (many large veins lie between muscles). Chest movements also have a syphon effect.

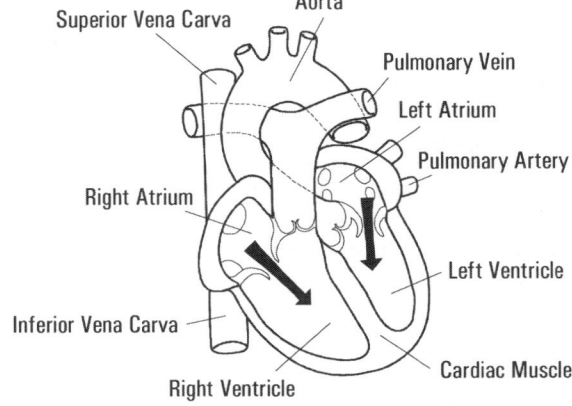

The muscle walls get their own blood from the *coronary arteries*. Cardiac muscle can contract rhythmically without nervous input, in a *myogenic rhythm*. Thus, the pumps do their work in phase, but deliver blood in series, throughout the body in one direction only.

Arteries carry oxygenated blood *from* the heart to the body (the *pulmonary artery* goes straight to the lungs) whilst veins return blood *to* the heart (again, the pulmonary vein has a direct connection from the lungs) at a lower pressure. Arteries eventually turn into *arterioles* which eventually break up into minute vessels called *capillaries* that allow the diffusion of small molecular substances like oxygen, vitamins, minerals, water and amino acids to nourish cells. Carbon dioxide and water pass the other way in a process called *capillary exchange.*

Note that, although blood from the heart is oxygenated, and that to the heart is de-oxygenated, the pulmonaries are reversed. In other words, pulmonary circulation carries deoxygenated blood from the right side of the heart to the lungs, and oxygenated blood back to the left side of the heart. The systemic circulation carries oxygenated blood from the left side of the heart to the head and body. The right side receives deoxygenated blood from the body, so oxygenated and deoxygenated blood is kept separate - the blood alternates between the two circulations.

The rate of contraction, or *pulse rate*, is around 72 (70-80) beats a minute when at rest. The pulse rate is influenced by *adrenalin*, *physical exercise* and the *treatment of glucose in the blood.* As the ventricle pumps about 70 ml of blood per beat, *cardiac output* is about 5 litres a minute (actually 4.9-5.3). Cardiac output is the volume of blood pumped per minute by each ventricle, and represents the total blood flow through the pulmonary and systemic circuits. It comes from the *stroke volume* and *heart rate* (increments in heart rate contribute more than stroke volume).

BLOOD

This is a liquid made up of:

- 55% colourless plasma, for transporting CO_2, nutrients and hormones, and

- 45% blood cells, which come in three varieties. *Red cells* transport oxygen via *haemoglobin*, and *white cells* (*leukocytes*) fight infection. *Platelets* are for clotting blood. All are produced in *bone marrow*, which capacity diminishes as we grow older

CO_2 in solution forms a weak carbonic acid which also helps to maintain the blood's acid balance. The amount of haemoglobin in the blood depends on the amount of oxygen in the lungs. Reductions in the amount of haemoglobin available reduces the blood's ability to transport oxygen (to cause anaemia). This could arise from either less red blood cells or the concentration of haemoglobin in them.

ANAEMIA

Anaemia means that you do not have enough functional haemoglobin, there being too few red blood cells, and a limited capacity to transport oxygen (more iron often cures it). *Anaemic Hypoxia* is the lack of oxygen resulting from anaemia.

BLOOD PRESSURE

This is the amount of force that the blood exerts on the vessel walls. It is sensed by bundles of nerves in cavities called *sinuses.* There are two sets in the main arteries to the brain, and another on the aorta, the *carotid* and *aortic sinus pressoreceptors,*

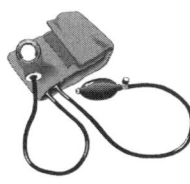

respectively, but you knew that already. The brain varies secretions of two hormones in response to their signals, to regulate blood pressure by narrowing the arteries. As with electricity, the rate of blood flow through a vessel depends on the pressure gradient from one end to the other, plus the resistance encountered (which works the same way, too, in terms of series *vs* parallel!) The resistance to blood flow depends on the *vessel dimensions* and *blood viscosity.*

The *systolic blood pressure* is the peak pressure as blood is pumped from the left ventricle into the aorta. The *diastolic pressure* is the lowest, produced when resting between beats - it is an indication of the resistance of the small arteries and capillaries to blood flow, or the load against which the heart has to work. The World Health Organisation says that "normal" blood pressure lies between 100-139 mmHg (systolic) and 60-89 mmHg (diastolic) - something like 120/80 (120 over 80). However, "standard" values are 100 and 60 mg, or 100/60, with the limits regarded as 160 and 100 mmHg, or 160/100. The higher the figures are, the harder the heart is working, and the greater is the risk of stroke and coronary heart disease.

As you get older, the systolic pressure should be roughly 100 plus your age in years. The arterial pressure in the *upper arm* is equivalent to the pressure in the heart, which is why it is used to check your pressure in medicals. The heart does not rest in the same way as do other muscles - instead, it takes a mini-rest for a microsecond or two in between beats. Heart muscles get their own blood from the *pulmonary arteries.*

Blood pressure has important links to diabetes (below).

HYPERTENSION & HYPOTENSION

This is known as a silent killer, as blood pressure is persistently elevated with no external symptoms - blood vessel walls, heart and other organs may be severely damaged without you knowing. It is the culmination of many factors, including your weight, diet, bad habits and family history. There is no cure, but prevention is possible.

Hypotension, on the other hand, is any blood pressure that is below the normal expected for given environment. It is a relative term because blood pressure normally varies greatly anyway with *activity, age, medications* and *underlying medical conditions*. Neurological conditions that can lead to low blood pressure include: changing your position from lying down to the more vertical (*postural hypotension*), stroke, shock, light-headedness after urinating or defecating, Parkinson's disease, neuropathy and simply fright. Non-neurologic conditions that can cause it include: bleeding, infections, dehydration, heart disease, adrenal insufficiency, pregnancy, prolonged bed rest, poisoning, toxic shock syndrome and blood transfusion reactions.

DEEP VEIN THROMBOSIS (DVT)

This is a blood clot (thrombus) that develops *inside* a deep vein, usually in the lower leg, but also the arm, where it can cause pain. Blood clots that form in superficial veins that lie under the skin are called *superficial thrombophlebitis* and are much less serious.

In most cases, the clots are small and do not cause any symptoms, as the body can gradually break down the clot. However, larger clots may partially or totally block the blood flow in the vein and cause symptoms such as:

- swelling of the calf, which is usually different from the mild ankle swelling that many people get during long haul flights

- pain in the calf, or calf pain that is noticeable, or worse when standing or walking

Although they are not always a sign of DVT, if you experience them, you should seek medical advice. There is evidence that long haul flights (i.e. lasting four hours or more) may increase the risk of DVT as a result of prolonged immobility, which can happen during any form of long distance travel, whether by car, bus, train or air. Potential complications include:

- *Pulmonary embolism*, when a piece of the blood clot breaks off and travels in the bloodstream to become lodged in the lungs and block blood flow, hours or even days afterwards. It may cause chest pain and shortness of breath

- *Post thrombotic syndrome* happens if a DVT damages the valves in the vein, so that instead of flowing upwards, the blood pools in the lower leg. This can result in pain, swelling and ulcers on the leg

Anticoagulant medicines are the most common treatment, which alter certain chemicals in the blood to stop clots forming so easily. Otherwise, you should:

- exercise your legs at least every 2-3 hours - starting with the muscles of your lower legs (which act as a pump for the blood in the veins) while sitting - pull your toes towards your knees then relax, or press the balls of your feet down while raising your heel.

- wear loose-fitting clothing

- keep hydrated with water rather than alcohol and caffeinated drinks

- wear graduated compression stockings

HEART DISEASE

Heart disease can be grouped into 3 categories:

- *Hypertensive* - from high blood pressure, working the heart harder so it gets enlarged (anxiety, etc.)

- *Coronary*, or *Arteriosclerotic*- hardening of the (coronary) arteries through excessive calcium, or cholesterol, which again makes the heart work harder (bad diet). The essential problem is that the coronary blood supply is blocked or restricted, and oxygen does not get to the affected cells, which die. Then you do, if enough are affected. This is known in the trade as a *myocardial infarction*. *Arteriosclerosis* exists where a build-up of fatty material in the linings of the coronary arteries makes them narrower. The fatty linings get harder as calcium deposits are added. The main result is *angina*, a symptom of which is a severe chest pain which radiates out to the left arm and up to the neck and jaws. The pain will go when you relax. Where the fatty lining disturbs the smooth blood flow, a clot may form to block the veins. The resulting *heart attack* would lead to *circulatory shock*, or a failure of the blood supply.

- *Valvular* or *rheumatic* - where valves are unable to open or close properly, allowing back pressure to build up (old age)

To reduce the risks of heart disease, double your resting pulse for at least 20 minutes 3 times a week. However, a recent US study has suggested that, although this will lengthen your life by around two years, that two years will be spent on the extra exercise! Otherwise, stop smoking, reduce stress and watch the diet........

The Digestive System

Digestion is the chemical process of breaking down the food you eat into substances that can be absorbed through the walls of the intestines, and transported to the rest of the body via the bloodstream, moving in a controlled fashion from the mouth to the other end. The stomach contains hydrochloric acid for this purpose, and the stomach lining is able to heal (from scratches, etc.) within 24 hours. The method by which energy is made available to the organism is called *Metabolism*.

The process starts in the mouth, where food is chewed and mixed with saliva that starts to break down starches.

CAPT

After being churned in the stomach, the food is moved through the intestines by a rhythmic muscular movement called *peristalsis*, which is controlled by numerous automatic reflexes. The centres that control hunger and appetite are in the hypothalamus and are closely related to pleasure and unpleasure. Since hunger and satiety are emotional states, the operation of the digestive system can be affected by other emotions, especially those that arise from stress - certainly, where anger, resentment and aggression are involved, the stomach will increase its production of hydrochloric acid.

Stress arousal will also affect peristaltic rhythm. You get diarrhoea if the food is moved so fast through the intestines that water cannot be absorbed, and constipation if the food moves so slowly that too much is absorbed.

DIET

The body's main fuel is glucose, which can either be converted from different types of food, or eaten directly. Levels of glucose are regulated by the *pancreas,* which secretes *insulin* to reduce blood sugar levels by getting it into cells or converting it into fat if there's no room.

The body's three sources of nourishment include:

- **Carbohydrates**, which are converted into glucose to provide energy and which consist of:
  - Simple sugars
  - Complex sugars
  - Starch
- **Fats** (and oils), which produce twice as much energy as carbohydrates for the same weight, but which are harder to digest
- **Proteins**, which are constructed from amino acids, not all of those required being carried in the body. Animal protein has to be broken down into peptides and amino acids before being reconstructed into what the body needs

Note that carbohydrates come in different varieties, according to the *glycaemic index,* which is a measure of how quickly they are absorbed into the body.

Trace elements should be obtained through a balanced diet, which is *not* a pint in either hand! *Breakfast should bring in about 25% of the daily calorie intake.*

Note: It should be pointed out that sugar is one of the most harmful substances we can put into our bodies on a daily basis, and there is almost no processed food that does not contain it - even baked beans. Certainly, there is hardly a cereal product without it (did you ever wonder why cereals are fortified with vitamins? It's because they are all taken out first! Manufactured ones are never as good as the real thing). Sugar that is not needed to maintain adequate glucose levels and replenish stored

glycogen in the liver and muscles is converted to fat, by insulin, which also tends to block the conversion of fat back to glucose, so a high insulin level makes it difficult to remove the fat it created in the first place. The problem is that, on the average Western diet, our insulin levels are almost permanently high, which is something that our bodies are simply not built to cope with - the pancreas needs a rest! Thus, we should try to eat so that large spikes of insulin are not generated, which can be difficult in a normal pilot's lifestyle. That is, insulin should be injected into the bloodstream under more controlled conditions - processed foods are converted into glucose *very quickly,* which is the real problem. The type of carbohydrate you eat will determine how this happens (the Atkins diet works because it doesn't trigger insulin). As well, sugar has no vitamins, so it is unable to process itself in the body, and has to borrow what it needs from other sources, which will create a deficit of Vitamin B.

After reading most of the diet books around, the following conclusions can be drawn:

- It is not necessarily the fat you eat, but the fat created from sugar that is bad for your health
- Don't eat anything processed - which is usually anything "white", or at least with white flour in
- Eat fruit by itself - although fruit contains sugars, they also contain enzymes and other beneficial substances, and don't stimulate so much insulin (around a third, in fact). However, once you combine fruit with other food, you get the full non-benefit. Also, fruit is digested mostly in the small intestine, and eating it after a large meal causes this to be delayed, with fermentation that causes indigestion
- If you drink alcohol (in moderation!), dry (low sugar) red wine is best
- Exercise, but not so much that you need to eat a lot to produce the glucose you need
- Don't eat a heavy meal just before going to bed - calorie consumption is different in the evening
- Drink lots of fluid (not with sugar or caffeine in! Caffeine can pull calcium out of your bones)
- Eat lots of fibre and water-based food, such as fruit, greens, tomatoes, etc. in their raw state - try for around 70% of your total diet

And if you thought sugar was bad - think about monosodium glutamate, or MSG, found in food under the name *hydrolyzed vegetable protein.* MSG is injected into rats to make them morbidly obese so they can be experimented on. It triples the amount of insulin created

*Less than 0.2 parts per thousand, around 20 mg of alcohol per 100 ml of blood

If this page is a photocopy, it is not authorised!

by the pancreas, so if you ever needed proof that insulin can be bad for you, this is it. MSG is addictive, and makes you want to eat the same stuff again, which is presumably why, after eating a Chinese meal, you want another one 2 hours afterwards (Chinese meals are notorious for MSG).

HYPOGLYCAEMIA

The most common problem (in the normal pilot's lifestyle, anyway) is low blood sugar (*functional hypoglycaemia*), or eating too much (*reactive hypoglycaemia*), caused by missed meals and the like. Although you may think it's better to have the wrong food than no food, be careful when it comes to eating choccy bars in lieu of lunch, which will cause your blood sugar levels to rise so rapidly that too much insulin is released to compensate, which drives your blood sugar levels to a *lower* state than they were before - known in the trade as *rebound hypoglycaemia*. Here, the sugar is pushed into all cells of the body and not specifically reserved for the Central Nervous System. Apart from eating "real food", you will minimise the risks of this if you eat small snacks frequently instead of heavy meals after long periods with nothing. Complex (slow release) carbohydrates are best, like pasta, etc.

Hypoglycaemia is bad enough in the short term, but long-term can be regarded as a *disease*. Although not life threatening, it is a forerunner of many worse things and should be looked at. The important thing to watch appears to be the suddenness of any fall in blood sugar, and a big one can often trigger a heart attack. A high protein diet will tend to even things out, as protein helps the absorption of fat, which is inhibited if too much insulin is about. Warning signs include shakiness, sweatiness, irritability or anxiety, difficulty in speaking, headache, weakness, numbness or tingling around the lips, inability to think straight (or lack of concentration), palpitations and hunger. At its worst, hypoglycaemia could result in coma, but you could also get seizure and fainting. Eat more if you exercise more.

HYPERGLYCAEMIA

This is the opposite of the above (and precedes it), an *excess* of blood sugar. Symptoms include tiredness, increased appetite and thirst, frequent urination, dry skin, flu-like aches, headaches, blurred vision and nausea. This condition causes dehydration, so have fluids around to help you. Also, decrease stress.

WATER & DEHYDRATION

You need water to:

- regulate body temperature
- circulate nutrients & oxygen and remove waste products from cells (there is 4 times more lymph than blood)
- prevent kidney stones, constipation and some urinary and colon cancers

The accepted figure is 8-10 glasses per day, which is around one for every two waking hours, plus more if you are exercising, as water is lost through respiration and sweating as well as urination.

Note: Hunger and thirst share the same signals, so try drinking water first!

DIABETES

Glucose in the blood provides energy, but sometimes the body cannot either produce the insulin in the first place that is required to get it into the cells (*Type 1* diabetes), or make use of it in the best way (*Type 2*). The former tends to appear in people under 40, and the latter in people over 40, although they can occur in either. Both can be treated by diet and/or insulin injections. Exercise is good, too, as it uses up blood sugar that would otherwise need insulin to get rid of it.

Since insulin is needed to get glucose into your cells, it follows that, if this is not done, blood sugar levels can be dangerously high. In the short term, you may be tired, thirsty, urinate frequently (and get dehydrated), have blurred vision, headaches and tingling fingers and toes. More long-term, blood vessels can get damaged from high blood pressure and cholesterol levels. So important is this, that, if you were on a desert island with a bottle of blood pressure pills and a bottle of diabetes pills, you'd better take the blood pressure pills first! High blood pressure will tend to push proteins through the kidney walls, to be detected in urine.

ALCOHOL

There is only one rule - **flying and alcohol don't mix!**

Although it appears otherwise, alcohol is not a stimulant, but an *anaesthetic*, which puts to sleep those parts of the brain that deal with inhibitions - the problem is that these areas also cover judgement, comprehension and attention to detail. In fact, the effects of alcohol are the same as hypoxia, dealt with elsewhere, in that it prevents brain cells from using available oxygen. One significant effect of hypoxia in this context is the resulting inability to tell that something is wrong.

It takes the liver about 1 hour to eliminate 1 unit of alcohol from the blood. Officially, alcohol leaves the body at 15 milligrams per 100 ml of blood per hour, but the answer for the exam is 0.01-0.015 mg% per hour. A blood alcohol level of 60 mgm/100 ml will therefore take 4 hours to return to normal. 1 unit is, or used to be, considered the same as 1 measure of spirit, a glass of wine or half a pint of beer. The number of units per week beyond which physical damage is likely is 21 for men and 14 for women.

You should not:

- Consume alcohol within 8 hours before the flight

- Start a flight with a blood alcohol level over 0.2 promille*

- Consume alcohol during the flight

Note: Most regulations are worded so that you can have a drink 8 hours before reporting time, but you must also not have alcohol in your system.

Australian researchers compared the effects of alcohol and fatigue on performance. They found that being awake for 17 hours in a row is as bad as a blood alcohol concentration of 0.05%. The limit for driving in Canada, for example, is 0.08%.

MEDICATIONS

Although the symptoms of colds and sore throats, etc. are bad enough on the ground, they may actually become dangerous in flight by either distracting or harming you by getting more serious with height (such as bursting your eardrums, or worse). If you're under treatment for anything, including surgery, not only should you not fly, but you should also check that there will be no adverse effects on your physical or mental ability, as many preparations combine chemicals, and the mixture could make quite a cocktail. No drugs or alcohol should be taken within a few hours of each other, as even fairly widely accepted stuff such as aspirin can have unpredictable effects, especially in relation to hypoxia (it's as well to keep away from the office, too - nobody else will want what you've got). Particular ones to avoid are antibiotics (penicillin, tetracyclines), tranquilisers, antidepressants, sedatives, stimulants (caffeine, amphetamines), anti-histamines and anything for relieving high blood pressure, and, of course, anything not actually prescribed. Naturally, you've got to be certifiable if you fly having used marijuana, or worse.

Note: Too much aspirin can cause gastric bleeding.

ANAESTHETICS

All procedures requiring local or regional anaesthetics disqualify you for flying for at least 12 hours.

DRUGS

A study of airline pilots landing in a simulator found that performance was significantly impaired up to 24 hours after smoking one marijuana cigarette with 19 milligrams of THC, although the pilots thought they were doing OK.

BLOOD DONATIONS

Pilots are discouraged from giving blood (or plasma) when actively flying, because it may lead to a reduced tolerance of altitude. Some dental anaesthetics can cause problems for up to 24 hours or more, as can anything to do with immunisation. If you do give blood, try to leave a gap of 24 hours, including bone marrow donations. Although your arm will fill back up in a very short time, and for most donors there are no noticeable after-effects, there is still a slight risk of faintness or loss of consciousness.

Having donated blood, you should *rest supine for about 15-20 minutes, drink plenty of fluid and not fly for 24 hours.*

SMOKING

There are over 200 harmful chemicals in cigarette smoke, which are more concentrated in *sidestream smoke*, or that which has not been filtered through the main body of the cigarette, so passive smokers face the worst risks (cigarettes release ten times more air pollution than a diesel engine - it is a Group A carcinogen). Here are some of the chemicals involved and the common places they may also be found:

- Carbon monoxide (car exhausts)

- Arsenic (rat poison)

- Ammonia (window cleaner)

- Acetone (nail polish remover)

- Hydrogen cyanide (gas chambers)

- Naphthalene (mothballs)

- Sulphur compounds (matches)

- Formaldehyde (embalming fluid)

- Butane (lighter fluid)

Otherwise, the addictive substance in tobacco is *nicotine*, and the substance that stops the alveoli doing their work is *tar*. There is also carbon monoxide (CO), described below.

Nicotine reduces the diameter of the arteries, which stimulates the release of adrenalin, to increase heart rate and blood pressure. The risk of heart attack or strokes is increased in the order of 100%, and gangrene by 500%.

CARBON MONOXIDE

Carbon monoxide (CO) is toxic gas that is created through the effects of incomplete combustion, when not enough oxygen has been available to create the proper waste product, which is carbon dioxide (CO_2). It typically gets into the cockpit from faulty engine exhausts, but other sources relevant to aviation can include cigarette smoke and cabin heaters. You can buy carbon monoxide detectors from most pilot shops that will act as an early warning, because it is colourless, tasteless, odourless and non-irritating, so is otherwise extremely hard to detect.

The precise way that the effects of carbon monoxide work on the body are complex and not yet fully understood, but when it is not ventilated it binds to haemoglobin* better than oxygen does, and makes it retain any oxygen it carries, so the blood oxygen content increases while the body does not get the supplies that it needs.

*The principal oxygen-carrying compound in blood.

The symptoms of CO poisoning can resemble those of food poisoning and the flu, but without the associated high temperatures. A headache is the most common symptom. Others include:

- feeling sick (nausea) and dizziness
- feeling tired and confused
- vomiting with abdominal pain
- shortness of breath and difficultly with breathing (dyspnoea)

The longer you breathe in CO gas, the worse the symptoms will get. You may lose your balance, vision and memory and, eventually, consciousness. This can happen within two hours if there is a lot of CO in the air, but the symptoms can occur over a number of days or months.

Later symptoms include:

- confusion
- memory loss
- co-ordination problems

To recover, turn off the cabin heat and open the air vents. Use 100% oxygen if you have it.

MISCELLANEOUS

Don't forget to inform the authorities (in writing) of illnesses, personal injuries or presumed pregnancies that incapacitate you for more than 21 days. Pilots in accidents should be medically examined before flying again.

PSYCHOLOGICAL FACTORS

Whatever influences the mind or emotions can alter the way we interpret the information on which we base decisions. For example, when under stress, because it's harder to concentrate, your judgement becomes impaired and you make rash decisions as you try to make the problem go away. In fact, during an emergency, people often go into denial - having been used to doing practice engine failures over wide open fields during training, it takes a while to get through the unfairness of it all as it happened for real over trees! By this time, the emergency will have rolled on.

In psychology, this is the **normalcy bias**, which causes us to underestimate the possibility of disaster and its effects. As something has never happened before, it never will! It is hard to prepare for and deal with new happenings.

Modern technology, in the shape of automation, allows us to achieve more in less time and has led to lifestyles of constant change, which is something that humans don't like in general. Just coping with change can be a major cause of stress, which can pull down your immune system and act as a catalyst for illnesses to take hold. It can all start with a simple mismatch between what you want and what you get.

Stress

Flying is stressful, but should that be a problem? A little is good for you; it stops you slowing down and keeps you on your toes; this is the sort associated with success.

However, the word *stress* is commonly used to mean both the source and an outcome of a problem. For example, we say we are *under* stress and that we are suffering *from* stress. In reality, stress is the outcome of being under pressure, which can either raise or lower your performance, depending on how it is perceived and/or reacted to, but eliminating pressure does not remove stress - the whole process, including the original pressure, must be managed. You do this by knowing when to use it to get things done. For example, you could batten down the hatches of a ship and ride out a storm (i.e. stay where you are), or set the sails properly and use the wind to get you along.

Negative stress (or *dis*tress) occurs when we react to pressure in the wrong way. It can lead to fatigue, anxiety and inability to cope, and is associated with frustration or failure. It can also make you ill - of the two systems that are designed to protect the body, only one can be active at any time. That is, when the adrenalin used for fight or flight kicks in, the immune system is suppressed, long term. Over your career, this can lead to failing medicals earlier. In fact, there is evidence to indicate that stress is behind many modern illnesses, certainly headaches, asthma, heart disease and hypertension.

CAPT

In short, stress disturbs the body's *homeostasis*, which is how the body maintains its comfort and efficiency. The word comes from the Greek *homeos* and *stasis*, meaning *similar* and *condition*, respectively, and describes a state of the body where the internal functions are in stable equilibrium. Homeostasis preserves the body's internal sameness, particularly with heat, by resisting and smoothing out changes. Since it allows the body's internal environment to be independent of the external environment, it gives you a great amount of flexibility, especially with time, so you can interact more freely with the outside world without being tied down.

The reason why stress is a problem for the human body is evolutionary - the autonomic nervous system, if you remember, works as a whole unit, which may have been OK when coming across a mammoth, but not for the more everyday stuff we have to cope with today that is present in a more or less relentless stream. That is, a physical response to an emotional or physiological threat is inappropriate, because the effects take too long to dissipate with no physical action. In other words, fight or flight as a mechanism for improved performance is now redundant, as most threats are now not physical.

Fight or flight stress (or pressure) is supposed to enable you to adapt to encountered situations - it is the body's response to a stressor, which is an internal or external stimulus that is *interpreted* as a threat to the body's equilibrium, and prepares it for action in various ways. Adrenalin starts to pump and many other changes take place as well, including a rise of sugar and fats in the blood (including cholesterol, from the liver), endorphins (from the hypothalamus), faster respiration, thicker blood (to carry more oxygen), tense muscles and the stopping of digestion (up to 70% of the immune system is in the gut), so more blood can be diverted to where it is needed. All this happens very quickly, but it cannot be maintained for long - if it is, the body can be adversely affected. Muscles can only contract or relax, and it takes a specific procedure to make them relax properly. The problem is that just thinking about a defensive action can cause you to adopt a posture without consciously realising it. This is how hidden fears or anger can create muscle tension, especially in the cardiovascular or digestive systems. Thus, stress disorders are caused by chronic, long term overactivity.

If a threat continues to be perceived as such, the imbalances in body chemistry will eventually no longer be sustainable, and our performance will eventually suffer. The cortisol and adrenalin (and other substances) combine to increase blood pressure, blood sugar and fats which, if continued over time, will result in the stress related illnesses above. The chemicals and hormones that help us in the short term will kill us long term.

Stress and preoccupation have their effects; a PA31 pilot was doing a cargo flight with three scheduled stops, but he did not refuel or even shut down at any of them, so both engines stopped after the last delivery. He was anxious to get home as his wife was in hospital. This illustrates how stress can cause a *narrowing of the focus*, or a fixation on one problem to the exclusion of others. It also illustrates some of the sources of stress (pressure), which can include:

- Personality
- Family
- Occupation
- Situation

and their combinations, which are discussed below. In a complex task, high levels of arousal narrow the span of attention and make you fixate on smaller areas.

This is because, with heightened awareness of a threat, you can get extreme visual clarity and tunnel vision - the mind shuts down all the stuff it doesn't need to deal with, including the bowels (yuk!) In fact, most people have one cerebral hemisphere dominant when under stress, as can be detected from their reactions. For example, a right-brain dominant person faced with a situation is more likely to want to run away from it. A left-brain dominant person, though, could get lost in the details - humour, a right brain activity, would be a good antidote in this case. Using only one brain hemisphere means that, on encountering a problem, you become less capable of solving it.

WHAT IS EXCESSIVE STRESS?

Anything that has a sufficiently strong influence to take your mind off the job in hand, or to make you concentrate less well on it. Not only are you not doing your job properly, but subconsciously feel guilty about it, too, which is enough to set up a little stress all of its own. We all like to feel we are doing the best we can possibly do, and it disturbs our self-image to feel that we're not. Consequently we get angry at ourselves for being in such a position, which increases the stress, which further takes us away from the job, etc.

Common situations causing stress include grief, divorce, financial worries, working conditions, management pressure, pride, anger, get-home-it is, motivation (or lack of), doubts (about abilities, etc), timetable, passengers' expectations, etc. In fact, there are many life events in a long list, with each item weighted with *Life Change Units* (LCUs) according to its stress-producing capacity. They range from death of a spouse (100 LCUs) to minor violations of the law (11 LCUs). A visit from the in-laws rates 29! The current list is called the *Life Change Events Scale*, which can be grouped for convenience as follows:

- *physical* (environment, temperature)
- *physiological* (fatigue, illness)
- *emotional/psychological* (divorce, death, etc.)

CAPT

All the above leads to anxiety, which is really based on fear (of people not liking you, of losing your job, etc.), but the common denominator is *change*. As anxiety itself can cause stress, you get a circulating problem. People have their own ways of dealing with stress, so what works for one does not necessarily work for someone else. This is possibly because of the evaluation of the stress that that particular person has, i.e. whether they feel they can cope and their perception of the problem. It is *perception* of demands and abilities, rather than actual problems that affect the individual. If you *feel* you are capable, or in control, your stress level will be relatively low. The more helpless you feel, the more stress.

Symptoms of stress include:

- Anxiety and apprehension, depression, gloom, mood swings
- Detachment from the situation
- Failure to perceive time
- Fixation of attention
- Personality changes
- Voice pitch changes
- Desire for isolation
- Reduced cognitive ability
- Poor emotional self-control
- Unsafe cavalier attitude
- Anger

STRESS MANAGEMENT

Referring back to the list of life events as stressors above, they all have one common denominator - change! You will cope with stress better if you learn to cope with change first, then modify *your* position relative to the stressor.

In fact, you can be affected by stress in these areas:

- **Adaptation**. Life is full of change, but this is a particular problem with customers, and the lack of planning on their part. Many pilots visualise a task up to a week before they get going, but it commonly changes at the last minute! Bad weather can also be included under this heading

- **Frustration** (too many people in the way, or thwarting of your goals). Pilots, in particular, have to reconcile the demands of two influential groups of people, namely customers and management

- **Overload**, so much to do, with so little time, particularly during a complex approach to an airfield. A level of demand that exceeds your capacity to cope (delegation helps)

- **Deprivation** (boredom or loneliness).

- **Biological/Personality** (anxiety, etc.)

- **Nutritional** (lack of proper diet). A stress prone diet includes sugar, caffeine and salt, and leads to vitamin depletion, especially B and C, because stress uses up the body's supplies that are needed to process sugar into energy. Salt regulates the body's water balance - too much leads to fluid retention, which leads to high blood pressure. Caffeine stimulates the body in the same way that stress does

- **Noise and vibration**

- **Smoking**

Since most of the above occur simultaneously, it can be seen that stress has a wide scope, with no simple solution - it is actually a *lifestyle* problem, which means that one of the most effective means of stress management is to switch to one that eliminates or avoids such stressors. You could change your daily routine, eat more healthy food, change your job or partner, or even your personality (however, you can never really get rid of them all).

Good cockpit stress management begins with what causes stress - in a crisis in the cockpit, for example, you must first identify the source. Then, try to relax and think rationally, and use all available resources to help.

Having recognised the situation, eliminate or deal with the factors causing your stress. I like black humour myself, and some people favour eating, meditation or biofeedback machines that help them reduce their heart rate, etc., but most either adjust to the situation, or change it, or their thinking about it, or walk away. Since the primary fight or flight response is physical, which takes hours to undo, one of the quickest methods would be to get enough physical exercise to use up the chemicals that have been placed in your bloodstream.

However, the willingness to recognise stress and to do something about it must be there; for example, if you don't admit there's a problem at home, there's not much you can do! It is not weakness to admit you have a problem - rather, it shows lack of judgement otherwise. As previously mentioned, it's your *attitude* towards stress that counts, not the situation itself, as other people may be able to cope with it very well. If you have the usual fight-or-flight symptoms over a relatively minor incident, you are stressed! This energy has nowhere to go and you end up in overdrive, with a very easily ignited short fuse to push you over the edge (see *Anger*).

Fatigue

Prolonged exposure to fatigue (mental or physical) can reduce the capabilities of your immune system and make you quite ill.

Fatigue is typically caused by delayed sleep, sleep loss, desynchronisation of normal circadian rhythms and concentrated periods of physical or mental stress or exertion. Working long hours, during normal sleep hours or on rotating shifts, all produce fatigue to some extent. As mentioned elsewhere, Australian researchers compared the effects of alcohol and fatigue on performance. They found that being awake for 17 hours in a row is as bad as a blood alcohol concentration of 0.05%, which is close to the legal limit for driving.

Symptoms of fatigue may include:

- diminished perception (vision, hearing) and a general lack of awareness

- diminished motor skills and slow reactions

- problems with short-term memory

- channelled concentration - fixation on single possibly unimportant issues

- being easily distracted by unimportant matters

- poor judgement and decision- making, leading to increased mistakes

- abnormal moods, erratic changes, depressed, periodic elation and energy

- diminished standards

Most people need about 8 hours' sleep, and you can do with less for a few days, creating a *sleep deficit*, but it's not only the amount of sleep you get, but *when* you get it that counts, so fatigue is just as likely to result from badly planned sequences of work and rest, or being too long away from base without a day off. A surprising amount (over 300) of bodily functions depend on the cycle of day and night - we have an internal (*circadian*) rhythm, which is modified by such things, which, oddly enough, is 25 hours, although there are actually several body clocks that might run for slightly more or less than that. You naturally feel best when they're all in concert, but the slippery slope starts when they get out of line. For example, one reason why people feel under par on Monday mornings is because they have let their body clocks run free over the weekend, instead of using the usual timegivers, like alarm clocks and observing the cycle of night and day. Thus, when your alarm clock says it is 7 o'clock on Monday morning, your body thinks it is around 4 o'clock and still wants to carry on sleeping.

The two types of fatigue are *acute* and *chronic*, the former being short-term, or more intense, and the latter arising from more long-term effects, like many episodes of acute fatigue, typically found after a long spell of fire suppression. Acute fatigue usually affects the body, and just needs a good nights' sleep to sort things out, whereas the chronic variety can have a mental element, where you might not want to see a helicopter ever again. It typically

happens after you've had no rest, food or recreation for some time, as mentioned in the example under *Error Management*, above. Symptoms are insomnia, loss of appetite, and even irrational behaviour. To control its effects, try rest, exercise and proper nutrition.

Foods low in carbohydrate or high in protein help fight fatigue, especially "healthy" ones, like fruit or yoghurt, or cereals, such as granola. Coffee, of course, contains caffeine, which keeps you awake (as does tea), but too much can lead to headaches and upset stomachs. People who drink unleaded coffee (decaffeinated) still report unpleasant side effects, as the process that removes caffeine is allegedly just as harmful, but in different ways. Caffeine has a half-life of about 3 hours, and although it might not stop you getting to sleep, it will affect its quality.

Trivia: ICAO Annex 1 excludes coffee and tobacco from the definition of psychoactive substance, but Coca Cola, Pepsi, Tea, and other substances containing caffeine, are not excluded.

SLEEP

Nobody really knows what sleep is for, but the current working hypothesis is that it is necessary to restore and replenish the body and brain. However, if that were the only reason, you would sleep less after a slack day and more after a busy day, but the amount does not seem to vary, although people do need different amounts - Margaret Thatcher only slept 5 hours a night as Prime Minister. As far as resting the body goes, you can do that in front of the TV, so it seems to be a mental thing.

Sleep is actually a state of altered consciousness, in which, although paralysed, you don't lose awareness of the external world, as any mother will tell you (it's actually where your brain focusses internally - consciousness seems to depend on certain regions of the brain stem for its function). It is part of a daily cycle which is 25 hours long - that is, the sleeping and waking rhythm is about an hour longer than the normal day of 24 hours, which itself is a mean figure anyway (*Moore-Ede, Sulzman & Fuller*, 1982). This is why flying West is easier on the system than flying East - the body's rhythm is extended the right way. Various factors, such as cycles of night or day, keep the natural 25-hour tendency in check. Normally, this *circadian rhythm* works with body temperature, so the body is coolest when it is hardest to stay awake, around 05:00. Thus, sleep is harder to achieve as body temperature rises.

1 hour of quality sleep equals 2 hours of activity, and you can accumulate up to 8 hours on a credit basis - that is, each sleeping hour gains 2 credit points and each hour awake loses one, to give you a *sleep debt*, which is the cumulative effect of not getting enough sleep. Although you can accumulate 30-40 hours of sleep debt, your performance will still suffer while under its influence.

CAPT

Thus, 8 hours' sleep overnight means you will be ready for sleep again 16 hours after waking. If your work pattern is disrupted, you can increase your "credit rating" with a short nap. Alcohol interferes with sleep because of its diuretic action - repeated use disturbs sleep on a long term basis, to give you insomnia. The British Army thinks that a shave is about equal to 20 minutes' sleep, in terms of refreshing you, and washing your face or brushing your teeth are also good, as is moving around for 5-10 minutes. A person suffering sleep loss is unlikely to be aware of personal performance degradation, which may be present for up to 20 minutes after a nap. The effects of sleep deprivation increase with workload and altitude.

Clinical Insomnia is being unable to sleep under normal conditions. *Situational insomnia* arises out of the circumstances, like sleeping in a strange bed or time zone (*circadian desynchronisation*). Although insomniacs may think they don't sleep at all, they actually spend their time in stages 1 and 2. *Sleep Apnea* stops people breathing for short periods up to a minute, and *Narcolepsy* makes them drop off at any time of the day.

The fact that how long you sleep depends on when you sleep also suggests that there are two components of the sleep system, and the former function is not an internal rhythm, but takes account of habits and routines - when these are taken away, people tend to sleep in shorter bursts. So, sleep can be resisted for a short time, but various parts of the brain will ensure that, sooner or later, sleep occurs. A Boeing 707 overshot LA International at 32,000 feet over the Pacific ocean after the whole crew had fallen asleep (one was only roused by ATC setting off alarms in the cockpit).

When we are asleep, the higher regions of the brain lose the ability to communicate - parts of the cerebral cortex which mediate perception, thought and action disconnect (*Science*, Sep 30 2005). It has been found that electronic signals do not pass beyond certain stimulated cells during sleep, so the brain "breaks down into little islands that cannot talk to one another." Conscious thought may therefore depend on the ability of the brain to integrate information, and REM sleep (see below), at least, may be a way of allowing the brain to defragment isolated pieces of information collected and processed during the day. Thus, the main role of deep sleep could be to allow for physical recovery and reconstitution of neural energy reserves.

TYPES OF SLEEP

The sleep process is characterised by 5 stages (4 + REM) that take place over a typical cycle of about 90 minutes.

Stage 1 sleep is the light sleep you get into just after dozing off. It only lasts a few minutes before you go into Stage 2, which takes up between 40-60% of total sleeping time. Stage 3 takes up 3-12%, while Stage 4 occupies 15-35% (you get to Stage 3 when delta waves are over 20% of

the total wave count, and Stage 4 when they get to 50%). In all this process, you get deeper and deeper into it and it is progressively more difficult to be roused to wakefulness. It takes about 15-30 minutes to get into Stage 4, and you stay there for about 30-40 minutes before going back up through to Stage 1, the whole process lasting about 90 minutes. After this, you enter the first stage of REM sleep, so the sequence is 1 - 2 - 3 - 4 - 3 - 2- REM - 2 - 3 - 4 - 3 - 2 - REM and so on.

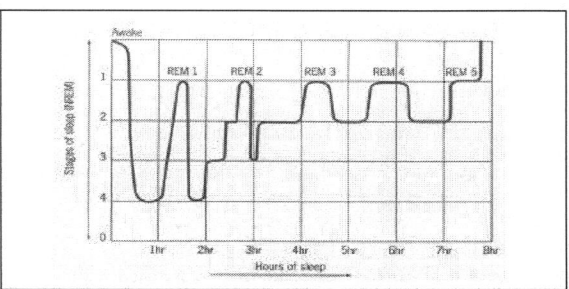

Figure 1   Typical Cycle of Stage 1-4 (NREM) sleep and REM Sleep in the Course of a Night

In *Rapid Eye Movement* (or *paradoxical**) sleep, the body and brain become active, heart and metabolism increase and the eyes shift, hence the name. The first REM period is between 5-10 minutes long, but the length of each period increases through the night (you could get up to four REM sessions per night, on average). Long term lack of REM sleep is not good for general health.

*Nathaniel Kleitman (1895-1999), the Professor of Physiology at Chicago University, is credited with discovering rapid eye movement in sleep experiments.

He wanted to study the rolling movements of the eyes that only occur during sleep (and speeches by politicians). About an hour after the eye-rolling ended, they began to move very rapidly, about every 90 minutes, coinciding with changes in brainwave activity as the long, slow wavelengths of normal sleep were replaced by fast frequency patterns which were close to those obtained when awake. As it is most difficult to wake people up then, it called paradoxical sleep. Signals from part of the brain stem (the reticular formation) paralyse the muscles.

It would appear that REM sleep refreshes the mind, and *Slow Wave* (NREM) sleep refreshes the body. With REM sleep, the brain is awake in a virtually paralysed body, so you are nearly awake anyway, and it is more difficult to get back to sleep for the next hour (but it is easier to wake up then). Alcohol degrades REM sleep which, in adult humans typically occupies 20–25% of total sleep, about 90–120 minutes of a night's sleep.

COMMUNICATION
••

The first cockpit tool that tends to suffer from stress is communication. Any relationship needs it to be successful. In fact, there is hardly any job in which it can be ignored. Lack of it can affect your physical health - in the 13th century, for example, Emperor Frederick experimented by cutting some babies off from all communication, instructing their nurses to stay silent. The babies all died. A study was once done on graduates of Stanford University, to find out what makes a great engineer. The responses indicated that technical expertise formed only 20% of the ingredients for success - the rest was due to people skills.

Communication in aviation is important because passengers, for instance, should know exactly what your aircraft can and cannot do or, more particularly, what you will and will not do!

The first requirement for communication is a common language, for which aviation uses English. However, we need something more precise, such as "Aviation English", which uses standardised, abbreviated, precise and agreed terminology. However, although aviation uses precise terminology, we still have to make certain assumptions, otherwise everything would grind to a halt as we continually ask for clarification. Such assumptions would certainly include peoples' levels of knowledge and how they think about things. This is one reason for clear briefings - to ensure that we are not operating on assumptions in the cockpit! The aim is that people should understand what they need to do without the need for detailed explanations.

Thus, your ability to communicate will account for over 80% of your success in any walk of life. However, your current methods of communication have more than likely been based on responses learned through childhood, and can almost certainly be improved. What happens is that you build a facade, either for emotional protection or because you have to behave in certain ways in order to get what you need (food, comfort, etc.), which does not necessarily have anything to do with the person that you really are. From that stems the playing of games and manipulation, hurting and punishment until you grow into a full-blown control freak. To be sure, personality plays some part, but most behaviour patterns are learnt. Luckily, communication skills can be learnt, too.

Communication is defined as the ability to put your ideas into someone's head and be sure of success, or to exchange information without it being changed. Or both. Unfortunately, even under ideal conditions, only about 30% is retained, due to inattention, misinterpretation, expectations and emotions. Your team needs to know what you want done, especially in an emergency, and requires feedback as to progress and satisfaction of your expectations. This could be through the spoken word or body language. Officially, around 80% of all communication is achieved by factors other than words, otherwise known as *metacommunication*, which consists of those tools, other than the words, which complement them in order to communicate, such as body language.

The ancient Greeks thought of communication between two people in three parts:

- *Ethos* - character (and credibility) of an individual. Its essence is in the degree of trust in the words the listener believes

- *Pathos* - emotional content

- *Logos* - the logical content, and the least influential part of the whole process - it will only be listened to when the other two are clear. You can be as correct as you wish, but if character and emotion are missing, your message will not get across

Implicit communication means that various interpretations may be placed on the information, whilst *explicit communication* has no ambiguity.

7% of all communication is accomplished verbally, 38% by unconscious signals, such as tone of voice, and the remainder (55%) by non-verbal means, i.e. body language.

Verbal communication may be either *social* or *functional*. The former helps to build teamwork, and the latter is essential to flying, or operating, an aircraft. For a spoken or written message to be understood, the sender has to make sure that the receiver is using the same channel of communication, and language, and can make out the message's meaning. The *channel of communication* is the medium used to convey the message. For the spoken word, this might be face-to-face, the radio or intercom.

So, communication is the exchange of thoughts, messages or information by various means, including speech. The elements of the process are the *sender*, the *message*, the *receiver* and *feedback* (alternative elements are the *Source, Message, Channel* & *Receiver*), which is the process of responding to a sender by confirming the reception of a message. It guarantees the understanding of a message without adding new information to it.

Body Language

The fact that somebody isn't talking does not mean they are not communicating (some female silences can be quite eloquent!) It is said that 7% of communication is accomplished verbally, 38% by unconscious signals, such as tone of voice, and the remainder (55%) by non-verbal means, such body language. In fact, before language was invented it was the only way to get your point across. It's certainly the most believed means of communication, since it will most likely reflect the true feelings of the person concerned.

CAPT

Non-verbal communication can accompany verbal communication, such as a smile during a face-to-face chat. It may be acknowledgement or feedback (a nod of the head). It can also be used when the verbal type is impossible, such as a thumbs-up when it's noisy. Body language can be very subtle, but powerful. For example, the word *No* with a smile will be interpreted quite differently from one accompanied by a smack in the mouth. Non-verbal communication may also include written information or notes, between pilots or the flight-deck and cabin crew, but technology makes this even more important - it is the main way that systems speak to you - newer displays present data graphically. Unfortunately, the side-by side seating arrangements in the cockpit tend to lessen the effects of body language, so the choice of words (and their packaging) assumes a greater importance.

Barriers To Communication

Barriers to communication include a reluctance to ask questions, the influence of authority, and difficulty in listening, not forgetting making assumptions, and anger, described below. You, therefore, have to put people at their ease and make them think they can talk to you or ask questions. In fact, there can be *lack* of communication and *poor* communication. The former might be a young first officer who is very computer-literate, but doesn't tell you what he's doing. The latter, someone that tells you there is a problem, but not what it is. However, an important component is speech - the words you say often have completely the opposite effect to what is intended, because they simply mean different things to different people. In addition, when people speak, the words become coded into some sort of indirect expression. This is because we grow up learning to be politically correct in order to get what we need from other people, thus hiding your real self behind some sort of language barrier and continual demands not to show emotion. For example, when a child asks questions at bedtime, the meaning behind the words is a request to stay a little longer. All too often, we take words at face value and confuse the real meanings for their presentation, if only because the real meat of any conversation tends to come at the end.

Listeners have problems, too, because people have filters through which words have to struggle to be understood.

ANGER

Anger has four elements, arising from the body, the mind, the situation and learned responses. Anger held in becomes resentment - the trick is not to express it destructively. When you are angry your body pumps out adrenalin, and cortisol, which depresses your immune system, so being angry can have long-term health effects. Although "losing it" in a grand firework display can make you feel better, it is only temporary and a huge exhaustive low follows as the hormones leave your system. You'll

probably also have to sort out the mess with the other people! Aggressive people are more susceptible to heart attacks, clogged arteries and higher cholesterol. However, anger is also an effective means of blocking communication. This is because there are four types of angry person, each with their own language:

- those who are generally non-malicious, whose anger is quick to boil and just as quick to dissipate
- those who are slow to anger, but keep a list of everything you did or said wrong since 1929
- those who just like being angry
- those who relish the after effects rather than the argument

If you learn more about your own makeup, you will be in a better position to avoid setting other people off. It will help you step back and *resolve* a conflict, if you can't avoid it in the first place. If you remember, the body is not built to be in fight or flight mode as much as it is these days. You will therefore not be surprised to hear that it takes very little effort to trigger off an angry reaction after even the most trivial event. Such emotional triggers can easily make people explode, but, at the very least, will affect the way you assess situations and react to them, or, more importantly, make decisions. Emotions carry so much force and influence that they rule your actions before you calm down enough to think rationally.

As for health, one study at the Ochsner Clinic in New Orleans reports high levels of hostility in many heart attack victims, who also had higher levels of weight, cholesterol, anxiety and depression. Stress brought on by rage can also affect memory, creativity and sleep. Bacterial infections can increase during angry episodes, and you lay yourself wide open to upper respiratory problems, like flu.

Radio Procedures

Professional languages use a limited vocabulary, to which the context provides meaning, reducing the risk of ambiguities. In Aviation, using non-standard phraseology can be fatal. The phrase:

"Advise ready for taxi, company pushing out of XYZ"

is not a clearance to pushback, even though it might sound like one. Similarly, an instruction to conduct runup checks on the other side of a runway you would have to cross to get there is not a clearance to do so. The words *"request Federal Aid"* in one message were interpreted to mean that a hijack was in process, rather than the intended request for FAA clearance expressed in a joking fashion. The figures 210 by themselves could mean a Flight Level, a heading, or a speed to be maintained.

JUDGMENT
•••

In short, judgment is process of choosing between alternatives for the safest outcome. Factors that influence the exercise of good judgment include:

- *Lack of vigilance* - vigilance (that is, keeping an eye on what's going on) is the basis of situational awareness. You need to keep a constant watch on all that is going on around you, however tempting it may be to switch off for a while on a long navex. Monitor the fuel gauges, check for traffic and engine-off landing sites, all the time

- *Distraction* - anything that stops you noticing a problem, for example, slowly backing into trees while hovering. Keep pulling back from the situation to keep the big picture

- *Peer Pressure* - we all like to be liked, whether by people in or outside your own company. Do they want you to fly overweight? Or fly in darkness, even though they are late back? Being too keen to please is part of a self-esteem problem. *Do not take on other peoples' problems!*

- *Insufficient Knowledge* - although you can look the regulations up in a book, this is not always the most convenient solution, so you need a working knowledge of what they contain, including checklists and limitations from the flight manual, etc. We don't all have an aircraft library, or have the time to refer to it if there was one

- *Unawareness of Consequences* - this is an aspect of insufficient knowledge, above. What are the consequences of what you propose to do? Have you thought things out thoroughly?

- *Forgetfulness of Consequences* - similar to the above

- *Ignoring the Consequences* - again, similar to the above, but more deliberate, since you are aware of the consequences of your proposed actions, but choose to ignore them

- *Overconfidence* - this breeds carelessness, and a reluctance to pay attention to detail or be vigilant. Also, it inclines you to be hasty, and not consider all the options available to you. This is where a little self-knowledge and humility is a great help

Attitudes & Personality

Flying requires considerable use of the brain, with observation and/or reaction to events, both inside and outside the aircraft. Psychology and aviation have been used to each other for some time; you may be familiar with selection tests and interviews. Part of why accidents happen is that some people are accidents waiting to happen! This depends on personality, amongst other

things, and we will look at this shortly. However, personality is not the only factor to be aware of on the flight deck. Status, Role and Ability are also important, discussed later.

Your *personality* is based on heredity, childhood, upbringing and experience. It could be defined as the *unique organisation of characteristics which determine the typical or standard behaviour of an individual toward the outside world*, although the word *attitude* also refers to how you respond to another person, situation or organisation, and is the way we look at life, or the sum total of the meaning and values we give to various events. Another definition of personality is *deep-seated characteristics that constitute the essence of a person*. Such characteristics are stable and resistant to change.

HAZARDOUS ATTITUDES

Your attitudes are the product of *personal disposition* and *past experience. Behaviour* is the outward result of attitude and personality combined, and is adaptable. These attitudes have been identified as undesirable for the accident-prone person to possess:

- **Impulsivity**. Doing things without forethought - not stopping to think about what you're doing and ignoring the consequences. For example, a pilot and passengers who are anxious to get to their destination for a business presentation when thunderstorms are reported to be in a line across the route exhibit this attitude when they want to hurry and get going, before things get worse. Apply your training! *Slow down and think first!*

- **Anti-authority.** These people don't like being told what to do. They may either not respect the source of the authority, or are just plain ornery (with a deep source of bottled-up anger). Very often there's nothing wrong with this - if more people had questioned authority, we wouldn't have had half the wars, or we wouldn't get passengers pressurising pilots to do what they shouldn't. However, regulations have a purpose. They allow us to act with little information, since everything is supposed to be predictable, although that doesn't mean that rules should blindly be obeyed - sometimes breaking the rules saves lives. The DC10 that had an engine fall off during takeoff could have kept flying if the nose had been lowered a little for speed, instead of being set at the "standard" angle of 6°, as per the simulator, which, in this case, stalled the aeroplane. An official example of anti-authority is a pilot who neglects to renew medicals or ratings, or maintain records and logbooks, but my own opinion is that there's an element of laziness in there as well. The real anti-authority person is the one who keeps ignoring the Chief Pilot's instructions and feels

CAPT

constrained by rules & regulations. This attitude is demonstrated when the passengers arrive almost an hour late for a flight that requires a reservation and the pilot considers that those rules do not apply. The antidote is to *follow the rules* (mostly!)

- **Invulnerability**. People like this think that nothing untoward can happen to them, so they take more risks, or push the envelope - humility is the antidote, or the realisation that it *could* happen to you. One instructor I know cures people who insist on flying VFR helicopters in IMC conditions by taking them up into cloud (in a twin) and showing them how incapable they are of instrument flying, even though they can do the occasional turn with the foggles on. The point is taken! *Repetitive tasks must be done as if they were new every time, no matter how tedious they may be* - you can guarantee that the one time you don't check for water in fuel, it will be there! You display this trait if, during an operational check of the cabin pressurization system, you discover that the rate control feature is inoperative and elect to disregard it and depart on the trip because you think you can handle the cabin pressure yourself

- **Macho** people are afraid of looking small and are always subject to peer pressure, which means they care a lot about what other people think of them - thus, they have a very low opinion of themselves and take unnecessary chances for different reasons than so-called Invulnerable people, above. These are typically the high-powered intimidating company executives who have houses in the middle of nowhere with no navaids within miles. Such people may subconsciously put themselves in situations where they push the weather to test their own nerve. This is demonstrated if, while on an IFR flight, you emerge from a cloud to be within 300 feet of a helicopter and fly a little closer, just to show him. The antidote is *don't take chances*, or think you can fix things on the fly. You must stick up for yourself, with management and passengers

- **Resignation**. The thought that Allah (or luck) will provide is OK, but the Lord only helps those who help themselves - you've got to do your bit! If you want help to win the lottery, buy the ticket first! The antidote is to realise you *can* make a difference, or to have more confidence in your abilities. *Complacency** (mentioned in some reference books) would come under this heading

*One definition of complacency is: "Self-satisfaction accompanied by a loss of awareness of danger." Once an activity is routine, you relax and reduce your mental effort, so the dangers are highest with the most skilled people. *Automatic behaviour* is most likely to result in complacency.

High performers *remain vigilant, cross-check* their performance and *correct errors* before they are significant.

As you can see when you compare the opposites, each side of each coin above is as bad as the other - we should be somewhere in the middle, with a possible slight bias towards anti-authority and paranoia (you don't want management or customers putting you in invidious positions, and neither do you want them trying to kill you).

The first step in neutralising a hazardous attitude is to recognise hazardous thoughts. Label the thoughts as such and correct them by stating the corresponding antidotes.

Pilots must also learn to avoid classic behavioural traps:

- *Peer Pressure*
- *Mind Set*. Allowing expectations to override reality
- *Get-There-Itis*. A fixation that clouds the vision and impairs judgment, plus disregard for other actions
- *Duck-Under Syndrome*. Sneaking a peek by going below minima, like descending below MORA
- *Scud Running*. Going VFR when you really should be IFR
- *Getting Behind the Aircraft*. Allowing events to control your actions, leading to.........
- *Loss of Situational Awareness*
- *Getting Low On Fuel*
- *Pushing the Envelope*. Exceeding design limitations in the belief that high performance will cover overestimated flying skills, or relying on manufacturer's fudge factors to go overweight
- *Poor Planning*

WHAT TYPE OF PERSON IS A PILOT?

Having decided what product we are selling (safe arrival), we can now talk about the best kind of person to produce it. We certainly have more intelligence than the average car driver. Or do we? Passing exams doesn't mean you're capable of doing a decent job or handling a crisis. There are stupid solicitors, professors, you name it. I have flown with 17,000-hour pilots who I wouldn't trust with a pram, and 1,000-hour types with whom I would trust anything.

I think it's fair to say that the public typically think of pilots (when they think of them at all) as outgoing types, often in the bar and having a lark, an image from all those World War II movies, and if you were cold, hungry, tired, frightened and inexperienced, you would probably behave that way, too, but life today is quite different.

A pilot should be a synthesis of the following headings:

- *Meticulous* - being prepared to do the same thing, the same way, every time, and not get bored, as that's the way you miss things

A skilled pilot who takes risks is a bigger problem than an average one who is prudent and cautious

- *Forward Thinking* - in just the same way that an advanced driver is ready to deal with a corner before going into it, the advanced pilot knows that the load underneath will carry on if the helicopter slows down, and positions the controls properly

- *Responsible* - the "responsible position" that you hold as a commander is one where you act with minimum direction but are personally responsible for the outcome of your activities. In other words, you are responsible for the machine without being directed by any other person in it

- *Trustworthy* - people must be able to *trust* you - all of aviation runs on it. You trust the previous pilot not to have overstressed the machine, or to really have done 4.3 hours and not 6. Signatures count for a lot, and, by extension, your word

- *Motivated*. Motivation* is a drive to behave in a particular fashion. It is an internal force which can affect the quality of performance, although excessive motivation together with high levels of stress will limit your attention-management capabilities. In short, you can get fixated

WHAT IS COMMON BETWEEN COMPETENT PEOPLE?

Competency is based on the knowledge, skill and ability of an individual pilot.

- *Intelligence*

- *Personality*. This can be defined as "The sum total of the physical, mental, emotional and social characteristics of an individual (when dealing with the outside world)". Generally, to be accident prone, you are either under- or overconfident. You might also be aggressive, independent, a risk taker, anxious, impersonal, competitive, and invulnerable, with a low stress tolerance, which, when you think about it, are all based on attention-seeking and fear. However, where personality really counts is during interactions with other people; behaviour breeds behaviour. Crews are frightened to deal with the Captain, and Captains won't deal with crews

- *Leadership vs teamwork*. Leadership has been defined as facilitating the movement of a team toward the accomplishment of a task, in this case, the crew and the safe arrival of their passengers. This is a better definition than "Getting somebody to do what you want them to do" which implies a certain amount of manipulation, something more in the realm of management as a scientific process.

- *Personal qualities* to passengers and colleagues

- *Knowledge*, and the ability to apply it.

RISK MANAGEMENT
• •

When the links in an error chain start to come together, the risk starts building, since error is one source of risk, and occupies the largest share of the total. Uncertainty about a situation can often indicate its presence.

One definition of risk is the chance that a situation, or the consequences of one, will be hazardous enough to cause harm, injury or loss. Another is that a *risk arises every time a person is in the presence of a hazard*. Health & Safety legislation defines a hazard as a condition, event or circumstance that has the potential to cause harm or damage to people or aircraft, equipment and structures (associated with the present, in that a hazard is always present). A **Risk** is the potential outcome from that hazard, expressed in terms of the likelihood of anything happening and its severity (and therefore associated with the future). In other words, the risk is a value judgment based upon the hazard.

Risk management is an important part of Decision Making because when good procedures are followed, risk is automatically reduced.

The goal of whoever operates a Safety Management System is to:

- Identify any hazards that might be encountered (e.g. wet helidecks)

- Identify the risks associated with them (spinning helicopters)

- The level of risk for each scenario

- Apply rules or design SOPs to minimise the risks

However, risks encountered in aviation do not always arise from being airborne. Ground operations pose their own problems. It's also worth pointing out that hazards need not be technical - there are business risks, too, such as when a company is growing quickly and can be exposed to cashflow problems, where safety might get a lower priority against simply surviving. There may be a high staff turnover, or you may have a disproportionate amount of inexperienced pilots that need proper supervision. A proactive safety manager will be looking for such problems before they start.

To have absolutely no risk, of course, we shouldn't take off at all, but that's not what we're here for (some communities in remote places *depend* on pilots taking risks), so we have to have some method of evaluating risk against a yardstick to get the job done, or balance profitability with safety. *Risk management* is the key, best used in an ample-time decision-making situation, where time is not critical. For example, in a helicopter, it can be more dangerous to avoid the height/velocity curve (say when coming out of a confined area) than to be in it for a few seconds. Part of the pilot's job is to decide which of

If this page is a photocopy, it is not authorised!

CAPT

the risks presents the least hazard - that is, is there a greater risk of colliding with something when coming out of the clearing than having an engine failure? Is it better to take off downwind into a clear area, or into wind with a lot of obstructions? Risk Management means measuring the degree of harm against that of exposure - the more you have to lose, the less risks you want to take.

Risk Management, therefore, is a decision-making tool that can be applied to either eliminate risk, or reduce it to an acceptable level, preferably before takeoff (things that stop you eliminating risk entirely would either be impracticality, or money). With it, you have to first identify a hazard, analyse any associated risks, make a decision and implement it (with a *risk strategy*) and monitor the results, with a view to changing things if need be. However, this depends on the *perception* of a risk, and the difference between yours, the management's and the customer's can be quite startling. Outside influences include weather, traffic and obstacles. Internal ones can be maintenance, fatigue, or the culture of the company.

Analysing Risk

There are two types of risk:

- **External** (or Objective) Risk is that of an accident in the current situation if no changes are made to the flight path or the operation of systems.

- **Internal** (or Subjective) Risk. A risk that reflects the inability of the crew to implement a solution due to lack of knowledge or time to apply it. Internal risk increases linearly as the deadline for making and implementing a decision approaches.

The **Risk Factor** can be defined as anything that may increase the likelihood of an accident occurring.

There are many aspects to analyzing risk:

- Where is it?

- How likely is it to happen? A *High Probability* means it is likely to happen. *Medium* means it has a fair chance of happening, *Low* means it is possible, but not probable, and *Very Low* means it will almost certainly not happen (but never say never!)

- How significant is it? That is, what are the consequences? *High* indicates irreparable harm. *Medium* means a significant impact, and *Low* means just inconvenience

- What are the priorities? An HH risk, meaning that not only is something likely to happen, but, when it does, will cause irreparable harm to people or property, needs attention first

The assessment of risk in a particular situation will be based on subjective perception and evaluation of situational factors. What this means in English is that the difference between perceived and actual risk depends on the amount of control you think you have, and familiarity. For example, it is a lot more risky to ride a bike through a busy city than it is to live near a nuclear power station, yet people still ride bikes along Main Street and don't want to live near nuckear power stations. The former situation allows you more control (you can always get off and walk) and is more familiar. Your perception of control is influenced by your fear of the unknown.

Features that reduce the risks associated with flight are:

- situational awareness

- problem recognition

- good judgment

- skill

Risk is equal to *probability* multiplied by the *consequences* of what you propose to do, and your *exposure*. You essentially have four choices, based on the TEAM acronym:

- **Transfer** the risk (maybe with insurance

- **Eliminate** the risk (don't do the job)

- **Accept** the risk (see *Risk Tolerability*, overleaf)

- **Mitigate** the effects of the risk. This means reducing a risk to bring it into a lower category. There may be three ways of doing this:

  - *Avoidance.* To be used when the risk exceeds the benefit gained.

  - *Reduction.* Don't take the risk so often, or reduce its consequences.

  - *Segregation.* Isolate the effects of the risk or build in some redundancy.

High risk means a high probability of death, damage or injury, requiring appropriate procedures - possibly with none available at all and you have to think on your feet, which is where your training comes in. *Low risk* is a normal situation, where normal precautions are enough.

A common attitude when exposed to risk is that of **denial**, which can typically show as a behavioural pattern:

- **Procrastination** ("I'll continue for a bit then decide")

- **Rationalisation** ("It'll work out fine")

- **Hope and Desires** ("It will be clear on the other side of these hills")

- **Refusal to Admit** ("It's not like that and anyway it can't happen to me")

- **Status and Reputation** ("I won't be beaten")

- **Refusal to Review** ("It worked last time")

Denial is a refusal to accept, admit, confront, change or decide and has been the cause of many accidents. For a good decision to be made, you should look at the world as it is, rather than how it should be!

You could always try and prehandle situations - that is, make as many decisions as possible ahead of time, as part of your flight planning - most important, though is to leave yourself a way out. For example, always be aware, when dropping water, that you may have to get out of a hot hole with the load on - don't assume that the bucket will work and you will be light enough to escape! Is the weather closing in behind you? Have you gone into a confined area and boxed yourself in? Mountain pilots *always* have a way out - even after they've landed!

You might find it strange not to accept a risk of engine failure and a possible wire strike after you've been in hostile terrain for the last 15 minutes, but this is the fine line in the world of aviation. In the words of one senior pilot: "We do what we have to do, when we have to do it, in the calculated risk sense, but we never take a single risk we don't have to…"

Risk Severity

The table below can be used to categorise the severity of the results if something went wrong.

Definition	Meaning	Value
Catastrophic	Accident, death or equipment destroyed	5
Hazardous	Serious injury, major equipment damaged	4
Major	Serious incident or injury	3
Minor	Minor incident	2
Negligible	Nuisance value	1

Risk Likelihood

The table below can be used to categorise the likelihood of something going wrong.

Definition	Meaning	Value
Frequent	May occur many times	5
Occasional	May occur sometimes	4
Remote	Unlikely but possible	3
Improbable	Very unlikely	2
Extremely Improbable	Virtually impossible	1

Risk Tolerability

Having determined the severity of the results and their likelihood, use the table below to determine whether the risk is acceptable or not:

Risk probability	Risk Severity				
	Catastrophic 5	Hazardous 4	Major 3	Minor 2	Negligible 1
Frequent 5	Unacceptable	Unacceptable	Unacceptable	Review	Review
Occasional 4	Unacceptable	Unacceptable	Review	Review	Review
Remote 3	Unacceptable	Review	Review	Review	Acceptable
Improbable 2	Review	Review	Review	Acceptable	Acceptable
Extremely improbable 1	Review	Acceptable	Acceptable	Acceptable	Acceptable

For example, if the risk taken would have hazardous consequences (a weighting of 4) and may occur frequently (a weighting of 5), it would be unacceptable. Usually, flexibility lies with the likelihood of an occurrence rather than its severity.

If the risk is unacceptable, the activity should be stopped immediately, or cancelled if it is not already under way. If it falls in the Review category, there is some concern and steps should be taken to reduce the risk to as low as is reasonably practicable (ALARP). A risk may still be acceptable in this category, provided it is understood.

Note: Even though a risk is acceptable, steps should still be taken to reduce it as far as possible.

"Carelessness and overconfidence are often more dangerous than deliberately accepted risks"

Wilbur Wright

CAPT

PRINCIPLES OF FLIGHT

Many of the definitions given below do not just apply to Principles of Flight, but originate from mechanics and can be used with many other aspects of aviation. For example, vectors can not only be used to describe the forces acting on an aerofoil, but can also show the relationships between heading and track when affected by the wind, which is useful in Navigation.

NEWTON'S LAWS

Sir Isaac Newton formulated three laws of motion that govern material bodies, which are also relevant to flight (especially 2 & 3 for helicopters):

- **1.** *An object at rest (or in motion) will remain at rest (or in motion at that velocity) until acted upon by an external force,* otherwise known as *Inertia.* In other words, the object is *neither accelerating nor decelerating,* although it might be moving, and you must apply a force to make it move or change direction (or if you observe an acceleration, there must be a force behind it. Obvious, really). Since air has mass, it can be seen as an object capable of applying force.

- **2.** *The rate of change of motion (of a body)* [acceleration] *is directly proportional to the force acting on it, along its line of action, and inversely proportional to the body's mass.*

  Put more precisely, acceleration is proportional to, and in the direction of, an applied force, so the acceleration of a stream of air when it is deflected by an aerofoil is proportional to its momentum - if its speed doubles, so does the air's acceleration in the direction it is forced to go. On the other hand, if the *mass* of air doubles, its acceleration halves. As a result of this law, the strength of a *force* depends on *mass* multiplied by *acceleration.* The other form of Newton's Second Law is the *Equation of Momentum and Impulse.* It simply means that the change of momentum of a system is equal to the impulse applied by a net force on the system.

- **3.** *If one body exerts a force on another body, the second body will exert an equal and opposite force on the first body,* popularised as: *For every action, there is an equal and opposite reaction.* This law is made use of by propellers and jet engines to drive aeroplanes (and autogyros) forward. In simple terms, the helicopter flies because it pulls down enough air through its rotors to lift it into the air. The tail rotor uses the same principle to stop the fuselage spinning the opposite way to the blades.

DEFINITIONS

Many of these are covered more fully elsewhere, but are here because of stray questions in the syllabus.

- **Vector** - A quantity that has size *and direction*, such as force or velocity (non-directional *scalar* quantities like mass have size only, and can be combined by simple addition or subtraction). The length of a vector is proportional to the quantity involved. For example, to represent a speed of 60 knots, you might draw a line 6 inches long, with each inch standing for 10 knots (all the other lines in the drawing must have the same scale).

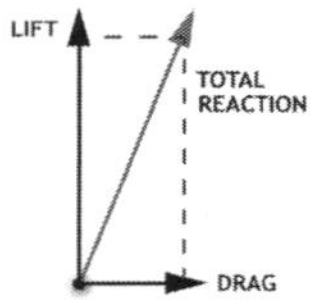

  Now you can work out problems with diagrams rather than complex formulae, because vectors can be combined to produce a *resultant* such as Total Reaction shown on the right. The single force which is exactly equivalent to two, or more, forces is called their resultant. When two forces are applied to or from a point, their resultant is the diagonal of a parallelogram based on that point. The resolution of a vector is the process of finding its effect in two mutually perpendicular directions.

- **Vector Diagram** - a picture of a vector with an arrow showing the direction the force is acting in.

- **Velocity** - The rate of change of position *in a given direction*, equal to distance divided by time. Unfortunately, this is often used synonymously with the word *speed*, as the units used are the same, but speed is only concerned with the time taken over a distance travelled, not the direction.

- **Inertia** - A resistive force that gives a body the tendency to remain at rest, or carry on with what it's doing - in other words, not to change its present state, or to maintain a constant velocity, and be hard to get moving (but see *Momentum* about stopping), as in Newton's first law. To do its work, air must possess the property of inertia.

Inertia should not confused with Momentum, as even bodies at rest have inertia. Inertia and momentum can both add stress to the materials used in aircraft construction, as found with aerofoils that flex on takeoff or landing.

When mass changes, inertia changes, too.

- **Mass** - the quantity of matter in a body, which is constant if the number of molecules remains unaltered. The word **weight** is often used instead, but that is described below.

  Newton defined mass in terms of inertia, in that the mass of a body can be a numerical measure of the inertia that it possesses - the greater its mass, the greater the force needed to move it.

  Note: The basis of flight is the *conservation of mass* (from Lavoisier) applied to a fluid. Conservation principles include:

  - *Continuity,* where mass can neither be created nor destroyed, but it may change form into something else, like heat with an engine, or chemical energy (from the engine) into kinetic energy (movement). In a steady flow process (where flow rates don't change over time) the inflow should equal outflow, or what goes in must come out, whatever might happen in the middle. This is similar to Kirchhoff's electrical law, and Daniel Bernoulli's *Venturi Effect.*

  - The *Conservation Of Momentum* is Newton's second law applied to a continuum.

  - The *Conservation Of Energy* applies to the First Law of Thermodynamics (see *Engines* for the second). It is similar to *Continuity,* above.

- **Weight**. This is the effect of gravity (g) on a mass that provides a force acting down, toward the centre of the Earth. This may not be constant, as gravity varies around the world, but as the atmosphere occupies only 1/600 of the space taken up by the Earth, its influence can at least be considered as constant. As weight is a force it should also be expressed in Newtons.

- **Force** - a dynamic influence that changes a body's state of rest to one of motion, or changes its rate of motion. In simple terms, a push (the only forces that truly pull are gravity, magnetism and electrical attraction). Force = mass x acceleration (f=m.a).

  Four forces act on an aircraft in flight, called *Lift, Weight, Thrust* and *Drag*. For now, lift makes a flying machine go up, weight makes it go down, thrust makes it go forward, and drag tries to stop it. Causing them to become unbalanced is what makes an aircraft go in one direction or another.

Under Newton's first law, a moving body will travel along a straight path (with *constant velocity*) unless a force acts on it from outside. With circular motion, the constant force pushing a body toward the centre is *centripetal force*, inwards along the radius of a curve. It is an accelerating force, as it changes velocity, and is proportional to the body's mass.

However, under Newton's third law the opposite reaction is *centrifugal force*, which is a fictitious one acting *outwards* from an axis of rotation. It increases with *mass*, the *square of rotational speed,* and the *distance from the axis,* and is inversely proportional to the radius of the curve in that, the smaller the curve is, the more influence centrifugal force has.

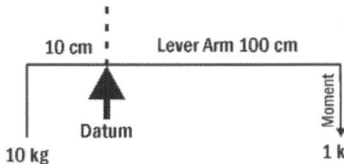

Note: Being fictitious, centrifugal force does not act on the body in motion - the only one actually involved is centripetal force. It is the *removal* of centripetal force that allows a blade to fly from the hub when it is released. "Centrifugal force" plays a significant part in the rigidity of rotor blades.

Force is not the same as Power! Forces are vectors.

- **Moment.** The product of a force over a distance, as used with Centre of Gravity calculations, or the turning effect of a force about a point, expressed in foot-pounds or Newton/Metres. **Torque** is similar, but is a continuous force in one direction.

  In the diagram below, the beam is balanced even though different weights are suspended from each end - the difference is compensated for by each one's distance from the fulcrum:

  10 cm | Lever Arm 100 cm | Moment

  Datum

  10 kg | 1 kg

  Clockwise movement of the beam is regarded as being positive, and anticlockwise is negative.

- **Centre Of Gravity**. The C of G is the point around which all moments arising from gravity are equal to zero. It is where an object's weight (or gravitational attraction) passes through, or where its mass is concentrated. When stationary on the ground, the total weight of an aircraft acts vertically through the Centre of Gravity, parallel to the gravity vector. The C of G could also be described as the average location of a body's weight force, or its point of balance.

- **Couple**. A combination of two equal, parallel and opposite forces that produces a rotation. For example, the couple formed by Thrust and Drag in the diagram will cause the nose of the helicopter to go down. It doesn't go down too far because, once they get out of line, the new couple formed by lift and weight pulls it back.

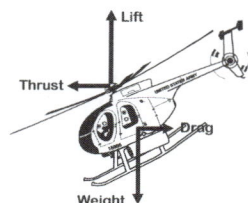

The *moment* of a couple is one of its forces multiplied by the distance between them both (this is relevant for tail rotor drift).

- **Acceleration** - the rate of change of motion in speed and/or direction (velocity), or the change in velocity, divided by time. If you change one or the other, or both, an object is accelerating, as with a turning helicopter affected by centripetal force, or a rotor blade. **Note:** Although the word *acceleration* refers to any change in velocity, the word *deceleration* is also used to indicate a decrease. Acceleration as G forces can affect the human body a lot in flight, as described in *Human Factors*.

Force and mass are related, in that doubling both produces the same value of acceleration. Doubling the force doubles the acceleration if mass stays the same, and doubling mass for the same force halves the acceleration.

- **G Forces**. *G* is shorthand for any force or acceleration that is equivalent to weight, so 2G is twice your body's weight. *g* shares the same units as acceleration which, for a falling body under gravity (g) is 32 feet per second, per second, but the SI unit is metres per second, squared (9.8 m/s²).

- **Equilibrium** - a state of balance between forces, where there is zero acceleration, like a helicopter in a steady vertical climb or straight and level flight.

- **Viscosity**. Fluids such as air behave differently when they are flowing because of internal friction between its layers. This is expressed by viscosity, which is also relevant for oil and lubrication, and the way air flows over an aerofoil. The higher the viscosity, the slower the flow.

- **Momentum** - the quantity of motion in a body, or its resistance to being brought to rest. As it is a vector quantity, momentum concerns the *velocity* of a body as well as its mass, so the relevant formula is *momentum = mass × velocity*, which denotes how much is moving and how fast (only bodies with velocity can have momentum). If either mass or velocity increase, the momentum increases and you need a bigger force to change the body's state of motion. For example, a heavy helicopter hover taxiing at a high rate of knots requires larger handfuls of power to stop than if it were going at walking pace. Of course, you could also use a relatively small force for a longer time - a bullet and a steamroller may have similar momenta, but they obviously have different masses and speeds. The small letter *p* signifies momentum.

Note: Momentum is not Inertia, and it is not the same as Kinetic Energy. The total momentum of an isolated system remains constant. Any change of momentum involves a force.

- **Energy** - the ability of a body (or unit of mass) to do work, in Joules (the unit of work) or 1 Newton metre. An aircraft can have three types of energy:

  - *potential energy*, which comes from a body's position in a gravity field (usually height)

  - *kinetic energy*, which comes from movement, and is actually a measure of the ability of a body to do work when it is brought to rest, where it can change to pressure energy

  - *chemical energy*, which comes from the engines

As an example, a hovering helicopter has no kinetic energy, miniscule potential energy and lots of chemical energy. One in straight and level flight has heaps of all three. A reduction in chemical energy (losing an engine) will cause a descent.

- **Work** is movement *against resistance*. It is done when a force moves a body in the direction that the force is acting, so it is equivalent to *force × distance*, or *force × velocity*, if you bring time into it. If an object doesn't move despite a force being applied, no work is done, although "work" in the casual sense obviously has. A hovering helicopter is not doing any work!

- **Power** - the *rate* of doing work, or how much is used over a period of time. It is measured in Watts.

- **Tip Path Plane**. The path taken by the tips of the rotor blades as they rotate. It can also be called the *rotor disc plane* or the *no-flapping plane,* as it refers to a plane with no variation in blade pitch (see *ACK*). The virtual rotation (no flapping) axis lies through the centre of the hub, perpendicular to the TPP.

- **Rotor Disc**. The area within the Tip Path Plane, rotating clockwise or anticlockwise when viewed from above. Anticlockwise rotation is also known as *North American Rotation,* and is assumed in this book, unless specified otherwise. Any effects are simply reversed if blades go the other way round.

- **Axis Of Rotation**. The line through the main rotor head about which the blades rotate. It does not always coincide with the main rotor shaft axis, as the rotor disc can be tilted in the flight direction.

- **Rotors** (rotor blades) - the lift producing surfaces of a helicopter, the same as wings on an aeroplane.

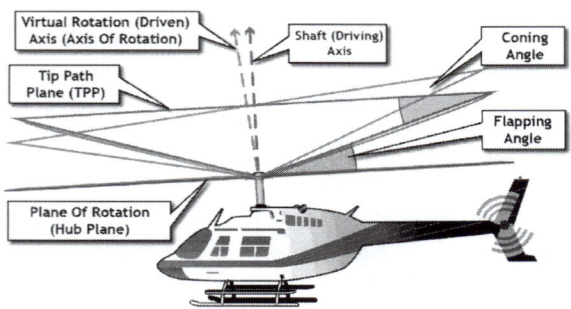

- **Plane Of Rotation**. A line extended from the rotor hub, through its centre, parallel to the Tip Path Plane*, and perpendicular to the Axis Of Rotation. On the ground, when the blades are not producing lift, the POR coincides with the Tip Path Plane. Once you increase the pitch and start creating lift, the blades (and TPP) rise into the air. The angular difference is the coning angle.

*Not completely true for fully articulated heads.

- **Angle Of Attack**. The angle at which the chord line (a straight line joining the front and rear edges of an aerofoil) meets airflow coming the other way.

- **Compressibility**. As soon as you start moving, air is compressed against the fuselage, and some areas change their density. This is ignored below 300 kts as the air manages to avoid being compressed and the factor is only around 2% but, above it, the effects can be significant, so any instruments or aerofoils relying on air pressure won't work so well without adjustment. Any speed above 300 kts needs compressibility to be accounted for.

To predict the effects of compressibility, you need to be able to determine the ....

- **Mach Number** - Compressibility effects depend on the relationship of airspeed to the speed of sound (M), but they can be experienced below that in small pockets of fast airflow (insignificant below M0.4). Although helicopters do not fly that fast, the tips of some rotor blades can approach the speed of sound if they rotate fast enough, or are affected by strong gusts of wind, which accounts for the "chopping" sound of mini sonic booms.

- **Pitot Static System**. A series of pipes around the cockpit through which air flows to feed three common instruments: the altimeter, airspeed indicator and vertical speed indicator. The difference between stagnation and static pressures allows speed to be indicated, plus altitude and its rate of change.

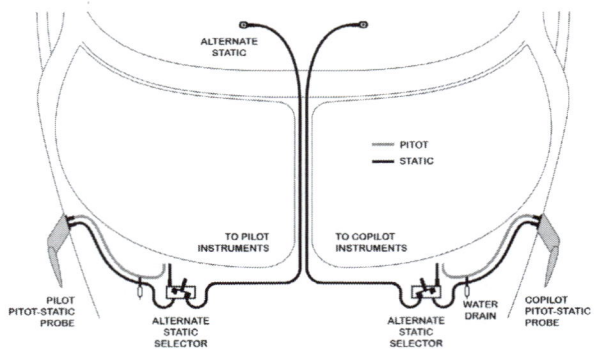

A static blockage causes an altimeter to stay at the height at which the blockage occurred. The VSI's pressure differentials will also disappear to make it read zero. If the pitot becomes blocked, the ASI will behave like an altimeter because it has only static information to work with - its readings (i.e. your airspeed) will increase as you climb. If the static gets blocked, this will reverse.

- **ISA Conditions**. A state of the atmosphere which is accepted as standard for the purposes of calibration and performance. For example, in the standard atmosphere, pressure is taken to be 1013.25 hectopascals and 15.5° Centigrade, reducing by 1.98°C per 1000 ft. **The only time pitot static instruments read accurately is in ISA conditions.** Otherwise they must be corrected, as conditions are hardly ever standard.

- **Indicated airspeed** (IAS) is read directly and corrected for instrument error.

- **Calibrated airspeed** (CAS) is IAS corrected for position errors*, which are highest at low speeds, and can be corrected out by the Air Data Computer in modern aircraft. IAS and CAS are about the same in the cruise.

*The effects of airflow around static vents and the pitot head.

- **Equivalent Airspeed** (EAS) is CAS plus compressibility.

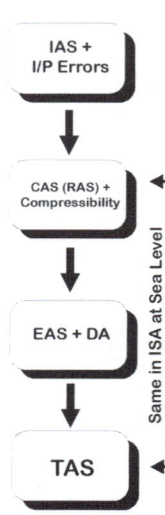

© Phil Croucher, 2013

CAPT

- **True Air Speed** (TAS) is the CAS corrected for altitude and temperature, or density. In ISA conditions at sea level, CAS = TAS. *It is the only speed* and the only figure used for navigation - the others are pressures and deal with aircraft behaviour! On average, TAS increases by 2% over IAS for every 1,000 feet. The difference between them decreases at decreasing altitude. Below sea level, TAS reduces compared to the IAS.

- **Indicated altitude** is what is shown on the dial at the current altimeter setting.

- **Calibrated altitude** is the indicated altitude corrected for instrument and position error.

- **True Altitude** is the actual one above mean sea level, taking the above errors into account, plus air temperature and density (absolute altitude is the actual height above the surface, and is produced by a radio altimeter).

- **Flight Controls**. A helicopter can move or turn in any direction, including up and down. To do this, the controls will move the aircraft in one of three axes - *pitching* (nose up or down around the lateral axis), *rolling* (wings up or down around the longitudinal axis) or *yawing* (nose left or right around the normal axis).

All three axes pass through the Centre of Gravity.

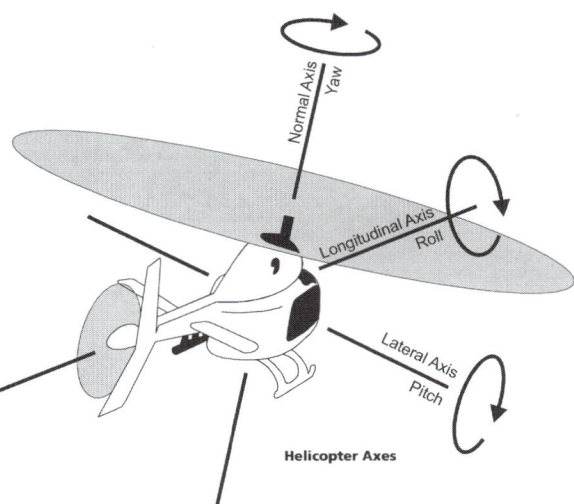

Helicopter Axes

Controls do not move in isolation, however - an adjustment in one causes a secondary effect in another and must be allowed for when you position them. In other words, you must learn to anticipate the movements and put in just enough control movement, which is hard on a machine that does not react instantly!

The flight controls are the *cyclic* and *collective* controls, the *throttle* and the *tail rotor pedals*, which all have much the same effect as they do in aeroplanes (once out of the hover), except for the collective, which isn't used in them at all.

- **Collective Pitch**. To the left of the pilot's seat, this control changes the pitch of all the rotor blades at the same time.

- **Rudder Pedals**. These control the pitch of the tail rotor blades collectively (i.e. all at once, but nothing to do with the collective control which affects the main rotors). In a helicopter with N American rotation, pushing the left pedal forward increases the pitch from the neutral setting* to make the nose turn left or keep it straight when power is applied, when the torque reaction increases. Pushing the right pedal decreases tail rotor pitch, so main rotor torque overcomes that of the tail rotor.

*This is not zero pitch, but a small positive angle that keeps the nose straight in the hover.

- **Cyclic Control.** Movement about the longitudinal and lateral axes is performed with the cyclic control, which only changes the pitch of one blade at a time, to raise the rotor disk (or, rather, the *tip path plane*) at one point and tilt it in the direction you want to go. In other words, it changes the *direction* of the lifting force, and not its *magnitude*, except in the one place required to lift the blade. When a cyclic control input has been made, the rotor blade pitch will be increasing for one half of a revolution and decreasing for the next half, to obtain *maximum pitch* on the *retreating* side and *minimum* on the *advancing side* in forward flight.

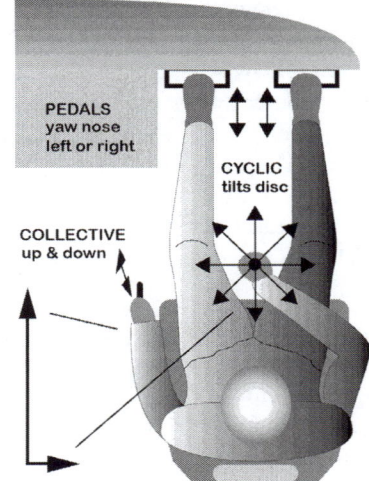

PEDALS yaw nose left or right

CYCLIC tilts disc

COLLECTIVE up & down

During flight, the cyclic determines *attitude, airspeed* and *horizontal movement*.

- **The Throttle** is usually on the end of the collective lever. Its function is to *regulate engine RPM*, and it is moved by the left hand outwards (away from the thumb) to increase 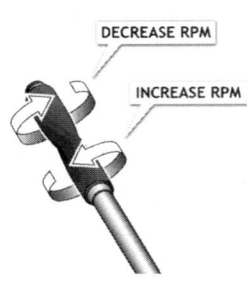 power, and the other way to reduce it. When engine RPM is maintained by a governor, the throttle isn't moved at all, except in some emergencies where it can control the directional attitude of the fuselage. Because they are usually left in one position, turbine helicopters may have the throttles in the roof or on the floor which, of course, restricts their use when such problems occur.

  Some throttle must be applied when the collective pitch is increased to keep the Rotor RPM up. In fact, the throttle in a piston machine should be applied just before, so the engine doesn't lag, a process of anticipation called *leading with throttle*.

AIRFLOW
••

Air is a fluid. Under the Archimedes Principle, an aircraft will be supported by a force equal to the weight of air displaced by it (buoyancy). Weight acts downwards and buoyancy acts upwards, so the two cancel each other out when the aircraft is in a steady, or unaccelerated, state, where the net force is zero.

However, in the diagram, the aircraft is moving at constant velocity (V) in air otherwise at rest. Looked at another way, the aircraft could be at rest, with the air streaming past it, at -V. In theory, the situation is the same in both cases, but air at rest has less turbulence than moving air, so there are practical limits.

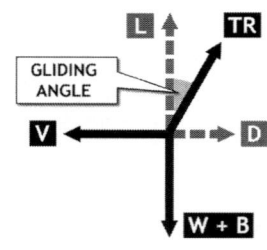

The speed at which an object moves through the air is called *airspeed*. It doesn't matter whether the air flows over it, or the object itself moves - the effects are the same, so even if you tie a rotor blade down, a strong wind will still make it want to fly up. The path an object takes through the air is the *flight path*, and the air going the other way is the *relative airflow, undisturbed airflow* or *relative wind* - they all oppose the flight path. As it is the resultant of two vectors, it may also be called the resultant wind.

To keep the vectors correct, you now need another force (labelled TR) which is caused by motion, and which is aerodynamic. TR (*Total Reaction*) can be resolved from two components, one **at right angles** to V, called *Lift*, and one **opposite** to V, called *Drag*. The angle between TR and L (the gliding angle) should be as small as possible to keep the drag vector short and the lift vector long. The smaller the gliding angle is, the more streamlined the aircraft is.

Note: Lift does not necessarily act upwards, and drag does not necessarily act in a horizontal direction.

As it has mass, air can exert force, do work and transfer energy. As a quantity, it is normally measured in cubic feet. The ability for air to do work is affected by air density, which reduces as you go higher or if the air gets warmer.

Aerodynamic effects depend on:

- **air pressure**, which acts perpendicular to the surface of a body, and

- **friction**, which acts parallel to it

As the friction is confined to only a small area (the boundary layer, described overleaf), the *pressure distribution* around the aerofoil is what does the work.

Streamlines & Streamtubes

The passage of air over an aerofoil in a steady path is called a streamline flow.

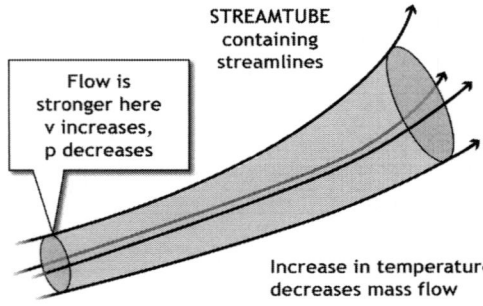

Streamlines are imaginary curves along which individual particles of fluid flow. Their density is proportional to their size (or strength), in that, the closer they are together, the stronger is the flow, so they can be used to illustrate increases and decreases in pressure and velocity by being drawn as converging or diverging.

If you draw a streamline through each point of a closed curve, you get a **stream tube**, which is a tubular region of fluid surrounded by streamlines.

If you reduce the cross-sectional area of a tube (or a pipe) and force the streamlines closer together, their velocity increases (notice how water flows faster if you squeeze the end of a garden hose).

DOWNWASH

Downwash is a good example of a streamtube.

Each blade displaces its portion of air downwards, so the ones that follow in quick succession are imparting downward motion to air that has already started in that direction. We now have a column of descending air.

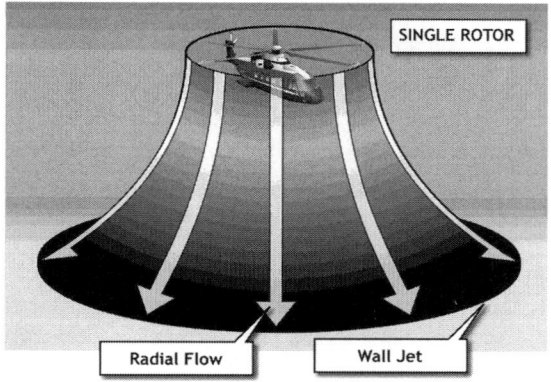

A **radial wall jet** develops when a helicopter hovers near the ground, when high velocity downwash hits the ground and changes direction by 90°, accelerating radially outward. It reaches its maximum effect about 1 rotor diameter away from the rotor axis, where the static pressure in the flow equalises to the atmospheric value.

When helicopters are flown in confined areas and near to people, structures or equipment (or other helicopters), there is a chance of a downwash related mishap, such as:

- Personal injury or equipment damage from flying debris, oil drums*, boxes, rocks, planking, trees, tents, etc.

    *An oil drum will blow over if it is within 45 feet of the centre of a rotor of a Bell 206L in a 9-knot wind. It will be 30 feet in a 5 knot wind.

- Rotor blade strikes on tailbooms and tunnel covers

- Doors and cowlings blowing off

The outward flow can also erode soil, blow things over and into other things, create rotor wake recirculation and wind hazards. When downwash hits the horizontal stabiliser, it pitches the nose up. It can also produce a downward force on the fuselage.

The Boundary Layer

Up to a certain critical airspeed, air flowing over or around a body will hug its shape and be quite well-behaved, flowing in a *laminar* fashion, after which it breaks up to form vortices that may interfere with any lifting action. Airflow is laminar if it follows a smooth path and its parallel layers do not interfere with each other. That is, it is non-turbulent, and its layers have different velocities.

The reason airflow hugs the body is that its pressure reduces because it speeds up as it goes round the object. Atmospheric pressure then pushes it against the surface.

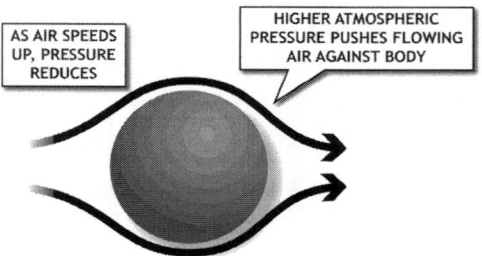

Note: The atmospheric pressure acts against *all* surfaces.

When a circular cylinder is at rest, and the velocity of the airflow as it meets the cylinder is given a value of V, the velocity will be twice that as it goes over the top (at A).

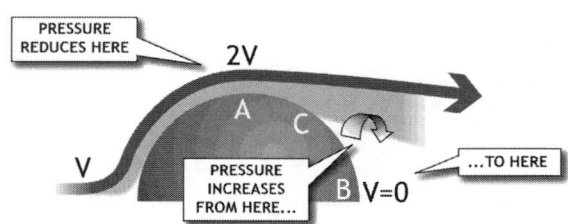

However, the pressure is higher at B, so the air cannot force its way there. This reverses the flow around point C, where it is about to break away. Beyond C it forms into an eddying wake, which increases the resistance. The shape of an aerofoil behind its thickest point tapers away to minimise this effect and ensure that the air breaks away as much as possible near the trailing edge, so the turbulent wake remains small.

If you go through a car wash, and your car is still wet, you will notice drops of water staying still on the bodywork, no matter how fast you drive. The layer in which this happens is called the *boundary layer*. Friction makes the air in the lower areas of the boundary layer slow progressively, until, at the surface, its relative speed could be zero, hence the water mentioned above being unaffected.

Looked at another way, an object moving through air pulls a few air molecules along with it, at around the same speed as the object. Molecules slightly further away will also be

pulled along, but at a slightly lower speed, and so on. The layer of air that extends from the surface of the object to where nothing is dragged along at all is the *laminar boundary layer*, which is typically about half an inch thick up to the *transition point*, somewhere near the thickest part of the aerofoil, where it becomes the *turbulent boundary layer*, and around three inches thick, and which has the strongest change in velocity close to the surface.

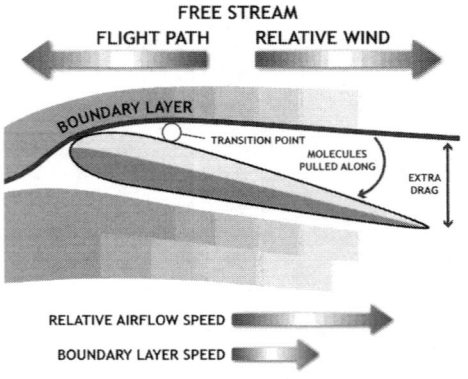

This creates a wedge of air that resists the aerofoil's movement in the shape of *drag*, which is dealt with in a few pages' time. The transition point moves *forward* with speed (and angle of attack), which is something to do with the Reynolds number*, and more of the blade becomes affected by the turbulent area, which increases the amount of skin friction. The point where turbulent airflow leaves the surface to create wake turbulence is the *separation point*.

Free Stream is air that has not been affected by the aircraft.

*The Reynolds number expresses the ratio of pressure against viscosity forces in the flow of a fluid - it is dimensionless, meaning that it has no units (it was developed to relate scale models in wind tunnels to their real-life counterparts). Fluid flow is turbulent when the RN is greater than 2000.

SUMMARY

The forces around aerofoils include pressure forces *against* or *from* the surfaces at right angles, and friction *along* them, so the airflow is slowed down to greater or lesser degrees, according to their smoothness. The layer of air immediately in contact with the surface is slowed down the most and subsequent ones less until it reaches the *free stream flow rate*. This boundary layer is divided into *laminar* (streamlined) flow and *turbulent* flow - the latter has more kinetic energy and the strongest change in velocity close to the surface. The point where it goes from laminar to turbulent is the *transition point*, where the layer thickens to create extra drag that will try to stop the aerofoil moving through the air.

THE AEROFOIL

An aerofoil is a wing, or a rotor blade, or any device that creates a lift reaction out of the air. It is shaped to produce a reaction at approximately right angles to the direction of flight (any angular differences are accounted for by the viscosity of the air below the aerofoil producing friction).

The aerofoil's purpose is to deflect air downwards, partly by making it go faster over its top surface. Newton's laws take over and the aircraft lifts up into the air.

The difference is that a wing has much the same airspeed flowing over its whole length, but a rotor blade has a different airspeed from inch to inch.

Note: The lower pressure above the aerofoil is not a vacuum, so the aircraft is not sucked up into the air. However, there is enough of a variation from normal surface pressure to start a reaction and allow atmospheric pressure from underneath to push the aircraft up.

The most effective part of the aerofoil in this respect is the upper surface, especially the first quarter, where pressure is decreased the most *relative* to the lower surface.

For it to go up, the lift created must be more than the weight of the aircraft - in the cruise, of course, when everything should be in balance, lift and weight will be equal. If the air becomes less dense (i.e. less thick), to maintain the mass airflow to keep the machine up in the air, you must increase the speed over the aerofoils to compensate. In an aeroplane, this means flying faster.

The Flat Plate

A flat plate held at right angles to a flow of air is impacted by kinetic energy. At slow speeds, nothing much happens but, at higher ones, a resistance is felt (inertia). This resistance can be diverted upwards by inclining the plate.

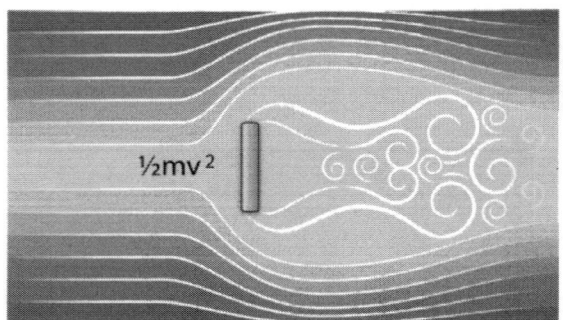

Pressure decrease behind flat plate is more than increase in front

Even though most of the air goes past the plate, its resistance to the air flow increases (almost entirely) because of the turbulence created behind it (form drag). The pressure in front of the plate does not increase as much as it decreases on the other side because the influence of atmospheric pressure is spoilt on that side.

CAPT

If the flat plate is held at 45° to the airflow, the drag is greatly reduced, but the plate will try to rise into the air.

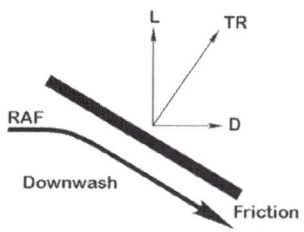

A flat plate in the airflow with a small angle of attack will produce some lift and some drag. If the plate is held edgewise, there will be no drag, but also no lift.

The flat plate now needs to be acquire a shape both to reduce drag and gain strength.

Profile

The side view of an aerofoil is its *profile*.

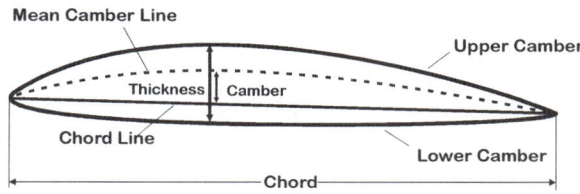

It can be changed in many ways. For example, collecting ice will change its shape and therefore its lift and drag characteristics, and their relative ratios, probably increase the stalling angle of attack, and make it heavier. In other words, if ice or snow, or any other contamination collects on the rotor blades, there is a reduction of lift, and extra weight makes things worse.

Heavy rain may wear the leading edge of a blade, and increase profile drag.

Planform

This is the shape of an aerofoil viewed from above. It could be *rectangular*, *tapered* (from root to tip), *elliptical* (see right), *delta* or *swept back*. Large, wide aerofoils, for example, are good for large transport aircraft, and short, stubby ones will be found on fast sports aircraft.

Helicopter rotor blades can have different shapes as well, in an attempt to reduce problems caused by flying near the speed of sound (see later).

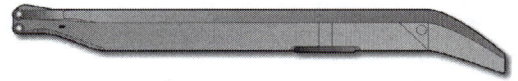

Aspect Ratio

The *aspect ratio* of a wing (or a rotor blade) is the relationship between its length and width, or *span* and *chord* (actually the square of the span divided by the wing area). You could have two aerofoils of equal surface area but different aspect ratios, depending on what they were designed for. The higher the ratio of length to width, the more lift you get (with *less* induced drag at the *tips*), but the blades are not so stiff and they may start to flutter.

Glider wings have high aspect ratios, as do rotor blades.

Thickness

Thickness describes the greatest distance between the upper and lower surfaces of an aerofoil. The Thickness/Chord ratio of an aerofoil section is expressed in *percentage of chord*. Using percentages allows you to change the size of the aerofoil without changing its shape. Somewhere near the point of maximum thickness, you get *maximum velocity* and *minimum pressure*.

The *fineness ratio* is the inverse of the thickness/chord ratio.

The Chord Line

The *chord line* is a *straight line* which joins the leading and trailing edges of an aerofoil (actually, the ends of the mean camber line, or the centres of curvature at each end), and it is the size of the angle that the chord line makes with the relative airflow that is so important in the creation of lift.

The mean chord is determined by dividing the gross wing area by the wing span.

The word *camber* is popularly used to mean the curvature of the aerofoil - an aerofoil is cambered when the line connecting the centres of all inscribed circles is curved. Technically, the word refers to the displacement of the *mean camber* from the chord line.

The mean camber line also joins the leading and trailing edges, but at an equal distance from its upper and lower surfaces. If the aerofoil is symmetrical, the mean camber line will follow the chord line. Otherwise, it will be a curve biased towards the thickest side. If it crosses the chord line, the aerofoil is *reflexed*. The maximum camber is just referred to as "the camber", because it is the only dimension worth bothering about.

The camber is there to smooth out the airflow, as there would otherwise be severe turbulence above the aerofoil if it were just a flat plate. Increasing the camber also makes the air speed up more to assist the reduction of pressure on the upper surface. There is more cross-sectional area above the chord line in a non-symmetrical aerofoil, so when lift is created, the forces in different places above and below create a twisting moment. A symmetrical aerofoil has no camber in the true sense.

Washout (Geometric Twist)

The tip of a blade rotates at a much faster speed than the root does, often approaching the speed of sound.

This causes a large difference between the lift force at each end. When a blade's speed doubles, as it might (and more) at the tip, the lift created is quadrupled because lift varies as the square of the speed (put another way, if you half the tip speed, you only get a quarter of the lift). To stop it bending upwards, the tip must be made stronger, which is expensive, so the lift (and drag) is evened out along the blade instead, by twisting it from root to tip.

This process is called *washout*, which affects the C_L part of the lift formula (described shortly), or by tapering* it towards the end, affecting the S component.

Unfortunately, the high twisting required for best hover performance produces vibration and oscillations at high speeds, so a compromise is made - between 6-12° of washout produces most of the advantages for hovering and avoids most of the disadvantages of speed. The Bell 206, for example, has a washout of -10° from root to tip.

*You can use washout and taper together, as is done with the Bell 412. Tapered blades have shorter chords at their tips, but this leaves less room for the weights usually placed near the end of the blade to reduce flutter and increase inertia.

Total Reaction

The complete force produced by an aerofoil is the *total reaction* which, on a fixed wing aircraft, can be split into two vectors, called *lift*, which acts at right angles to the airflow, and *drag*, which acts in line with it. On a helicopter, they are usually called rotor thrust and rotor drag.

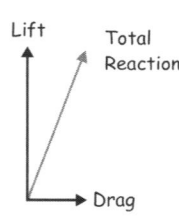

In the hover, rotor thrust is virtually the same thing as lift, and the lift formula applies, except that the equivalent of $\frac{1}{2}\rho V^2$ (IAS) is the combination of air density and RRPM. As RRPM are constant for a helicopter, air density variations can therefore have a significant effect (maintaining IAS in aeroplanes is the same as maintaining RRPM in helicopters).

In any case, the TR should be as near vertical as possible, to keep the drag value low.

Note: This drag produces a resistant torque (moment) on the shaft, plus another acting from the centre of the hub in the opposite direction to the helicopter, called rotor profile drag (H*). Rotor profile power is used to overcome the torque + H.

*It is called the H force because it acts around the hub. The drag of the retreating blade is less than that of the advancing blade, and the difference between the two opposes the movement of the aircraft. It arises from the unbalanced profile and induced drag of the MR blades.

Angle Of Incidence

The wing on an aeroplane is often fitted at an angle to the length of the fuselage (it is the way that is it rigged). The end result is that the aerofoil is able to start altering the velocity of the air coming the other way as soon as it moves. The angle at which the chord line meets this axis is called the *angle of incidence*. The helicopter equivalent is the *blade pitch angle*, where the chord line intersects with the plane of rotation of the rotor blades. Both are *mechanical* angles, affected by the flight controls.

Angle Of Attack

The *angle of attack*, on the other hand, is an *aerodynamic* angle*, controlled by the relative airflow.

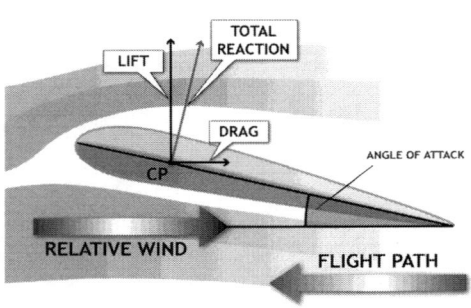

A **non-symmetrical** aerofoil will produce lift at a zero angle of attack because of the excess upper surface exposed to the airflow (that is, the bulk of its mass is above the chord line). It must be at a negative angle of attack to produce zero lift ($C_L = 0$). A **symmetrical** aerofoil needs a small angle of attack to produce lift because the upper and lower surfaces are equal, which is why they are less efficient at producing lift than asymmetric ones, although they are easier and cheaper to make. *A symmetrical aerofoil at 0° produces no lift and some drag.*

*The angle between the chord line and the free stream is the *Geometric* angle of attack. That between the zero lift line and the free stream is the *Aerodynamic* angle of attack. They are both the same in a symmetrical aerofoil.

You can fly at a high speed with a small angle of attack, or a slow speed with a high one, up to the accepted maximum of around 15° but, as the angle of attack increases, there is more frontage to the airflow, increasing drag markedly, and lift decreases again.

The generally accepted optimum angle of attack is between 3-4°.

Stalling

The stall is a condition where an aerofoil cannot support an aircraft in flight because either not enough air is flowing over it, or it is turbulent, or without energy. When its upper surface is mainly covered in separated airflow, an aerofoil is stalled.

An aerofoil starts to be less efficient at producing lift when it is inclined sharply upwards and its speed is too low, so, instead of cutting its way smoothly through the air, as it would normally do at a higher airspeed and a lower angle, it leaves a turbulent partial vacuum behind.

The stall always happens at the same angle of attack for a particular shape of aerofoil. However, the *speed* at which it occurs can vary according to air density, mass and other factors. As well, because the angle of attack can vary along the blade, some parts of it can stall before others. The *stalling angle* is that *above which* the aerofoil stalls, or above the point where lift is at its maximum. Although lift is still being produced after that angle, the aerofoil has a hard time producing it.

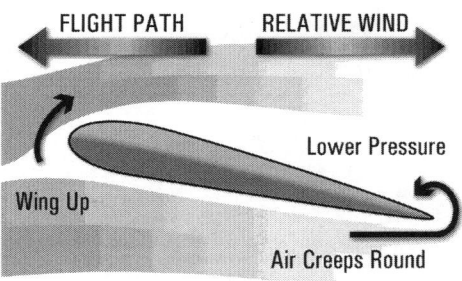

The reason the stall happens in the first place is because the air under heavier pressure beneath the blade finds it easier to creep *forwards* over the upper surface from the trailing edge as the angle against the relative airflow increases, because the upper air has started to slow down and now has an unfavourable pressure gradient, past the peak. It has longer to travel and more surface friction to cope with, so it doesn't have the energy to keep flowing and create the same pressure differential, and the amount of lift is reduced (the pressure at the trailing edge is atmospheric anyway). As the boundary layer has less momentum, it works harder keeping to the surface.

Boundary layer separation is therefore produced from the *adverse pressure gradient*, when air starts flowing in the *reverse* direction to the free stream, forcing itself under the normal airflow which has started to slow down. If you

were to attach some wool to the trailing edge, you would see it point *forwards*, well before the stall. As the aerofoil comes into the stall, it starts to pitch down as the airflow starts to react about the midpoint of the lower surface instead of at 25% of chord.

When an aeroplane's wing stalls, the Centre of Pressure moves rapidly aft, to a point behind the Centre of Gravity, which pitches the nose down into an attitude favourable for recovery from the stall (helicopters can do without the blades pitching!) However, as its rotors are not rigidly attached to the fuselage, **when a helicopter rotor blade stalls, there is no recovery!**

Stalling can be alleviated by increasing the speed of the aerofoil. Retreating Blade Stall is one of the limiting factors in the forward speed of a helicopter, and is discussed under *Dissymmetry Of Lift* and V_{NE}.

Centre Of Pressure

The pressure created by an aerofoil at any point may be represented by a vector at right angles to its surface, whose length is proportional to the difference between absolute pressure at the point and the free stream static pressure. The greatest decrease in pressure occurs forward of the thickest part of the aerofoil, due to *leading edge suction*.

All of the vectors can be represented by a single resultant acting at a particular point, called the Centre of Pressure.

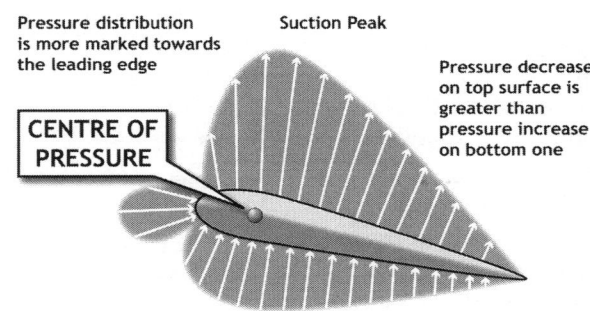

The C of P is a theoretical point on the chord line through which the resultant of all forces (i.e. the total reaction) is said to act, so the sum of all moments around it is zero.

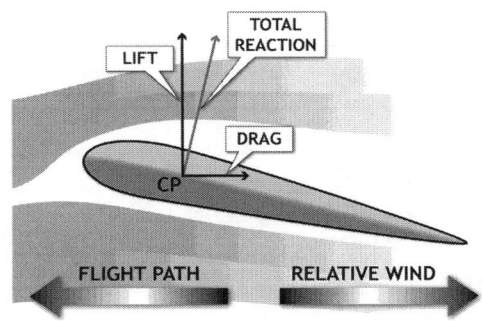

It is around 25% of the way from the leading edge, simply because more lift is generated there but, on **asymmetrical aerofoils**, it moves steadily forward along the chord line as the angle of attack is increased, until just before the stalling angle, when it moves rapidly backwards (the C of P's most forward point is just before the stalling angle).

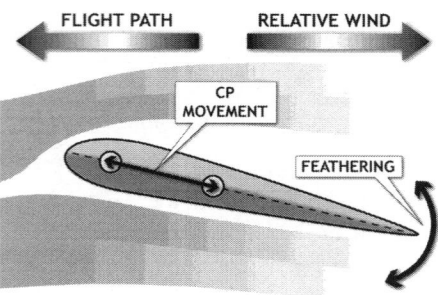

As upper surface lift can act through a different point than lower surface lift, there can be a Centre of Pressure for the upper and lower surfaces (the lower one tends to be forward of the upper one), and a couple may result

Forward movement of the C of P is classed as unstable, because it ends up forward of the aerofoil's C of G and makes things worse.

On **symmetrical aerofoils**, the position of the C of P is (more or less) fixed because the upper and lower surface lifts act through points opposite each other, so its position is independent of the angle of attack for its usual values (i.e. below the stall). This is why they are useful on helicopters, to prevent twisting moments and extra loads on the control links. The Centre of Pressure should therefore be as close to the feathering axis as possible.

On the TH-57 (SeaRanger), the rotor blades have a symmetrical blade with an asymmetrical nose (the "droopsnoot"), which is lowered relative to the rest of the blade. Thus, there are low pitching moments and the retreating blade can have a high stalling angle.

Bernoulli's Theorem

Put simply, in the initial stages, the airflow will hit the underside of an aerofoil, to be forced downwards, which is similar to carrying a large piece of plywood in a strong wind. That the air flows downwards can easily be proven by flying low over some ground fog or a field full of wavy crops, where you will see a disturbance that can only have come from downflowing air (see *Stick & Rudder*).

Downwash also comes from wingtip vortices. These curl inwards from the tips as the higher pressure from underneath an aerofoil interacts with the lower pressure air above, to produce a downward flow that is stronger at the tips than it is at the root (*source*: NASA).

Picture: from DARK BLUE WORLD (2001) by Jan Sverak

As the direction of the airflow shortly behind the trailing edge is not parallel to that shortly ahead of it, the amount of downwash (which is proportional to the lift coefficient) has an effect on the angle that the upwash makes with the leading edge - the more downwash there is, the higher that angle is (because the relative wind angle changes), and the more the lift vector leans back (Point B in the picture below. The difference between A and B is induced drag). The new angle created by the upwash produces a lower true angle of attack, and you need a bit extra to make up for the difference, called the *induced* angle of attack.

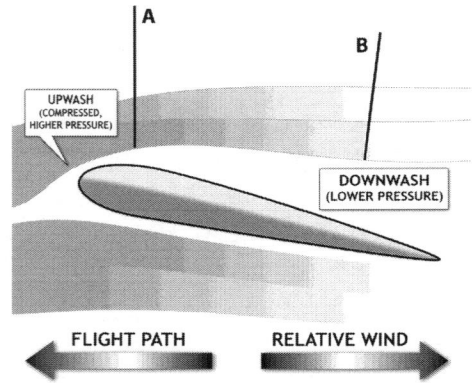

The plank of plywood is a bit of a brute force solution, so the aerofoil will also be shaped to help things along to reduce the turbulence and create a better reduction of pressure. It takes advantage of the *venturi effect*, which is credited to *Daniel Bernoulli*, a Swiss mathematician who died well before the first balloon got into the air.

It is also used in carburettors and air-driven instruments.

Bernoulli stated that *in the streamline flow of an ideal fluid* (i.e. non-turbulent), *the quantity of energy remains constant,* consisting of potential, kinetic and pressure energy.

Ignoring potential energy, as we have no height to deal with, if air is at rest, it is subject to *static* pressure, and if it is moving, *dynamic* pressure. Thus, as the fluid speeds up, static pressure becomes dynamic pressure, so it reduces, because the sum of the two must remain the same.

If this page is a photocopy, it is not authorised!

CAPT

As dynamic pressure depends on velocity, we can say that the pressure of a fluid decreases where its speed increases, or that an incompressible fluid speeds up through a restriction in direct inverse proportion to the reduction in area, which is balanced by a decrease in pressure. In a moving stream of fluid:

```
density x area x velocity = constant
```

but at low speeds, you can disregard the density, so the total amount of energy remains constant, although its form may change.

If you take a tube with a smaller diameter at its centre than at either end, and blow air through it, the pressure in the centre becomes less because the speed increases and the pressure decreases.

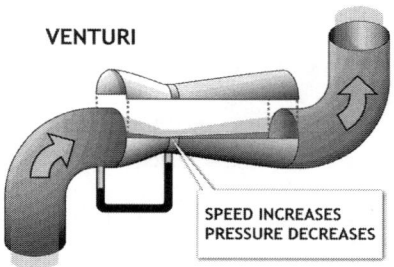

If you take the top half of the tube away, the phenomenon is still supposed to work on the remaining (lower) half, which looks like the top surface of an aerofoil. A layer of undisturbed air is supposed to replace the missing part of the tube, as the cross-sectional area is reduced by the space taken up by the aerofoil (it is reduced more over the top surface, so the pressure there is reduced more). The imbalance of pressure allegedly creates an upward force we call lift.

You can see this yourself by taking a large piece of paper and folding it back over the top of your hand, keeping hold of it with your fingers. If you blow across the top, you will see the paper rise. Similarly, a high wind will lift the roof from a house rather than blow it off. Used sideways, this is how yachts use the wind to get along.

As the Titanic was proceeding at high speed, it may have invoked the venturi effect to pull the iceberg towards it.

Note, however, that this applies to *subsonic air*, which is assumed to be incompressible, so such pressure changes can take place without apparent changes in density. Also, this is a closed system, and assumed to be frictionless. The molecules of air taking the longer route may be up to 30% of the distance away from their original fellows, depending on the angle of attack. This means that the faster flow over the top has the effect of bending the airflow downwards. For exam purposes, though, since the speed of the flowing air (on top of the aerofoil) is increased, its pressure is reduced. This is because, when the airstream

meets the curved upper surface, its tendency to stick to the aerofoil is interrupted when it is diverted upwards. It cannot immediately get back to where it wants because of inertia, so there is a partial vacuum on the upper surface.

To reinforce the point - as air flows around an obstruction and does not pile up against it (like sand would), the same mass must flow away as flows towards it. As the obstruction makes the distance longer (over the top), the flow must accelerate, exchanging *potential energy* for the *kinetic energy* of movement. The reduction in potential energy shows up as a reduction in pressure. The net result is a cocoon of lower pressure (created by the aerofoil) surrounded by atmospheric pressure, with a bias to the upper end. The aerofoil has no choice but to go up.

Note the *stagnation point* at the point of impact just under the leading edge:

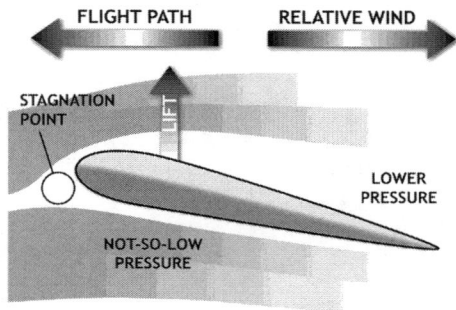

That's where the air molecules are brought to rest for an instant before being given the choice of going over or under an aerofoil, so between the top and bottom edges, there is only a difference of one molecule. The essential point to note is that the flow does not divide precisely at the tip of the aerofoil, but at some point under the leading edge, which effectively increases the upper surface of the aerofoil, and will carry on doing so as the angle of attack is increased, up to the stall point. That is, as the angle of attack increases, the stagnation point moves downwards on the profile, to increase the size of the upper area.

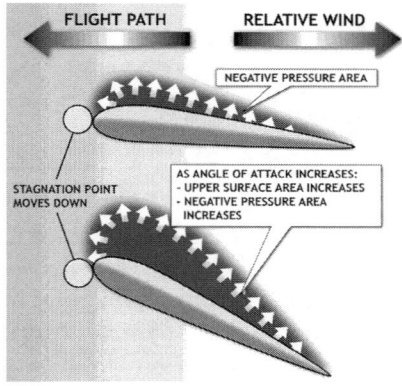

This explains why an aerofoil will still produce lift when it is upside down, although it will require a much higher angle of attack. The stagnation point can also be used as a trigger for stall warning devices.

In terms of laminar flow, the molecule that is sent under the wing just goes with the flow and is held against it by air pressure. The one that goes over the top, however, tends to get pulled away by the lower pressure, and has a harder time keeping next to the surface. The inertia that prevents it doing do creates a partial vacuum.

This is not helped by the dents, scratches, rivets and generally rough surface of the average working aerofoil, which help give it a bumpier ride. The creation of circulation in the first place is sometimes called the *Magnus Effect*, which is a mechanically induced circulation familiar to golfers, where lift can be generated by the spinning ball, but the dimples will keep the air close to the surface (the ball flies twice as far with dimples than without).

The pressure at the stagnation point is *static + dynamic pressure*, meaning *total pressure* (static pressure will be at its maximum value at this point). In fact, Bernoulli's equation can be written like this, where *pt* = total pressure, *ps* = static pressure and *q* = dynamic pressure:

$$pt = ps + q$$

q is measured in N/m^2.

Of course, all this can be proven mathematically. In physics, the formula for kinetic energy (that arising from movement, and measured in Joules) is:

$$\tfrac{1}{2}\text{Mass} \times V^2$$

Where *V* stands for *Velocity*. In other words, the faster an object of a given mass moves, the more kinetic energy it has. We know that air has mass, because it consists of molecules that can exert pressure (against your hand in a wind, for example), so we can replace *Mass* in the formula above with *air density*, which uses the Greek symbol *rho*:

$$\tfrac{1}{2}\rho V^2$$

The above formula with a fixed wing would relate to Indicated Air Speed. On a helicopter, it is a combination of air density and rotor RPM, so variations in air density can have a great effect on performance.

The more dense the air is, the more molecules that are available to push against an object. Combine that with speed, and you get *dynamic pressure* (q), which is represented by the above formula. Given that the total pressure is constant, if you increase speed, the dynamic pressure will automatically increase, if density remains constant. Therefore, static pressure will decrease (total pressure - dynamic pressure = static pressure). Static pressure, of course, acts in all directions. The difference between the two is how airspeed is measured.

Around two thirds of the total lift is said to come from the reduced pressure effect across the top of an aerofoil, not forgetting the less-reduced (therefore higher) pressure underneath. That is, the pressure above a wing is a *lot* lower than ambient pressure, and that below is *only slightly* lower, although they are signified by - and +, respectively (the not-so-low pressure underneath becomes a positive pressure area at higher angles of attack, helping the pressure differential). Officially, half the lift from a wing is typically produced in the first ¼ of the chord length.

The Coanda Effect

In 1910, Henri Coanda built an aircraft which used an air compressor powered by a reciprocating engine. He injected fuel into the compressed air and obtained an afterburner which provided thrust. Metal plates were installed in order to deflect the exhaust flames away from the plywood fuselage, but they drew the flames toward themselves instead. Theodor Von Karmen, one of the foremost aerodynamics theorists of the time, at the University of Gottingen, realised that this was a new discovery and named it the Coanda effect. Coanda later found that a sheet of fluid discharged through a slit onto an extended and rounded lip will attach itself to the curved surface and follow its contour, and that a shoulder made of a series of short flat surfaces, at specified angles to each other and with a certain length, can bend a jet stream around a 180° arc. This is in keeping with Newton's laws, which also dictate that an attractional force exists between all masses, which gets stronger as the masses are increased, and weaker as the distance between them increases, although the bodies concerned do not automatically move towards each other, as they may be prevented from doing so with other forces that are greater.

As well, the deflected airstream sucks up air from the surroundings - as the jet flowed around the shoulder, it pulled in up to 20 times the air in the original jet.

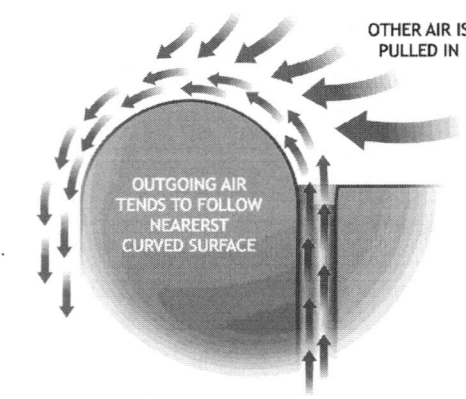

Thus, a stream of air (or other fluid) emerging from a nozzle tends to follow a nearby curved or flat surface, if it is gentle, which is why teapots tend to dump their contents anywhere but in the cup if you try to pour slowly. If you had a stream of water coming out of a tap, and held the bottom surface of a spoon against it, the flow of water would follow the spoon, whether you used the concave or convex surface, and if you held the spoon lightly, you would find the water would exert a force on it.

The fluid follows the curved surface on top because of viscosity, or resistance to flow (remember the boundary layer). The viscosity of air is small but it is there, and enough for air molecules to stick to the surface of a wing.

This effect is made use of for directional control in the NOTAR (No Tail Rotor) helicopter, but it could also explain how a wing shifts so much air. Here, the air speeds up *because* the pressure is lower, and not the other way around - Bernoulli's process may start things off, but something else takes over.

For example, the length of the path taken by air flowing over the top of the wing of a Cessna 172 is only about 1.5% greater than it is under the wing, so only about 2% of the needed lift would be developed at 65 mph (indeed, 2% is the figure calculated by aircraft modellers as to the complete contribution to lift from Bernoulli). On those figures, it would appear that the minimum speed for the wing to develop enough lift to keep the 172 in the air is over 400 mph, or, looked at another way, the path length over the wing would have to increase by 50%. The wing would then be as thick as it is wide!

Assuming the Cessna weighs about 2300 lbs, and is moving at 140 mph with an angle of attack of 5°, the vertical velocity of the air its wing deflects is about 11.5 mph. Taking half of that (from the lift formula), Newton's second law shows that the 172 in the cruise must shift about 5 tons of air (about five times its own weight), of air per second to keep flying. That means it must accelerate all the air within 18 feet of the top of the wing.

That's a lot of air! The air bending around the top of the wing is accelerating the air above it downwards, leaving a gap, or a lower pressure until the air pressure is equalised. This lower pressure will suck air from the front of the wing and shoot it down and back toward the trailing edge. It is still the top surface of the wing that is the critical part, but the magical force called "lift" is really the opposite of the downward trend of the air.

FORCES IN FLIGHT

The forces acting on an aerofoil are commonly specified as Lift, Drag, and the location of the Centre of Pressure from the leading edge (around 25%). Thrust and Weight are also part of the equation, however, and all must be balanced for straight and level flight. In an aeroplane, they would resolve into something like this:

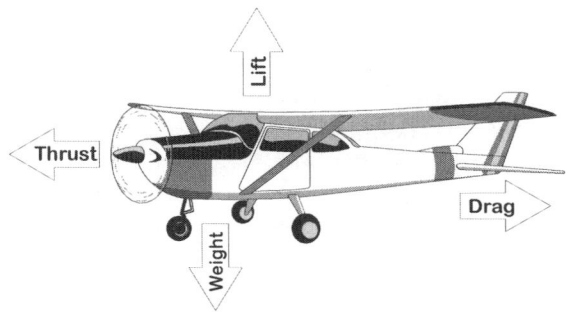

They are not in line with each other, because the idea is to produce a couple if one of them is removed, to create a suitable aircraft attitude.

However, things are slightly different for a helicopter, since it uses many aerofoils (in quick succession) to create the downwash that raises it into the air. In addition, each aerofoil is subject to ~~two~~ three airflows once the helicopter starts moving.

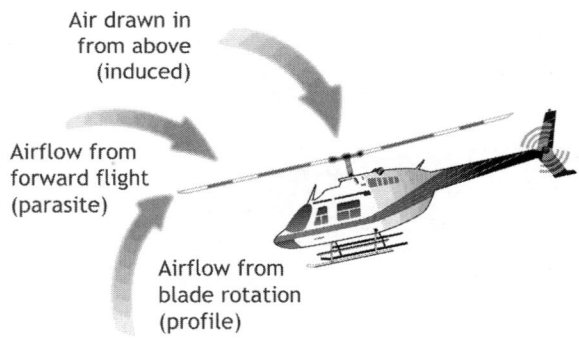

There are many theories about how lift is generated, but none of them really explain the facts. First there is the flat plate at an angle that deflects air downwards, assisted by its tip vortices, then the aerofoil shape that smooths out turbulence and helps the pressure differential. Even the formula used to calculate Lift (described later) has only been constructed to explain certain observed effects. For helicopters, the *Momentum* and *Blade Element* theories have turned out to be the most relevant.

The Momentum Theory

Under the Momentum theory, based on Newton's 2nd and 3rd laws (as originally applied to ship's propellers), the upward thrust from the rotor disc is the reaction to the downward movement of air that has been accelerated and therefore had its momentum changed.

However, it assumes a uniform induced velocity, and falls down under certain flight situations when the throughput isn't there, such as Vortex Ring, so we also use the Blade Element theory to explain what's going on.

The Blade Element Theory

This allows the integrated thrust and drag forces on infinitely small parts of a rotor blade to represent those of the whole blade*. The term *blade* means its length between the root and tip, as attached to a hub with hinges or flexible elements. Its rotational velocity around its axis is an angular velocity usually expressed in RPM, but could be degrees or radians per second.

*As based on the behaviour of a section at 75% of the radius. This is because a blade with washout has the same thrust coefficient at that length as a full length one (i.e. 100%) with no twist (a constant blade pitch angle). The correct downwash is found by assuming that the quantity at the 75% point applies along the whole blade.

TIP LOSSES

There is a reduction in thrust near the blade tips because air flows from underneath to the top, so around 10% of the blade area is wasted. Thus, both the above theories become suspect as they assume a constant downwash over the whole disc.

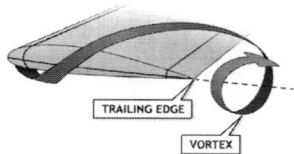

Tip losses destroys the pressure difference, and the lift. They vary with the square root of the thrust coefficient and inversely with the number of blades. Another form of tip loss is the fountain effect at the hub - see *Rotor Blades*.

They can be reduced with blade tip caps.

BLADE SECTIONS

A cross section of a blade along its chord is a *blade section*, which would be at a distance of radius *r* from the centre of the hub or the shaft axis.

Note: The pitch angle of a blade section is the angle between its chord line and a reference plane (usually the hub plane).

A blade section has a contour, leading and trailing edges, a chord line, a chord, a camber line, a maximum thickness and a thickness to chord ratio, as described below (strictly speaking, blade sections do not have upper and lower surfaces, but curves, although *surface* is popularly used).

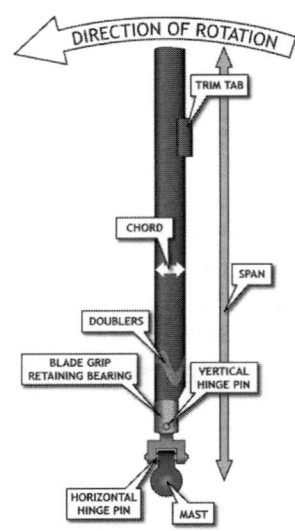

BLADE ELEMENTS

A blade element is a spanwise piece of a blade, or a collection of sections along its length. Aerodynamic forces on an element produce lift, drag and pitching moments.

Otherwise, the blade reacts to a combination of rotational velocity (V_r) and induced flow (V_i) creating a resultant called Relative (or resultant) Airflow (RAF). On the ground, with the rotors running, the only airflow is that over the rotor blades as they rotate (V_r).

So everything starts from this diagram:

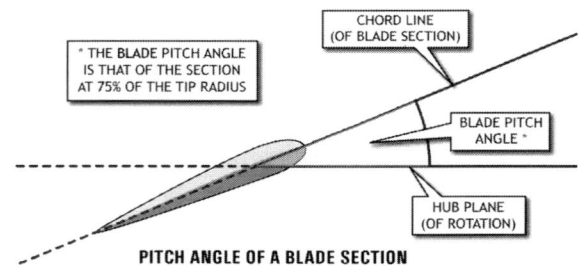

PITCH ANGLE OF A BLADE SECTION

The Blade Pitch Angle lies between the chord line and the Plane of Rotation (although technically the angle is between the chord line and a reference line based on a datum mark on the rotor hub for engineering purposes - the POR is parallel to it). The Blade Pitch Angle is varied by the cockpit controls. On the ground, it is the same as the Angle of Attack.

Once you get into the hover, however, air coming down through the rotor disc (induced flow, or V_i) has to fit into the Blade Pitch Angle, so the angle of attack must reduce to accommodate it. Thus, V_i modifies V_r to produce the Relative Air Flow, which is now not parallel to the plane of rotation, but somewhere between it and the chord line. It is also producing a little drag of its own.

CAPT

The angle of attack of a rotor blade is never equal to the pitch angle during powered flight. The Total Reaction from each blade, at right angles to the chord line, is split into two vectors. One is Rotor Thrust (Lift), at right angles to the relative airflow. The other is (induced) drag, in line with it, being overcome by engine torque. Rotor thrust is that part of Total Reaction which acts through the hub, in line with the shaft axis.

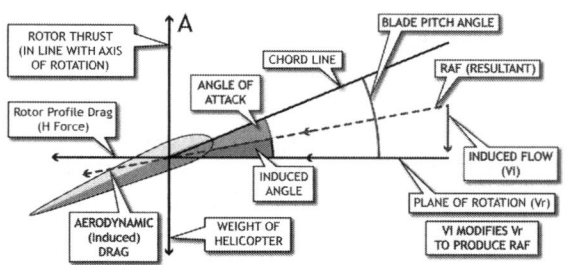

If you look at the components in the diagram below, you will see that the lift at right angles to the Relative Airflow does not produce a force in direct opposition to the weight of the helicopter as it would in an aeroplane. This function is actually performed by the Rotor Thrust in line with the axis of rotation (Point A). All the Rotor Thrusts together produce the Total Rotor Thrust that keeps the machine up in the air.

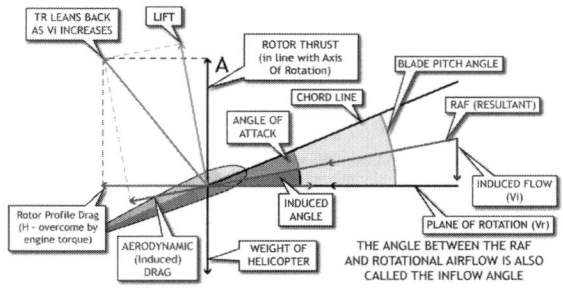

That is, the TR vector is resolved into a vertical element that overcomes *some* of the weight of the helicopter (rotor thrust), and a horizontal element (rotor drag).

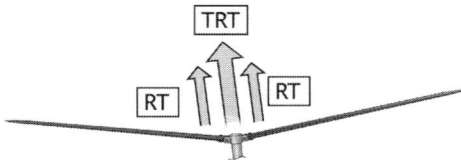

The sum of all the rotor thrusts as shown above makes up the Total Rotor Thrust, or TRT, which keeps the machine up in the air. It acts through the centre of the hub, perpendicular to the plane of rotation.

TRT decreases with larger disk areas. Also, as the coning angle increases, the RT from each blade inclines more into the disc and the TRT reduces.

THE CLIMB

Note: Climbing in a helicopter is mostly straightforward, but descending involves various vortices, turbulence and separated flow.

When starting a vertical climb from the hover, you apply collective pitch and the Total Rotor Thrust increases until it equals the helicopter's weight, at which point the machine is resting lightly on its skids (or wheels). A little more collective increases the TRT until it is greater than the weight of the machine so it accelerates vertically upwards. The induced flow increases, and makes the induced angle bigger, which makes the angle of attack smaller, so the rate of acceleration decreases until the helicopter is in a steady vertical climb.

Meanwhile, the change in angle of attack causes the relative airflow to change and tilt the Total Reaction further away from the axis of rotation to increase the drag - so you need more power. Parasite drag equals the excess of lift over weight, until it reduces to zero with the rate of climb. The helicopter is now in a free hover.

FORWARD FLIGHT

The forces acting on a helicopter in forward flight can actually be reduced to three, namely:

- Weight
- Parasite drag
- Total, or main, rotor thrust (TRT), split into:
  - vertical (vTRT)*
  - horizontal (hTRT)*

*For convenience, they are often labelled the traditional way. vTRT (i.e. lift) opposes the weight of the helicopter, and hTRT (thrust) opposes the various types of drag.

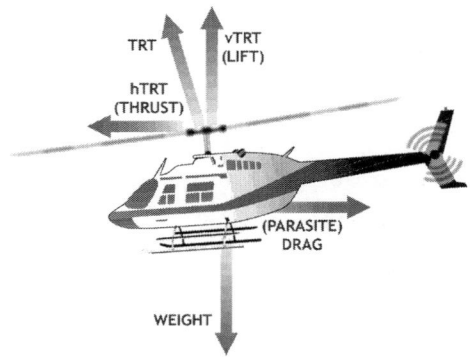

The main rotor shaft axis lies through the main rotor shaft. The (virtual) axis of rotation of the blades, on the other hand, is through the *centre of the main rotor head* about which the blades rotate, so the two are only in line when the rotor disk is in a neutral position.

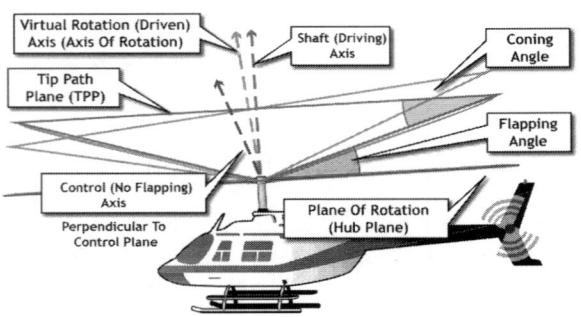

DESCENT

There are four states of vertical descent:

- **Normal Thrusting**. The induced flow velocity (downwards) is more than the rate of descent.

- **Vortex Ring.** The flow is upward in the inner part of the disc and downwards in the outer part. This creates a second set of vortices along the blades.

- **Autorotation**. The airflow is upward, providing enough power to stop the RRPM getting lower, and extracting enough to stop them getting higher. In other words, the central part of the disc is keeping the machine up in the air. The outer portion is driven and the inner part is stalled.

- **Windmill Brake**. There is so much upward airflow that the rotors must be braked to stop them overspeeding.

All are discussed later. Those for forward flight are similar, but their rates of descent and symptoms are different.

Lift

Lift is "generated" when a mass of air is accelerated downwards. You could therefore argue that it is not a force, but a *reaction*. With reference to an aerofoil, or a single rotor blade, it is said to act through the Centre of Pressure at 90° to its relative wind.

Technically, you can increase lift in 4 ways, in this order:

- Increase speed

- Increase the size of the lift producing areas

- Increase the angle of attack (up to the stalling point), with collective pitch

- Fly in denser air (lower, or in a colder air mass)

As the first two are constant for a helicopter, and you have little control over the density, the only way you can vary lift is through the Coefficient Of Lift (C_L), which means altering the angle of attack, by moving the controls.

LIFT FORMULA

There is a formula for calculating lift, which is:

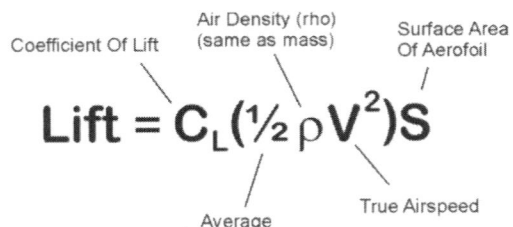

$$\text{Lift} = C_L \left(\tfrac{1}{2} \rho V^2 \right) S$$

- The lift actually created by an aerofoil is measured by the **coefficient of lift**, which is a unit-less number that is the product of design (thickness and camber) and angle of attack, or relative pressure distribution above and below the aerofoil. It is unit-less because it is a percentage figure that expresses how much dynamic pressure is harnessed by the aerofoil to create lift. If it is all converted, the C_L would be 1.

Because of wing loading considerations, we need just the right amount of lift, or components would be stressed. For example, the dynamic pressure in the free stream flowing past the average Cessna in the cruise would be around 29 lbs per sq ft. The wing loading of the Cessna 172 is 14 lbs per sq ft, so its wing only needs to capture around half the free stream to do its work, a C_L of 0.48. In contrast, something like a Learjet would require a C_L of 0.39, and Concorde 0.22.

The value will be maximum at, or just before, the stall, which you can see from the formula - if C_L increases on one side, the other side (L) will also increase, until lift can no longer be produced. Similarly, reducing speed (V) decreases lift. Thus, to keep the same lift, you must change the aerofoil shape and/or angle of attack if you change the speed, and *vice versa*.

- ½. Thinking in terms of drag for a moment, a flow of air hitting the front of an object bounces off it and creates a back pressure, which turns out to reduce the proper value by about half, especially in a pitot tube.

- ρ (rho) = air density. $\tfrac{1}{2}\rho V^2$ = IAS (in the hover).

- V = **TAS**, and by extension, rotor RPM, and more or less constant, as it arises purely from the rotation of the blades, and the maximum and minimum limits are very close together. The rotor speed is constant because the blades are too heavy to react properly to speed changes. True Airspeed depends on Indicated Airspeed (IAS) and air density, which decreases with altitude, so you need a higher TAS to get the same lift as you go up (even if IAS stays the same). At height, the aircraft

encounters less resistance, or drag, in front of and around it. In a descent, the air gets more dense, so you get more drag, more friction, and the aerofoil decelerates. Thus, TAS could be seen as a function of the resistance found when flying in the air. If the angle of attack does not change, other things being equal, lift varies with the square of the IAS - if airspeed doubles, lift is multiplied by 4, so doubling IAS in level flight reduces C_L to ¼.

- **S** = the surface area, which won't change during flight for a helicopter, although it can be affected by any taper in the rotor blades.

Weight

The opposite of lift, and a force acting through the Centre of Gravity, parallel to it. In a climb, however, it will acquire a rearward component which is below, parallel to and in the same direction as drag, and

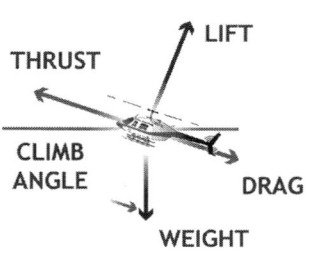

must be added to it, which is why you need more power. In a steady vertical climb, after the initial increase in induced flow, which reduces the angle of attack and requires you to increase collective pitch, the TRT eventually becomes equal to the gross weight, assuming enough power is available, which is similar to straight and level flight, but in a different direction. If you remember Newton's laws, once the helicopter is in a steady vertical climb, it is not accelerating.

Thrust

This is the force that makes the aircraft move through the air, being the horizontal component of TRT.

Drag

It's not all plain sailing for anything forced to move through air, as a certain resistance tries to prevent it, caused by friction from air molecules as they are forced out of the way when all they want to do is cling to the body that is moving (*skin friction*). This tendency to stick is called *drag*, which both absorbs energy and produces heat, so it needs to be reduced as much as possible. Drag is a force that tends to slow an aircraft down, acting in the opposite direction to thrust, parallel to the relative airflow. As it retards motion and increases fuel consumption, it also affects range, endurance and maximum speed.

In order of priority, drag is split into various components:

- **Induced Drag**. Sometimes called *Vortex Drag* or *Lift Dependent Drag* (LDD), this comes from the

air's reaction to the rotor blade, or is induced from the creation of lift, when air at different pressures mixes at the trailing edge to produce tip vortices, so it only comes from lift-producing surfaces (rotors and stabilisers) and varies with the angle of attack. The slower the aerofoil is moving, the more induced drag you will get because of the pressure differential. *If no lift is induced, there is no induced drag.* It is inversely proportional to the square of the velocity, that is to say, halving air velocity increases induced drag four times.

The induced drag forces from the blade elements lead to a resistant torque on the shaft that needs induced power to overcome it, i.e. that required to induce velocities at the rotor disc.

Induced drag is reduced by:

- increasing airspeed
- long, narrow blades (with high *aspect ratios*)
- reducing the lift coefficient, which can be done with *washout* or by *blade design*. A *blade tip anhedral*, on the Sikorsky S-92 (see below), captures some of the lift lost to tip vortices forced below the plane of the next one:

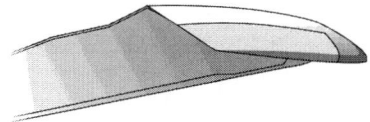

The slight difference between the upwash and downwash angles is due to induced drag.

- **Parasite Drag** comes from anything moving through the air that is not actually creating lift, like the fuselage, undercarriage, or an underslung load. Unlike induced drag, it *increases* with speed (the square of the velocity) and is zero in the hover.

The largest single element comes from the rotor head (hub drag). In fact, even though its components are small, their combined drag can be larger than that from the fuselage! An articulated head can produce as much as 40-50%, compared to about 30% from a hingeless head.

Parasite drag consists of:

- **Interference Drag**, or the result of the interaction between components and the fuselage. In other words, if you added the various types of drag together, the result would be less than the total - interference drag is the difference.

- **Profile Drag** (or *zero lift drag*) which arises from the action of the blades passing through the air, so it is like parasite drag but only for the blades, as it is present even in the hover. It depends on the cross sectional characteristics of the aerofoil (i.e. its profile) and consists of:

  - **Form Drag**, or *Pressure Drag*, from the differences in pressure between the high pressure in the front stagnation region and the low pressure in the rear stagnated region, acting normal to the surface. Eddies form when the streamline flow is disturbed, as when a flat plate is held at 90° to the airflow, where you would get 100% pressure drag. Form drag is minimised by *streamlining* - the best shape for a streamlined body is round at the front and sharp at the rear so the airflow does not separate quickly.

  - **Skin Friction** (or *surface friction drag*) from the boundary layer, tangential to the surface, due to surface roughness from shear forces over the aerofoil. It arises from the surface area, viscosity, and rate of change of velocity.

Profile Drag is therefore the result of the smoothness or otherwise of surfaces, proportional to, and increasing as, the square of the speed, but as rotor RPM are usually constant, it can be regarded as a static figure in a helicopter, if you ignore airspeed (where the advancing blade is affected much more than the retreating blade by the V^2 bit in the lift formula). It is also greater near the tips of rotor blades, rather than the roots, and increases moderately with airspeed.

DRAG FORMULA

Guess what? There's a formula for drag, too, which is similar to that for lift:

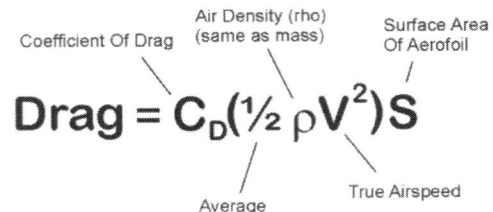

$$\text{Drag} = C_D(\tfrac{1}{2}\,\rho V^2)S$$

You can see that drag also increases with speed, although it is virtually unchanged with altitude (that is, it does decrease, given the same angle of attack, but you need more lift at height, so more angle of attack, and more drag, so what you gain, you lose). See also *Power*, discussed later.

Note: The V^2 factor takes it out of all proportion once you get out of the low speed regime - at 150 kts you encounter 100 times the drag found at 15 kts. This means that small increases in speed need disproportionately larger amounts of thrust. Where drag is squared, power required (see later) is *cubed*.

C_D, being the drag coefficient, represents the potential of a body to interfere with smooth airflow over it, or how much of the force produced by dynamic pressure gets converted to drag. Like with lift, shape is the most important factor, not size, plus the dynamic pressure, and the angle of attack must be considered. The remainder of the formula works as it does for lift, except that the force is measured parallel to the airflow, so S is the frontal area, and we want it to be as low as possible.

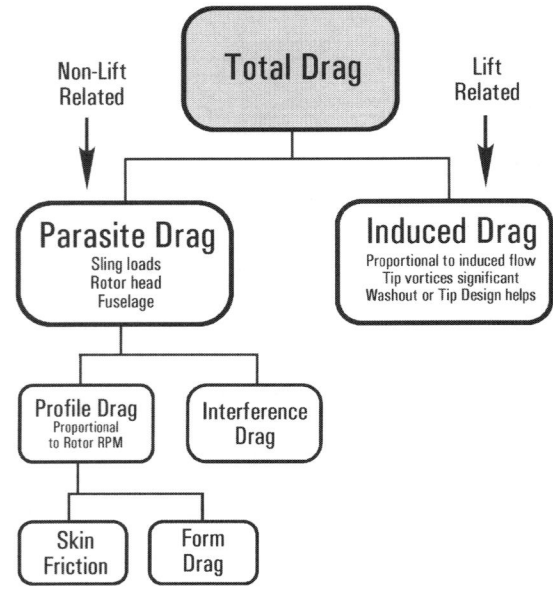

CAPT

LIFT/DRAG RATIO

The airspeed where drag is at a minimum can be seen from a graph which compares total drag to parasite, profile and induced drag.

As airspeed increases, parasite drag increases as the square of the velocity (it is zero in the hover), but as airspeed reduces, induced drag increases (never quite reaching zero) so, going either way increases total drag. Profile drag rises slightly with speed because of the extra lift created by the advancing blade.

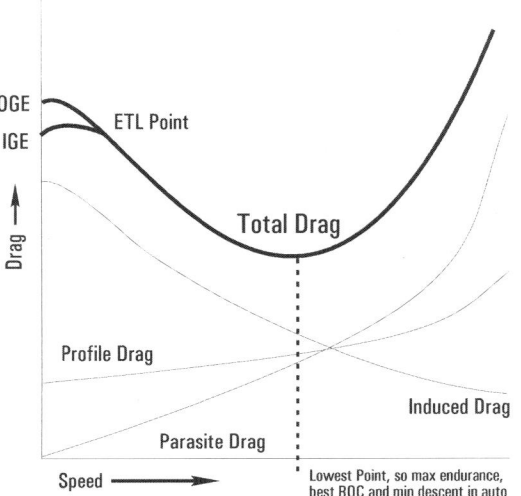

As the lift is remaining the same, the lowest point where Induced and Parasite Drag cross is the best lift/drag ratio, or L/D_{MAX}. It is the most amount of lift you get against the least amount of drag, and it is used to determine the efficiency of an aerofoil for particular angles of attack, so you can calculate such items as max cruising or gliding ranges. It is not necessarily the lowest point on the curve, which simply represents the least drag. Typically the best C_L/C_D ratio occurs at an angle of attack of 4°. It is degraded when the whole helicopter and possibly a slung load is taken into consideration.

Good L/D characteristics are needed for a helicopter because the power to weight ratio is important. The blades cannot act at L/D_{MAX} in the hover because forward flight would then be inefficient. A reasonable ratio of thrust to weight (or load factor) must exist to stop the blades from stalling. In the hover, the load factor would be unity.

Note: The total drag curve may look similar to the Power Required curve (discussed later), but it is plotted against IAS, as opposed to TAS.

STABILITY & EQUILIBRIUM

A helicopter is in a state of equilibrium (or trimmed*) when the vector sum of all the forces involved equals zero. There is no acceleration, either from a speed increase or turning, which could be from climbing, descending, or whatever. If this equilibrium should be disturbed, in an ideal world, the machine should revert to what it was doing before. The significance lies with turbulence, or wind gusts, which have the most to do with your machine being knocked off its flight path.

*In steady flight, the balance of *forces* determines the orientation of the main rotor in space. The balance of *moments* about the C of G determines the airframe attitude. When both are in balance, the aircraft is trimmed.

So, the stability characteristics of an aircraft describe its ability to return to its flight path after a disturbance without any input from the controls. For example, in an aeroplane, the dihedral of the wing (where the tips are higher than the root) allows a greater angle of attack to be created on the downgoing wing if the aircraft is disturbed by a gust. This creates more lift on that side to straighten things up.

If the Centre Of Gravity is forward, the machine will fly nose-heavy, and if it is aft, it will fly nose up. In a helicopter, this will restrict the control available from the cyclic, which is used to restore the equilibrium. If you run out of cyclic control because the C of G is too far forward or aft, the machine will be uncontrollable. Forward speed can also make the nose pitch down, as the airflow is working against the top of the fuselage.

Stability is usually divided into *static* (immediate) and *dynamic* (subsequent) stability. An aeroplane must be statically stable, but the helicopter is unstable in nearly all flight regimes (including when carrying slung loads), so it must always be controlled, either manually by the pilot (requiring a high workload), mechanically by stabiliser bars or paddles or electronically by a Stability Augmentation System (SAS). All methods use available control power (see below) to return the rotor disc to its former state.

Stability and controllability are opposite sides of the same coin - the more of one you have, the less of the other you get. With excessive stability, control response is slow. That is to say, a stable aircraft would resist both desired and undesired changes.

Control Effectiveness

This refers to the ability to respond to control inputs and move from one flight condition to another, or the degree to which control inputs achieve the desired effect aerodynamically. It is expressed in terms of two ways: *Control Power* and *Control Sensitivity*.

TEETERING HEAD
(zero offset)

The only sideways
force is from hTRT

The greater the distance from the
Centre Of Gravity
(i.e. the longer the mast),
the greater the control power
and C of G range

ARTICULATED
HEAD

Offset Gives
More
Leverage

Blade centrifugal force
pulls against rotor hub

HINGELESS HEAD
(Rigid Hub)

Virtual Hinge

CONTROL POWER

This describes the maximum initial acceleration against displacement of the cyclic (e.g. the rate of response for a given control input, or how quickly and effectively the rotor disk responds to cyclic movement to achieve a change in fuselage attitude). It is affected by:

- the distance of the rotors from the C of G*

- the rotor configuration, whether *Teetering, Articulated* or *Rigid*.

*Older machines have their rotor heads high above the C of G to maximise this effect, although *hinge offset* (see centre picture, above) allows the rotor head to be closer to the fuselage. It also allows positive control movements at relatively low RPM, which means greater sensitivity. In the Hughes 500, offset flapping hinges provide around two thirds of the control force, with the rest from the horizontal part of TRT.

- On the **teetering** (zero offset) **head**, the only force for pitch and roll is the horizontal component of TRT, which you get by tilting the thrust vector, so there is relatively poor control power. The forces arise only at the hub, and are proportional to the lift created . No lift, no Control Power!

- With the **articulated head**, the blades are attached to extension arms which stick out a bit from the rotor head, so a little extra force is produced around them, instead of just at the rotor head, so you need less cyclic movement to make an attitude change, and the fuselage tends to remain more parallel with the disc. Put another way, the flapping blade pulls up or down on the extension arm, and not the rotor hub, to rotate the fuselage, after the aerodynamic forces have started. As this does not depend purely on what the lift vector does, but is assisted by centrifugal force, it works at low pitch and load factors. Blade centrifugal forces also help the fuselage to cope with a wide C of G travel.

- The **rigid rotor** shifts the forces from the extension arms to around halfway down the rotor

blade, since this is where they flex. It is the equivalent of placing the flapping hinges of an articulated head at a 17% radius from the shaft. Rigid rotors have the most control power - the direct moment is 4 times larger than with articulated heads.

Control Sensitivity refers to the relationship of control power against the natural damping effect of the disc (the maximum rate of roll or pitch per unit of control movement). High control sensitivity is due to low rotor damping, so control power is large relative to damping, and a large angular velocity is reached before the damping kicks in. Large diameter rotors have greater damping.

Types Of Stability

If *positive stability* is a tendency to return to the flight path, *negative stability* is increasing movement away:

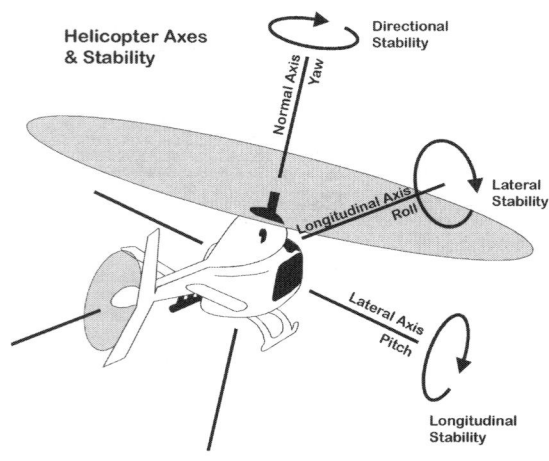

Neutral stability occurs where the oscillations are of constant amplitude around the original flight path, or the aircraft maintains the new attitude.

Helicopter Axes
& Stability

Directional
Stability

Normal Axis
Yaw

Longitudinal Axis
Roll

Lateral
Stability

Lateral Axis
Pitch

Longitudinal
Stability

CAPT

Stability is always discussed against a variable. For example, most helicopters have negative static stability with respect to the angle of attack, but positive static stability with regard to airspeed. It can also be related to an aircraft axis. Stability in the pitching, rolling and yawing planes translates to *longitudinal*, *lateral* and *directional*.

The roll angle in a steady hover without wind comes from forces and moments around the *longitudinal* axis.

Stability is also discussed with reference to low and high speed regimes, both concerning the main rotor. The helicopter is naturally unstable at low speeds, but is more stable at high speeds due to the effects of various stabilising surfaces, such as fins and horizontal stabilisers.

STATIC STABILITY

Static stability is the *initial* tendency to return to the desired attitude:

- If an aircraft returns to its original position by itself after a disturbance it is **statically stable**, or has positive static stability.

- If an aircraft moves further away from its original position, it is **statically unstable**.

- If it takes up a new position a distance away from the first position it is **neutrally stable**, or has negative static stability.

Overall static stability can be measured by comparing the cyclic stick position against speed behaviour. Once trimmed in straight and level flight (at a constant airspeed), move the cyclic forward to gain a new speed without moving the collective or using trim. A more forward (final) position indicates positive (longitudinal) static stability, and a further aft position is unstable.

Helicopters are designed to be as close as possible to positive static stability in as many cases as possible. The next priority is neutral static stability, adjusted to react as slowly as possible.

CYCLIC STICK REVERSAL

The cyclic is not necessarily at its most central point in the hover. It is more likely to be central at around 40 kts. The *cyclic control stick plot* is an engineering graph that shows the stick positions for various steady-state airspeeds.

The restrictions for flying with front doors off in some helicopters are partly because aircraft response may not always follow a predictable pattern for a given cyclic input. In other words, the anticipated rate of speed increase or decrease when moving the cyclic forward or backward may not be achieved with doors off, due to disturbed airflow over the horizontal stabiliser, to reach a state of *negative static stability*.

In forward flight on a Bell 206, for example, with all the doors on, the air flows evenly over the horizontal stabiliser

to create the lift required. However, if you remove the doors (especially the rear ones) the airflow at higher airspeeds (above 69 kts) now burbles back toward the tail and disrupts the lift over the stabiliser. Thus, as your speed increases, the lift created by the stabiliser decreases, which means that the nose will be too far down, requiring *aft* cyclic to correct it.

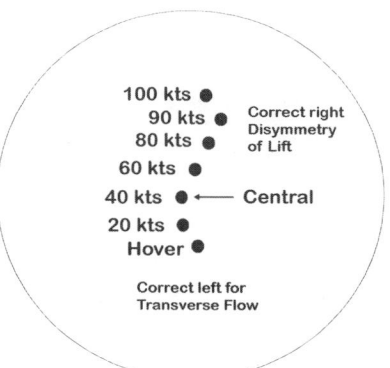

Now, from 60 KIAS, if you accelerated to and held 70 KIAS, the longitudinal cyclic position could be slightly *behind* the original 60 KIAS position. As a result, the problem got called *Cyclic Stick Reversal*, but there has never been a situation where you had to push the stick forward to make the nose go up.

THE MAIN ROTOR

A helicopter's overall static stability is dominated by what happens to the main rotor, especially in terms of:

- **Angle of attack**. The rotor will continue away from the trimmed condition if disturbed (negative static stability). When the disk gets a change in angle of attack (say from an updraught or a collective movement), all blades experience an increase in local angle of attack, but the advancing ones end up with more upward acceleration because there is more lift on the advancing side of the disk, due to its relative airspeed, discussed later. Because of the disk's "gyroscopic" properties, the disk flaps back (i.e. up at the front), and the nose pitches up, but the angle of attack increases further because the airflow comes from under the disk (reducing induced flow), so the motion is unstable.

In general, a more forward C of G produces more stability as the main rotor's contribution to angle of attack stability is reduced.

- **Airspeed**. The rotor will try to provide a positive moment to return towards the trimmed airspeed. An increase in forward airspeed also increases dissymmetry of lift, and flapping of the disk backwards, as above, but the thrust line moves in front of the C of G, and the nose pitches up.

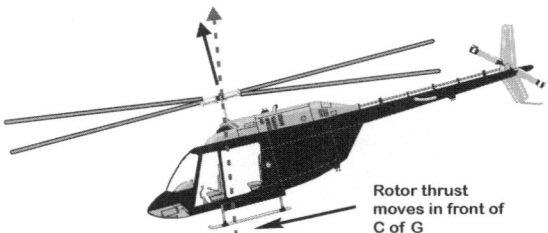

Rotor thrust moves in front of C of G

This is positive static stability because the tendency is to decelerate and cancel out the speed increase. If speed decreases, you still get a stable response, as the aircraft pitches nose down and accelerates.

- **Changes in relative airflow**. The rotor will move away from a change in sideslip - i.e. it will continue.

At high forward speeds, some helicopters can gain enough stability from the horizontal stabiliser to overcome the unstable tendencies of the main rotor.

THE TAIL ROTOR

Taking the Bell 206 as an example (whose tail rotor is a pusher), if a gust of wind hits the helicopter in forward flight, the tail rotor's angle of attack will decrease, causing a yaw to starboard. However, the weather cock action from the helicopter's inertia as it continues along its flight path keeps it going in the original direction. Therefore the helicopter is statically (and dynamically) stable in the yawing plane in forward flight.

IN THE HOVER

A hovering helicopter is mainly disturbed horizontally in the short term. If a gust of wind hits the rotor disc, it flaps away and the helicopter follows. As airflow is now coming the other way, the rotor disc reacts to it. The helicopter slows down, but the fuselage carries on, tilting the disc further so the helicopter returns to its original position faster than it moved away. The helicopter is statically stable in this condition, but because the amplitude of the oscillations continues to increase, it is also dynamically unstable, in the pitching and rolling planes.

The helicopter is statically stable in this condition, but because the oscillations increase, it is also dynamically unstable, in the pitching, rolling and **yawing planes**.

The tail rotor's angle of attack would also be affected, depending on the direction of the gust of wind. If the angle of attack is reduced, as it would be on a Bell 206 with the wind from starboard, the helicopter will yaw into wind, assisted by the weather cock action of the fuselage.

In moving away from the gust, the effect on the tail rotor is reduced, so the helicopter will yaw to port, based on the new airflow from its own movement. Thus, the helicopter will continue yawing from left to right with successive sideways movements. In this situation it is statically stable, but dynamically unstable in the yawing plane.

DYNAMIC STABILITY

Dynamic stability concerns the overall, or long-term, tendency to resist oscillation, so you cannot have dynamic stability without some form of static stability. It is governed by the mass or inertia characteristics of the aircraft - once a motion is in progress, other forces and moments influence what happens next, such as damping.

You get damping whenever a force is produced on a body that is proportional to its velocity. If the force opposes the motion, it is positive, like that exerted by a spring, and which contributes to static stability. A spring, however, will not return to the equilibrium point, but will oscillate back and forth around it, depending on its strength.

Adding a damper, such as a hydraulic one, adds another force, proportional to velocity in the opposite sense to the direction of moment. Fighting this force reduces the amplitude of the oscillation with time.

Aerodynamic damping forces work in the same way. Side forces on a vertical fin proportional to the sideslip angle provide a restoring spring-like moment, where the oscillations get smaller and smaller.

- If oscillations are damped out, the aircraft is **dynamically stable**.

- If the amplitude of the oscillations increases (as with ground resonance, for example), the aircraft is **dynamically unstable**.

- If oscillations continue at a constant amplitude, the aircraft is (dynamically) **neutrally stable**.

However, with any aircraft, a movement in one plane induces a movement in another. You hardly ever get a pure yaw, since it produces a sideslip and a roll.

LONGITUDINAL (PITCH) STABILITY
IN THE HOVER

The helicopter is not affected much by changes in longitudinal airspeed, but as the C of P of the fuselage is usually ahead of the C of G, it is a negative contributor to longitudinal stability.

If disturbed in the hover with the cyclic in a fixed position, the helicopter will slowly oscillate translationally and move back and forth with larger and larger movements. The helicopter is therefore dynamically unstable in the hover, but as the periods of oscillation are long enough to allow the pilot to counteract them, it is not considered to be a serious problem.

There are three aspects of movement to consider:

- **Up and down**, which is more isolated in the hover. There is vertical damping that comes mainly from the main rotor, but also from aerodynamic forces on the fuselage, according to how fast you are going up or down. For example, when going up, each blade's angle of attack is effectively reduced*, which cancels out the initial thrust. There is no spring-like force when out of ground effect, but there is in ground effect, so there might be an oscillatory plunging (this is why it is hard to maintain height).

  *Induced flow is increased. Also, when the rate of climb equals the updraught velocity, the relative velocity is zero.

- **Fore and aft.** See below.

- **Pitching**. This is coupled to the above, because pitching nose up will cause an aft translation.

In the short term, the dynamic longitudinal response of a helicopter in the hover is usually non-oscillatory and heavily damped. Long term, it is oscillatory and divergent, and similar to the phugoid** of a fixed wing aircraft (see below). It must be corrected by the pilot, so hovering with your hands off is not possible without some help.

IN FLIGHT

There are two common oscillatory modes. One is short term and the other long term, the phugoid mode**. The short term response to a gust or a longitudinal cyclic input should be rapid and heavily damped, as the helicopter should respond promptly and smoothly.

**A phugoid is the path a particle takes when it is subject to gravity vertically, but is acted upon by a force at right angles and proportional to V^2. Put another way, it refers to the size of the oscillation for dynamic stability (you could loosely call it porpoising). There is a large-amplitude variation of airspeed, pitch angle, and altitude, but almost no angle-of-attack variation. It is really a slow interchange of kinetic energy (velocity) and potential energy (height) about some equilibrium energy level as the aircraft attempts to re-establish the steady flight condition from which it was disturbed. The motion is so slow that the effects of inertia and damping are very low. Although the damping is very weak, the period is so long that you normally correct for it without realising. Typically it lasts for between 20–60 seconds.

Dynamic stability (in helicopters) produces a convergent phugoid, whilst dynamic instability produces a divergent phugoid. Dynamic neutral stability has a neutral phugoid.

Because of angle of attack stability, vertical motions are coupled to pitching, and there is no uncoupled plunge mode. As mentioned previously, initially, there is a nose down moment, but the stronger flapback makes it nose up. If a gust of wind hits the helicopter on the nose, the disc flaps back to reduce the forward thrust. The helicopter will slow down, but inertia makes the fuselage follow through to bring the nose up, tilting the disc more to the rear and slowing the helicopter down more. At some lower, stabilised speed, the fuselage will pitch down again, below its original position because of the pendulous effect. The disc will now flap forward, from reduced flapback, due to the lower speed.

The speed will now start to increase while the helicopter descends in a shallow dive. There will be more flapback, and the cycle will repeat, increasing in magnitude. Unless you apply cyclic early enough, the helicopter will pitch outside its control limits.

In summary, during forward flight, the helicopter is statically stable (because it returns to its original position), but (mildly) dynamically unstable in the pitching plane, because it carries on oscillating.

ROLL (LATERAL) STABILITY

The fuselage contributes most to lateral and directional stability, particularly the vertical stabiliser which keeps it aligned with the relative airflow. Otherwise, lateral airspeeds (side winds) are corrected by lateral cyclic and tail rotor positioning (the rotor will move away from a change in sideslip). However, with zero airspeed in the hover, the helicopter has no directional stability - it will settle in any direction.

Lateral-directional static stability is affected by dihedral effect, directional stability (weathercocking) and side forces. In the hover, the yaw motion does not usually affect the other axes, as it is only controlled with the pedals. The other two are coupled, as roll moments cause side forces and *vice versa*.

DIHEDRAL

This refers to the rolling moments arising from sideslip.

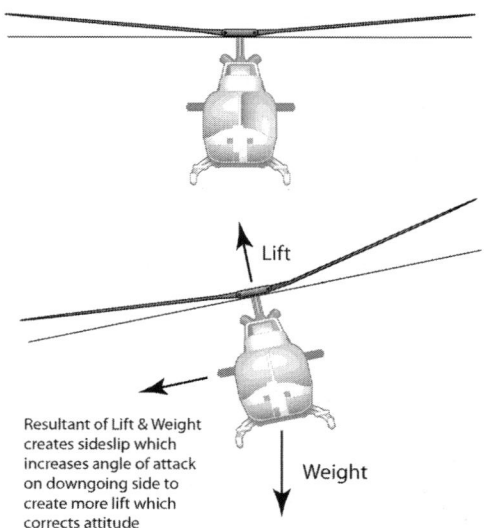

Lift

Weight

Resultant of Lift & Weight creates sideslip which increases angle of attack on downgoing side to create more lift which corrects attitude

Dihedral is the angle between the wings (or rotors) and the horizontal, looked at from the front, where the blade tips are higher than the roots. It is an angle that raises the centreline of the blade tip above the centreline of the root (because the rotors are not fixed, in helicopters this is better called *effective dihedral* as it is really a preset coning angle). A moderate amount of positive effective dihedral is needed for good flying qualities, meaning a right lateral displacement of the cyclic to maintain the bank angle in sideslips and *vice versa*. A sideslip to the right (i.e. with the relative wind from the right) is regarded as positive, so a rolling moment to the right is also positive. A positive dihedral effect is exhibited if, in a right sideslip, the helicopter rolls left. How much lateral cyclic into wind you uses gives you an idea of the size of the force.

In the hover, tail rotor roll needs a bank to the left, which is still needed in forward flight, but the same effect can be achieved with a little sideslip if you keep the disc level. The sideslip to the right creates forces on the fuselage that, at the correct angle, just balance the tail rotor thrust at that speed. *In straight and level flight, you cannot fly a helicopter in equilibrium without a steady bank and/or sideslip angle.*

Any sideward velocity tilts the disk away from the wind that creates a rolling moment in the stable direction (to the left). If the centre of pressure of a vertical surface (including the fuselage) is above the centre of gravity, a further positive dihedral effect is gained (it is negative if the C of P is below the C of G).

DIRECTIONAL STABILITY

Also known as *weathercock stability*, static directional stability concerns yawing around the normal axis, and is a measure of the size of the restoring moments generated by sideslip. Instability is greater longitudinally than laterally, due to the tail's inertia, so most helicopters are directionally stable.

After a yaw, momentum keeps the aircraft going in the same direction, while generating a sideslip. An angle of attack is created on the fuselage. The C of P's position ahead of the C of G increases the sideslip angle. Thus, the fuselage contributes negatively to directional static stability. The greatest contributor is the vertical fin.

Static directional stability has three main sources:

- **Aerodynamic moments on the fuselage**, which are destabilising as for longitudinal static stability

- **Side forces on the vertical tail**, which are stabilising, and which are the reasons for the vertical tail in the first place. As the tail is behind the C of G, a right yawing moment is produced that tends to negate the initial disturbance

- **Tail rotor thrust changes with sideslip**, which is also stabilising (there are no spring-like oscillations in the hover). More lateral velocity from the right

reduces tail rotor thrust, and *vice versa*. With North American rotation, a left yaw increases the induced velocity through the tail rotor because of the increased airflow. The angle of attack reduces, and so does the rate of yaw. With a right yaw, the opposite happens. This restoring moment is the major source of static directional stability in single rotor helicopters, especially at low speeds where the vertical fin doesn't work.

In forward flight, sideslip generation (through yawing moments) immediately creates rolling moments, so the yaw mode, which is uncoupled in the hover, now has some effect. In the lateral-directional sense, there are three dynamic modes of motion:

- **Roll mode** - non oscillatory. After a lateral cyclic input, a steady roll rate would eventually be achieved. The roll is opposed by roll damping up to where they equalise.

- **Spiral mode** - non oscillatory. Increases in bank increase inside sideslip, to increase yaw rate, etc.

- **Dutch Roll**. This is an uncomfortable oscillation of the tail in a combination of up & down and left & right, so it combines roll and sideslip at the same frequency, but not in phase, so the maximum sideslip does not occur at the same time as maximum roll, which is why it is uncomfortable.

SIDE FORCES

These determine what bank angle you need to hold a specific sideslip angle at constant increasing forward speed. The higher the airspeed, the more bank angle you need. The static yawing moment for equal bank angles is much greater for an aircraft with low side force effects because of its larger sideslip angle (if two aircraft have the same static directional stability, but one has zero side force per unit of sideslip, and the other produces a very large side force for a very small sideslip, the first one will quickly slip into a large sideslip, whilst the second will not sideslip for more than a few degrees).

Side force characteristics are very important for slow speed operations.

CROSS COUPLING

This is the effect on one axis caused by motions in another, from the gyroscopic qualities of the rotor disc, or aerodynamic effects from control surfaces. A right turn will make the nose go down, or up in a left turn, for example, so some manoeuvres are not the mirror image of their opposites (a single positive dihedral tail surface can generate more lift in a sideslip). The yaw plane is relatively unaffected because the plane of rotation (of the main rotor) is essentially in the yawing plane.

STICK FORCE STABILITY

This refers to the stick forces required to achieve a given change in airspeed from a trimmed condition. As well, there is a lateral force that would cause the aircraft to roll if it were not corrected, from the reaction of the control orbit to the forces acting on the pitch operating arms. In forward flight, for example, if the control orbit is tilted forward, the pitch operating arms reach their highest and lowest points in line with the longitudinal axis, which means that the maximum forces imposed on them are midway between them (i.e. lateral). Otherwise, the principal factor is the longitudinal distance between the Centre of Gravity and the Neutral Point on the longitudinal axis of the aircraft. If the aircraft C of G is located on it, the aircraft will be neutrally stable. In this condition the stick forces required to achieve any change in g load or airspeed is zero.

If the C of G is in front of the Neutral Point, the aircraft is positively stable. The further forward the C of G, the greater will be manoeuvre and stick force stability. If the C of G is behind the Neutral Point, the machine is unstable, so stick force stability and manoeuvre stability are positively affected by forward movement of the C of G. However, in pull-up manoeuvres, the downward sweeping motion of the stabiliser increases its angle of attack. This produces a nose down moment which opposes the nose-up pitching motion which temporarily increases longitudinal stability, so during such a manoeuvre the C of G could be slightly further aft than the Neutral Point without resulting in neutral stability. This further aft point is the Manoeuvre Point.

SUMMARY

The helicopter is (mostly) *statically stable* and *dynamically unstable* in pitch and roll in the hover (if the controls are held in a fixed position after a disturbance*), except when in forward or rearward flight, where the tailboom affects the yaw axis. This means that a helicopter would normally try to return to its normal position after a disturbance without necessarily staying there, but would actually increase its oscillations afterwards. The differences are:

- It is statically and dynamically stable *directionally* in forward flight. Whereas the tail rotor will yaw into a gust it receives in the hover when its angle of attack is reduced, in forward flight, inertia maintains the flight path and weathercock action restores the original position of the fuselage.

- It is statically and dynamically unstable *directionally* in rearward flight. This is because there is airflow on the tailboom to move it further away from the original position, instead of a weathercock effect to restore it. The horizontal stabiliser doesn't help.

*With hands off, helicopters are statically and dynamically unstable.

REMEDIES

As well as using the pilot, there are many mechanical ways of assisting stability.

STABILISER BARS

Bell helicopters use these on some rotor masts to which the control rods from the cyclic and swashplate are connected, through *mixing levers*.

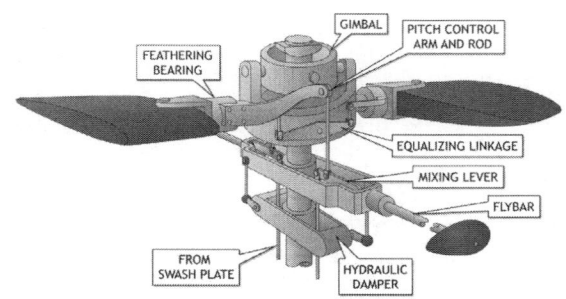

The rotating bar (stabiliser) has a weight on each end that has all the properties of a gyroscope, including rigidity in space, so it tends to maintain the same plane of rotation. This has the effect of isolating the rotor head from the mast, and hence the fuselage, so the rotors can almost operate by themselves. So, if a gust or flapback changes the disc attitude, the pitch change rods push against the stabiliser bar, which resists the movement, and nobody inside the fuselage should notice. However, this also means that your control movements are interpreted as disturbances, so dampers destabilise the stabiliser to make the machine easier to fly.

So, the cyclic moves the stabiliser bar, and the stabiliser bar moves the rotors. The bar is therefore a gyroscope that can be steered by the cyclic, and when not being steered, tends to maintain its position.

On a two bladed main rotor, a stabiliser bar at 90° to the rotor blades will *increase stability* and *decrease control forces*.

PADDLES

Hiller helicopters use paddles to produce the same effect, but the difference is that the cyclic is connected only to the paddles. The disc tilts purely as a result of their flight path. This, unfortunately, produces a significant delay in control response, so a *lot* of pilot anticipation is required. In the Bell system, a portion of the cyclic control goes directly to the rotor head.

OFFSET FLAPPING HINGES

By setting the hinges further out from the axis of rotation (i.e. outboard from the hub), the movement takes place further away from the fuselage's C of G, so a turning force is created when flapback occurs, which reduces any fuselage pitch-up. See *Control Power*.

INCLINED HINGES (DELTA 3)

Inclined hinges combine movements about more than one axis. If the flapping hinge is set at an angle, rather than at right angles, with the blade, the blade can feather and flap at the same time. Thus, it automatically changes to a lower pitch angle when it flaps up, because there is a slight twist with the movement.

The Delta-3 hinge allows blade pitch to *decrease* on the upwards flapping blade (in fact, it flaps up and moves forward). In this way, dissymmetry of lift should not cause such a large inclination of the disc from flapping. The R22 has 17° of Delta-3 on its main rotors, but Delta hinges are more commonly found on tail rotors, which can cope better with the stresses involved. They control the flapping caused by dissymmetry of lift.

Delta-3 is also known as *pitch-cone coupling*, since it provides automatic pitch reduction with increases in coning angle.

You can get the same effect by offsetting the pitch change horn at the root of the blade, as used in the pitch/flapping coupling of the AS350/355 (the K-Link). The front of the horn is fixed, and resists the blade's flapping movement at the front, slowing down its rate of change relative to the rear, reducing the flapping angle.

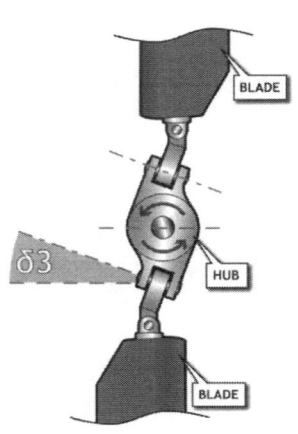

UNDERSLUNG HEADS

Here, the majority of the head is below the top of the mast. Refer to *Hooke's Joint Effect*, later.

THE HORIZONTAL STABILISER

TRT, etc., operate through the rotor head, while weight and drag work through the C of G (pendulosity).

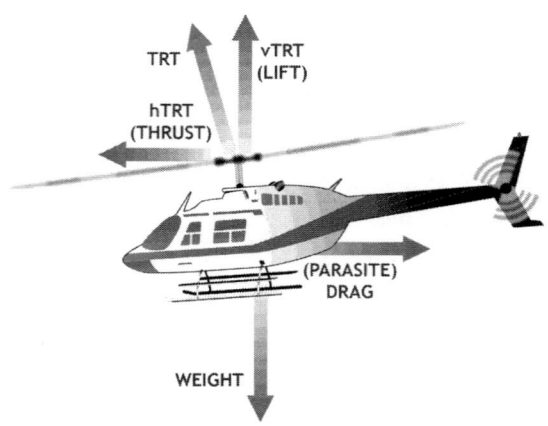

This means that the *H component of TRT is above* (i.e. at a higher level than) *parasite drag*, and a couple is produced that pulls the nose down in forward flight, which is why some helicopters have a horizontal stabiliser on the tailboom. The stabiliser (on the Bell 206, at least) is an inverted aerofoil that creates a downward force to pull the nose up to keep the fuselage more level, so that the controls remain within their ranges of operation.

Another reason for a stabiliser is that more fore and aft cyclic movement is needed to achieve the same fuselage response that you would get with an equivalent amount of lateral (sideways) cyclic movement, due to the extra inertia from the fuselage that has to be overcome. Some helicopters, such as the Bell 206L, also have a cyclic-controlled synchronised elevator at the rear of the stabiliser to increase the force required. Some stabilisers may also have inflatable de-icing boots. In the Hughes 500, the "stabiliser" is actually a horizontal tailplane which meets the airflow at an increased angle of attack if the nose pitches up to produce a nosedown pitching moment that improves stability.

A stabiliser on the tail will stop the fuselage following through when a gust of wind makes the rotor disk flap back. As the fuselages pitches nose-up, the increasing angle of attack at the stabiliser damps the movement and reduces the rearward tilt of the disc.

Without a horizontal stabiliser, gravity keeps the fuselage stable in pitch. Part of the reason for the V_{NE} is so that the helicopter is not flown near unstable speeds.

The effectiveness of a stabiliser is proportional to the square of the forward speed, so it corrects for instability at all speeds, once the right size has been decided on.

CAPT

CONING ANGLE

Centrifugal force keeps rotor blades stiff when they are rotating, which means you can use lighter blades and reduce the stress at their attachment points. When lift is generated, the thrust created makes them rise and form a *coning angle* between the blade and the Tip Path Plane, the size of which arises from the lift (thrust) produced and the centrifugal force applied, plus the weight of the blade.

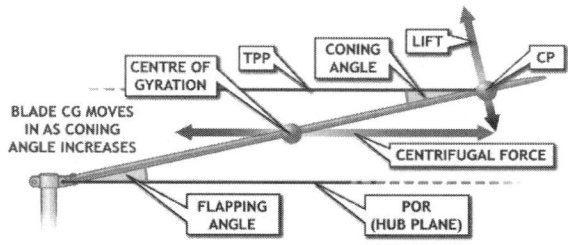

Centrifugal force and lift are proportional to the square of the RRPM, but as the RRPM do not change in normal flight, the coning angle tends to vary only with collective pitch or, effectively, angle of attack.

Centrifugal force is measured in tons*, as opposed to pounds for lift, thrust, weight or drag. In forward flight, if rotor RPM increases above those specified, the large centrifugal forces impose severe and possibly excessive loads on the hub. It also affects the blade grips and the turbine speed - in the Bell 206, 1 extra RPM on the blade is good for around an extra 300 on the N_2 turbine.

*The S-76A, with its blades rotating at 300 RPM, has to cope with 33,818 lbs at the attachment points. 40 tons of centrifugal force balanced by 4 tons of lift has a coning angle of 6°.

The coning angle is that at which the blade's weight is supported by the lift it creates. Excessive coning can occur with low RRPM, high aircraft weight, turbulence or high G conditions. The more mass the blade has, the lower will be the TPP. If one blade has more mass than others, it will be out of track and will cause a vibration.

Increasing the coning angle makes the C of G of each blade move inboard, to make the rotor disc smaller and less able to generate lift. The bigger pitch angle also means more drag and more power required - once your engine is putting out maximum power, the blades may slow down and start to overpitch.

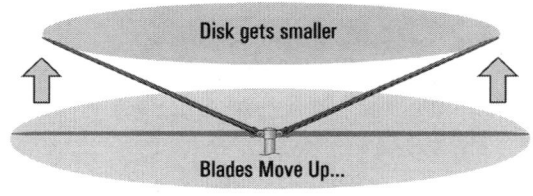

The blades also spin faster as their relative Centres of Gravity move towards the hub. 5° or 10° of coning decreases the disk size by 0.7% or 3%, respectively.

Disk Loading

This is the effective weight (or mass) of the helicopter (you could be using more G in a turn) divided by the area created by the rotor disc:

$$\frac{M \ (or \ W)}{\Pi R^2}$$

It doesn't stay constant, because the rotor disk size can vary with the coning angle (disk loading increases as coning angle increases, because the disk area gets smaller and it must carry more weight per unit area). The higher the disk loading, the higher will be the induced power and the downwash velocity.

The disk loading for a piston engined helicopter, for example, is normally quite low, around 10 kg/m^2 (the R22 has 2.5 lbs/sq ft). This is because piston engines are heavy (compared to turbines), so you need a larger rotor disc. Turbine-engined machines can use smaller disc sizes and shorter fuselages for a typical disc loading of between 30-40 kg/m^2.

Blade Loading

Aerodynamic Blade Loading, on the other hand, is the coefficient of thrust (equal to weight) divided by the total area of all the blades (solidity), which is *not* the same as the disk area, so it does not alter, as the blades themselves stay the same size.

Blade loading is the mass of the helicopter divided by the blade area. It is measured in N/m^2, and increases from root to tip, which is one reason for using washout. It falls to zero at the tip of the blade, and just inside. The area at the tip that produces no lift is given a tip loss factor which is expressed as a fraction of the blade radius.

Overpitching

When the power required is greater than the power available, and rotor RPM are decaying, the rotor is *overpitched*. In other words, you don't have enough engine power to overcome rotor profile drag and keep the RRPM up, leading to the rotor disc area reducing in size as the coning angle increases. The problem is, if you apply more collective, and thus increase drag without adding engine power, the situation will only get worse. It's the nearest equivalent a helicopter has to stalling in an aeroplane, and mostly affects piston-engined machines, because transmission torque limits on a turbine machine should be reached well beforehand.

Unintentional overpitching may occur at low airspeed in a transition to or from, or even in, the hover, especially when manoeuvring. Otherwise, you are simply applying too much collective at high power settings. Get out of it by reducing drag, by reducing the collective pitch (if you are landing, don't try to hover). You cannot increase power, because the definition of overpitching is that RRPM are so low that even full engine power will not restore them.

Centrifugal Turning Moment

Centrifugal force emanates from all points, rather than just along the length of the blade:

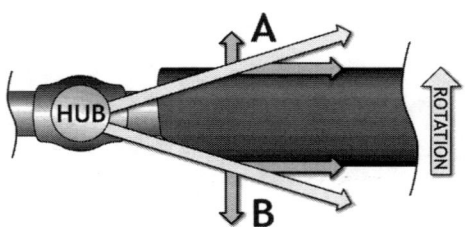

The outgoing vectors can resolve into two components - one parallel to the blade axis and one perpendicular which creates a moment around the feathering axis.

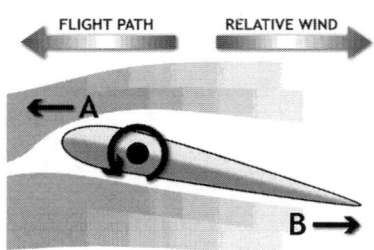

Because of the angles involved, the moment at the trailing edge of a blade (B) is longer than the one on the leading edge (A), and it is lower than the other in flight, so a couple is created that feathers the blade and makes it throw off pitch (or return to fine pitch). This effect is also called the *Zero Pitch Return Moment*. It is a particular problem with tail rotors.

Ways of alleviating it include:

- hydraulic controls. If they fail, the blades can take up a basic pitch setting (Gazelle)

- springs in the control run to help you apply pitch (R22). The collective may need to be locked down so that pitch does not increase with low RPM

- a counterweight above the pitch change axis, as is used on the Bell 47 or the tail rotor of the AS 350/355. The *Chinese weight* is perpendicular to the aerofoil to create a moment to counteract the zero pitch tendency. Such weights are called *Preponderance Weights*.

MANOEUVRING
● ●

To maintain height in a balanced turn at high angles of bank, collective pitch and power must be *increased* because the machine gets artificially heavier. Once you start to turn, you must balance the increased centrifugal force with centripetal force to keep the machine in the turn. This draws from TRT, which will ultimately require more collective pitch and engine power, although this will be limited by maximum blade pitch angles.

If you slip or skid in a turn, the fuselage presents more of itself to the airflow, meaning more parasite drag, so you will need even more power to maintain the same airspeed. The radius of the turn is also affected - slipping reduces it and skidding increases it, while the rate of turn will increase and decrease, respectively.

The maximum angle of bank is achieved at maximum rate of climb speed.

Load Factor

The Load Factor is the measure of extra weight added to the fuselage due to centrifugal force when manoeuvring.

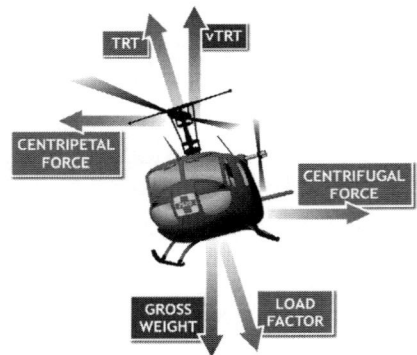

The actual weight varies according to what you do. A steep turn, for example, will "increase" the aircraft's weight more than a slight turn will. In other words, the greater the angle of bank, the greater the load factor is, compared to weight:

Bank	Load Factor
30°	1.2 (20% more)
45°	1.4 (40% more)
60°	2 (100% more)
75°	4 (400% more)

In a 30° banked turn, the apparent increase in mass is around 15%. The table is derived from the cosine of the angle of bank against the vTRT vector.

Unlike an aeroplane, which develops more lift with speed, and therefore has a greater load factor, the helicopter's

CAPT

greatest load factor is at zero speed, because less lift is produced in forward flight than in the hover. This is due to the retreating blade and the correction made with cyclic to reduce the pitch on the advancing side.

It can be expressed as the ratio of the total load supported by the rotors divided by the weight of the aircraft, in lbs/square foot.

$$\frac{\text{Actual Weight}}{\text{Normal Weight}}$$

The Load Factor is the resultant of the vectors for centrifugal force and gross weight in a turn, which opposes TRT. It is small below 30° of bank (around 20%) but soars otherwise:

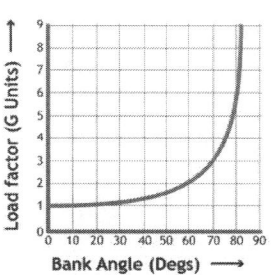

Note that, in a 60° bank turn, the effective weight of your aircraft has doubled. Your Bell 206, which normally weighs 3200, now weighs 6400! At 80°, it is 6 times the weight!

This is the reason (when performance planning) for restricting bank angles to 15°, because you will otherwise need more power (and fuel) than you planned.

If you increase the airspeed in a coordinated turn while maintaining a constant angle of bank and altitude, the rate of turn will decrease resulting in no changes in load factor (the bank angle, not speed, affects the load factor, which remains the same because the rate of turn decreases to compensate for added centrifugal force).

Control of the aircraft is also directly related to the load factor. For example, at zero G, and therefore zero load factor, in a teetering-rotor helicopter, the cyclic control will have no effect (see *Mast Bumping*, below).

MAST BUMPING

Mast bumping occurs with helicopters with teetering rotor heads that may come into contact with the main rotor mast under certain conditions. 20 strikes per second is not impossible, each one of which could weaken the rotor mast enough to snap the top off (although other helicopter types have their blades attached to the mast, fully articulated rotors can suffer from a similar effect called droop stop pounding).

Mast bumping is characterised by an unusual airframe vibration with the sound of sharp metal-to-metal contact, and you are vulnerable when the fuselage does not follow the tilt of the rotor disc (even in the hover, if the mast is tilted to counteract tail rotor drift).

Low-G manoeuvres are most dangerous, because the fuselage will carry on with its original flight path when the

disk is tilted and push the disk towards the airflow, markedly increasing the induced flow. Such manoeuvres might occur when you push the nose down into a dive after a steep climb, maybe when contour flying, or having dumped some water onto a fire, but turbulence* can also put you in a bad position, as can low RRPM and slope landings. Essentially, the angle of attack reduces to zero because there will only be induced flow through the rotors. As TRT disappears, and the apparent weight of the helicopter reduces, so does the couple between the rotor head and the C of G, and the fuselage will not follow the disc as you move the controls. That is, as control depends on lift, you can't move sideways because there is none.

*Although turbulence is not a severe problem, if you get into it, slow down and avoid excessive control movements.

In fact, as the torque from the engine and tail rotor thrust are unaffected, it will want to drift to the right and yaw to the left on its way forward because, in normal powered flight, the rotor disc is displaced slightly to the left to counter the effects of tail rotor drift. In addition, when the nose is pushed forward far enough, the tail rotor will be above the main rotor thrust line and the C of G. The end result in both cases is a rapid roll to the right.

If you try to correct this with left cyclic, as you would instinctively, the lack of TRT (from increased induced flow and zero angle of attack) means that the helicopter will not respond and the distance between the rotor mast and the head reduces drastically to where they could touch. *Opposite cyclic will not stop a roll under low, zero or negative G conditions.* Apply aft cyclic first to load the disc. Review the discussion on *Control Power* under *Stability,* above.

To make sure you always have some control, a minimum G-loading is established above where loss of control would occur, say between -1 and +0.5G, although you may get further limitations from aircraft systems (i.e. oil, fuel).

ROTOR BLADES

Helicopter rotor blades behave in the same way as any other aerofoil, in that they attempt to mechanically create a partial vacuum across their top surfaces in order to produce an upwards force (lift) that makes the machine rise into the air, whilst shovelling a sizeable amount of air downwards. However, airflow across them can also be *backwards* in forward flight, depending on their position in the rotor disc's rotation.

Blades are usually symmetrical in cross section, which means that they have the same shape above and below the chord line which, if you remember, is a *straight* line joining the leading and trailing edges. This means that the movement of the Centre of Pressure will be restricted, and there will be less of a tendency for Ground Resonance

(see *ACK*). Unsymmetrical blades are used when extra performance or different flight characteristics are required, but they should always be kept at their design RPM to keep the C of P under control (in the Bell 412 it also stops you wearing out bearings in the rotor hub). Variations in pitch (i.e. twisting or tapering to incorporate washout) along the blade will allow it to operate with a relatively constant angle of attack, and therefore lift distribution, along its span, or length.

Induced Flow

One source of airflow that affects a blade is that being pulled in from above and forced vertically downwards to pull the helicopter into the air, and called the induced flow. The induced angle thus created is the difference between the plane of rotation and the relative airflow. If the controls are not moved, there is less room for the angle of attack, and you will lose lift, so you need more power because the drag vector gets longer.

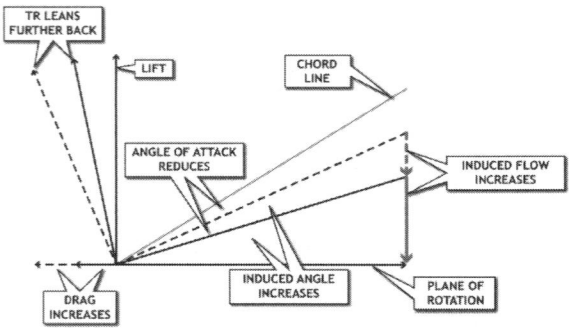

The induced flow comes from the repeated downwards displacement of small puffs of air as the blades rotate in quick succession.

Despite washout, which is supposed to balance the lift along the span of the blade, induced flow is still greater at the tips simply because washout isn't perfect and that part of the blades is going so much faster. Tip vortices, which arise from higher pressure air curling around to the top surface, increase induced flow anyway.

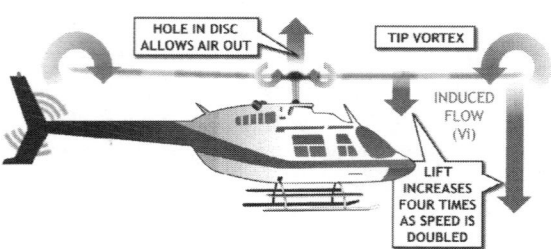

The upward-going parts of the vortices are outside the blades, so induced flow isn't affected, but the downward-going flow is inside the rotor disc span, adding to the induced flow and, ultimately, increasing induced drag. The

vortices not only affect the blade they belong to, but the ones following as well (*Blade Vortex Interference*, or BVI). The creation of vortices in the first place and their ingestion by others are the main reasons why a lot of power is required to hover.

There are also vortices at the root of the blades, where there is a gap in the rotor disk, because the blades do not go completely to the hub. The root vortices induce an upward flow through the centre of the disk which helps to reduce the aerodynamic download (vertical drag) caused by the downwash hitting the fuselage. This reduces the effective weight of the helicopter. The production of induced flow is overcome by induced power, which is that needed to induce velocities at the rotor disc.

In level, forward flight, induced flow velocity is smallest at the front of the disc.

V_i and V_r ultimately determine the angle of attack, because they modify the relative airflow.

Note: Induced flow takes a split second to increase its velocity, so if you are rough with the controls, and move them too quickly, you will get all the drag without the lift, and require more power until the induced flow has a chance to build up.

GROUND EFFECT

This is a condition of improved performance in the hover, within about one rotor diameter of the surface (at a height of half a rotor diameter, thrust increases by about 7%). It can also be achieved in forward flight, when very low over the ground, but the maximum effect is at zero airspeed (the reason why ground effect does not show very well at 100 knots is that induced power is very low there).

The slowing down and stagnation of the downwash as it hits the ground underneath the helicopter and changes direction opposes and reduces the induced flow, and reduces the effect of the tip vortices.

The vortices normally reduce the efficiency of the rotor disc so that some of the lift "leaks away" at the edges of the disc - in Ground Effect, the leaking away is reduced.

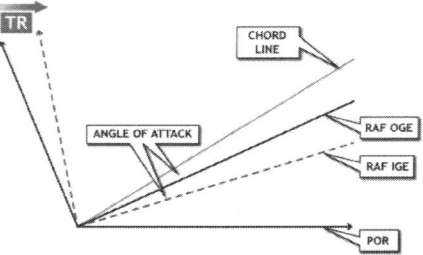

Put more simply, the velocities of the various forces are altered enough by the surface to reduce induced flow and increase the angle of attack. The TR vector becomes more vertical, and longer, resulting in less induced drag and a

If this page is a photocopy, it is not authorised!

CAPT

subsequent reduction in the power needed to hover (a Bell 206 will typically need 15% less in the ground cushion). In a typical hover (around 4 feet), the power required reduces by about a third. Because you have more lift, you have to lower the collective to maintain your position, so the blade pitch angle is lower.

As ground effect depends on a streamline flow, it can be reduced by:

- the **surface you are hovering over** (the harder and smoother the better, and the more level)

- the **wind**, which will vary the direction of the downwash from under the blades. Any wind above about 10 kts will produce translational lift

The effect of ground cushion on a hovering helicopter is greatest on level ground with a hard surface and no wind, and is most effective at a skid height below 4 ft. Over long grass, the power required to hover will be greater than that required over a smooth surface because of greater recirculation of air through the rotor disc.

RECIRCULATION

When hovering near the ground, some downwash comes back on itself and goes through the rotor disc twice, which reduces the lift because it does so at a higher speed and the angle of attack has less space available (more induced flow, larger induced angle). This is usually more than compensated for by the power reduction from the ground cushion, but when hovering over long grass, for example, it can go the other way.

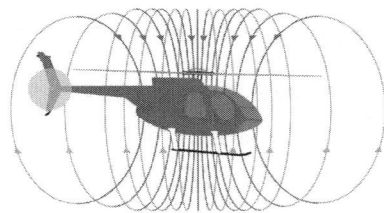

If the effect of recirculation becomes greater than ground effect, more power and collective pitch is required. A non-standard control position should give you a clue.

Where the downflow is prevented from escaping properly, as when hovering near an obstruction, the effect will be to tilt you 90° from where recirculation was introduced, or even pull you down if all sides are affected (like in a courtyard), so a lot more power will be required. Thus, when hovering in front of a building, the recirculation occurs at the front, but the disc will tilt to the left and make the left skid hover lower than usual which, if it catches you unawares, might cause dynamic rollover (see later). If you are closer than a third of the disc diameter, the advancing blade is also affected, in the above example, *pulling you towards the building* because the lift is disturbed on that side and becomes less effective.

The effects of recirculation are at their worst close to obstructions. Be particularly careful within 1 rotor diameter of another helicopter.

Dissymmetry Of Lift

In forward flight, the advancing blade develops more lift because the forward speed of the helicopter is added to its rotational speed.

On the other side of the disc, however, the blade going backwards (the retreating blade) generates *less lift* because of its relatively *reduced* speed (rotational speed *minus* forward speed). This makes it fly down because it is trying to increase its angle of attack to maintain the lift.

The result is that one side of the disc produces more lift than the other. In the picture below, there is a 200 kt difference in airflows, which is reflected in the lift produced on either side. The main lift is actually taken by the fore and aft positions.

At low speeds, this imbalance tends to cancel out but, at higher speeds, it becomes more significant because lift varies as the *square* of the speed. If you increase collective pitch in forward flight, the advancing and retreating blades get the same increase in angle of attack, but the advancing blade develops more lift than the retreating blade and nose-up flapping results.

Note: The advancing blade is the one with an increased relative wind from its airspeed, and it goes in the same direction as the helicopter, so if you are hover-taxying sideways to the left in a machine with N American rotation, the advancing blade is in front of you. Similarly, if you are hovering with a wind from the left. Going backwards with a clockwise rotor, it will be on the right. In a stationary hover (relative to the ground), the position of the advancing or retreating blades relative to the pilot depends on the direction of rotation of the main rotor and the wind. In flight, it just depends on the direction of rotation of the main rotor.

The areas in reverse flow on the retreating side are not actually stalled - the back to front airflow still produces some sort of venturi effect, and it is not turbulent, although it does try to pitch the blade up and develop unwanted twisting moments (blades with a cut-out in the trailing edge near the root try to reduce this effect).

Dissymmetry of lift, therefore, is the difference in lift between the advancing and retreating blades, in forward flight. If nothing were done to compensate for this, the helicopter would just roll towards the retreating blade and flip over, were it not for "gyroscopic" effects that result mainly in the nose pitching up. However, arrangements are made for the blades to flap to equality so that the lift generated by the whole rotor disc equalises on both sides, although it does result in *flapback*, which is an

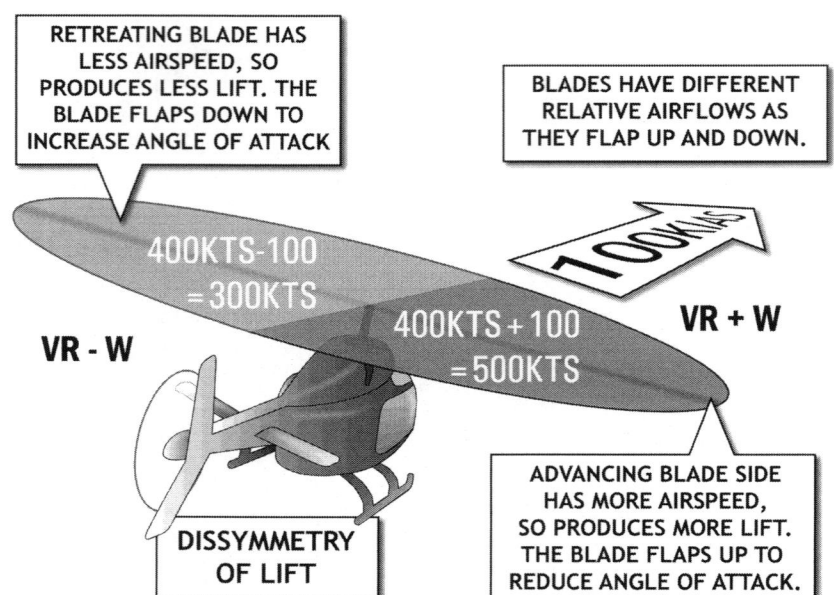

uncommanded change in disc attitude away from the wind, or direction of flight, discussed elsewhere.

There is no dissymmetry in the hover with nil wind.

RETREATING BLADE STALL

The size of the reverse flow area on the retreating blade increases as you go faster. To compensate, it flaps down more until its stalling angle is reached.

The term *Retreating Blade Stall* refers to the tendency of the *tip* of the retreating blade to stall as it tries to keep things going, once the reverse airflow starts, and is one of the limits on the helicopter's forward speed, assuming you don't run out of power first (the rest are under V_{NE}).

The stall starts at the tip, then moves inboard because the blade is flapping down. Thus, you will get a nasty surprise if you exceed maximum speed (V_{NE}) in a dive with low power applied, then pull collective! The tip of the retreating blade *reduces* speed as the helicopter's forward speed *increases*, yet it must still try to produce the same lift as the advancing blade, especially as the root is in reverse flow and produces little, if any.

Retreating blade stall occurs at high collective pitch angles at high mass, high altitude, temperature and humidity. In a level, balanced turn, it will occur at a lower IAS.

You can expect roughness and a low frequency vibration equal to the number of blades, the nose will pitch up, and there will be a roll to either side, but mostly to the retreating side, because the other blades are still producing lift. For example, in a fully-articulated system, with more than two rotor blades, only one will be in a stall condition, so you can expect a 1:4 (or 1:3 or even 1:5) vibration that increases in intensity with the stall. Departure from

controlled flight can therefore happen fairly rapidly and sometimes violently - this is from Dave Williamson who had it demonstrated in the OH-58 (Bell 206) in the army:

"At V_{NE}, the nose will gradually try to climb, and when you push the cyclic forward more to maintain level flight, it will continue to do so. Just before the max forward cyclic, the fuselage panels begin to oil-can, at which point the nose will come up* and force the machine into a vertical climb, before breaking sharply, similar to a hammerhead stall."

This is not something to fool with!

*The maximum angle of attack is at 270°, so the lowest blade position is at 0° (the rear), and the nose pitches up. This is a typical representation of the airflow and angles of attack around the disc:

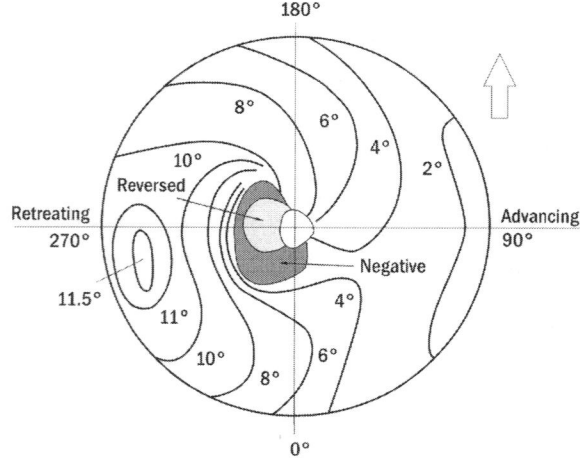

As forward speed increases, the no-lift area moves out to the left, covering more of the retreating bladed sector. Thus, the helicopter stalls as a function of going too fast,

CAPT

rather than too slowly - the retreating blade flapping down to increase its lift ends up with a very high angle of attack.

With modern helicopters that have specially designed rotor blades, you might not get the pitch up or roll behaviour described above because the blades produce a strong pitching moment as lift moves aft during the stall.

The vibration occurs because a rotor blade cannot dip in the stall (as a wing would in an aeroplane) because one end of it is attached to the rotor mast.

Recover by:

- *lowering the collective*, and/or
- increasing the rotor RPM*
- reducing forward speed and reducing manoeuvring* - fly slower than normal in:
  - high density altitudes
  - high drag configurations (such as with external loads)
  - turbulent air

*These are mostly effective beforehand.

Note: Trying to slow down with cyclic will only make things worse, as will easing the nose forward to stop the pitch up. The high airspeed puts the retreating blade at such an angle of attack that it has no choice but to stall, if you only use the cyclic, and if you throw the machine around or have a low RPM, the airspeed at which the blade stalls is even lower.

Note: The advancing blade can stall as well, but from compressibility and high speed buffeting near the speed of sound, which also limits forward speed.

DYNAMIC STALL

This concerns the alteration of the stalling characteristics of aerofoils that are rapidly pitched beyond the static stall angle of attack, which explains why the retreating blade doesn't stall as quickly as you might expect - its angle of attack changes very quickly as it rotates round the disk.

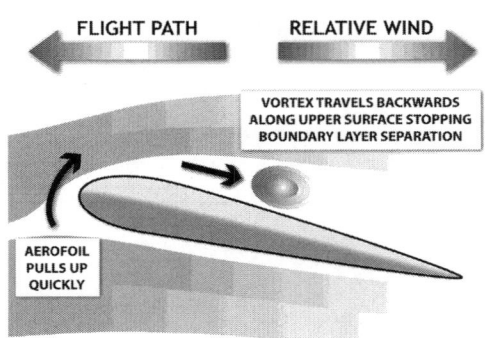

In a quick pull-up, an aerofoil can temporarily produce lift* beyond the static stall because flow reversals in the boundary layer can take some time to show in the free stream. Thus, separation takes a little more time to complete, during which a transverse vortex sweeps back from the leading edge, temporarily increasing the lift available (*Source:* NASA). In fact, the max C_L may be 30% higher than the static level.

*In action, the angle of attack may be different from that in the static condition.

Note: If the angle of attack does not change quickly enough, you only get *G stall*, which does cause loss of lift.

As a result, in a vertical autorotation into a tight spot, it may be possible to pull the collective hard enough to nearly double the normal lift for a second or two (from an article in *Helicopters Magazine* by Dennis Venturi).

FLAPPING

The rolling moment on the main rotor hub from the asymmetrical airflow on the blades in forward flight is reduced by flapping hinges, which allow the blades to move up and down by themselves (there are no flapping hinges on a teetering head, because the blades move as one unit, like a seesaw). Lift on each side of the disc is approximately equal because this allows the angle of attack on each side to change, and the lift produced by the blade.

Flapping is the angular movement of the blade relative to the hubplane, above or below the plane of rotation (i.e. up or down).

Equalisation of lift is further improved because the advancing blade causes more air to move downward (because it is creating more lift), which has the same effect as increasing the induced flow, which reduces the angle of attack enough to cancel out any expected lift increase from increased air velocity across the blade. Similarly, but in reverse, for the down-flapping blade.

Because of flapping, more lift is produced over the nose and tail than abeam the helicopter (see *Flapback*). This results in bouncing, which is a vertical oscillation of the rotor hub at a frequency equal to the number of blades multiplied by the RPM. This is why the R22 has a third flapping hinge at the centre of the hub (the other two are really coning hinges that relieve blade bending stresses).

DRAGGING

Limited movement of blades *horizontally* is the equivalent of the coning angle in the lead-lag sense, using dampers or dragging hinges. Also known as *lead-lagging*, *dragging* is the angular oscillation, or movement, of a rotor blade forward or backward in its mounting, horizontally, perpendicular to the axis of rotation.

*When a blade is ahead of its normal position, it is *leading*, and when behind, it is *lagging*.

The lead-lag (drag) hinge compensates for Coriolis effect, and avoids blade bending stresses. Drag dampers may control the rate of damping. The greatest lead and lag movement occurs as you gain or lose translational lift, hence the vibration.

Dragging hinges are only found in articulated heads. In a hingeless rotor head (often called a rigid rotor), the blades (or their attachments to the hub) bend instead.

Bearingless heads (as with the AS 350) have a flexible (elastomeric) coupling that allows fore-and-aft (and flapping) movement - instead, either the coupling or the blades flex. Two-bladed rotor systems are built strongly enough to keep the stresses within limits anyway.

CORIOLIS EFFECT

Flapping causes the centre of mass of the blades to move inboard and outboard as they move up and down, making them speed up or slow down relative to each other. This is the *Conservation Of Angular Momentum*, or *Coriolis Effect*.

When the cyclic is moved, and the disc tilts, the axis of rotation stops coinciding with shaft axis, so the centres of gravity of the blades will not coincide all the way round the disc. When they get to be more inboard, the blades will speed up, and when they move outboard, they will slow down, rather like the centrifugal governor in a fuel injection system. Thus, the blades can speed up or slow down according to whether the radius of the disc is reducing or increasing.

The underslung design of the teetering head can reduce the lead-lag tendency by keeping the C of G of each blade within bounds.

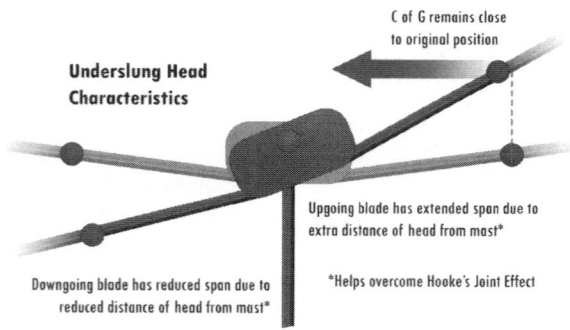

Underslung Head Characteristics

C of G remains close to original position

Upgoing blade has extended span due to extra distance of head from mast*

*Helps overcome Hooke's Joint Effect

Downgoing blade has reduced span due to reduced distance of head from mast*

It effectively eliminates geometric imbalance because the plane of rotation of the feathering hinges is set below the shaft attachment point, and there is some preconing* to ensure that the plane of rotation of the Centres of Gravity of the blades passes through the attachment point (or a common flapping hinge), regardless of the rotor tilt. This ensures that the Centres of Gravity vary equally in distance from the centre of rotation during flapping, and that they do not move too far inboard.

*Preconing is the setting of a blade angle to a slight incline when the helicopter is level - on the Bell 206, it is 2½°.

In this way, most of the bending stresses in the lead-lag plane caused by coriolis effect and geometric imbalance when flapping are relieved (according to Bell). That is, the difference in Coriolis force between the blades is minimised, so the tendency for an accelerating blade to speed up the decelerating one is reduced. Although this eliminates the need for drag hinges, there are still uneven drag forces on the individual blades in the speed range where transverse flow occurs, meaning vibration as you go through *Effective Translational Lift* (covered later).

HOOKE'S JOINT EFFECT

In the hover, or when stationary on the ground, the C of G of a blade will be the same radius from the axis of rotation all the way round the disc. When you move the cyclic to change the disc attitude, the changed radius will make the blade lead or lag about the dragging hinge as it flaps up or down, due to Coriolis.

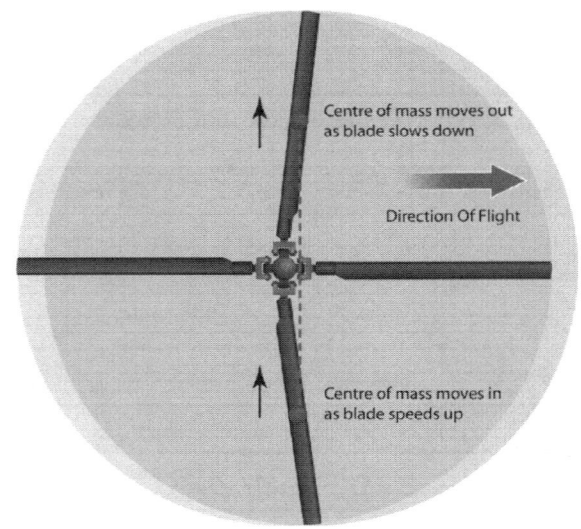

Centre of mass moves out as blade slows down

Direction Of Flight

Centre of mass moves in as blade speeds up

In forward flight, the advancing blade speeds up and moves *forward* on its drag hinge or bearing as it flaps up (if there isn't a hinge, the blade will just bend). Similarly, the retreating blade moves *back* slightly as it starts to slow and flap down. As the advancing blade accelerates, its C of G will move inboard. At the same time, the C of G of the retreating blade will move outboard as it slows down, which is one reason for using an underslung rotor head. A the head tilts, the gap between the head and the mast changes in size and extends or reduces the size of the disc on the relevant side.

The end result is that both blades (and their Centres of Gravity) lie forward of a line drawn laterally across the rotor hub as they try to reposition themselves, as well as moving towards the retreating side.

CAPT

So, whenever the driving and driven axes (the shaft axis and axis of rotation) are not in line with each other, the C of G of the whole rotor system is placed forward of the mast in the direction of flight, which will give the mast a tendency to bend.

This imbalance creates *Hooke's Joint Effect*, which looks like the picture below from the side.

A Hooke's joint allows a drive shaft to bend whilst it is rotating - in other words, it can allow power transmission to go round corners, within certain limits, by using two rotating joints at 90° to each other. Thus, it can compensate for misalignments and relative movement between the shafts they connect. Hooke's Joint Effect only applies to gimbal mounted heads, such as that on the Bell 47 which had two hinges at 90° to each other in the rotor hub, gimbal fashion.

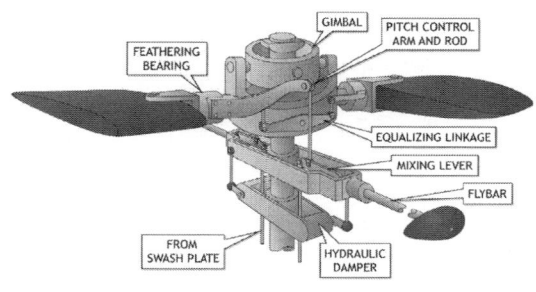

It does not affect other teetering heads, as there is no gimbal ring, just one hinge (the teetering one).

GROUND RESONANCE

In flight, the assorted rotors, engine(s) and drive shafts transmit their own vibrations to the structure which are generally stabilised because there is no real focal point for them to attach to. Sometimes, however, a coupling can occur between the lead/lag tendency of a blade against fore and aft or sideways movement of the shaft, which results in the rotor head (or at least the top of the mast) whirling round in a circle. This can focus through the landing gear when it touches the ground.

Although they are there to counteract vibration caused by movement of the centres of mass of the blades, dragging hinges can also allow those centres to get closer and unbalance the disc as a whole (its C of G moves slightly to one side of the mast, where it should be over the centre). Thus, because of the *lead/lag tendency* of the blades, shocks from the landing gear can be transmitted to the rotors, where the blades across the contact point with the ground will be forced closer together and unbalance the disc. That

is, the blades hunt back and forth and take up abnormal positions, so that the rotor C of G moves off-centre, to cause an imbalance that starts an oscillation which can be further aggravated when the wheels or skids touch the ground. They are not properly damped as they lead/lag, so the problem is blade motion that resonates with the fuselage rocking motion. Most causes of ground resonance are due to one bad damper and one bad blade. The required condition for the initiation of ground resonance is a *deliberate or unintentional oscillation of the helicopter in contact with or resting on the ground.*

This is especially a problem if the C of G of the rotor disc is away from the mast and creates a wobble, and if any damping effect from the undercarriage is not available (the oleos may be fully extended). Peculiar to helicopters with dragging hinges, Ground Resonance is indicated by an uncontrollable *lateral* oscillation (roll inertia is lower than for pitch) increasing rapidly in sympathy with rotor RPM.

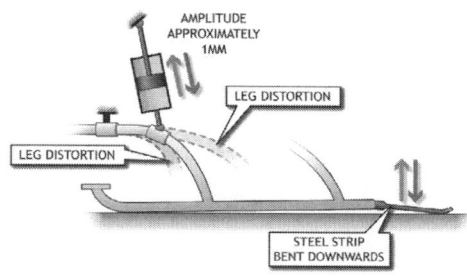

On the AS 350, there is a flexible steel strip that is bent downwards at the rear of the skids that increases the gear's flexibility and changes its natural frequency so that ground resonance should not occur (it does). The shock absorbers do their bit by absorbing the vibrations and eliminating divergent oscillations.

Ground resonance could also be caused by blades not being in balance, unequal tyre pressures or finger trouble, but will only occur if the gear is in contact with the ground, most typically on three-bladed helicopters with wheeled undercarriages (two-bladed helicopters do not have dragging hinges, and therefore no lead/lag tendency, so they don't suffer from ground resonance. Those with *fully articulated* rotor systems do). As the rotor spins up, it passes through two regions where resonance can happen, about 30% and 60% N_R. Blade dampers and oleos are designed to eliminate the vibrations, and ultimately ground resonance, so there is some mis-adjustment or mis-maintenance if you get it.

Ground resonance is best avoided by landing or taking off as cleanly as possible, but, if it does occur, either lift off, *if you have enough rotor RPM*, or lower the collective and **close the throttle** if you haven't. Cutting the throttle(s) immediately makes the blades all go to the lead position. Applying the rotor brake straight away pins them, from the deceleration.

Note: Some helicopters have spots where the main rotor dampers are less effective while on the ground, and they shuffle or bounce in yaw, roll or pitch enough to be noticed. This is not ground resonance.

Phase Lag

The rotor disc is tilted with the help of the *swashplate*, which consists of two circular plates that surround and can move up and down the main rotor mast, altering the pitch of all the blades when the collective pitch control is moved (see Section 3). The bottom half remains still and the top half rotates. The bottom part of the swashplate is also free to tilt, as influenced by the cyclic control, which is copied by the rotating part, and is eventually reflected in the tilting of the rotor disc in the desired direction.

As you can only directly control feathering with the cyclic (flapping and dragging follow the pitch changes), there is a slight time lag between the original movement of the swashplate and the subsequent movement of the rotor disc. In other words, the blades have some inertia and it takes them a little while to realise that there has been a change. This happens with any change of lift.

The difference between the tilt of the control orbit (swashplate) and the rotor disc, measured in degrees, is called *gamma*, or *phase angle*, which is not a constant figure and can vary between helicopters. **Phase angle is 90° for a system that is hinged at the axis of rotation.**

*This refers to how far away from the rotor hub the flapping hinges are (see *Control Power*). Where the hinges are only slightly offset, the phase lag can be in the order of 80-90°. It might be between 75-80° for a semi-rigid rotor.

ADVANCE ANGLE

The compensation for phase lag can be built into the control run as an *advance angle*, so that when you push the cyclic forward, the rotor disc tilts in exactly the right direction. In fact, the size of the advance angle depends on how well the blade responds to flapping, in terms of timing, or inertia - if the blade responds quickly to control input (i.e. it may be lighter or shorter), the gamma can be smaller, and even less with Delta 3.

The advance angle is the difference between the position of the pitch operating arm on the swashplate and where the blade pitch actually changes. It is not affected by rotor RPM. At one time, Bell used blades on a Bell 206 that were double the normal weight and they ended up with an advance angle of 180°! However, for simplicity, most helicopters (particularly those with teetering heads) have a gamma angle (or phase lag) of 90°, which has led some books to describe this behaviour in terms of a gyroscope*, which is subject to *precession*, meaning that an input doesn't have an effect until 90° later in the direction of rotation (see *Instrumentation* for more).

*The aerodynamics involved mean that a rotor disc is not as stable as a gyroscope, so there the similarity ends. Also, as mentioned, the gamma angle can change.

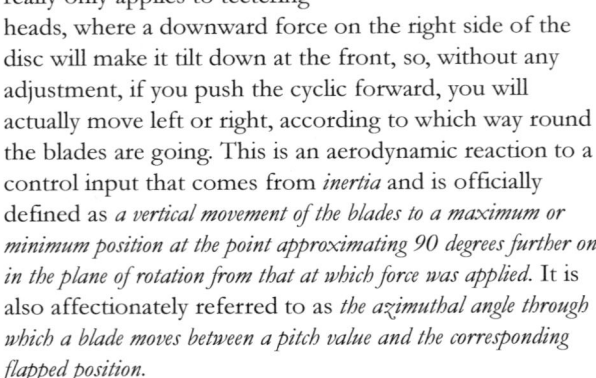

This is purely coincidental and really only applies to teetering heads, where a downward force on the right side of the disc will make it tilt down at the front, so, without any adjustment, if you push the cyclic forward, you will actually move left or right, according to which way round the blades are going. This is an aerodynamic reaction to a control input that comes from *inertia* and is officially defined as *a vertical movement of the blades to a maximum or minimum position at the point approximating 90 degrees further on in the plane of rotation from that at which force was applied*. It is also affectionately referred to as *the azimuthal angle through which a blade moves between a pitch value and the corresponding flapped position*.

What this means in English is that the blade has moved up or down (i.e. flapped) a certain amount between position A and position B. It also means that the helicopter behaves differently in turns - it will try to put the nose up in a left turn, and down in a right turn.

Flapback

Dissymmetry of lift and phase lag cause a pitch-up tendency as the helicopter increases speed, and *vice versa*.

This is a side effect of trying to cure the problems due to dissymmetry of lift with flapping, and is the real reason for phase lag, as opposed to "precession". It is a change of disc attitude (away from the wind) that occurs without any control movement, as might be found when hovering, where a small gust will lift the disc up from that direction without altering the TRT. If you use the cyclic to move the disc back, only the control orbit (the plane in which the pitch links move) is affected, meaning that the only thing that will change is the cyclic position - the fuselage attitude will stay the same, so you lose a little cyclic range (the loss of cyclic range is another limitation on forward speed).

If you initiate a control input, the disc responds, then flaps back *the other way*, so you have to keep applying the original control input to keep going until everything equalises.

Luckily, forward speed should be limited by other factors (discussed under V_{NE}) before you reach the end of your cyclic travel.

As the advancing blade passes over the tailboom, it gets faster and produces more lift, which means that it climbs.

Because of the V^2 part of the lift formula, the lift produced is way more than that of the retreating blade, and its maximum relative airspeed (and therefore lift) is

gained at the front of the disc, because the climb starts 90° after it starts to increase its relative speed, and its maximum lift point is 90° after that, which is a shift of 180° overall. There is a 90° difference between maximum flapping *velocity* (abeam) and *displacement* (at the front).

As well, there is more induced flow at the rear of the disc which increases the difference between the front and rear angles of attack.

Note: This is why the nose lifts when you apply collective pitch, or drops when you reduce it, so if the engine fails and you don't apply rear cyclic to correct this tendency, you could get into an unrecoverable situation. The moral: don't take your hand off the cyclic!

This is also why some helicopters have a horizontal stabiliser on the tail, to produce an upward force from an increased angle of attack as the nose lifts after inputting forward cyclic, in order to bring the nose down again.

Picture: One reason for following through with cyclic:

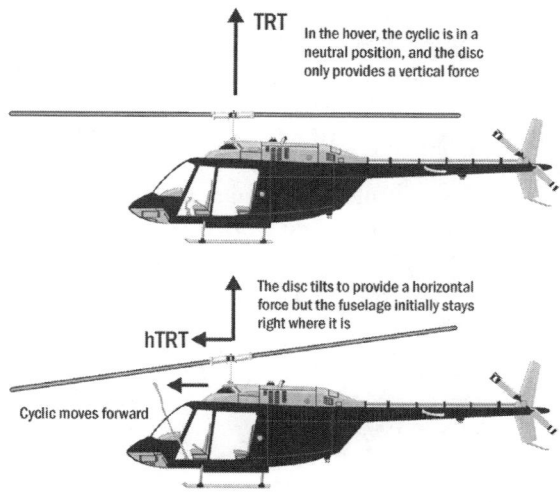

TRT — In the hover, the cyclic is in a neutral position, and the disc only provides a vertical force

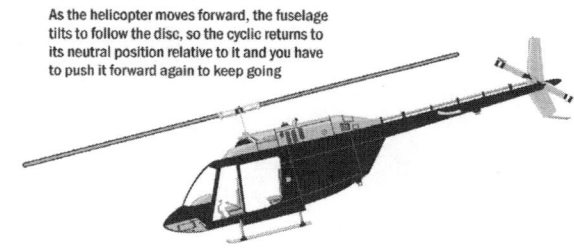

hTRT — The disc tilts to provide a horizontal force but the fuselage initially stays right where it is

Cyclic moves forward

As the helicopter moves forward, the fuselage tilts to follow the disc, so the cyclic returns to its neutral position relative to it and you have to push it forward again to keep going

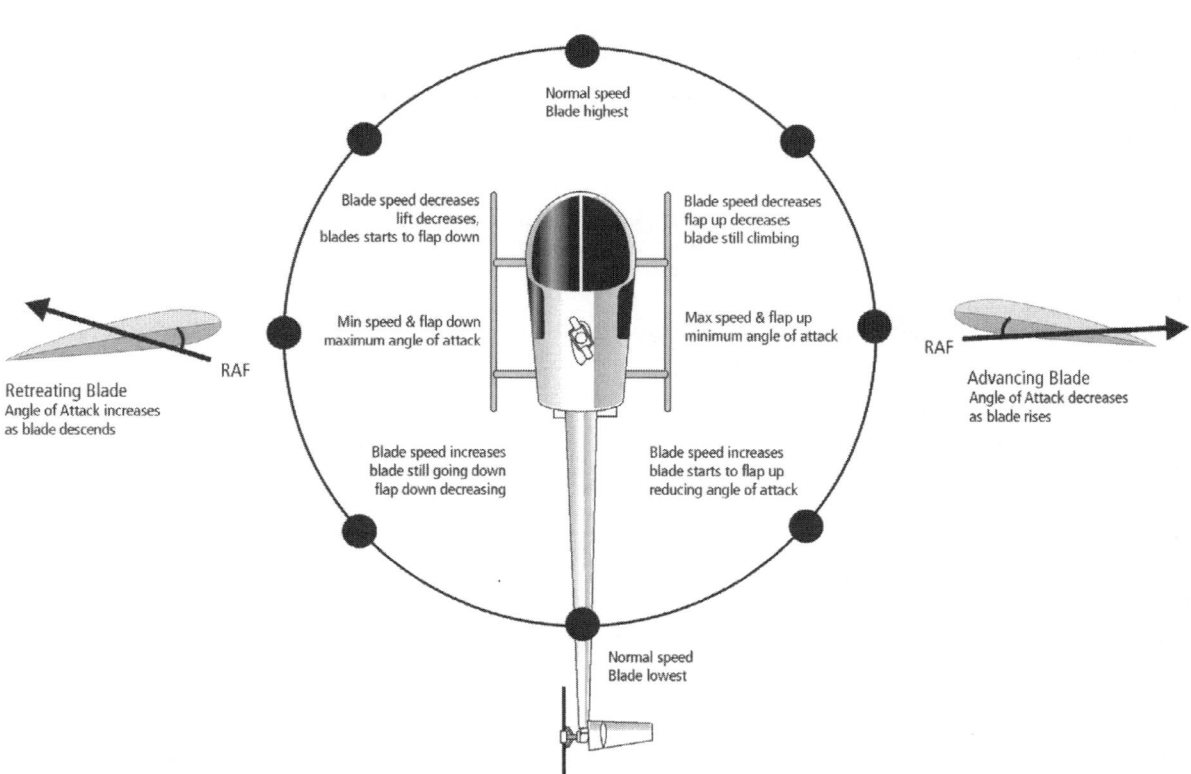

Normal speed
Blade highest

Blade speed decreases
lift decreases,
blades starts to flap down

Blade speed decreases
flap up decreases
blade still climbing

Min speed & flap down
maximum angle of attack

Max speed & flap up
minimum angle of attack

Blade speed increases
blade still going down
flap down decreasing

Blade speed increases
blade starts to flap up
reducing angle of attack

Normal speed
Blade lowest

RAF

Retreating Blade
Angle of Attack increases
as blade descends

RAF

Advancing Blade
Angle of Attack decreases
as blade rises

TRANSLATIONAL LIFT

You get the same amount of lift from applying a large acceleration to a small mass of air (as you would in the hover), or a small acceleration to a larger mass. In the case of the hover, the air entering the disc from above will already have gained some speed. In forward flight, on the other hand, it only gets a relatively small acceleration, as it has not had much of a chance to get out of the way, which makes the rotors operate more efficiently (up to a point, where it is offset by an increase in drag).

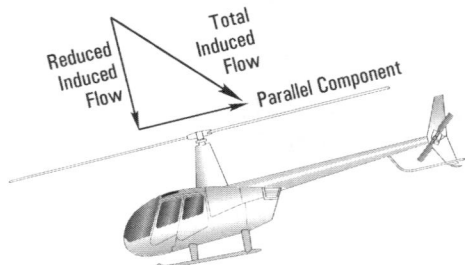

As forward speed is gained (or windspeed in the hover is increased), much of the air starts to miss the rotor disk and reduce the induced flow going through the rotors.

Now, without increasing power, the helicopter will climb and continue its acceleration. This extra lift (or reduction in the power required) is called translational lift. It occurs because the mass flow decreases when you ease into the transition*, . The subsequent reduction in induced flow allows the angle of attack to become larger, within the blade pitch angle. In the picture above, the Total Induced Flow is moved from its original position, leaving a reduced inflow behind.

*All changes in velocity from cyclic movements are transitions but they are often just regarded as changes in the flight condition from or to hovering flight.

Translation is the conversion from hover to forward flight, where the helicopter is supported by other means than its own power. *Translational lift* is extra rotor efficiency from directional movement, when the new horizontal airflow reduces the amount of air entering the disk from above.

The speed at which a helicopter moves from translational lift into forward flight varies, but it is generally equal to around ½ the rotor diameter in knots, or 25 knots for a 50-foot rotor disc. The effects of translational lift first become noticeable at around 12 kts.

Because there is less induced drag, *the same TRT is produced for less power* (not extra lift). Put another way, *as airspeed increases during the transition from the hover to the climb, the rate of climb improves due to a reduction in induced drag*. The speed where there is a rapid change in the direction of airflow and a rapid increase in rotor efficiency is called the *Effective Translational Lift* speed, around 10 knots.

Transverse Flow (Inflow & Coning Roll)

Whilst dissymmetry of lift involves the advancing and retreating sides of the rotor disk, causing it to move up and down at the front and rear (from flapback), Transverse Flow affects the front and rear halves, and causes the helicopter to roll to the advancing side. It arises **from coning** and the forward tilt of the rotors, where the horizontal airflow hits the blades at different angles.

During forward movement, the air going into the rear of the tilted disc has a more perpendicular flow, meaning it has had time to accelerate and become part of the induced flow, so the induced angle is more, the angle of attack is less and the thrust is reduced (the more time the disc has to act on the airflow, the greater the deflection at the rear).

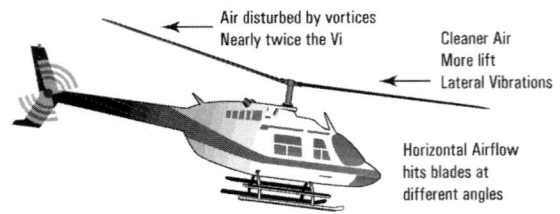

The airflow into the disc is more horizontal at the front, however, so there is less induced flow and more angle of attack, and more lift, so the disc rises at the front. Phase lag means that the maximum upwards blade displacement occurs to the left, and the maximum downwards displacement to the right, which tilts the rotor disk to the right to change the direction of the thrust vector to the advancing side.

Thus, when you pull more collective *in forward flight*, the helicopter will roll towards the advancing blade, and *vice versa*, so you need opposite cyclic to compensate as airspeed increases. In a tight spot, such as going into a confined area, you could get some unexpected sideways movement if you don't watch out, especially when you add the effects of tail rotor drift (although inflow roll increases with increasing speed, the effect on roll is greater at low speed as there is less flapback to offset it).

The point of greatest differential between the front and rear halves of the disc is just before ETL (*Effective Translational Lift*) on takeoff and after passing through it on landing, signified by vibration from increased induced drag on the blades as they pass over the tail. That is, drag is unequal between the fore and aft parts of the disc, giving noticeable vibration between 10-20 kts.

At higher speeds, the lift differential will decrease and allow you to use less left cyclic movement to compensate.

Note: The combination of inflow roll and flapback causes the disc to move up or down at a point just left of the nose, but they have their greatest individual effects at different speeds (the effect of inflow roll is greatest at low

CAPT

speeds, and flapback is greatest at high speeds). Thus, the amount that the disc tilts, and the position at which it does so, varies with forward speed. Inflow roll starts when leaving the hover but decreases, coning roll slightly increases with airspeed.

Because of inflow roll and coning, the blades crossing the nose produce more lift than those at the tail, so the induced drag is not the same between the two sides of the disk. This creates a Y force that acts at right angles to the direction of flight.

Note: Transverse flow doesn't produce vibration, the onset of ETL does. They often happen at the same time, but transverse flow is most noticeable in the early stages of the transition from the hover. Transverse flow can happen across the whole flight envelope, which is why the R22 has a knob that you pull up to offset any lateral cyclic loads in forward flight.

TAIL ROTOR DRIFT

In the hover, the tail rotor provides more of a force in the relevant direction than is actually needed to counteract the main rotor torque, and a single-rotor helicopter with North American rotation (anticlockwise viewed from the top) will drift laterally to the right if not corrected.

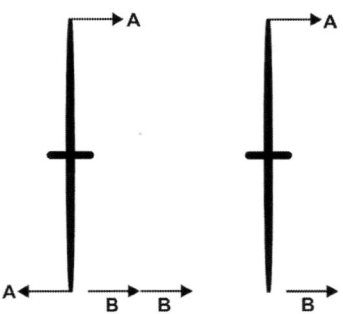

The tail rotor is doing more work because it is impractical to place any part of the force at the front. In the example on the left, above, the blades rotate around the centre, and points A are counterbalanced with a double force BB, as with a typical tail rotor. If you cancel out one each of A and B at the bottom, you are left with a side loading that causes movement in the direction of the anti-torque force. Also, the tail rotor is out on the end of the tailboom, and has a moment arm, and leverage, to increase the effect as it produces thrust of its own. Thus, the *moment* of the tail rotor force is used to overcome the couple of torque reaction - when a couple is opposed by a moment, there is a residual translation force.

The correction for this residual movement can be done simply by holding the cyclic control slightly off-centre. Other ways include offsetting the mast in the first place, rigging the controls (a mixing unit moves the cyclic proportionally to the collective), or causing the disc to tilt when the collective is raised. None, however, eliminate it completely, and it will not work for semirigid heads because the trunnion bearings are centred at the mast.

The amount of anti-torque from the tail rotor depends on the power setting - more will be required in the hover, for example, so the "power pedal" will be more forward than normal. The power pedal is the left one for a helicopter whose blades go round anti-clockwise when viewed from above (*North American rotation*). It is called that because, not only does it apply more anti-torque in the required direction, but its use also uses power from the engine and may cause the RRPM to droop (see *Overpitching*), which is why a little throttle application is needed when you use it, otherwise the helicopter would descend.

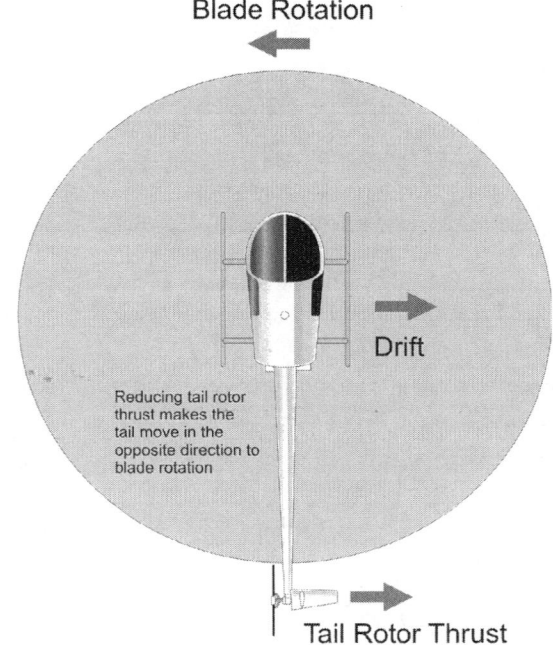

Note: Tail rotor drift is why the helicopter will go one way or the other (depending on which way the blades go round) when the engine fails in the hover. It is also why, when slinging, you need a clear space on that side so you can go there safely, and the ground crew need to be taught to go the opposite way.

This is also known as *translating tendency.*

Tail Rotor Roll

A helicopter will normally fly nose down when the disc is tilted for forward flight, so some are designed to hover tail-down, to make the cruise more level, and comfortable (and with less parasite drag), so you can get more speed for the same power.

Unfortunately, if the tail rotor is below the level of the tip path plane in the hover, the horizontal component of TRT which is the correction for tail rotor drift mentioned above (in this case a tilted main rotor) will cause a couple around the C of G with the tail rotor thrust going the other way, causing one or other of the skids to be lower in the hover, depending on the direction blade rotation (you can have them level in the cruise or hover).

It is therefore totally normal for one skid to be lower than the other, unless you've left the refuelling hose in (actually, this is quite useful when landing on sloping ground, as long as the slope goes with the skids). On some helicopters (e.g. the AS 350) the downwash can cause translational lift in the tail rotor that causes a yaw-roll couple which gets worse closer to the ground.

To combat this, you could raise the tail rotor on a boom or lower the rotor head, as is done with the Brantley, but the C of G position could screw that up anyway. Mostly, it is adjusted with left cyclic input.

If the C of G is above the tail rotor, the roll is accentuated, and if it is below, it is lessened. High tail rotors produce a rolling moment that subtracts the left lean. For a given helicopter, if the tail rotor is centered on the tail cone, the left lean is about 5 - 6°. If it is moved up a few feet to the top of the tail, it is reduced to 3° or so.

When hovering, for a single rotor helicopter whose main rotor turns *clockwise* from above, the thrust of the main rotor is mainly vertical with a slight orientation to the *right*, and *vice versa*. A helicopter in the hover, with anti-clockwise rotating blades, if not corrected (i.e. with a vertical rotor mast), would tend to drift to the right with power on.

TAIL ROTOR FAILURE

Losing a tail rotor is a problem because of the potential for extreme and rapid loss of control. There are two types:

- **Tail Rotor Control Failure**, where the blade pitch cannot be changed although the tail rotor may still be spinning (it may at least help with yaw stability)

- **Tail Rotor Drive Failure**, where the tail rotor simply ceases to rotate, perhaps due to a broken drive shaft or a gearbox failure

The problems associated with the failure can include:

- Those associated with recovering control

- Those associated with manoeuvring

- Those associated with landing

The first two need to be sorted fastest.

When the tail rotor fails, it will be in varying degrees of positive, neutral or negative pitch, depending on what you were doing at the time, so if you can remember what it was, you will have an idea of the state of the pedals. Unless it's a drive failure, or you lose some of the components, the chances are that you won't discover the problem until you change your power setting. It's very unlikely that you will be flying along in the cruise, for instance, and find a pedal forcing itself completely over to one side, as simulated by instructors on test flights, unless you have something like a motoring servo, in which case your problem has something to do with hydraulics as well. More typically, you will be in a descent, climb, cruise or hover, with the pedals where they should be and won't move when you want to do something else. When descending, for example, in the AS 350, you will have more left pedal (more right in the Bell 206), both of which will aid the natural movement of the fuselage against the main rotors. The pedals would be in a neutral position if you were flying at medium to high speeds, and the power pedal would be forward in high-power situations, like hovering. In any case, the spread between the pedals is not likely to be more than a couple of inches either way, certainly in a 206 - try an autorotation properly trimmed out to see what I mean. The same goes in the hover.

In fact, landing with a power pedal jammed forward is relatively easy, since the tail rotor is already in a position to accept high power settings, so you may be able to come in very slowly and even hover. If the pedals jam the other way (right in a 206), look for more speed, as there will not be enough antitorque thrust.

A *drive failure*, on the other hand, or loss of a component, will cause an uncontrollable yaw, and maybe an engine overspeed, so the immediate reaction should be to enter autorotation, keeping up forward speed to maintain some directional control (which is difficult in the hover, so try to

© *Phil Croucher, 2013*

CAPT

get one skid on the ground at least), if you have time. If you lose a component, the C of G may shift as well.

Pilots who have been there report there is a significant increase in noise with a drive shaft failure, and that the centrifugal force in the spin is quite severe. Anyhow, an autorotation is certainly part of the game plan, and as speed is reduced towards touchdown, you will yaw progressively with less control available in proportion, so it may be worth trying to strike the ground with the tailwheel or skid first (if you've got one), which will help you to keep straight - according to the JetRanger flight manual, you should touchdown with the throttle fully closed, as you would if the failure occurs in the hover, to stop further yaw when pitch is pulled to cushion.

Reducing the throttle and increasing collective pitch would reduce the effect of the tail rotor, as would beeping down to the bottom of the governor range (difficult in most AS 350s or Gazelles, where the throttle is not on the collective). The tail rotor is there to counteract torque, so if you give it less work to do, you will be more successful.

Otherwise, you might find a power and speed combination that will maintain height until you find a suitable landing area, then you've got as much time as your fuel lasts to solve the problem - you don't necessarily have to get down first time, although it's also true to say that you don't really know what's going on mechanically, so you shouldn't hang around, either. The cyclic can be used to change direction and allow you to fly sideways to create drag from the tail boom and vertical stabiliser.

If you want to run-on for landing, get the wind and/or nose off to the retreating blade side, so the fuselage is crabbing, and control your (shallow) descent with a combination of throttle and collective, applying more of the latter as the throttle is closed just before touchdown so you run on straight. Note that some helicopters (such as twins, or the AS 350) won't let you use the throttle as precisely as that. Not only that, you may well be so busy that worrying about minor details like the wind's exact quarter will be the last thing on your mind. For a running landing, on most machines, about 30% torque (power) at 30 kts will put you in a good position for landing at 30 ft, and a little power at the last minute will put your nose nicely straight. For the non-power pedal, keeping straight involves either more speed or less power, and you have to accept more of a run-on.

Loss of Tail Rotor Effectiveness

This is a phenomenon that was discovered and studied by the US Army in relation to the OH-58 (Bell 206). They found that under certain wind conditions on low speed missions (below about 30 kts), the machine would be subject to an unanticipated yaw to the right that could not be stopped with full application of the opposite (left) pedal. As a result, it is sometimes also known as *tail rotor breakaway*, or a stall, which is not strictly correct, as thrust is still being produced - it's just not enough for the task in hand. The problem is that the aircraft will yaw uncontrollably *within its published flight envelope*, due to a tail rotor that can just about cope with benign conditions losing thrust from interference by the main rotor wake, which brings its anti-torque capability to less than zero.

Loss of Tail Rotor *Authority*, or LTA, on the other hand, exists when the power required exceeds the power available and the nose yaws to the right. This is because thrust required is a function of main rotor torque - TR thrust available depends on RPM^2.

Note: When main rotor RPM reduce, demands on the tail rotor are higher.

The difference is subtle, though - LTA is a *mechanical* effect. LTE is aerodynamic, due to wind, and is more of a problem where the tail rotor's top blade goes forward.

However, it is important to realise that, in both cases, the tail rotor has not suddenly stopped working. Typical situations where LTE might be encountered include powerline patrol, low level survey, spraying, herding, traffic watch, EMS, or anything that involves operating in a high-power, low-airspeed environment with an appropriate crosswind or tailwind, and right turns.

When winds are encountered from the critical areas given below, they exert a force on the fuselage and tail section. The higher the windspeed, the more force is applied. If the tail rotor has very little or no additional power left in reserve, the force will cause the aircraft to yaw, which you will be unable to stop. Responding in time to an uncommanded right yaw is critical - the yaw is usually correctable if left pedal is applied *immediately*.

Your helicopter can be more susceptible to LTE if the tail rotor is masked by a tail surface, like a vertical fin, which will reduce the cubic footage of air going through the system, and it can be especially triggered by tail and side winds (this is actually a good reason for maintaining main rotor RPM - as the tail rotor runs at a fixed speed in relation to it, lower N_R will reduce tail rotor effectiveness). Remember that the initial investigations were done on a machine that has its tail rotor on the left (a Bell 206), which means that its tail rotor is a *pusher*. It also looks as if the phenomenon affects only those machines, but see also *Fenestron Stall*, below.

Note: In steady winds, the azimuths given below can be demonstrated with safety, but gusts can cause problems when rotor RPM can vary from moderate collective changes. The tail rotor thrust is varied, and if it is reduced just when the wind increases from the right, you could reach the left pedal stop.

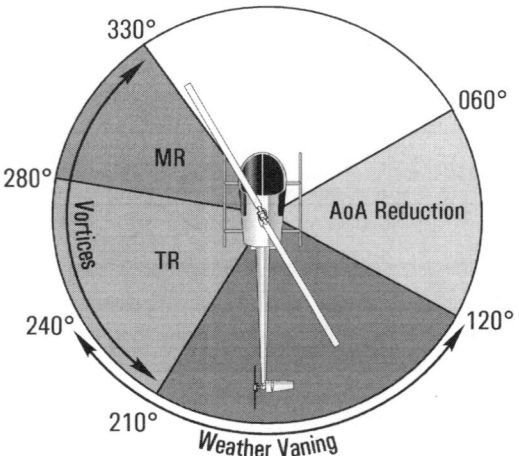

The wind azimuths concerned are:

- **120-240°** (the rear). The machine's weathercocking stability is affected. The nose is pushed towards the relative wind by the fuselage and vertical fin. If a yaw rate has been established it will be accelerated in the same direction.

- **210-330°** (the left). Possibility of tail rotor vortex ring state, which varies the tail rotor thrust spasmodically to create yaw rates, so you need to be quick. If a right yaw rate develops, the machine can get into the rear region described above where the rate of turn will increase.

- **285-315°** (forward left). Main rotor vortex interference helping to create a tail rotor vortex ring state, as described above.

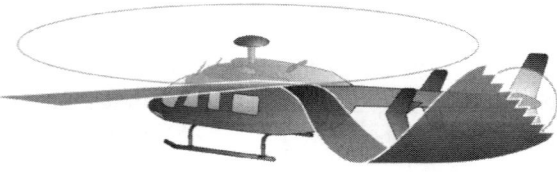

You would get the same effect if you were turning right from a flight situation with the wind from the front - as you turn, the wind will start to come from that quarter. *LTE is a particular problem when turning right at slow speed with the wind from the left.*

With reference to the 210-330° region, at windspeeds between 5-10 kts, the tail rotor is just entering its own vortex ring* state, and the vortex

rings start forming between 10-20 kts. Above 20-35 kts, they start disappearing again.

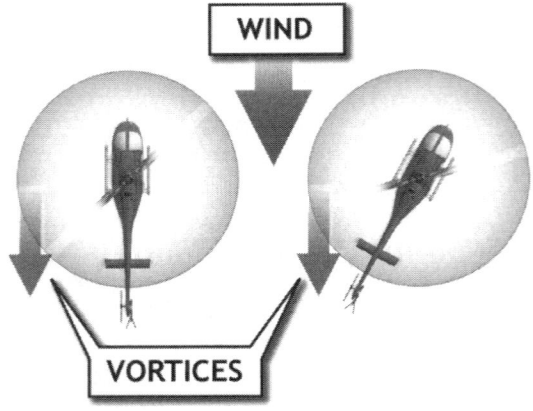

*The vortex ring mentioned here (*falling in a hole*) is not from the main rotor, except when dirty air from them is blown into the tail rotor, but from simple movement of the tailboom to the left, whether you're putting in right pedal or are hovertaxiing to the left (or sitting in the hover with a wind from the left). In a pedal turn to the right (e.g. right pedal forward), the tail rotor pitch is reduced at the same time as induced airflow is increased through the tail rotor, which is another reason why the pedals should be moved smoothly, to prevent the possibility of vortex ring through the tail rotor.

- **All areas**. Loss of translational lift.

The characteristic is most significant when at or near maximum power.

You must try to maintain translational lift - if you do not maintain airspeed during a right downwind turn, you can experience an increasing right yaw rate as the power demand increases and a sink rate develops.

Recovery comes from a combination of full power pedal*, forward cyclic and reduction in collective**, or autorotation. Prevention lies in keeping into wind and always using the power pedal (left in a 206 or one with similar blade rotation), and being *smooth on the controls.*

If you use the other pedal, not only will the fuel governor ensure that the aircraft will settle after a short time (using the power pedal by itself makes it climb), but a large bootful of the power pedal in a fast turn the other way will create a torque spike. In addition, as mentioned before, there is a danger of the tail rotor encountering its own downwash and entering the vortex state.

*Remember that the tail rotor is not stalled, so the corrections to be applied are always in the normal direction, that is, opposite to the turn.

CAPT

**Although this helps to stop the yaw rate, it may also cause a greater rate of descent which may need larger collective movements to stop, increasing the yaw rate further and decreasing rotor RPM. Don't do it too near the ground!

FENESTRON STALL

Fenestron Stall is another misnomer which arises from similar circumstances - a high pedal input in the hover or at low speed with low winds has been known to start the aircraft rotating so rapidly that it looks like control has been lost. It seems to occur on SAS-equipped aircraft (i.e. with stabilised controls), because the SAS masks the initial feel required for the pilot to react early enough.

AUTOROTATIONS

You are in autorotation when the rotors are driven purely by the airflow coming up through the disc as you descend in a stable condition - the engine does not contribute towards keeping the machine up in the air, because it has either failed or been disengaged (whenever engine RPM becomes slower than rotor RPM, the freewheeling clutch allows the rotors to turn by themselves).

Note: The state of ideal autorotation allows the main rotor to produce thrust that is approximately equal to aircraft weight. As profile power is still needed to overcome the drag of the blades, a real autorotation has a higher descent rate.

The rotor profile drag that is normally dealt with by engine power is now handled by the upcoming air, which is called the *Rate Of Descent Flow*, and associated with an inflow angle. In short, potential energy is used up.

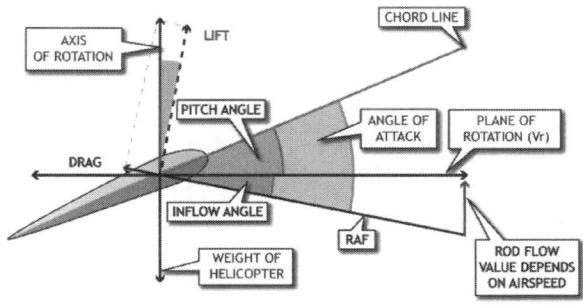

The angle of attack is now the *combination* of the blade pitch and inflow angles, so it can be rather large. The rate of descent (or the inflow) is the same for all sections of the blade, but the rotational velocity (hTRT) is not, so the relative airflow along the blade will vary, depending on the section being discussed, and so will the position of the TR vector, forward or behind the axis of rotation, according to the amount and type of drag produced.

In fact, the rotor disc behaves like a parachute as the air bunches up underneath it:

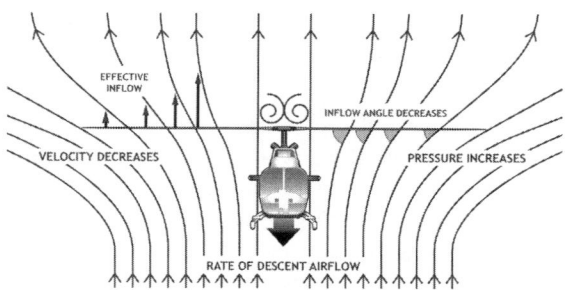

Again, the flow is curved to satisfy the Continuity Equation. As the inflow angle reduces from root to tip, due to washout and characteristics of the airflow (it is being slowed down by the retarded air passing through the rotor), the effective inflow decreases (as the rotational flow increases) until it becomes lower than the ROD flow, so there is relatively higher pressure below the disc. The momentum theory states that the disc is absorbing energy from the flow and slowing it down, and to satisfy Bernoulli, the pressure must increase.

Note that the Lift vector will always be forward of the Axis of Rotation - the Lift/Drag ratio positions the TR forward or behind, because it governs the angle between the Lift and TR vectors.

Vertical Autorotation

In autorotation, the rotor disc area splits into three concentric regions. It is the middle part (the driving region) that does the work. The problem is that the blade washout normally established for flight is the opposite of what is needed for autorotation.

- In the **stalled** region (at the roots), there is little lift so the long drag vector pulls TR behind the axis of rotation. The TR then produces some rotor thrust, which reduces the rate of descent, and rotor drag, which slows the blade down

- In the **driving** region, it is forward of the axis, because the drag vector is short. This creates a force that turns the blade. The wing of a gliding aeroplane provides lift and a forward pull, and this quality is made use of to keep the blades rotating, since, if you tie one end of a blade to the hub, the remainder will want to turn in a circle. The higher L/D ratio here balances the rotor profile drag from the rest of the blade

- In the **driven** region (at the tips), the TR vector lies behind the axis of rotation, due to profile drag from the V^2 factor and induced drag from vortices. This area is behaving as it would in normal flight

At the neutral points, the TR vector is vertical, producing zero shaft torque. These are therefore the only two points on the blade that are autorotating. The driving region is technically windmilling, as some shaft torque is needed to drive the tail rotor.

The size and position of each area changes with pitch angle, rate of descent and RRPM, so you can alter the driving region size and position to control the speed of the rotors (increasing ROD increases RRPM and *vice versa*). For example, raising the collective lever (in a vertical descent) makes the neutral points move together due to the alteration in relative airflows, which reduces the size of the driving region.

Constant RRPM is therefore achieved by balancing the accelerative forces from the driving region against the decelerative forces from the stalled and driven regions, plus any drag from hangers-on, such as the tail rotor. This is done by raising or lowering the collective lever.

At constant rotor RPM, rotor drag = autorotative force, so there is zero torque at the hub if you ignore hub bearing friction, and the tail rotor does not need to produce an anti-torque force. If an outside disturbance (such as an updraught) increases the RRPM, the neutral points move towards the root, the autorotational force works on a shorter arm and RPM decrease to compensate.

If rotor RPM are maintained, the rate of descent will be constant regardless of altitude or weight, although the collective lever might sit a little higher.

If an autorotative descent is started from high up, and the collective position is not changed, TRT will increase and RRPM and ROD will decrease as the air gets denser.

DRIVING REGION POSITION

This depends on air density, weight, and airspeed.

If the air is less dense, the rate of descent and inflow (and hence inflow angle) must be increased to maintain the mass flow into the disc from beneath. This changes the angle of attack so that the neutral points move outward, to give them a longer moment arm, so RRPM will increase.

The same result arises from greater weight. A light helicopter at low rates of descent may not produce enough autorotative force to keep the blades spinning.

As a helicopter accelerates away from a zero speed autorotation, the ROD initially decreases, then increases.

Forward Flight

The amount of ROD flow varies in sympathy with forward speed. For example, as speed is increased, there is less resistance to the air passing through the blades, so the upward flow increases, as does the angle of attack. The rate of descent reduces. There are three factors involved:

- **Factor A (or X)**. If you tilt the disc forward, the POR approaches the RAF and the inflow angle will decrease, as will the angle of attack. This produces a decrease in rotor thrust, and an increased rate of descent. You must keep tilting the disc forward to gain the airspeed required to overcome parasite drag. Factor A gives a continuously increasing rate of descent throughout the helicopter's speed band.

- **Factor B (Y)**. This introduces a horizontal airflow on top of the ROD flow. The induced angle is reduced, for the same effect as Factor A

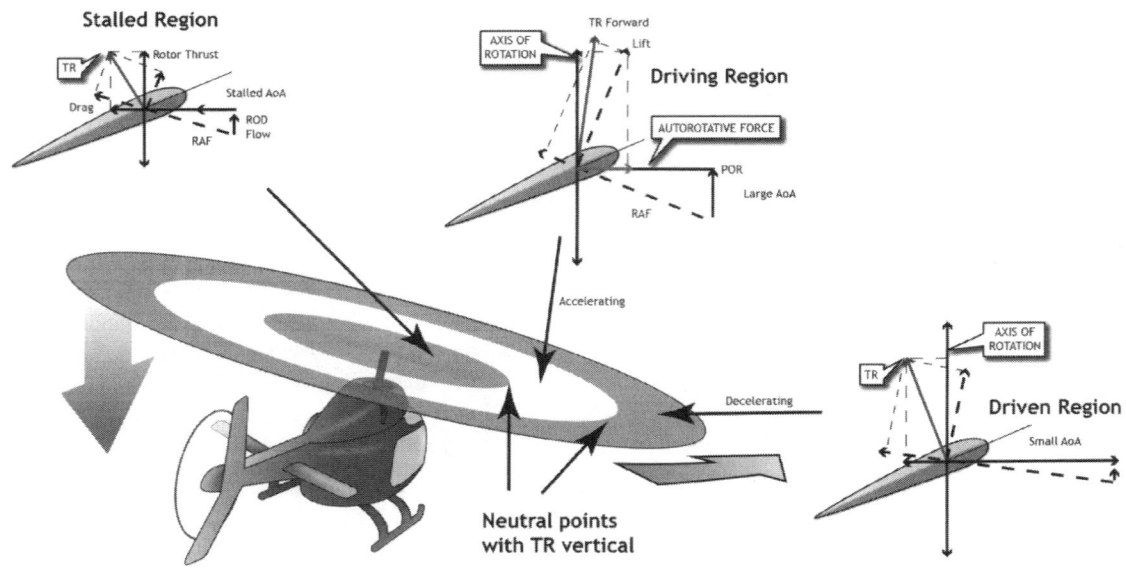

BLADE SECTIONS IN VERTICAL AUTOROTATION

CAPT

- **Factor C (Z)**. The disc is moving into new air that has not been slowed down by any downwash from the rotor disc, so the ROD flow will increase, which increases the induced angle and the angle of attack. This reduces the rate of descent. The reduction is largest at slow forward speeds where the ROD flow is slowed down the most.

At low forward speeds, Factor C is greater than the combined efforts of A and B, as the disc is only tilted a little way. As forward speed increases, however, Factor C's influence diminishes as the effects of parasite drag have to be overcome. Eventually, A + B will equal C at minimum rate of descent speed. At higher speeds than this, A + B will be more than C and the only way you can maintain the induced flow is with a higher rate of descent.

The best lift/drag ratio is at minimum endurance speed (most helicopters use about 45 kts), when the driving region of the disc is exactly centred. As you increase speed, it moves towards the retreating blade side (together with the stalled region) until it touches the edge, where the angle of attack is larger. This is your power-off V_{NE} because once the driving region goes beyond the edge of the disc, the surface area of the driving region is reduced, resulting in rotor decay. It moves left because of dissymmetry of lift.

At this point, the advancing blade contains a higher proportion of the driven region and the retreating blade contains more of the stalled region, with a reduction in the size of its driven region.

Autorotation Procedure

The purpose of a good autorotation is to put you in a position for a safe engine-off landing. Proper control of the rate of descent is critical, for which airspeed is the primary factor, as controlled by the cyclic (the collective controls the lift produced by the main rotor, to keep the RPM within the normal power-off range*). For example, a higher or lower airspeed than that for minimum rate of descent will result in the helicopter going down faster. Going too fast also means a longer or more aggressive flare to reduce the forward speed just before touchdown. Too slow means little flare and very high rates of descent.

*If rotor RPM are allowed to build above the top range, you raise the collective to keep the RRPM as normal. If it decreases below the normal range, collective pitch must be reduced. One phenomena that can occur is ground rush, which produces a sensation that the ground is coming up faster than expected. This can make you flare or increase collective too early, resulting in rotor energy management issues, and may jeopardize a safe landing.

If the engine in a single-engined helicopter fails in the cruise, the recommended immediate actions are:

- lower collective and counteract yaw with pedals
- select attitude with cyclic
- select landing site
- transmit Mayday
- position helicopter for an into wind landing

Your average autorotation is split up into various phases, with each having different aerodynamic characteristics.

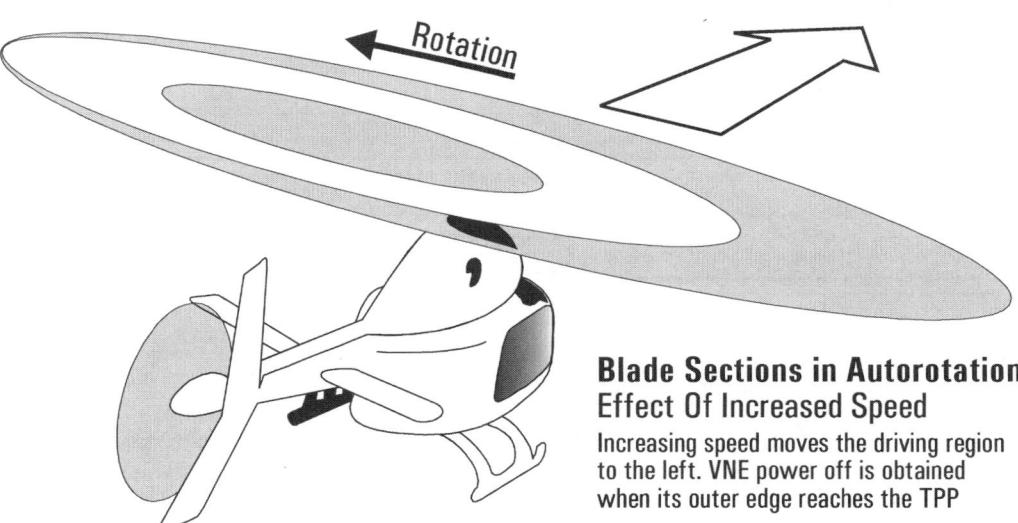

Blade Sections in Autorotation
Effect Of Increased Speed
Increasing speed moves the driving region to the left. VNE power off is obtained when its outer edge reaches the TPP

ENTRY

RRPM decays most quickly when the helicopter is heavy, in thinner air, or travelling at high speed, because higher collective pitch and engine torque are needed. Rotor RPM will also be slowed down by the tail rotor and other bits attached to the main rotor gearbox.

Rotor profile drag must be reduced as quickly as possible, together with adjusting the angle of attack. If you allow the blades to slow down, the centrifugal force lessens, the coning angle increases, the rotor disc gets smaller, TRT reduces and you have a high rate of descent.

Loss of RPM at the entry into autorotation is therefore the most significant problem, especially if your weight is high or the air density low. This is why as little power as possible is used on takeoff, so that, if the engine fails, your rotor blades are not already at a high angle of attack, and producing more drag to slow them down.

 The only way you can maintain blade speed in autorotation is by controlling the aerodynamic forces around them, by raising or lowering the collective (the cyclic controls speed).

 When the rotor speed decays, the tail rotor speed will decay as well, and it will become less effective, so more right pedal will be needed than usual.

Otherwise, there is an initial loss of airspeed, and the collective is lowered, both of which cause the rotor disc to flap forward. Because you are using some left pedal, there will also be a yaw to the left, and a roll to the left because you are using some cyclic to cancel out inflow roll.

DESCENT

In a power-off autorotation in still air, for a minimum rate of descent, you should fly close to V_Y (Best Rate Of Climb) with minimum rotor speed (within limits). The maximum glide range is close to best range speed with minimum rotor speed (without exceeding power off V_{NE}). At high gross weights, in high density altitudes, or when the wind is strong, increasing the airspeed slightly will give better autorotative performance. In light winds or at low density altitudes, decrease the airspeed slightly.

- Set minimum descent speed (60 mph in the Bell 206). The rate of descent is large at low airspeeds (most at zero), decreases until minimum descent speed, then increases again after that.

- If undershooting, stretch the glide by increasing airspeed slightly and/or pulling collective within the RRPM range - use the low RPM beeps.

- If overshooting, you have to manoeuvre the aircraft with S-turns, etc., keeping to minimum descent speed.

RANGE & ENDURANCE

The best speeds for autorotation mirror those for powered flight (see later). The idea for the longest glide is the same as best range speed - expending the least energy for the most ground covered. Similarly, for least rate of descent, expending the least energy to stay up, so the speed is very similar to the best rate of climb speed.

For maximum time in the air, or endurance, you need the speed that gives you the least rate of descent, which is at the bottom of the ROD curve. Flying for range needs a higher forward speed, but that reduces your time aloft.

If you raise the collective, lift increases and RoD decreases, which allows you to travel further in the same time. This can be increased further if you use the best glide speed. This is called Stretching The Glide.

Tip: Only use best glide speed *after* entering a good autorotation (rotors in the green range and steady, pedal trimmed, speed about right), *after* the turn into the wind.

The correct speed is found by drawing a tangent from the origin to the curve.

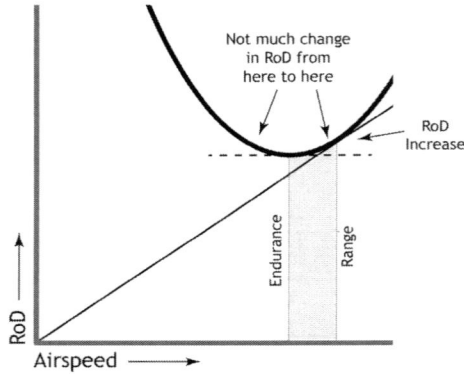

It is actually the max ratio of speed to ROD, which is the equivalent of the distance covered.

The maximum glide ratio for the average helicopter in forward autorotative flight at range speed in still air is about 4:1 (forward:descent). For minimum ROD, it's 3:1 - i.e. around 17°. So, from 5,000 ft, at 85 kts (for example), you would glide for about 19,000 feet (at 2200 fpm). At 60 kts, the glide would be for 15,500 ft (at 1870 fpm).

Thus, the speed is always faster in an autorotation for range, **with a higher rate of descent**, so get used to it. Add half the wind speed if you are battling against a headwind. The rate of descent is always lower in an autorotation with normal forward speed, as compared with a vertical autorotation in still air.

© *Phil Croucher, 2013*

Note: In theory, low RRPM should be used (the bottom of the green range), but higher RRPM should be used for lower speeds to ensure that kinetic energy is available.

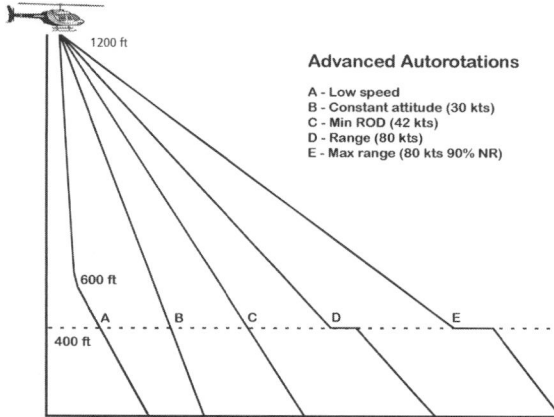

The picture above shows the various types of autorotation for a Bell 206, but the same principles apply for other helicopters.

Note: If collective pitch is increased and rotor RPM is reduced to a safe minimum during autorotation, the ROD *decreases*. If the cyclic is pulled back, speed will reduce and the rate of descent will *decrease*, and coning angle and RRPM will *increase*.

FLARE AND TOUCHDOWN

When about 70 feet from the ground, (depending on whether you think you are descending or moving across the ground too fast), use rearward cyclic to slow down vertically and horizontally, to trade airspeed for lift, with judicious timing. The amount is proportional to your speed and serves to increase the total lift reaction (which stops the sink) and shifts it to the rear (which stops forward movement). It also increases the rotor RPM. Continue the flare progressively (and sharply), to be at the correct speed for landing at 10 feet, applying collective as flare effect decreases to check the descent more positively, watching for drift towards the retreating blade side (the "check" is the application of some collective to brake the descent - in the 206 it can be a positive movement; in the 407 and AS 350, it can just be a pause). As the flare ends, and the kinetic energy of the rotors is used when the collective is raised, the airflow through the rotors is reversed, assisting you to level (the amount depending on the model), ready to cushion the landing as you apply collective pitch. This is where correct use of airspeed during the descent will have had the most beneficial effects - as the kinetic energy stored in the blades is what slows you down, it follows that any you have to use to slow an unnecessarily fast rate of descent is not available for the final stages of touching down.

In every flare there is a point called the *apex*, which is where the trading off of airspeed for lift is essentially all over and you just have to get yourself on the ground. Put another way, it is the point where there is no further benefit from the flare manoeuvre, so you may as well pull the pitch. The *variable flare* is used for a low or zero speed touchdown. It is started at a slightly lower height than the gentle flare, with a progressive raising of the nose until you reach the touchdown speed at 10-15 feet (the tail is lower than normal). Level the aircraft and cushion the touchdown with collective, remembering that a more positive application will pitch the nose up.

FLARE EFFECTS

Although the flare is mostly associated with the final stages of autorotation, it is actually used in every landing, when you reduce speed to zero. It can slow you down horizontally and vertically because, not only does the horizontal component of TRT reverse when the disc is tilted back, the airflow from underneath increases the angle of attack and creates more lift (thrust). The coning angle also increases to increase RPM.

Characteristics of the flare include:

- **Thrust reversal**. The disc is tilted in the opposite direction to that of the helicopter's travel, and the TRT now points in the same direction as the parasite drag vector. The nose will pitch up.

- **Increase in TRT**. The airflow from underneath increases the angle of attack and TRT.

- **Increased rotor RPM** in spite of the increased angle of attack and drag because:

  - Collective is lowered as you try not to climb.

  - Coriolis effect* - increased TRT causes coning angles to increase and the C of G of all blades to move inwards.

  - Increased load factor.

  - The TRT vector is more forward of the virtual rotation axis (because the RAF is shifted downwards) to increase the autorotative force.

Note: Be careful when flaring downwind, as the pressure against the horizontal stabiliser will pitch the nose up.

THE LANDING

From about 50-70 feet, the landing can be split into four distinct phases:

- The flare

- Pulling collective

- Check & Level (in some aircraft - could be a pause)

- Cushion with collective

IN THE HOVER

If the engine fails in the hover, at 3' skid height in still air, in a single-engined helicopter, the recommended action is to counteract yaw with pedals, maintain position with cyclic, and cushion touchdown with collective.

The Height/Velocity Curve

Otherwise (wrongly) known as the *Dead Man's Curve*, this is a chart for helicopters that compares speeds against heights for areas of increased vigilance, or where not to be if you want to maximise your chances of successful recovery from an engine failure; that is, you don't want to be at high altitudes with low speeds, or low ones with high speeds. For example, it is unwise to fly at low speeds between 15-400 feet above the ground, so the best place to be is in the gap between the shaded areas.

In other words, the graph shows initial combinations of speed and height that the average pilot would find it difficult to land safely from in an autorotation (it has a lot to do with the design limits of the landing gear). More precisely, it is where *continuous operations should be avoided*, as engine failure is likely to result in damage to the helicopter. It should still be observed when flying a twin-engined helicopter, in case an engine fails (it is *critical* for the Bell 212), but some machines (e.g. the AS 355) do not have a height/velocity curve at all for some flight regimes.

Note: This does not mean that, if you do not land safely from the "safe" areas, that you are a below average pilot! Neither does it mean that an above average pilot will be able to execute a safe landing from the avoid areas! Average pilots are not used to establish the curve!

Check if the chart is in the *Limitations* or *Performance* section of the Flight Manual (it moves to the limitations section with more than 9 passenger seats). If it's in the latter, its requirements are *recommended*, not mandatory.

The curve is valid only when it is inside the limits for Weight, Altitude and Temperature. It is *not* valid for approaches*, as it is actually calculated for *level flight conditions* (i.e. *a steady state constant airspeed & attitude*), but lawyers and juries don't often appreciate the niceties, so it would be prudent to take note of its requirements, since engine failure while climbing through any of the shaded areas *will* result in airframe damage, as you are using higher power settings and angles of attack. You also have a fair amount of inertia, so RRPM will decay nicely while you wait for airflow to start going up through the disc after you have continued going up a short way before descending. On approach, your hands are on the controls and you are using less than cruise power, so the figures don't work the same way.

*The expression *not valid* does not mean that the curve should be ignored - it just means that it has not necessarily been validated for those conditions, so the figures will be

different. Also, the aircraft will naturally be climbing in the takeoff corridor, so it is the *power used* (or rotor blade pitch) that is important, because that increases rotor decay when the engine fails, as your collective pitch is higher.

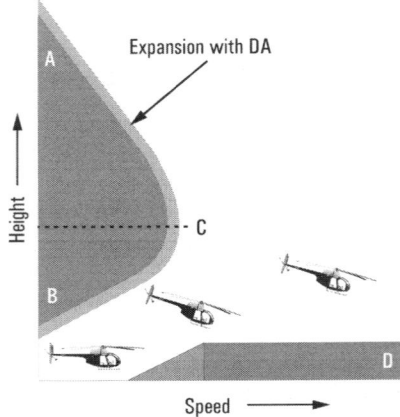

The vertical shaded area in the diagram above is the *low speed section*, which takes account of:

- The rate of descent required to drive the rotor

- Rotor inertia characteristics or RRPM decay rate from the time of engine failure until the pilot wakes up, plus reaction time (to give the average pilot a chance, a one-second delay is factored in for minimum skill levels)

- Landing gear design limitations and hard landing risk to the occupants

- Translational lift values and sink rates

Point A is the minimum height that you need to establish a steady descent velocity and build up rotor speed from the hover. Point B is the maximum height at which you can use the kinetic energy stored in the rotor. At point C, you can still use the kinetic energy of motion to maintain rotor speed. At point D you are too high for a run-on landing, and there is a risk of ballooning and/or a tail strike when you flare. The clear area between the high and low speed areas is the takeoff corridor.

While we're on the subject of real engine failures:

> *I have yet to see anyone who has had a real, unannounced engine failure from 100' not have damage to the helicopter and their body. There's a good reason for avoiding that area (I've probably done close to 100 demonstrations of the HV curve to budding test pilots and flight test engineers, as well as participated in a few real world HV curve demonstrations for certification, just to establish my bona-fides). If you've convinced yourself through lots of training for autorotations that you can do a zero airspeed entry from 100' and got away with it, you're deluding yourself that when the real, unannounced failure happens that you can survive - the important part you're not thinking about is the surprise, it can't happen to me, this isn't true part of the real*

engine failure that deprives you of the very important two to three seconds that the training aspect doesn't consider. You're ready for the engine failure, know what's going to happen and are spring loaded to react to the first twitch of the throttle.

.....and for those of you who think that you can get away with it from a 20' hover, much the same applies.

Everyone I've talked to who's had a real engine failure has said the same thing- the surprise factor caught them big time.

And just to round this out - when doing a zero airspeed entry from a high hover in a Jet Ranger (one of the more forgiving machines to do this in), it takes a minimum of 250-300 feet for the airspeed to start approaching something that will let you flare and have the rotor start to get back into the green. This is with a one second delay between rolling the throttle off and lowering the collective - a very short time.

Shawn Coyle

DYNAMIC ROLLOVER

Every object has a *static* rollover angle, to which it must be tilted for its Centre of Gravity to be over the roll point, for most helicopters being 30-35°, but it can be smaller (that is, the helicopter can then roll without any power being applied, and will typically need quite a steep slope for it to work). The static rollover angle arises when the lateral C of G is over a skid or wheel.

Dynamic rollover, on the other hand, can occur on a fairly shallow slope or even on flat ground if you mishandle the helicopter. As the name implies, it occurs *when power is applied*, within normal roll rates. A helicopter will roll over if you carry on landing or taking off after you reach the cyclic control limits - the first clue is mast bumping.

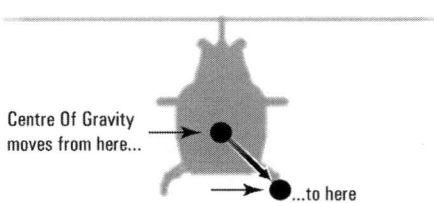

Centre Of Gravity moves from here...
...to here

At this point, there is a horizontal component to TRT which, though small, is enough to rotate the helicopter around any skid that is unable to move, especially as the main rotor thrust is not vertical but leaning into the direction of the roll. Thus, dynamic rollover can occur when your helicopter has a tilted main rotor thrust vector with respect to the C of G, commonly encountered with some side drift when you have one skid or wheel on the ground acting as a pivot point, but you can also get a problem when your lateral C of G falls outside the width of the skids or wheels (you might get caught on a cable, or snagged on a tree root in a clearing).

In other words, with one skid or wheel on the ground (flat or sloped), the roll centre will be transferred from the C of G to the skid (or whatever is contacting the ground).

Because of the fulcrum effect, roll momentum will be multiplied by the square of the distance from the C of G to the new roll centre, so the controls, particularly the cyclic, will be less effective, as roll momentum is increased by between 4-8 times. The moment arm from the pivot point becomes longer, to give it more leverage.

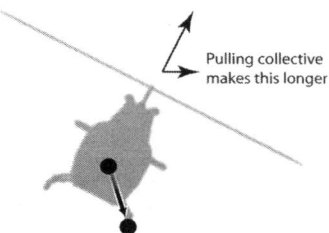

Pulling collective makes this longer

As your lateral cyclic control at that point is a lot less effective than if you were hovering, because it is not rotating around the C of G, but the rollover point, you are less able to get out of trouble, and the only real control is through the collective (do *not* raise it!), especially with teetering heads, because their control power is poor.

Past a certain point, *the rolling motion will not be correctable with cyclic*. Lower collective *immediately* and *smoothly*.

Dynamic rollover is worst with the right skid on the ground (counter clockwise main rotor) because tail rotor drift to the right makes it roll anyway. A crosswind from the left, with left pedal applied and thrust about equal to the weight (i.e. hovering) doesn't help either, as the left pedal pushes the right skid further into the roll. Keep away from tail winds, and land and take off vertically.

Note: Dynamic rollover occurs longitudinally as well!

Sloping Ground

Because the effective Centre Of Gravity can end up outside the skids or wheels, a helicopter can roll upslope if you apply too much cyclic into it or downslope if you apply too much collective, that is, enough to make the upslope skid rise too much for the cyclic to control.

During sloping ground manoeuvres, the rotor disc must be kept level so that the main rotor thrust is vertical, otherwise you will introduce a horizontal component that will rotate around the skid on the ground. As collective pitch is increased and the helicopter becomes light on the gear, adjust the cyclic position to compensate for winds, aircraft loading and translating tendency, making further adjustments as each wheel or skid leaves the ground.

Do not commit to landing until you get both skids on the ground. If you start sliding downwards with full cyclic applied the opposite way, use the cyclic *in the direction of the slide* as you pull up off the ground with collective.

VORTEX RING

A vortex ring (or toroidal vortex) is a region of rotating fluid moving through the same or a different fluid, where the flow pattern takes on the shape of a doughnut. In aviation, they are typically found in microbursts or in the combustion chamber of a turbine engine.

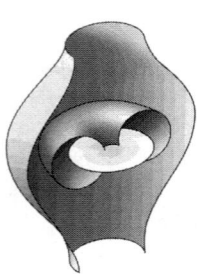

When applied to helicopters, the vortex ring state describes the recirculation of airflow around the tips of the rotor blades, so you are descending in descending air. In a vertical descent, the stream velocity is negative, whilst induced velocity remains positive. At some stage, they will both meet at the rotor blades.

Vortex Ring is often confused with *Power Settling* where, above a certain rate of vertical descent, the descent can only be arrested by moving into forward flight. This is because an alternative name for VR is *Settling With Power*. It really depends on which side of the Atlantic you are on. Either way, it is an unstable condition which may result in an uncontrolled rate of descent.

Just to make it clear:

- The **Vortex Ring** State exists when your forward speed is slow enough (below about 12 knots) and your descent is steep enough (faster than 700 fpm for modern helicopters) for the rotor to consume its own downwash, if power is applied. That is, the main rotor tip vortices are being recycled into the induced flow, typically existing when your vertical rate of descent is greater than half its velocity The torque will oscillate, and the aircraft will bump, pitch and roll, because the rotor is pumping air into a large bubble underneath. The bubble bursts every couple of seconds, which causes large scale disturbances in the surrounding airflow. Beyond about 1200 fpm, the rotor will be more or less in autorotation, even though there is still enough induced flow to qualify as the vortex ring state (the real difference is in your collective position). VR is most when the descent rate is ¾ of the induced velocity found in the hover. When it is about twice the rate, with an upward flow, you are in the **windmill brake state**, similar to autorotation. The **turbulent wake state** exists when the ring moves just above the plane of the rotor disc, and is like the wake behind a circular disc, hence the name.

- **Power Settling** means that the engine produces less power than is needed for the conditions. The aircraft descends and must be accelerated above translational lift to recover. At lowish rates of

descent, without power applied, this is more likely what you will be affected by. It is like driving at high speed towards a stop light. If you try to brake at the stop line you won't do so in time. Settling with power is not an aerodynamic condition, but a result of poor power management. It's what happens when you take off at sea level at gross weight and try and land at 8000 ft ASL and 35°C! However, SWP can lead to vortex ring if you don't do anything about it. This condition is most noticeable by the lack of tail rotor effectiveness because it is running slower with the main rotor.

You can get into Vortex Ring, or at least the incipient stage, quite unawares - you could be coming into a nicely set up approach to a hotel car park, for example, and a bunch of people come out to watch, standing right where you were going to land. So you raise the nose and lower the collective, to steepen the approach angle so you can land in front of them, and when you apply power at the bottom end, you add the third ingredient to the requirements for Vortex Ring, as described below.

You could also be bringing yourself into a hover on a mountain peak or the top of a building, into an updraught (which has the same effect), or you could be taking off into wind towards a slope near a glacier, planning to turn downwind when you have enough height, and not having enough airspeed when you do so. If you are landing in a tailwind, the downwash will be blown under your rotor system instead of trailing behind you.

In a quickstop, what starts off as horizontal airflow becomes nearly vertical when the disc is tilted back, which is similar to what happens in a powered recovery from autorotation if you pull in collective before levelling and people have even been known to get the initial symptoms when dropping down for fuel after longlining.

The essential problem with Vortex Ring is that there is no pressure differential between the top and bottom parts of the rotor disc to produce lift, because the blades fly through each other's dirty air, and you fall out of the sky. The inner and outer sections of the blade also begin to produce less lift, for different reasons.

In the descent, the vertical upflow alters the direction of the relative airflow, which is in the plane of rotation at the root, and causes an increased angle of attack because there is no induced flow. When the root stalls, the already small downwash is effectively cancelled out by the upwash.

At the tip, the vortices are strengthened, to increase the induced flow and *reduce* the angle of attack.

Eventually, the only thrust that balances aircraft weight comes from the middle sections, which is very erratic.

Thus, once into the Vortex Ring state you would be very lucky to get out of it, since the controls become

significantly less responsive*.

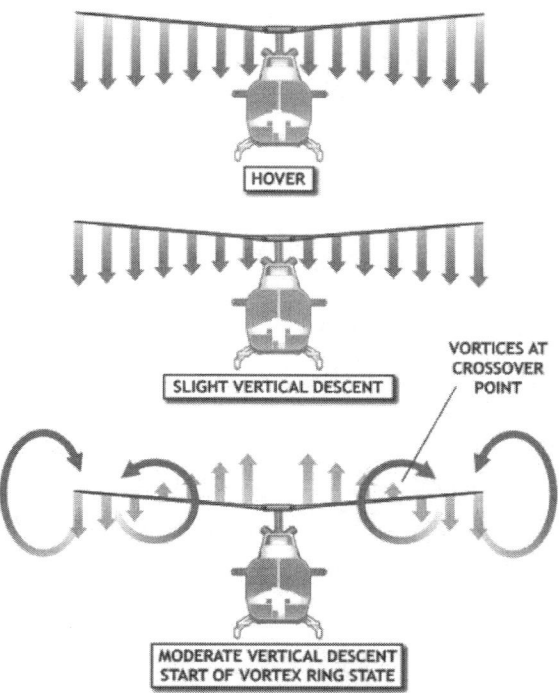

HOVER

SLIGHT VERTICAL DESCENT

VORTICES AT CROSSOVER POINT

MODERATE VERTICAL DESCENT START OF VORTEX RING STATE

However, you can get out of the incipient stage by removing one of the three ingredients that cause you to catch up with your own downwash, namely:

- Low speed (typically less than translation, 10 kts)
- Over 30% power applied
- 300-500 fpm ROD

*Fenestron-equipped helicopters could also suffer from *Fenestron Masking*, where the airflow goes up either side of the fenestron, but not through it.

The implication of the low speed above is that the column of air created by the applied power remains *more or less underneath the helicopter,* and you are not getting translational lift, although there is some evidence to suggest that a 70° glideslope is worse than being vertical (US Navy). Also,

300 feet per minute is not very fast, so you won't need much power to match the ROD, especially when lightly loaded, although some experiments suggest that you need to be descending at a rate of at least 50-75% of your downwash speed, which really means around 800 fpm in an R22. This is because modern helicopters have higher rates of downwash than when the above limits, for older helicopters, were formulated.

However, 300 fpm is taught because VRS can be started off easily by entering into the hover with too little power, slip into overpitching and enter VRS.

A heavy (or high) helicopter has a higher disc loading, as does one with a smaller rotor diameter, so it needs a higher rate of descent to match its downwash. Thus, as long as you are not overpitching, it can be *more difficult* to get into Vortex Ring, because the downwash velocity required is higher, and you will have to descend faster to catch up with it. For example, the onset of Vortex Ring in a heavy Bell 206 occurs around 900 ft/min rate of descent, with the real stuff at 1500 ft/min.

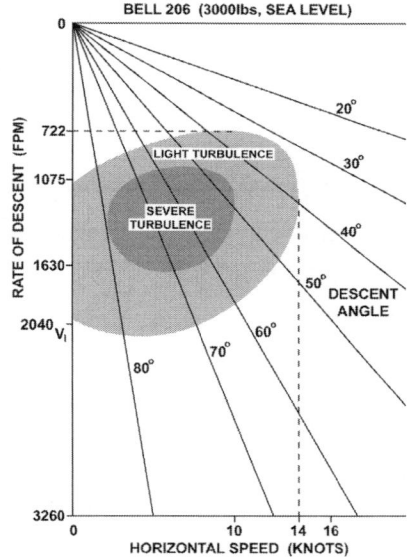

BELL 206 (3000lbs, SEA LEVEL)

As a further example, a V-22 Osprey (tiltrotor) once had a VRS accident after a descent at 2700 fpm at 285 ft AGL at 32 kts, whilst decelerating rapidly on a hot night with a quartering tail wind. Subsequent testing proved (as the mathematics had predicted) that it takes a higher rate of descent for a tiltrotor to get into VRS than a helicopter of equal size because of the high proprotor loading, which results in a much higher downwash. Because VRS occurs when the descent rate equals the downwash, a helicopter would have experienced VRS earlier.

You can avoid vortex ring by descending on flight paths shallower than 30°, or faster and slower speeds for steeper approaches because the turbulent wake does not lie near the rotor disc. At shallow angles, it is shed behind the helicopter, and at steep angles it is below the helicopter at slow rates of descent and above it at higher rates.

So, because the RoD and downwash velocity must be more or less equal for VR to occur, you won't get into it if you have a high rate of descent with a low power setting, or *vice versa*, or have some airspeed on, sideways or forwards, or are at altitude, or are in a heavy helicopter. Also, the stronger the wind, the less likely it is to occur - light and variable conditions are the worst, especially in mountains, where it's difficult to tell where it's coming from anyway, especially at the top of a sling line.

The key to avoiding VR is to recognise the symptoms:

- *Harsh vibration*, often felt through the controls, because the stalling of the blade at the root increases the control forces, but the vortices forming and breaking at the tip have an effect, too

- *Random yawing*, pitching and rolling from the machine trying to compensate for dissymmetry of lift). Yawing can also occur because the tail rotor is in the unstable airflow from the tip vortex region

- *Fluctuating power demands* and torque fluctuations from large increases in rotor drag

- *Reduced control response* caused by the reduced length of rotor blade that is producing thrust and therefore able to respond to control inputs

- *Rapid increase in rate of descent*

Note: The airflows in Vortex Ring have to build up - momentary combinations will likely not produce it.

To recover, you must eliminate one of the ingredients that contribute to VR, and low airspeed is usually the only one you have any influence over that does not involve significant height loss. However, this is not as easy as it sounds, because the controls can be very inefficient, especially in a machine with low control power.

If you feel a shudder, lower the nose and increase the airspeed, after which you can apply power, without letting the nose come up. If you have enough height, you could reduce power to zero, then gain airspeed, always watching your rotor speed. What you have to do is stop the blades flying directly into the vortices created by the others. If you have lots of power, simply climb out, as the idea is to remove the blade tips from the recirculating vortices. However, the power required for this will rise up to 40%! Lastly, if you have enough height, you could go with the rate of descent until you are in autorotation.

Note: Vortex Ring can also affect the tail rotor.

POWER
••

Power is needed to overcome the various types of drag (such as parasite, profile and induced), and to run various bits of the engine, plus the tail rotor. You need force to overcome drag, so you can say that:

$$\texttt{Force = Drag}$$

Because work is equal to:

$$\texttt{Force x Distance}$$

It is also equal to:

$$\texttt{Drag x Distance}$$

Power is the rate of doing work, so:

$$\texttt{Power} = \frac{\texttt{Work}}{\texttt{Time}}$$

or:

$$\texttt{Power} = \frac{\texttt{Drag x Distance}}{\texttt{Time}}$$

But distance divided by time is Velocity, so:

$$\texttt{Power = Drag x Velocity}$$

But the formula for drag is:

$$\texttt{D = C}_\texttt{D}\texttt{½}\rho\texttt{V}^2\texttt{S}$$

Now we get:

$$\texttt{Power = C}_\texttt{D}\texttt{½}\rho\texttt{V}^2\texttt{S x V}$$

or:

$$\texttt{Power = C}_\texttt{D}\texttt{½}\rho\texttt{V}^3\texttt{S}$$

This means that, while drag might increase as the *square* of the speed, the power to overcome it varies as the *cube* of the speed. If you double your speed, you will quadruple the drag and require 8 times more power, hence the steep rise in the parasite drag curve.

There are three types of power needed:

- **Induced Power** is the force opposing weight, or that associated with accelerating air downwards, with a value in the hover of about 60-85% the total possible. It decreases rapidly with forward flight, to reduce by about a quarter at maximum speed. It is the power needed to overcome the rise in drag as air is induced into the rotors. Induced power is maximum at the hover, increasing in a level turn, depending on disk loading and forward speed.

- (Rotor) **Profile Power** is used to maintain RRPM (plus the tail rotor and ancillaries), because it overcomes friction drag on the blades when the collective is fully down. Put another way, it is the power required to maintain a given rotor RPM at

CAPT

the zero thrust condition to drive the tail rotor, etc. This accounts for 15-40% of power, or around ¼ of the total possible. Note that power for the ancillaries and rotors will remain relatively constant, while that for the tail rotor will decrease with speed as translational lift and the vertical fin start to have an effect (up to a point). However, the RRPM figure will be affected when retreating blade stall and compressibility on the advancing blade start to kick in. The drag is different for the advancing and retreating blades because of V^2, but the bias is to the advancing blade, so there is a net increase in power required with speed, slowly at first, but steadily increasing.

With weight on the wheels or skids, and takeoff rotor RPM set, rotor profile power only is required. Profile power will be reduced at altitude because the air is less dense, but induced power will be up because the thinner air must be accelerated more to produce the same thrust. Thus, rotor profile power only changes with air density and RRPM.

- **Parasite Power** concerns itself with all parts of the helicopter except the rotor blades, and is only required in flight. It provides the horizontal component of TRT, and is equal to parasite drag multiplied by velocity, so it is least in the hover.

Induced power forms most of the power consumption in the hover.

Power Required

Performance of a helicopter is essentially the difference between power available and the power required to maintain a constant rotor RPM. It is adversely affected by Density Altitude. The power curve is the resultant of:

- Induced Power +
- Rotor Profile Power +
- Parasite Power

The total power required in level flight at constant speed is the sum of:

- Total power for the **main rotor**. In level flight at constant speed, main rotor induced power, rotor profile power and parasite power combine to provide the total power required to drive the main rotor, notated as $P_{tot\ MR}$.

- Power for the **tail rotor** (induced and rotor profile power). Tail rotor drag is included in parasite drag.

- **Accessory** (ancillary) **power**, covering generators, oil pumps, etc., and friction in the transmission.

The amount required depends on the air pressure, the temperature and the amount of moisture in the air.

Below is a graph that shows the relationship of power required against various forward speeds.

You can see that a little power is needed at first to prevent the machine sinking as the lift vector is tilted and reduced, and you transition into forward flight out of the ground cushion. Then power required reduces drastically until the effects of parasite drag require much more power for forward speed than the benefit you get from translation (it increases as the cube of the speed). The curve is like the resultant of the drag curve, except that is it based on TAS, and is more relevant for finding range speeds, for example.

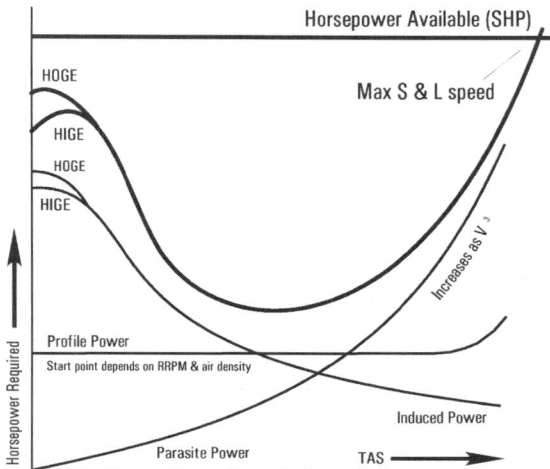

TAS is used because that is the only speed that gives a measure of the ground distance covered (power is the rate of doing work, or *force × distance*).

Note: Helicopters use *Shaft Horse Power* (SHP) which is the power available *to* the rotor, and not *from* it, since rotor efficiency is automatically taken into account (with a propeller, efficiency varies with forward speed). This is unaffected by speed, so constant power is usually available. This is why the horsepower available curve is a straight line. The point where it intersects with the power required curve is the maximum straight & level speed.

The lowest point of the curve is the *TAS* at which the *least power is needed* (as opposed to *producing the least drag*) and is therefore the best for endurance in level flight, for piston-engined machines. It is also the maximum rate of climb speed because the gap between power required and power available is greatest. This is not the same as the *minimum drag point*, which is the lowest point on the total drag curve.

The point on the power curve which shows the least amount of power for the greatest amount of TAS (i.e. the best L/D ratio) is slightly to the right of the bottom point and is found by drawing a tangent* to the curve from the origin, to find the *range speed*, which is therefore slightly higher. Note that is not a specific speed, but a range of speeds covered by the tangent's broad intersection point.

Note also that the range speed for turbine helicopters is greater because the power output remains constant within the helicopter's authorised altitude range. The HPA curve for a piston engined machine can move according to altitude and the efficiency of the engine and supercharger.

The origin itself can be moved forwards or backwards to take into account the effects of headwind or tailwind.

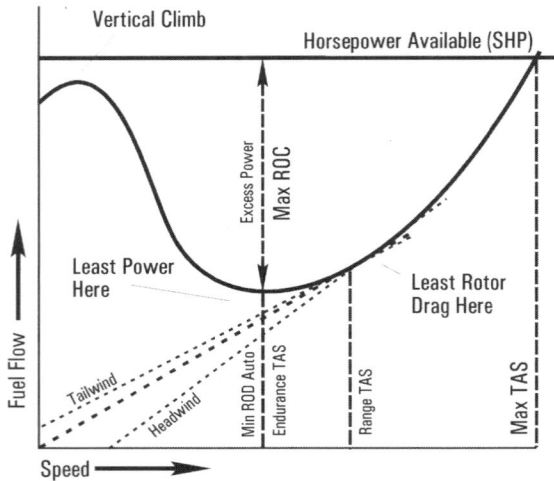

*A lower tangent means lower angle, for the least force.

The decrease in groundspeed is represented by moving the origin to the right by an amount equal to the wind speed. Thus, the velocity for maximum range in a headwind is automatically increased by an amount roughly equal to somewhere between ¼-½ of the headwind component. If you move the line left to cope with a tail wind, the speed is reduced because you don't have to fly so fast. The more the tailwind, the closer you come to endurance speed, so you can keep up in the air as long as possible and let the wind do the work. You get a greater range of speeds in a headwind, because of the flatness of the connection of the line with the curve.

The best rate of climb speed gives the maximum altitude in the shortest range, and because the maximum power is also available then, is the same as the endurance speed. In other words, the best ROC is obtained when there is the greatest difference between the power required for level flight and that available from the engines, which is the meaning of the power check before you go into a confined area. *The speed for max ROC (V_Y) is higher than that for best angle (V_X). A headwind will increase the angle of climb path - there will be no effect on rate of climb.*

Normally aspirated piston engine power available will *decrease* with altitude and rotor power required will *increase*. High density altitude reduces engine and rotor efficiency. In calm wind conditions, in a helicopter with north American rotation, a left pedal turn requires most power.

If you climb at a constant IAS, you must increase TAS to maintain it, therefore power required *increases* as you climb. This comes from the formula:

```
Power Required = Drag x TAS
```

It derives from the fact that *Power* (the rate of doing *Work*) is equal to *Force* x *Distance* (i.e. Work) divided by *Time*.

See also *Fuel Management* in the *Performance* chapter.

Limited Power

If you don't have enough power to hover*, the best angle of climb speed is found by drawing the tangent *down* from the horsepower available line to the power required curve.

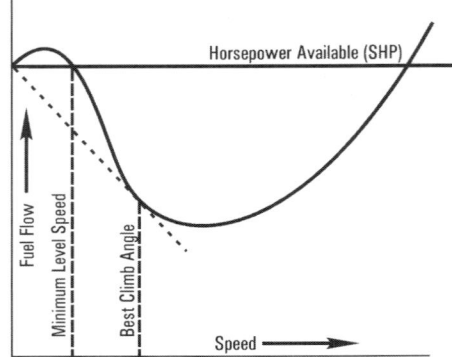

Limited Power means that the total power required to hover OGE is greater than the available engine power.

As this is the best ratio of power margin for climbing against minimum forward speed, it is the steepest angle available. When operating with limited power, the speed giving the steepest or maximum angle of climb is less than the best endurance speed.

Note: The best *angle* of climb speed increases with altitude. The best *rate* of climb speed stays constant. Normally, climb angle does not change because it is taken relative to the air mass, but a headwind increases the angle, and a tailwind decreases it.

Compared with a hover in ground effect, a helicopter hovering out of ground effect has the same total rotor thrust and increased rotor required power.

V_{NE}

This decreases with altitude for two reasons - firstly, the thinner air means that the rotor blades need a higher angle of attack to get the same lift, and the ASI reads incorrectly. Things that impose V_{NE} in helicopters include:

- **Retreating Blade Stall**, where the retreating blade flaps down, but not to equality - it actually stalls further, inboard from the tips, as that is where the angle of attack is highest, even with washout. As your forward speed increases, the margin for the angle of attack required to stall gets much smaller.

The *tip speed ratio* defines the percentage of RBS against forward speed - a figure of 0.45 means 45% of the retreating blade is stalled at cruise speed

- **Airflow Reversal** (over the root of the retreating blade). At 100 kts, about a quarter of the retreating blade is subject to this

- **Cyclic range**, from weight and altitude (both can affect RBS by angle of attack) and C of G position

- **Blade stresses**

- Advancing blade **compressibility**

- **Engine power available**

- **Density Altitude** and **All Up Weight** (the higher these factors, the lower the V_{NE})

The first three are the main ones.

Best Rate Of Climb (V_Y)

This speed occurs when the power curve is at its lowest point, when there is the most excess power available. It represents the maximum altitude gain against time.

As you increase altitude, the power curve moves up and to the right, firstly because TAS increases relative to IAS, but also (as power is drag x TAS), the power required increases as well. Because TAS increases, V_Y must also increase because the graph moves.

As air density decreases, IAS reduces against TAS quicker than TAS increases, so the indicated speed for V_Y decreases slightly (V_Y is based on IAS). It also increases with weight, because you need more TRT, so more collective means more induced power, more tail rotor thrust, increasing profile power. V_Y is not affected by wind, provided it is steady.

Best Angle Of Climb (V_X)

This concerns the best ratio of height gained to forward speed, or the change in height over distance.

The rate of climb for a helicopter is related to excess power. If you have more power available than that required to hover OGE, you can climb at 90°.

Note: OGE Power plus about 1% is the minimum power needed for a vertical takeoff.

Otherwise, you need to know the point where excess power divided by the airspeed is at its maximum.

The climb angle is:

```
Sin = ROC
      IAS
```

V_X is always lower than V_Y (by about 25%) until the absolute ceiling, where it is equal.

WAKE TURBULENCE

A by-product of lift behind every aircraft, (including helicopters) in forward flight, arising from induced drag, particularly severe from heavy machines, and worst at slow speeds, as on takeoff or landing.

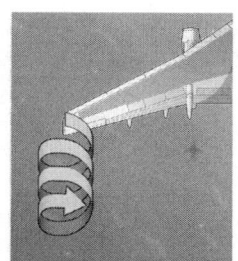

Wake vortices are horizontally concentrated whirlwinds streaming from wingtips, from the separation point between high pressure below and low pressure above the wing. Air flowing over the top of the wing tends to flow inward due to the reduced pressure sucking it in, while that under the wing tends to flow outwards because it is of higher pressure and pushes outwards. Where the lower air curls over the wingtip, it combines with the upper air to form a clockwise flow (on the left wing - on the right it is counter clockwise - see left).

Wake generation begins when the nosewheel lifts off (i.e. as lift is generated) on takeoff and continues until it touches down again after landing:

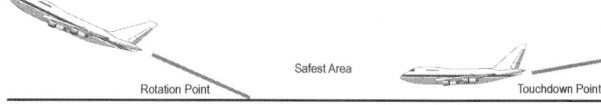

Vortices (one from each wing) gradually sink into the flight path of aircraft operating below at about 400-500 fpm for larger aircraft, levelling out at about 900 feet below the altitude at which they were generated. Eventually they expand to occupy an oval area about 1 wingspan high and 2 wide, one on each side of the aircraft. The distance between them will be about ¾ of the wingspan or rotor disc:

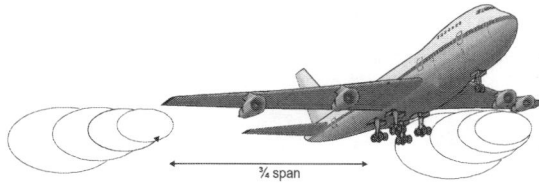

The heavier and slower the aircraft, the more severe the vortices will be, and flaps, etc. will only have a small effect in breaking them up, so even clean aircraft are dangerous. The worst combination for an aircraft producing vortices is *heavy, clean* and *slow*.

Inside a vortex core, you could get roll rates as much as 80° per second and downdraughts of over 1500 feet per minute, so avoid them. The effects become undetectable after a time, varying from a few seconds to a few minutes

after the departure or arrival, although they have been detected at 20 minutes. Vortices are most hazardous to other aircraft during takeoff, initial climb, final approach and landing, but you should be careful any time you are within 1,000 feet below and behind a heavy aircraft.

Those from large aircraft tend to move away from one another so, on a calm day, the runway itself will remain free, depending on how near the runway edge the offending wings were. They will also drift with wind, so your landings and takeoffs should occur upwind of moving heavy aircraft, before the point of takeoff and after that of landing.

A crosswind will increase the movement of the downwind vortex and decrease that of the upwind one. A light wind of 3-7 knots could mean the upwind one actually stays in the touchdown zone and the downwind one moves to another runway. Since a tailwind can also move the vortices of previous aircraft into the touchdown zone, a light quartering tailwind is the most dangerous hazard.

Although there is a danger of shockloading, the biggest problem is loss of control near the ground. You are safest if you keep above the approach and takeoff path of the other aircraft, or land beyond its touchdown point (or lift off before its takeoff point) but, generally, allow **at least 3 minutes** behind any greater than the Light category (especially widebodies) for the effects to disappear.

Aircraft are grouped as follows:

Category	ICAO & Flt Plan (kg)	UK
Heavy (H)*	136,000 or more	136,000 or more
Medium (M)	7,000-136,000	40,000-136,000
Small (S)	Not ICAO	17,000-40,000
Light (L)	7,000 or less	17,000 or less

Note: ICAO does not split the Medium category nor do they recognise Small (it is a UK classification).

For timed approaches (non-radar), for **landing** aircraft:

- MEDIUMS behind HEAVY aircraft - 2 mins
- LIGHTS behind HEAVY or MEDIUM - 3 mins

For takeoff, it's 2 minutes behind anything, or 3 minutes if you are taking off from an intermediate part of the same or a parallel runway separated by less than 760 m. For displaced thresholds and opposite direction runways, separation is 2 minutes.

If an arriving aircraft is making a straight in approach, a departing one may take off in any direction which differs by at least 45° from the reciprocal of the direction of approach, if the takeoff is made at least 3 minutes before the arriving one is estimated to be over the instrument runway. Or in any direction 5 minutes before the arriving.

Helicopters

For helicopters, the effects are similar to fixed wing, in that you get vortices from each side of the rotor disc, but the lower speed means they are more concentrated.

The rotor wake changes within three distinct speed ranges:

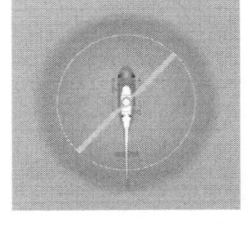

- *Up to 20 mph*, the air moves primarily downwards, most of it descending from the outer edges of the blades, so you get a relatively calm area around the fuselage (in other words, you are in the middle of a ring, like a doughnut - you can see this by hovering over water)

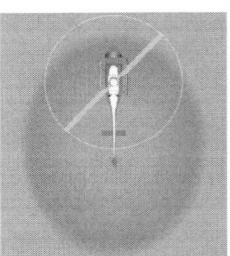

- *At 18-22 mph* (on a Bell), the annular ring shortens in the direction of movement to become an ellipse, coinciding with translation. Above 20 mph, the annular ring disappears, and a large amount of separate, small airflows coalesce to provide an area of ill-defined downward airflow

- *Above 35 mph*, two distinct rotating vortices are formed from directly behind the machine (they are fully developed about 1 rotor diameter behind the mast, and can be sustained for up to 2500 feet). Each vortex starts from where the annular ring would be in the hover, and is relatively calm in the centre (in fact, the centre-to-centre distance between them is just under the rotor diameter, and slightly displaced from the centre towards the retreating blade). Regard them as large funnels extending rearward and downward, getting bigger as they go. There is still a downward flow.

Photographer unknown

CAPT

"The pilot who masters the simple engineering principles of his aircraft, who understands the why behind the reaction - immediately elevates himself to a new level of competence and safety"

AIRFRAMES & SYSTEMS

3

This section should be read in conjunction with *Principles Of Flight*, as some of the items required by the syllabus are covered there.

HELICOPTER TYPES   082 03 01

The helicopter is a flying machine that uses two opposing forces to stay airborne, and whose wings go round instead of remaining still, cynically referred to by some as 50,000 rivets in loose formation! This means that the lift-producing surfaces (i.e. the rotors) are (sort of) separate from the body, unlike with an aeroplane (the word *helicopter* comes from the Greek words for *rotating wing*).

Aside from being much more fun to fly, there are many differences between aeroplanes and helicopters.

For example, the engine in a helicopter is not directly related to the machine's forward speed - its function is to *drive the rotor system* which is really what makes it move through the air. On an autogyro, lift is certainly provided by the rotating blades, but the *thrust* comes from the propeller, which is the only item driven by the engine, so engine power output is used to ensure forward motion. Thus, the autogyro is permanently in autorotation because its rotors are driven by the airflow from forward speed, and *not the engine* - it is not capable of true vertical flight, so *lift ultimately comes from the speed of forward movement.*

Even the use of power is different - on takeoff, it tends to be used as required on helicopters, whereas full throttle is mostly used with aeroplanes.

Single Main Rotor

Helicopters with one main rotor have a tailboom with a tail rotor on the end, or some other arrangement, such as the NOTAR or fenestron. This configuration is simpler and lighter than others, needing less maintenance. As the tail rotor uses some of the available power, the single-rotor system has a smaller centre of gravity range.

The main rotor provides lift and thrust while the tail rotor opposes the torque from the main rotor. As the blades turn under engine power, the body wants to rotate the opposite way, which is where the tail rotor produces the second force that is so important. So, the main rotors keep the machine in the air, and the tail rotor stops it spinning uncontrollably.*

The tail rotor also provides directional control during hovering and engine power changes.

Power to operate the main and tail rotors comes through a gearbox, which is driven by the engine.

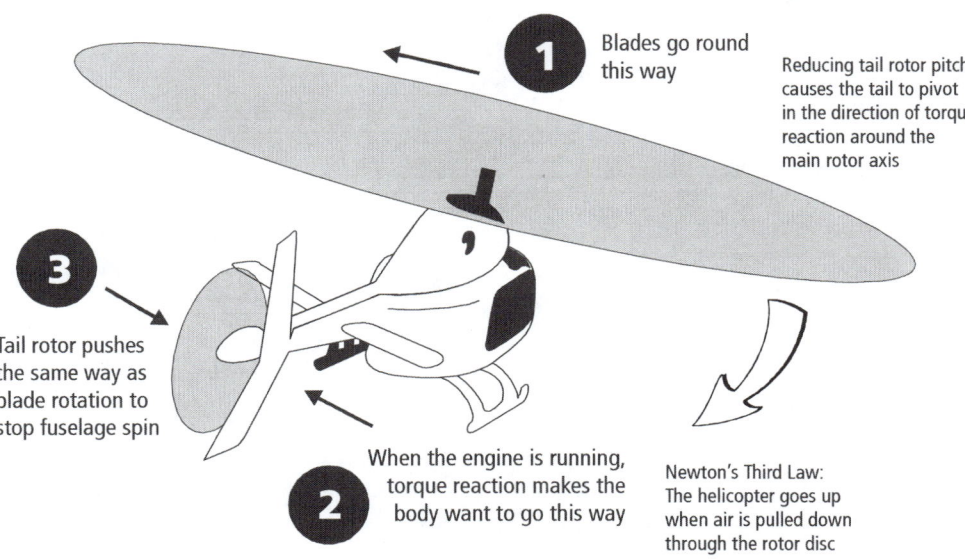

1 — Blades go round this way

Reducing tail rotor pitch causes the tail to pivot in the direction of torque reaction around the main rotor axis

3 — Tail rotor pushes the same way as blade rotation to stop fuselage spin

2 — When the engine is running, torque reaction makes the body want to go this way

Newton's Third Law: The helicopter goes up when air is pulled down through the rotor disc

If this page is a photocopy, it is not authorised!

CAPT

© Phil Croucher, 2013

Private Helicopter Pilot Studies   **3-1**

THE AIRFRAME
021 01/02

The *airframe* is the complete structure of an aircraft, without engines and instruments. It is as light and as strong as possible, because of the stresses found in flight, such as *compression*, *tension*, *torsion*, *shearing* and *bending*.

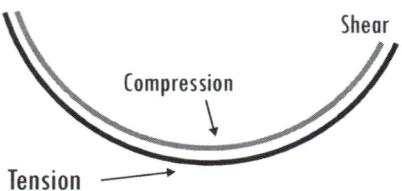

When a material is subjected to an external force, the bonding forces that hold its atoms together act like springs to oppose it.

When stretched, it is *in tension*. Its ability to withstand the tension is a measure of its *tensile strength*. When the material is squeezed, it is subject to *compression*, and it has a *compressive strength*. Torsion is a twisting force. If one face of the material is forced to slide against another, it is *in shear* - in a stressed skin pressurised aircraft, the rivets holding the fuselage together are under shear loads.

A structural member subjected to bending stresses is a *beam**, one subject to compression is a *strut* and one under tension is a *tie*.

*A beam supported at both ends, carrying a load at the centre, has its top in compression, its bottom in tension, with a shear force at each end trying to slice it in half.

If the beam is supported at one end, as with a wing or a rotor blade when the aircraft is still on the ground, the tension is at the top, the compression at the bottom, and only one end, namely the supported end, has a shear force (this is otherwise known as a *cantilever*).

Note: Beams, struts and ties can change places, depending on the loads applied to them. For example, the wing strut in the aeroplane below is only a strut when the aircraft is on the ground. In flight, it becomes a tie, because the presence of lift reverses the loads.

Struts have to be designed with compression in mind, and are often hollow tubes, for lightness. This is because the

centre part of a strut subject to compression is in the neutral plane, being neither in tension nor compression, so the material in that location can be removed and made to serve a more useful purpose elsewhere.

Thus, rotor masts are hollow because they primarily carry torsion loads, and the highest stress is carried on the outer sides. The shear stress varies linearly from zero in the centre to the maximum at the outer radius, so there's no point in carrying the extra weight in the middle.

A tie is often just a piece of cable or wire, rather than a tube, to save weight.

The mixture of struts, ties and beams that make up the structure of an aircraft is called the *framework*, with the components inside being *structural* or *non-structural*. Structural items are load-bearing, meaning that they directly absorb the loads of flight. The *primary* structure takes the most stress, the *secondary* structure takes not so much, and the *tertiary* structure takes minimal stress.

Structural failure can occur through the forces that arise from normal flight manoeuvres, plus turbulence and landing, etc., but threats to structural integrity also include overstressing, and operational hazards, such as bird strikes and corrosion.

Stress is discussed later, under *Fatigue and Stress*.

The Fuselage

The *fuselage* is where the pilot, passengers and cargo are placed, and to which tailbooms and rotors are attached. It is completely useless aerodynamically, so its design is a compromise between the need to protect its occupants and to be aerodynamically shaped. Helicopter fuselages are built on the same principles as non-pressurised fixed wing ones, but the loads they carry are different, and go in different directions.

Older aircraft are made of a *truss construction**, or *frame and skin*, where aluminium or steel tubing is joined in a series of triangular shapes, like the tail boom of the Bell 47:

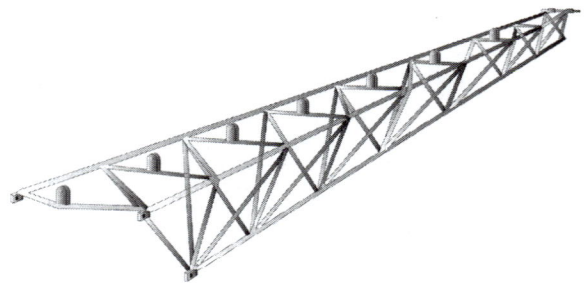

*Now mainly used for light training aircraft.

Then the tubing might be covered with metal or fabric, which will act merely as a cover, making no contribution towards the strength of the assembly. Instead, each part is made strong enough to take a certain load (mostly tension or compression) by itself. Unfortunately, this makes them relatively heavy - another disadvantage is that the crossbracing takes up a lot of space.

More modern machines use *monocoque*, a development of *stressed skin*, where the outside covering takes all the stress, and supporting devices inside, like *formers* held together by *stringers* (or *longerons*), just help keep it in shape. It uses magnesium alloy or aluminium to cope with normal bending and tangent stresses, and torsional moments.

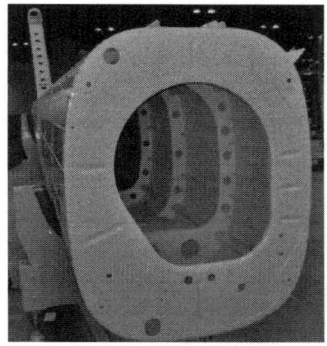

Bulkheads are at either end of a fuselage, or a compartment, and are used when more strength is required. A *firewall* can be a bulkhead, being a fireproof partition that separates an engine compartment from the cabin or from another engine.

An egg is a good example of a monocoque structure, which is handy, as *cocque* is French for *eggshell*. Monocoque therefore means *single shell*. Aside from saving weight, the big advantage of monocoque is that it leaves more space inside the aircraft.

Methods of attachment include:

- **Riveting**. Aluminium alloy rivets are light, small and strong *in shear*. The condition of the covering paint is a good indication of that of the rivet underneath - black stuff is powder from *fretting* against the aircraft skin. Loose rivets can indicate excessive vibration.

- **Welding**

- **Bolting**

- **Pinning**

- **Adhesives** (Bonding), as with composite materials

COMPONENT LOCATIONS

Because so many parts of a helicopter rotate, the terms *left* and *right* can be meaningless. As a result, colour coding determines the location and position of components:

Picture Below: AS 355 Construction & Materials Used

KEY:	
1 - CANOPY	4 - TAIL BOOM
2 - BODY STRUCTURE	5 - TAIL UNIT
3 - REAR STRUCTURE	6 - LANDING GEAR
	7 - BOTTOM STRUCTURE AND CABIN FLOOR

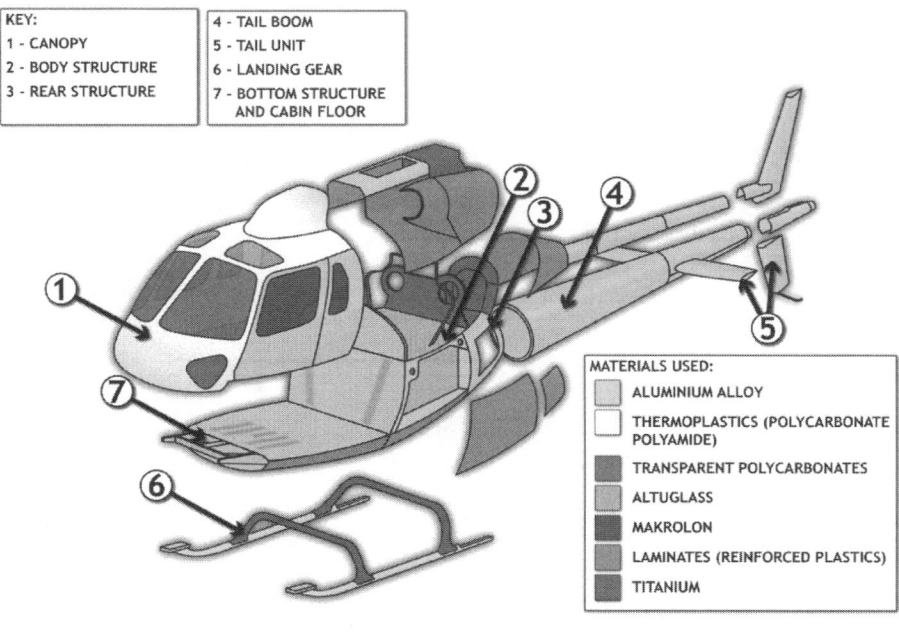

MATERIALS USED:
ALUMINIUM ALLOY
THERMOPLASTICS (POLYCARBONATE POLYAMIDE)
TRANSPARENT POLYCARBONATES
ALTUGLASS
MAKROLON
LAMINATES (REINFORCED PLASTICS)
TITANIUM

Components are also located within an airframe against *reference lines* and *station numbers*, which are used with centre of gravity calculations. The *zero datum is* at a given point on the fuselage, and numbers are allocated a distance forward or aft of it (see *Mass & Balance*). If the datum is forward of the nose, station numbers are positive.

Materials Used

To be commercially viable, an aircraft must be light, yet strong enough to cope with the forces of flight. For this purpose, materials such as wood, aluminium, titanium, fabric and carbon fibre are used.

Many metals cannot be used by themselves. For example, aluminium is too soft, so it is mixed with other metals for strength (AL2024 is a mix of aluminium and copper). Aluminium alloys are light, easily machined and have good wear resistance. *Duralumin* is the brand name for an alloy of aluminium, magnesium, manganese and copper (4%) which is hard to weld but has good thermal conductivity (it is commonly used with engine cylinders). Although it is a third of the weight of steel, it has only a third of the strength, so it is easy to work but prone to fatigue.

When bulk is needed, a **honeycomb construction** helps keep things light. This is a framework made of short hexagonal tubes covered over both open ends by metal or laminate sheeting. It is commonly used in rotor blades, but will also be found in cabin floor panels, in a sandwich, with aluminium, Kevlar™ or Nomex™.

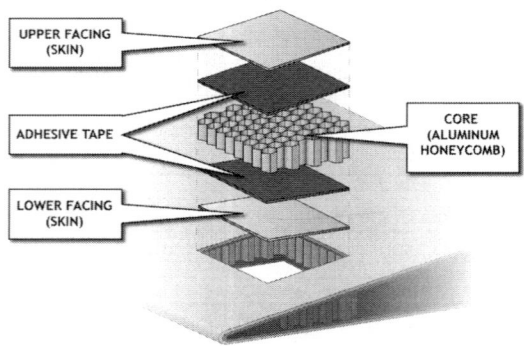

Laminated honeycombs have a core made on metal, glasscloth or Nomex™, each face of which goes against one or more impregnated layers. The assembly is then oven cured.

Doors & Windows

Helicopter windows are usually made from perspex, but they can use sandwiched laminated glass, with embedded heating elements, for preventing ice on small areas and protecting against birdstrikes, because the windscreen becomes flexible with the heat (it takes about 15 minutes to warm up). An electrically heated windscreen is actually made from glass and *polycarbonate laminate*, with the inner surface being made of soft polycarbonate.

Tip: Some helicopters have windscreen wipers, but they are best not used at all, unless the windscreen is made of glass. This is because, if the wipers are operated when the windscreen is dry, a perspex one will get scratched and marked and reduce visibility during normal weather. There are rain repellent products that work better, although these should be used with caution.

The Undercarriage   021 04

The landing gear is there to take the shock of landing, so that it isn't transferred to the airframe. The most common type is skids, which will consist of 2 aluminium alloy main skid and cross tubes, to provide some sort of flexing and therefore suspension.

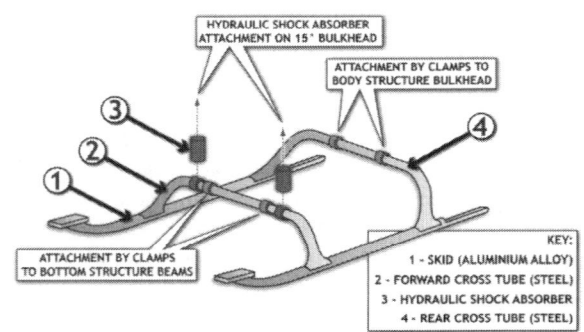

They may or may not be covered with fairings for streamlining, but stainless steel shoes will likely be fitted along the bottom to prevent wear and tear when landing on hard surfaces.

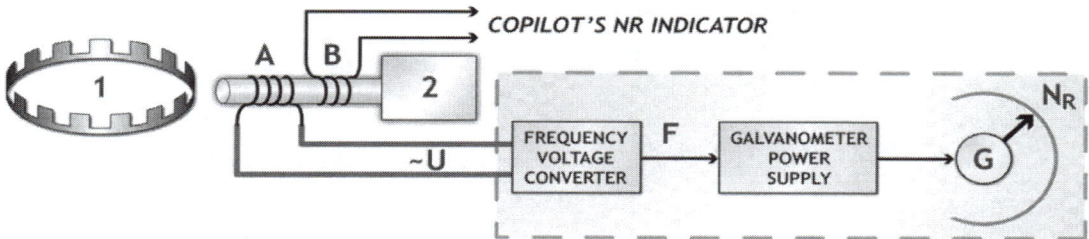

Rotor Blades

Rotor blades can be made of many   021 17
materials, including fabric in the early days
(for the Saunders-Roe Skeeter), or wood (early Bell 47),
but modern ones are either of metal or composite
construction. Those for the Bell 206, for example, are
made of metal, with an aluminium honeycomb core,
aluminium skins, main spar at around 25% of chord, and
trailing edge strip, all joined with metal-to-metal bonding.

Erosion strips on leading edges are usually made from
Tungsten Nickel or Stainless Steel.

Many blades also have a washout (or taper).

Composite blades are a lot more flexible, and may even
bend nearly double before any breakage is detected (their
main advantage is much greater fatigue life). Some fibre-
covered blades have an aluminium mesh within the skin to
protect against lightning strikes.

The weight, lift and balance of each blade must be equal,
which is the reason for the high degree of accuracy during
manufacture. See *Blade Alignment & Tracking*.

BLADE SPEED

The picture above shows a system for measuring rotor
RPM, which is sensed by a magnetic probe by a toothed
wheel, called a **phonic wheel**.

When a tooth passes in front of the sensor, the magnetic
flux is maximum (it is minimum when a slot passes by).
The pulses have a frequency equal to the number of
variations per second. As the number of teeth stays the
same, the signal frequency is proportional to rotor RPM.

A frequency-voltage converter transforms the signals into
DC so that the tachometer receives a current proportional
to rotor RPM.

CONTROL STOPS

There are two types of control stop, sometimes called
Primary & *Secondary*. Primary stops usually limit the degree
of control movement, and secondary stops prevent
overruns before damage is done to external control
surfaces, so there should be a clearance between the
surface and the secondary stop. This is similar to the
relationship between droop stops and flapping retainers.

BLADE SAILING   082 05 05

High winds and gusts can cause the
main rotor blades to flap up and down during starting and
stopping and be a danger to both people near them and
the helicopter itself, as the droop stops (see below) could
be damaged, or a particularly flexible blade could hit the
tail boom or people walking about (two-bladed helicopters
at low RRPM in gusting winds are especially vulnerable).

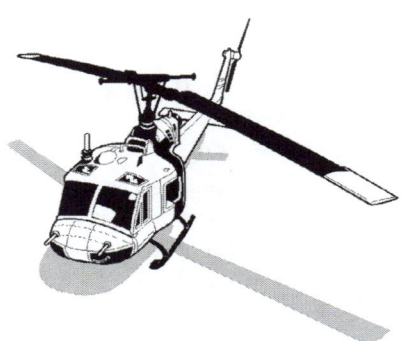

Note: Dissymmetry of lift still applies, even at low speeds.

At certain critical speeds (50-100 RPM), the blades will pass in and out of the stall. Holding the cyclic in the direction of the wind (and applying the rotor brake) will keep the pitch of the advancing blade to a minimum and stop it lifting in the first place.

However, the cyclic is less effective at low RPM, so other ways of minimising the effect include parking away from the downwind side of obstructions or the downwash or slipstream of other machines, keeping the collective down, or accelerating and decelerating the blades as quickly as possible. In addition, *point the nose out of wind*, so the lowest deflection is away from the tail boom.

With clockwise-rotating blades, have the wind coming from the port side, and *vice versa* - the blades will then start to rise as they pass over the tailboom and the wind will lift the blades over it when slowing down or starting up (but they will be down at the front, so warn your passengers). Having the wind from the rear helps you keep an eye on the low blade at the front, but it means landing downwind.

DROOP STOPS   082 05 05 03

Droop stops, or droop restrainers, work inside the rotor head to keep the blades horizontal at low RPM, or when stopped. They are held *out* of their position by centrifugal force, so are inactive during flight.

They also depend on friction for their proper operation, so if you use the collective to slow the blades down after cutting the engine, all you will be doing is lightening the load and stopping them from working properly.

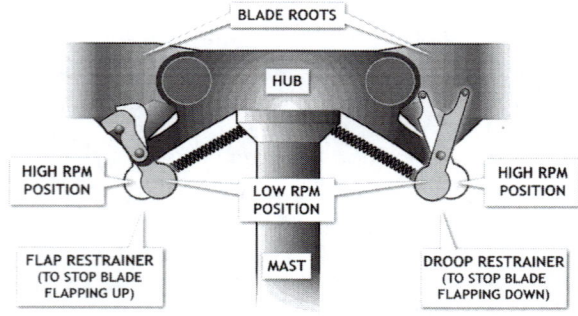

FLAPPING RESTRAINERS

These work in a similar way to droop stops, but their purpose is to stop the blades from flapping up too much.

THE SWASHPLATE (CONTROL ORBIT)

The movements of the collective and cyclic controls are often transmitted to the main rotors through a swashplate (or *star assembly*) on the main rotor mast. The control orbit (or control plane) is the plane of rotation in which common points on the pitch change links (or pitch operating arms, which are attached to the swashplate) are

rotating. This is to cover for manufacturers using different systems for control, such as the spider (overleaf).

With the swashplate, two circular plates are (usually) on top of each other, directly connected, but the bottom one does not rotate, although both can move up and down the rotor mast. The bottom one is held in place by *non-rotating scissors* which are attached, at their lower attachment point, to the rotor gearbox. This stops the lower swashplate from moving, without bending the control arms connected to it. The *rotating scissors* perform the same function for the upper part of the swashplate, connected to the main rotor mast.

Picture: Agusta 109 Swashplate Assembly

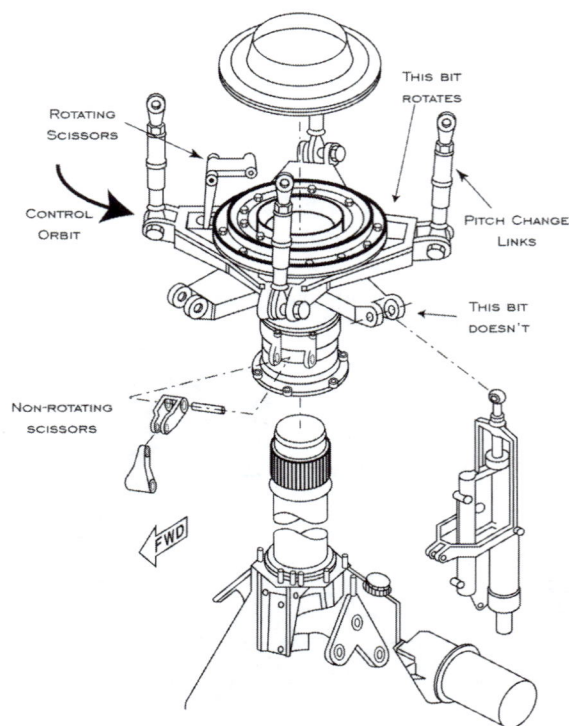

The scissor links also extend and contract, which moves the swashplate up and down, to allow collective control movements to be made. The Bell 47 and 212 bypass the swashplate with a sleeve that surrounds the rotor mast, inside the swashplate. Other designs allow the whole swashplate to be moved.

Movement of the bottom plate caused by control input is reflected directly in the upper one, so the swashplate converts stationary push-pull movements of the controls into rotating ones, 90° before the reaction is required, because of *phase lag*, described elsewhere.

The vertical position of the non-rotating part is altered through the collective pitch control, and its tilt is altered with the cyclic. The movements are duplicated in the rotating part. The pitch horn is where the rotating control rods are connected to the blade, and its position will vary between the leading and trailing edges of the root.

In the hover, when the disc is level, the control orbit will be level. When transitioning from the hover to forward flight, the swashplate is moved so that the pitch operating arms start to move upwards on the left hand side of the swash plate (for North American rotation). The fixed scissor link on the gearbox resists the rotational force applied to the lower swashplate (i.e. stops it moving), while the rotating scissors transmit the drive from the rotor hub to the rotating swashplate.

THE SPIDER SYSTEM

This uses a control rod inside the rotor shaft that is connected to pitch change arms on the blades.

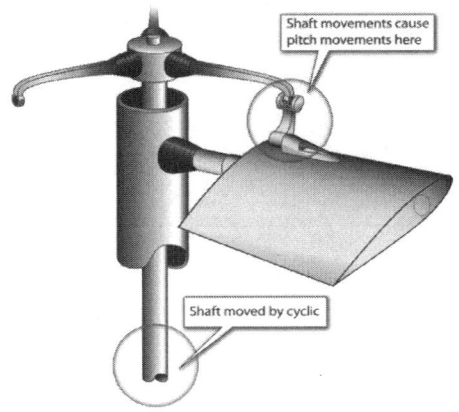

Somewhere inside the rotor shaft, the control shaft is connected to a universal joint which allows it to tilt and alter the angle of the control arms to affect cyclic pitch. The universal joint allows the blades to rotate while the connection to the flying controls stays still. The *inverted spider* is the same, but upside down, on older machines.

The spider can produce less cyclic movement as you pull collective, hence its use with tail rotors, as they don't use any cyclic movement.

Rotor Systems

082 05 04
021 15

Rotor heads are time-limited because of the stresses and strains imposed on them.

FULLY ARTICULATED

A fully articulated head is one in which the blades can move up and down, forward and back, and around their centres independently of each other, although they will be more complex and expensive.

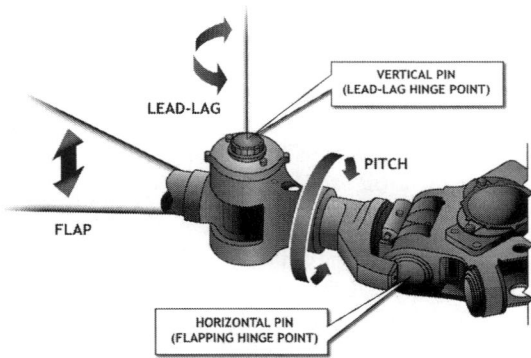

Each blade is attached to the hub with a *flapping hinge*, for up and down movement, which is some distance from the hub (see *Control Power*, in *Principles Of Flight*), and a *dragging hinge*, that allows the blade to move back and forth horizontally (i.e. in the plane of rotation), also some distance from the hub. *Main rotor freedom of movement* includes *feathering, flapping* and *dragging*.

Feathering allows the blade to rotate around its longitudinal axis so that the angle of attack can be altered.

Note: The only direct control is feathering - flapping and dragging follow automatically. As well, blade root bending, stress and rolling moments are only eliminated by flapping if the hinge is on the axis of rotation - if it is offset, there are residuals, especially with hingeless heads.

Movement about the dragging hinge avoids stress from the blade bending - it is normally dampened, because it helps to absorb the acceleration and deceleration of the blades, about the chordwise axis. *If one blade on a fully articulated head is not equidistant from the others in the lateral plane, the blade damper is suspect.*

THE HINGELESS ROTOR (EUROCOPTER)

Hingeless Rotors have flexible elements (elastomerics) instead of flapping and dragging hinges, although they do have feathering bearings. They lie somewhere between fully articulated and semi-rigid, so you could probably also call them semi-articulated (Eurocopter calls them semi rigid).

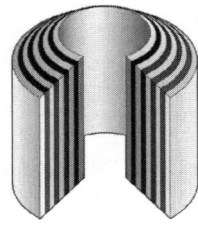

The idea is that you cannot place a moment across a hinge, but you can across an elastomeric bearing. For example, if you lifted the blade of an articulated head, all that would move is the blade around its flapping hinge. If the blade was attached to the hub with elastomerics, it would place a force on the whole head.

The core of the system is a three-bladed *starflex* which moves upwards and downwards to cope with flapping, but not horizontally, so dragging forces are dealt with by elastomeric flanges which distort when the blades feather, flap or drag (see picture below).

The purpose of the rectangular-shaped bits sandwiching the blade roots is to hold the blade to the hub. They can flap and lead-lag to some degree, and can allow the blade to rotate about its axis for desired pitch change, which is why the pitch change horns are attached to them.

The star flexes to allow for coning and pitch changes, but is as close to inflexible as possible in the lead-lag (dragging) axis. The tip on each point of the star is a cylindrical machined bearing surface that plugs into the centre of an elastomeric *frequency adapter* (coloured green). These allow lead and lag by springiness on their leading and lagging sides (as appropriate) and applying a re-centring force when aerodynamic forces are more equal (these composite parts need good inspections to check that they aren't breaking down, as they are completing at least one flexing or bending cycle per turn of the head).

SEMI-RIGID

Semi-rigid heads do not have flapping and drag hinges. The term refers to blades with roots designed to flex instead, such as the blade grips on the Bell 206.

TEETERING HEADS

The blades on a teetering rotor can flap up and down as one unit because the whole head is allowed to teeter around a *trunnion bearing*, or a *gimbal mounting* like a seesaw.

Note: The trunnion bearing actually relates to the Bell 206 - the R22's head moves around a central flapping hinge which reduces hub oscillations arising from bouncing, but the effect is the same.

Teetering heads tend to have an underslung design. See *Coriolis Effect* in *Principles Of Flight*.

Wind gusts have a greater adverse effect on semi-rigid rotors due to their seesaw flapping.

Picture: Eurocopter AS 350 rotor system

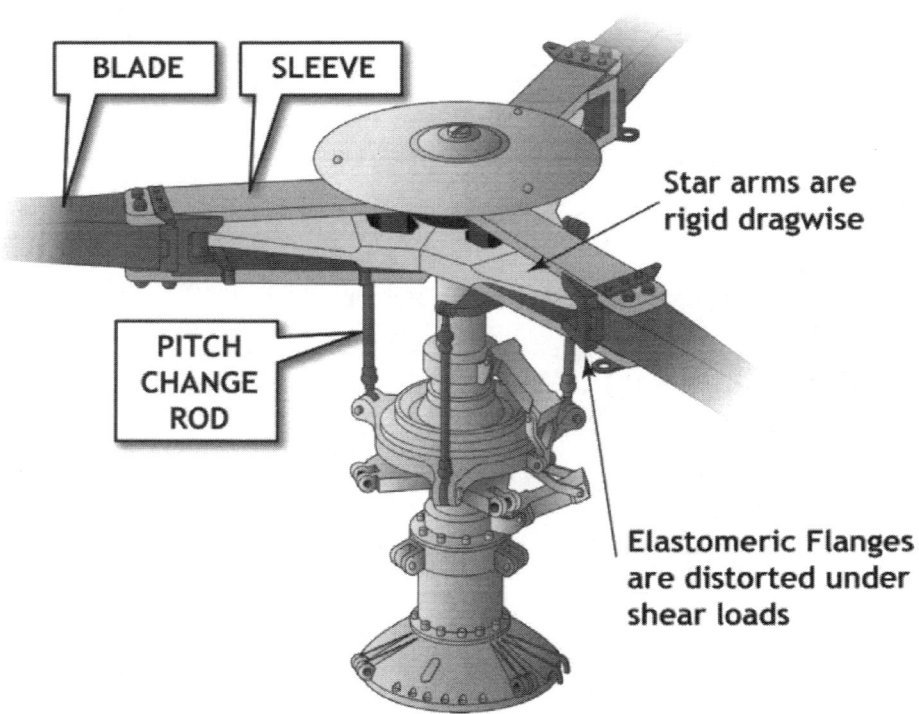

BLADE   SLEEVE

Star arms are rigid dragwise

PITCH CHANGE ROD

Elastomeric Flanges are distorted under shear loads

BEARINGLESS ROTORS (RIGID)

These have no bearings at all. A rigid rotor (or, more accurately, a rigid hub) only allows feathering, but the blades are more flexible towards their ends, so they bend when absorbing the forces of flight, producing the same effect as flapping and dragging hinges, but removed from the root. This is why some helicopters have mast torque gauges to measure the bending of the mast (see *Control Power*) from the longish moment arm. Blade centrifugal forces hold the fuselage level to allow a very wide C of G tolerance, both fore and aft and laterally.

Transmissions

This is how you get power from the engines to the main and tail rotors, plus all the hangers-on, such as the generator, hydraulic pump, etc. Because engines work at higher speeds than the blades, there is also an element of reduction. When the engine and rotor needles are in their correct places on the tachometer, the ratio of engine to rotor RPM is the same as the gear reduction ratio.

The (torque) output from piston engines can vary widely during a single rotation of the crankshaft because of its intermittent combustion. Depending on the number of cylinders and the firing order, the instantaneous output torque can be up to twice as great as the mean value. Since the engine and rotor drive train must be able to cope with them, the drive train on a piston engined helicopter has more robust margins than that on a turbine engine, whose output is much smoother.

Transmission attachments must be able to handle at least twice the aircraft's maximum weight. They must also carry the twisting moments of the control force from the rotor head, plus any forces that arise when you crash.

Metal tail rotor shafts are usually made of aluminium or steel tubing (on small helicopters). Multi-segment ones are joined with flexible couplings that allow for bending and flexing of the tail cone during flight, and slight changes in length from thermal expansion and contraction.

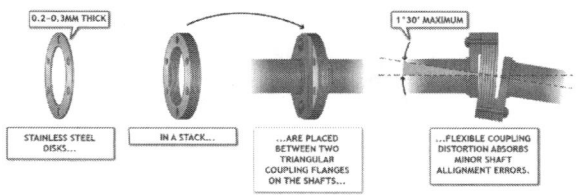

The engines and transmission ride as one element so that the drive shaft is not deformed - for this reason they are both structurally tied to the transmission mounts.

A drive shaft between two engines should be protected by a firewall, or be fireproofed (CS/FAR 29). Fire detection lines will also be in there somewhere.

MAIN ROTOR GEARBOX

The input speed from the engine is too high for a 1:1 drive to the main rotor gearbox, so step-down gearing must be used. In doing this, more torque is produced (stepping up the speed to the tail rotor reduces the torque to an amount the dive shaft can stand).

Below is a typical twin-engined transmission arrangement from the AS 355.

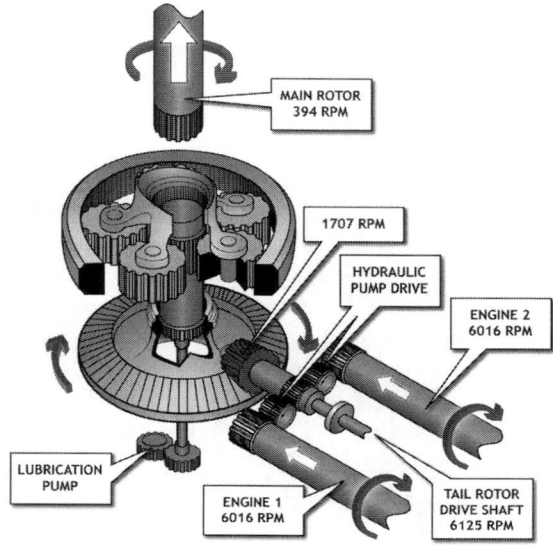

It is impractical to step down a ratio between the engine and gearbox of (for example) 15:1 in one go, so the first stage is where the input from the engine meets the bottom large gear. The second stage comes from the central sun gear surrounded by planetary gears which rotate inside a stationary ring gear on the gearbox casing. The planetary gears play no part in the reduction ratio, but act as idlers and spacers between the sun and ring gears.

Gearbox casings are usually made from magnesium alloy. The design of a gearbox needs to take into account the heat generated by all the gears meshing around in contact with each other inside.

THE TAIL ROTOR

082 06 01
021 02 05

The more work the engine has to do, the more anti-torque force is required, and the more power is required to drive the tail rotor, which must balance the main rotor torque at full power with enough thrust left over for directional control. The combination of sideways flight, autorotation and climb requires a pitch range in the order of 40°, including negative pitch for autorotations, because the fuselage wants to turn the same way as the blades.

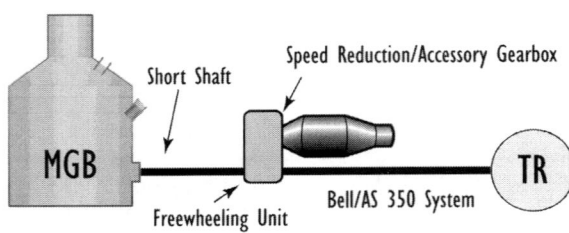

Tail rotors operate at greater speeds than the main rotor and different speeds than the driveshaft and intermediate gearbox, if they exist, to reduce vibrations. However, they have no cyclic variation. The blades all feather at the same time when the tail rotor pedals are moved. This is known as moving collectively, but it is nothing to do with the collective control for the main rotor.

The direction of rotation is usually chosen to account for the higher flow at the top and the lower flow at the bottom, meaning rotating backwards at the top.

During flight, the yaw pedals control heading, balance, slip and skid. The amount of pedal needed to maintain heading increases in the hover as density altitude increases because the tail rotor is less effective. In straight and level flight, or above about 60 knots, they can nearly be ignored, as the tail boom and fin will do the work (up to about 100 kts in the Bell 206).

A tail fin reduces the engine power required in forward flight by offloading the tail rotor. On the Bell 206, it is offset 5½° to the right to provide a movement of the tailboom in the appropriate direction. The fin is often asymmetric as well.

The purposes of the tail rotor include:

- Balancing the fuselage torque reaction, and stopping it from spinning the other way

- Altering the heading in the hover

- Maintaining balanced forward flight

- Stopping the fuselage rotating in autorotation, for which it needs to go into negative pitch

To make sure that the tail rotor still works after the engine fails, there must be a connection between the main and tail rotors. On some older helicopters, such as the Bell 47 (and the Hiller), the engine drives the gearbox directly from underneath through a mechanical centrifugal clutch, and the tail rotor takes its drive directly from the main gearbox. The engine and gearbox share the same engine oil and pumps. Otherwise, the oil system is self-contained.

In other words, the main gearbox usually drives the tail rotor, as shown in the upper part of the diagram at the top of the page. The speed at which the tail rotor drive shaft rotates is determined inside the main rotor gearbox by the number of teeth per bevel gearing. Very often, the drive shaft runs at a higher speed than the tail rotor, which means that the drive shaft can be slimmer and lighter because less torque is required to drive the tail rotor.

However, in the Bell 206 (and the AS 350), an accessory gearbox is driven by the engine, and the main and tail rotor gearboxes are driven directly from that (see the bottom part of the diagram above). The tail rotor is driven by the engine in powered flight and by the main gearbox in autorotation, as it normally would be, but the arrangement is not ideal.

Although it saves the weight and cost of an extra drive shaft, there are disadvantages. One is that, if the short shaft to the main gearbox fails, the only power to the tail rotor now comes from the engine, so if you shut it down, the tail rotor will stop working. One symptom will be a loss of rotor RPM while the engine is still running - with a typical Bell tachometer, where the rotor needle is normally superimposed on the turbine needle, you will see the split

right away (the opposite way round to the picture shown), but this is not so easy on some machines with the needles in separate instruments, as with early AS 350s.

THE FENESTRON

082 06 02

The traditional tail rotor is simple to construct and is very efficient, particularly as a stability device. It also needs many components, is fragile, less safe for people walking around and sits in the dirty airflow from the main rotors - it can therefore live a stressful life. The fenestron, as used by Eurocopter, is a different solution, consisting of a series of very small blades enclosed in a shroud which is inside a relatively large fin.

The shroud reduces the tip losses normally present with a traditional tail rotor, and creates a pressure difference between the up- and downstream faces of the fin, which produces a force that aids directional control. The force is around 30% of the total available from the fin.

The fan's disc area can now be less. In fact, it is as effective as an unducted tail rotor that is 30% larger.

As the diameter of the fan increases, the weight of the duct goes up by the cube of the amount of increase.

The blades are not equally spaced, to help with noise.

Because the blades are rigid (to keep tip clearances small), they are also less susceptible to vibration. They can also work closer to the stall, and their service life is longer because they are not so stressed - this applies to the rest of the transmission. As the blades are smaller, they have a higher disk loading, and you need hydraulic assistance to move them. Without it, you need about 66 lbs of pressure.

As the airflow goes through the vertical fin rather than around it, you can use less engine power or produce more speed. 100% of the mature wake is available after going through the blades, as opposed to the more normal 70-80%. If the outbound duct has some divergence, the wake is slower and needs less power.

Note: The acceptance angle (for the airflow) at the shroud can allow the yaw rate to accelerate significantly, enough to make the aircraft rotate well in excess of its operating limit.

The loading on a Fenestron is greatest when hovering at low altitude. As forward speed is increased in level flight, the loading reduces, due to increased aerodynamic effects from the fin, which has an unsymmetrical profile with a linear twist for that purpose.

Although the fenestron largely removes dissymmetry of lift and the need for cyclic feathering of the tail rotor, it is heavier*, more complex and ultimately not as powerful, especially for heavier machines - it is certainly not suited for those weighing more than 12,000 lbs. The AS 350 (a serious lifter) uses a conventional tail rotor.

*The fenestron uses more power in ground effect, possibly for airflow reasons (11.5-13% as opposed to 10-12% OGE, which is presumably why the AS 350 doesn't have one). However, it absorbs less than 1% of the total power in forward flight, even though the fin is wider and produces a lot of cruise drag.

Note: *The fenestron only has feathering hinges,* where a normal tail rotor will feather and flap. It also responds to *collective pitch control,* meaning that the blades move all at once. It does *not* mean that the collective lever is involved!

NOTAR

082 06 03

NOTAR means *No Tail Rotor,* describing a design that uses low pressure*, high volume air inside the tail boom before it is fed out of the end through a moveable nozzle, aided by tangential slots on the side. In other words, the "tail rotor" is inside the tailboom, and is similar in construction to that found in the fenestron. Control is provided in the usual way through the pedals.

*Low pressure reduces the risk if it is lost.

Originally, the air inside the tail boom was fed only out of *tangential slots,* which are located on the starboard side.

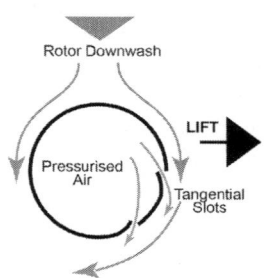

They eject low-pressure air at 250 fps (and 2 psi) onto the outer surface of the tailboom to energise the boundary layer and delay separation so that the downwash flows around the tailboom to create a sideways component that helps counteract the torque and reduce the engine power requirement enough to allow you to use a jet of air instead of a tail rotor. There is also a downwards component from induced drag, but the upthrust from the jets cancels it out.

This is the *Coanda effect,* as mentioned in *Principles Of Flight,* which describes the tendency of a fluid to cling to a gently-curved surface that is near an orifice from which it is emerging, and which has a tendency to *entrain* a larger volume of the same fluid and cause it to be drawn along with the primary stream.

However, the effect only works when the downwash flows directly down over the tailboom, so yaw control is reduced markedly in a crosswind. A tip nozzle was added later.

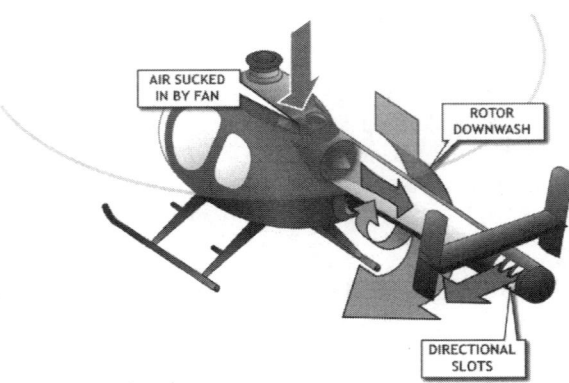

Note: The directional nozzle (or *direct thruster*) is now the primary yaw control. It consists of a fixed cone with air outlets to the left and right, plus an outer moveable cone with one air outlet to deflect the air to port or starboard. The moveable cone is controlled by the pedals. About two thirds of the force required comes from the slots.

NOTAR helicopters are safer with regard to passengers walking into tail rotors, and produce less noise, but the effects of the pedals are not so precise - they can feel a bit mushy. The system also draws a lot of power - in some conditions, it will take over 200 horsepower just to drive the fan. The Explorer takes even more. In addition, they are less useful at high Density Altitudes - above 4000 feet, they are reported to lose about 300 pounds of useful load.

CLUTCHES   021 16 06

The clutch allows the engine to start with a low inertial loading, meaning that the gearbox is only driven after a certain RPM, so the engine is not loaded so much, aside from the usual generators, pumps, etc.

A centrifugal clutch (on the Bell 47) is automatic and will have more effect as speed is increased so, if the engine stops, the blades are free to rotate. A set of shoes driven by the engine impinge against the casing of a drum. Centrifugal force keeps the shoes against the drum and drives the transmission. The system runs in oil, on which it depends for cooling.

Some belt driven helicopters use a belt tightener as a clutch, which simply increases the tension of the V-belts until everything starts to rotate. The tightener is the small set of wheels on the left overleaf, that moves outwards.

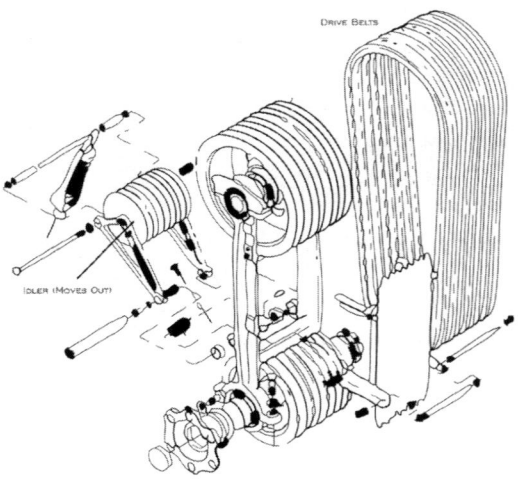

An electrically operated solenoid may be used to move the belt tightener, but in the Enstrom, the clutch is manually operated with a lever at the right side of the pilot's seat, on the forward side of the seat structure.

The rotor system is engaged by pulling the clutch lever upward, then rearward, until it hits the stop and the light on the annunciator panel goes out. The clutch can be disconnected by lifting the lever straight up, then pivoting it down to the floor.

The overrunning clutch is a sprag-type free wheeling unit.

FREEWHEEL UNITS   021 16 07

The freewheel unit is part of an overrunning clutch. It is there to allow the blades to continue rotating when the engine drive shaft stops for whatever reason. Freewheels are mostly lubricated from the main rotor gearbox.

Two common designs include:

THERMO BYPASS VALVE

COOLING AIR COMES FROM TAIL ROTOR DRIVE FAN

COOLER

MAIN MAST

FILLER CAP AND VENT

JET NO. 1

JET NO. 2

PRESSURE REGULATING VALVE

SPRAY

FILTER

DRAIN PLUG AND MAGNETIC CHIP DETECTOR

PUMP

FILTER

CHIP DETECTOR

DRAIN PLUG AND MAGNETIC CHIP DETECTOR

OIL

TO PILOT'S PANEL GAUGE AND LOW PRESSURE WARNING SWITCH

- The **sprag clutch** tends to be used for higher speeds. It has inner and outer races with an annular space between them, supported by ball bearings, but filled with sprags. Theoretically, the inner race is driven by the engine, but on a helicopter the outer race typically does the work.

On one design, the sprags are figure-of-eight shaped lumps of metal (tumblers, with springs) which don't quite fit into the gap between the sections (they are slightly longer), so they are pushed up, or wedged, by the springs against the outer race, forcing it to move. If the drive is taken away, the outer race overruns, past the sprags.

- The **ramp and roller** is used for lower speed applications. It has ramps on the inner race, up which rollers move until they are stopped by the outer race, forcing it to move. When the engine

drive is taken away, the rollers move down the ramps and allow the outer race to move freely.

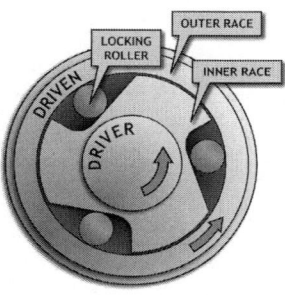

Picture Above: Bell 206 Gearbox Lubrication

LUBRICATION

Transmission systems have their own, self-contained oil supply, except for some earlier helicopters that have their gearboxes on top of the engine and share the engine oil.

Gearboxes are most often lubricated by *splash and mist* methods. In the picture of the Bell 206 transmission lubrication system above (and typical of many others, such as the AS 350 on the left).

A gear-type pump pulls the oil from the bottom of the main gearbox and delivers it under pressure to a cooler, via a filter. The cooled air enters the main gearbox where it is sprayed onto gears and bearings through oil jets. Gravity is used to drain it down to the bottom of the case.

FATIGUE & STRESS
••

Maintaining the structural integrity of aircraft is important for flight safety, aside from reducing maintenance and minimising costs. *The statistical probability of losing an aircraft through structural failure should not exceed 0.001.*

Design Philosophy   021 02 05

This will determine the life of an airframe. For example, you could establish the *safe life* as 25% of the time taken to destructive failure, so that the equipment is retired well before it becomes a problem. Destructive testing naturally destroys the object being tested, so it cannot be used afterward. Non-destructive testing (which is more normal) includes measuring for wear and tear, leak testing, x-rays, etc. The length of the safe life may depend on such items as:

- the **number of landings** (stress on the gear or rotor mast and head, as with the Bell 212).

- **hours flown** (components wear out).

- **calendar time**. The TT straps in the rotor head of the Bell 206 must be changed every 2 years regardless of the hours flown, because of possible corrosion. Some turbine engines have 3000 hrs TBO, but also a date limitation of 10 years.

- **cycles**, which are usually more relevant with pressurised aircraft, but the number of times you move the collective above & below predetermined points must be counted to preserve engine life in the AS 350. On the Bell 212, you must also record the number of landings for rotor head wear.

With *Hard Time Maintenance,* the known deterioration of an item is limited to an acceptable level by maintenance actions at certain periods of time. For example, a part might be changed every 2 years regardless of hours flown.

On-condition Maintenance is a preventive process in which an item is monitored continuously or at specified periods. Its performance is compared against an appropriate standard in order to determine if it can stay in service. In other words, as long as the item meets the required standards, it will not need any maintenance.

Strains & Stresses

STRENGTH

The strength of a material lies in its ability to resist the application of a force without fracturing.

When opposing forces are applied to an object, its size and shape can alter. An object's ability to return to its original size or shape when external forces are removed is called *elasticity*. For example, a rubber band usually returns to its original shape after being stretched, but if it is overstretched will be unable to (the strain that remains is called permanent set). This can also happen to metals used in aircraft. When a substance is on the verge of permanent change, it has reached its *elastic limit.*

The elastic limit of a material is reached at a lower load than its ultimate strength, so a member used in an aircraft must be stronger than the normal working load. The relationship between the strength needed to carry the load and ultimate strength is the *factor of safety*. The minimum required is 1.5*, so a part that is meant to have a normal working load of 100 lbs must be strong enough to carry at least 150 lbs.

However, the loads on an airframe in steady flight are calculated and multiplied by a *Load Factor*. The airframe is then built to withstand the new figure. How high the load factor must be mostly depends on how the aircraft is handled, or what its task is. A change of one unit in the load factor means a 1% change in the weight of the aircraft, so one designed for aerobatics will be heavier than one for normal duties, as it must withstand higher stresses.

Metal Fatigue

Applying a load to a metal produces a stress, measured from the load itself divided by the cross-sectional area. *Ultimate stress* is where the metal will fracture, after applying a single load, but repeated loads *well below* the level of ultimate stress will eventually have a similar effect, called *metal fatigue*. Because an aircraft has to be as light as possible, and the metal it is made of has to work harder, it will be subject to *alternating loads* and *load reversals.*

Essentially, if a material is continuously loaded and unloaded, it will eventually break. An aircraft designed for long distance travel cannot simply be used for short haul flights at higher frequencies because the lifetime of the components will have been based on a predetermined spectrum of loading (the fatigue life of such a fuselage is based on pressurisation cycles. Repetitive cycles induce hoop stresses which can cause fatigue cracks).

Metal fatigue is the *initiation and propagation of microscopic cracks, due to the slippage of atomic planes within a metal component*. It occurs from repeated application of stress and can be caused by flight and landing loads, and vibrations. However, an applied load only needs to be around 30% of the ultimate load or stress for a fatigue crack to occur, although it is true to say that a load this small needs to be applied many thousands of times to become significant.

Note: These fatigue cycles are cumulative and non-reversible throughout the life of a component!

This is why a helicopter's total number of hours in service, as opposed to time since new, is so important. The most significant factors include:

- the type of operation

- the magnitude and frequency of loads
- the quality of the material

The points where fasteners are used to join parts together will be even more exposed. The local stress at any round hole in a sheet of metal under tension is 3 times the average. Fatigue cracks have three stages - *initiation, growth* and *final fracture*. Once started, corrosion helps a crack grow faster. A small hole is usually drilled at the end of a crack to stop it spreading (called *stop drilling*).

With metal, cracks almost always start on the surface of a structure that has anything out of the ordinary, such as sharp corners, fastener holes or just discontinuity of shape. With composite materials, fatigue is not a consideration at stress cycles around 80% of ultimate stress, because the individual elements tend to fail rather than the structure itself. In this case, cracks will not appear, but the structure will weaken gradually, as opposed to suddenly, as with metal.

GOLDEN RULES

Metal fatigue can now be controlled and predicted, and airworthiness can be extended to the maximum if certain rules are followed:

- Maintain accurate records
- Keep within Flight Manual limitations
- Do not use the wrong parts
- Report all exceedances

Corrosion   021 01 04

You can get corrosion where dissimilar metals are used together. Corrosion happens where a metal breaks down into various compounds, either by chemical or electrolytic action, or movement, such as fretting, stress or erosion. The condition of the covering paint is a good indication of that of a rivet underneath - black stuff is powder from fretting against the aircraft skin. Loose rivets can indicate excessive vibration.

Where a steel bolt is used to hold an aluminium panel together, for example, you will get galvanic corrosion when moisture or some other electrically conductive substance acts as an electrolyte to form a "battery", where the aluminium, which is an anode, deteriorates when it receives metal ions from the steel bolt, or the cathode (see *Electricity & Magnetism*). In this case, you would see a white, powdery surface. This effect gets worse with temperature and humidity, so the worst thing you can do with a wet aircraft in this respect is put it into a warm hangar (the same goes for your car, which is made up of panels dissimilar enough to cause a reaction when they get wet. Salts from the road conduct electricity better and only make things worse). This is a lesser reason why good bonding between aircraft surfaces is so important.

Engineers can prevent such corrosion with zinc-based paints, or by using a suitable jointing compound, or electrically isolating the panels. For example, if your battery is held against an aluminium firewall with a steel bracket, and the battery leaks, corrosion will start as soon as the battery's electrolyte meets the two metals, so a barrier between them will be cheap preventive medicine.

Also, copper and cadmium are relatively close in terms of electrical potential, so steel terminals should be cadmium plated if you want to use them with copper cabling. On the other hand, aluminium and magnesium will corrode easily because they are far apart electrically.

Oxidation is the loss of at least one electron when two or more substances interact, which may or may not include oxygen. Oxygen is actually very caustic - with iron, for example, the oxygen creates a slow burning process, which results in rust. When oxidation occurs in copper, on the other hand, the result is a greenish coating called copper oxide. The metal itself is not weakened by oxidation, but the surface develops a patina after years of exposure to air and water.

On aircraft, the outside paint is constantly exposed to air and water. If it is not protected (say by a wax coating or polyurethane), the oxygen molecules in the air will eventually start interacting with the paint and the finish will become duller and duller.

Destructive oxidation cannot occur if the oxygen cannot penetrate a surface to reach the free radicals it craves.

Vibrations   082 05 06

The manufacturer designs an aircraft to behave itself within a certain flight envelope. If this is exceeded, you will incur strains and stresses.

One way to increase precision and reliability is to eliminate vibration, part of which can be done by ensuring that as many parts of the helicopter as possible are in balance, particularly the main rotor blades. There can also be harmonic vibrations induced in components from others - this is one reason why inputs to and outputs from gearboxes are made to run at different speeds.

There are two sources of vibration on a helicopter - the main rotors, from unequally balanced or tracked blades, or faulty drag dampers, so you can get lateral and vertical vibrations at the same time (low frequency vibrations in the vertical plane in high speed flight are mostly due to a badly adjusted trim tab). Then there are vibrations from the fuselage, possibly induced by the pilot, or from unequal tyre and oleo pressures.

The dominant vibration comes from the flapping of the blades as they create their part of the total lift, together with their centres of pressure moving back and forth as they rotate, and the fact that more lift will be produced over the nose and tail than abeam - the number of blades determines the principal frequency at "N per revolution" where N is the number of blades. The more blades you have, the higher the frequency (for 1-per revs, it also depends if the centre of mass is on the axis of rotation). It gets worse at high blade pitch settings and forward speeds.

For a rotor system operating at 360 RPM, the frequency corresponding to 1 per revolution is 6 Hz (360 RPM is 6 cycles per second). At 2 per revolution it is 12 Hz, and so on. As rotor RPM are changed, so are the frequencies, which can cause complications, which is why a constant speed is used.

One good source of vibration is being downwind, but various components can induce vibrations in others; for example, a tail rotor can produce them in the main rotors (a 1 per on the tail can be very close to an N per on the head). They may be felt as lateral, longitudinal or vertical, or a combination. One way of testing which types are affecting you is to sit in the cockpit and rest your wrist on your knee to see which way your hand moves.

VERTICAL VIBRATIONS

Because of flapping, more lift is produced over the nose and tail than abeam the helicopter (see *Flapback*). This results in bouncing, which is a vertical oscillation of the rotor hub at a frequency equal to the number of blades multiplied by the RPM. This is why the R22 has a third flapping hinge at the centre of the hub (the other two are really coning hinges that relieve blade bending stresses).

An out-of-track blade can cause a vertical vibration, as it produces different lift, particularly when it becomes the advancing blade.

LATERAL VIBRATIONS

If one blade is heavier, the C of G of the rotor head can move away from its ideal position at the centre and force the main rotor shaft to oscillate in a circle that follows the offset C of G. Because the helicopter has less mass on the sides than fore and aft, this is felt as a lateral shake as the oscillation transfers to the fuselage.

BLADE TRACKING & ALIGNMENT

A rotor system is out of balance when the loads are not equal on all of the blades. A well balanced one runs true, which means that, at stabilised pitch and rotational speed, its weight and aerodynamic loads are equal, especially lift and centrifugal forces, which should be equal on each blade so that they have an identical path on the tip path plane*. As well, the rotor head should not be unbalanced. Because the rotor system is operating under high stress loads, this should mean less vibration and maintenance.

*To prevent 1:1 vertical vibrations, blades should fly within the same tip path plane, or exactly in line with each other. In theory, if they are made within the proper

tolerances they should not need adjustment, but if one flexes more than the others, or another is warped, they will need to be adjusted. Tracking is also necessary when the blades, the main gearbox, or the main rotor head have been replaced. Thus, although manufacturing processes are tight, not all blades coming out of the factory are identical. The differences must be compensated for by static and dynamic balancing.

In the early days, tracking was achieved on the ground by standing underneath the rotating disk with a paintbrush or a wick containing engineer's blue on the end of a broom handle, pointing upwards. The blades were adjusted until they got an equal amount of blue on the end - the blades with lighter marks had to be lowered.

Things got more sophisticated by placing a different-coloured substance on the ends of the blades, and seeing which colour was in the lowest notch on a length of vertical tape (a *flag*) that was gently pushed towards the edge of the disk:

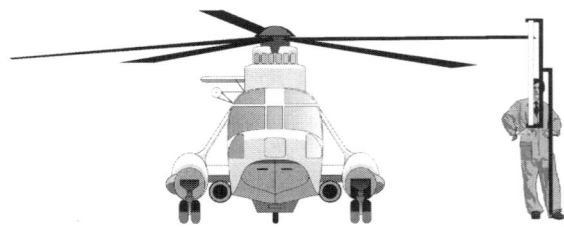

However, blades move differently in flight, and *dynamic tracking* is done with *strobe trackers*, with which a coloured reflector (or a tab with a number on) is placed on the end of the blade and a strobe light used from inside the machine, flashing in sequence with rotation of the blades, so the reflectors appear to be stopped or the numbers easily read, with their relative vertical positions noted.

A soft iron sweep on the rotating swashplate passes close to a magnetic pickup on the stationary swashplate, to cause a once-per-revolution pulse, for synchronisation. *Dynamic balancing* is done by adding or subtracting weights to the blade or its attachment pins.

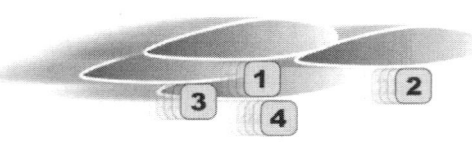

Otherwise, aside from being either lateral or vertical, vibrations fall into four ranges:

© Phil Croucher, 2013

CAPT

- **Extremely Low**, which essentially concerns pylon rocking at 2-3 cycles per second, from the rotor, mast, or transmission. The rocking is absorbed by transmission mount damping.

- **Low**, with large amplitude, between 100-400 cycles per minute, generally associated with loose or worn components, such as gearbox mountings, but could concern one blade of the main rotor developing more lift at a given point than the others. A *wumper* is 1 kick per revolution (*one per*), and a vertical one-per is usually from a blade out of track. A lateral means a blade is out of balance.

- **Medium**, 1,000-2000 cycles per minute, or 4/rev and 6/rev, usually concerning multiple main rotor blades or loose components, such as landing gear. These can usually be felt through the cyclic.

- **High**, over 2000 cycles per minute, usually from items that rotate or vibrate at the same speed as the tail rotor or engine. Vibration through the tail rotor or yaw pedals may indicate wear in either the tail rotor gimbal or the pitch change link bearings (or that you are downwind!)

The most likely causes of rotor head vibration are:

- faulty drag dampers

- incorrect blade tracking

- blades of unequal weight or balance

so you can get laterals and verticals at the same time.

RESONANCE

Most of the parts of a helicopter vibrate at their own natural frequency. *Sympathetic Resonance* is a harmonic beat created between components or assemblies that is usually designed out by making them run at different speeds, a common practice with tail rotor gearboxes.

When vibrations cannot be designed out, there will be ranges that should be avoided - you will often see yellow marks on the gauges on the instrument panel. For example, on the Bell 206, you should accelerate the rotors through 50-60% RRPM as the old one-piece tail rotor drive shaft (when fitted) starts to whip.

GROUND RESONANCE
Covered in *Principles Of Flight*.

AIR RESONANCE

This comes from interactions between the main rotor and various parts of the fuselage when in flight. It is usually designed out, so that if you keep within Flight Manual limitations, nothing untoward will happen.

FLIGHT CONTROLS   021 05 03

The effectiveness of any control depends on its *distance from the Centre of Gravity*, the *size of the control surface*, its *speed through the air* and the *degree of movement*.

Control surfaces can be activated by cables and pulleys, rods, tubes, hydraulics or electrical signals. Because of the high loads, helicopters often need hydraulic assistance to move them, and some form of feedback system (artificial feel) so you can gauge their movement correctly.

Movement of the controls in the cockpit causes the push/pull rods and bell crank levers to move and tilt the bottom (non-rotating) part of the swashplate. The movement of the bottom half of the swashplate is directly transmitted to the top (rotating) part, and then to the pitch operating arms on the rotor blades.

A typical range is 15° for the collective, greater than 20° for longitudinal cyclic and 15° for lateral cyclic. The tail rotor requires 40°.

The primary response to a control input contains a mix of effects from all axes, with strong cross-couplings. The quality of control response degrades at the edges of the flight envelope because the aerodynamics are stronger than the structure.

Picture: Bell 206 control linkage (not to scale!)

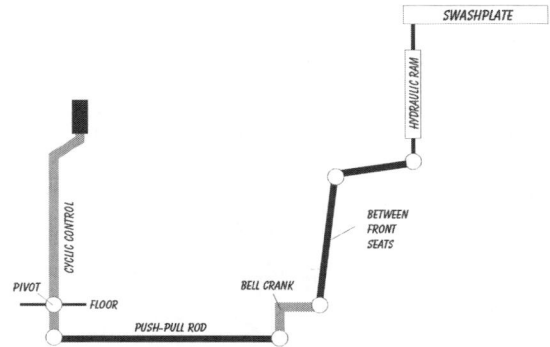

Bell cranks turn control movement through 90°.

Note: The point about flying controls, especially in helicopters, is that they should always be moved *smoothly*. Good helicopter flying is essentially downwash management, which has some lag built in. If you jerk the controls, you will get all the drag without the lift when the blades get into position before the induced flow has a chance to catch up.

The various aerodynamic surfaces at the rear (fin & stabiliser) are there to provide stability above a minimum speed of about 45 knots in most helicopters, but around 76 knots in a Dauphin. They are not there to provide lift in the proper sense, although some horizontal stabilisers have a moveable surface at the rear that is controlled by fore and aft movement of the cyclic. Its controlling force becomes larger as airspeed increases.

Enstrom Collective System (Courtesy, Enstrom Corp)

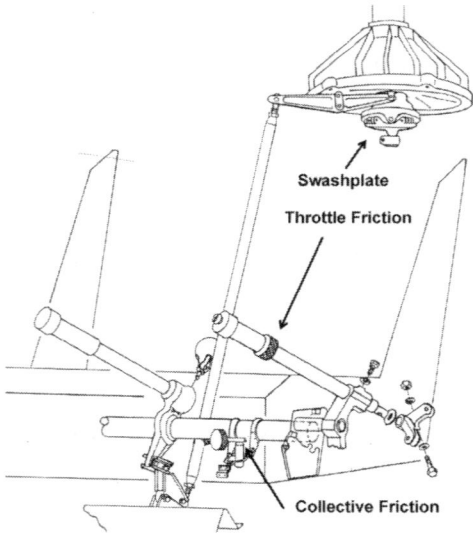

Throttle Correlation

There is some sort of automatic linkage between the collective and throttle on most machines but, with pistons, this is rudimentary at best, and may not exist at all, as on the Hiller 12E. In such cases the job is done by the pilot.

The *correlation box* does most of the work, but fine tuning is still left to the pilot because the box cannot factor in atmospheric conditions. On the Bell 47, for example, the throttle rotates a shaft inside the collective lever, which drives various cams and push-pull tubes that operate a cam box. A cam is needed because the power output is not linear, meaning that power increments do not correspond with main rotor pitch changes. The cam is actually a curved slot cut into a metal plate.

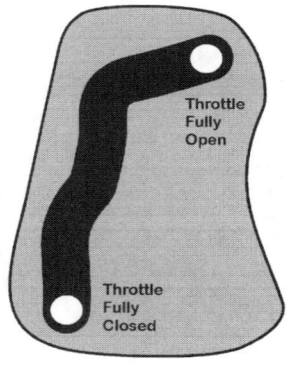

Robinson helicopters tend to use an electronic RPM governor that requires no pilot input in normal flight conditions. It takes over once you get past 80% power.

Note: Should you get carburettor icing, the RPM loss that would naturally occur is compensated for by the governor system. If you do not detect any throttle movement, you will be unaware of the RPM trend because one of the main indications of carburettor icing has been removed.

Control Mixing

In helicopters that have their collective pitch changed by moving the whole swashplate up and down the rotor mast, there must be some way of making sure that the cyclic is not affected. Otherwise, moving the collective would alter the height of the cyclic setting on the swashplate, and alter the disc attitude. Moving the cyclic would also screw with the collective.

A *mixing unit* allows the cyclic and collective to operate without interfering with each other, so a change in collective pitch does not affect the tilt of the swashplate and a cyclic movement tilts the swashplate but does not affect its height. In other words, it maintains the cyclic angle by superimposing collective inputs onto cyclic inputs, keeping the disc angle constant. It consists of a series of summing bellcranks and torque tubes.

Upward movement of the collective moves the swashplate as well, and the cyclic input that was already there moves the same amount in the same direction. In the picture below, cranks A, B and C will all move at the same time.

When fore and aft cyclic is used, however, only crank B moves upwards to tilt the swashplate in the desired direction. Lateral movements will move only A & C in equal and opposite directions.

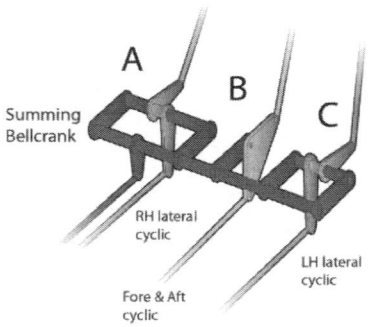

A similar arrangement can be used to increase or decrease tail rotor pitch as the collective is moved, particularly on some helicopters with automatic flight control systems.

Control Friction

Frictions, to increase or decrease the "feel", or to keep the controls still while you change a radio frequency, are fitted to cyclic and collective controls, but only that for the collective is normally adjustable in flight.

Throttle frictions can also be fitted, but are usually set at the beginning of a flight and left alone.

ELECTRICITY & MAGNETISM

Note: Much of this section is background knowledge for your later flying life - it helps sometimes to know what an engineer is talking about! The examiners don't ask much about electricity in exams, but examples of questions are:

- why is an alternator better than a generator?

- what device changes DC current to AC current?

Electrical formulae are not questioned.

The term *electricity* comes from the Greek word for amber, *elektron*. As far as pilots (and engineers) are concerned, its basic function is to transmit energy (or data, with electronics) from one point to another, possibly remote. For this, it has to be produced, transmitted, applied and controlled, with switches and/or computers.

As you cannot see electricity, some imagination must be used in order to understand it, but the whole process is very like the movement of water (current) in a hose. The difference is that you have to put the water into the hose, whereas the charge is already present in an electrical cable - all you have to do is set it in motion.

Some airmanship points first:

- Take care not to overheat electrical equipment when it is switched on (for checking) during a preflight check (there is no airflow to cool it)

- Do not start or stop engines with unnecessary electrical equipment switched on

- Avoid using the starter motor for too long - there is usually a limit of one or two attempts for around 30 secs each before you have to let it cool down before trying again. Also, starters don't have fuses - make sure the warning light is out after starting!

- Check that the generator or alternator is working properly after starting, and often during flight

- Make sure the Battery Master Switch is off before you leave the aircraft after flight (many pilots leave the anti-collision light on to remind them)

Atomic Theory

Matter is anything that has mass and volume which, for our purposes, exists as a solid, liquid or a gas.

The atom is the most basic building block of matter. The diagram on the left is a loose depiction of the inside of an atom. The large ball in the middle is the *nucleus* and the smaller ones spinning rapidly round it are a cloud of *electrons*, which are **negatively charged particles** and around 2,000 times smaller in size.

There are an equal number of electrons to protons, to make it electrically neutral, which is why an extra electron (or a hole caused by one leaving), is balanced immediately. An atom with one extra electron is *negatively* charged, because electrons are labelled as negative, and an atom with one missing is *positively* charged, or "carrying a positive charge", which is a bit of a misnomer as all it has done is lost an electron. This is called *ionisation*, because an unbalanced atom is called an *ion*, which we will come across later when we discuss the *ionosphere* that surrounds the Earth. Some components, like transistors, depend on the movement of electrons or holes (missing electrons) one way or the other.

Insulators & Conductors

Some atoms don't have much of a hold on their free electrons, and allow them to move around easily because their shells overlap. The materials made from these atoms (i.e. copper) are called **conductors**, and they have a low resistance to the flow of current. Silver is best, and copper is next by 6%, but gold is commonly used because it doesn't corrode and cause bad connections. Even a gas can conduct electricity, as with fluorescent lighting, or the ionosphere. Conductors therefore contain *charges* (electrons or holes are *charge carriers*), which only need to be set in motion to do work.

Helium atoms, by contrast, have all their shells full, and do not overlap, so they allow no movement of electrons. This makes them good **insulators**, and useful for keeping conductors from touching each other, otherwise electricity would flow where you don't want it.

Good examples of insulators are glass, or plastic coating round a cable.

SEMICONDUCTORS

A substance that is normally an insulator but which can become a conductor when it gets hot is a semiconductor.

As semiconductors can produce changes in circuit conditions, they are known as *active* components, as opposed to the more passive capacitors and resistors, which is why they are also called **solid state devices**, meaning no moving parts.

Electricity

If you line up a series of atoms in an electrical cable, and remove an electron from one end, the resulting hole is filled by a free electron from the previous atom, because the others are trying to repel each other, and so on.

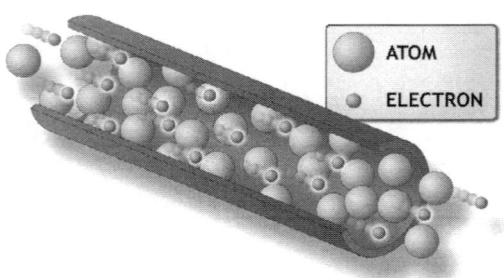

That is, you have created a (very) slight difference in pressure, or potential, between each end of the cable, which causes the movement of free electrons, or an electric current, to the area with less electrons. However, this won't happen unless you have a complete circuit, which is described later.

You can separate electrons from their atoms and make them move in 6 ways:

- **Heat**. The usual way of using heat is to apply it to the junction of two dissimilar metals, such as iron and copper. How much electricity you get depends on the temperature difference between the ends of the wires. The *thermocouple* is a component built like this that detects the heat coming from the back of a turbine engine. The electricity it produces drives a temperature gauge in the cockpit. As you don't need batteries for this, you have at least one gauge that works when the electrics fail. A heated element is also used in Cathode Ray Tubes (as used on radar screens) to emit electrons.

- **Friction**. When rubbing two materials together, such as glass and silk, electrons may be forced out of their orbits in the glass and transferred to the silk, which then acquires a negative charge of static electricity, described overleaf. The glass, of course, acquires a positive charge.

- **Chemical Action**. Used in batteries.

- **Light**. Photo-electric or solar cells create reactions between two substances when exposed to light.

- **Pressure**. Certain substances, such as quartz, can produce an electric charge when pressure is applied to them. This principle is also used in carbon pile voltage regulators (described later) to control the amount of electricity fed into a battery by a generator. Applying electricity to such a substance can also make it expand or contract.

- **Magnetism**. This is the most common method, using relative motion between a coil of wire and a magnet. It is described later on in this section.

THE ELECTRONIC TIDE

The energy behind the work needed to create a difference in potential is *electromotive force*. They are both expressed in volts, so the terms tend to be used synonymously. In reality, emf is a cause and p.d. is an effect.

- **emf** is the *open circuit* pressure, or the total voltage a battery or generator is *capable* of generating (open circuit means that it is not connected to anything).

- **p.d.** is the "pressure" difference between two points, say across a component such as a lamp. The voltage measured in a circuit when current is flowing is smaller than the maximum, because of internal resistance and the work required to overcome it. Put another way, p.d. involves the conversion of electrical energy into another form, such as heat, having first been converted from, say, chemical energy to get emf. The coulomb (quantity of electrons) and the joule (work done by them) are used to derive a unit of p.d. called a volt, so if the electrical energy converted when a coulomb passes between two points is a joule, the p.d. is 1 volt. If 2 coulombs produces 5 joules' worth of work, the p.d. is 2.5 volts. So, **the voltage coming out of a component is not the same as that going in**. Kirchoff's second law (later) states that all the voltage drops in a closed circuit equal the total voltage applied to the circuit, or emf.

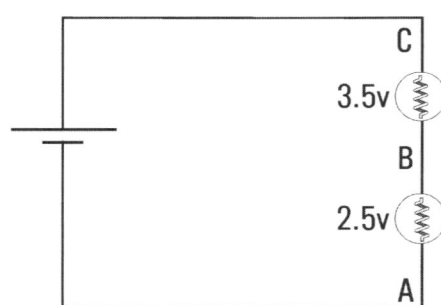

In the picture above, the emf from the battery divides between two lamps so that a voltmeter connected across the top one reads 3.5 volts, and one across the bottom one reads 2.5 volts.

If point A has zero potential* (otherwise known as Earth), the p.d. at B is 2.5 volts, and at C, 6 volts. The battery is therefore a 6 volt one (3.5 + 2.5). So, although the number of electrons flowing at each point of the circuit is the same, the pressure behind them (voltage) can vary.

TYPES OF ELECTRICITY

There are three:

- That which stays right where it is, or **static electricity,** although it can jump across small gaps, (this can be a problem with underslung loads on helicopters, especially in dry snow). As this force does not move, it is called *static*, meaning electricity that goes nowhere in particular, but which can build up on a point to create a charge that can be attractive or repellent (no conductor is needed).

  You discharge static electricity by providing a path for the electrons to move. *Static discharge wicks* are used on aircraft for this purpose, because the airframe can develop its own static potential. They allow the charge to concentrate, then discharge to air (the visible discharge of static electricity to the air is called *St. Elmo's fire*). A conducting bead in the tyres will do the same job on the ground. Skids do it automatically, unless you are on ice or snow. Static (and sparks) are why you bond an aircraft and a refuelling vehicle together, and aircraft surfaces to each other, hence the use of bonding strips between parts of the fuselage.

- That which goes in one direction, usually at one speed, called **Direct Current**

- That which flip-flops back and forth, called **Alternating Current**

It is AC which concerns us when it comes to radio.

Voltage

Voltage is a measure of how much energy a charge has. It is like the head of pressure behind the movement of water in a hose.

Current

One electron has such a small charge that it is hardly detectable. You need a larger unit to work with, such as the *coulomb*, which consists of 6.28×10^{18} electrons (think of a coulomb of electrons in the same way as you would a pint of beer). The symbol for a coulomb is *C*.

The flow of charge (electrons) in a conductor is called the *current*. The rate of current flow is the number of electrons passing any section of the conductor in one second, expressed in terms of *amperes*, or *amps* (an ampere is the movement of 1 coulomb per second). Small currents may be measured in *milliamperes* or *microamperes*.

The more electrons that move along a wire in a given time, the higher the current that is measured, so if you increase the voltage, current will automatically increase, other things being equal. It follows that to control the current, you can vary either the voltage or the resistance.

Resistance

A waterwheel produces work when it is turned, but it also slows down the flow of water. Electricity is affected in the same way. For best economy, you must therefore move the most current with the least waste, in a circuit with as little resistance as possible.

A conductor has a low resistance to current, and an insulator has a high one, but even a good conductor slows electrons down, because a new electron joining an atom is repelled by the atoms already there, and some energy is lost. This increases the temperature. The more work you make electricity do, the hotter things get, which is how electric fires work. If you make it work harder, you get light as well, hence light bulbs.

If your conductor is thick and short, you won't meet much resistance (just imagine a large water pipe). If it is long and thin, on the other hand, you have to force the current along, which takes more work (a thin water pipe).

Thus, resistance is *directly proportional* to *temperature* and *conductor length*, and *inversely proportional* to *cross-sectional area*, so the warmer, longer and thinner a cable is, the more resistance it has.

So if resistance is such a drag, why use it? The answer is that resistance can generate heat, limit current, or control voltage*. It is therefore associated with the *dissipation* of energy, and power is used up (as heat) when it is present. Power used against resistance cannot be recovered.

*A switch is a very crude way of controlling current. Resistors used properly can allow much finer adjustments. For example, a volume control is a variable resistor.

The symbol for resistance is Ω (omega), but in diagrams the zigzag symbol given below is used.

Note: The symbol can mean either a specific component or the amount of resistance present. In circuit diagrams, connecting lines are assumed to have no resistance.

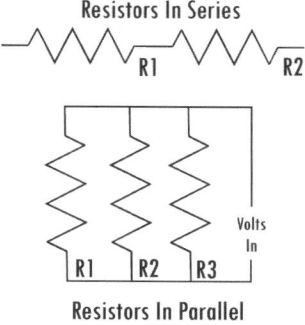

Ohm's Law

The ratio of the voltage across, and the current flowing through, a resistance is constant, and equal to the value of the resistance.

If you increase the voltage (pressure) in a circuit, you increase the current automatically. On the other hand, given a constant voltage, current flow decreases if you increase the resistance. Current flow is therefore *directly proportional* to voltage and *inversely proportional* to resistance. The ratio of *voltage across* a circuit to the *current flowing through it* is a constant known as resistance.

Ohm's Law describes the fixed relationship between voltage, current and resistance, and is therefore very useful for finding the unknown factor in a circuit if you know the values of the other two and have forgotten the relevant measuring instrument (actually, it's very hard to measure current, and it is most often calculated anyway). Ohm's law does not apply to all conductors, but is valid for practically all metals if the temperature remains constant.

The symbols for the elements in the formula are *I* for current (amps), *R* for resistance (ohms), *V* for voltage, and they come together in this formula:

```
V (or PD) = I x R
```

or (rearranged slightly):

$$I = \frac{V}{R}$$

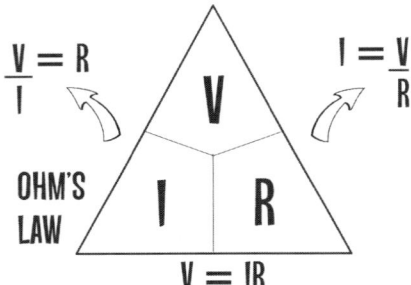

So, if you have a 24 volt battery, and a load has 12 ohms of resistance, there are 2 amps of current:

```
24 = I(2) x 12
```

Aircraft systems typically use 24-volt systems because of the weight savings you get when using a higher voltage and lower current (you can use lighter cabling).

This formula can be useful in many ways - if you had a break in a cable run, your ammeter would indicate a different current than if the cable were unbroken. Since you know the voltage, you can divide it by the current to get the resistance. As the cable will have a known resistance per foot (engineers have a book with them all in) you can calculate how far down the fuselage you need to start looking.

Note: If you connect a heavy load to a battery (i.e. a low resistance), the battery's voltage will drop as it tries to satisfy Ohm's Law, due to its internal resistance. If the required current cannot be produced, it pushes out as

much as it can and the voltage will reduce to whatever Ohm's Law says it should be.

Circuits

There must be an unbroken connection between the components for electricity to flow, or a complete circuit, which is any combination of a conductor and a source of electromotive force that allows electrons to travel round it in a continuous stream. The energy supplied to the charges in a circuit is changed into other forms of energy by any appliances connected to it that have resistance.

If a circuit is broken (usually with a switch), it is known as an *open* circuit (as opposed to *closed*), and no current will flow. With an open circuit, the loss of continuity stops everything in the circuit from working.

A cable going to a component must have one returning to the switch as an earth return, to create a *dipole circuit*. However, you can use the fuselage as a return path, which means that you only need one length of cable (the battery will be connected by its *negative* pole). This saves weight and space, as you don't need two cables to complete a circuit. Further weight savings can be made with busbars, and alternating current, both described later.

SERIES CIRCUITS

A series circuit exists when its elements are connected end to end, creating *one path* for the current to flow in, so if one fails, everything stops (as with Christmas tree lights). An identical current flows through the whole circuit.

PARALLEL CIRCUITS

In a parallel circuit, components are on separate paths in which current can flow - you could think of them as being connected side by side - that is, *across* the voltage source (a common term for this is a *shunt* connection). In this case, the *voltage* across the components is the same, while the current may change with individual values of resistance.

In a parallel circuit, the loss of one component does not result in the circuit failing (that's why parallel circuits are used in buildings).

COMPLEX CIRCUITS

Simply a circuit where the components are connected in combinations of series-parallel.

CIRCUIT PROTECTION

A **short circuit** exists when the full current comes into contact with the grounded part of the circuit. This can be more than the circuit is built to handle, so electrical equipment may be protected in many ways.

Note: The *Battery Master Switch* controls the power to all circuits, and others will control smaller groups of equipment, such as the *Avionics Master Switch*, for the

radios and navaids. The Battery switch may well be in two parts, one for the battery itself, and the other for the alternator circuit, which needs DC for the electromagnet that makes it work.

Circuits will be otherwise protected by *fuses* or *circuit breakers*, which are designed to interrupt the flow of current where specific conditions that generate a lot of heat exist. One difference between the two is that a fuse will blow *before* the full fault current is reached, and the circuit breaker will trip afterwards, in which case both it and the item protected must be able to take the full fault current for a short time. Circuit breakers are not designed to protect equipment as such - rather, they are there to protect the cabling and connectors which are not easy to replace and may be old and/or inaccessible if a fire starts.

Circuit protection devices should only be reset or replaced once, after allowing them to cool. This especially applies with the fuel system! Only reset it if the item is needed for flight safety. There are a lot of instruments in the average aircraft that do not need electricity with which to function.

FUSES

A fuse is a deliberately weak part of a circuit that is designed to fail if a problem occurs, thus protecting the rest of the circuit, so instead of replacing wiring in odd places, all you do is change the fuse. Technically, a fuse is a *thermal device wired in series with the load protected*, meaning that all the current passes through it, and it *melts* because it *overheats* from *excess current*. Fuses are placed as close to a power distribution point (busbar) as possible to minimise runs of unprotected cable.

Note: As the current is large, there is *no fuse protection for starters*, which is why there is a starter warning light.

Fuses are rated according to the number of amperes they will carry, which must be lower than that of the lowest rated equipment. As well, fuse capacity should be double the amperage requirement. So, in a 100-watt circuit using 25 volts (i.e. 4 amps), you need an 8-amp fuse. Generally, the lowest rated fuse is selected consistent with reliable operation, but for emergency equipment (anything that will affect safety), the highest rating is used consistent with cable protection.

CIRCUIT BREAKERS

A circuit breaker is a combination of a relay and a solenoid, both described later. It is relatively slow acting, and can be used in AC and DC circuits, being a button that pops out when a fuse would otherwise break, so it is a *resettable mechanical trip device,* activated by the heating of a bimetallic strip element, where one metal expanding more than another pops it open.

A *trip-free* circuit breaker will trip even if it is held in, and therefore does not remake a circuit, so pilots don't make the situation worse!

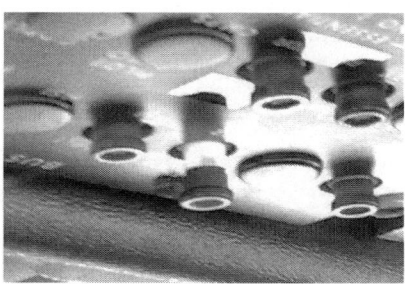

Note: Although they are the most commonly used method of circuit protection, try not to use a circuit breaker as a switch. This cannot always be avoided, but it is still not good practice.

Generally, circuit breakers are resettable, fuses are not.

Capacitance

Where two separate, nearby, conductors have a current flowing through them, there is an electric field flowing through the insulation (dielectric) between them. Even two wires close together can have this property. A circuit has capacitance if it can store energy as an electric field.

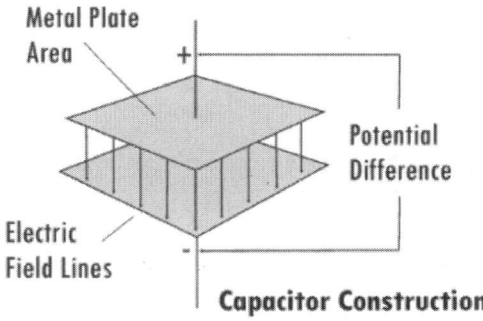

Capacitor Construction

Whereas resistors can control the amount of current in a circuit, capacitors can control how quickly the p.d. across a component changes, so they allow you to design circuits that involve timing. Potential energy is also associated with *elasticity*, which can be represented by a stretched spring, or a hydraulic accumulator, including smoothing fluctuations and absorbing surges. Electrically, you can do the same thing with a capacitor.

Normally, electrons cannot enter a conductor unless there is a path for an equal amount of them to leave, which is why you need a circuit. However, a conductor can hold a greater charge if it is near another one with an electric field in the space between them, as with a capacitor.

STORAGE

In electronic circuit, you often need to store small quantities of electricity for short periods for later use.

Because they can store electricity (or energy), capacitors can make a circuit dynamic. If you had two circuits, each with a battery, a switch and a light bulb, but one with a capacitor, the capacitor can introduce a time delay before the bulb goes on or off (as can a coil, or solenoid for different reasons). This is because capacitors tend to resist changes in voltage drop.

Capacitance is the ratio of the stored charge to the applied voltage. The larger the capacitance, the larger the charge you can store from a given voltage. It depends on:

- the **dielectric** used. Glass, for example, has 5.1 times the capacity of dry air and fuel has double. The reason that solids are more effective than air is that, when the charge starts or stops, a momentary flow of electrons begins or ends. This wouldn't happen if there was nothing there at all.

- **distance** between the plates (they cannot touch or there would be a short circuit)

- the **parallel surface area**

Thus, capacitance is more when the plates are nearer to each other, or larger. If they are relatively far apart, you will get more leakage from the field, which is the basis of radio transmission, discussed in *Radio Navigation*.

The unit of capacitance is the *Farad* (F), named after Faraday. It represents 1 amp for 1 second with a change of 1 volt stored as 1 joule of energy. As it happens, this is too large to be used in most circuits (the capacitor concerned wouldn't even fit into a room), so *microfarads* (μf), representing millionths, are used instead.

CURRENT FLOW

When voltage is applied across a capacitor, one plate becomes negatively charged. At the same time, electrons leave the other plate to resupply the battery, leaving that plate positively charged.

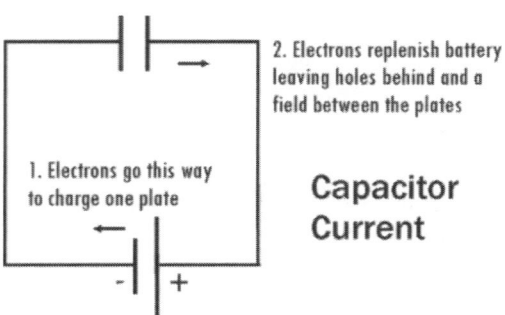

2. Electrons replenish battery leaving holes behind and a field between the plates

1. Electrons go this way to charge one plate

Capacitor Current

This effect is called *polarisation*. The current flows until the charge across the capacitor is equal to the battery emf, at which point everything stops. However, you now have an electric field of force (charge) between the plates, which carry equal and opposite charges, attracting each other. In other words, there is a "strain" across the dielectric (hence the word "tension", as in *High Tension*). DC will not normally pass across the gap, unless the voltage is very high and the gap very small, in which case there may be a spark. Thus, once a capacitor becomes fully charged, it acts as an open circuit to DC because, as it reaches the maximum charge and therefore matches the supply voltage, the current becomes zero. **No current will flow if you simply charge the capacitor** (with DC).

If the source of voltage is taken away, the voltage across the capacitor stays where it is, but will leak in the reverse direction over time so, until this happens, capacitors behave like miniature batteries, since they preserve a difference of potential between the plates for a short time. This is how you can change the batteries in your mobile phone without backup power. Capacitors are also used in computer memory cells to store information, and as suppressors on electric motors, or in magnetos.

Alternating current appears to pass through capacitors because the plates change between positive and negative on each cycle as the charge on them builds up and decays. The "flow" is allowed because of the rapid change of p.d.

Measuring Instruments

THE AMMETER

Current is measured in series* using *ammeters*, or *loadmeters*, both presenting the information in different ways.

*They need a low resistance so they don't affect the current they are measuring. Ammeters measure coulombs per second, and there is one per generator.

An centre-reading ammeter's needle (right, above) is typically associated with DC generators and light aircraft and should always be in the + side of the gauge (not too much!), to show a positive charge going into the battery. It is connected to the battery's positive lead. With the battery on and the engine off, the needle will show a negative reading in the minus range, or a discharge. If a discharge is shown with the engine running, the generator is not up to the job and the difference has to be made up by the battery. Switch things off until you get a positive reading.

The other type (left, above) is also called a *loadmeter*. It is often associated with AC generators and/or turbine engines, and measures electrical loads rather than battery charging. The display starts at zero, and shows positive numbers, sometimes as a percentage. With the battery on and the engine off, it will read zero.

Components draw more current in the initial stages, until the flow settles down. Typically, when you switch on the generator after starting an engine, the loadmeter will read high at first, then decrease as the battery becomes topped up. Only after reaching a certain figure on its way down (say 0.7) should you switch the electrical services on.

A high rate of charge after starting an engine is only allowed for a short period.

THE VOLTMETER

A Voltmeter is connected in parallel, so the current does not pass through the meter instead of the circuit and affect the readings. A good voltmeter therefore has a very high resistance.

Power (Watts)

The *rate* at which electrons are moved about is called *electrical power*, represented by the letter P, which is measured in *Watts*, after James Watt (the Watt is the SI derived unit of power, equal to the transfer of one joule per second. 746 Watts equal 1 horsepower). As Watts are very small units, we tend to use Kilowatts (KW) instead. Power consumed (Wattage) is determined by voltage multiplied by the current (in amps):

$$P = V \times I$$

Or Power is a product of Amps x Volts.

In general, for maximum power transmission, V and I (voltage and current) must be as large as possible, but the current is limited by the size of the wire and the voltage by the insulation. It is easier and cheaper to make a line with good insulation, so you can transmit a higher voltage, than to make one able to carry high current, as power loss is proportional to the square of the current, which should be as low as possible. This is one reason why we use alternating current, as high voltages are easier to achieve.

Power Distribution (Busbars)

The lighter an aircraft is, the better, so it's impractical (if only for weight saving) to run a wire from the battery (and back) to every component it supplies. A better solution is to run a single (big) wire to a distribution point and then (via fuses or circuit breakers) to any electrical appliances, to serve all of them from the end of that line, and use the fuselage as an Earth return, which is what a busbar system is all about.

Physically, an electrical busbar (*bus* for short) is a metal bar with provisions to make electrical contact with a number of devices that use electricity. Electrically, it's a conduit between components, like the memory bus in a computer. There's nothing to stop you having main buses supplying secondary ones, but the system must ensure that problems on or near it do not endanger any components connected to it, so services connected to a busbar are normally in parallel, to enable isolation and keep voltages equal.

Below is a theoretical example of a busbar system. It shows the possible location of typical components.

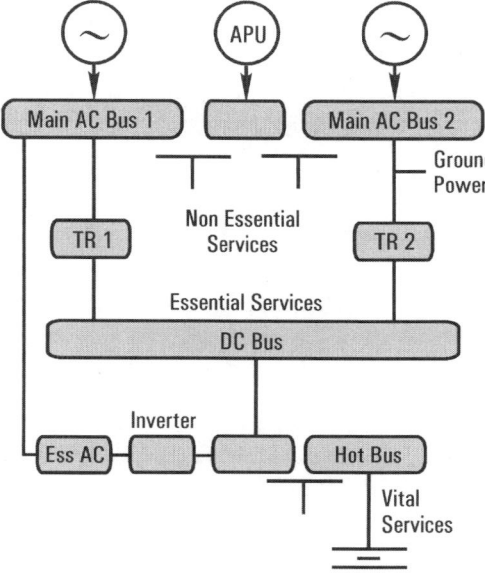

Each generator has its own busbar with non-essential services connected to it, or those that don't matter if it fails. Both are ultimately connected in parallel to a central (combining) busbar which carries the essential services, so they will always have at least one source of power.

The combining busbar could also be split so that each side runs independently (they can be connected with a *bus tie*). The battery is connected to the combining busbar, so it can be charged, yet still supply essential components if both generators fail.

Busbars can be split, so that isolation is possible, to protect delicate equipment from large variations in electrical power, such as found when starting. In many aircraft, something like the Avionics Master Switch would serve as the link between two busbars (a *bus tie*), but you could also use a relay, which would open automatically when the starter switch is activated.

Note: The Avionics Master Switch would also be a circuit breaker, and is also useful for reducing wear and tear on the switches of the radios and navaids.

For isolation purposes, components are graded in order of importance in an emergency: *vital, essential* and *non-essential*.

- **Vital** services include items that are wired directly to the battery, so they will carry on working when the generators fail. The term *hot bus* or *direct bus* means that the bus is always live, so you must switch devices attached to it off when you close down, as with the fuel boost pumps in some aircraft. There may be a secondary battery switch for this purpose. The hot bus not only allows items to be powered if alternators or generators fail, but also allows the engine(s) to be started when they are not working anyway. All aircraft need standby electrical power systems, in case the normal one goes down. For small ones, this is usually the main battery, which is oversized for this reason. The problem is, it's time-limited to 30 minutes.

- **Essential** services are those needed for safe flight that can still be run by a generator or the battery.

- **Non-essential** services are things like galleys which can be isolated for load-shedding purposes.

Batteries

Certain chemicals, when they are combined with some metals, can cause electrons to flow as direct current, until all the electrons disappear from the metal, causing it to eventually get eaten away - since the atoms comprising the metal lose electrons, they cease to be the same atoms and therefore cease to exist in their former state - if you could put the electrons back, you would regain your metal plate, and recharge the battery.

A primary, or dry, cell, is one enclosed in a metal case which gets eaten away as the battery discharges. This process is not reversible. Primary cells are typically used in flashlights as a throwaway item.

A secondary cell can be recharged, and usually has a liquid involved in its construction.

A "battery" is a *collection* of secondary cells, which have a charge of about 2.1 volts each (lead-acid), or 1.2 (Ni-Cad), hence the need to combine them to do anything useful. Lead-Acid batteries will have 12 cells, and Ni-Cads 19 or 20 to produce the 24 volts needed for aircraft.

Note: If one cell is dead, the battery is unserviceable.

A cell consists of alternating positive and negative *plates* surrounded by *electrolyte*. Different materials are better or worse at this job, so you might get more or less voltage out of one type of battery compared to another. The two types used in aircraft are *lead acid*, as found in cars, and *NiCad*, as found in portable computers. People who use both will already understand the difference but, in simple terms, the lead acid's output tends to fall off steadily with discharge, whereas a NiCad can pump out a constant power until it can do no more, meaning that its *closed-circuit voltage* remains nearly constant until it is nearly discharged.

In addition, a NiCad recovers more quickly, and has a low internal resistance, so it's good for starting turbines.

In the early days, say, up till the 1950s, *vented* lead-acid batteries were used almost exclusively, until vented NiCads came along, with their superior performance at low temperatures. *Sealed* lead-acid batteries were subsequently invented, for better reliability, and are now more common.

An aircraft battery's purpose is to maintain a power supply under transient conditions, help with short term heavy loads, supply total power for a short time in emergencies, and start the engines, where it also has to excite the alternators. However, it needs the right conditions - at minus 30°C, your battery has less than half its power to start an engine that needs 350% more effort to get going! This is because, when it is cold, a battery's internal resistance increases (in the Arctic, you often take them out at night to keep them warm).

A flat battery has maximum internal resistance, which will generate lots of heat when an attempt is made to charge it (on a bench, only a very small current is used). It is therefore not a good idea to continue flight if your battery gets discharged! In any case, it should be replaced before the next flight. One problem is, for it to work, an alternator needs current from a battery, and your machine's electrics won't work if it isn't there.

BATTERY CAPACITY

The capacity or holding power of a battery is a measure of its ability to produce a flow of current. The number of cells will determine the voltage it produces, but the area of the plates inside, the amount of active material in the plates and how much electrolyte there is determines the *ampere-hour* capacity, or amps multiplied by hours.

This means that a battery is supposed to provide enough current to drop the voltage down to 1.2 volts per cell in 5 hours when fully charged, though it is never wise to rely on any battery for more than about 20 minutes (officially, they should last for at least 30 when the electrics fail).

To get an idea of your aircraft's capabilities, add up the number of devices that use power and divide them into the amp/hour rating. So, if your devices collectively use 45 amps, and your battery supplies 45 amp-hours, you should be able to get an hours' use out of it. When faced with such an emergency, it is usual to use the navaids, for example, to get a position fix, then turn them off until you start feeling a little lost, then turn them on again until you are once more certain of your position. The same with radios. This will get a little extra time out of your battery.

The definition of electrical current is the amount of charge flowing down a wire per second, expressed as:

$$\text{Current} = \frac{\text{Charge}}{\text{Time}}$$

CAPT

Therefore current is a time-derived value, meaning that its value takes time into account, so a current of 45 Amps = 45 seconds' worth of electrical charge. A battery delivering 45 Amps for 2.5 hours could then deliver 90 Amps for 1.25 hours (double the current, but only for half the time) or 22.5 Amps for 5 hours (half the current, but for twice as long). Or any combination in between. The battery's rating is therefore 112.5 Ampere-hours.

POLARITY

The polarities of a battery are positive and negative, marked plus (+) or minus (-), or coloured red and black, respectively, and electrons flow from the negative (-) electrode, through the circuit the battery is connected to, back to the positive (+), because the negative end has the most electrons (the terms are indeed misleading, and the words *positively charged* even more so, but they were coined a long time ago and it's a hard thing to change). If you join batteries in *series*, that is, one after the other, with the positive of one connected to the negative of the next (left, below), you will get a voltage which is the *sum* of them both, but with the *current capacity* of *one*.

If you join them in *parallel*, with the positive and negative connected to each other (right, below) you would get the *voltage* of *one* battery, but the *current capacity* of *all* of them, so you can use them for longer.

This is because anything connected in series keeps the same current, and anything in parallel keeps the voltage. Since a typical aircraft runs on a 24-volt system, you would therefore connect two (12v) car batteries in series (better yet, two sets in parallel). Be aware, though, that terminals are different sizes to stop them being confused, so you need an adapter to connect them up in the middle (jumper cables may open up and spark when a load is applied).

Ensure that batteries have an electrical load on them before completing a circuit.

CHARGING

During engine operation, the battery is recharged with a *generator* or an *alternator*, based on DC or AC, respectively, using the constant voltage method via a voltage regulator.

An alternator will charge at low RPM (a generator doesn't much), but some aircraft use a *starter/generator* to save space, despite this advantage. The same unit spins the engine on startup, and switched over when it's running to become a generator. If an alternator were used, you would

need yet another item attached to the engine. Alternators and generators are discussed later.

LEAD ACID

The lead-acid battery is made of alternating lead peroxide (+) and lead (-) plates, with separators in between, and an electrolyte made of sulphuric acid (37%) and water (63%), which can be neutralised with sodium bicarbonate (bicarbonate of soda). The oxygen in the lead peroxide has an affinity for the H_2 in the sulphuric acid and the other plate likes the SO_4, so there is a tension between the plates which would create lead sulphate on one plate and water on the other, if the battery were part of a circuit. The formation of water dilutes the electrolyte and reduces its specific gravity, which is why the state of charge of a lead-acid battery is measured with a hydrometer (see below).

One plate turning into lead sulphate as electrons are lost is the reason for the term *sulphated*, which describes a fully discharged battery.

NICKEL-CADMIUM

When uncharged, the positive electrode of a NiCad cell is nickelous hydroxide, and the negative is cadmium hydroxide. In the charged condition, the positive electrode is nickelic hydroxide, and the negative metallic is cadmium, meaning that the chemical reaction is in the plates. The electrolyte is *potassium hydroxide*, which is only there to provide a path for the current flow - it plays no part in the chemical reaction. If you spill any electrolyte from a NiCad, you can neutralise it with *dilute boric acid*.

To be the equivalent of a 12v lead-acid battery, a NiCad must have between 10-11 cells. The cell voltage is 1.2 V when charged, with a nominal voltage of 1.0v.

However, NiCads have short memories, in that if you keep charging them up when they have only discharged a little way, they will begin to think they have a lesser power rating*, so to stop them causing hot starts they need regular *deep cycling* to keep them awake. Thus, although it's good practice to start an aircraft, for example, from a battery cart, to preserve the ship's battery for better reliability in remote places, occasionally a battery start is good for the system as it will help to eliminate the memory effect. The actual term is *voltage depression*, where there is a slight dip in the voltage near the end of a discharge. The dip goes below the normal output voltage, which makes you think the cell has actually discharged - a common occurrence with home movie cameras! As the battery is charged, the voltage depression point moves toward the beginning of the discharge period.

*This is only noticeable when you try to use all the charge, so you can fly for some time believing a full charge exists.

Another problem with NiCads is that they can catch fire when too much current is drawn and then replaced, a process called *Thermal Runaway*. This is why some aircraft have a *Battery Temp* caution light on the warning panel which means you must land *immediately*, before the battery catches fire and takes other stuff with it, if it doesn't actually burn its way through the airframe and fall out. Yet another problem is that a NiCad cell will lose about 1% of its charge per day.

CAPACITY CHECKS

Battery capacity checks should be made every 3 months. The minimum acceptable is 80%. Because the electrolyte remains unchanged, there is no way to tell the real state of a Ni-Cad's charge by checking its relative density. Checking the voltage is no good, either, because a NiCad can produce a constant voltage for some time, even when discharged, and closed-circuit voltage changes very little.

On the other hand, a *hydrometer* (see right) can be used to check the specific gravity and hence the state of charge of a lead-acid battery, but not when it is installed in the machine, in case the (acidic) electrolyte gets spilled. The specific gravity of electrolyte is 1.25 fully charged, and 1.3 when cold.

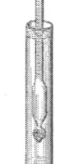

If you have to measure capacity whilst the battery is in the aircraft, the open and closed circuit voltages can be compared (e.g. on-load and off-load). The voltage will fall significantly as charge diminishes. Otherwise, you can use a *voltmeter* while a load is applied.

Switches

Switches control the flow of electricity round a circuit. They can be mechanical, electrical, thermo, or based on time or proximity (for doors or panels). Switches are also often relays, or based around solenoids, both discussed later.

Mechanical switches can be operated by toggle (above).

Multiple switches can be lined up in a gang of several together, like these rocker switches:

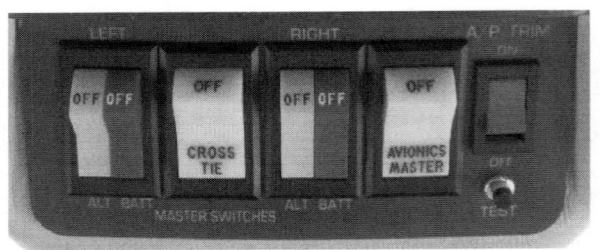

Switches can also be guarded to ensure that they are not switched off by mistake.

A button is also a (push-pull) switch. Buttons are used for short duration purposes only.

Magneto switches are often rotary switches.

Mercury switches are typically used inside electrical gyroscopic instruments.

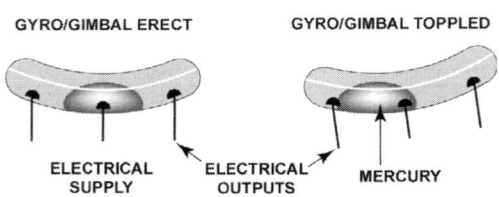

Magnetism

The study of magnetism is important because, without it, we would not have electricity.

Magnetism is an invisible force which is defined as the property of an object to attract certain metallic substances, mostly ferric (iron based).

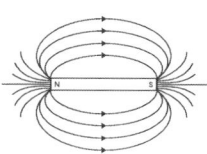

A magnet is therefore a ferrous substance, typically a soft iron bar, that has lines of magnetic force running through and around it in the shape of a *magnetic field* (the Earth is a magnet as well). The lines are called the *magnetic flux*, expressed by the Greek letter φ (phi). The *flux density* is the number of lines within a magnetic field, and the flux is stronger when the lines are closer together (at the ends). The picture on the left is often used to show what iron filings do in a magnetic field. It is assumed that the lines of force flow from the North to the South Poles.

Magnets can be permanent or temporary, whose magnetism is lost after the magnetising force is removed. However, there is always a small amount left, called *residual magnetism*, which is useful for getting generators and motors to work in the initial stages. Even when a material is permanently magnetised, it can only be driven back to zero by a field in the opposite direction. This is called *hysteresis*, and is used widely in the recording of information on disks or tape.

Lines of magnetic flux always form closed loops and behave like stretched elastic bands, in that they are always trying to shorten themselves. This property is made use of in electric motors to turn the moving parts. As an example, the lines of flux between the North and South poles in the bottom magnet below are as short as they can be. On the top one, however, where the two poles are the same, the flux lines are pushed out towards the sides and do not shorten.

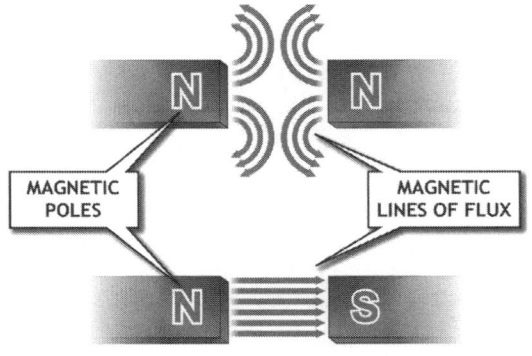

All magnets have a North and a South pole, and like poles will repel each other - unlike poles attract. If you therefore had a bar magnet, its South Pole (traditionally red) would point towards the Earth's (magnetic) North pole. This is what a compass is all about, discussed under *Instruments*. The thing to remember is that the South Pole is marked as North, because that's the end that points North.

Iron and steel (and nickel and cobalt, slightly) are the only elements to be attracted by a magnet, and which can be magnetised. In their non-magnetic states, the theory is that the molecules in such metals are arranged at random, and their poles cancel each other out. When stroked with another magnet, the molecules align with each other and their magnetic fields combine to create the magnet as a whole. Heat or rough treatment can destroy this effect.

Through *magnetic induction*, an unmagnetised iron bar held close to a permanent magnet will attract iron filings in its own right, without being permanently magnetised.

ELECTROMAGNETISM

When a current flows through a cable, there is a magnetic field associated with it, moving clockwise* if you look at it from the rear. An electromagnet is created when such a cable is wrapped round an iron bar, which becomes a magnet for as long as a current flows, although the iron bar doesn't actually have to be there, but the field from the coil without it is much weaker. An iron bar has a greater permeability than air, so it can concentrate the flux better.

*The movement of electrons creates the field - it is nothing to do with the conductor. Although the flux lines have a clockwise action, they do not actually rotate.

If a conductor, particularly soft iron, is moved within a magnetic field, or if a magnetic field is moved around a conductor, current can be made to flow in the conductor. This is called *electromagnetic induction* (from Faraday).

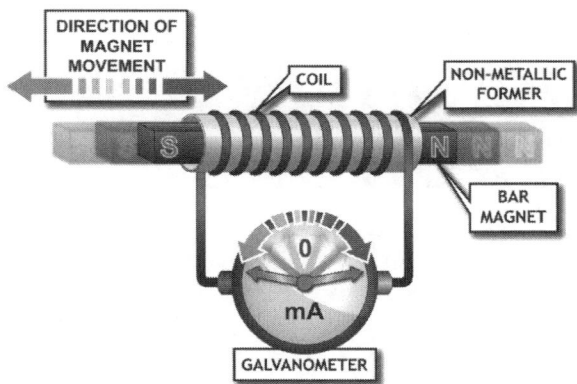

In the picture above, as the magnet moves, a current is induced in the coil and the needle moves according to which way the bar is moved.

The strength of the induced emf depends on the size of the magnetic field, the number of turns in the coil or the speed of movement of the bar.

A changing magnetic field (as produced by an alternating current) around a stationary conductor also produces an electric current in the conductor, with the size of the voltage proportional to the rate of change of the field.

Mutual induction occurs between two coils close enough to each other to have currents induced in them. In the picture below, because there is a current flowing through the bottom coil, there must be a magnetic field around it, which will interact with the other coil and induce a current into it. Mutual inductance is greatest when one coil is wound round the other, as found inside a magneto, and least when they are at right angles to each other.

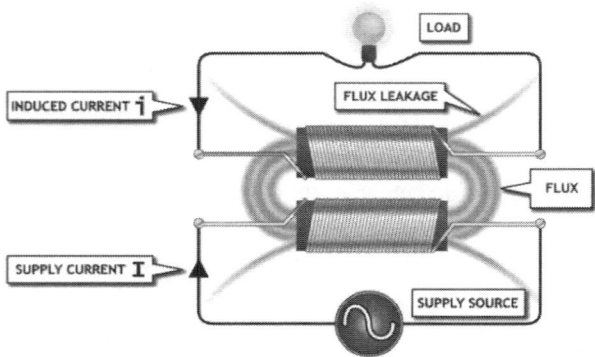

INDUCTANCE

An inductor is a coil (solenoid) of insulated wire, possibly wound over a ferrous metal former. The flow of current turns the coil into an electromagnet that will induce its own current in the opposite direction (sometimes called *back emf*). Inductance can oppose a change in current flow or induce a voltage when there is a change. All conductors have this property, but for best results you need a coil.

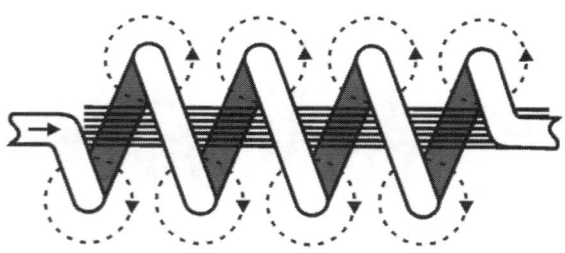

SOLENOID FIELD MERGING

To produce back emf, the magnetic field that is produced around the wire of which the coil is made cuts the next loop in line as it grows and spreads, and induces a current the other way, stopping the main current from rising too quickly. The separate fields merge to produce a magnetic field through and around the whole coil, resembling that of a bar magnet.

Inductance is the degree of this self-induction, and it can also happen between complete circuits that are near to each other (see *Transformers*). Note that there is no induction if the current is steady, so if DC is used, there will only be an effect as the switch is closed and opened, and the current rises and fall, hence the use of contact points in magnetos.

The effect obtained is that, when you first apply the current, the inductor appears to have a high resistance (that does not generate heat), which drops after the flow becomes constant, leaving you with the normal resistance you would find in any wire. In this respect, the inductor is the opposite of a capacitor. Practically, an inductor will slow down the rise and fall of current, and will behave like the flywheel in an engine.

This ability to "store" energy in a circuit is due to inertia, because the current is moving as it does its work (it is like kinetic energy). Thus, the circuit discharges quicker if you apply the brakes, or add resistance. A capacitor, on the other hand, stores energy electrostatically, as nothing is moving, so the discharge rate increases when you *release* the brakes, or remove resistance.

This is proportional to the rate at which the current changes, so when it collapses to zero very quickly, as when you use the contact breakers in a magneto, the back emf will be very large, and enough to jump across a gap.

In conjunction with capacitors, inductors can produce electrical resonance at particular frequencies, which is useful with radio.

The unit of inductance is the *Henry*, and its symbol is *L*.

TRANSFORMERS

Transformers can convert alternating current at one frequency and voltage to AC at the same frequency, but a different voltage. In this respect, they work like gears. They can be used for three purposes:

- Isolating parts of circuits from others, with a *one-to-one* transformer

- Raising or lowering voltages. A *step-up* transformer has more windings in the secondary coil and will increase voltage. A *step-down* is the opposite

- Matching impedances, particularly with headphones and amplifiers (both use coils and alternating current)

Transformers are a special application of inductance, commonly used in magnetos to boost voltage from 24-28v to whatever is needed to jump across the gap of a spark plug, but they have other uses, such as electrical isolation, because they are able to create electricity without any wires, as mentioned in *mutual induction*, above.

Transformers consist of electrically separate coils on a common laminated iron core which are *magnetically coupled* when an induced emf is created in one (the *secondary*) by a change of current in the other (the *primary*).

That is, an alternating current (or fluctuating DC) in the primary coil sets up an alternating magnetic flux. Self-induction in the primary creates an opposite voltage that is nearly the same as the original. The difference between the two is just enough to set up an alternating magnetic flux in the core. Mutual induction then allows a voltage to be established in the secondary (a load on the secondary reduces the opposition current in the primary).

In this way, we can get an electrical current without moving conductors and magnetic fields around each other, as you would have to with a generator or alternator.

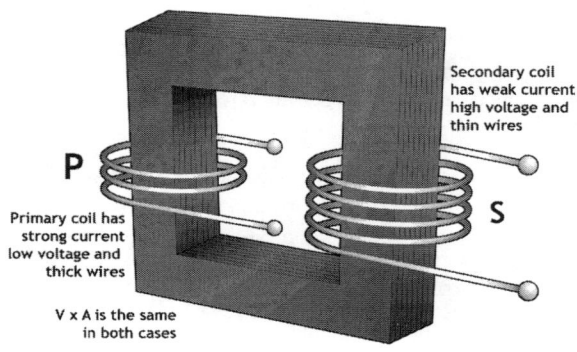

Secondary coil has weak current high voltage and thin wires

P

Primary coil has strong current low voltage and thick wires

S

V x A is the same in both cases

The voltage induced depends on the relative number of turns between the windings, or the *turns ratio*. For example, a transformer with 1000 turns on the primary coil and 500 on the secondary will have a turns ratio of 2:1 and an output voltage that is half of the input, but Ohm's Law says that there will be more current, so the secondary windings will have to be thicker.

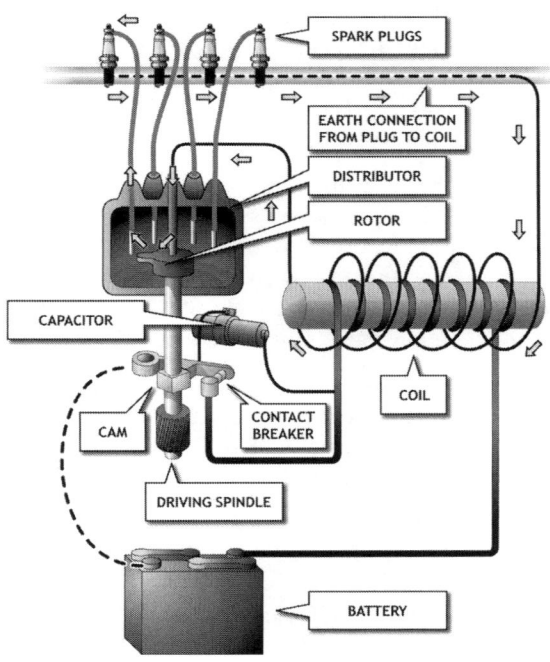

SPARK PLUGS

EARTH CONNECTION FROM PLUG TO COIL

DISTRIBUTOR

ROTOR

COIL

CAPACITOR

CAM

CONTACT BREAKER

DRIVING SPINDLE

BATTERY

IGNITION CIRCUITS

The above principles are made use of in ignition circuits, where the current generated from a battery (in a car, as shown below) or a rotating magnet is fed into a primary coil, which is wrapped within a secondary one, to make a transformer. The supply to the primary coil is interrupted by contact breakers when a spark is required.

Because the second coil is larger, it produces an emf large enough to jump the gap of the spark plug to ignite the fuel. However, although the voltage might be large (in the order of 15 000 volts), the current is reduced to keep the outgoing amount of energy the same as what went in.

THE SOLENOID

The word *Solenoid* actually refers to a coil of insulated wire, but as they are often wrapped around a moveable metal core, thus creating an electromagnet, its common usage means a *solenoid switch*, or *solenoid valve*, such as those used to operate starter motors, or valves that switch fluid around a hydraulic system. A speaker uses a solenoid.

When electricity is passed through the coil, a magnetic field is created, and the core is drawn in to the centre, which movement can be used to do work. Thus, a solenoid could be defined as a device that turns energy into linear motion, typically used as a remote switch, that might be used to operate a starter, for example, because a starter draws so much current that a normal switch would burn out. The cockpit starter switch therefore operates a relay which triggers a solenoid (which can handle the current) and which operates the machinery concerned. As well, you don't need to lay large cables everywhere - you only need them thick enough to operate the solenoid. In this way, a small switch can start a large reaction in a remote location. The core is pulled back against a spring, so when power is switched off and the magnetic field collapses, it returns to its original position.

Some aircraft use switches in the cockpit to operate a solenoid that controls the hydraulic system. They are held on by the solenoid as long as current flows. When it stops, the switches revert to the off position.

THE RELAY

This does a similar job to a solenoid, but it is used for low-current switching or interruption of electrical current, typically used with a voltage regulator. Relays were among the first electrical components to be used for amplification and were widely used in telegraph networks.

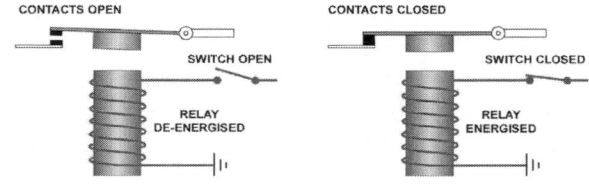

CONTACTS OPEN

CONTACTS CLOSED

SWITCH OPEN

SWITCH CLOSED

RELAY DE-ENERGISED

RELAY ENERGISED

A relay consists of an electromagnet with a non-moveable soft iron core that does not retain magnetism easily. The force produced by the electromagnet moves switching contacts back and forth, either automatically or manually.

Direct Current

As previously mentioned, this is current that flows in one direction only. It can be produced in many ways, but aviators are concerned with electromagnetism and chemical action (see *Batteries*).

THE GENERATOR

The electrical equipment on an aircraft may only be run by the battery for a short while, otherwise you would have to keep stopping to recharge it. Long term, the power must come from the aircraft itself, using a self-contained generating device. For DC systems, this is a generator, or dynamo - for AC, an alternator, although the term *AC generator* is used instead. The battery's function is really for short-term storage and to act as a reservoir when the generator's output fluctuates.

Generators use magnetism to create DC. Faraday found that the magnetic field had to be *changing* to induce a current in a nearby circuit. A simple generator exists when a coil of wire (i.e. a conductor) is spun between the poles of a magnet to induce a current in the loop.

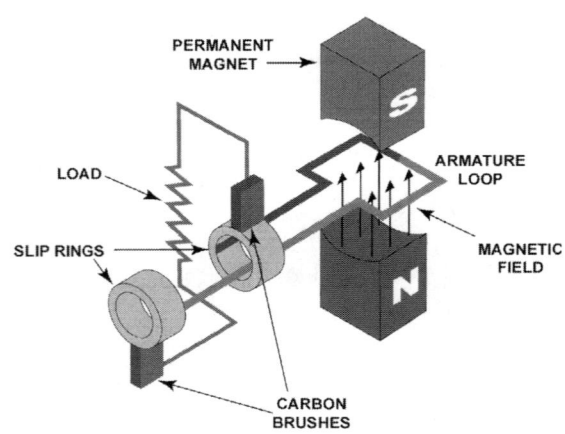

The magnet can be permanent*, or an electromagnet formed from battery current or the generator's own, of which more in a moment. The current so generated is actually AC, and can be converted to DC with a *rectifier* or by mechanical means at source, in which case the ends of the rotating coil are attached to a *commutator*. To produce a current in the first place, the generator does not need any help from the battery (as the alternator does) because there is residual magnetism in the field winding poles.

Note: The blue and red blocks in the diagram above are magnetic poles.

The generator is constructed as shown below.

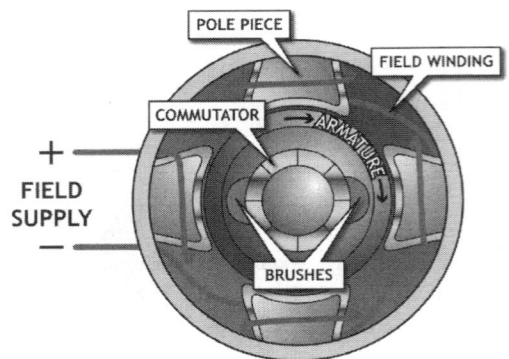

The major parts are a field frame (or yoke), a rotating armature (which includes the commutator, described below) and a brush assembly.

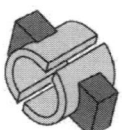

The commutator is really an adapted pair of the slip rings used in an alternator, combined and split into two halves which are placed opposite and insulated from each other, each being attached to one end of the rotating loop through *brushes*, so called because the original designs used copper ones as contacts, but which have now been replaced by spring-loaded carbon blocks which simply wear out and are replaced from time to time. Thus, a commutator is a *mechanical means of periodically reversing current*, or an automatically reversing switch, which is ideal for converting the AC from the loop into DC, otherwise the current would keep reversing. As the rotor spins, the brushes contact each segment in turn, just as the current flow stops and is about to go in the other direction (actually twice per cycle). In this way, the polarity of the brushes remains constant, as does that of the commutator, and DC voltage is produced.

However, the supply in the simple generator is a series of positive pulses, which can be quite jerky (called *commutator ripple*), which can be minimised with more loops and connections, or more poles through which the coil(s) can rotate. Complex generators have several commutators to ensure a smooth output and a constant supply.

Problem 1 is that the generator is driven by an engine, which will run at different speeds, so the next step is to vary the field current in sympathy with the engine to try to keep the voltage constant (see *Voltage Regulation*, overleaf).

When the field current is taken from the generator itself, it is *self-excited*. It can also be provided through the Master Switch, although this facility is normally associated with an AC generator, which must have a battery on the bus bar as it cannot self-excite.

*Any small generator using a permanent magnet is commonly called a magneto.

VOLTAGE REGULATION

The voltage from a DC generator is controlled by regulating its field current, because you can't change its speed independently or the number of wires in the coil. The output line of the generator or alternator is sensed, and the regulator tries to maintain it at a constant value.

If an overvoltage occurs, for example, the regulator will change the resistance of the field circuit to lower the output voltage from the generator. In this case, the voltage regulator acts as a variable resistor between the external field connection and the ground. If the alternator output is low, it will increase the field strength.

A reverse current relay between the generator and the bus stops the battery discharging through the generator, putting the generator online again as soon as its voltage rises above that of the battery.

DC MOTORS

These are essentially the reverse of DC generators - note the resemblance in the picture below. As before, the field winding is carried around the inside of the casing, around pole pieces. The armature, which is magnetised and revolves inside, has a commutator, to which brushes are pressed. A simple motor with a single armature coil would be impractical, because it will have neutral current positions and a pulsating torque, so a large number of coils is used instead, and the commutator is split into a corresponding number of pieces.

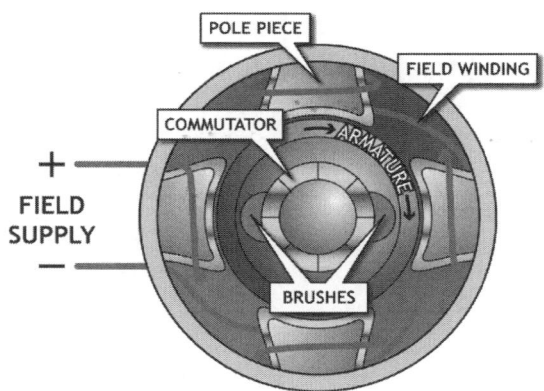

The commutator plays a very important part in the operation of a DC motor because it causes the current going through the loop to reverse just when unlike poles are facing each other, which causes a reversal in the polarity of the field, so that repulsion exists instead of attraction and the loop carries on rotating.

Since every current has an associated magnetic field, the one produced in the field winding as it is energised is repelled by the field already on the armature and the motor starts to spin. As mentioned previously, lines of magnetic flux behave like elastic bands, in that, when they are displaced, the tendency is to push back and create a force which starts the movement.

Just as the generator has a reverse motor effect, the DC motor can behave like a generator. This leads to a self-adjusting characteristic, in that, as the load is increased, the motor will start to slow down.

STARTER/GENERATORS

These units combine two functions, those of a generator and a DC motor, which saves both weight and space. The DC motor function is used to start the engine, then the unit is switched over to be a generator at a predetermined speed, after a short wait (say 1 minute), to allow the system to stabilise and the battery to recover before it receives a charge. A *changeover relay* is used for the process.

Alternating Current

Most modern aircraft (large ones, at least) now use AC as their primary power source, employing a transformer-rectifier unit (T-R unit) to get any DC they require (there are no AC batteries, so you still need DC for backup systems!) AC is typically used for flight instruments and fuel quantity systems, and its advantages include:

- **Better performance** from AC generators (more amps per unit weight), which are also brushless, so there is less wear and fire risk. An AC generator can be even smaller (and lighter)

- **Ease of converting** voltage and current, either to different values (with transformers) or rectification between AC & DC

- **Lighter cabling**. There is a point beyond which the size and weight of DC components become a disadvantage, as well as the power loss you get when transmitting electricity over longer cable runs. For example, with DC, you would have to have a high starting voltage to get only a relatively small one at the other end, even between the nose of an aircraft (where many batteries are installed) and the engine starter motor.

As an example, if you transmitted 250 volts of DC over a cable with a resistance of 1 ohm, the current would be 80 amps, if the generator had a capacity of 20 KW. This gives a voltage drop over the cable of 80 volts, so the receiving end only gets 170. The power loss would be in the order of 6400 watts (20 000 - (170 x 80). If you raise the voltage to 10,000, the generator would only need to produce 2 amps of current. Ohm's Law now gives a voltage drop of 2 volts and a power loss of only 4 watts.

The problem is that DC cannot be stepped up and down readily. AC, however, can, with *transformers*, described previously, which don't work with DC because the current is not changing.

Aside from the lack of batteries, about the only disadvantage is that AC requires frequency control*.

Alternating Current is electricity that continually reverses its polarity (and direction), and magnitude. That is, while the "positive" wire is negative, the "negative" wire is positive, and so on, alternating between the two. Because of the potential for confusion, in AC circuits the positive wire is called *live*, and the negative wire is called *neutral*.

As a result, the free electrons don't actually move very far because they simply move back and forth. With AC, moving half a coulomb back and forth produces the same current (1 amp) as moving 1 coulomb in one direction for the same distance. The essential point is *movement*, and many devices, such as light bulbs, only care that electrons move, and not which way they move, in order to work.

Changing the connections to a battery very quickly from one terminal to the other would achieve the same effect, but the results would be jerky, and the waves virtually square, because there would be a near 90° rise when on, and a near 90° drop when off. In contrast, transitions from an alternator are smooth and like *sine waves*, as shown below (AC current is assumed to be in the form of a sine wave unless otherwise stated).

*A *cycle* is a complete transition from zero through a peak, down to a trough and back up to zero, so the more cycles you can fit into a particular time scale (the higher the frequency), the shorter the length of the wave is.

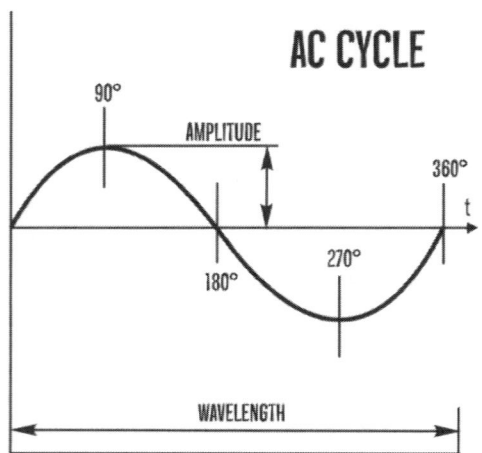

One cycle per second is called 1 Hertz (Hz).

The difference between the peak (or crest) and the base line of a wave is the *amplitude* (or, loosely, volume).

POWER CONVERSION

DC FROM AC (RECTIFIERS)

AC is used when it comes to generating large amounts of power, but most radio and computer equipment uses DC, and 12v at that. That part of the problem is easy - a transformer can be used to step the voltage down (or up) as required. Then a *rectifier* is used to convert the AC into DC by extracting the peaks from the AC waveform.

AC FROM DC

Inverters produce AC from DC supplies. This might be because an older aircraft using DC has new equipment fitted that requires AC.

THE ALTERNATOR

Aside from using an inverter to create AC, you can use an alternator, or an AC generator. These are similar in construction to DC generators, but use *slip rings* instead of commutators, so the current reversals are not modified, and radio interference is less. Each end of the rotating loop connects to a separate ring.

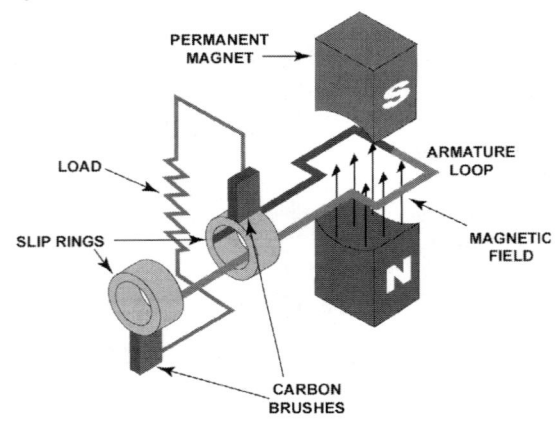

ENGINES

••

An engine is a device for converting the stored energy of fuel into useful work. In a steam engine, for example, the fuel is burnt in a separate furnace, which boils water and produces steam to drive the pistons. It is therefore known as an external combustion engine. In an internal combustion engine, the fuel is burnt in a confined space, and the increase in temperature produces an increase in pressure which is used to operate the engine, thus converting chemical energy into heat energy, and then into mechanical energy (the mechanical energy may drive electrical, hydraulic and pneumatic systems as well, which is why engines are also called *powerplants*).

In doing this, air is sucked in, mixed with fuel, compressed, set on fire and slung out (*suck, push, bang, blow* for short or, more technically, *induction, compression, power* and *exhaust*). Piston and jet engines use more or less the same sequence of events, but the difference is that the power comes from the ignition stage in the piston, and the exhaust stage in the turbine, which is always ignited. The piston only ignites when the spark plugs operate (the turbine is also lighter, and spins a lot faster).

Aside from the engine itself, there are a few subsystems:

• Cooling

• Lubrication

• Ignition

• Fuel supply and carburation, which mixes the fuel with the air, ready to be burnt

Engine Power

Power from an engine driving rotor blades is measured in *horsepower*, which has a standard value of 33,000 ft/lbs per minute, or 550 per second.

When you lift a weight, you work against gravity and the power you need depends on the weight of the item concerned and how high you raise it. So, if you lift 10 lbs over 55 feet, or 55 lbs over 10 feet, you require 550 ft-lbs, the product of weight multiplied by distance. However, the horsepower is a measure of *the rate of doing work*, so time is a factor. That 550 ft-lbs must be used within 1 second to qualify as a horsepower.

• The raw power developed inside the cylinders is **indicated horsepower**

• **Friction horsepower** means accumulated losses

• **Brake horsepower** is indicated power minus friction horsepower (a prony brake places a known resistance against the engine's motion)

Piston engines use brake horsepower.

If this page is a photocopy, it is not authorised!

EFFICIENCY

Mechanical efficiency is the ratio of brake to indicated horsepower, or power output to input. You can expect about 80% from a piston engine from friction and pumping losses. **Volumetric efficiency** is covered later.

Thermal efficiency is the ratio of useful work to the heat put in, expressed as a percentage. The first law of thermodynamics states that energy may be changed from one form to another, but cannot be destroyed.

However, the second law says (more or less) that: *Heat flows from a hot substance to a cold one unaided, but energy from an external source is needed for it to flow the other way.* That is, you might be able to convert most of your work into heat, but turning heat into work will incur serious losses, which is another way of saying that engines are grossly inefficient - if it were otherwise, exhausts would be cold!

In fact, engines waste as much energy in heat as the power they produce - the approximate thermal efficiency of a 4-stroke engine is 33% (0.33). About 40% is lost through the exhaust gases, and another large chunk is lost through the cooling mechanism (although allowing the engine to run hotter will stop some of this loss, the lubricating oil and other parts need to be kept within certain temperature limits to do their work properly). In addition, not all the fuel is burnt properly in the first place.

Reciprocating Engines

A typical piston engine consists of a series of identical cylinders which can be arranged in many ways, according to what the engine is going to be used for. The difference between engines designed for cars and those designed for aircraft is mainly the power to weight ratio, or the power delivered relative to their size. Aircraft engines undergo much more in terms of development to ensure that the materials are just strong enough for the job, having due regard for safety and reliability.

Aircraft engines also have more cylinders, which reduces vibration and allows for smooth operation, an important factor if the aircraft itself is lightly built. Having more than four cylinders means that you don't need a flywheel*, which saves further weight, but this also means that if the engine stops you need a propeller to keep it going. This is one reason why helicopter engines are set to run a little higher, typically 3000 RPM, or 1700 at idle.

*The flywheel is a large heavy disc designed to keep the engine turning through those cycles where energy is not produced, as only one stroke out of four per cylinder produces any.

Another difference is that aircraft engines are built to run continuously at 60-75% power, or more when taking off. A car engine typically uses only 15% of its maximum power even on the motorway, and very rarely tops more than 80%. In addition, car engines produce their

maximum power at high RPM, whereas a helicopter engine would do this between 2500-3000 RPM. That is, they are designed to run slower (to reduce internal stresses) and are made of sturdier construction, so the chances of mechanical failure are minimised. Because they have to run within a narrow speed band, helicopter engines are subject to higher power settings than aeroplanes are, particularly when taking off or landing.

A helicopter engine may also be placed vertically, which requires a dry sump lubrication system. It will also be outside the regular airflow, so it will need special cooling arrangements as the downwash by itself is not enough.

On top of all that, an aircraft engine is expected to work at high altitudes (in low temperatures), which will require some form of adjustable mixture control.

The most common piston engine used in modern aircraft is the four-stroke petrol, with an even number of cylinders (typically 4 or 6) arranged opposite each other, to cancel some opposing forces out:

Photo: Lycoming Horizontally Opposed Engine

The *cylinder* in which the piston slides up and down is just that, being a large hole drilled in the engine casing and lined with steel for increased wear resistance, but it is closed at the top end by the valves (one for the *inlet* and one for the *exhaust*), to provide an airtight seal. Inside are also two spark plugs, and a *piston*, which slides up and down to provide an action like a pump, since it pulls air and fuel in, and pushes the burnt exhaust gases out.

As the piston is meant to be gastight, and no fit is perfect, there are two or three metal rings round it (the *scraper* ring at the bottom is for cleaning) to mate against the cylinder wall and stop movement of anything from one side of the sealed portion to the other because, on the one hand, the engine will not produce full power if the burnt gases leak out and, on the other, oil will get through to the head from the lubrication system, mix with the fuel and air and cause a lot of bluish grey smoke (if you are getting mysterious oil

leaks from your car, and everything seems to be done up underneath, check your piston rings, as they may be allowing pressurised gases through to the sump to force the oil out). The piston is very slightly tapered towards the top, so its sides will be parallel with the cylinder walls when it gets hot. In this respect, the piston's crown and skirt do not have the benefit of the cooling that the cylinder wall gets from the system is in use, so heat can only escape from the piston to the cylinder wall through the intervening film of oil, or the air inside the crankcase.

Picture: Inside a typical 4-stroke engine

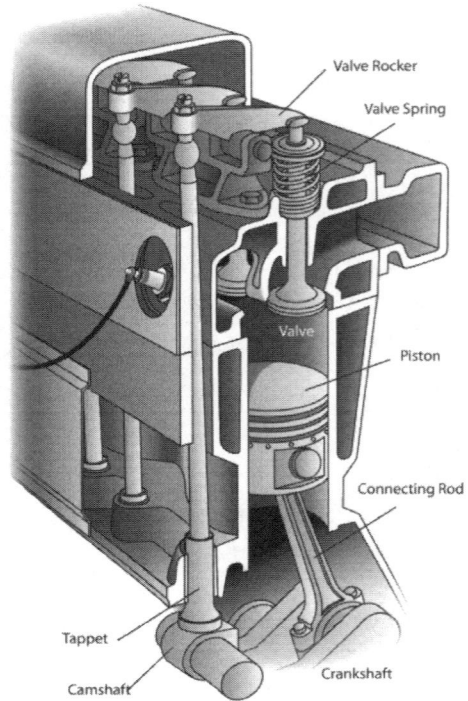

The piston is attached by its big end to the *crankpin* on the *crankshaft,* via the *connecting rod* (or conrod, for short), which goes to the *small end* at the top (if either end goes, the engine will suddenly start clattering loudly). The piston is attached to the small end with a *gudgeon pin.*

The conrod turns the back and forth (reciprocating) motion of the piston into the rotary motion at the crankshaft, which is not straight, but is offset for each piston connected to it, one after the other.

There will be one throw for each piston, so a six cylinder engine will have six. Each throw has two webs and a crank pin to which the big end of the piston is connected.

Throws are separated by journals, which are placed into *main bearings*, in which they rotate. As there is a main journal at each end, there is usually one more journal than there are throws. The stroke of a piston engine is equal to twice the crank throw.

CAPT

The crankshaft rotates clockwise (from the front) as the piston is pushed downwards to the lowest point of its travel, where the centres of the gudgeon pin, crank pin and crankshaft will all be in a straight line (the crank pin will be directly under the centre of the crankshaft). As any pressure from the piston will have no turning effect on the crankshaft, this position is called a *dead centre*, in this case the Bottom Dead Centre, or BDC). The Top Dead Centre (TDC) exists at the other extreme of the piston's travel. The TDC is an important factor in the timing of the spark that ignites the fuel/air mixture, mentioned later.

Movement of the piston from one dead centre to another is known as the *stroke*, and there are two strokes of the piston to every revolution of the crankshaft. A *short stroke* engine (i.e. most aircraft engines) allows lighter construction and reduces vibration.

THE 4-STROKE (OTTO) CYCLE

In simple terms, pressure is introduced on the upper surface of the piston by burning a mixture of fuel and air in the confined space at the top of the cylinder. One complete stroke of the piston is used for each of the operations involved, namely *induction, compression, power* and *exhaust*. The problem is that, if you have only one cylinder, the power stroke is the only one that does any useful work - the other three simply wear the engine out. It makes sense, therefore to have more than one cylinder, at least four, so that you get a power stroke somewhere in the engine for each cycle. With six cylinders, some power strokes will overlap, but the power stroke is not used for the full run of the piston anyway. The overlap also helps remove the need for a flywheel, which saves weight.

It all starts with the piston at *Top Dead Centre* (TDC), ready to start moving down to decrease the pressure in the cylinder, and suck in a fuel/air mixture from the carburettor, through the inlet valve, which has just opened (left, below). Atmospheric pressure also helps to force the fuel and air in.

Left: Induction **Right:** Compression

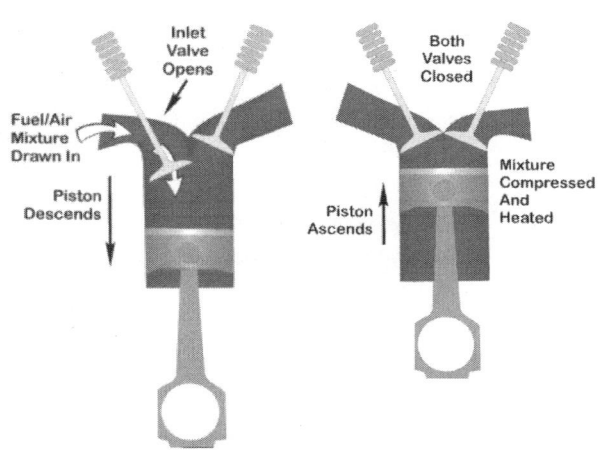

The valve closes as the piston reaches Bottom Dead Centre (BDC), so the chamber is filled to maximum. With both valves closed, the piston starts moving up again (right, above), compressing and therefore heating the mix, as well as increasing its density, which helps the flame ignite quicker because the particles are closer together (the heating helps to increase the pressure).

Note: The weight of charge remains the same.

For a very short period the volume remains relatively constant while the spark plug fires and causes the pressure and temperature to increase rapidly as the fuel ignites.

Left: Power **Right:** Exhaust

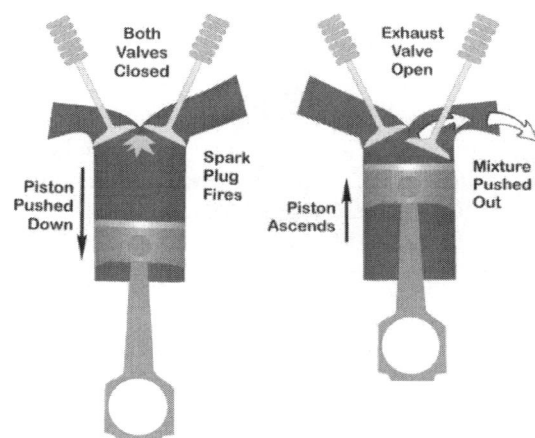

The spark plug actually fires just before TDC, with a spark from a high-voltage electric current provided by the magneto, which is rotating in sympathy with the engine. It is timed this way to give the fuel time to catch fire, and produce the optimum expansion at 10° *after* TDC, which is when it is actually required. Under power (i.e. at high speeds) the spark can occur as much as 30° beforehand (when idling, it is more like 10°).

The ignited gases expand adiabatically, and the temperature drops because the volume increases as the piston is forced downwards, in a smooth movement, making the crankshaft rotate, plus whatever is attached to it (left, above). Then the crankshaft's rotation, assisted by a flywheel, if there is one, forces the piston up again with the exhaust valve open to let the burnt gases escape.

Note: Although there were four cycles, the crankshaft only went round twice (and the camshaft once). Valves open and close once each for every two revolutions of the crankshaft. At 2400 RPM, that's 20 times a second.

V_1 (TDC) represents the space above the piston at the top of its stroke (the clearance volume).

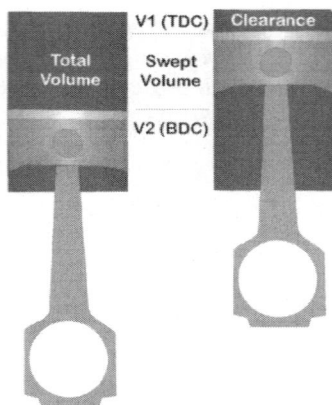

V_2 (BDC) is the volume enclosed when it is at the bottom. V_2 minus V_1 is the *swept volume*. The ratio of V_2 over V_1 is the *compression ratio*, which is an expression of the number of times the volume above the piston *before* compression is greater than that *after* compression, or the big space divided by the small space. The *total volume* above the piston at V_2 is the clearance volume plus the *swept volume*.

The induction stroke takes place at A. In theory, the pressure should be the same as atmospheric, but it's actually lower. The compression stroke occurs from A to B, where both valves are closed. The compression is adiabatic, and no heat enters or leaves the cylinder.

Ignition occurs at C, where the gases resulting from the ignition expand adiabatically, leading to the power stroke.

From D to A, the gas is cooled instantaneously.

At A, the exhaust stroke occurs and the gases are removed at constant pressure to the atmosphere.

Note that the Otto cycle takes place very quickly, so the gases will swirl. There are also considerable temperature gradients, so the gas cannot be treated as if it had constant temperature. As well, ignition takes a finite time, and takes time to propagate through the fuel-air mixture, so pressures will vary within the gas.

DIESEL ENGINES

Formerly known as *compression ignition* engines (Rudolf Diesel patented one in 1892), these engines do not require spark plugs or carburation - instead, fuel is injected at high pressure (so you need a strong pump) just as the temperature increases at the end of the compression stroke, which means that the induction stroke only pulls in air, and only air is compressed.

The original idea was to operate the engine at constant pressure, but this is difficult, so part of the fuel is burnt at constant volume, as with the Otto cycle, and the rest at constant pressure.

The diesel engine has a higher thermal efficiency than the petrol engine, but it is noisier, heavier, and bigger for a given power. Incomplete combustion also makes for considerable pollution.

COMPRESSION RATIO

The space between the crown (top) of the piston and the cylinder head, into which the fuel/air mixture is pulled and later compressed, is also called the *combustion chamber*, which naturally gets larger and smaller as the piston goes up and down. Piston crowns are generally concave, but they may be convex if you intend to reduce the size of the combustion chamber to produce more power.

More power is obtained with a higher compression ratio because the compression pressure is higher - as the mixture ignites, the pressure rises to about four times its previous value, which naturally, up to a point*, increases the Mean Effective Pressure. At higher compression ratios, temperature increases at a slower rate than pressure, so at pressure ratios of say, 16:1, the small temperature gain is lost in the inefficiencies introduced by the rise in pressure. 16:1 is good for diesel engines - petrol engines must have a typical ratio of 8:1 (with 100 octane fuel) because the heat from compression would cause pre-ignition, described above.

*There is a limit to the compression ratio, because the fuel/air mix ignites too early, and you get detonation.

In a reciprocating engine, to measure the power exerted on the pistons (indicated horsepower), you need to know the pressure acting on them, the cylinder dimensions, and the RPM of the crankshaft (the time element).

VOLUMETRIC EFFICIENCY

Whatever power you get from an engine ultimately depends on how much fuel (and air) mixture you can cram into the cylinders. Volumetric efficiency is the measure of how much mass charge *is* pulled in against what *could* be taken in, in standard conditions, or how well the engine can breathe (if you restrict its air supply it will not work so well). It is typically about 75% for an unsupercharged engine, due to various leakages and losses, or even the nature of the passages through which the mixture has to pass*, hence the need for supercharging. However, it will improve with increased atmospheric pressure (i.e. flying in denser air) or compression ratio.

*The bigger the valve openings and the smoother the passages, the less lag there will be from the gases (this inertia is the reason why valves are made to open and close early, as explained elsewhere). In addition, if the mixture is too hot at the inlet valve, or the scavenging is poor, you will not get a full charge.

© Phil Croucher, 2013

VALVES & TIMING

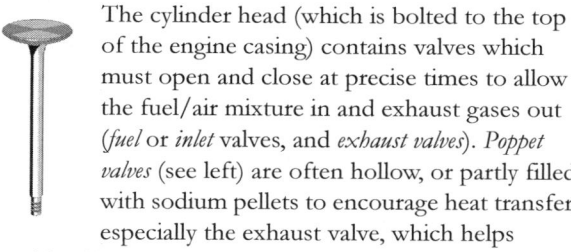

The cylinder head (which is bolted to the top of the engine casing) contains valves which must open and close at precise times to allow the fuel/air mixture in and exhaust gases out (*fuel* or *inlet* valves, and *exhaust valves*). *Poppet valves* (see left) are often hollow, or partly filled with sodium pellets to encourage heat transfer, especially the exhaust valve, which helps considerably with minimising pre-ignition. They will be made of a steel tough enough to take the hammering as they open and close, and the extreme temperatures.

Valves have two springs around the shaft to return them to their original positions - the second reduces *valve bounce*.

As it turns, the crankshaft will turn a smaller version of itself, called a *camshaft*, which rotates at *half the crankshaft speed* (i.e. once per cycle), and is linked directly to the valve rocker at the top of the cylinder by a long metal rod, the bottom end of which is enclosed in a *tappet* (to save wear). The top end of the rod hits the valve rocker directly, pushing the valve open. As the engine gets hotter, these rods expand, so there is a little clearance to allow for this, called the *valve rocker clearance* (valve rockers are *not* tappets). If the valve rocker clearance is too large, the valve will not open so much, which will reduce volumetric efficiency. If the gap is too small, there will be loss of compression because the valves won't close properly. Hydraulic tappets take up the slack automatically so you don't have to keep adjusting the valve rocker clearance.

Valve design is actually very important for efficiency. If the inlet valve is too small, or it doesn't lift high enough, volumetric efficiency is reduced. Its position is also important, because you need some turbulence inside the cylinder to spread the flame more rapidly. For this reason, there should be no obstructions to the flow of gases after they have passed through the inlet valve. Too small an exhaust valve stops the burnt gases escaping quickly and creates a back pressure that heats the engine up.

Note: A *hydraulic lock* (hydraulicing) occurs when there is some liquid in the cylinder when you start up that is equal to, or greater than the swept volume, and which stops the piston moving during the compression stroke, when both valves are closed. Damage (usually a broken connecting rod) occurs once the preceding cylinders have fired since the piston is forced against the liquid, which is incompressible. In a radial engine, the fluid is likely to be oil, in the bottom cylinder. In a horizontally opposed engine, however, the liquid is more likely to be accumulated fuel, in one of the forward cylinders. Be careful when operating the fuel boost pump during a failed start, and do not over-prime on sloping ground.

In theory, the fuel/air mixture should enter the cylinder during the piston's travel from TDC to BDC (top to bottom), with the exhaust gases leaving it between BDC to TDC, but things are not quite as simple as that! In practice, a small part of the piston's up and down movement is immaterial relative to the work done - this is called *ineffective crank angle*. In other words, it is a short period where the valves may as well be open as not.

As an engine is complicated, with a lot happening in a short time, some anticipation here and there doesn't go amiss. Opening valves early (in the *modified* Otto Cycle) is called *valve lead*, and being late is called *valve lag*. When they are both open at the same time, you get *valve overlap*, where the exhaust gases on their way out reduce the pressure in the manifold, which helps to pull in the incoming fuel/air mix (this is more effective at altitude, where the atmospheric pressure is lower).

Valve overlap also promotes easier valve timing. Opening the inlet valve early means it is fully open as the induction stroke starts, which overcomes the fuel/air mix's inertia, so there is no time lag between the piston moving down and the mix actually moving. Its momentum when the piston finally stops at BDC means that as much of the mix as possible is crammed in and the valve closes *after* BDC to make sure. At the end of the power stroke, as its force weakens, you may as well open the exhaust valve early so that the remaining internal pressure can force the gases out early. It closes late to use of the gas's momentum.

ADVANCING & RETARDING

The engine is spinning relatively slowly in the initial stages, something like 120 RPM, which means that the magneto is spinning at 60 RPM. Unfortunately, it needs to spin faster at around 200 RPM to produce a proper spark. In addition, the spark would occur too early, since, at normal RPM, it typically occurs about 25° before TDC. If the piston is pushed down too early, it might try to turn the crankshaft in the wrong direction, resulting in a kick-back. We therefore need something to temporarily make the spark occur later in the cycle. An *impulse coupling* attached to the left magneto provides a high energy *retarded* spark during startup, as the engine is rotating very slowly at that point, and the spark needs to occur *later* than usual to ensure that the piston is beyond TDC as the gases start to burn and exert their pressure.

In the coupling, flyweights react against two stop-pins in the magneto housing as the engine (and magneto shaft) is turned over. The locked flyweights hold the magneto still whilst a spring is wound up until a certain amount of rotation has occurred, when projections on the housing release the flyweights. The spring unwinds and spins the magneto to produce the spark. Once the engine fires, a centrifugal clutch disconnects the mechanism and spring. The spark is produced normally with the engine rotation.

Ignition is automatically *advanced* as RPM increases, and *retarded* when starting up (the spark is intensified as well).

IGNITION

Near the end of the compression stroke, you need a spark with enough energy to ignite the fuel/air mixture in the cylinder **just before** Top Dead Centre (where the piston gets to the top of its stroke), because the burning fuel needs to build up to its maximum pressure. In early engines, any timing adjustments (advancing or retarding) were done by the pilot, but now they are done automatically. Magnetos have fixed timing, meaning that any settings must be a compromise, which is not the best for low or high RPM.

The whole mechanism that provides the spark at the critical moment consists of spark plugs, leads and magnetos, etc., in duplicate (one magneto will serve one plug per cylinder, and the second the other). The duplication is actually for efficiency, as the magneto doesn't work that well at low RPM, but a side benefit is, obviously, safety. Two sparks provide two flame fronts within the cylinder, which decreases the time needed for the complete fuel charge to start burning, so most of the fuel can be already burning at a lower temperature and pressure. In a cylinder with only one spark plug, lower octane portions of the fuel mixture far from the original flame front can explode, lighting off another flame front in a different part of the cylinder at a different time, leading to engine knock. Thus, two flame fronts can help to decrease the octane requirement for any given engine.

The magneto, which is actually a small generator that uses a permanent magnet, contains a transformer and all the circuitry needed to boost the low primary voltage (24-28 volts) to one large enough to jump across a small preset gap at the plug electrodes (around 20,000 v - this is dependent on the amount of turns in the secondary coil). A car has a similar system, but not all in one unit.

The magneto is a precision instrument. It needs to generate several hundred sparks per second, timed to occur at a precise instant on the compression stroke.

When doing power checks before takeoff, they are checked against each other for power and whether they actually are independent - there should be a discernible drop in RPM (around 100) when one magneto is switched off. If the RPM stays the same, they are interconnected somehow. When running up, set the magnetos to *Both* between testing each one singly to allow the engine to stabilise at the proper RPM and to burn off oil and fuel that may have accumulated on the plugs that have been switched off. Any rough running at this point usually indicates fouled plugs which are typically cleared by leaning the mixture for a while.

Note: The ignition switches in the cockpit, when selected OFF, ground the magnetos to Earth through the *primary circuit**. As any connection can fail, magnetos should always be regarded as being live as far as safety is

concerned. In normal operations, **magnetos will always work when the rotor inside is being spun**. They do not need any external influence or power.

*This means that, if one magneto fails, you will get a dead cut if you switch the other one off.

The magneto uses *magnetic induction*, which requires that a conductor (or a wire) moves in a magnetic flux, or a magnetic flux moves past a conductor, whichever is convenient. In this way, current flow is induced in the conductor, if it is part of a complete circuit. It does not matter whether the flux field is developing or collapsing; the induction effect is the same. If the conductor is part of a coil, the induced current can be used to step up the voltage, as would be done with a transformer.

The most efficient induction of current into the conductor is when the conductor moves at 90° to the plane of the flux field, where the conductor cuts more lines of flux per unit of distance travelled, as explained under *Electricity & Magnetism*. The ends of the magnet are concave to keep the coil as near perpendicular to the flux field as possible.

The components of a typical magneto consist of:

- a permanent magnet
- primary and secondary windings on a core.
- a way of making the magnet or the core move (by rotating either one)
- contact breaker points
- a capacitor
- a distributor

ROTATING ARMATURE

In a *rotating armature* magneto, a rotor (armature) rotates in the gap between two ends of a horseshoe-shaped permanent magnet. The rotor is actually an engine-driven shaft, which is surrounded by two sets of coils, a *primary* then a *secondary* winding. As the rotor spins, the conductor, which is the primary coil, moves within the flux field of the permanent magnet. This induces an alternating current into the coil and its associated circuit. The coil produces its own flux field which starts to build up.

The distributor rotor contacts a spark lead, which completes the secondary coil's circuit. At the right moment, the contact breaker opens, to break the primary circuit, whereupon the flux field of the primary coil collapses and induces a current in the secondary coil windings. The number of windings in the secondary coil, or the ratio of its windings to the primary, determines the voltage you get at this point, but it is in the order of 20 000 volts, so that it spark can jump across the spark plug gap and produce a spark that ignites the fuel/air mixture.

ROTATING MAGNET

For engines needing more powerful magnetos (maybe they have more than 4 or 6 cylinders), a rotating magnet is used. Here, the primary and secondary windings are around the horseshoe-shaped former, or core (in other words, they are stationary). The rotating shaft spins a permanent magnet, which has as many lobes as there are cylinders, so the core and primary windings (because they are nearby) have currents induced in them.

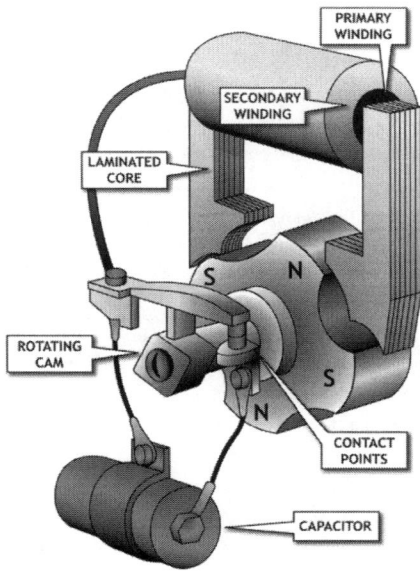

This arrangement makes the magneto more robust as you can use it at higher speeds without the coil breaking up from centrifugal forces. The alternating pulses create an alternating flux in the primary coil that produces current.

CONTACT BREAKER

A voltage is only generated in the secondary coil when the current through the primary is changing. With DC, you only get such changes when the circuit opens and closes.

Inside the primary circuit of both types of magneto is a set of contact points that do just that, making the flux reversals more abrupt when they open and close at critical moments. When the points are closed, current flows in the primary coil and a flux field builds up around it. When a spark is needed, the points open, and the field also collapses across the secondary, inducing a current which is fed to the spark plugs through the distributor.

The current created by the collapsing magnetic field is large enough to jump a small air gap, like the one between the just-opening points. This stops the magnetic field from collapsing quickly as the electrical activity continues until the points are far enough apart to stop it happening.

The points are opened by a *rocker arm*, which is moved by a cam as many times per revolution as there are lobes on the cam. The rocker arm returns to its normal position with a spring.

CAPACITOR (CONDENSER)

The more sudden the breaking of the primary circuit, the greater will be the voltage swing and the more current will be induced in the secondary coil. The purpose of the capacitor across the contact points is to help create a good strong spark at the plug, and it does this by absorbing the charge that would otherwise go across the points and slow down the collapse of the field. This is a *spark quench*.

When the capacitor discharges back into the primary, its collapsing field is more rapidly suppressed and a higher secondary output is produced.

In doing this, damage to the points from arcing and pitting is also prevented. Without the capacitor the spark only ceases when either the voltage drops or the points open enough to stop an arc forming, about ten times as long as it would otherwise take to stop.

The condenser and coil, when the points open, form a tuned circuit, which makes the current in the primary oscillate rapidly back and forth with a peak-to-peak voltage swing of about 400v, sustaining the spark for about 2 thousandths of a second (2mS), or several degrees of crankshaft revolution.

DISTRIBUTION

The high voltage generated is fed (from the secondary coil) to the plugs by a *distributor*, which is essentially a rotor spinning inside a cap at the end of the magneto holding heavy screened cables going to the plugs. The rotor contacts each cable in turn, but they are not matched to the plugs in order, as one cylinder would receive the spark at the wrong time. Instead, the cables are out of order, on a four-cylinder engine as 1342 or 1243).

Note: If the internal half-speed wheel that drives the distributor fails, you can expect extreme rough running because the sparks will be delivered to the plugs in the wrong order. The solution is to turn off the offending magneto, which will allow you to land without turning the engine off - include it in your engine failure checks. If one magneto does not work, the engine will run, but will not develop full power.

The leads to the spark plugs together form an *ignition harness*. They are shielded with braided wire to minimise radio interference (one reason for checking them on a preflight inspection).

ABNORMAL COMBUSTION

Note: Popping back is most likely to occur in a running piston engine at low RPM with a weak mixture.

DETONATION

In being compressed, the mixture gets warmer, making it more disposed to ignite when the spark plug fires. Unfortunately, some mixtures get so warm that they can ignite without the spark, which will not only increase the operating temperature unnecessarily, but cause harm to the engine from shock waves, because the piston gets the effects of the power stroke when it doesn't expect it (fuel is more explosive than dynamite).

Having said that, ignition normally happens just before Top Dead Centre, to allow the flame to build up. In other words, burning of the fuel/air mixture starts in the latter part of the compression stroke and carries through to the early part of the power stroke. The flame front is accelerated by using two spark plugs so that heat is released more rapidly and the pressure rise is quicker.

Where the last portion of the mixture burns almost instantaneously (i.e. too fast), rather than expanding smoothly, you get detonation. It is a product of the fuel characteristics and engine design, which will ultimately limit the compression ratio. It takes place *after* ignition has occurred, at high pressure and temperature in the unburnt part of the mixture ahead of the flame front, where many isolated areas of ignition may exist at the same time. Although it is similar to pre-ignition, mentioned below, the two are intertwined and detonation can occur at any time.

Detonation is otherwise known as *pinking*, because it sounds like that. You will hear it in your car if you make it work too hard (try going uphill in high gear). It can cause the temperatures inside the cylinder head to rise to the melting point of the components inside, with the piston usually going first. The hot gases will leak past the piston rings, pressurise the crankcase and blow the oil out. Net result: seized engine and holes in pistons. Open the wallet!

Detonation can be caused by:

- using low grade fuel
- too lean a mixture
- too high a manifold pressure
- an overheated engine

When detonation is recognised (through rough running, high cylinder head temperatures, or loss of power), you should *reduce manifold pressure* or *richen the mixture,* or cool the engine (or even increase engine RPM). The long-term cure is to use fuel with a higher octane rating.

PRE-IGNITION

Ignition of the charge by hotspots in the combustion chamber is called *surface ignition*. It is also called *pre-ignition* when it happens *before* the charge is supposed to be ignited by the spark plug. Put another way, the piston receives a "hammer blow" on its way up the compression stroke, i.e. early, rather than when it is going down on the power stroke. Gases may leave the combustion chamber while still burning, producing local hotspots and detonation.

Thus, pre-ignition is a product of overheating, especially where the mixture has been leaned too much (meaning that the engine is not being cooled adequately), and deposits inside the combustion chamber that are glowing bright red (more from misuse of the throttle than the mixture control, as when increasing power without adjusting the mixture). This is why engines sometimes won't stop (this is called *dieselling)*.

Pre-ignition tends to affect only one or two cylinders.

OCTANE RATINGS

Because of the above problems, piston engines use fuel with an *anti-knock additive*, which used to be lead, to ensure that fuel ignites smoothly, and doesn't explode, and to stop it igniting before it's meant to. In the days before carburettors, fuel was much more volatile, and could be ignited ten feet away. Lead, of course, is no longer politically correct so, in cars, at least, the timing of engines is adjusted to produce the same effect with unleaded fuel.

The aviation industry still uses it, though. The "LL" in 100LL stands for *low lead*, but there is still about four times more than is needed. As well as the lead (as TEL - *Tetra-Ethyl Lead*), a scavenging agent (*Ethylene DiBromide*, or EDB) is added to ensure that the lead is vapourised as far as possible, ready to be expelled from the cylinder with other gases, otherwise the lead deposits would stick to the insides. This is not 100% successful, but the results are best at high temperatures and worst at low ones - the unwanted extras result in fouling of spark plugs, heavy deposits in the combustion chamber, erosion of valve seats and stems, sticking valves and piston rings and general accumulation of sludge and restriction of flow through fine oil passages, so it makes you wonder which is worse (in fact, petrol is not the only fuel you can use - Japanese Zeros used to outfly American aeroplanes because they used ethyl alcohol). The *octane rating* reflects the ability of fuel to *expand evenly.*

Higher octane fuels allow higher compression ratios than are possible with "normal" fuels without detonation. If fuel of a lower octane rating than is recommended in the Flight Manual is used, you should never use full throttle.

Trivia: TEL is actually a liquid gas, which forms lead oxides *when it is compressed.* It was developed by a subsidiary company (Ethyl, Inc) of General Motors and I G Farben sometime before WWII, although the basic idea was

If this page is a photocopy, it is not authorised!

CAPT

thought of around 1921. In June, 1940, just before the Battle of Britain, you could only get TEL through the Anglo-American Oil Company, or Esso - the fuel concerned was called BAM 100. When British fuel was changed from 87 octane to 100 after working around the US *Neutrality Act* which banned its sale, German pilots got a real surprise, because British aircraft could suddenly climb a whole lot quicker (German planes could use 80-ish octane fuel anyway).

More Trivia: The unstable elements of petroleum have more hydrogen than carbon in their molecules. Octane (named after eight carbon atoms) results from reordering the atoms of a hydrocarbon. When stored for long periods, the octane rating will decrease slightly if there is a lot of evaporation. Also remember that it isn't the fuel that burns, but the vapour given off from it - a lot of fuel is actually wasted, even in modern engines, because the fuel droplets going in are not fully vapourised.

COOLING

The gases burning in the engine can produce temperatures as high as 2500°C. This will be absorbed by the various engine parts according to the temperature itself, the surface area exposed and the duration of the exposure. If left unchecked, this heat could cause those parts to distort and malfunction, or even cause pre-ignition or detonation. The function of the cooling system is therefore to remove heat from the engine at a high enough rate to keep its temperatures within safe working limits (note that overcooling can produce as many problems as undercooling - you need heat to vapourise the fuel, for example, and you don't want water vapour condensing on the insides). Liquid contaminants, such as water, have to be boiled off, at over 100°C.

AIR COOLING

Heat radiates directly into the air from the warm parts. Fins on a cylinder head, for instance, increase the surface area through which this can happen. The best engines for this tend to be those that allow the same amount of airflow over each cylinder, such as radials, but others, such as in-lines or those with a V formation may need fans and shrouds to assist the process, or their cylinders would have to be very far apart to let air through.

LIQUID COOLING

You need around 2000 times more air to remove a given amount of heat from an engine than you would if you used water or a suitable liquid.

There is a jacket around the warm parts, and the space between them is filled with a liquid such as water, with ethylene glycol added to solve certain limitations (such as boiling at low temperatures at high altitudes). This is pumped through a radiator which sticks out into the airflow to cool it down before it recirculates. Because all this has to be heated, the engine takes a little longer to

warm up, and there is also the extra weight of the liquid and fixings to consider, not to mention leaks, extra maintenance and the possibility of freezing in cold weather, which is why water is not generally used, but a liquid that does not freeze in low temperatures or boil at high ones. The boiling problem can also be solved by operating the system under pressure, for which you also need a *thermostat*, which is a bypass valve that regulates the movement of fluid in and out of the radiator.

Plain water is not used because it freezes on cold nights and expands, which can crack the engine. It also has a corrosive effect. Instead, it is mixed with glycol to increase its boiling point and lower its freezing point.

THE CARBURETTOR

It is not the fuel, but its vapour that burns, so you need a means of ensuring that it is vapourised rapidly enough to feed an engine, and mixed with air in the right proportions. The carburettor does just this and delivers the mixture to the inlet manifold* for its onward journey to the cylinders. It does this with a small bore jet in its choke tube that allows fuel to spray in a fine mist.

*A channel that serves manifold, or many, cylinders.

Carburettors in aircraft engines typically contain more than one complete carburation unit (i.e. float chamber, jets, butterfly, etc.) In fact, one carburettor will usually serve three or four cylinders to ensure that each one gets its fair share of the fuel/air mixture.

The carburettor uses the Venturi principle. As the speed of the air increases through the choke, the pressure reduces., enough to pull fuel into it via the main nozzle, which is connected directly to the fuel system through a series of pumps and jets. As the main nozzle is inside the low pressure area, the fuel is forced to expand, which cools everything, so be careful with carburettor icing, which can form well in advance of any other type. In fact, if you could make one small enough, there's no reason why an air conditioning unit could not achieve the same effect. It would certainly work better than a carburettor.

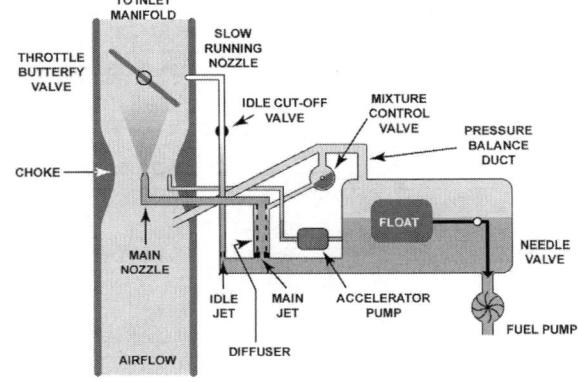

There is a fuel strainer upstream of the needle valve (not shown). The diffuser ensures that the fuel flow is kept directly proportional to the volume of air flowing through the choke, preventing the main jet from supplying excessive fuel as engine speed is increased.

Just before the carburettor ends and the inlet manifold begins is a *butterfly valve*, which is best compared to a coin in a tube - when the throttle is closed, the butterfly valve is closed, and *vice versa*. One problem is that fuel splashes against it and condenses, which doesn't help with vapourisation or atomization much.

Even when the butterfly is fully open, though, there is still resistance to the flow of fuel from its sideways presentation. New car engines have eliminated it altogether by making the throttle increase the inlet valve opening time to get the same effect.

All the above is fine, but a small complication arises, in that we pilots keep wanting to change the speed of the engine. For example, when the butterfly is closed, the engine still needs fuel, but the pressure differential between the venturi and the float chamber is very small, so there is an *idle jet* that bypasses the butterfly to keep the engine ticking over (the jet is actually a hole next to the butterfly, and it's sometimes called the *slow running jet*).

Also, when you need power in a hurry, there is a small lag from inertia between the time you open the throttle and the time the engine starts to speed up, because the air supply responds more quickly than the fuel does, which gives you a *weak cut* (a momentarily weak mixture), so a small squirt of fuel is delivered separately to compensate, from an *accelerator pump*. When starting an engine from cold, therefore, resist the temptation to pump the throttle, because all you will do is flood it with large drops of fuel. A better tactic is to open the throttle v e r y s l o w l y, so that the pump doesn't kick in.

To start a flooded engine that has a carburettor, place the mixture control in cutoff, with the ignition switch off, and the throttle open until the fuel has been cleared.

Because aircraft go up, and air gets less plentiful at height, there is a danger of the fuel/air mixture getting out of balance as you climb - the engine will not work at all if the ratio of fuel to air is not correct. A mixture that has too much fuel against air is *rich*, while one the other way round is *weak*. The *mixture control* is provided to adjust for this as you increase altitude - for example, you would set it fully rich for takeoff and landing. The "normal" mixture is about 15:1 of air to fuel by *weight*, but this is not critical over a wide range. However, 18:1 would be considered weak. The *mixture ratio* is that between the *masses* of *fuel* and *air* entering the *cylinder* (air to fuel).

The mixture control's main purpose is to adjust fuel flow to get the correct fuel/air ratio - it corrects for variations resulting from reduced air density at altitude. Leaning makes the engine run hotter and give you more power for less fuel; a 112 hp aircraft cruising at 4000 feet and 85 knots might burn 5 gallons an hour when rich, but only 4.5 when leaned, giving a range of 116 miles as opposed to 100 - a saving, or an increase, of 16%. The mixture control's secondary function is to cut fuel from the engine on the ground when you want to stop it (you don't just switch the magnetos off). The *Idle Cut Off* (ICO) in the carburettor is joined to the mixture lever with a *Bowden cable*. When the lever is operated at the end of a flight, the engine is starved of fuel, and stops.

Note: Most normally aspirated engines can be leaned at any altitude when the power is set *below* about 75% (cruise power for Lycomings is normally between 55-75%). Thus, leaning off at more than cruise power (i.e. in the climb) should *not* be carried out, as many engines rely on a rich mixture for cooling. It may save fuel, but petrol has a high latent heat content, and the excess fuel reduces the temperature when it evaporates.

MANIFOLD PRESSURE

The Manifold Absolute Pressure (MAP) indicates the power output of a piston engine, being a measure of the pressure of the fuel/air mixture in the inlet manifold.

The instruments below are typical of what you might see in the cruise:

 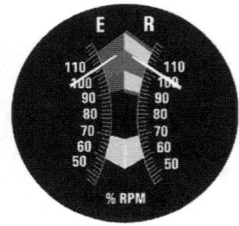

In an unsupercharged engine, the reading will drop with height for a given throttle setting, because there is less atmospheric pressure to push the useful charge into the cylinder, and you must keep opening the throttle to compensate. When the engine is stopped, the MAP gauge will read atmospheric pressure, just below 30 inches (1013 hPa). It will indicate lower than atmospheric pressure when the engine is running, because it is showing the engine's *suction*, and the MAP sensor is in the induction system, upstream of the throttle butterfly. At idle, the figure is about 12 inches.

Eventually, you will get no more power, at the *limiting altitude*, which is kinda fun when you still have to get into a landing site at altitude when the throttle has no effect.

The *service ceiling* is the altitude at which you can achieve 100 fpm rate of climb. The *absolute ceiling* is when you can only (just) maintain level flight.

You can extend the service ceiling by *supercharging* or *turbocharging*, discussed below. High MAP and low RPM makes an engine work too hard, and means severe wear and damage, and detonation, so observe the limits.

Humidity has an effect, too, although it is less with turbines. The more water there is in the air, the less air gets into the engine, therefore the mixture is richer and burns slower. The point is that performance graphs do not show this, so factor them by around 10% if the air is wet, say after a shower. You will get the most engine power when it's cold and dry, in high pressure conditions.

Note: *Boost pressure* is generally considered to be any manifold pressure above 30 ins Hg. The boost gauge has one side connected to the induction system and the other to a sealed chamber which is kept at sea level pressure.

FUEL PRIMING

A *fuel primer* is a small hand pump that puts neat fuel directly into either the induction manifold (near the combustion chamber) or the inlet valve port before you start in the cold to promote the presence of fuel vapour (very rarely do you need to prime a warm engine). They are not there with fuel injection systems.

Tip: As the primer injects fuel into the manifold, you can put fuel into your engine if it quits because of carb icing.

Aside from the fire hazard, excessive priming should be avoided because it washes lubricant off the cylinder walls.

CARBURETTOR ICING

This is actually one aspect of *induction system icing*. The other two are *fuel icing*, arising from water suspended in fuel, and *impact ice*, which builds up on the airframe around the various intakes that serve the engine.

Even on a warm day, if it's humid, carburettor icing is a danger, especially with small throttle openings where there's less area for the ice to block off in the first place (as when descending, etc.) Also, the temperature drop (between the OAT and that in the venturi) can be anywhere between 20-30°C, so icing (in an R22, anyway) can happen even when the OAT is as high as 21°C (70°F), or more. Tests have produced icing at descent power at temperatures above 30°C, with a relative humidity below 30%, in clear air. Because it is more volatile, and likely to contain more water, you can expect more fuel and carb icing with MOGAS than AVGAS.

Carb icing usually arises from the action of the venturi in the throat, just before the butterfly valve, which regulates the amount of fuel into the engine, so it is most likely to occur in the *venturi* and the *throttle valve*.

You will remember the venturi's purpose is to accelerate airflow by restricting the size of the passageway, which has the effect of reducing the pressure and pulling the fuel in. Unfortunately, this process also reduces the temperature, as does the fuel vapourisation, hence the problem (the lower temperature means greater relative humidity, and closeness to the dewpoint, and the vapourisation takes its latent heat from the surroundings, making the situation worse). In fact, the vapourisation (and cooling) can carry on most of the way to the cylinders, causing the problem to persist, especially with the butterfly semi-closed, which produces another restriction and more of the same. Any water vapour under those conditions will turn directly to ice. Note also that warm air produces *more ice* because it holds more moisture.

CARBURETTOR HEAT

If you pass the air going into the carburettor past the hot air coming from the exhaust manifold, you can warm it up and prevent icing from occurring. This is controlled by a carburettor heat control in the cockpit.

With smaller engines, use full settings for every application - that is, carb heat either on or off, with no in-betweens - the greatest risk is at reduced power.

Rough running may increase as melted ice goes through the engine. Also, be careful you don't get an overboost or too much RPM when you reselect cold. Of course, aeroplanes have some advantage if the engine stops from carb icing, as the propeller keeps the engine turning, giving you a chance to do something about it.

Usually, a gauge is used with a yellow arc on it, showing the danger range. Use carb heat as necessary to keep out if it.

Carb heat reduces air *density*, so the mixture gets *richer*.

FUEL INJECTION

Most of the above problems with the carburettor are avoided with fuel injection, where fuel is metered directly in an atomised state to the cylinders according to power requirements, automatically taking air density into account. Ice is not formed because there is no venturi to cause temperature drops (there's no carburettor in the first place, as it is replaced with an engine driven pump).

The fuel is also atomised more thoroughly as it is forced through a small nozzle at high pressure. The whole process is more precise than a carburettor, which uses a more scattergun approach when it comes to delivering fuel to the cylinders - some would get excess fuel in the process of ensuring that each one gets a minimum amount. As a result of fuel injection, engine response is quicker and smoother, fuel efficiency is improved (you

If this page is a photocopy, it is not authorised!

need less fuel for the same power output), and exhaust emissions are cleaner.

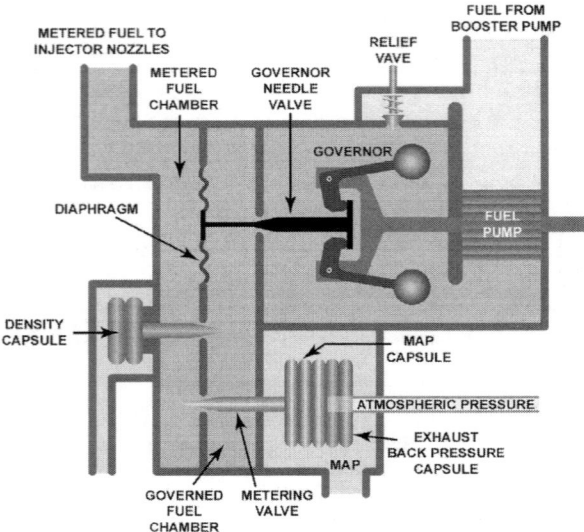

The fuel injector consists of a nozzle and a valve. The mechanics of the system exist much further back, and the process of delivering the fuel is known as **fuel metering**.

More fuel than is required is forced into a **governed fuel chamber**, which is separated by a diaphragm from the **metered fuel chamber**. Thus, the pressure in the governed chamber is always constant (any excess goes through a relief valve).

As the governor rotates, its bobweights fly out to open a **needle valve** to allow the fuel to proceed into the **metered fuel chamber** where the difference in pressure between the governed and metered chambers acting on the diaphragm is used to try and close the needle valve and balance its movements. The pressure across the diaphragm is proportional to the square of the RPM, so the fuel flow through the jets ends up varying with engine speed. The fuel flow through the **main jet** is governed by *boost pressure* and *exhaust back pressure*. Increasing the boost (with the throttle) compresses a series of evacuated **MAP capsules**, which makes the main metering needle withdraw from the main jet to increase the fuel flow through it because the hole gets bigger (the needle is tapered to automatically control the mixture strength).

Normally, as atmospheric pressure falls with altitude, the exhaust gases find it easier to escape, as the pressure differential between the inside and the outside of the engine is larger. This improves volumetric efficiency because more of the fuel/air mixture can be pulled in. In a carburettor, the extra depression automatically pulls more fuel into the throat to keep the mixture correct but, in an injected system, some compensation is needed, otherwise the mixture would be weak (the improved volumetric efficiency makes more air in the manifold available to be

drawn into the cylinders). This is provided by **back pressure capsules**, which are connected internally to atmospheric pressure, and externally to the MAP capsules. As altitude increases, the back pressure capsules are compressed by the greater difference between MAP and atmospheric pressure, opening the main needle valve.

To compensate for the reduction in density of the inlet charge when the temperature increases, a thermometer bulb in the inlet manifold controls the position of a second capsule-controlled needle valve. The capsule chamber is connected to the thermometer bulb by a liquid-filled capillary tube. When the manifold air temperature increases, the liquid expands, compresses the capsule and closes the needle valve, reducing the fuel flow to match the air density.

A common problem with fuel injected engines is blocked jets, from dirt in fuel.

SUPERCHARGERS

As the supply of air (and therefore oxygen) reduces with height, less air gets in and not all the fuel will be burnt, so your power will be less than it could be.

If you can force air into a cylinder under a pressure that is higher than atmospheric, you can artificially increase its density, and the volumetric efficiency of the engine. The amount of pressure above atmospheric pressure is called *boost* pressure. Ambient pressure is *static boost*.

The extra oxygen also allows you to add more fuel.

Compressing the air like this increases its temperature, which means you can use a smaller compression ratio because the engine doesn't have to work so hard. However, if it gets too high, detonation could occur, so the compressed air is fed into the manifold *after* the carburettor so that the fuel, as it vapourises, will cool it.

Also, at high altitudes, when throttled back to avoid overboosting, the temperature in the carburettor may drop low enough to cause ice to form at the butterfly, even at full rated power. This is why many supercharged aircraft have a carburettor air temperature gauge.

With the reduced drag at high altitude, and the engine producing its rated power, a supercharged aircraft can fly much faster.

 A supercharger is a centrifugal air pump (e.g. it has a *radial compressor*) run directly from the engine, (at 6-12 times the crankshaft speed) between the carburettor and the inlet manifold. The supercharger's function is to *extend the service ceiling of the aircraft*, by compressing the fuel/air mixture to *maintain sea level power at altitude*, or to increase normal power lower down.*

It gives the air a high velocity which is gradually reduced as it passes through diffuser vanes, which provides the higher pressure (it is greatest at the supercharger outlet, indicated on the MAP gauge). The essential point to remember is that the extra air is sucked through the carburettor, and *then* blown into the cylinder, so fuel does not go through the supercharger.

Although some work is wasted and the efficiency of the cycle is reduced, and the supercharger adds weight to the aircraft, the overall result is an improvement in power of around 40% for the same fuel consumption.

*This is not quite correct. The air pressure coming out of the supercharger depends on the pressure going in - even with a supercharger, this falls with an increase in height. Thus, the power *available* from a supercharged engine will also fall with height as it would with a normally aspirated one. It is more accurate to say that a supercharged engine, at whatever height, will give out as much power as an unsupercharged engine of similar capacity and RPM would give at ground level. If you allowed it to, the supercharged engine would give much more power at ground level, so you either have to restrict what it can do or make it super strong, which will make it heavier.

The former option is cheapest, with........

AUTOMATIC BOOST CONTROL
The crude method of restricting the power output is simply to place a gate on the throttle, which can be over-ridden in an emergency. A more elegant way is to place an evacuated capsule between the throttle and the butterfly valve which opens the butterfly automatically until it is fully open at the rated altitude. In other words, the length of the throttle linkage changes as the capsule contracts or expands, which ultimately controls the weight of charge entering the cylinder. The capsule is exposed to inlet pressure while being linked to the throttle via an oil operated servo piston. When the capsule is compressed, the throttle is partly closed, and *vice versa*. The oil comes from the engine lubrication system.

When the engine starts, the induction manifold pressure falls to a low value which is sensed by the capsule, which expands, to make oil flow below the servo piston, which is forced to the top of its stroke. If the throttle is opened any more, the capsules compress and the oil supply is eventually cut off, then directed above the piston, to make it go down and close the throttle. In this way, the boost cannot rise above the *Rated Boost,* which is the maximum continuous boost that can be selected (it can be exceeded with an override system for takeoffs and emergencies).

When things are in equilibrium, any tendency for pressure to fall in the inlet is counteracted by a progressive opening of the throttle because more oil is introduced underneath the servo piston until you reach the altitude where the throttle is fully open. This *rated altitude* is that, above

which, the induction manifold pressure *falls*, just like it does with a normally aspirated engine. The *full throttle height* is the altitude up to which a given boost setting can be maintained at a given engine RPM, so the lower the boost pressure you select, the higher it can be maintained by the automatic system. The rated altitude is also full throttle height at rated boost and normal RPM for that boost.

HANDLING
With superchargers, engine speed should be kept as low as possible to minimise losses from friction and adiabatic heating, which will cause the charge's density to reduce, followed by the engine power. You get maximum efficiency with the throttle fully open and the engine RPM as low as it can be without causing detonation. Two-speed superchargers, which use variable gearing, are an attempt to overcome the problems of operating the engine at high speeds at high altitudes.

Note: Superchargers (and turbochargers) need special attention, particularly when they are older, as under- or overboosting (when applying full power or descending rapidly) can cause significant damage.

TURBOCHARGERS
Because they are internal devices, and driven by the engine, superchargers can use up a lot of power (150 HP in a Merlin) and therefore fuel, increasing costs and reducing the range of the aircraft. They must also be controlled and continually adjusted by the pilot.

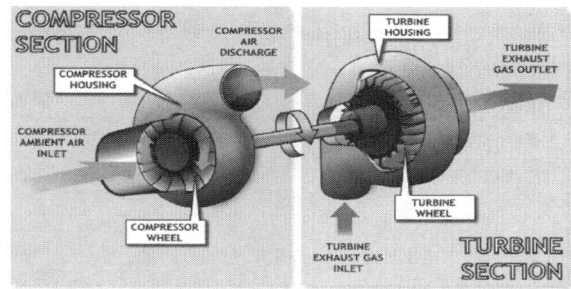

Turbochargers use the engine's spent exhaust gases to operate an automatic *wastegate*, so turbochargers are external exhaust-driven superchargers. In fact, *turbocharger* is a contraction of *turbosupercharger.*

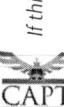

A turbo charger is an external device that operates *before* the carburettor or fuel metering device. The *critical altitude* is the pressure altitude at which the wastegate is fully closed. Above that altitude, power will fall in line with the manifold pressure.

The amount of power in the exhaust gas depends on the difference between the exhaust pressure and the outside air pressure, which increases with altitude, allowing a turbocharger to compensate for changing altitude without using up any extra power by driving all that machinery. In other words, the manifold pressure is controlled within preset parameters, and as long as the system is working properly and the pilot is smooth on the controls, a turbocharger will not overboost the engine and damage it.

Note: As the exhaust is involved, preflight checks should include security of the exhaust pipes, so that carbon monoxide doesn't get into the cabin.

Turbochargers provide a constant air *pressure* to the engine, but the air temperature is increased from the compression so, at higher temperatures, the density provided to the engine is less anyway, which is why you will never be able to obtain the full theoretical capability of the turbocharger. The reduced density reduces volumetric efficiency, which can be partly restored by using an aftercooler.

BOOTSTRAPPING
This is a condition that occurs at high altitude and low engine RPM, which can be made to disappear by increasing RPM or descending a bit. It is an over-reaction to rapid throttle movement, leading to large pressure fluctuations and overboosting. A pressure relief valve in the induction manifold also cures it.

Cessna defines bootstrapping as "The unstable manifold pressure condition that occurs when the wastegate closes at high altitude under low RPM operation." In other words, it occurs when the manifold pressure begins to fall off as the RPM is reduced. The wastegate has fully closed and the turbo is not spinning fast enough to produce desired manifold pressure. Controls should be moved smoothly and not too rapidly, and in the correct sequence.

Tip: To preserve turbocharger life, let the engine run for a little while before shutting it down (check the flight manual for minimum times - usually 2 minutes), to stabilise the temperature and reduce the chances of distortion or having the engine oil which lubricates it coking (caking) on hotspots.

THE WASTEGATE
With a wastegate, once the engine produces more exhaust pressure than the system will allow, a flap opens to redirect excess exhaust away from the turbine blades. That is, when the waste gate is open, the exhaust gases are being dumped overboard before reaching the turbine blades.

There are two types of wastegate:

- An **internal** wastegate lives on the turbo unit itself. The gate is opened via an actuator which driven by a diaphragm. Excess exhaust is then fed directly into the exhaust system.

- An **external** wastegate is separate from the turbo unit and does not require an actuator. Excess exhaust can either be fed into the exhaust system or it can be vented straight out and into the atmosphere. External wastegates generally use a valve like the poppet valve in the cylinder head. However, they are controlled by pneumatics rather than a camshaft and open in the opposite direction

Most modern turbocharged aircraft use a hydraulic wastegate control with engine oil as the fluid. A wastegate is closed by oil pressure and opened by spring pressure.

On the oil output side of the wastegate actuator (i.e. *downstream*) sits the density controller, an air-controlled oil valve which senses upper deck pressure and controls how fast oil can bleed from the wastegate actuator back to the engine. As you climb and the air density drops, the density controller slowly closes the valve and traps more oil in the actuator, closing the wastegate to increase the speed of the turbocharger and maintain rated power.

If the waste gate seizes with the throttle open in a descent, Manifold Air Pressure may exceed maximum value.

Turbine Engines
The same principles apply to jet engines as reciprocating ones, only they're applied in a different way. For example, in the piston engine, part or all of the functions of induction, compression, power and exhaust happen in the combustion chamber, which is not necessarily the best place for them all. A turbine engine's components can be designed specially for the task.

Turbines also use cheaper fuel, because compression is not a factor in producing the power, although avgas can sometimes be mixed with jet fuel (see the Flight Manual), at the expense of reduced maintenance periods, because it doesn't lubricate the fuel pumps so well (also, there is a lot of crud left on the turbine blades from the anti-knock additives and, being a thin fuel, avgas will "bubble out" quicker at lower altitudes). Since compression can be ignored, and most of the airflow is used for cooling anyway, a high relative humidity has little effect on the output of a jet, which is a hot, thin and fast stream of air.

Whereas a piston engine relies on a precisely timed sequence of individual events, with all the bits flying back and forth violently, jet engines just spin round, although their "simplicity" depends hugely on their quality of design and manufacture. Also, jet engines run on a continuous cycle (the *Brayton Cycle*), with everything happening at the same time. A typical air-fuel ratio is 60:1.

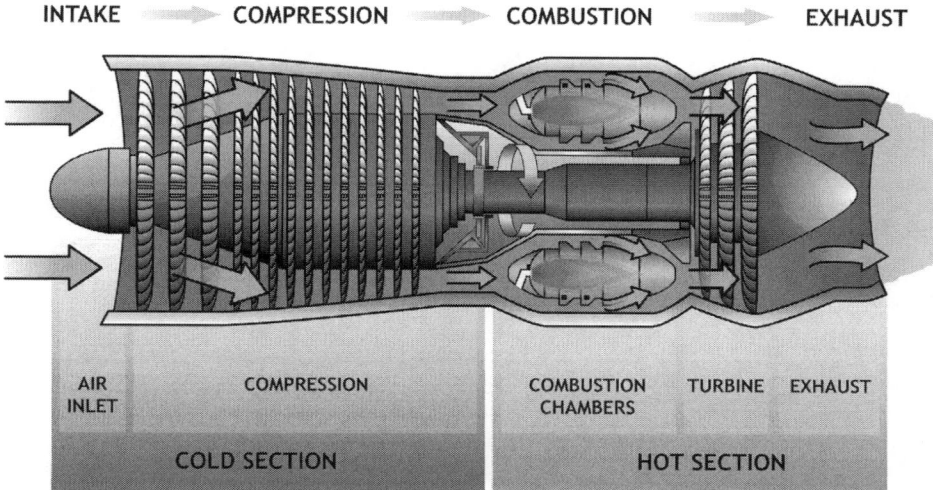

INTAKE ⟹ COMPRESSION ⟹ COMBUSTION ⟹ EXHAUST

| AIR INLET | COMPRESSION | | COMBUSTION CHAMBERS | TURBINE | EXHAUST |

COLD SECTION | **HOT SECTION**

A turbine is lighter and produces more power than a piston engine, although it is much more of a precision instrument because it spins faster, and needs to be handled more gently. The bearings inside are not loaded as much as they are with a piston engine, because there are no loads from reciprocation.

In a jet aeroplane, thrust is used to propel the machine forward directly. In a helicopter, the stream of hot gases is intercepted by a *turbine*, which drives a rotor gearbox. Unfortunately, about two thirds of the energy thus produced is simply used to keep the engine running. Most of the rest is used by the power turbine to drive the gearbox and rotors, leaving just enough energy to ensure the hot gases fall out of the engine by themselves, so you don't need extra components to drain more energy. As hot air is used in this way, the engine in a helicopter is called the *gas producer*, and the output is measured in shaft horsepower. In other words, the engine's function in a helicopter is to produce enough hot air to spin the turbines that drive the main rotors.

Note: The first point for the transitioning pilot to grasp is that the payback for mistreating a piston engine is immediate, and likely to affect you directly, whereas that with a turbine engine may affect a pilot further down the line, as any damage is cumulative..

Due to thermal wear and shock, starting up puts more wear and tear on a turbine engine than any other operation, within certain limits. Consequently, *start cycles* on the engine are counted, meaning that you count the number of starts you do during the day and put them in the Tech Log when you finish flying. Cycles can be more important than total hours, if you fly shorter missions. If you divide the cost of an engine by the start cycles you are allowed, it will give you an idea of how much it costs just to start the machine up.

Tip: One of the biggest things to unlearn when moving from piston to turbine is to keep your finger on the starter button once things start happening (with a piston, you tend to take your finger off straight away when the engine starts) - now you *don't* take your finger off *until the engine becomes self-sustaining*. Before then, it relies heavily on the battery to keep it turning. It follows that, if the battery is weak, the engine won't spin as fast, the cooling airflow is reduced, the whole process becomes hotter and you could melt the back end with a *hot start*, aside from losing the instruments if you have an EFIS display, so you won't see what's going on to stop it anyway. **Always** check the voltage from the battery before starting a turbine engine!

Hot starts are mainly due to:

- finger trouble
- a weak battery
- suspect fuel control

You can help avoid the finger trouble by making sure the throttle is fully closed *before* you press the starter button.

A *hung start* exists when the fuel has been introduced before the engine has been accelerated enough by the starter. It just sits there, weakening the battery, and the throughput of fuel is not enough to accelerate the engine, so the temperature increases. You get a *wet start* when the engine doesn't light off at all (e.g. it's flooded), in which case you should wait a while and vent the engine before starting again. It is even more important to have airflow for cooling, so an external start is also recommended under those circumstances.

Learn to recognize a weak battery by how rapidly the igniter snaps and how quickly the engine pitch increases as it spins up. Also, watch how much the fuel pressure drops as you hit the starter. If it drops to near zero, the battery is weak. When in doubt, *use external power*.

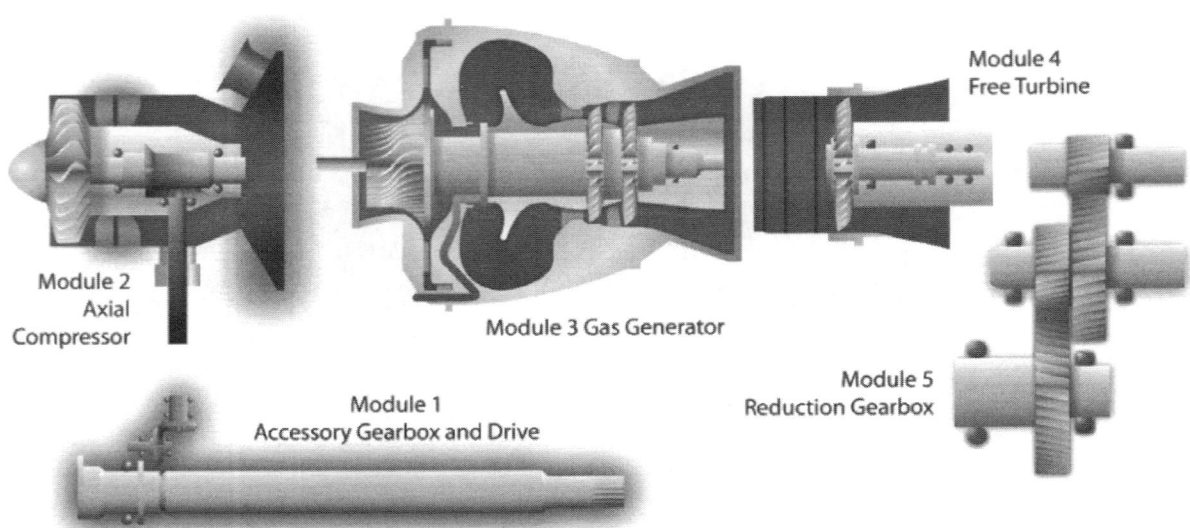

Module 4
Free Turbine

Module 2
Axial
Compressor

Module 3 Gas Generator

Module 5
Reduction Gearbox

Module 1
Accessory Gearbox and Drive

Picture Above: Components of Arriel 2B Engine

If, for any reason, you believe a hot start is imminent, the procedure is to roll the throttle closed, past the idle stop *while continuing to motor the starter!* **Read that again**. Release the starter in such a case and the TOT will skyrocket, and there's nothing you can do to stop it - remember, *the starter motors the compressor stages*, which channel cool air through the engine.

Unless cool air keeps moving the exhaust gases on their way out, the turbine will suffer damage.

Tip: When you reduce power in normal flight, the engine RPM will slow down as less fuel is pumped through it, and if you want to increase power, there will be a slight delay as the engine spools up to the speed required. In fact, as you make the demand for power, the engine will continue spooling *down* for a short while, then start spooling up. It is therefore important to learn to anticipate power demands to reduce the chances of the engine surging (see *The Compressor*, below).

Turbine Engine Components

The five basic parts of the average jet are the *inlet*, the *compressor, combustion chamber, turbine* and *nozzle*, for the exhaust, and they could be combined or reversed, to save space. In the Allison 250, the combustion chamber is at the rear, with the turbine near the centre, although the air at least goes in the front:

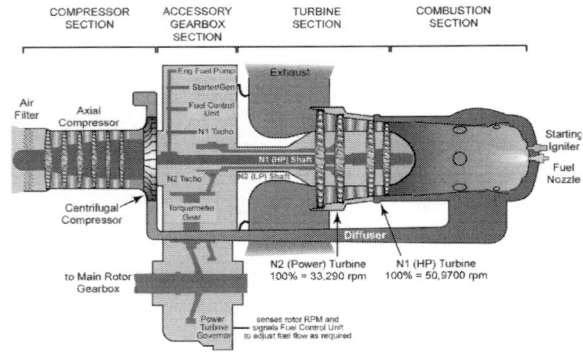

The Pratt & Whitney PT-6, found in the Bell 212, has the air getting into the engine at the rear.

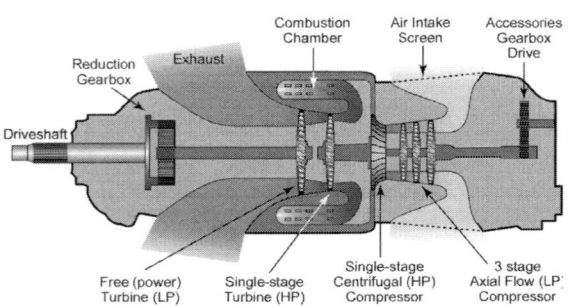

CAPT

THE INLET

This is where air enters the system. Its function is to convert ram-air pressure (from forward movement) into static pressure, ready for the compressor, for which inlet ducts should be as straight and smooth as possible, producing a minimal boundary layer, and delivering the air to the compressor with an even pressure distribution. In fact, the air enters the nozzle at less than the flight speed and is further slowed before the compressor (below) causes a substantial rise in pressure and temperature.

The amount of air needed by a gas turbine engine is around 10 times that needed by a reciprocating engine. The inlet is designed to conduct incoming air to the compressor with minimum energy loss from drag or ram pressure loss, that is, the flow of air into the compressor should be free of turbulence for maximum efficiency. Proper design contributes materially to performance by increasing the ratio of compressor discharge pressure to duct inlet pressure.

The amount of air passing through the engine depends on:

* The speed of the compressor
* The forward speed of the aircraft
* The density of the ambient air

PARTICLE SEPARATORS

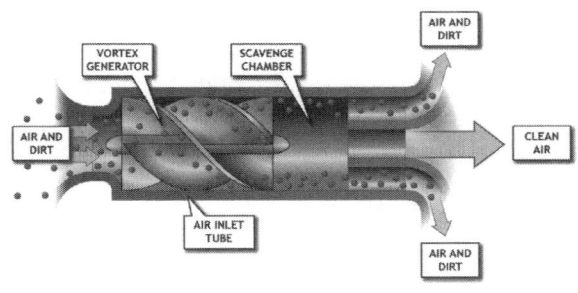

The air travelling through the inlet may well include other odds and ends, like sand (in the desert), dust, leaves, etc. Various methods are used to combat this, but they do restrict the airflow and have an effect on performance, as filters and separators at the inlet reduce the efficiency of the air intake.

A particle separator uses centrifugal force from inlet air to create small swirls that pick up small particles and drop them into a *sediment trap*.

They work with snow as well. The crude method is simply to stick a piece of gauze over the inlet.

THE COMPRESSOR

This is a rotating mass of impellers or blades, designed to take vast quantities of air, compress it (and therefore heat it) for direction to the combustor (see below), so it's an air pump, sometimes with the weight of air delivered determined by the engine RPM. That is, for any specified RPM, the air volume will be a definite amount.

For maximum efficiency, a compressor must have the least possible pressure loss, to save the turbine from driving it so hard. This requires aerodynamic stability, so the tip speeds of the compressor blades should not be close to the speed of sound - 0.9M is about right. A high compression ratio allows a higher pressure in the combustion chamber, which will allow a greater pressure differential to the atmosphere, so you get a higher nozzle velocity and more thrust for the same amount of fuel. The compression ratio could be nearly 10:1 for a centrifugal compressor, and 25:1 for an axial compressor. The higher the ratio, the more thrust for the same frontal area.

The temperature rise in the compressor could be 555°C, or more - in the Bell 407, it is 750°C. High temperatures may restrict the maximum output because less fuel is burnt before the maximum temperature limits at the turbine inlet are reached.

Note: The air being so hot has some significance if the fire detection system in your machine is set to trigger off at a similar temperature, as a compressor leak could give you a false fire indication.

The compressor is an ideal place from which to tap small amounts of bleed air for other purposes, such as anti-ice, cooling or sealing, where back pressure is used to stop other gases going the wrong way. However, when doing this, the exhaust temperature will tend to rise slightly. For anti-ice systems, the bleed is taken from the back end of the compressor (that is, compressor discharge air) that has already been heated from compression. It will typically flow through the compressor shell and hollow struts, and the inlet guide vanes.

Only 40% of the total air leaving the compressor is used for combustion.

The two types of compressor (axial or centrifugal) both give high kinetic energy to a quantity of air with a high speed rotating element, then convert the energy into pressure through a diffusing stage. Some engines, particularly the Allison 250, use both types, so the engine can be made shorter without greatly affecting the cross-sectional area. Also, as the combustion chamber is usually a reverse-flow annular type, the transition stages for the airflow can be made smoother as it will already have gone through a 90° change of direction.

CENTRIFUGAL COMPRESSORS

The centrifugal compressor uses impellers to fling air *outwards* into channels leading to the combustion chamber, being a development of those used in superchargers. It has a *high compression ratio by stage* and a *large diameter*, so it makes an engine shorter, but wider.

However, the large frontal area makes it hard to create engines with multiple stages. You can place impellers one after the other, or back to back, but in the latter case the rear face is less efficient due to pre-heating of the air, although it does produce a greater mass flow without an increase in diameter, therefore producing less drag. As air is accelerated across the face of the impeller, a low pressure is created at the eye, which pulls more air in (air enters at the eye and leaves tangentially at the periphery).

The rotating guide vanes on the impeller form divergent air passages, and they are curved in the direction of rotation to ease the pick up of the air as it comes in from the front and has to change direction. Before it gets here, the air will have passed through a *plenum chamber* which reduces the air's velocity with *swirl vanes*, which also direct the air to the rotating guide vanes at a suitable angle.

After the compressor, the air is forced into a diffuser, whose vanes form **divergent passages** that slow the air down and increase its pressure, turning kinetic energy into pressure energy. In the diffuser, velocity decreases, while pressure and temperature increase. The pressure rise is shared between the impeller and diffuser.

The passages are arranged to form the most suitable angle under *running conditions*, so there could be some turbulence outside these. If the clearance between the impeller and diffuser is too small, there could also be aerodynamic buffeting to cause an unsteady flow and turbulence (the clearance is normally about an inch). Clearances between the impeller and its casing also stop leakage.

Cascade vanes turn the air properly into the combustion chamber(s), as well as providing further diffusion.

AXIAL COMPRESSORS

Because the air in a centrifugal compressor has to be bent at high speeds (supersonic in places), there are losses that become more apparent as higher pressures are required.

The axial compressor has rings of rotating blades called *rotors* followed by rings of stationary ones called *stators*, or *stator vanes*, whose purpose is to slow the air down to compress and heat it by bending and shaping it into the right position for the next compressor wheel.

Inside the casing, pressure is gradually increased as the air is forced into smaller spaces created by further blades downstream. In other words, the blades get shorter towards the discharge end to form a convergent duct of

the casing as a whole. This is to maintain the air velocity as the pressure *increases,* and to better suit the air density.

Each rotating wheel with its set of stators is one stage of compression, so several together (on a shaft) constitute a *multistage compressor*, used because the heat increase is relatively small and needs boosting. The pressure increases across each stage are quite small (between 1.1-1.2), to keep the rate of diffusion and deflection angles of the blades small. This keeps any turbulence within limits.

Because the clearance between the casing and the blade is so critical, blades are often made with a *knife edge tip*. As the blade heats up, the edge rubs against the casing and the knife edge beds in to provide a minimal clearance.

The power output of a gas turbine engine depends on mass airflow (with constant temperature at the entry to the turbine). The axial compressor handles more air for the same frontal area, so it produces less drag (if you want more air, just make it longer). It is also slightly lighter.

The axial compressor has a higher percentage of efficiency over a wider range of compression ratios, so it has a better specific fuel consumption. It is also more expensive.

COMPRESSOR SURGE

For maximum efficiency, and because engines have to react quickly, you need to operate the compressor blades as close to the stall as possible - turbine engines work best when the air is flowing smoothly through them, although the airflow within a compressor tends to be especially unsteady near the blade tips - typical flow problems can include vortices, separations, secondary flows, shock and boundary layer interactions, and turbulent wakes. However, the stalling involved is not quite the same as that on an aerofoil, as compressor blades cannot change their position relative to the airflow they meet. They are affected by an *effective* angle of attack, which depends on the velocity of the airflow and the speed at which the blades are moving. In a centrifugal compressor, for example, there are normally more impeller vanes than

CAPT

diffuser vanes, so not all the diffuser passages will have smooth airflow. Pressure will therefore be less in the more turbulent ones, and air may turn back on itself and flow from the smooth channels into turbulent ones, and back.

In an axial compressor, the various stages have dissimilar airflow stages, especially at lower speeds, where the air has more of a tendency to break away from the blade contours and cause a stall because its volume reduces so little - it is therefore too fast and chokes the compressor. If the throttle is closed too quickly, the mass airflow reduces quicker than the RPM does, so the angle of attack of the blades in the early stage increases beyond the stall.

If the throttle is opened too quickly, the extra fuel increases the velocity of the gas too fast through the turbine, which chokes, so pressure in the combustion chamber is greater than that leaving the compressor and everything backs up. You can also upset airflow inside an engine by manoeuvres and turbulence, where the air at the intake is disturbed. Below its design speed, an axial compressor tends to surge in its front stages.

Energy wasted in simply churning air in this way is called *compressor surge*. It is not restricted to jet engines - it can also be encountered in supercharged piston engines, although it is fair to say that centrifugal compressors suffer less because they tend to have lower compression ratios. In mild cases, the engine will keep running, but if the engine gets starved of air it will stop.

A compressor stall reduces engine efficiency, meaning less power. A *cold stall* only affects a few blades, whereas a *hot stall* involves them all, and may mean severe damage from the hot gases coming out of the combustor when the airflow becomes reversed inside the engine (as the air is being compressed, it will try to spring back the way it came, as might happen if the intake gets blocked). In a *transient stall*, you will just hear the odd bang (and a bigger one when a blade flies through the side), but in a more steady stall, there will be a roaring sound and severe vibration with a sound like a machine gun, but mostly, you should just hear a coughing sound from the engine. In the extreme, compressor surge is accompanied by loud banging noises and severe engine vibration. The only things you can do are to reduce the fuel flow and angle of attack on the compressor blades, or increase speed.

Common causes of surging (which ultimately lead to less air relative to fuel) are:

- Rapid increase in fuel flow when RPM increases
- Low engine RPM
- Air going into the engine from the wrong direction, say in a crosswind, or restricted (say from icing)
- Contaminated or damaged compressor blades

Symptoms of surging include:

- Loss of thrust
- Odd noises & vibrations
- RPM fluctuations
- Increased TOT
- Burning gases out of various orifices

Some engines have a small valve (a *compressor bleed*) in the late stages of the compressor (or between the axial and centrifugal compressors) that opens at low RPM (when the engine cannot shift as much air) to dump air overboard to correct the airflow.

A bleed air system makes the compressor see less restrictions by staying open until a certain pressure ratio is obtained. In other words, it aids acceleration without stalling, because the engine is made to use a higher pressure and the excess is bled out. The valve closes when acceleration is required so that the additional pressure better matches the increased fuel flow.

Bleed valves can be operated hydraulically (using fuel pressure) or pneumatically. In the pneumatic system, the valve is spring loaded in the open position. At low RPM, the airflow through a venturi creates a depression that operates a linkage to close the valve when required.

Compressor surge and stall tend to affect older engines with mechanical fuel control units - newer ones use those with quicker response times, including hydromechanical and electronic fuel control systems such as a FADEC.

Note that the cause of compressor stall are not necessarily internal - there could be ingestion of debris or otherwise dirty air (smoke, etc.), distorted flow through the intake during abrupt manoeuvres or hovering in adverse winds (or ice, water or snow), re-ingestion of exhaust gases (downwash can do this, as can flying near oil rigs), etc. Eroded compressor blades can cause blades to stall. An axial-centrifugal engine increases an engine's resistance to this by about 10 times as the centrifugal compressor is essentially not affected by sand and dust erosion.

How severe the stall is dictates what to do about it. In general, slowly reduce the power. Keep an eye on the temperature (one reason why there are limitations in the flight manual). However, the Bell 206 L-3 manual states that, with stalls of a less-severe nature (one or two low-intensity pops) continued operation may be allowed, but with reduced power and by avoiding the conditions that started the stall in the first place. If flight is continued, it prescribes reducing power, switching engine anti-ice off, maintaining slow cruise flight, checking the TOT and gas producer rpm for normal indications, slowly increasing the collective to achieve a desired power level, rechecking the TOT and gas producer rpm, and landing as soon as practical. A compressor stall in the Eurocopter AS 350 requires an overhaul of the tail-rotor gearbox due to the oscillating loads. In the extreme, compressor surge can potentially lead to total destruction of the engine.

THE COMBUSTION CHAMBER (COMBUSTOR)

The combustion system's purpose is to provide a smooth stream of uniformly heated gas, with the least loss of pressure and the maximum release of heat. It adds heat energy to the gases so they accelerate to produce thrust.

Although the pressure is meant to be constant, in practice about 5% is lost through the turbulence that is needed to mix the air and fuel properly in keeping the flame stable.

Once the flame is lit by the spark igniter during the start, it stays that way till the engine is shut down (you could say that the engine is on fire all the time, and it's only when it becomes uncontained that it becomes an emergency).

As the combustion chamber has a fixed size, the hot gases must increase speed to escape. They are delivered to the turbine below the limiting speed of its blades.

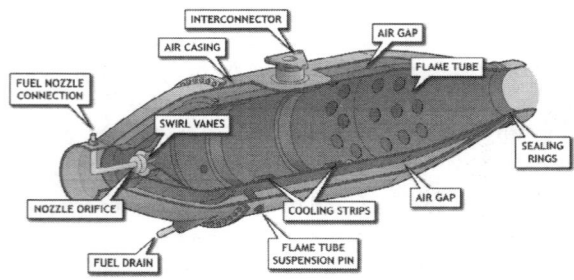

The combustion chamber is made from two tubes - one is the flame tube, which is inside the air casing. Between the two is an air gap, through which any air that does not go into the combustion chamber passes (secondary air).

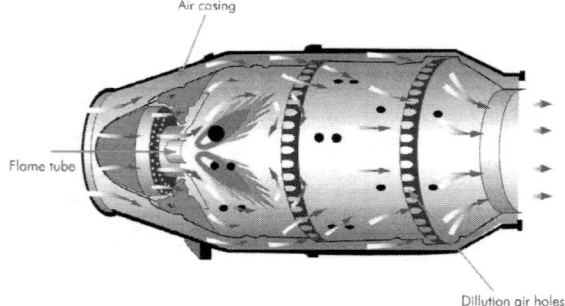

Air enters the combustion chamber at around 500 ft/sec, and is diffused to around 80 ft/sec. Even at this speed, the slow flame (at 1-2 ft/sec) would be blown away, so a region of low pressure is created round it to keep it alight.

AIRFLOW

Airflow in a combustion chamber is classified as *primary*, *secondary*, or *tertiary*. The overall air/fuel ratio can vary between 45:1 and 130:1.

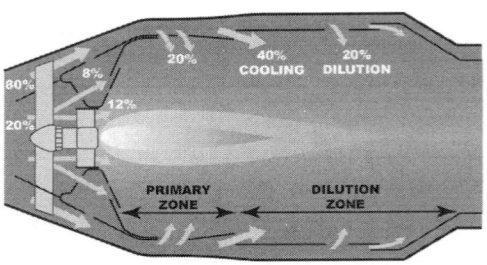

Primary air comes directly in through the snout of the combustion chamber. About 10% of it passes through the swirl vanes, which creates a toroidal vortex, that resembles a ring doughnut or a smoke ring - low static pressure in the centre encourages the air to reverse back into the incoming flow, so once ignition starts, the flame is fed back to the burner head, shortening and concentrating it. The centre of the vortex is also where the conical spray of fuel intersects the airflow, so the fuel is broken up and mixed with the air. *The highest temperature in a running turbine engine is in the primary zone of the combustion chamber, which is where the flame, or air used for combustion, is.*

Maximum flame temperature is between 1800-2000°C.

The remaining 90% of the primary air passes through the colander, where it meets the fuel spray at right angles to the spray cone. This shapes the flame and keeps it from touching the flame tube.

Secondary air is mainly concerned with cooling the gas flow before it enters the NGVs and turbines and the flame tube and casing material.

It gets into the air gap between the two casings and comes back into the combustion chamber through holes a little way downstream. This both cools the hot gas and provides more oxygen for the burning process.

Tertiary air, also from the air gap, cools the flame tube before it is mixed into the gases downstream of the secondary air. Aside from diluting the high temperatures, it helps to distribute the heat uniformly throughout the gas so that it reaches the entry to the turbine at a more acceptable level, as local hot spots could damage it.

Some cooling air enters the flame tube through windows or corrugations which are shaped to form a skin of cooling air over its inner face.

Multiple combustion chambers (cannular) were used on early engines, particularly those with centrifugal compressors. The separate tubes were interconnected so that the pressures within the various chambers were equalised, but 2 igniters were needed, to ensure that as much fuel as possible is ignited at the same time.

Axial flow engines now tend to have annular combustion chambers, with a single concentric flame tube around the spools (that is, continuous circular casing around the compressor drive housing, open to the compressor at one end and the turbine at the other). This provides better use of volumetric space and control of the primary airflows, and better distribution of fuel, air, pressure and temperature, for more stable and even combustion (no hot spots). It also allows the engine to be made shorter, and the diameter of the engine can be reduced.

THE TURBINE

The turbine's purpose is extract energy from the hot gases and expand them to a lower pressure and temperature, to drive the compressor and maybe some accessories. As the gases are hot and fast, the turbine has to withstand a lot of stress, particularly when starting, where the temperature rise is very quick. The temperature over the blades can be anywhere between 850-1700°C, and the pressure against them can be in the order of 50 tons per square inch, so the operating temperature is limited by the materials used.

Turbine blades are usually of the impulse/reaction variety (50% impulse from the root, 50% reaction for the rest) because each type is inefficient when used by itself. In an *impulse turbine*, the gases pass through without changes in velocity or pressure, but they do change direction - it is the reaction from this that makes the blades rotate. Newton's second law applies. Reaction types use a narrowing (convergent) gap between the blades to react to the *pressure* of the airflow. Newton's third law applies. The two can be combined to create an impulse-reaction turbine.

In a **free turbine** engine, the exhaust gases go through two turbine stages, a compressor turbine, which drives the compressor directly, and a power turbine, which is connected to the transmission. **There is no direct connection between the engine and the gearbox it drives**, which is important for autorotation (and helpful when starting, as one less turbine needs to be driven). The compressor is allowed to run at different speeds while the power turbine is maintained at a constant RPM for any value of collective pitch. This means that the power delivered to the rotors depends only on engine torque, and that the free turbine is better for multi-engine systems because only the compressor speed needs to be adjusted to maintain rotor RPM.

With a **fixed turbine**, all parts of the engine run at the same speed, and fuel flow is changed to alter the temperature and velocity of the air. This makes the engine a little less responsive, and the compressor might not necessarily run at its optimum speed.

75% of the pressure energy from the exhaust gases is converted to mechanical energy. 25% is used for thrust.

TURBINE BLADES

Turbine blades wash in, and are mostly held in place with *fir tree fittings* (centrifugal force ensures a tight fit).

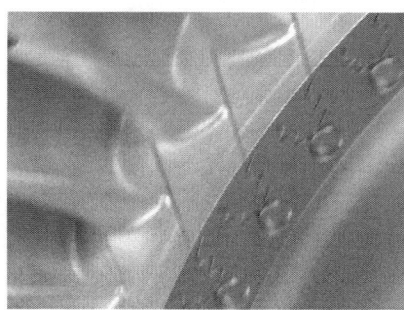

Creep is the continued plastic deformation of a component subjected to stress, such as heat. If the stress lasts for a long time, the stress continues. Turbine blade creep is a change in blade length from a combination of heat and centrifugal force when spinning too fast. If you overtemp the engine, the change will be permanent. **Creep is cumulative and irreversible.**

There are three stages of creep:

- **Primary**, with rapid expansion, as when starting (because the engine is not spinning fast you are allowed more TOT as there is less risk of creep).

- **Secondary**, which is more or less constant after the initial elongation

- **Tertiary**, where rapid and fundamental changes occur, until the blade fractures.

The greatest risk created by a free turbine overspeed is bursting of the free turbine disk.

Sealing

The turbine engine does not have as many closed areas as a piston engine does, so how are the different regions sealed off? One method is to use air pressure that stops air of lower pressure getting past, and another is to use a labyrinth seal, which is a mechanical seal that fits around a shaft to prevent leakage between the fixed and rotating parts of a turbine.

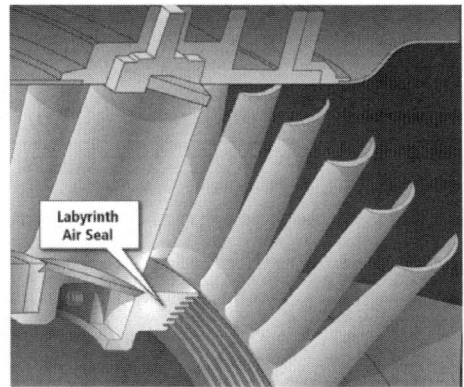

Labyrinth Air Seal

The seals have fixed and rotating parts, consisting of solid wheels on the rotating part that interlock with stationary gates, so that whatever fluid is being blocked has to pass through a long and difficult path to escape. The stationary part has a material that allows the rotating knife edges to fit into it. Thus, there is a non-contact sealing action - at higher speeds, centrifugal motion forces the liquid towards the outside and away from any passages.

Similarly, any liquid that escapes the main chamber becomes entrapped in a labyrinth chamber, where it is forced into a vortex-like motion to prevent its escape and repel any other fluid. Because labyrinth seals are non-contact, they do not wear out, and can cope with the high speeds associated with turbines.

Fuel

To make fuel, crude oil is boiled up in what is effectively a giant still. The heavy stuff drops to the bottom, whilst the lighter parts (gasoline & kerosene) are distilled off the top. This is repeated at higher temperatures until complete.

Jet and piston fuels mix differently with contaminants (particularly water), which is due to variations in their specific gravities and temperature. The specific gravity of water, for example, is so close to Avtur that it can take up to 4 hours for it to settle out, whereas the same process may take as little as half an hour with Avgas. As a result, there is always water suspended in jet fuel, which must be kept within strict limits, hence two filtration stages, for solids and water. The latter doesn't burn, of course, and it can freeze, but it's the fungi that gather round the interface between water and fuel that is the real problem - it turns into a dark-coloured slime which clings to tank walls and supporting structures, which not only alters the fuel chemically, but will block filters as well. Not much water is required for this - trace elements are enough, although, in reduced temperatures, dissolved water will escape as free water, and look like fog. Water in jet fuel is the reason for *icing inhibitors*, which will combine with the water and lower its freezing point, so that ice crystals do not form and block the lines, although this is really more relevant for aeroplanes at high altitude. However, helicopters operating in the Arctic can be affected too, and fuel heaters or filters are more popular these days anyway.

Each day before flying, or after a long turnaround time, and when the fuel is settled, carry out a water check in aircraft and containers. Collect samples in a transparent container and check for sediment, free water or cloudiness - if there is only one liquid, ensure it is not all water. Aviation fuel is "clean" if a one-quart sample is clear of sediment when viewed through a clean, dry, clear glass container, and looks clear and bright. Cloudiness indicates the presence of water, which is heavier then fuel, so it will sink to the bottom eventually.

Aircraft parked overnight should ideally have their tanks completely filled to stop condensation, although the amount of water found under these circumstances in a small aircraft is unlikely to be more than a tablespoon.

The reason why long-term storage is not good for fuel (up to two years for drums is the accepted maximum) is partly because of daily temperature changes. When it is warm, the fuel expands and some of the vapour-air mixture is driven out. When it gets colder, the fuel contracts and fresh air is sucked in, to mix with more vapour. As the cycle repeats itself, the fuel inside gradually loses its effectiveness. Humidity means that water vapour will get in, too, and condense into liquid. The presence of oxygen will also cause a soluble gum to form, and insoluble black particularates, which become more apparent when fuel evaporates. TEL will oxidise into an insoluble white mass. Containers should be filled to 95% (to allow for expansion), and sealed tightly, in a temperature mostly below 80°F, out of direct sunlight.

Fuel's volatility increases with altitude and temperature, so it will evaporate away quicker. This can cause *vapour locking*, where a bubble may form in the pipes and stop the fuel flowing. Increasing the pressure in the pipes helps with this, which is why boost pumps are installed.

The *flash point* is the lowest temperature at which fuel can produce a flammable mixture when vapour forms, so a volatile mixture has a low flash point. The *Reid vapour pressure* is that required to keep a liquid as a liquid, or the pressure measured where only a small fraction of the fuel vapourises, so a volatile fluid has a high vapour pressure.

AVGAS

Aviation gasoline is made of lighter hydrocarbons and has a specific gravity of around 0.72. It is coloured this way:

Colour	Fuel
Red	80/87
Blue	100LL
Green	100/130

AVGAS fuelling points on aircraft are painted red with white lettering.

If you cannot use the recommended fuel (in the flight manual) you must use a higher grade. Too low a grade causes detonation and increases cylinder head and oil temperature indications.

MOGAS

Motor Gasoline, for road vehicles, is colourless, and should not be used in temperatures greater than 20°C or at altitudes greater than 6000 feet. An aircraft using MOGAS is likely to be affected more by vapour locking and carburettor icing.

CAPT

JET FUEL

This is less volatile than AVGAS, but will still catch fire, given the chance - technically, it has a higher flash point, but a lower freezing point, and it gets more viscous as it cools, so gets harder to pump. At the freezing point, the hydrocarbons turn into waxy crystals. The specific gravity of jet fuel is between 0.75 to 0.84, but most flight manuals peg it down to 0.79.

Jet A, standard for commercial and general aviation (in the USA, at least), is narrow-cut kerosene, usually with no additives. **Jet A1** has a lower freezing point than Jet A, and possibly (but rarely) something for dissipating static, and inhibiting fungus. It is used for long haul flights where the temperature gets very low. **Jet B** is a naphtha-type fuel made by blending straight-run kerosene with lower-boiling distillate, so it's wide-cut, lighter (i.e. less dense) and has a very low flash point (it's actually 2/3 kerosene and 1/3 naphtha, but in an emergency you can swap the naphtha for avgas to get pretty much the same thing). It contains static dissipators, and is mainly used by military aircraft - **the FCU may need to be adjusted** if you want to use it, although it is being phased out, at least by Esso. Its only significant demand these days is in really cold places.

Try not to mix Jet A and Jet B - the mixture can ignite through static in the right proportions, as Air Canada found when they lost a DC-8 on the ramp in the 70s. The static can come simply from movement of fuel through the lines (it has to cross many materials). Jet A weighs about 5% more per litre than Jet B, but it gives you a longer range, as turbines work on the weight of the fuel they burn, not the quantity (hence the use of kg/hr for fuel flow, for example). So, if you load the same amount of fuel, your machine will weigh more with Jet A, but if you fill the tanks, you will use fewer litres and less money (this is one reason, aside from lubrication qualities, for not using AVGAS - its specific gravity is lower. However, AVTUR has more water in suspension and residual wax that must be heated to stop it blocking pipes).

JP4 is like Jet B but also has a corrosion inhibitor and anti-icing additives. It was the main military fuel but is being superseded by JP8, at least in the USA, for the Air Force. JP5 has a higher flashpoint than JP4, and was designed for US navy ships. It is similar to Jet A.

AVTUR is pale yellow in colour (like straw). Its markings are white on a black background.

Note: Aircraft and refuelling vehicles must be bonded together before the fuel cap is removed (see *Operations*).

Fuel Control

FCU

The *Fuel Control Unit* does pretty much the same job as a carburettor on a piston engine by providing the proper amount of fuel to the combustion chamber, using hydraulic pressure, springs and centrifugal bobweights (hydromechanical) to meter fuel according to demand.

$$\downarrow \begin{matrix}\text{Rotor}\\\text{Droop}\end{matrix} \xrightarrow{\begin{matrix}\text{Detected}\\\text{By}\end{matrix}} \textbf{PTG} \xrightarrow{\begin{matrix}\text{Signal}\\\text{To}\end{matrix}} \textbf{FCU} \xrightarrow{\begin{matrix}\text{Flow}\\\text{Increased}\end{matrix}}$$

Too much fuel causes too much pressure in a centrifugal compressor which blows back to cause a stall. Too little fuel may cause a flameout.

On the Bell 206, for example, the FCU reacts to signals from the *Power Turbine Governor* (PTG), which senses the load on the rotors in the form of rotor droop - if more pitch is applied, the PTG signals the FCU to increase fuel flow, and the velocity of the hotter gases will increase through the gas producer turbine to increase N_1 and through the power turbine to maintain rotor speed.

The FCU is protected from debris damage by a fine filter between it and the high pressure (engine) fuel pump.

The turbine governor's job is to keep the speed of the free turbine (and rotor blades) constant, irrespective of the fuel flow and power demands.

Although it detects RPM variations and issues control orders, it doesn't get much feedback, so the rotor RPM is not always constant in the true sense of the word - it will drop slightly as power is increased and rise when power demands decrease. This slight difference in RPM is called *static droop*, and

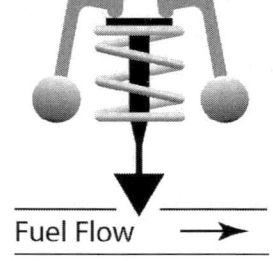

Fuel Flow ⟶

it can occur whenever a flyweight centrifugal governor is used on a free turbine engine. Its value depends on the spring tension.

The free turbine drives bobweights which fly outwards as engine RPM is increased, which compresses the spring that pushes a needle into the fuel flow to restrict its movement through the hole. If, at a stabilised RPM, RRPM decreases (say after an increase in collective pitch), the centrifugal force will decrease and the spring will move the flyweights closer in to each other. This will pull the needle out of the hole and allow the fuel flow to increase, and increase the rotor RPM.

THE FADEC

The initials stand for *Full Authority Digital Electronic Control*. It's just a computer that controls the fuel system, based on information from various sensors, such as exhaust temperature, engine RPM, control movement, etc. (typical inputs are TOT and N_1). On the Bell 407, for example, data is always flowing from the engine sensors to the computer, and is stored in temporary short term memory. When anomalies are detected, the previous 10 seconds' worth is captured, and the next 50 seconds' worth is recorded. This data is tagged by time and date.

The end result is a more precise control of rotor speeds under varying flight conditions, particularly for overspeeding. Other benefits include automatic starting, optimal fuel metering, faster response to power demands, better care of the engine (more time between overhauls) and reduction of pilot workload through automation. It is also better at limiting. On a piston engine (with fuel injection) it can automatically set the mixture and timing.

Being a computer, it is software-based, and one preflight check is to ensure that the right software is loaded. Also, as it's a computer, it can monitor many parameters, which is why you might see more caution lights. With a single FADEC, there will also be a backup Hydro Mechanical Unit (HMU), which works like the old-style FCU when the FADEC is disabled.

A double FADEC has no backup system, but all types must have their own source of power.

There will also be sensors and relays for the transmission of information around the system. Many signals will be repeated to the relevant instruments.

A FADEC has the following functions:

- Flow regulation
- Automatic starting sequence
- Transmission of engine data to pilot's instruments
- Thrust management and protection of limits
- Prevent overtemperature or overspeed

With the FADEC, corrective changes can be made before droops or overshoots occur.

The fuel metering valve is positioned by a torque motor.

Engine Handling   021 10 10

Pulling full power just because it's there is not always a good idea. Limitations may be there for other reasons - for example, the transmission might not be able to take that much, so excessive use of power will ruin your gearbox well before the engine (and will show up as metal particles in the oil). Many turbine failures are the result of pulling too many cycles from minimum to maximum N_G (gas producer RPM), so if you don't need 100% torque, it's

best not to use it. With some turbine engines (as on the AS 350), you must keep a track of the number of times you fluctuate between a range of power settings because of the heat stress. It's also best not to reduce the collective to the bottom stop when descending, either, and to make power changes gently, avoiding over- and undershoots.

Maximum Continuous Power is the setting that may be used indefinitely, but any between that and maximum power (usually shown as a yellow arc on the instruments - see left) will only be available for a set time limit, typically 30 minutes. There may also be a "takeoff" or "emergency" rating that is valid for 2-5 minutes. The 30-minute rating is typically 20% above Max Continuous and the short-term one 10% above that.

Note: If, by the time you reach the beginning of the yellow arc on your torque or temperature gauges, you are not off the ground, you are too heavy!

While I'm not suggesting that you should, piston engines will accept their limits being slightly exceeded from time to time with no great harm being done. Having said that, the speed at which the average Lycoming engine disintegrates is about 3450 RPM, which doesn't leave you an awful lot of room when it runs normally (in a Bell 47, anyway) at 3300! Turbines, however, are less forgiving than pistons and give fewer warnings of trouble because of the closer tolerances to which they are made. This is why regular power checks should be carried out on them to keep an eye on their health. The other difference is that damage to a piston engine caused by mishandling tends to affect you, straight away, whereas that in a turbine tends to affect others down the line.

Apart from sympathetic handling, the greatest factor in preserving engine life is temperature and its rate of change. Over- and under-leaning are detrimental to engine life, and sudden cooling is as bad as overheating - chopping the throttle at height causes the cylinder head to shrink and crack with the obvious results - the thermal shock and extra lead is worth about $100 in terms of lost engine life. In other words, don't let the rotors drive the engine, but rather cut power to the point where it's doing a little work. This is because the reduced power lowers the pressure that keeps piston rings against the wall of the cylinder, so oil leaks past and glazes on the hot surfaces, degrading any sealing obtained by compression. The only way to get rid of the glaze is by *honing*, which means a top-end overhaul. For the same reasons, a new (or rebuilt) engine should be run in hard, at least at 65% power, but preferably 70-75%, according to Textron Lycoming, so the rings are forced to seat in properly. This means not flying above 8000 feet density altitude for non-turbocharged engines. Richer mixtures are important as

well. Also, open the engine compartment after shutting down on a hot day, as many external components will have suddenly lost their cooling.

After flight, many engines have a rundown period which must be strictly observed if you want to keep it for any length of time. As engines get smaller relative to power output, they have to work harder. Also, in turbines, there are no heavy areas to act as heat sinks, like the fins on a piston engine, which results in localised hotspots which may deform, but are safe if cooled properly, with the help of circulating oil inside the engine (75% of the air taken into a turbine is for cooling). If you shut down too quickly, the cooling air is not blown over the turbine blades and the oil no longer circulates, which means that it carbonises on the still-hot surfaces, and can build up enough to prevent the relevant parts from turning, which is why you walk the blades backwards on a preflight check to see if there is a problem. This coking up could seize the engine in 50 hours or less.

Because starter systems on piston engines don't have fuses (too much current), if the starter light remains on after you release the starter button on a piston engine, it means that the starter is still engaged. There is a small gear on the starter motor and a very large one on the engine, so the starter motor will be driven at a very high RPM. You must shut down *immediately* to avoid serious damage.

Engine Instruments

A turbine engine has to operate within certain limits - it must not be run too fast, or too hot, or have too much strain imposed on it. The relevant gauges (in a helicopter, anyway) are:

- the **N₁**, or *compressor RPM*

- the **TOT**, or *Turbine Outlet Temperature*, and

- the **torquemeter**

Stop raising the collective when you reach the first of these limits.

ENGINE FIRST LIMIT INDICATOR

To get around the problem of watching too many instruments at once, a trend is to combine critical readings into one, as is done with some Eurocopter machines:

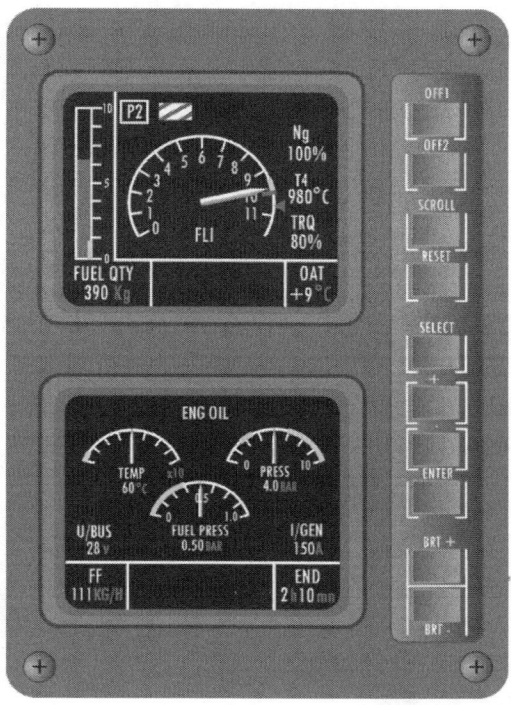

In the top display (FLI) the readings from the instruments are displayed down the side, but the needle points to whichever one is reaching the first limit.

THE TACHOMETER   022 01 05

Engine RPM indicate power directly, so the tachometer is a primary engine instrument. Turbines rotate so fast that the numbers are too large to make sense of, so percentages are used instead (that is, 100% means full power), so that engines can be compared better.

In a helicopter, the engine and rotor RPM (R) needles are near each other in the same *dual tachometer*. They can be separate, as in the Robinson R22 on the left:

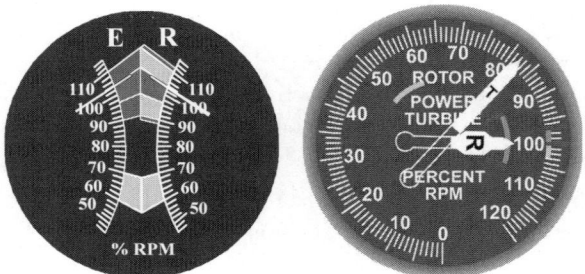

Or sitting on top of each other, as with the Bell 206 on the right, above. In powered flight, the needles will be joined; in autorotation, they will be split, as shown.

On a helicopter with a free turbine engine, the big needle labelled T above represents the turbine RPM (N_2). The other big needle (R) is for Rotor RPM. There will also be a smaller gauge showing "gas producer", or N_1, RPM (right). Its small pointer moves in 1% increments.

A fixed turbine engine has only one indicator because the engine has only one rotating unit.

MECHANICAL TACHOMETERS

These are found on older piston-engined aircraft, where the feed is taken from the crankshaft (on a turbine, the measurement is taken from compressor speed).

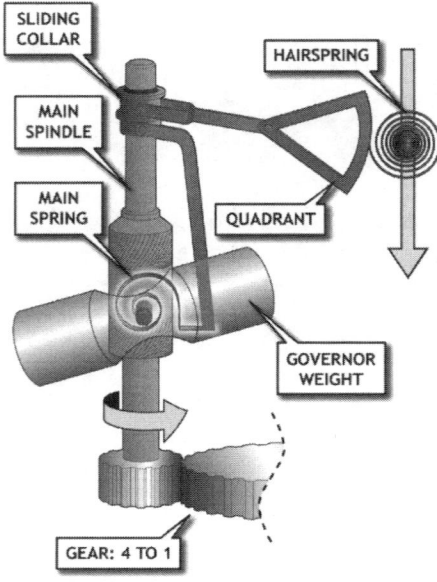

There is a long, flexible drive shaft from the engine to the indicator, which runs at a quarter of the engine speed to reduce wear and tear. This is the reason for the 4:1 step-up gear in the base of the instrument. The longest practical length for such a cable is 30 feet.

A governor weight assumes a more horizontal position as the speed of the engine is increased, which makes a sliding collar move up and down the shaft, driving a suitable linkage to the indicator. The governor moves against a spring that moves it back to its home position when the engine speed is reduced.

Another type uses the flexible shaft to turn a magnet inside an aluminium drag cup to set up eddy currents that make the cup turn at the same speed as the magnet. The cup is supported on a shaft to which is attached a pointer and a controlling spring which opposes the turning force so that, for any one speed, the eddy current drag and spring tension are in equilibrium, and the pointer is steady.

ELECTRICAL TACHOMETERS

On more modern aircraft, tachogenerators driven by the engine can put out DC, or single- or three-phase AC, which can drive a voltmeter calibrated in RPM over electrical cabling. The lack of moving parts allows engines to be further away from the cockpit, and you don't need separate power supplies. With the DC version, output voltage varies with RPM, and drives a moving coil indicator which needs a commutator and carbon brushes, so there is wear and sparking which can cause radio interference (or fires). Also, voltage loss in transmission leads to indication errors.

A single-phase brushless AC generator, on the other hand, has its output rectified to DC, so the mechanical problems are not there, but indication errors are. One disadvantage of a single phase AC generator tachometer is that the values transmitted may be affected by line resistance, but spurious signals from a DC generator's commutator are avoided and the information is independent.

A Three-Phase AC tachogenerator has its AC frequency varying with RPM, to drive a squirrel cage motor at the instrument. Frequency is proportional to transmitter drive speed and the speed indicating element is an asynchronous motor driving a magnetic tachometer. These normally rotate slightly slower than the generator, with the slip depending on the torque required. Motors that rotate at the same frequency as the AC generator are synchronous squirrel cage motors. Because frequency is sensed rather than voltage, voltage losses are not a problem, but extra wiring is needed to carry three phases.

ELECTRONIC TACHOMETERS

It is not always possible to drive a tacho generator from some points in a turbine engine. In these cases, a system with fewer moving parts is used (alternating current is required for the system to work).

The picture below shows a system for measuring rotor RPM, but the principles are the same for engines. RPM is sensed by a magnetic probe using a toothed wheel, called a phonic wheel.

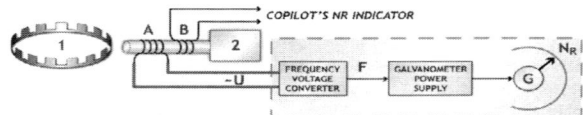

The probe counts the passage of teeth on the wheel as it rotates by changes induced in its magnetic field, which creates an electrical current whose frequency changes in proportion to the speed of rotation. This is fed to an indicator in the cockpit.

CAPT

MANIFOLD PRESSURE GAUGE

The *Manifold Absolute Pressure* (MAP) gauge shows the pressure inside the inlet manifold, in inches (mostly in supercharged engines). The theory is that the higher the pressure, the more the amount of fuel/air mixture that is potentially available. The power we can extract from the charge is proportional to the manifold pressure. The equivalent in a turbine helicopter is the *torquemeter*.

When the engine is stopped, the MAP will be at atmospheric pressure. When the engine is running, MAP is below atmospheric because of the pressure drop across the butterfly valve (the engine is sucking air in). For a non-turbocharged engine at maximum power, the manifold pressure is very close to atmospheric, so you get maximum power by letting the engine breathe freely. The manifold pressure can be higher than atmospheric if you use a turbocharger.

A break in the line between the MAP gauge and the induction system is shown when the gauge registers atmospheric pressure. A MAP gauge uses a bellows.

The *critical altitude* is the highest that a given MAP can be obtained, or the pressure altitude at which the waste gate of a turbocharger is fully closed. Thus, a turbocharger will maintain ISA sea level pressure up to the critical altitude.

The maximum horsepower output you can get from an engine when it is operated at safe continuous RPM & MAP is the *rated power*. Full throttle height is the maximum height for rated boost.

Remember, the throttle controls the horsepower, and engine RPM is concerned with the load (if you kept the throttle setting constant, and increased the load, you will find that the engine RPM will drop). Engine power is not proportional to RPM alone.

THE TORQUEMETER

The torquemeter indicates the twisting force of the engine against the transmission, or the loads applied to the transmission shafts and gears, so that limitations can be observed. As rotor speed is more or less constant, it also shows the engine's power output.

The power turbine runs at so high a speed (typically 30,000 RPM) that reduction gearing is necessary to drive a transmission at something like 6000 RPM. Part of the reduction gearing can be used to measure the engine's power output because axial thrust (movement) is generated when helically cut gears are used to transfer power from one shaft to another. Put another way, ss the gears rotate they move slightly, the amount being proportional to the torque applied.

Turbine engines in helicopters (and in turboprops) have a smooth and uniform torque output due to their continuous combustion. Torque is the measure of power being used, being a force applied at a distance by a turning point. It is measured between the engine and the reduction gearbox, and can be expressed in Newton metres, brake or shaft horsepower and inch or foot pounds. It may be shown on a torque gauge (above) as a percentage.

$$\text{Power} = \text{Torque} \times \text{RPM}$$

The torquemeter needs to be on the output shaft because the driveshaft connecting the power turbine assembly is designed to be as light as possible, so it only has a little margin of strength for excessive torque, or twisting, loads. Having the torquemeter on the *output* shaft allows engine torque to be closely monitored (Manifold Pressure is measured on the input side of the engine). Changes in the N_1 or TOT will be the only way of telling whether the engine is off specification, as the torque indication will always be the same. MAP is at best a predictor of engine power output, torque is a measurement of it.

One method of measuring torque is by oil pressure.

On the AS 350, for example, engine torque is measured at the intermediate pinion of the engine reduction gear. As it has helical teeth, it produces a sideways thrust and reaction proportional to engine torque as the gears try to separate (because engine torque and the resistance of the rotor drive system oppose each other).

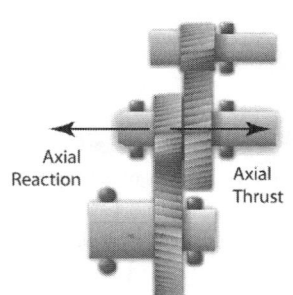

Axial Reaction

Axial Thrust

TEMPERATURE

Operating at higher than intended temperatures will cause *loss of power, excessive oil consumption and damage to the engine.*

PISTON ENGINES

In a piston helicopter, the *Cylinder Head Temperature* (CHT) gauge (which uses a thermocouple) shows the temperature of one selected cylinder, usually a rearmost in a horizontally opposed engine, which is not necessarily the one that reaches peak temperature first, even though it may end up as the hottest, so a margin of 25° rich of peak may still not be enough to stop another cylinder from getting too close to peak for comfort, or even lean.

Knowledge of the *Exhaust Gas Temperature* (EGT), on the other hand, is needed for leaning the mixture efficiently. The probe is in the exhaust manifold.

Tip: An EGT gauge is a fast-reading instrument that lets you know what the flame in the combustion chamber is up to. It responds almost instantly to changes in power and the fuel/air mixture. The CHT gauge, on the other hand, measures the core temperature near one of the combustion chambers, so it reacts more slowly and may not represent the whole picture, especially when there is only one carburettor supplying several cylinders and one may be hotter than the others. The *oil temperature gauge* (which reacts very slowly to changes) is the best measure of how heat is balanced around the engine, which means that having the correct amount of oil in it is essential, if only for cooling purposes. However, having too much oil can be just as much a problem as having too little, as it can creep up the pushrod tubes and pick up heat directly from the cylinders.

One consideration with using low power when it's very cold is that the engine may not warm up properly and water that forms from combustion may not evaporate, so oil won't lubricate properly.

The reason the temperature cools either side of the peak reading is that on the one hand (rich), there is too much fuel and, on the other (lean), there is too much air (having said that, the hottest CHT is between 25-50° *rich* of peak EGT, because that's where the peak cylinder pressure occurs, with a high rate of heat transfer to the cylinder head, so you need to lean past it). However, although being lean of peak works, there is much more potential for causing damage to the engine if it is mismanaged - it needs more monitoring to be used effectively, as the temperature at the exhaust will still be high, which is not good for the valves, and particularly acute with high performance turbocharged engines - The Australians found that leaning causes lead oxybromide deposits to cling to parts inside the combustion chamber, which could become hotspots and cause detonation (the lead appears as a result of chemical changes in avgas as it burns). At richer settings, the lead either doesn't form or is swept out of the cylinder.

Tip: Don't forget to enrich the mixture before increasing power when at peak EGT, or when increasing to more than 75% power. Move the engine controls slowly and smoothly, particularly with a turbocharger. Harsh movements (on older engines) will result in a cough and splutter and having no power can be embarrassing.

Although many flight manuals state that, as soon as an engine is running without stuttering, it's safe to use it to its fullest extent, try warming up for a few minutes before applying any load, at least until you get a positive indication on the oil temperature (and pressure) gauges. This ensures a film of oil over all parts, and no excessive

wear. In addition, when the oil is cold, its pressure will be higher, and too much throttle will only ensure that the pressure valves will let unfiltered oil into the system (high oil pressure spikes are also bad for the oil cooler).

Even better, warm the engine before you start it, because the insides contract at different rates - in really cold weather the cylinders may have the grip of death on the pistons and cause some strain when you turn the starter (manufacturers tend to suggest preheating around -10°C, but many pilots do it around 0°C. Don't forget the oil cooler, as warm oil from the engine meeting cold oil inside might also cause a burst). In addition, a cold engine absorbs the heat required for ignition.

Equally important is not letting an engine idle when it's cold, as it must be fast enough to create a splash of oil inside (about 1,000 RPM is fine).

TURBINE OUTLET TEMPERATURE

On a turbine-engined helicopter, depending on where it is measured, the temperature gauge may be called any of the following names:

- TGT - *Turbine Gas Temperature*
- EGT - *Exhaust Gas Temperature*
- TOT - *Turbine Outlet Temperature*

It can also be called the ITT (*Integrated Total Temperature*).

One of the most important instruments in your cockpit is the *Turbine Outlet Temperature* (TOT) gauge, which shows the heat coming out of the back end.

A red triangle, or dot, or diamond on an engine instrument face or glass indicates the maximum limits for high transients, as found when starting

It is particularly important during starting because, if the battery is too weak to spin the engine properly, there will be less airflow through it, and not as much cooling available, leading to a hot start and an expensive repair as the back end melts. During flight, on hot days, this temperature may well be the limiting factor in the payload you can take, even if you have lots of torque left.

High temperatures in the 700-1000°C range are measured with *thermocouples*, which are based on the idea that dissimilar metals welded together can create an electrical potential at their junction, proportional to the temperature (the very small voltages are detected by a *galvanometer*). In other words, the voltage output is determined by the

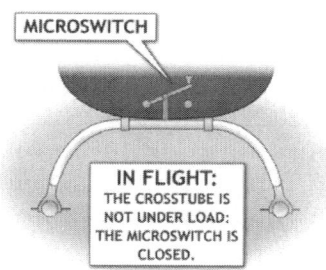

difference in heat between the two ends, if the cold end is kept at a constant temperature (intermediate metals in the circuit will not modify the emf either if their contact points are kept at equal temperatures). Thermocouples are wired in parallel so the failure of one does not stop the whole system. External power is not needed, so when you shut down on some helicopters, you can check that the TOT is not moving rapidly out of limits. In a gas turbine engine, the thermocouple is found at the turbine outlet.

For higher temperatures, a *radiation pyrometer* measures the frequency of emitted radiation, and can deduce the actual turbine blade temperature. Its advantage is that it can perform measurements independent of the supply voltage.

The reason why the Turbine Outlet Temperature is measured after the turbine wheels is because it is simply too hot for a thermocouple to survive anywhere else (although, in the Allison 250, as fitted to the Bell 206 and many other helicopters, the temperature is actually measured *between* the turbine wheels). Instead, a more severe limit is imposed on the TOT to protect the turbine(s) at the other end. The heat is kept within limits with cooling air extracted from the compressor, which is driven by the turbine through a connection.

An instrument may contain *overspeed detectors* in the form of pointers or warning lights. These may only be reset by engineering, for obvious reasons. Sometimes, exceeding temperature limits may cause the rotor RPM to droop.

TIME MEASUREMENT

An hourmeter records the operating time of an engine, machine, or mechanism to monitor and log its service life.

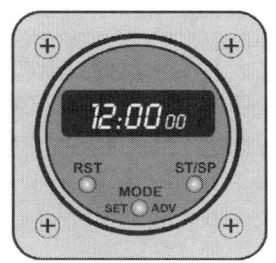

In a helicopter it is typically started by a switch that operates when the collective lever is lifted a certain distance, and stopped when it is lowered again (see above).

Electric clocks, or semiconductor or magnetic devices driven by a constant-frequency quartz or other master oscillator, may be used as timers for aircraft engines.

Lubrication

Friction can be quite handy, but not inside an engine! Without some way of making the various surfaces rub smoothly against each other, they would get hot, and suffer from scoring damage. Oil actually does many things, including:

- **Cooling**. Hot oil is cooled in an oil cooler, which is exposed to the airflow, so cooling the engine. A high temperature means too little oil in the system. Low oil pressure could be due to a worn pump.

- **Cushioning.** A film of oil has three distinct layers, the outside two of which cling to each surface, and the middle one moves between them, providing some sort of buffer

- **Flushing & Cleaning**. Oil carries contaminants to the oil filter where they are blocked

- **Lubrication**. Reduces friction in two ways:
  - *Film Lubrication*, where a thin film of oil between two surfaces stops them touching. The thinner the oil is (i.e. the less viscous), the easier the movement is
  - *Boundary Lubrication* is a state of near breakdown where the film above is reduced to next to nothing.

- **Sealing**

- **Prevention Of Corrosion**

ENGINE OILS

An engine that is not used enough develops corrosion very quickly on the inside, and rust flakes, which are very abrasive, will circulate when the engine is started, which is why you have to change the oil even when you don't fly a lot. Another reason is an increased water content, which will have an acidic effect once it mixes with the by-products of combustion. The most wear takes place in the

first seconds of a cold start, after the oil has been allowed to settle. Priming will wash whatever oil is left off the cylinder walls, so don't do too much, and maintain minimum RPM to let the oil circulate. The pressure will be high just after starting, but will reduce to normal once the engine warms up. Excessive oil pressure is acceptable *for a few seconds* on a cold day. In fact, after starting a cold engine, particularly in winter, you can allow the oil pressure not to rise for about 30 seconds, because it may be too thick to get through the passages until it gets warm. Otherwise, you should shut the engine down immediately.

Note: If you use high power before the engine is warmed up, bearings and other parts will suffer from oil starvation.

When flying, the oil temperature and pressure gauges work with each other (they are measured after the pump and before the engine). If the pressure is low, you can generally expect the temperature to rise because it is working harder. Oil is hot when it comes out of an engine, and to preserve its lubricating qualities it must be cooled. This is why monitoring oil temperature is so important.

With Hiller 12 and Bell 47 helicopters, the main rotor gearbox is lubricated with engine oil, because it is bolted directly to the top of the engine. An engine oil pressure problem with these machines (or any similar) is therefore quite serious.

VISCOSITY

Oils come in various thicknesses, or *viscosities*, which indicate their resistance to flow. The lower the viscosity number, the thinner the oil is, so you would use 120 oil in Summer, 100 in Fall or Spring, 80 in Winter and 65 in the Arctic. To keep the oil thin, in the cold, one trick is to pour a few litres of petrol into the oil system just after closing down at night, so it is very thin in the morning and you can start the engine. By the time the oil has warmed up, the petrol has evaporated and you can carry on (but check your flight manual to see if *Oil Dilution* is acceptable.

MINERAL OIL (RED BAND)

Mineral oil (castor oil) has no additives and is now only used in new or overhauled engines, to help them bed in. This is because it can oxidise when exposed to high temperatures or when it gets frothy, and form a sludge in low temperatures, and there are better modern oils for long term use. Look for a label on the oil filler to make sure that you only use this type of oil.

DETERGENT OIL

This has chemicals that help with cleaning, etc., including keeping particles suspended, but it is no longer available.

ASHLESS DISPERSANT (AD) OIL

This does not form carbon like mineral oil does, although it does get dark soon after an oil change. It has an additive that causes the components of sludge to repel each other and remain in suspension until they reach the oil filter, where they are screened out. It is the most used oil.

SYNTHETIC OILS

Synthetic oils have been developed to cover wide temperature ranges, for jets at high altitudes and reciprocating engines operating at high temperatures. However, synthetic oil is expensive, and another drawback is that it holds contaminants longer.

MIXING OILS

The official stance is that you should not mix oils, period, especially mineral oil. However, within their basic groups, there is an element of compatibility, but you should never use motor vehicle oil, because it is designed for liquid cooled engines that operate at lower temperatures.

AD oil is compatible with mineral oil, at the expense of some of the advantages offered by AD oil. Not enough data is available to confirm that the same situation exists with synthetic oil, so it would not be a good idea to mix it.

TYPES OF LUBRICATION SYSTEM

The lubrication system's purpose is to supply oil to critical parts of the engine under enough pressure to force it between the various surfaces.

WET SUMP

This is very simple, because the engine oil is kept in a sump which is under (and part of) the engine, where the crankshaft and other moving parts rotate, splashing it all around (*splash and mist lubrication*). When you start the engine, the oil is sucked from the sump through a filter to the galleries around the engine casing.

It is generally thought that wet sump systems do not use a pump, but they can, as with the Piper Cherokee. Wet sump systems tend not to be used on modern aero engines, as the bearings are starved of oil when the aircraft is inverted, and temperature control is difficult as it is contained inside the hot engine.

In addition, more oil changes are needed because of the continuous churning.

DRY SUMP

A dry sump system (see above) keeps the oil in a tank *outside* the engine (sometimes above it for gravity feed), and the oil is force fed under pressure to where it is needed - the sump in this case is used merely as a collector for stray oil dripping off the components inside. Because the engine parts aren't having to make their way through oil in the sump, it has less work to do and more power is therefore available. Less oil is also needed.

The "oil pump" is actually two pumps running on the same shaft - the scavenge pump and the engine oil pump.

The scavenge pump (which pulls oil *from* the engine) has the greater capacity in order to keep the sump dry, or to stop oil accumulating in the engine, especially after an unusual attitude, where oil might not necessarily be in the collection area until the machine is righted again, and the pump must cope with the surge (also, overnight, the

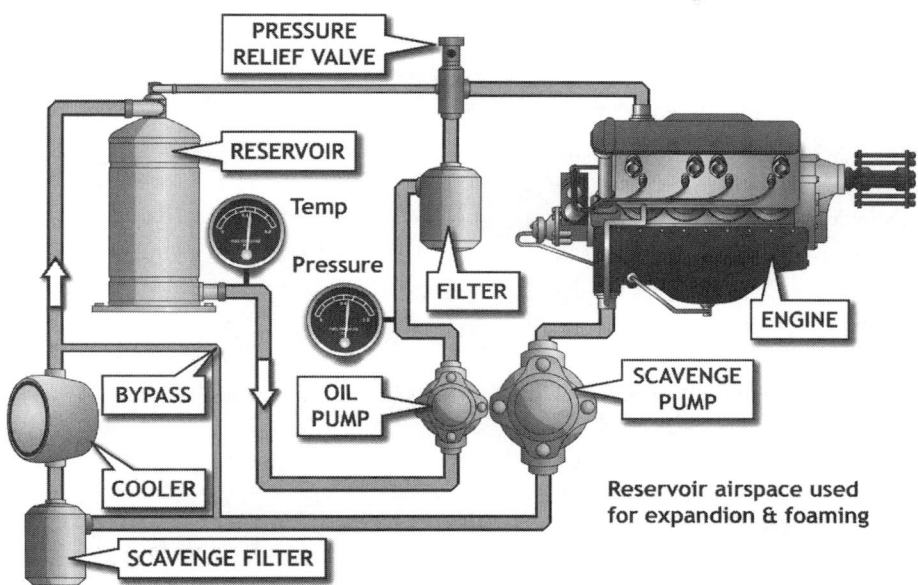

crankcase drains into the sump and there will be oil remaining when the machine is started if the pumps were the same size). In addition, because air gets mixed with oil as it does its work, it becomes frothy, gaining a greater volume, which the scavenge pump has to handle.

Pumps are usually mesh gear types, where one gear is driven, which drives the other, to force oil round the outside of the gears within their housing. In practice, the scavenge pump is 25-30% larger than the pressure pump.

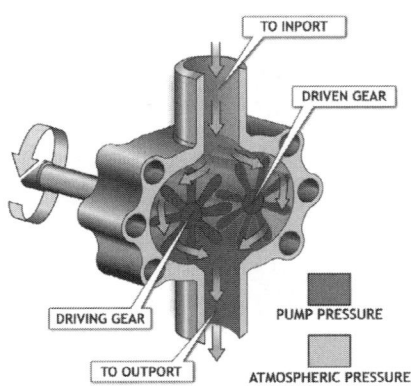

Engine oil reservoirs are often at the front of the engine because the hot oil can be used to heat the air intake.

Pressure is regulated by the *oil pressure relief valve*, which compensates for oil pump speed and viscosity variations with engine speed changes through the tension on its spring - in fact, engine oil pressure is adjusted by changing the spring pressure*. If oil pressure gets too high here, the pressure relief valve dumps it back to the reservoir. One symptom of problems with the relief valve is *lower than normal oil pressure*, with *steady oil temperature*.

*The reading on the oil pressure gauge is the pressure of the oil on the *outlet* side of the pressure pump. In other words, the oil pressure in a piston engine is measured immediately downstream of the oil pump.

An oil cooler in the return line to the oil tank cools things down after the oil has passed through the scavenge pump (that is, the oil cooler is *downstream* of the scavenge pump), if it is above a certain temperature. If not, it is fed directly to the engine. The bypass is triggered by high oil pressure.

Chip Detectors

Modern helicopters, especially their engines, work at the edge of technology in terms of speed and temperature. They have to deliver maximum performance, reliably and safely, while being as lightly constructed as possible. For example, the main engine bearings need to cope with internal engine speeds and pressures on top of any loads generated by what we do with the aircraft. The contact areas between the balls or rollers and the bearing races they run against are only microns thick, and repeated stress can lead to flakes of metal breaking off the bearing surfaces (this is known as *spalling*). The resulting rough contact surfaces will ultimately result in the bearing breaking up and the engine seizing.

Inside engines (and transmissions) are magnetic chip detectors, which are designed to pick up stray bits of metal floating in the oil. They provide warning of impending failure without having to inspect filters.

Chip detectors should be as close as possible to the element being monitored, but always upstream of filters and coolers. When enough metal has built up, an electrical contact is bridged, with the aim of illuminating a light in your cockpit to warn you of the situation. Metal particles not picked up should be trapped by an oil filter. Naturally, if all this is detected early enough, costly repairs or even the loss of the engine should be avoided.

Fine particles occur during normal engine operation, and more frequently during running in (in the first 50 hours or so) but larger ones that occur more frequently can indicate some sort of failure. The problem is that multiple particles can give the same continuity as a single large particle, so you still don't really know what's going on round there.

Tip: Push-to-test buttons in the cockpit typically only test the bulb. If you connect a jumper wire or ground out the chip plug at the engine sump, you can check the whole circuit when the indicator light comes on.

The magnetic detectors are there to *warn of impending failure*, and are designed to be removable for frequent checking, but can often not be put back.

In machines such as the AS 350, it's fair to say that chip lights almost never come on. In other machines, such as the Bell 206, they come on much more frequently, particularly after maintenance, or the installation of a new engine, which leads many pilots to give them less attention, if not disregard them altogether. Certainly, a typical reaction in such a machine would be to extend the flight a little further than would be done with the 350.

However, a chip light is still a chip light, and should still be given due respect, because the situation may be a little more involved. How about oil starvation? If a chip light comes on, take a look at the oil pressure as well. You may have been losing oil for some time.

A transmission chip light can also mean the impending failure of a sprag clutch, assuming that the freewheel chip plug is wired to the light, with results not unlike an Input Drive Shaft failure, but there is no loud noise to make you start putting the collective down.

CAPT

SYSTEMS

The motive power for the systems used to operate the aircraft comes mostly from the engine (with independent backup), and they may work singly, or in combination, frequently with one type of system controlling another (electric switches controlling hydraulic rams, for example). It is important to know which way any system goes when it fails - that is, does it fail open or fail closed? A basic system of whatever type will consist of a *reservoir* (e.g. a fuel tank or a battery) to contain whatever flows around it and ensure that the delivery is constant and consistent, with no highs, lows, or shocks.

To keep things clean there will be a filter and, finally, some sort of motor could be powered by the system to do work. There are two variables in any system - the amount of stuff in it and its pressure. You can use a small amount at high pressure or a larger amount at a lower one.

Fuel Supply

The purpose of the fuel system is to deliver clean fuel to the engine.

The simplest way is to use gravity, which needs the fuel cells to be above the engine, but fuel may also arrive through booster pumps in the tank or suction from an engine driven fuel pump.

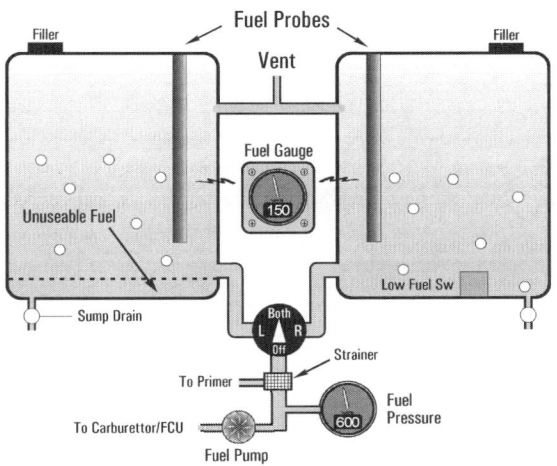

Integral fuel tanks are part of the aircraft which are sealed. They could be as simple as a metal container inside a monocoque structure, with baffles inside to stop the fuel sloshing around during manoeuvres (and equalise pressure). The lowest point of the tank will contain a sump and a drain point to allow dirt and water to be drained off before you go flying. The line supplying the fuel will be higher than this to stop contamination being drawn into the engine.

The tank will be vented to allow atmospheric pressure in. This is to ensure that the rate of flow to the engine is not restricted by a vacuum inside the tank. There may also be an overflow drain (with a check valve) to cope with increased pressure inside the tank. From the tank, the fuel goes to the selector valve (so you can choose tanks, if you have more than one), then the filter, the pumps and the carburettor/fuel injector. The filter will have a collector bowl to trap any contaminants that are heavier than the fuel. It will also contain a drain point that should be inspected before flight.

Otherwise, tanks are normally found in the *lower fuselage* with the C of G coinciding with a line extending from the main rotor mast. This is to reduce any effects of the C of G changing as fuel is used up. In fact, fuel cells can be in very strange places, and be in many different shapes and sizes (together with their own C of G system).

This means that various methods may be used to get the fuel from the tanks to the engine, all involving fuel pumps and filters. Each engine will have its own high pressure pump, but there will also be a *boost pump*, in the tank, to pressurise the fuel slightly and prevent vapour locks*, or *cavitation*, providing an excess-to-requirements quantity of fuel at low pressure (usually 20-50 psi), to the engine driven pump, which typically operates at 400-600 psi.

In other words, boost pumps work at low pressure, and their job is to *push* the fuel into the pipes (i.e. under pressure), to stop any bubbles forming at the input to the high pressure pump, which is usually next to or inside the fuel control unit, and is *sucking* the fuel up.

*Vapour lock occurs when the pressure in the fuel system is low enough to allow fuel to vaporise and interrupt the supply of fuel to the engine. It may unprime the pump.

Boost pumps are lubricated by the fuel they work on, so don't run them dry or you will burn them out. Any pumps submerged in the fuel tanks of a multi-engined helicopter are *low-pressure centrifugal types* powered by AC induction motors. They are submerged to keep them cool, and to ensure they are primed, and they can also be used for fuel jettison and transfer.

There is always *unusable fuel* in the tanks and fuel lines. This is fuel that cannot be used for combustion and which will be allowed for in the Dry Operating Mass, but under certain conditions, unusable fuel can be increased. If one fuel boost pump fails in the Bell 206, for example, unusable fuel increases to 10 US gallons. Unusable fuel can be minimised by using *tank sump pads*.

Many helicopters, such as the Bell 206, require boost pumps on for all normal operations, so don't turn them off until after closing down the engine. The reason they were installed in the first place is because the most common fuel at the time was JP4, which had a vapour pressure of 6,000 feet, a lot lower than that of JP5, which is somewhere between 8000-9000 feet.

This is why, if a boost pump fails, you must descend below 6,000 feet PA in that machine (the need for a boost pump is therefore really to cater for older technology).

Hydraulics

Note: Although the word *hydraulics* technically refers to water (i.e. hydro), it is commonly used to refer to any system operated by a fluid, particularly oil.

Moving the controls directly on some aircraft is physically impossible, so hydraulic components called *Power Control Units* (PCUs) are used instead. Movement of the controls operates control valves that allow a metered amount of hydraulic fluid through to move the controls a specific distance. As there is no feedback to tell whether you are moving the controls too much, artificial feel units are built in to do this in proportion to the control movement.

Power for a hydraulic system can be mechanical or electrical, or be driven by an engine or gearbox. Standby systems are usually driven by electric motors or a gearbox.

Flight deck indications include *temperature*, *pressure* and *contents*. If only the temperature changes, for example, and the contents and pressure stay the same, you have an internal leak. Other indications would mean external leaks.

Liquids have minimal compressibility, meaning that, when pressure is applied, it is taken up throughout the whole system. It is the *height* of the fluid that matters, not the shape of the container:

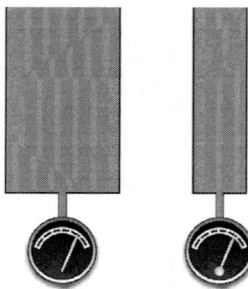

In fact, *Pascal's Principle* states that static pressure exerted by a fluid is the same on all surfaces touched by it, or, when pressure is applied to an enclosed fluid, it is transmitted uniformly in all directions, assuming the fluid concerned is confined and doesn't compress.

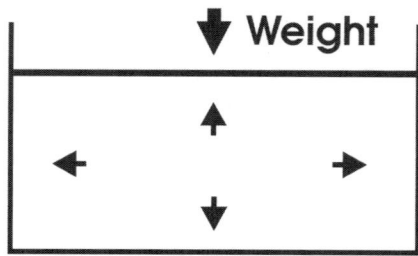

This makes it a useful way of transferring movement round corners and into strange places, as the forces produced by a hydraulic system can be very powerful, hence their use in aircraft to reduce the forces that would otherwise be required to move the flying controls. If you input 20 lbs of force into a piston with an area of 1 square inch, the output on a 10 square inch piston will be 200 lbs, so the total pressure in the system remains equal. However, the smaller piston would have to be moved for 10 inches to make the larger one move for 1 inch.

As well, cables stretch and linkages wear. If you add friction to the mix, much of your control input, with traditional methods, will not even get to the control surface concerned.

Hydraulics can therefore provide an alternative, lighter weight solution to moving large or difficult to move control surfaces.

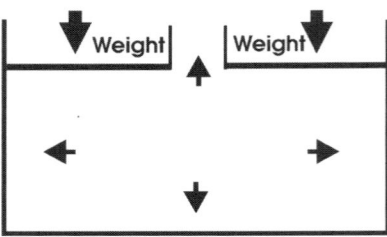

If a tube is placed into the middle of the piston in the diagram above, water will fill the tube until the weight of water in the tube equals the weight placed on the piston, equal to the sectional area of the tube, in pounds per square inch. If the weight is atmospheric pressure and the tube is long enough (36 feet) with a vacuum inside, and one square inch in cross-section, eventually the weight of the water in the tube would equal the pressure outside, in pounds per square inch (14.7).

Hydraulic power is a function of *system pressure* and *volume flow*. Thus, *high pressure* and *large flow* are symptomatic of a hydraulic system - 3,000 psi is typical.

Such high pressure allows more energy to be transmitted with smaller piston areas, so it saves weight. The trade-off is the potential for leaks and the need to protect against line bursting.

SYSTEM COMPONENTS

Let's try to build a system with some of the components described later, using a Bramah's Press.

If you move the force of 20 Newtons downward by 4 cm, the other piston will be moved upwards by 1 cm.

When you let the force go, however, both pistons will move back to their original locations, so you need something to stop that happening.

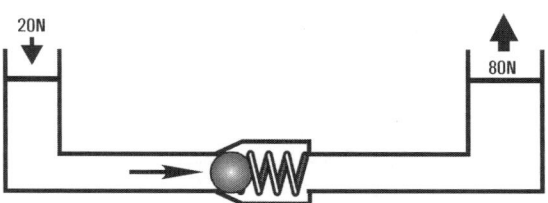

A non-return valve is a spring loaded device that allows fluid to flow in one direction only. It will be marked with an arrow to show which direction that is. Now, when the piston on the right has been pushed up, it will stay up, due to the pressure trapped between it and the NRV. However, you can only do this once, because pulling the left hand piston back up will leave a lower pressure between it and the NRV unless you can let more fluid through, which you need to be able to repeat the process.

Enter the reservoir, with another NRV between it and the other side of the piston. There will be a hole in the piston to allow the fluid through, with yet another NRV to keep it in the system. When you push the piston down, the NRV in it closes, and the one in the pipe allows fluid through to push up the second piston. At the same time, the depression above the first piston allows fluid to flow in from the reservoir.

On the upstroke, the delivery NRV closes, trapping fluid above the first piston until pressure increases enough to open the NRV in the piston and allow fluid through again.

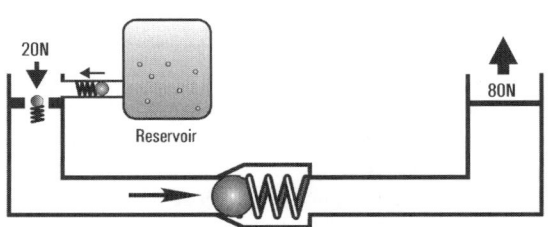

To reset the system, by allowing fluid from underneath the second piston back to the reservoir, add a pipe between them, with a release valve to act as the switch.

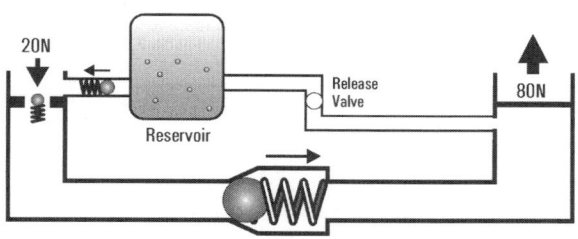

Now replace the first piston with an engine driven pump, attach the second piston to a component that is required to do some work, and you have the workings of a rudimentary hydraulic system.

A couple of extra components now need to be mentioned.

The engine driven pump is running all the time, and when the jack is fully extended the pressure may be too high for the system to cope with. A pressure relief valve will dump fluid back to the reservoir in this case.

In between the pump and the system itself, a filter will keep any foreign bodies out of the fluid.

Lastly, the jack cannot return to its original position by itself, so you need a selector valve to deliver fluid under pressure to the other side of the piston so it can move the other way.

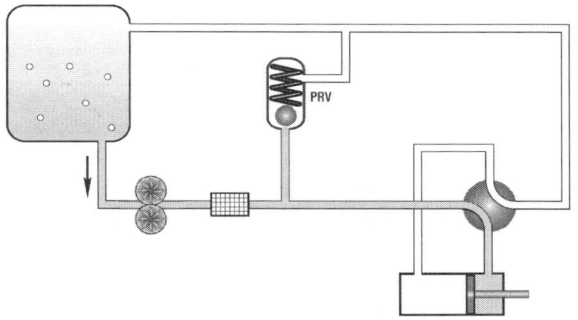

JACKS

The purpose of the jack is to transform hydraulic pressure into linear motion.

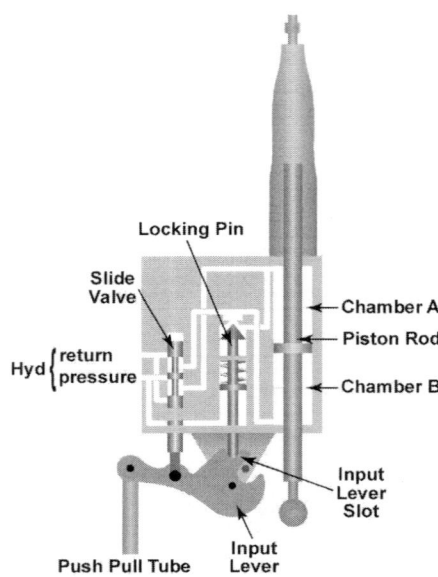

- *Single-acting* jacks move in one direction only, and are pulled back to their original position non-hydraulically, maybe with a spring. They are usually used as locking devices, where the fluid pressure overcomes the spring tension. A typical use is to keep undercarriages locked in the up position.

- *Double-acting* jacks can move either way according to where hydraulic fluid is injected - the spool/slide valve diverts system pressure to the side of an actuator where it is needed. However, because the piston is only connected on one side, you can exert more pressure on one side than the other. This could be used to raise an undercarriage against gravity, which would assist it the other way.

- *Balanced jacks* have a connecting rod either side of the piston, so you get an equal force whichever way the piston is moved, useful for steering and flying controls.

The power from the actuator depends on system pressure and the size of the piston.

In a *fully powered* system (i.e. power operated), the controls only activate the spool/slide valve, and the fluid pressure will move the actuator concerned. When the servo moves, a feedback linkage closes the spool valve pistons over the two actuator ports to trap hydraulic fluid inside the working cylinder. With such an **irreversible** flight control system, the trapped fluid causes a hydraulic lock that freezes the controls so they cannot be moved by the control surface. In this case, there is no feedback to the controls, so artificial feel systems need to be introduced.

For a *boosted* system (i.e. power assisted), the input and output are connected to the control linkage, as shown below, so the pilot's efforts will be assisted by a set percentage, such as 4:1, which will apply 4 units of servo power for every one from the cockpit.

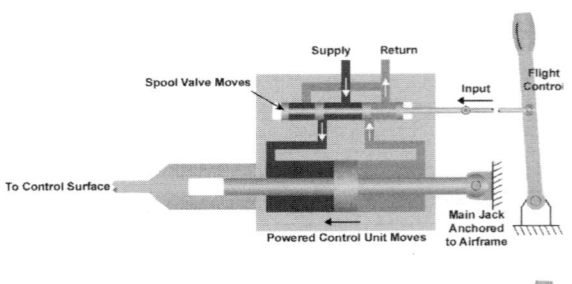

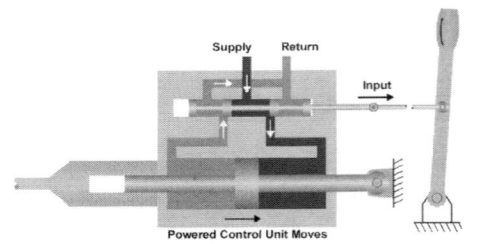

If a jack is *compensated*, the area either side of the actuator piston is identical. An uncompensated jack is used in situations where the force required to do the job is more one way than the other, for example, with undercarriages, which are harder to pull up than to let down.

SELECTOR VALVES

Otherwise known as Directional Control Valves in the real world, these send system pressure to either side of an actuator, or jack, and provide for a return path for the unused fluid. In some systems, selector valves are operated electrically (by a solenoid) and are fail safe, so the hydraulic switch in the cockpit, when switched off, turns on the solenoid, so that, if the electrics fail, the solenoid reverts to the position where fluid can flow again.

A rotary selector valve spins to direct fluid into channels:

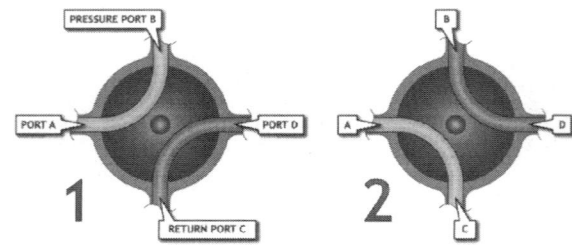

The above picture shows a closed centre valve. When it is in the Off position, the flow of fluid is blocked, and the system stays at its operating pressure at all times. The four-way, closed-centre selector valve is the most commonly used valve in aircraft hydraulics. There are two types, rotary (as shown above) or spool valve.

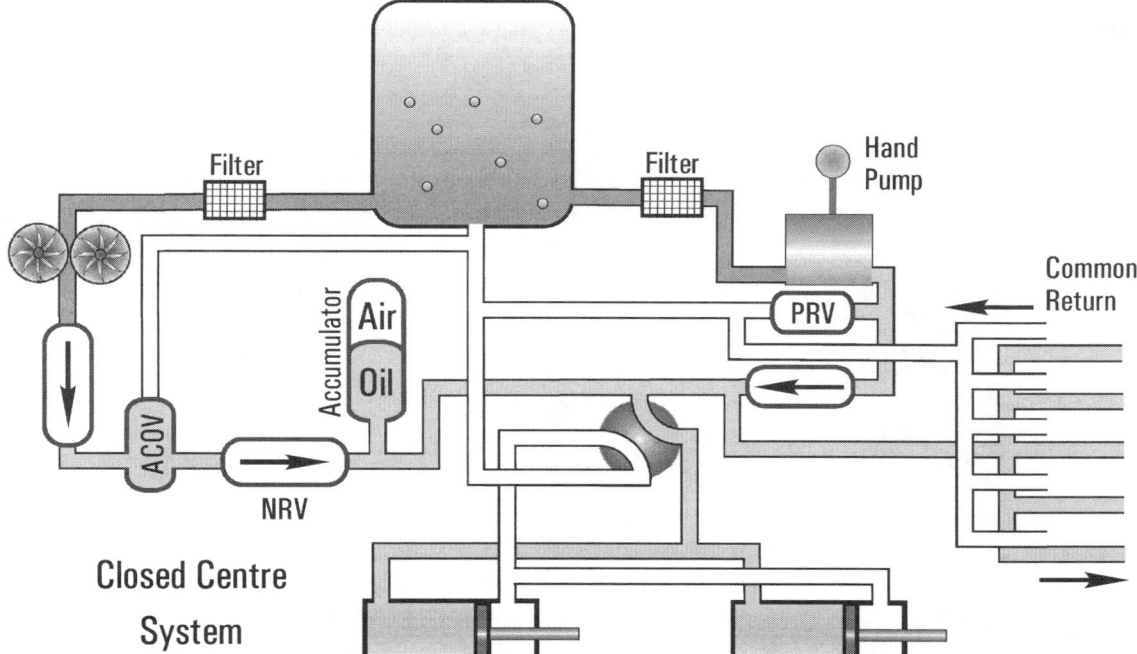

Closed Centre System

A spool valve uses a sliding piston:

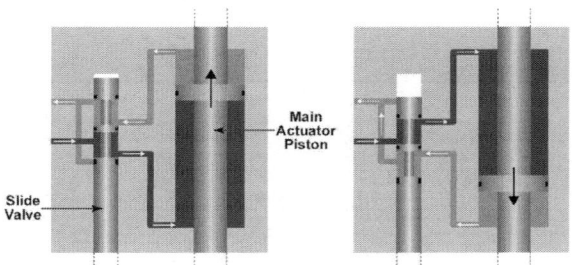

Open centred selectors have an open centre, or third pathway, in the neutral position to allow fluid to flow when nothing is selected (this allows the system to idle). In either On position, they work like closed-centre valves.

Hydraulic systems are classified according to the selector valves they use. In an open centre system using more than one selector valve, the valves are arranged one behind the other, in series. The open centre is needed so that fluid can reach all jacks when only one is being operated.

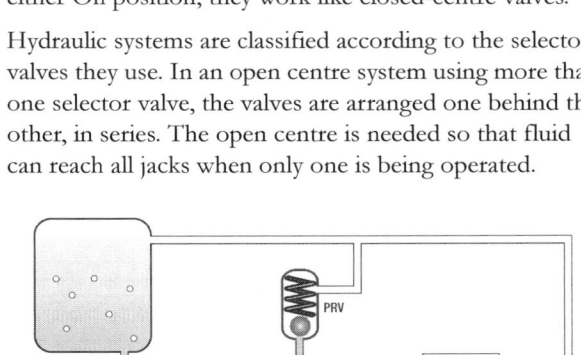

An open-centre system has fluid flow but no pressure when the selector valve is off, as there are no restrictions. Pressure is only present when an actuator is operated.

In a closed-centre system, fluid is under pressure all the time the pump is operating (with no flow, hydraulic pressure is equal throughout the system), and pressure varies in direct proportion to system demands. A relief valve is needed in case the pressure gets too high when all valves are off.

A closed centre system allows you to run several items at once - that is, things are done in parallel.

A **servo** is a combination of a selector valve and an actuator in one unit. Servos are used when precise control is needed over the distance a component moves.

When the pilot valve of a servo is opened, it is automatically closed by the servo's movement because the pilot valve housing moves as well (the two are attached). The pilot valve itself is being held stationary by the operator, and the ports again become blocked by the lands of the pilot valve stopping the piston when it has moved the required distance.

A **Sloppy Link** is the connection point between the control linkage, pilot valve, and servo piston rod. It allows the servo piston to be moved either by fluid pressure or manually by providing a limited amount of slack between connecting linkage and pilot valve. Now the pilot valve can be moved to an On position by the connecting linkage without moving the piston rod.

THE RESERVOIR

The reservoir stores the fluid at the highest point in the system (there is one reservoir per system). It may be pressurised (from the engine), but typically not for light aircraft, as they do not fly high enough to need it. Pressurisation, when used, provides a positive supply of foam free fluid at the pump inlet. The pressure comes from reduced engine bleed air.

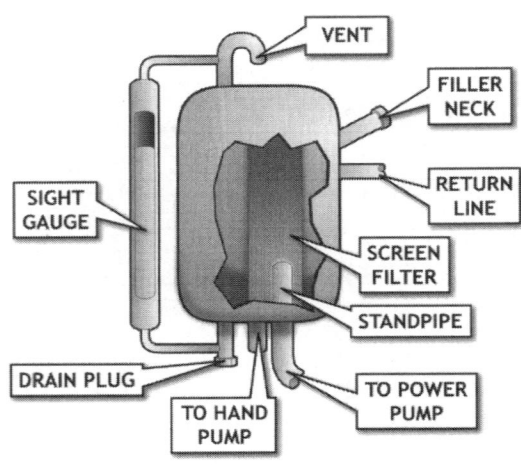

A de-aerator will remove air bubbles from the fluid.

When you have a reservoir, if the system starts to leak, there is a ready supply to replace it. There will be some airspace above the normal fluid level to allow for expansion and to let any trapped air escape. Thus, the fluid level in a reservoir will fluctuate according to system demands, accumulator pressure and jack displacement.

If there is only one reservoir, and there is an emergency hand-powered hydraulic facility, the fluid from the reservoir will be taken from a standpipe *at the bottom*, so there will always be fluid for emergencies.

A reservoir may also have baffles to stop the fluid from sloshing around, and a sight gauge to allow you to check the fluid level before flight (using a dipstick could introduce impurities, even if there is a filter in the system).

Fluid temperature will typically be measured in the reservoir. Overheat detectors are at the pumps.

THE ACCUMULATOR

Some helicopters (like the AS 350) use an accumulator instead of a second hydraulic system, to save weight (and expense). Part of an accumulator's job is to store energy in the form of hydraulic fluid under pressure that can be used for a short time if the main system fails or needs help at peak times - that is, in a failure, you can still move the controls for a few seconds, at least enough to bring the speed back to where the forces are controllable. The stored pressure also allows an initial impetus to be given when a selection is made (i.e it reduces lag). You can also

think of an accumulator as a shock absorber, since a valve opening in a highly pressurised system makes quite an impact on the hydraulic lines. Yet another function is to use the stored pressure to reduce the number of times the hydraulic pump has to switch on and off when there is low demand, which saves wear and tear. As the output from an accumulator can be more (temporarily) than that from the system anyway, you can then save weight and expense by using pumps of lesser capacity, and size.

An accumulator is a container in which a piston or a diaphragm separates hydraulic fluid under normal pressure from an inert gas (usually nitrogen or dry air) which is ay about half system pressure. An inert gas is used because oxygen and oil can explode if you combine them under high pressure.

The bladder (diaphragm) is thinner and larger in diameter at the top (near the air valve) tapering to a smaller diameter. The accumulator's operation is based on Barlow's formula for hoop stress, which states that the stress in a circle is directly proportional to its diameter and wall thickness. Thus, for a certain thickness, a larger diameter circle will stretch faster than one with a small diameter or, for a certain diameter, a thin wall hoop will stretch faster. The bladder will therefore stretch at its largest diameter and thinnest wall (that is, at the top), pushing itself outward against the walls.

Bladder-type accumulator from the AS 350 series

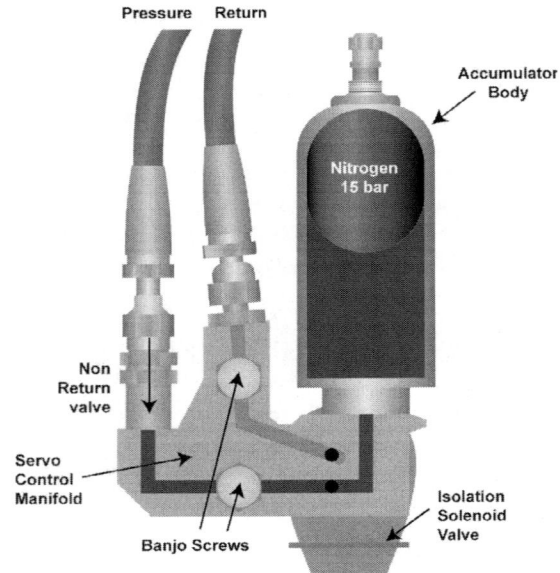

As pressure builds up in the system, the gas in the accumulator is compressed until the fluid and gas pressures equalise inside it at normal system pressure, at which point the pump runs down to idle speed and pressure is maintained by the accumulator. As soon as the system pressure drops, the nitrogen expands against the

bladder to force out the fluid on the other side, which keeps the system pressurised for a short while, until the pump kicks in again. Depending on how much and how harshly you use the controls, the accumulators will usually bleed off their stored pressure inside about 20-30 seconds. The capacity of an accumulator is what it can supply during discharge.

If an accumulator is precharged to, say, 1000 psi (as usually found on large transport aircraft), and the system is pressurised to 3000, the pressure on the gas side should read 3000 psi, i.e. system pressure.

If gas pressure is too high, there will be less fluid in the system, and more on/off cycles as the pump kicks in and out. If gas pressure is too low, you can expect rapid fluctuations in fluid pressure as surges are not absorbed. A piston would also hit against the stops and cause *hammering*, which should be investigated immediately. A *cutout valve* sits between the pump and the accumulator. When the pump is keeping system pressure up, the valve will be closed. When the accumulator is doing the work, it will open, so fluid can be dumped back to the reservoir.

A low pressure switch sets off an alarm if pump output pressure is not enough. A non-return valve upstream of the accumulator stops fluid going back to the reservoir.

Most new systems do not use an accumulator but a constant speed variable displacement pump. Or both.

Note: The system used for demonstration purposes on this course belongs to the AS 350 series, from Eurocopter. Not only is it fairly complex, as compared to, say, the relatively simple one on the Bell 206 shown before, it is also one that will bite if it is not understood properly. The sooner you get to grips with it, the better!

HYDRAULIC FLUID
Speaking of shocks to the system, hydraulic fluids are specially made to withstand high pressures and temperatures without vapourising, so make sure you use the proper stuff. The ideal hydraulic fluid should be:

- incompressible.
- have a low viscosity (to minimise power consumption and resistance to flow). Viscosity is dependent on temperature.
- have good lubrication properties.
- be non-flammable and non-toxic.
- have a low freezing point and a high boiling point, with no foaming, plus a high flash point.

It should also be compatible with the seals and materials used, that is, it should not cause corrosion. Being coloured helps as well, so that leaks show up better. Did I mention stability? I thought not.

You can recognise the correct type of fluid by colour* (and can). The three main types are:

- **Vegetable** (Castor). May be yellow or almost colourless (i.e. straw) and must be used with pure rubber seals and hoses. It is found in some braking systems, but not often in power systems.
- **Mineral**. Normally red, for synthetic rubber seals and hoses in braking systems, power systems and shock absorbers. Mineral-based fluid can be flammable, so if it leaks out, it can catch fire, especially if the leak is in the form of a spray
- **Synthetic**. Phosphate Ester based, may be green, purple (Skydrol*) or amber and must only be used with Teflon, Ethylene Propylene or Butyl Rubber seals and hoses, as it is hostile to rubber. It is **fire and cavitation resistant** and has a wide temperature range, but it becomes acidic if overheated, and will attack electrical insulation. It will also be harmful to the skin and eyes. It is the most common fluid used in modern hydraulic systems.

They cannot be mixed, because using incorrect fluid could damage the seals. You must use the fluid specified in the Flight Manual.

*DTD 585 and MIL-H-5606 are red.

PUMPS
High pressure and *large flow* are symptomatic of a hydraulic system. The S-76, for example, uses 3,000 psi. This high pressure allows more energy to be transmitted with smaller piston areas, so it saves weight. In fact, 3,000 psi is now considered old hat! The S-92 uses 4,000 psi, and the V-22 (Osprey) 5,000. The trade-off is the potential for leaks and the need to protect against line bursting.

Hydraulics systems are *passive* when they don't use a pump, and *active* when they do. A high pressure system typically works higher than 3000 psi (as used in large transport aircraft), and a low pressure one at 2000 psi or below.

Systems will typically have at least 2 pumps in parallel. After the pump will be a pressure switch that operates a light if the pump output pressure falls below a given value.

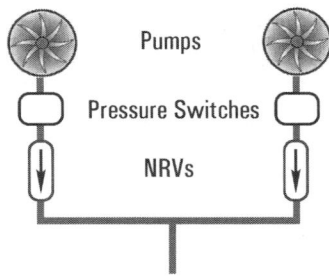

After the pressure switch comes a non-return valve, which stops any back flow of fluid through the pump which could happen if it fails.

With 2 pumps running, normal pressure will be the same as if 1 pump was running, but the flow rate will be doubled. Should a pump fail, the pressure remains the same but the flow rate will be halved. This will not affect smaller components, but larger ones may operate at a slower rate giving longer operating times.

Modern aircraft may have many hydraulic systems that are colour coded for ease of identification.

Major services will be supplied by at least 2 systems to protect against their loss. For example, a hydraulic motor in one system may be used to drive a hydraulic pump in another, also known as a *Power Transfer Unit*.

A hydraulic pump's mechanical action first creates a vacuum at the pump inlet, which allows atmospheric pressure to force liquid into it from the reservoir. Then it delivers the liquid to the outlet, forcing it into the hydraulic system. The fluid may be slightly pressurised as it enters the pumps to prevent vapour lock. *Pressure gauges show the outlet pressure from the pump.*

Note: A pump only produces the flow necessary for the *development* of pressure, which you will only get when you try to compress the fluid, as when it is obstructed in some way, and even then it will only rise to the level necessary to overcome the load's resistance. In other words, the pressure of the fluid at the pump outlet is zero when it is not connected to a system.

There are many types of pump - constant or variable *volume*, or constant or variable *pressure*. They can also be piston or gear based. Hand pumps allow for ground servicing and emergencies, and are usually double acting.

Variable displacement pumps adjust the amount of fluid pumped to the amount of fluid required, so fluid only moves when necessary.

Constant Volume (or constant delivery) pumps deliver a fixed amount of fluid, which means that you need to dump excess fluid back to the reservoir when it is not required (the combination of pump and valve creates a constant pressure source). The wasted output from the pump shows up as heat. An Automatic Cut Out Valve (with an accumulator) provides an idling circuit when no hydraulic service is selected or when the accumulator is full. When the pressure gets high enough, the pump cuts out and system pressure is maintained by the accumulator until another service is selected. Constant volume pumps mean less engine wear.

The gears are turned by a shaft which has a shear pin or section that will break under excessive loads (something might get jammed. If a hydraulic pump seizes, the quill

drive will shear to offload and protect the gearbox). The inlet port to the pump is fed straight from the reservoir, and the outlet is connected to the pressure line. As the teeth pass the inlet port, fluid is trapped between them and the housing, and carried round to where the teeth mesh again to displace the fluid into the outlet port. This produces a positive flow under pressure into the line.

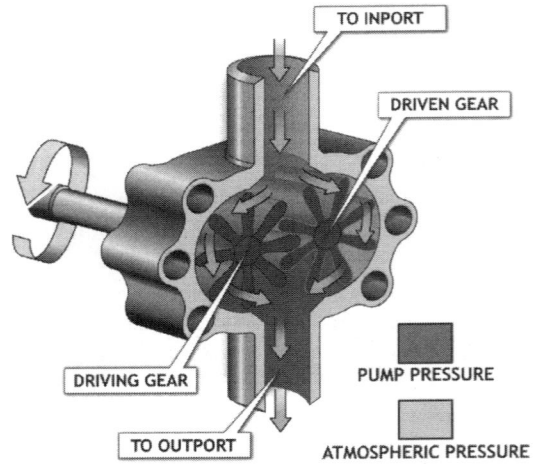

One rotation of the shaft displaces a fixed quantity of fluid that is determined by the geometry of the motor (i.e. the rate of flow determines it speed). The pressure drop across it is determined by the torque it is applying. A constant delivery type pump requires a pressure regulator.

CAPT

NON-RETURN (CHECK) VALVES

These allow fluid to move in one direction only. In the USA, they are known as hydraulic fuses.

HYDRAULIC FUSE

See above. This is designed to limit or check the flow of fluid that is leaking at some distance from the main circuit. A leak has the effect of decreasing fluid temperature.

One type shuts off the flow when pressure drops enough across it. Another type shuts of the fluid when enough has flowed through it, when the flow rate is too high. An arrow on the housing points in the direction of flow.

THE SHUTTLE VALVE

Sometimes, fluid must come from more than one source to meet the demands of a complex system. At other times, an emergency system might be needed to provide pressure if the normal system fails (the emergency system will usually only actuate essential components). The shuttle valve can isolate the normal system from an alternate or emergency one, or provide best pressure to a service.

A typical shuttle valve contains three ports— normal system inlet, alternate or emergency system inlet, and an outlet. Inside, there is a sliding part predictably called the shuttle, whose purpose is to seal off an inlet port, which itself will contain a *shuttle seat*.

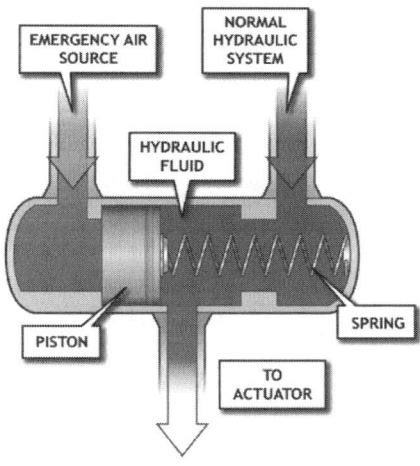

When a shuttle valve is in its normal position, fluid can flow freely from the normal system inlet port, through the valve, and out through the outlet port to the actuating unit. The shuttle is seated against the alternate system inlet port and held there by normal system pressure and the *shuttle valve spring*, where it remains until the alternate system is activated. Fluid under pressure is then directed from the alternate system to the shuttle valve, forcing the shuttle to seal off the normal inlet port. Fluid from the alternate system then has a free flow to the outlet port.

PRESSURE RELIEF

Relief valves are pressure limiting or safety devices that prevent pressure from building up to where it might blow a seal or burst or damage the container in which it is installed. They are installed within hydraulic systems to relieve excessive pressurized fluid that may arise from thermal expansion, pressure surges and other failures.

For example, when a jack gets as far as it can go, a *pressure relief valve* may allow fluid to bypass the jack and unload the pump. The *cracking pressure* is that at which the PRV opens.

Main system relief valves operate within certain specific pressure limits to relieve complete pump output when in the open position, from where it directs excess fluid to the reservoir return line. In systems designed to operate normally at 3,000 psi, the relief valve might be set to be completely open at 3,650 psi and reseat at 3,190 psi.

A coil spring at one end of a piston retains it against a stop on the valve housing, and the poppet valve, just inside the pressure port, is spring seated over a passage through the valve. When fluid pressure reaches 3,650 psi (for example), the piston is forced to depress the coil spring and move clear of the poppet valve, so the fluid can flow through the valve into the return line. When pressure is reduced to 3,190 psi, the coil spring reseats the piston against the poppet valve, and fluid flow ceases.

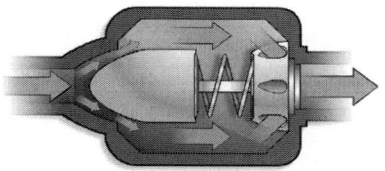

Pressure relief valves may be separate components in their own right, or be found within others, such as filters. The simplest form is a ball or piston held in place with a spring, whose tension can be adjusted to change the cracking pressure. If the fluid pressure gets too high, the ball is moved against the spring to allow fluid past.

JACKSTALL

Also called *servo transparency,* or *control reversibility,* this occurs in the AS 350 when the forces from the rotor blades (possibly from Retreating Blade Stall) overpower and stall the hydraulic jacks, to lock the controls (officially, jackstall in an AS 350 means an uncommanded aft and right cyclic and down collective motion together with the helicopter pitching up and rolling right, which tends to be self-correcting since the rapid loss of airspeed should cause an equally quick reduction in feedback forces). It happens during manoeuvres that increase the loading on the rotor system, where the hydraulic system essentially reverts to manual operation for a few seconds. As the rotor blades come into the stall from the manoeuvre, they start to pitch down, as does any aerofoil in that state, as the airflow starts to react about the midpoint of the lower surface instead of at 25% of chord.

The pitch down moment presses down on the controls and can overpower the hydraulics. It is unlikely to happen on any machine in the normal flight envelope, but if you pulled up and to one side to avoid a bird, for example, you could get a surprise.

In some aircraft, such as the Gazelle, jackstall can be reproduced consistently under given conditions, such as pulling the controls hard in a descending, fast right turn. In others, such as the AS 350, it is less predictable and can occur at 40 kts flying round a fire on a warm day, or coming off the top of a mountain in low temperatures.

Some pilots flying around the Grand Canyon have experienced the phenomenon just on breezy days when the relative airflow is changing constantly. Usually, the corrective action is just to release the pressure on the controls to unlock the jacks.

CAPT

INSTRUMENTS

Aircraft instruments base their readings on the measurement and comparison of the different temperatures and pressures found inside and outside the aircraft. They will cover four areas of aircraft operation - *Control, Performance, Navigation,* and *Miscellaneous,* which includes voltmeters, gear position indicators, etc.

Instruments must be able to be read easily, in terms of position, lighting and clarity. They can have up to four sub-systems, not all of which will be in the same case:

- Detection (e.g. temperature probe)

- Measurement (aneroid capsule)

- Coupling (suitable linkage between measurement and indication)

- Indication (Pointer, or digital display)

At the point of measurement, a measuring body absorbs some energy and converts it to a quantity that has a functional relationship with the measured quantity. As some energy is absorbed, the measured quantity will never be the same as the true value. Corrections are usually included with any amplification signals.

Displays can be *circular,* as shown on the right, or *straight* (like a tape) or *digital,* or even a combination, as with this display from an AW 139):

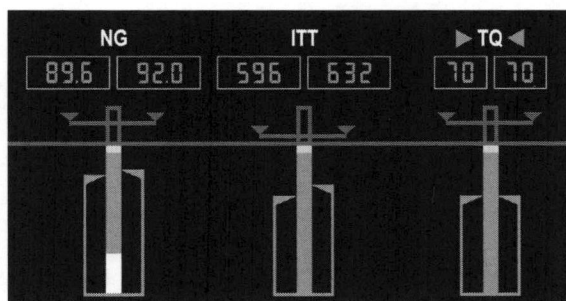

Instruments can also be classified into four groups, after the variations in properties of certain materials against variations in temperature:

- Expansion

- Vapour-Pressure

- Electrical, based on:

  - Resistance, or

  - Increase in electromotive force

- Radiation

Most will be electrical.

Right: Circular Instrument

Lighting

White lighting is usually combined with grey cockpit interiors because:

- you have unrestricted use of colour

- warning indicators become more prominent

- black instrument cases against a grey background will emphasize their size and shape

Individual instruments may be lit by:

- integral lighting, which is built into the instrument

- ring, eyebrow, or post lighting, all of which are fitted to the outside of the instrument case

- floodlighting

PRESSURE   022 01 02/02 02

In many systems, the pressure of a liquid or gas must be measured and indicated, either directly, where the source of pressure is connected to the instrument (mostly Bourdon tubes), or remotely, where it can be some distance away, with electrical signals being sent instead. Such systems would have a transmitter at the pressure source and an indicator on a panel. This means you won't have yucky fluids in the cockpit, and you don't have to carry a lot of plumbing. Indicators can be based on *synchronous receivers, DC* or *AC ratiometers* or *servos.*

Pressure is the *force per unit area,* or the force exerted on an area divided by the size of that area:

$$P = \frac{F}{A}$$

where *F* is Force (N) and *A* is the Area in m^2. The result:

$$\frac{N}{m^2}$$

is equal to 1 *Pascal* (Pa), which is the standard unit of pressure under the SI system, described in *POF.*

ot measured directly - rather, the instruments
measure *differences* of pressure, usually between
the relevant fluid and that of the atmosphere at
point, hence its use as a reference or datum. The
difference of pressure indicated is predictably called:

- **Gauge Pressure**, as measured against ambient air
  pressure, so it is absolute pressure (below) minus
  atmospheric pressure. In other words, any variance
  from atmospheric pressure is called gauge
  pressure. For example, fuel and oil pressure
  instruments indicate the amount that the pump
  has raised the pressure of the fluid above that of
  the atmosphere. Note that it can be positive or
  negative. If the absolute pressure stays constant,
  gauge pressure varies with atmospheric pressure.

- **Absolute Pressure** is the difference between the
  pressure of a fluid and absolute zero (a vacuum). It
  is usually measured in inches of mercury, as on a
  Manifold Air Pressure gauge. It would be the sum
  of gauge pressure and atmospheric pressure, and is
  what forces the fuel and air charge into the
  cylinders of a piston engine.

- **Differential Pressure** is just the difference in
  pressure between two points, as represented by the
  airspeed indicator. Two inlet ports may be used,
  with each connected to one of the sealed volumes
  whose pressure is to be monitored.

Pressure Sensing

Aneroid gauges use a metallic pressure sensing element
that flexes under pressure. *Aneroid* means *without fluid*, or
not wet (depends on which book you read), to distinguish
between aneroid and hydrostatic gauges, which do use
fluid, although aneroid gauges can be used to measure
liquid pressure. The pressure sensing element may be a
Bourdon tube, a diaphragm, a capsule, or bellows, all of
which will change their shape in response to the pressure.
The deflection is transmitted by a suitable linkage that will
rotate a pointer around a graduated dial, or activate a
secondary transducer that might control a digital display,
the most common of which measure changes in
capacitance that follow the mechanical deflection.

In order of sensitivity, you have:

DIAPHRAGMS

Diaphragms are simply circular metal discs that are
corrugated to give them strength, to provide larger
deflections. They are used to detect low pressures. One
side of the disc is exposed to the pressure to be measured,
and the other is linked to the indicating mechanism.

ANEROID CAPSULES

A capsule consists of two diaphragms placed face to face
and joined at their edges to form a chamber that may be
completely sealed or left open to a source of (absolute)
pressure. They are also used for low(ish) pressures, but are
more sensitive than diaphragms.

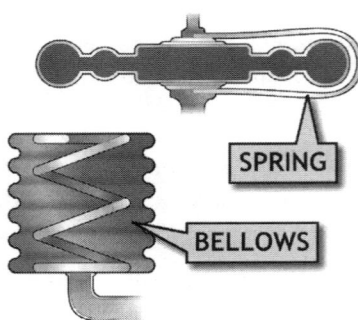

BELLOWS

In gauges that sense small pressures or differences, or
require an absolute pressure to be measured, the gear train
and needle may be driven by an enclosed and sealed
bellows chamber, called an *aneroid*, as used in aneroid
barometers, altimeters, altitude recording barographs, and
the altitude telemetry instruments used in weather balloon
radiosondes. The sealed chamber is used as a reference
pressure and the needles are driven by the external
pressure. Bellows are an extension of the capsule (think of
them as several unsealed capsules joined together), but
operate like a helical compression spring - indeed, there
may even be a spring inside to increase the *spring rate* and
to help the bellows return to its normal length once the
source of pressure is removed.

THE BOURDON TUBE

The most common pressure sensor was invented by
French watchmaker Eugene Bourdon in 1849, in which a
C-shaped elliptical hollow spring tube is sealed at one end,
with the other end connected to a source of pressure. The
pressure differential from the inside to the outside causes
the tube to change from an elliptical to a more circular
shape, and to straighten out, rather like an uncoiling hose.
Which way it moves is determined by the curvature of the
tubing, as the inside radius is slightly shorter than that on
the outside, and the ratio between the major and minor
axes depends on what sensitivity you need - the larger the
ratio, the greater it is.

CAPT

The pressure range is governed by the *tubing wall thickness* and the *radius of the curvature*.

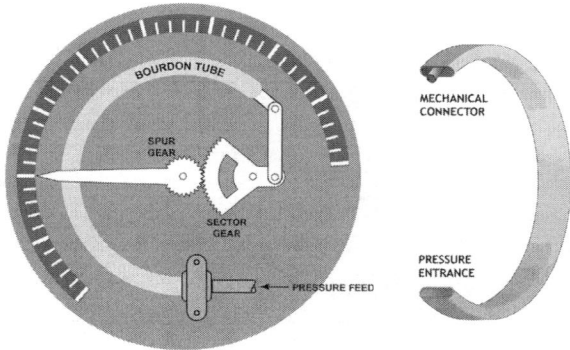

The end result is that a specific pressure causes movement for a specific distance. When the pressure is removed, the tube returns to its original shape. To do this, the material used requires a form of heat treating (*spring tempering*) to make it closely retain its original shape while allowing some elasticity under a load. Beryllium copper, phosphor bronze, and various alloys of steel and stainless steel are good for this purpose, but steel has a limited service life due to corrosion, stainless steel alloys add cost if specific corrosion resistance is not required, and beryllium copper is usually reserved for high pressure applications. Most general use gauges use phosphor bronze.

In summary, a Bourdon-based gauge uses a coiled tube which causes the rotation of an indicator arm connected to it, as it expands due to pressure increase.

MANOMETER

The term *manometer* is often used to refer specifically to liquid column hydrostatic instruments (as described above). These consist of a vertical column of liquid in a tube whose ends are exposed to different pressures, with the difference in fluid height being proportional to the pressure difference.

However, the simplest design is a closed-end U-shape, with one side connected to the region of interest. A force equal to the applied pressure multiplied by the area of the bore will force the liquid downwards until, eventually, the two levels will stand the same distance above and below the original level. If you take into account the area of the tube bore and the density of the liquid, you can calculate pressure from the difference in the levels. Any fluid can be used, but mercury is preferred for its high density and low vapour pressure, so the tube can be shorter.

Manometers are used for calibration purposes.

TEMPERATURE

Knowledge of the air temperature is needed for performance calculations, anti-ice control and calculation of true airspeed (TAS), amongst other things.

The quantity of heat contained in a substance is a measure of the kinetic energy of the molecules it contains, depending on the temperature, mass and nature of the material concerned. For example, a bucketful of warm water will melt more ice than a cupful of boiling water because it contains more heat. Thus, two bodies containing the same amounts of thermal energy may not have the same temperature, because temperature is a measure of the *quality* of heat (or the rate at which molecules are moving), which means it cannot strictly be measured, but only compared against some form of scale.

There are two ways of measuring temperature (or rather the average kinetic energy of molecules), called *Fahrenheit* or *Celsius*, and it's a real pain to convert between the two. The quick and easy way is to use the scale on the back of a flight computer:

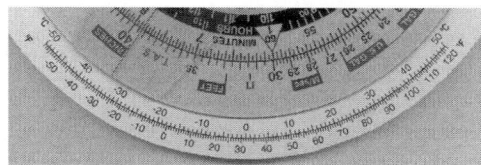

Here are the calculations:

$$\text{F} - \text{C} \quad \text{Tc} = 5/9*\text{Tf}-32$$

$$\text{C} - \text{F} \quad \text{Tf} = 9/5*\text{Tc}+32$$

16°C is equal to 61°F, 20°C is 68°F and 30°C is 86°F, for gross error checks and quick conversions - however, given the standard of performance charts in the average flight manual, doubling Celsius and adding 30 to get Fahrenheit, or subtracting 30 from Fahrenheit and dividing the remainder in half to get Celsius is probably good enough!

The Fahrenheit scale assumes that water freezes at 32°, and boils at 212°. Celsius starts at 0° and finishes at 100°, which is more logical, but the scale is coarser. The differences are 180/100 or 9/5.

The *freezing level* (in flight) is where the temperature is 0°C.

Thermometers

BIMETALLIC STRIP THERMOMETER

Below about 150 kts, a thermometer like the one shown below is good enough for getting the OAT. The probe sticks out directly into the airstream, and the dial is inside the cockpit. The works consist of a helical (coil-shaped) bimetallic strip in a tube, which twists as the temperature changes, and moves the pointer.

The probe cannot be shrouded from the Sun, and it is necessarily mounted next to the fuselage skin, so its readings can be affected by kinetic heating, even at the low speeds associated with helicopters - at 150 kts, the rise can be in the order of 3°. The OAT probe measures the total air temperature minus kinetic heating effects to obtain the static temperature.

Being crude instruments, they are also subject to other errors, so a professional rule of thumb is to assume an error of about 2-3°.

Errors

Instrument error comes from the usual imperfections in manufacturing and can be sorted out by fine calibration. *Environmental error* is caused by solar heating or icing, for which the Rosemount probe has a heater. Probes are usually mounted on the underside to keep them in shadow, but the residual effects of environmental error can only be minimised, and not corrected for. Some heating is caused by compression as air is brought to rest, which is the difference between SAT and TAT, so it is only a problem when you need to find SAT. There is also frictional heating in the boundary layer, but both heating errors can be fully compensated for, either automatically or by calculation.

TEMPERATURE COMPENSATION

Various methods can be used to make an instrument over- or under-read according to which way the temperature is going. For example, a thermal junction can get hot by itself, which will vary the emf it produces and give you false readings. In mechanical terms, a bimetal strip made of invar and brass or steel can be attached to a capsule to make it expand or contract slightly, or you could arrange to vary the resistance of an electrical current.

FLIGHT INSTRUMENTS

Flight instruments are grouped in a *T arrangement*.

The artificial horizon is in the centre, because it is a primary instrument (it tells you which way is up), the heading indicator is below, No 1 altimeter at the top right, the vertical speed indicator below that, and the airspeed indicator at the top left with turn coordinator underneath.

The idea is to have the most important instruments as close together as possible to reduce the scanning distance.

As mentioned, instruments cover four areas of aircraft operation:

- **Control**, such as the artificial horizon and engine instruments
- **Performance**, that show you what the aircraft is doing (ASI, VSI, altimeter, compass)
- **Navigation** (VOR, ADF, DME)
- **Miscellaneous** (Warning flags, gear position indicators, pressure and temperature, etc)

A *primary instrument* is one which gives instant and constant readouts (also called *direct*). A *secondary instrument* is one that you have to deduce things from, such as the altimeter increasing, telling you that the pitch must have changed* (you might also say that the altimeter gives you an indirect indication of pitch attitude). The ASI and VSI also give indirect indications of pitch, and the HI and TC indicate bank. Note also that a primary instrument will tell you at what rate things are changing, but a secondary one will only indicate that change is taking place.

*The needle, ball and airspeed method of instrument flying refers to the Sperry turn indicator - as long as the needle and ball were centred, you were flying in a straight line. In a turn, keeping the ball centred meant you were not slipping or skidding, and holding the correct airspeed meant you were either flying straight and level or climbing or descending at a constant rate. In this case, the primary instruments were the ASI, turn and bank indicator and the VSI. However, using such slow, indirect indications was

CAPT

mentally tiring, as aircraft attitude had to be continually deduced, which led to the development of the artificial horizon and DGI, that gave more instantaneous readings (once gyros became more reliable!)

Instruments are further grouped under the headings of *pitch*, *bank* and *power*.

Pitch

- **Artificial Horizon** (Attitude Indicator). The most important pitch instrument, because it gives direct, instantaneous readings

- **Altimeter**. Although it indicates pitch indirectly, it is a primary pitch instrument. Its readings will lag more at higher altitudes

- **Airspeed Indicator.** Secondary pitch instrument, although its value becomes less at higher airspeeds, as changes are more pronounced and the range indicated by the needle is less and more difficult to read. Any given power setting has only one pitch attitude where altitude and airspeed are constant

- **Vertical Speed Indicator** (VSI). A secondary pitch instrument, to be used with the altimeter. Don't forget that it will give a brief reverse indication if you jerk the controls

Bank

- **Artificial Horizon** (Attitude Indicator). Also the most important bank instrument, for similar reasons under *Pitch*, above

- **Heading Indicator.** An indirect instrument, because if you change heading, bank must be involved somewhere

- **Turn Coordinator**. Shows a rate of turn (3°/sec for rate 1), so it is an indirect indication of bank

Power   022 01 03

Power instruments are not strictly in the traditional T, but you have to check them anyway. The Airspeed Indicator is a secondary power instrument, as it changes in relation to power application.

Engine and temperature instruments have already been covered under *Aircraft General Knowledge*.

FUEL GAUGES

Fuel quantity is measured by the level in the tank, but may be shown in volume or weight. The measurement can be done by *float type* (resistance) or *capacitive* contents gauges.

Note: Although many fuel gauges are accurate, they should never be relied upon as the final guide to what you have in the tanks, especially if they are calibrated with lbs or kg - fuel weight (per gallon) varies with specific gravity

and temperature, so instrument readings will vary as well. Reading the book *Free Fall*, about the Gimli Glider is very instructive about this - a 767 had to make a dead stick landing at Gimli (in Manitoba, Canada) after running out of fuel in the cruise, from a combination of circumstances, including misleading fuel gauges and confusing lbs for kg (the whole episode is very instructive about CRM).

Fuel system indications available to the pilot normally consist of contents, fuel low, pressure, flow, transfer status and filter condition.

FLOAT TYPE (RESISTANCE)
This consists of a resistive circuit using floats connected to a Wheatstone Bridge circuit, typically powered by DC. The float may be made of specially treated cork, or a sealed lightweight metal cylinder. It is attached to an arm that is pivoted to allow angular movement that is transmitted to an electrical element consisting of a wiper arm and a potentiometer (variable resistance), so, as the fuel level changes, the float arm's movement alters the resistance. Ohm's Law determines the current flow, which is fed to an indicator.

Float type indicators provide information on *volume*, whose indication varies with the temperature of the fuel.

One advantage of float-type fuel gauging systems is their easy construction. Neither are they affected by voltage variations (if a galvanometer is used), but they are influenced by *attitude, acceleration*, and *temperature variations*.

On their own, the detectors can only measure the height of fuel (volume), so a datum or *reference capacitor* compensates for *density* to ensure that weight is indicated correctly (if not told otherwise, assume you have a compensated system, as most aircraft use them).

PITOT-STATIC SYSTEM   022 02 01

This consists of a series of pipes around the cockpit through which air flows to feed three common instruments: the altimeter, airspeed indicator and vertical speed indicator. The difference between stagnation and static pressures allows speed to be indicated, plus altitude and its rate of change to be indicated.

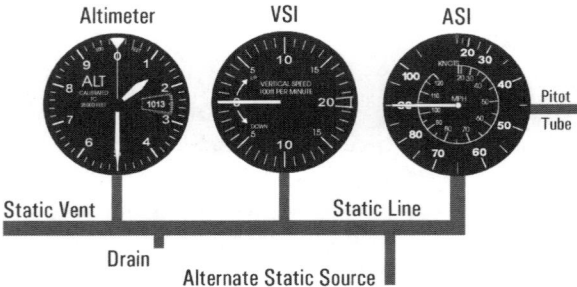

An aircraft is acted on from all directions by *static pressure*, which is fed into the system through static lines that are connected to static ports or static vents on *both sides* of the machine, to ensure that they balance out when it yaws, or does strange manoeuvres. They may or may not be heated (generally not on smaller machines). The static pressure is so called because it remains pretty much the same all the time. It's actually the normal barometric pressure that decreases with height, so any changes in it are relatively slow. Information from the static ports may also be fed to non-flight systems, such as an autopilot or a flight director.

An *alternate static source* takes its feed from inside the aircraft in case the main one starts leaking or gets blocked, either through ice, a bird strike, or whatever. When used, some error will be introduced into the instrument readings because the cabin air pressure is lower than that on the outside due to airflow over the cabin (there are also different pressure errors), so indicated airspeeds and altitudes will read *higher* than normal (that is, the altimeter and ASI will over-read). The VSI will show a momentary climb as the alternate source is selected, then it will stabilise and produce "normal" readings. If the alternate source gets blocked, or you don't have one, smashing the VSI glass (preferably not the ASI or altimeter) will have the same effect.

Otherwise known as the *Total Pressure Probe*, the *pitot tube* (pronounced pee-toe) is used to detect *total pressure* (as mentioned by Bernoulli). It is connected to the airspeed indicator. Total pressure (sometimes called *stagnation pressure*) is the pressure

obtained when a moving gas is brought to a stop through an adiabatic process - in this case, it includes the static pressure that affects the aircraft from all sides, and an extra element that comes from forward movement, since the pitot tube is pointed towards the direction of flight (within 5°). If the fluid (air) is an ideal one (meaning not viscous), total pressure is equal to the sum of potential energy, kinetic energy and pressure energy, but the first is ignored in a pitot tube, and the kinetic energy is converted to pressure energy anyway.

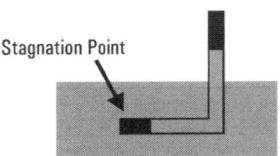

This creates an equal volume above the level of the flow, which is *dynamic pressure*, and the difference between it and static pressure is a measure of airspeed. In simple terms, dynamic pressure of the air against the front surfaces of an aircraft (as detected by the pitot tube) is greater than the pressure of the undisturbed air sensed through the static ports. The difference is proportional to the square of the speed, so instruments can be calibrated in units of speed, such as knots.

The pitot tube may be heated to stop it icing up, so watch your hands (tell the passengers). If it's not at the front, it will be in another relatively undisturbed place, parallel to the relative airflow for best effect. Sometimes, a static source will be incorporated in a pitot head, as a small hole or series of holes around the side of the base.

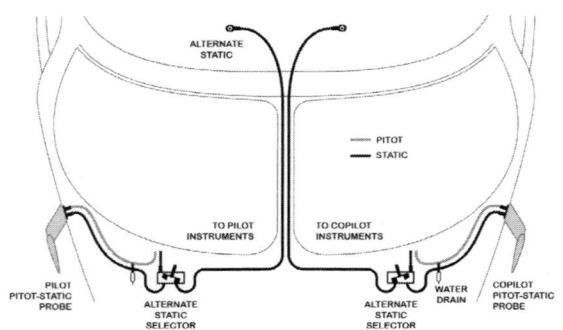

Pitot-static systems are checked during regular maintenance, usually something like every 2 years for IFR machines. Preflight checks will be simpler, usually just making sure that nothing is blocking the holes (take the red covers off!) and that the heating works. Do not blow into the holes, at least, not with instruments connected.

Errors

Errors in measurement will affect displayed speed, height and vertical speed. Accuracy depends on the shape of the probe and where it is placed. The total *pressure error* comes in two categories, *position* or *configuration error* (inherent from the design), and *manoeuvre error,* from the way you handle the machine, which mostly affects the VSI. Position error is defined as the *amount by which the local static pressure differs from that in the free stream airflow.* The ASI and altimeter can develop positive or negative position errors.

Configuration errors will have been established during flight testing, and can be displayed on calibration cards or programmed out by electronics, if you have them. Standby instruments, however, will not have the luxury, and will have uncorrected errors given on a calibration card.

The greatest pitot-static system errors are found when manoeuvring. If the left static port becomes blocked, the altimeter over-reads when sideslipping to the left but is otherwise OK.

THE ALTIMETER
. . . .

Static pressure is inversely proportional to altitude, so if you know the static pressure, you can figure out how high you are (in the standard atmosphere).

The altimeter is a barometer with the scale marked in feet rather than millibars. It does not measure the true height, but the weight of the air above the aircraft, which compresses the capsule inside.

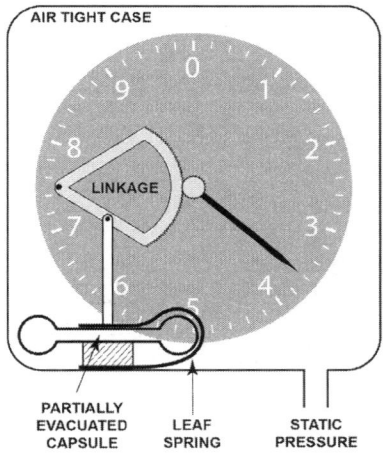

As you go up, pressure is less, so the altimeter translates air pressure into an *estimate* of altitude, although it will be better sealed than a barometer, so that air pressure in the cockpit doesn't affect it - the only pressure that should be there is static pressure from the pitot-static system. The readings could be inaccurate due to temperature and pressure variations from standard.

Inside a *sensitive* altimeter are *two* aneroid capsules (vacuums), which are corrugated for strength and kept open with a large leaf spring (a *simple* altimeter is a little more basic, with only one capsule - they are commonly used as cabin altimeters on pressurised aeroplanes since, at high altitudes, the capsule's movements are difficult to detect). The capsules' movements as you go up and down are magnified through the spring by a "suitable linkage" that connects directly to the pointer, using jewelled bearings. If the capsules expand, as they would when you go up, the pointer increases the reading. There is also a temperature compensation system to correct any spring and linkage tensions. Outside, there is a small knob, linked to a subscale which is visible through a small window. Rotating the knob causes the subscale to move and adjust the instrument to an *altimeter setting* (see *Meteorology*).

Caution: The three-needle display (on the right) can be easily misread:

True altitude is shown from pressure altitude, so only in standard ISA conditions will the true altitude be indicated directly. When it is extremely cold (below about -16°C), it will be a lot lower than shown, so corrections must be applied (altitudes given with radar vectors from ATC are corrected already). If this is something you need to take note of, you could perhaps mark the corrections directly on to the approach chart, next to the heights they refer to (you must recalculate *every* significant height).

The dials work like a clock. The long, thin pointer indicates hundreds of feet and the short, wide one, thousands. A very thin one, maybe with an inverted triangle at the end, as above, shows feet in ten thousands.

Encoding Altimeter

An *encoding altimeter* is used with a transponder in Mode C so that your altitude can be shown on a radar display.

The encoding assembly is mechanically activated by the aneroid capsule. Older versions consist of a light source, various lenses and an encoder disc with a special pattern on it (in eleven concentric circles) that works like a bar code when the light is reflected from it to produce binary inputs that correspond to 100-ft increments in altitude. One turn of the disc covers the complete range of the altimeter. Naturally, there are now digital versions of the same thing that can also be fitted externally.

Note: The adjustment knob on the altimeter does not affect what ATC see on their radar screens! All encoding systems transmit your altitude corrected to 29.92 inches, or 1013.25 hPa. The ground equipment makes any regional corrections directly. You won't get into trouble for small deviations, say, of 200 feet or so, but you may be treated as an amateur and directed around their airspace, rather than being allowed a more direct routing.

Datums

Height is the vertical distance from a particular datum, usually in the case of aviation from the surface of an airfield (QFE is used more in Europe - it is the airfield datum pressure, which makes the altimeter read your height above the airfield). *Altitude* is height above sea level. *Elevation* is the vertical distance of a point on the Earth's surface from mean sea level. *Indicated altitude* is what is shown on the dial at the current altimeter setting. *Calibrated altitude* is the indicated altitude corrected for instrument and position error. *True Altitude* is the actual one above mean sea level, taking the above errors into account, plus air temperature and density (absolute altitude is the actual height above the surface, and is produced by a radio altimeter).

You can calculate true altitude with a formula. First, subtract the ground elevation from the indicated altitude, and divide by 1,000 feet to get a single decimal number. Next, multiply that figure by the difference between the ISA temperature and the indicated one. Multiply that figure by 4 ft to get the amount to be subtracted from the indicated altitude. Thus:

$$\frac{\text{Ind Alt-Elevation x OAT-ISA x 4 ft}}{1,000}$$

On the flight computer, put the PA against the OAT in the altitude window and read the true altitude on the outer scale against the indicated one on the inner scale.

Pressure altitude is the height of a particular pressure setting, usually 29.92" or 1013.2 mb, but could be any other, such as 700 mb, as on high level weather charts. QNE (1013.2) makes your altimeter read Flight Levels. *Density altitude* is the pressure altitude corrected for non-standard temperature. The *altimeter setting* (QNH) is the pressure at a point (or *station*, to be technical), corrected for temperature and reduced to mean sea level under standard conditions, so if you set it on your scale, you will see altitude (your height above mean sea level), or the airfield elevation if you are on the ground.

Errors

Altimeters suffer from:

*   **Mechanical errors**, which include:

    *   *Scale error.* The difference between the indicated altitude and the basic altitude at which the measurement is taken

    *   *Friction error.* Causes irregular or jerky movement of the needle because the inner workings are sticking together. It is fixed by gentle tapping or vibration

    *   *Position error* arises from unusual attitudes. It is sometimes confused with Installation error, and is generally greater at low airspeeds as the angle of attack is abnormal, but manoeuvring doesn't help. On an aircraft with 2 altimeters, and only one compensated for position error, in straight symmetrical flight, the lower the speed, the greater the error will be between them, but an ADC should compensate (a non-compensated altimeter, however, will indicate a higher altitude). If the static source on the right gets blocked, in a sideslip to the right, the altimeter will over-read

*   **Temperature error**, caused by linkages in the instrument shrinking or expanding, but this includes the temperature of the atmosphere, particularly when cold (see the *Meteorology* section). If the temperature is lower, *you* are lower! It will be around 4 ft per thousand for every degree of deviation from ISA, and the same deviation is assumed to apply for all heights. At a constant indicated altitude over a warm air mass, the altimeter reading will be less than true altitude. Going into a colder air mass, it will over-read

*   **Elastic error**, which includes:

    *   *Hysteresis,* an irregular response to pressure changes (technically where changes lag behind the force that produces them). This varies a lot with time passed at an altitude and is measured by the difference in two readings, when increasing and decreasing. The effects are negligible in slow climbs or descents, but a rapid descent will cause a delay, fixed with a vibrator. Indicated readings will lag behind true altitude, and the aircraft will be lower than indicated.

    *   *Drift.* A slow increase in readings without an increase in altitude after levelling off from a climb - after descending the readings should return to normal. Drift should not be more than around 0.2% for every 15 000 ft change in altitude for flights over an hour long

© *Phil Croucher, 2013*

CAPT

• *Secular error.* The slow change over time of the entire scale error curve, mainly from internal stresses in the metal. Fixed by resetting zero

• **Time lag** from the distance a pressure change has to travel in the pipes, at its worst during steep altitude changes. Due to lag, the altimeter will under-read in a climb, and *vice versa*

• **Reversal error**, a momentary display in the wrong direction after an abrupt attitude change

• **Installation or Position error.** This appears when the altimeter is not exposed to true static pressure, because there is no perfect place to put the static ports (or the pitot tube, for the ASI). *The error in altimeter readings caused by the variation of the static pressure near the source is position error*

Between areas with different pressures, you could be at a different height than expected. For example, flying from high to low pressure, your altimeter would over-read (from HIGH to LOW, your instrument is HIGH), so you would be lower than planned and liable for a nasty surprise, especially in the lee of a mountain wave. Conversely, going from low into high pressure, without the altimeter setting being adjusted, the altimeter will indicate lower than the actual altitude above sea level. The same goes when you move between areas with different temperatures.

A static blockage causes the altimeter to stay at the height at which the blockage occurred. A partial blockage would cause a significant time delay.

Altimeter Settings

• **QFE** makes the altimeter read zero at the airfield elevation. *Airfield QFE* is measured at the highest point of the airfield surface, and *Touchdown QFE* at the touchdown point of the precision runway

• **QNH** makes the altimeter read altitude above Mean Sea Level, and airfield elevation on touchdown (it is QFE reduced to a sea level value under ISA). *Airfield QNH* must be set when departing in controlled airspace. **Note:** The Regional QNH is the *Lowest Forecast Pressure* for a complete Altimeter Setting Region, which changes on the hour, is valid for an hour and is available for an hour before that, so don't expect accurate height indications!

• **QFF** is like QNH, but uses actual station temperature instead of ISA (it's for meteorologists and is plotted on sea level pressure charts). It should read zero feet at sea level.

• **QNE** is the height at touchdown with 1013 mb set on the subscale or, in other words, the pressure altitude of the touchdown point. It is used at very high aerodromes where QFE is so low that it cannot be set on the subscale

Notes: When *en route*, Regional QNH should be set, unless below a TMA when the Zone QNH, or suitable Aerodrome QNH can be used. Alternatively, aerodrome QFE may be used on finals, in which case it should be on the No 1 when single-pilot, and on both otherwise. When single crew, No 2 may remain on the relevant QNH. A third altimeter must be set to relevant QNH at or below MOCA (*Minimum Obstacle Clearance Allowance*).

Altimeter Checks

Rotating the knob through ±10 hPa must produce a corresponding height difference of about ±300 ft in relevant directions. At a known elevation on the aerodrome, vibrate the instrument by tapping, unless mechanical vibration is available:

• Set the scale to the current QNH. The altimeter should indicate the elevation, plus the height of the altimeter above it, within ± 20 m or 60 ft for altimeters with a test range of 0-9 000 m (0-30 000 ft) and ± 25 m or 80 ft for altimeters with a test range of 0-15 000 m (0-50 000 ft)

• Set the current QFE. The altimeter should indicate the height of the altimeter in relation to the QFE reference point, with the same tolerances

• Both should be set to the aerodrome QFE and should indicate within ±80' of zero, within 60 or 80' of each other. Thus, they can misread by up to 120 or 160 feet and still be "serviceable"

• With No 1 on QFE and No 2 on aerodrome QNH, the difference should equal the aerodrome altitude AMSL, to within 80 feet

• With both on aerodrome QNH, indications should be within ±80 feet of aerodrome elevation, and 80 feet of each other

Note: No 1 is the handling pilot's primary instrument and No 2 the secondary.

According to JAR 25 the tolerance for an altimeter at MSL is ±30' per 100 kts CAS.

AIRSPEED INDICATOR   022 02 06

To find airspeed, you need to compare the general pressure outside the aircraft (the static pressure) with the pressure created from its movement through the air, so this instrument is connected to both the static and pitot pressure systems. The ASI is similar to the altimeter inside, except that the capsule is fed directly with pitot pressure, and its size will vary in direct proportion to any increase or decrease. The ASI is a *differential manometer that measures the difference between total (pitot) and static pressures.* That is, it is a pressure gauge with its dial marked in knots or mph instead of PSI. It captures total pressure then subtracts static pressure to get dynamic pressure, which indicates speed because the needle is connected to the capsule through the usual suitable linkage.

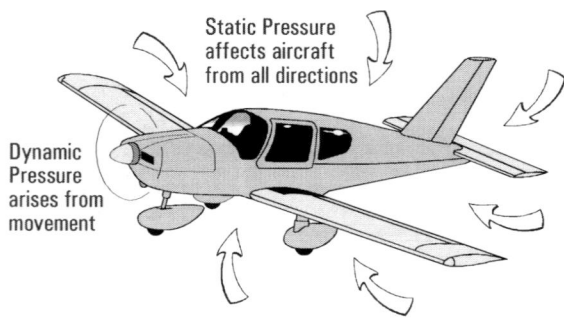

Dynamic pressure varies with the square of the airspeed.

The combination of static and dynamic pressure is the *stagnation pressure*, because airflow is being brought to rest inside the pitot tube, or stagnating.

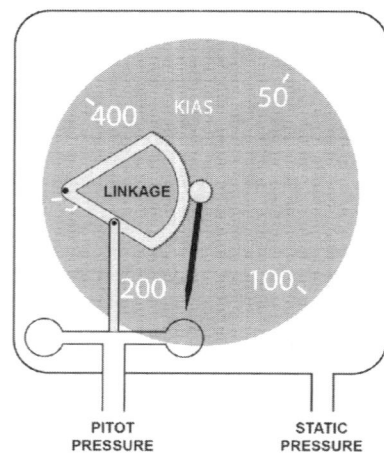

Note: Some aircraft, such as the Bell 407, have a dampened needle, which will indicate the speed you have been, and not the speed you are at.

Because the atmosphere gets less dense as you climb, the IAS must be corrected. The rate is 1.75% per 1000 feet.

There are several variations on the airspeed theme:

- **Indicated airspeed** (IAS) is the direct reading, corrected only for instrument error - turbulent flow around the pressure head accounts for 95%). Modern instruments have little error, so the direct reading is effectively IAS.

- **Calibrated airspeed** (CAS) is the IAS corrected for pressure (system) errors, which are highest at low speeds (IAS and CAS will be about the same at speeds above the cruise). It's known by older pilots as the *Rectified Air Speed* (RAS), and is a measure of the dynamic pressure at *low speeds*. Instrument and position errors can be corrected out by the Air Data Computer in modern aircraft. *An aircraft always takes off at the same CAS.*

- **Equivalent Airspeed** (EAS) is CAS compensated for compressibility, or factors arising from high speeds. It does not consider density error, and is effectively IAS/CAS where such errors are small, such as in helicopters (below 200 kts and 20,000 feet it will be in the order of 1-2 kts). EAS is always lower than or equal to CAS, because, as the air is compressed inside the pitot tube, the dynamic pressure is greater than it should be, and the correction is a negative value, so it could be regarded as a form of error. EAS explains the aerodynamic behaviour of an aircraft - it is what keeps the aerofoils in the air, and is what you would feel on your face if you were in an open cockpit. It compares flight at altitude to that at sea level, so if you have an EAS of 250 kts at 20,000 feet, you have the same dynamic pressure as if you were at sea level in ISA conditions. The bridge between EAS and TAS is Density Altitude.

- **True Air Speed** (TAS) is the CAS corrected for altitude and temperature, or density (its original calibration is based on the standard atmosphere). *It is the only speed* and the only figure used for navigation - the others are pressures and are to do with aircraft behaviour! The slide rule part of the flight computer is used to calculate these, discussed below. On average, the TAS increases by 2% over the IAS for every 1,000 feet. Refer to the *Performance* chapter for a discussion on the effects of air density on TAS.

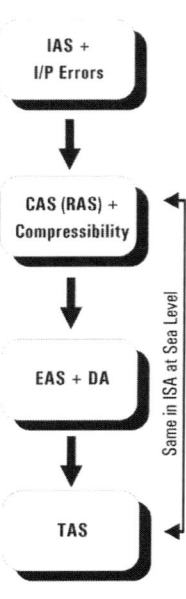

© Phil Croucher, 2013   CAPT

You can find TAS from the CAS and Air Density, which can be derived from Pressure Altitude and temperature which, in an exam, may involve a conversion from Fahrenheit to Centigrade (and from miles per hour to knots). Thus, in ISA conditions at sea level, CAS = TAS. However, as an example, given an altimeter setting of 30.40", an indicated altitude of 3450', an OAT of 41°F and an IAS of 138 mph, find the TAS in knots.

For the moment, take CAS as 118 kts, having converted 138 mph to 120 kts and looked it up on an imaginary graph (if there isn't one, the question will contain the information required). 41°F also converts to 5°C. The PA is found in the usual way, remembering that 1" equals 1,000'. The difference between 29.92" and 30.40" is 0.48, or 480 feet, which gives 2970' when subtracted from 3450' (29.92 is the "higher" figure in terms of distance above ground).

The TAS is 122 kts, and the Density Altitude (out of interest) is 2500'. If the TAS were over 300 kts, you have to apply a compressibility correction, which will bring TAS and CAS closer together.

If the pitot becomes blocked, the ASI will behave like an altimeter because it has only static information - its readings (i.e. your airspeed) will increase as you climb. If the static gets blocked, this will reverse.

If you maintain a constant CAS and level, flying from warm air to cold air, TAS will *decrease* as air density *increases*, and *vice versa*. In the standard atmosphere, therefore, when descending at constant CAS, TAS decreases.

If you climb at constant IAS, you will be climbing at a constant dynamic pressure, but air density decreases, so you need more V^2 to produce the same dynamic pressure.

At 40,000 ft for example, rho is about ¼ of its sea level value, so V^2 must be 4 times its own sea level value to keep dynamic pressure constant. In fact, TAS is twice the IAS.

To find out what happens to various speeds in the climb or descent, remember this picture:

The initial letters stand for *Equivalent, Calibrated* and *True* airspeeds, and *Mach number*. In the climb, select which one remains constant, and the speeds to the right will be increasing, with the ones to the left decreasing. The reverse for the descent.

022 02 05

Colour Coding

JAR 23 specifies various colour codes for ASIs, which are handy if you don't have the flight manual to hand.

The *green arc* covers the range of speeds for normal operations, the yellow arc is the caution range (that is, not to be used for long periods of time, and the red line is the speed not to be exceeded, V_{NE}. The blue line on a helicopter ASI is V_{NE} in autorotation.

The "normal" V_{NE} varies inversely with altitude, decreasing as you go higher. For example, on the Bell 206, when below 3000 lbs MAUW, you have to decrease V_{NE} by 3.5 kts per 1000 feet. On a Bell 212 at 9,000 feet, it could easily be as low as 80 kts.

Errors

The ASI suffers from position and attitude errors, plus those from the instrument itself, and lag. It is very susceptible to position error, which can be up to 10 or 20 kts at low speeds (check the flight manual), because the instrument will be calibrated for greatest accuracy in a particular flight condition (i.e. straight & level), otherwise the stagnation point will move to a different position.

However, density error is also important, since changes in air density affect the dynamic pressure, and make the ASI under-read at altitude (the ASI only reads TAS when density is standard, so to find it you have to apply a correction to CAS). The effect of temperature extending and contracting the linkages is fixed by a bimetallic strip that distorts to correct the expansion.

At high speeds (over 300 kts TAS, or 200 kts IAS) a further correction is made for compressibility, from air being compressed as it is brought to rest in the pitot tube.

If the pitot tube and its drain get blocked, the airspeed indicator will read high in the climb, low in the descent and not change at all when airspeed varies. This is because only the static pressure is changing, so they are behaving like altimeters (a typical icing situation). Thus, as you get higher, the instruments will over-read, and there is a danger that you will try to bring the speed back until you stall (without knowing why) which is what happened when the crew of one large jet missed the checklist item for the pitot heat. As static pressure *increases*, the ASI reading will *decrease*, and *vice versa*. If the drain hole remains open, however, IAS will read zero, as there is no differential between static and dynamic pressures, due to the drain hole allowing pressure in the lines to drop to atmospheric. A leak in the pitot total pressure line of a non-pressurised aircraft would cause an ASI to under-read.

If the static port gets blocked, the pressure inside the instrument (but outside the capsule) remains the same. The ASI will still read correctly in the cruise as long as the OAT doesn't change but, in the descent, it will over-read because the static element of pitot pressure increases inside the capsule - you will be closer to the stall than you think. In the climb, the static element of pitot pressure decreases, which causes a partial collapse of the capsule, so the instrument will under-read.

SQUARE LAW COMPENSATION

ASIs work on a differential pressure that varies with the square of the airspeed, and if you plotted the results linearly, the graph would look something like this:

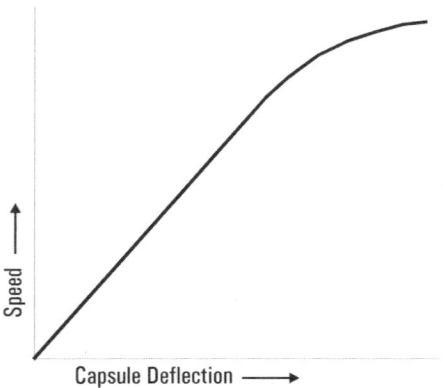

If you translated that to the instrument, you would end up with a logarithmic scale that would be difficult to read at low speed, and the whole speed range would be too big to fit in the display. In order to create a linear display, either the capsule or the linkage must be adjusted to produce the correct results or, rather, that the indication moves at the same rate as the airspeed. Usually, the length, or more accurately, the point of leverage of a lever, is adjusted to produce increased pointer movements for small deflections and decreased ones for large deflections. It is known as the *principle of variable magnification*.

V-Speeds

More in *Performance*!

Speed	Explanation
V_{LE}	Max gear extended
V_{LO}	Max gear operating
V_{NE}	Never Exceed speed. A red line on the ASI of a helicopter is the V_{NE} for power on, and a blue line is that for power off. V_{NE} may not be exceeded under any circumstances because it concerns aerodynamic and structural limitations.
V_{NO}	Normal Operations. 10% less than V_{NE}.

VERTICAL SPEED INDICATOR

There is a capsule inside this, too, but it is connected only to the static system. However, there is a *restrictor*, or *calibrated leak* between the inside and outside of the capsule that makes the pressure outside it lag behind, so the VSI measures the *rate of change* of *static pressure* with height, based on pressure difference between the inside of the capsule and the inside of the casing. It is also a *variometer*.

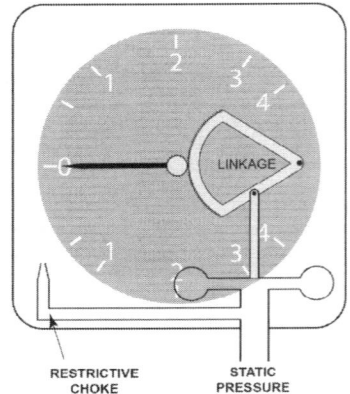

In other words, the difference of pressure between two chambers is measured, with one chamber (the capsule) being inside the other (the case). Static pressure goes to the capsule, then through the metering unit to the case, so that the pressure inside the case is always lagging behind that in the capsule by about 10 seconds.

During level flight there is no pressure differential across the metering unit, but in a descent (for example), static pressure increases and flows into the capsule and case. The capsule will expand as normal, but the restrictor will keep the pressure inside the case relatively low and create a differential that distorts the capsule one way or another and the suitable linkage transfers the movements to the dial to show climb or descent. However, the case pressure must be kept lower than the capsule pressure and made to change at the same rate to obtain a constant differential.

Increased velocity through the restrictor means decreased pressure, after Bernoulli, and the case has a greater volume than the capsule, so the process is slow enough to allow the aircraft to stabilise before anything needs to be done. In fact, the capsule leads the case by about 4 seconds.

A complex choke system self-compensates for temperature, density and air viscosity, using two capillary tubes to give a laminar flow and two sharp-edged orifices for a turbulent flow. Errors that result from the two types are of opposite sign and cancel each other out.

The VSI is a trend *and* a rate instrument, showing the direction of movement (up or down), and how fast you're going, in hundreds of feet per minute on a logarithmic scale, with zero at the 9 o'clock position, so it is horizontal

CAPT

during straight and level flight. Any movement up or down is shown in the relevant direction.

The advantage of a logarithmic scale is that, at low rates of climb or descent, the pointer movement is much larger and easier to read.

About 10% of indicated vertical speed should be used to determine the number of feet to lead by when levelling off from a climb or descent.

Errors

Aside from the usual position error, the VSI suffers from lag, which may last up to 6-8 seconds before the air inside and outside the capsule stabilizes. This means that, for example, once you level off and the altimeter is stable, the VSI takes a few more seconds to settle to neutral. There is also *reversal error*, which occurs when abrupt changes cause movement briefly in the opposite direction. In the hover, the VSI often shows a slight descent.

If the static source becomes blocked, pressure differentials disappear and the instrument reads zero.

IVSI

An *instantaneous VSI* uses two accelerometers in the static line, or a static input to an acceleration pump, to reduce lag errors, which unfortunately introduces turning errors. The accelerometers consist of two small cylinders with weights inside (they act like pistons), held in balance by springs and their own mass. The weights are centralised when stabilised in the climb or descent, but, when levelling, they act in opposing directions to sharply reduce instrument indications by puffing air into the appropriate places (inertia causes an immediate differential pressure).

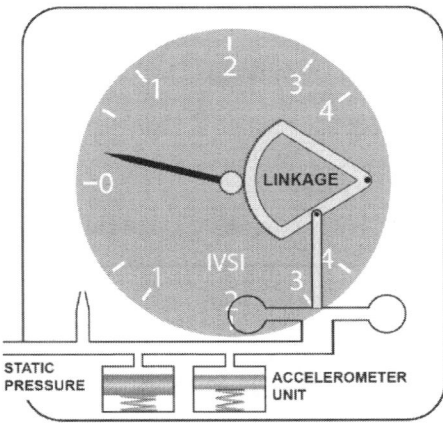

When returning to level flight from large angles of bank, the IVSI will initially show a climb. If the turn is maintained it will stabilise to zero, and then indicate a descent on rollout. Thus, IVSIs should not be relied upon while initiating or ending turns at bank angles of more than about 40°.

THE COMPASS 022 03/061 02

The Earth has its own magnetic field, which resembles a doughnut, in that the lines of force are more or less parallel with the curvature of the Earth but increase their angle towards the Poles until they move vertically downwards in a circle surrounding the true pole.

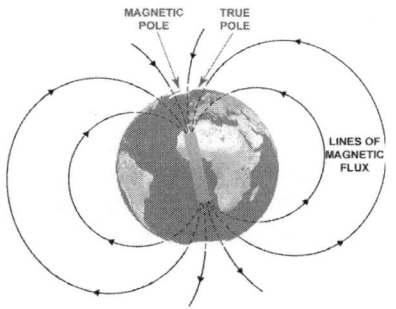

Although the origin of the Earth's magnetic field is not known, the Earth is regarded as a magnet with its blue pole near the North pole and the direction of the magnetic force pointing straight down to the earth's surface. In fact, the geographic North Pole is magnetically a South Pole, and *vice versa*, which is why the North end of a compass needle points to it.

A direct reading compass has a pivoted magnet that is free to align itself with the horizontal component of the Earth's magnetic field.

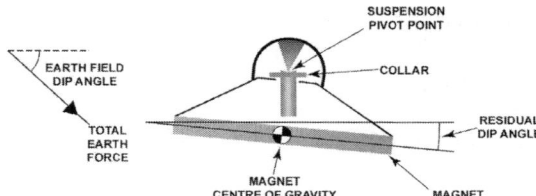

It must have certain properties to do this, namely:

- **Horizontality**. The needle must dip as little as possible. The centre of gravity lies below the pivot point, with pendulous magnets, which opposes the vertical component of the Earth's magnetic force (Z). Although there is still a residual dip, if it is less than 3° at mid-latitudes, it is OK. There is a collar and sleeve that stops it falling apart when inverted

- **Sensitivity**. This can be improved by increasing the length and/or the pole strength of the magnet. However, multiple magnets will do just as well, and they can also be employed as the weights under the pivot point mentioned above. Pole strength can be increased by using special alloys. In addition, you could use a jewelled pivot to reduce friction, and a suspension fluid which both lubricates it and reduces the effective weight of the whole assembly. Modern compasses are sensitive, down to 0.01

gauss, but even that gives excessive hunting (in fact, you need gyro assistance when the magnetic field is below about 0.06 gauss)

- **Aperiodicity**. The ability to settle quickly after a disturbance, without overshooting or oscillating, which is helped by the (transparent) suspension liquid and a wire spider assembly. The two magnets above are also useful here, as they keep the mass of the assembly near the pivot, reducing inertia. Light alloys reduce inertia even more. Thus, *the mass of the assembly is kept close to the compass point, and damping wires are used*

Being magnetic, the compass will be affected by all the fields generated by the aircraft itself, causing a phenomenon called *Deviation*, which is discussed under *The Compass Swing*, below. To try and eliminate errors, particularly magnetic dip, a remote indicating gyrocompass may be used, which is slaved to a DGI (discussed later). The master unit is mounted near the rear of the aircraft, so it is removed from as much influence as possible (hence the term *remote*). It contains a gyroscope under the influence of a magnetic element.

One purpose of using a fluid in a compass is to reduce friction at the pivot points.

E2B

A typical E2B direct indicating *standby* compass, as used in most aircraft today, consists of a floating inverted bowl suspended on a pedestal in kerosene, for damping (aside from allowing you to see the compass card through it, the purpose of the transparent liquid is to increase sensitivity and aperiodicity). The bearings are marked on the outside of the bowl, and there are two parallel magnetised needles inside, suspended under the pivot point, as mentioned.

Here is what the insides look like:

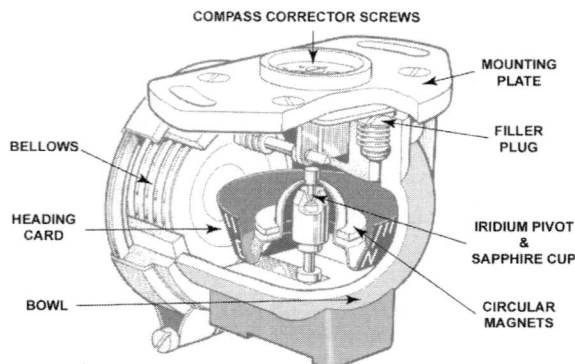

COMPASS CORRECTOR SCREWS

MOUNTING PLATE

FILLER PLUG

BELLOWS

HEADING CARD

IRIDIUM PIVOT & SAPPHIRE CUP

BOWL

CIRCULAR MAGNETS

Dip

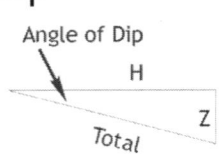

Angle of Dip

H

Z

Total

As the compass needle tries to follow the lines of force, it dips near the Poles, to where it is vertical (and unreadable), due to the vertical component of the Earth's magnetic force, which is called *Z* (in UK, the dip angle is around 67°). The bit we are interested in is *H*, the directive component, which is zero at the poles. At the Equator, there is no dip, so H is maximum, but as soon as you move away, and dip commences, the compass's Centre of Gravity becomes misaligned with its pivot point, and will move towards the Equator, or away from the nearer Pole.

H is about the same at magnetic latitudes 50°N and S.

Dip should obviously be minimised as much as possible, and is the reason why true tracks and headings are flown in Polar areas - the North and South magnetic Poles are the only places on the Earth where a freely suspended magnetic compass will stand vertical. On Northern routes, the dip effect causes a compass to turn much slower than you are used to in lower latitudes.

Magnetic dip is the angle between the horizontal and vertical forces acting on a compass needle toward the nearer pole. Its existence is why the limits of a magnetic compass lie between 73°N and 60°S (it is most effective about midway between the magnetic Poles). An *aclinic line* is a line representing points of zero magnetic dip. As the magnetic pole and lines of force do not coincide with either the true poles or lines of longitude, there is a way of accounting for any magnetic variation, discussed below.

Unfortunately, although the centre of gravity's position below the suspension point assists with minimising Z (and dip), it also gives rise to errors. before you start relying on the compass (either to navigate or align your DGI), make sure you are in steady, level flight. Also, make turns gently, because the swirling fluid will keep the compass moving afterwards.

ACCELERATION ERRORS

These are caused by inertia on East-West headings. Because the C of G of the compass is under the pivot point, accelerating displaces the C of G behind the pivot point and makes the bulk of the compass lag behind the machine. If you were just going N-S, all you would get is extra dip, but because you are going East or West, the displaced C of G, not being vertically in line with the pivot point, creates a couple that makes the compass turn in the direction of the acceleration (clockwise when heading East) to read less than 90° during the turn. A deceleration has the opposite effect.

CAPT

Acceleration errors are maximum on East/West headings and near the magnetic Poles, and nil on North/South headings, and at the Equator.

The watchword here is ANDS - *Accelerate North, Decelerate South*, or SAND in the Southern Hemisphere.

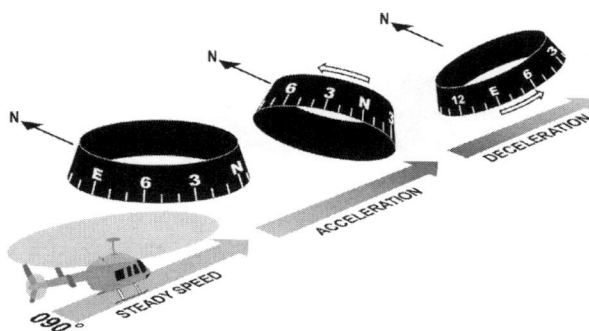

In the Northern Hemisphere flying East, for example, if you accelerate, the needle deflects to the nearest Pole (North, for an easterly deviation) and to the South when you decelerate.

- During deceleration after landing on runway 18 (a Southerly direction), a compass in the Northern hemisphere would indicate no apparent turn

- During deceleration after a landing in an Easterly direction, a magnetic compass in the Northern hemisphere indicates an apparent turn South

- During deceleration after a landing in a Westerly direction, a magnetic compass in the Southern hemisphere indicates an apparent turn North

TURNING ERRORS

A Mr Keith Lucas discovered that a simple compass under-estimates turns on Northerly headings, and over-estimates them on Southerly ones in the Northern hemisphere (UNOS, and ONUS in the South). This makes it look as if you are turning slower through North and faster through South as the compass moves with or against the aircraft. To put it another way, to eliminate the hemispheres from the equation, during turns through the *nearest* Pole (within 35°), the compass is sluggish, so you need to roll out early. During turns through the *furthest* Pole, it will be lively, so roll out late. The errors are maximum (30°) at the Poles and decrease by 10° towards East and West, where they are nil.

Turning errors can have two elements, both of which work in the same sense:

- **Magnetic**, which depends on the angle of bank. In a turn from North to East, for example, the North-seeking end will move down towards Earth, so its readings will decrease and a turn in the opposite direction will be indicated. The more the bank, the more the error*.

Turning error actually depends on the tangent of the angle of dip multiplied by the cosine of the heading and the angle of bank. It is nil on E-W headings because the cosine is nil. For a 5° angle of bank, the error will be in the order of 30°.

*Thus, it will be more apparent with a fast aircraft for the same rate of turn.

- **Dynamic**, which depends on speed and the rate of turn. In a flat turn, the dip makes the C of G of the compass move toward the Equator and it moves to the outside of the turn, producing a clockwise movement as above.

A rough calculation as to how much to overshoot or anticipate by when turning to the North or South comes from this formula:

$$\frac{\text{Bank Angle + Latitude}}{2}$$

So, to turn right on to a southerly heading with 20° bank at 20°N, you stop on an approximate heading of 200°.

Direction

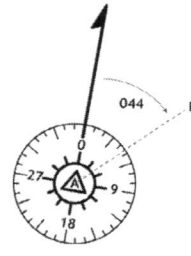

Direction (for us) is the position of one point relative to another, regardless of distance between them, measured in an angular fashion with reference to True, Magnetic or Grid North, using up to 360 numerical degrees*.

*The complete circle of direction (or *compass rose*) is split into 360 *degrees*, which are split into 60 *minutes* and 60 *seconds*, so the complete expression of an angle is in degrees, minutes and seconds - 30° 45' 53". North is 0°, so, going round the clock, East is 90°, South is 180° and West is 270° (the *cardinal* directions. NE, SE, SW & NW are intercardinal).

A *bearing* is a direction obtained by observation. It is the horizontal clockwise angle from a North baseline, or the angle between whichever North you use and any line between two points, such as that between A and B in the diagram above. The bearing is 044°, and the opposite is the *reciprocal*, found by adding or subtracting 180°, or 224°. Because you go clockwise, and the largest number is 360°, 355° is less than 010°.

Note: This is not the same as the *relative bearing* from your aircraft, which is measured from the longitudinal axis!

The bearing starts at the centre of an imaginary circle (A).

*   **True North** is a line from any point on the Earth's surface to the North Pole (i.e. up, towards the top of the Earth), along the local meridian. Modern navigation systems such as INS/IRS output True North and their readings are changed to magnetic according to a lookup table.

*   **Magnetic North** is the direction to the North *magnetic* pole, as shown by the North-seeking needle of a magnetic compass. Its usual symbol is a line ending with half an arrowhead.

*   **Grid North** is a line established with vertical grid lines drawn on a map, explained later. It may be symbolised with the letters *GN* or *y*

All meridians run North to South.

MAGNETIC BEARINGS

The North *Magnetic* Pole was discovered by Soviet explorers to be the rim of a magnetic circle 1000 miles in circumference, around 600 miles from the True Pole.

Both magnetic Poles move slowly around their respective True Poles, over a period of around 960 years. The North magnetic pole and various lines of force described below change their positions to the West.

That there is a True and a Magnetic North indicates that a compass will not point towards True North, since it relies on magnetism for its operation, and the two Norths (or Souths) do not coincide at their respective Poles. This is because the Earth generates its own magnetism, which may be varied by local deposits of metals under the

ground, for example, which bend the magnetic flux lines. The way to Magnetic North will therefore vary across the ground from place to place, and a freely suspended compass will turn to the direction of the *local* magnetic field (the *Horizontal Component* is toward Magnetic North). As well, the lines of force will be vertical near the poles.

VARIATION

To find the direction of the geographical Pole, or True North, you have to apply a correction called variation, which is the angle between the magnetic and true meridians (that is, variation is the correction that must be applied to magnetic headings or courses (at the same place) to make them true. It is technically called *declination*.

If the magnetic meridian is to the right of the true one, variation is easterly and has a plus (+) sign (think of what it makes the compass rose do). If it is left, it is Westerly and has a minus (-) sign So, -8 is really 8W.

Remember: The **Magnetic Track Angle** (MTA) is the direction of the path of an aircraft across the Earth's surface referenced to *Magnetic North*.

The phrase to remember is *Variation East, Magnetic Least, Variation West, Magnetic Best*, that is, if the variation on your map is, say, 21° West, the final result should be 21° *more* than the true track found when you drew your line.

*   If you travel over many variations, use an average about every 200 miles.

*   Variation on a VOR bearing is applied *at the station*, and on an ADF *at the aircraft*.

Note: Magnetic information in a Flight Management System is stored in *each IRS memory* - it is applied to the true calculated heading.

Variation can change temporarily from sunspot activity or magnetic storms. This is more of a problem in the Arctic or Antarctic areas, where the change can be ±5° for an hour or more.

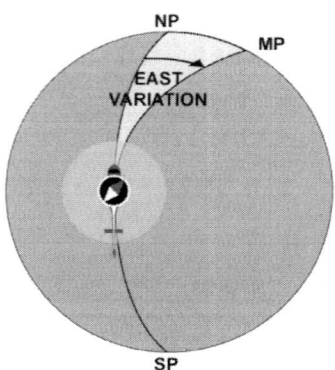

Compass needle pointing
east of true North

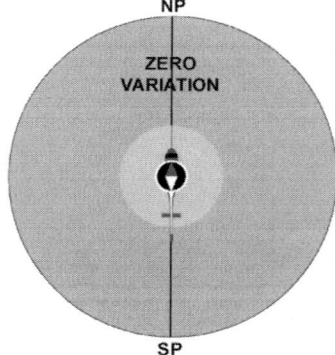

Compass needle pointing
to true North (along agonic line)

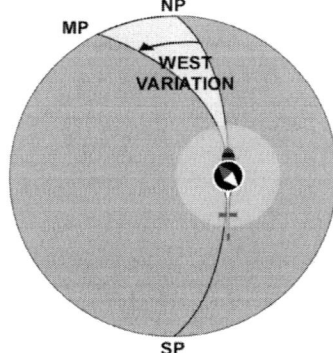

Compass needle pointing
west of true North

On a map, or chart, which would be drawn initially for True North, there is a dotted line called an *isogonal* that represents the local magnetic variation to be applied to any direction you wish to plan a flight on.

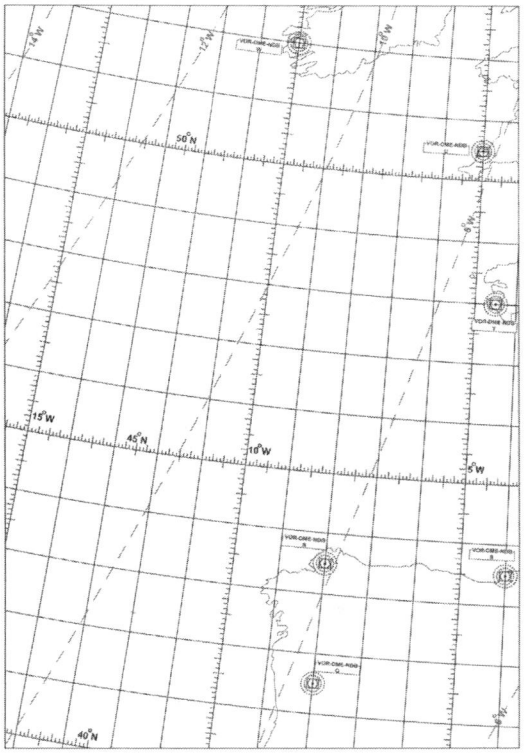

The charted values of magnetic variation normally change annually due to magnetic pole movement, causing values at all locations to increase or decrease. When plotted, isogonals are accurate worldwide to ±2°.

An *agonic line* exists where magnetic variation is zero, or where True and Magnetic North are both the same. There's one near Frankfurt, running North/South.

DEVIATION

Errors in the compass, plus the aircraft's own magnetism, created from large amounts of metal mixed with electrical currents, and any residual magnetism from hammering, etc. during manufacture, makes the compass deflect from Magnetic North, a process called *deviation*, which is unique to an aircraft. It is applied to the compass heading to get the magnetic heading.

The net result of an aircraft's magnetic forces is represented by a dot somewhere behind the wings or rotor head. On Northerly headings, the dot lies behind the South part of the needle and merely concentrates the magnetic force. On Easterly headings, however, the dot is West of the South part of the needle and causes an Easterly deviation, and *vice versa*. It is proportional to Z and inversely proportional to H.

Deviation is the difference between a heading measured from the magnetic meridian and the same heading measured by a compass, at the same place. It is defined by the number of degrees which must be added (algebraically) to the observed reading to get the True magnetic bearing. Two aircraft flying in formation would have slightly different headings due to their deviations.

When deviation is West, compass North is to the West of magnetic North. When deviation is East, compass North is to the East of magnetic North. The phrase here is *Deviation West, Compass Best, Deviation East, Compass Least,* similar to Variation. This means that if the compass is reading 005° when it should be reading 360°, the deviation is 5° West, or -5°, as it must be "added" to the observed reading to get the proper reading. If it is reading 346°, the deviation is 14° East, or +14°.

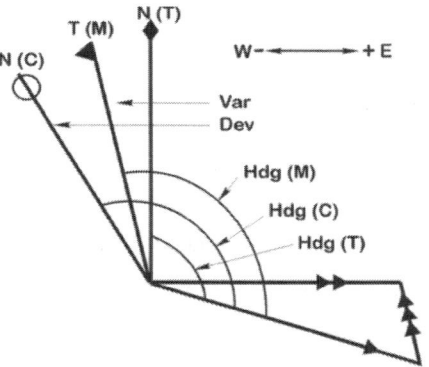

Thus, positive deviations deflect the compass needle to the right, and will have a plus sign even though the heading reads less. Negative deviations deflect the needle to the left and have a minus sign, although the heading increases. The key is to realise that they are based on what the deviation does to the heading on the compass rose.

Deviation varies with the heading and its values are displayed on a correction card next to the compass (they should not exceed 1° after correction). The values are obtained after a *compass swing*, a complex procedure normally done by an engineer. Every aerodrome has an area well away from buildings, etc. for the purpose.

For	Steer
000	001
045	043
090	089
135	133
180	184
225	223
270	269
315	316

Allowing for deviation is called *compensation*. So:

$$HDG(T) \pm VAR \pm DEV = HDG(C)$$

EXAMPLES

1. With a compass heading of 030°, deviation of 3°W and variation of 8°E, what is the true heading?

C	D	M	V	T
030	3W	027	8E	035

The Compass Swing

The magnetic compass is incompatible with aircraft, if only because it needs to be placed where it can be seen, which is typically in the middle of any stray magnetism.

A compass swing allows you to find out by how much a compass reads differently from the proper figures on any heading, then make corrections that cancel out as many deviations as possible. Airfields and have clear areas in which this can be done. The aircraft is taxied there and everything electrical that would be used in flight turned on. Then the aircraft compass is compared against a landing compass on several headings by an engineer standing out in the rain (you need to find the errors on the cardinal and quadrantal points, so the aircraft is placed on each one in turn). The deviations are reduced by adjusting the magnets inside the compass and a calibration swing is done to see what deviations or residuals, are left. The figures are written on the deviation card.

A compass swing should be done:

- on installation of the compass in the first place
- as per maintenance schedules
- whenever there is any doubt about accuracy
- after a shock to the airframe or a lightning strike
- if the aircraft has been left standing for some time or has moved to a significantly different latitude
- when major components or electrical installations change

Aircraft themselves have built-in magnetism, whose influence on a compass can be classified broadly into 3 components, *hard iron*, *soft iron* and *electrical*.

HARD IRON

This is a more or less permanent effect that arises because the aircraft will have been on a particular heading* at a particular latitude for some time when it was being made, and will have absorbed some of the earth's magnetism at that point. The effect is increased by hammering, and it will weaken when the machine starts flying, but some permanent magnetism will always remain. It is therefore unlikely to change.

In summary, hard iron magnetism is permanent, and does not change with latitude, but the deviation caused by it increases with latitude because the H force is weaker, and the compass magnets are more easily deflected.

SOFT IRON

This is a temporary influence that only appears when the metal in the aircraft is affected by the Earth's magnetic field and, to a lesser extent, aircraft electrical systems (i.e. induced magnetism). In other words, all ferrous metals that are not permanently magnetised. The effect of soft iron depends on the heading and attitude of the aircraft, and its geographical position.

In other words, as your heading changes, so does the soft iron magnetism.

ELECTRICAL

Current flowing through a conductor produces a magnetic field. There can also be effects from lightning strikes.

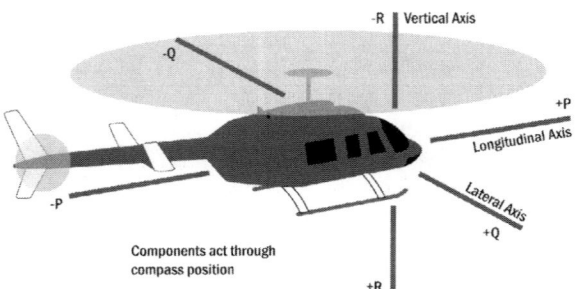

-R Vertical Axis
-Q
+P
Longitudinal Axis
Lateral Axis
+Q
-P
Components act through
compass position
+R

CAPT

GYROSCOPES

Gyros (and accelerometers) are also called *inertial sensors* because they use resistance to a change in momentum to sense angular motion (gyro) and linear motion (accelerometer).

Usually, three cockpit instruments are under gyroscopic influence, the *Attitude Indicator* (artificial horizon), *Directional Gyroscopic Indicator* (DGI) and *Turn Indicator or Coordinator*. The first two are typically suction-powered and the last by electricity, but many are now all electric.

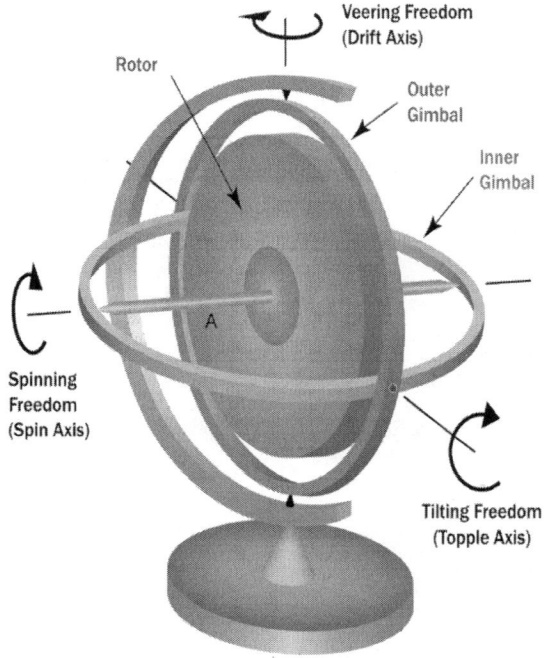

A gyroscope is a heavy rotating mass on a vertical or horizontal axis*, suspended in inner and outer *gimbals* which are in *frames*. Its operation depends on the resistance to deflection of a spinning wheel or disc.

*A gyroscope's axis of rotation defines its orientation. A vertical gyro has its axis in *Earth Vertical* (as opposed to aircraft vertical) and a horizontal gyro is in *Earth Horizontal*, but more properly aligned with North.

You need a gimbal for each axis to be measured, so an artificial horizon has 2, because it measures pitch and roll.

Tip: During startup checks, pull and hold any erection or caging knobs *before* turning the power on, as the parts inside can clash against each other as they spin up (just one of those little things a pilot can do to save long-term maintenance costs).

Also, don't move the aircraft after flight until all the gyros have stopped running (takes about 15 minutes), otherwise they will go unserviceable more often. This particularly applies to autopilot equipped machines.

Rigidity

The spinning allows the gyro to maintain its own position in space, regardless of whatever it is attached to is doing. In other words, it resists attempts to displace it from its position. If you attached one to a camera in a helicopter, the helicopter could be bumping around all over the place due to wind or pilot input, and the camera would not move from where the operator put it. The same applies with the instruments mentioned above, as we shall shortly see. In fact, the gyro does not move, but the Earth moving around the gyro gives you that impression. The magnitude of this apparent movement depends on your latitude or, rather, the sine (drift) or cosine (topple) of your latitude.

Rigidity can be improved with:

- faster spin speeds

- increasing the gyro's peripheral mass

- increasing the gyro's radius

The greater the rigidity, the more force will be required to move the spinning gyro, which is an example of the *Law of Conservation of Angular Momentum*.

Precession & Wander

Any movement of the gyro's spin axis from its initial alignment is called *precession*. A force applied to a gyroscope's spinning mass is felt 90° away from where it is applied, in the direction of rotation.

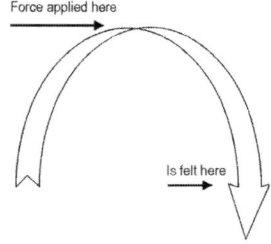

A mundane example comes from riding a bicycle - when you apply a force to turn one way or another, it is done at the top of the wheels, but the turning movement appears 90° later, hence the turn. More technically, precession is the *angular change in the plane of rotation under the influence of an applied force*.

The rate of precession depends on:

- the strength and direction of the applied force

- the rotor's moment of inertia (degree of rigidity)

- the rotor's angular velocity

WANDER

When a gyro moves from a preset position because of precession, it is said to wander (see also *DGI*).

The gyro is *drifting* when the axis wanders *horizontally*, and *toppling* when it wanders *vertically*. Thus, a gyro with only a vertical axis cannot drift. Both types are affected by real and apparent wander, described in the DGI section

Drift is the horizontal rotation of the spin axis around the drift axis, which is 90° from the spin axis in the vertical plane. Topple is the vertical rotation of the spin axis about the topple axis, is 90° from the spin axis in the horizontal plane (the word *topple* also refers to the tumbling that occurs when a gyro reaches one of its limit stops and a rapid precession occurs around a misaligned axis).

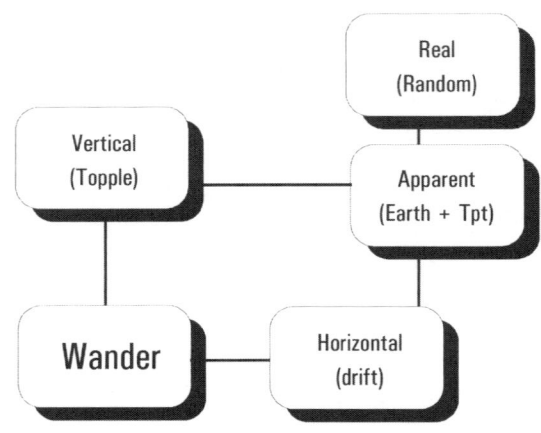

Types Of Gyroscope

3 PLANES OF FREEDOM

Gyros with 3 planes of freedom have 2 gimbals and total freedom of movement around 3 axes. There are 3 types:

- **Space Gyro**. Free to move in all directions with reference to space. Theoretical.

- **Tied Gyro**. As above, with the spin axis tied down in one local plane. 2 *degrees* of freedom (see below).

- **Earth Gyro**. As above, but the spin axis is tied *Earth vertically* by gravity.

2 PLANES OF FREEDOM

These show a rate of movement rather than a position:

- **Rate Gyro**. One gimbal, free to move around 2 axes (including the spin axis). Turn indicators.

- **Rate Integrating Gyro**. These are used in Inertial Navigation Systems. They have a gyro mounted inside two cans, one inside the other. The outer one is fixed to the INS platform and the inner one is free to rotate within it, behaving like a gimbal. There is a viscous fluid between the cans that stops the inner one toppling and reduces friction on the gimbals*. Precession from aircraft movement generates movement between the cans, and an error signal which is measured to determine the rate of movement.

*The fluid's viscosity is affected by temperature, so a warm-up period is required.

DEGREES OF FREEDOM

An older method of classifying gyroscopes uses the numbers of axes *not* including the spin axis, so one with 3 *planes* of freedom has 2 *degrees* of freedom. A degree of freedom is the ability to move around an axis - for example, a fuselage can pitch, roll and yaw. A turn indicator has 1 degree of freedom. An airborne instrument, with a gyro that has 2 degrees of freedom and a horizontal spin axis could be a DGI.

- *Spinning* freedom is about an axis perpendicular through the centre

- *Tilting* freedom is about a horizontal axis at right angles to the spin axis

- *Veering* freedom is about a vertical axis perpendicular to the spin and tilt axes

Degs	Gyro	Purpose
1°	Rate Rate Integrating	Turn Indicator Inertial Navigation
2°	Earth Tied	A/H DGI
3°	Space	Theoretical

Attitude gyros use rigidity in space for their operation, while rate gyros use precession.

Power

As mentioned, gyroscopic instruments are made to spin through suction or pressure (heading and attitude indicator) or electricity (turn instruments) although many are now all electric (even then, there should be separate and independent power supplies. If there is only one, you need suction, too).

SUCTION

With suction, air is usually *sucked out* of the casing, to create a vacuum that will be indicated on a gauge in the cockpit. It is part of the checklist before flight to ensure you have enough for the instruments to work properly, typically 4-5 inches of mercury. If it is reading low, the filters are blocked or equipment is worn, and the gyros will run too slowly. If the reading is too high, the gyros will run too fast.

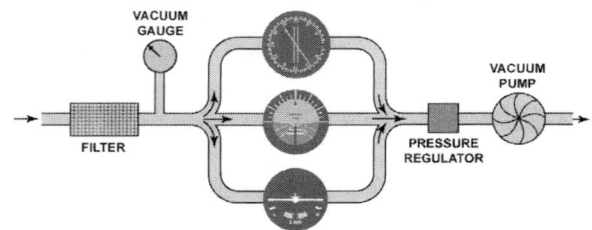

If this page is a photocopy, it is not authorised!

Vanes (small bucket-shapes) on the gyro mass catch the air movement and force it to go round. at several thousand RPM. The rest of the vacuum system has a pump driven by the engine, a relief valve, an air filter, and enough tubing for the connections. Older aircraft may have a venturi tube on the side to create the initial vacuum.

ELECTRICITY

At high altitudes, suction-driven gyros can lose rigidity because they cannot produce so much vacuum. They also require large amounts of plumbing. These can be resolved with electrical gyros, whose advantages include:

- Faster spin speed, therefore greater rigidity

- Spin speed is easier to initiate and maintain, as aircraft power is regulated, and you don't need other systems running first

- The container can be sealed to keep dirt out - suction driven instruments necessarily have a hole in them to let air in

- More stable operating temperature

- The ability to work at higher altitudes

- Acceleration errors are minimised because there is no heavy mass underneath the gyro, but if there are, they will be due to the mercury sloshing around in the switches

The motor is usually a squirrel cage, using a power supply of 115v 400 Hz 3-phase AC in large aircraft, while smaller ones can have an inverter built in to produce 26 V (AC motors tend to be used in artificial horizons, while DC is used in turn and bank indicators). There must be some form of failure indication to show loss of power.

Fast erection involves giving the motors a higher error signal, which can be done in unaccelerated flight.

ARTIFICIAL HORIZON

Otherwise known as the *attitude indicator*, this instrument represents the natural horizon and indicates the pitch and bank attitudes, that is, whether the nose is up or down, or the wings are level or not.

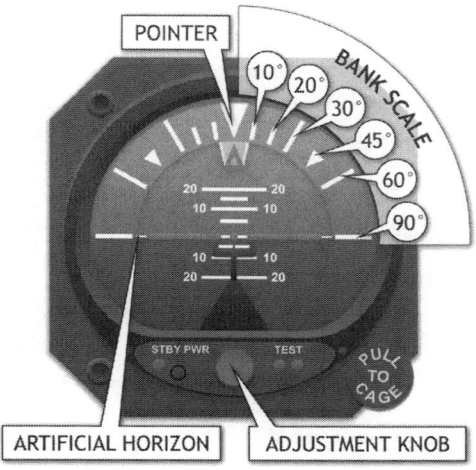

As the main rotor provides lift and is also the control surface in pitch and roll, the helicopter is very attitude-conscious. Acceleration and deceleration produce large changes in attitude at the same time, so the artificial horizon is very important.

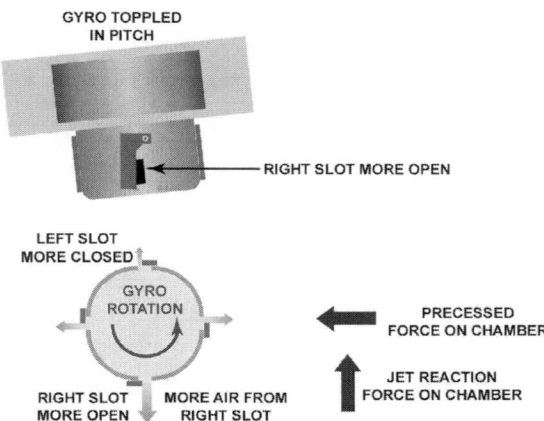

The spin axis is *vertically mounted* (in line with Earth Vertical) so the housing (and the aircraft) can rotate around its vertical axis, at right angles to the one in the DGI. The whole assembly is inside an *outer gimbal*, which is Earth Horizontal. There are two degrees of freedom.

The instrument's C of G is below the suspension point, so it is nearly vertical when it is switched on, which reduces the erection time. In the suction-driven version, four *pendulous vanes* cover holes through which air tries to pass, but is blocked by the vanes as long as the instrument is vertical. When it is not vertical, the vanes, which are suspended from a pivot and kept vertical by gravity, open the hole by differing amounts to let more or less air through as required, to provide the correcting force.

In other words, the pendulous vane stays vertical, but more of the hole is exposed as the instrument moves.

The aircraft symbol is attached to the casing and therefore the aircraft. The *horizon bar* (which stays in line with the Earth) is connected to the rear of the frame and to the housing with a *guide pin*, so when the nose pitches up, the outer gimbal comes off the horizontal. The movement is amplified by the beam bar and the guide pin is driven down - in a descent it goes up. Rolling rotates the instrument case.

Aircraft Pitched Nose Up

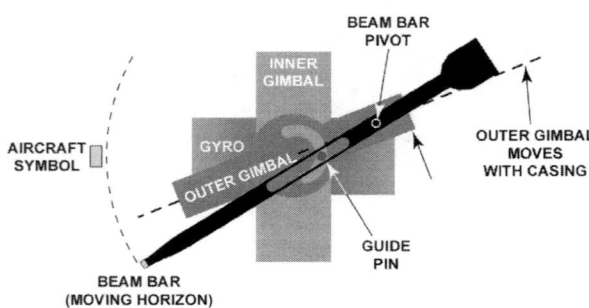

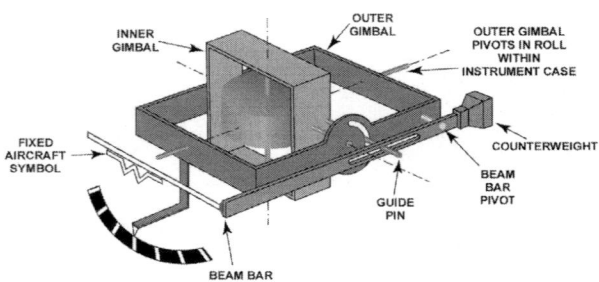

Errors

With all the rotating parts, there is bound to be friction, which will cause some errors in the readings. Others include *acceleration error*, during forward movement (as in a takeoff) which gives a false climb to the *right* - this is because of the pendulous mounting - the heavy bottom of the (suction) gyro suffers from inertia and creates an imbalance between misplaced centres of gravity (roll error) and closing one of the suction ports (pitch error) - the effect is similar to the compass. The resulting forces precess 90° away for false readings. Deceleration shows a false descent and roll to port.

Centrifugal force created during a turn will also displace the mass of the instrument's heavy bottom, but modern designs minimise turning errors at low rates of turn.

Electrical artificial horizons will show a climbing turn to the *left*, because they normally spin the opposite way.

Thus, an instrument showing a climb to either direction indicates *pitch* and *roll* errors. This has some significance when, for example, taking off from an oil rig at night. If you were not aware of this problem, you would fly nose down and to the left, and pitch yourself into the sea.

When an aircraft has turned 360° with a constant attitude and bank, both will be correct on a classic instrument. When it turns 90° with a constant attitude and bank, you will observe too much nose-up and bank too low.

Electrical Version

In an electrical artificial horizon, two *torque motors* are used, one parallel to the lateral axis, and one to the longitudinal axis. The laterally mounted one detects movement in roll, and a correction from the torque motor is applied to the pitch axis. Displacement in pitch is detected by the longitudinal switch which corrects around the roll axis.

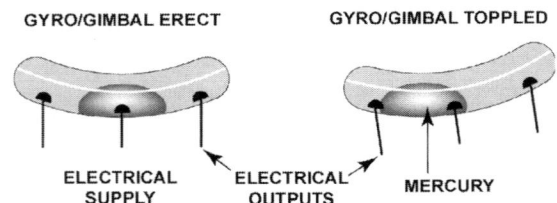

The torque motors are squirrel-cage type laminated iron rotors mounted concentrically round a stator, with two windings - one provides a constant field and is called the *reference winding*, and the other is in two parts so it can be reversible, called the *control winding*.

Levelling switches are sealed glass tubes containing 3 electrodes (one at each end and one in the middle) and a small blob of mercury. An inert gas is also present to stop any arcing as the mercury comes into contact with the electrodes. The glass tubes are set at right angles to each other on a switch block behind the gyro housing.

In the normal operating position, the mercury is in contact with the centre electrode, which is connected to the reference winding. If a displacement happens, the mercury makes contact with one of the side electrodes which completes a circuit to the relevant part of the control winding to apply the necessary torque correction. In fact, the voltage to the reference winding is fed via a capacitor and, as we know, this will cause the current to lead the voltage by 90°. As there is no capacitance in the control winding, it lags the reference winding by 90°. The resulting magnetic field rotates the stator in the required direction, at the same time cutting the conductor in the squirrel-cage winding and inducing a further magnetic field that makes the rotor follow the stator field.

This is immediately opposed because the rotor is fixed to the case, so a reactive torque is set up to cause the required amount of precession to correct the instrument.

© *Phil Croucher, 2013*

CAPT

Remote Vertical Gyro

Older artificial horizons are subject to gross errors when being accelerated, as when taking off or landing. As they must be small to fit into most instrument panels, there are practical limits to the size of the gyros inside them.

A remote vertical gyro is placed somewhere on the airframe that can take the size of the gyros and the information is fed to the cockpit over electrical cables.

HEADING INDICATOR (DGI)
••

This is used to give a stable heading reference free from compass errors. It works in a similar way to the artificial horizon, except that the spin axis is *aircraft horizontal* in the *yawing plane*. The casing turns round a horizontally tied gyro, which has a compass card mounted on it, so the aircraft rotates around the compass card:

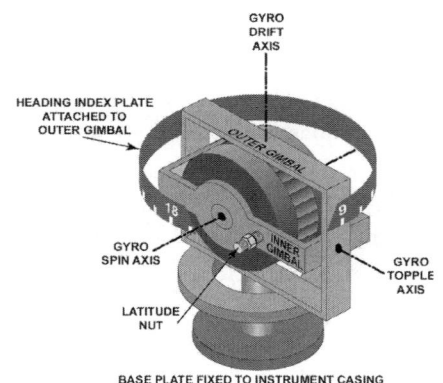

GYRO DRIFT AXIS
HEADING INDEX PLATE ATTACHED TO OUTER GIMBAL
OUTER GIMBAL
GYRO SPIN AXIS
INNER GIMBAL
GYRO TOPPLE AXIS
LATITUDE NUT
BASE PLATE FIXED TO INSTRUMENT CASING

The instrument is an air driven horizontal axis tied gyro, with typical limits of 55° in pitch and roll. To help with re-erection after toppling, the mass of the gyro is spun at 10,000-12,000 RPM, with air jets from twin sources, very close to each other (below left). When the gyro does not lie in the yawing plane, one jet (the drive component) will be pushing the gyro round, but the other (erection component) will strike the rim and cause a precession force at the top which will tend to re-erect it (below). Electrically driven gyros use a *slip ring and commutator*.

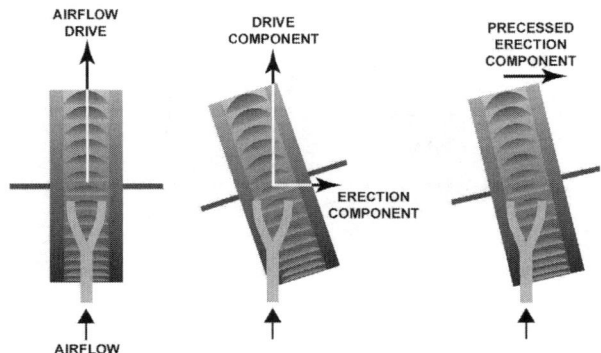

AIRFLOW DRIVE
DRIVE COMPONENT
PRECESSED ERECTION COMPONENT
ERECTION COMPONENT
AIRFLOW

DGI indications are only valid for limited periods due to:

- rotation of the Earth
- aircraft movement over the surface of the Earth
- mechanical imperfections, plus low rotor speed
- geometry of the gimbal system (gimballing errors)

The above are the reasons why we align the DGI with the compass every 15 minutes or so remembering, of course, to do it in level, unaccelerated flight, otherwise you may get erroneous readings.

Gimballing errors arise when the airframe does not move about one of the gyro axes. It is affected by banking, and goes away when the aircraft straightens up again.

Wander

If you just sat in your aircraft and watched the DGI, you would see it change from its original setting at a rate of 15° per hour, all by itself (not forgetting the sine of the latitude), if you applied no compensation. When flying, this would be compounded, because your gyro may be rotating by more or less than the speed of the Earth's rotation, as you cross lines of longitude.

There are two main types of wander:

- **Real**, or mechanical, which comes from friction in the bearings, power fluctuations and other imperfections, although this is less than 1° per hour in modern systems and may be considered negligible. However, it is unpredictable and can be measured only by checking your heading. This is sometimes called random wander as the effect is supposed to be unintentional. A perfect gyro has no imperfections, and no random wander.

- **Apparent**, where the spin axis remains aligned to a point in space as the plane of reference changes, making the gyro *appear* to precess. It consists of:

  - **Earth Rate** (N-S), from the Earth's rotation. Although there is a vertical component, the horizontal component is meant when talking about this (assuming you are stationary). So, at the Pole, the gyro will appear to move at 15.04° per hour (in the horizontal plane) because that is the rate at which the Earth is spinning and orbiting round the Sun. The only time this won't happen is at the Equator if the gyro's axis is aligned with a meridian and is parallel to the Earth's axis. Thus, it varies with the sine of the latitude for the DGI, to the right in the Northern hemisphere and the left in the Southern hemisphere. The sign is negative in the Northern Hemisphere because the gyro under-reads as the Earth rotates. Apparent drift is corrected with a latitude nut.

- **Transport Wander** (E-W). Here, the spin axis appears to move because you are crossing meridians and convergency is added to the mix. With transport wander, flight to the West causes over-reading, and Eastward flight causes under-reading* (in the Northern hemisphere), so if you held a steady heading of 090°, because the gyro is under-reading, you will be turning away to the *right* of earth track and your *true heading* is *increasing*.

This is not normally corrected for in light aircraft, but is minimised by resetting the gyro every 15 minutes or so.

*Eastward flight increases apparent drift because the gyro is rotating faster than the speed of the Earth, and Westward flight reduces it, so errors will be more than 15° per hour, and less, respectively.

TURN COORDINATOR

This is actually a combination of two instruments, one power driven, and the other not. The idea is to measure the *yaw* rate for low *bank* rates, and since yaw and bank have to be measured, the instrument is made sensitive to both by having its axis (i.e. the gimbal ring) *tilted upwards* by about 30-35°, though it is less sensitive to roll.

The roll is sensed first, and the rate increases when the correct angle of bank is set. This is what the instrument is sensing. Displacement remains constant for a given bank, regardless of airspeed. A small aircraft tilts to indicate whether you are banking, so it is a useful backup to the artificial horizon, especially since the gyro is electrically operated and not affected if the suction system fails (although it gives you a rudimentary indication of bank, turns without the other instruments are done with timing). It becomes very useful when you are not able to use the full panel, as the amount that the wings of the aircraft move also indicates the rate of turn.

Note: The slip indicator does not indicate true slip in a helicopter.

When the wings in the little aircraft hit one of the lower marks you are in a Rate 1 turn, which takes two minutes to go through 360°, making 3° per second (you can also add 7 kts to 10% of your airspeed to get a rough guide to the bank angle required). Underneath is a ball in a clear tube containing fluid, for damping purposes, called an *inclinometer*. It is subject to gravity (weight) and centrifugal force, and will be thrown one way or another if the aircraft is not in a coordinated turn. In a *slip* (left, below), the rate of turn is too slow for the bank, so centrifugal force will be less, and the ball will not be thrown out so much. It will therefore be on the *inside* of the turn (decrease the angle or increase the rate to correct). In a *skid*, the turn is too fast, so more centrifugal force causes the ball to be displaced more, to the outside of the turn (right, below).

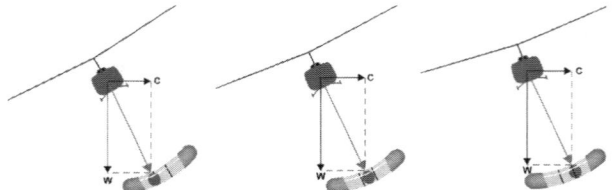

Correction is the opposite of the slip. If you are out of balance, the instrument under-reads, so you will go past your turn.

Under normal operating conditions, when an aircraft is in a banked turn, the rate-of-turn indicator indicates:

- angular velocity of the aircraft about the yaw axis
- the direction of the aircraft turn

At low bank angles, the measurement of rate-of-turn consists in measuring the yaw rate.

Rate of turn indications are only accurate at the speed for which the instrument has been calibrated, though these are not serious (around 5%). The angle of bank to obtain a given rate of turn increases with TAS, but you shouldn't need to make any calculations - the instrument reads correctly automatically. If the gyro rotates too slowly, the device will have less inertia and be less rigid, so it will tilt less and indicate a slower rate of turn than you are actually doing. Turn radius is directly proportional to TAS, and inversely proportional to the rate of turn.

CAPT

Turn And Bank (Slip) Indicator

This instrument has a vertical needle instead of a horizontal small aircraft. As such it will only give you the *rate* of turn, since it is only sensitive to yaw. It has the spin axis athwartships (across the aircraft, so it spins up and away from you), with each end of the spindle held in place with a spring, so it can only move in two axes (one degree of freedom), none of them vertical. The spin rate is 10,000 RPM, and there are mechanical stops to keep it from going more than 45° either side of the centre.

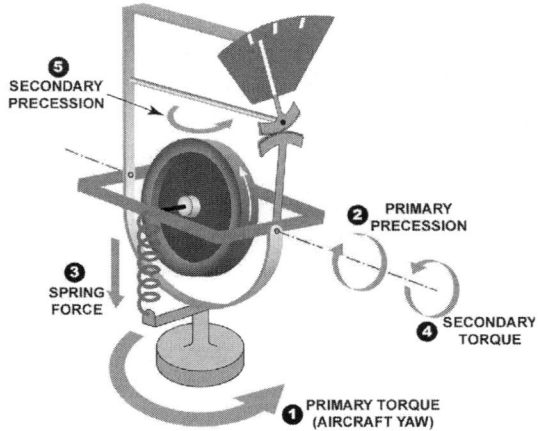

The gyro is aircraft horizontal with 2 planes of freedom. During normal operation, the spring keeps the spin axis horizontal so the turn pointer is at zero, and the gyro's rigidity will tend to keep it there. The yaw induced when you turn is precessed to the top and bottom of the gyro. As the springs stretch to cope with gyro movement around the longitudinal axis, they apply a force that produces a *secondary precession* equal to and in the same direction as the rate of turn. In other words, a turn makes the gyro move, to create a primary precession that stretches a spring that creates another in the same direction as the original force.

Without the spring, you would still see a turn indication, but would have no idea of its magnitude, so the spring controls the angular deflection of the gimbal ring and introduces its own precessing force. As the precession is equal to the rate of turn multiplied by the angular momentum, the force is a measure of the rate of turn.

All errors cause the instrument to under-read, except when the rate of turn is less than rate 1, when rotor speed is faster than normal, and the springs are slack. The ball is sensitive to gravity and centrifugal force.

WARNING & RECORDING

Warnings should be attention-getting (audio) without being startling, while informing you of what is wrong. They should also guide you to the correct actions (visual).

Warning systems should be reliable, that is, they respond to all genuine problems without generating false alarms.

Alerting for all important failures should be fulfilled by an audio warning. Ideally, there should be a single one to alert the crew and direct their attention to a single central warning panel that announces the nature of the problem with a suitably illuminated caption.

Otherwise, the standard methods of bringing unusual occurrences to the notice of pilots include:

- **visual** (lights, gauges, displays)
- **aural** (bells, sirens, and sometimes voice)
- **tactile** (stick shakers)

The three levels of alerting are:

- **Warnings** (Level A) - Red in colour, could be flashing
- **Cautions** (Level B) - Amber in colour
- **Advisory** (Level C) - White in colour

Some warnings may be turned off (or muted) so as not to be a distraction during an emergency, or a nuisance during a normal procedure. This includes the Master Caution light, which can be cancelled so you can see if another warning appears on the Central Warning Panel:

Off flags signify whether an instrument is working properly.

They might come on if:

- electrical power is lost
- a gyro is operating at too low a speed
- the signal received by a navigation instrument is non-existent or too weak

TCAS/ACAS

Airborne Collision and Avoidance Systems (ACAS) provide you with an independent backup to your eyes and ATC by telling you if you are likely to hit another aircraft. The system was developed after the increased use of Area Navigation systems which allowed more direct routings away from specific airways.

TCAS (the T stands for *Traffic*) is actually the system developed by the FAA, whilst ACAS is the generic name used by ICAO. Your aircraft's ACAS capability is not normally known to ATC, unless you mention it on a flight plan. Basic systems (TCAS I) just provide warnings of traffic without guidance.

However, TCAS II, the current equipment, provides advice in the *vertical* plane, as a:

- **Traffic Advisory** (TA), or a warning, telling you where nearby *transponding aircraft* are, or a
- **Resolution Advisory** (RA) which suggests avoiding action *in the pitch plane only*.

This is because all systems depend on azimuthal accuracy, which is not all that good (TCAS I leaves it up to you to work out any avoiding action and hope the other guy does the same!) In view of the above, TCAS I can be regarded as a VMC aid.

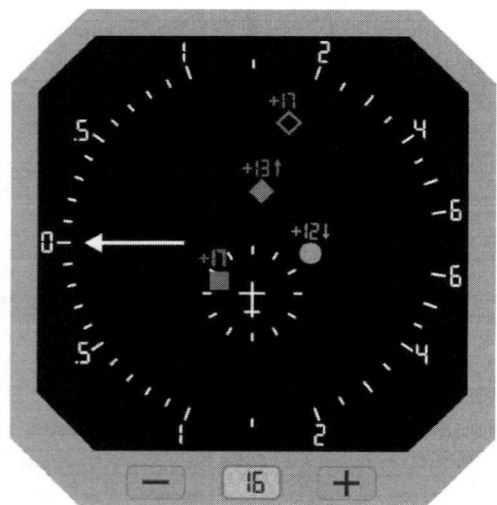

TCAS 1

The system interrogates other aircraft, so it is independent of ground facilities. It uses four antennae, a computer *and a transponder* to continually survey the airspace around you and predict the flight paths of likely intruders, based on Mode C (TCAS I) transponder signals from other traffic. *It will not see obstacles or non-transponder equipped aircraft.* TCAS scans a small amount of airspace around your aircraft (at least 8 nm) in which it thinks a collision is possible. An *intruder* will show up on the display with a symbol

representing the grade of threat, plus numbers representing their height above or below your aircraft in hundreds of feet with + or - signs. An up or down arrow also gives you a vertical trend.

A hollow diamond (white on EFIS) indicates non-threatening traffic over 6 nm away horizontally. A shaded diamond indicates proximate traffic within 6 nm horizontally and 1 200 feet vertically.

A Traffic Advisory (TA) is given when an intruder comes with 30 seconds of your aircraft, as a *potential* threat, when the symbol changes to a solid amber circle. When it becomes a red square the intruder is an *immediate* threat - red for danger and a box because if you don't follow an RA that's where you will be. An RA would normally come about 20 seconds after the TA.

CAPT

Although Great Circles are the shortest distance between two points on the Earth's surface, when you fly along one, the angle between North and the meridians keeps changing, so your course is continually under review. In other words, as you change meridians during your travels around the Earth, your relationship to True North is changing by the amount of *Convergency*, which is discussed shortly. Thus, your track direction is defined by the local meridian, so you must keep altering track if you want to fly long distances along great circles. This, of course, is a pain, and there are solutions, discussed later.

Note: The change in Great Circle track direction is the difference between the angles of inclination of the meridians at each end. See *Convergency*, below.

RHUMB LINES

Rhumb Lines, on the other hand, cut each meridian at the same angle, and, in so doing, maintain a constant direction with respect to True North. They are not straight (being concave toward the nearer Pole), because the meridians converge, so they are longer in distance than Great Circles (170 miles between San Francisco and New York, for example). However, the difference between them is not worth worrying about below about 1,000 miles, for the convenience of steering one track.

A rhumb line (or *loxodrome*) always spirals toward a Pole unless it is actually going East, West, North, or South, in which case it closes on itself to form a parallel of latitude (small circle) or a pair of meridians.

All lines of latitude are rhumb lines, as are meridians, but the Equator and meridians are great circles as well.

Trivia: The word *rhumb* comes from the angle measurement representing the "point" on old-fashioned compass cards. With 32 rhumbs in 360°, a rhumb is 11¼°. Rhumb lines are also called *loxodromes*, which comes from the Greek for *slanting path*.

Speed & Distance

Distance is the length of a line separating two points, although this becomes more complicated on a sphere, where the line becomes curved.

Horizontal distance is measured in metres, kilometres or nautical miles, and speed is a *rate of change of position expressed in those units*, per hour, minute, or whatever. For example, a **knot** is 1 **nautical mile** per hour. It was originally measured by allowing a long rope to stretch out behind a ship with knots tied in it at regular intervals, hence the name. For aircraft, we need *airspeed*, *groundspeed* and *relative speed*, discussed elsewhere in this section.

For navigation, a typical length can be expressed as:

- A **kilometre**, which is 1000 metres, and was originally 1/10,000,000 of the distance between the Equator and either Pole on a meridian passing through Paris (thanks to Napoleon). 8 km equals 5 statute miles. As a rate, it is expressed in km/hour

- 1 **nautical mile** (nm) is 6080 feet, or 1852 m (as a reminder, check out your calculator - see right).

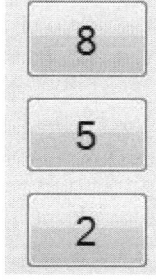

- A **statute mile**, which is 5280 feet and is an Imperial measurement. In aviation, it is used only in visibility reports in some countries. 1 nautical mile is equal to 1.15 statute miles. In this book, it is used without qualification, i.e. 25 miles.

The distance between parallels of latitude is 60 nautical miles, because 1 nm is the distance subtended by 1 minute of latitude, although it varies between the Poles and the Equator because the Earth bulges in the middle. The length of a nautical mile at these points is 6108 and 6046 feet, respectively, but 6080 is used for calibration and navigation in general, and is actually only correct at 48° latitude. One minute of longitude, however (i.e. along a parallel), will only be 1 nm *at the Equator*, due to convergency, where the distance between meridians gets smaller toward the Poles.

CHANGE OF LONGITUDE

Distance along a parallel of latitude is also known as *departure*, or *change of longitude*. Here is the formula:

$$\alpha \text{ (nm) = ch long (mins)} \times \cos \text{lat}$$

In English, it means that the distance between two points on the Earth's surface **in nautical miles** is equal to the difference in longitude between them **in minutes** multiplied by the cosine of the latitude.

TIME & TIME ZONES
••

As it happens, the principles of modern time-keeping have evolved from the needs of navigation, in particular the problem of finding your longitude when at sea, since it is not fixable by natural means. The standard used is the interval between two transits of the same heavenly body over some place on the Earth, otherwise known as a *sidereal day*, or one which is related to the stars. All other methods of recording time (clocks, watches, eggtimers, etc.) reflect regular divisions between those transits.

However, sidereal time is only used in observatories, because it doesn't fit naturally with the Sun's motion, which is what we base our lives on. The Solar day is longer than the sidereal day by about 4 minutes (it varies), and it is noon when the Sun is over the meridian you are on. Note that this is *local time* unless you know when it is noon at some standard meridian, like Greenwich.

To recap, a sidereal day concerns one revolution of the Earth against a particular star. A solar day relates to one revolution against the Sun. This irregularity of the solar day is the result of several circumstances, one being the *obliquity of the ecliptic*, and another being the Earth's orbit.

The Earth does not spin vertically, like a top, but is inclined at 23½° from the vertical over a 41,000-year cycle, so the Equator is not in line with the Celestial Equator (for the fixed stars). This *obliquity of the ecliptic* actually ranges over 22.1-24.5°, so the Earth, in this respect, behaves rather like a ship caught in the swell of the sea as it nods back and forth. When the inclination points towards the Sun, the Northern Hemisphere days are long and the nights are short - it's Summer. The day when this is at its maximum value is the *Summer Solstice* on June 21 (Solstice is Latin for *Sun Stand Still*). In other words, the Sun sets further South each day, until, on

December 21st, it stops, then starts moving North again. On June 21st, it stops going North to go South.

Kepler's Laws Of Planetary Motion

We know that the Earth, with 8 other planets (making 9), revolves round the Sun, although, to be picky, Pluto is no longer considered to be a real planet, because its orbit intersects with Neptune's - it is referred to by astronomers as a dwarf planet. There are also about 2000 minor planets and asteroids. 1 year is the time it takes a planet to go once round the Sun, in the Earth's case being 365¼ days (the odd quarters are consolidated every four years into one day in a leap year, and 3 leap years are suppressed every 4 centuries). While it is going round the Sun, the Earth spins on its axis once nearly every 24 hours, and the Solar System itself is creeping towards the star Vega, but that need not concern us right now. The speed of the Earth's orbit around the Sun is 66,600 mph, or 18.5 miles per second, much faster than a bullet. Because the Earth rotates from West to East, the heavenly bodies appear to revolve about the Earth from East to West.

Copernicus first proposed that the planets revolved around the Sun, but Johannes Kepler determined that:

- each one moves in an ellipse, with the Sun at one focus (it's an ellipse rather than a circle because there are influences from outside the solar system)

- the radius vector (the straight line joining the Sun and any planet) sweeps equal areas in equal time, so they speed up and slow down to compensate

The *perihelion* (1-10 Jan) is where the Earth is closest to the Sun, and the *aphelion* (1-10 Jul) is where it is furthest away.

At perihelion, Earth is about 91 million miles from the Sun; it moves outward to around 95 million miles at aphelion, so the difference in distance is only about 3%.

The degree to which an orbit is elliptical is known as *eccentricity* - 0 means a perfect circle

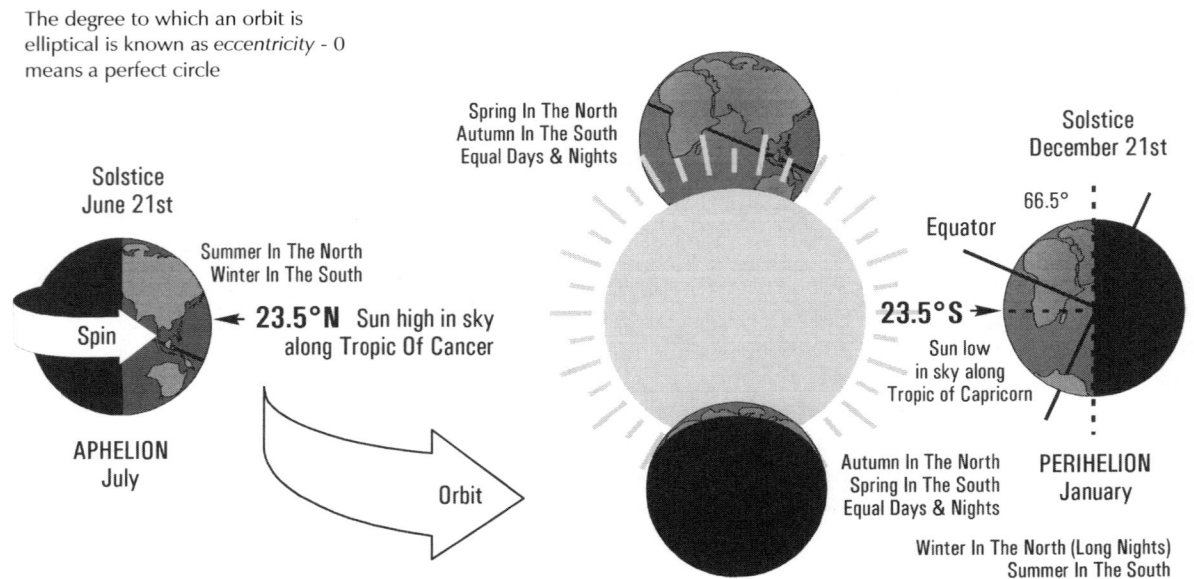

CAPT

The problem with the elliptical orbit and the different speeds is that the length of the *apparent solar day* varies. For example, in Summer in the UK, a sundial in Cornwall could be as much as an hour and a half away from the Greenwich time signal, so the *mean solar day* is used as an average, at 24 hours (the apparent solar day is the time between successive transits of the real Sun).

Thus, a (non-existent) Mean Sun actually transits any meridian at noon, hence the expression *Local Mean Time* (LMT), which is an averaged time at a particular meridian. On the other hand, the time of transit of the real Sun over a meridian is *Local Apparent Noon*. Your watch must change speed continually if it tries to track the real, or apparent (visible) Sun.

Remember: The Mean Sun is a fictitious (or hypothetical) Sun moving at a uniform rate along the Celestial Equator at the average speed that the real Sun apparently moves along the Ecliptic.

The difference between a solar and a mean day is never more than a minute, but the results are cumulative - the real Sun is about 16 minutes ahead of the mean Sun in November and 14 minutes behind it in February. The Air Almanac uses mean Solar time. The difference between clock time and Apparent Solar Time (or between a clock and a sundial) is called the *Equation Of Time.*

In summary, the word *transit* means the passage of a heavenly body over the meridian of a place on the Earth (or through the field of a telescope) - the time difference between two transits is called a *day*, and we have to cope with transits of the Sun and the fixed stars, so we have two types of day. *Sidereal time* (star time) is kept with regard to the fixed stars, which appear fixed only because of their distance from us (it's actually time measured by the apparent diurnal motion of the vernal equinox, which is very close to, but not identical with, the motion of stars. They differ by the precession of the vernal equinox relative to the stars, but you knew that already ☺).

To all intents and purposes, therefore, the Earth rotates 360° in one *sidereal day*, which is regarded as a constant figure against the stars, even though, technically, it isn't. A sidereal day lasts 23 hours and 56 minutes (of solar time), which is about 4 minutes less than a solar day, because the Earth's direction of rotation and its orbit round the Sun are the same. To make up the time, the Earth must rotate an extra 0.986° between solar transits, so in 24 hours of solar time, the Earth will actually rotate 360.986°. In other words, during the course of one (solar) day, the Earth has moved a short distance along its orbit around the sun, and must rotate a little bit more before the Sun reaches its highest point again at any given place.

The Earth spins slower every day, enough to be detected by the atomic clocks in satellites which must be resynchronised every 20 years or so (1000 weeks).

Time

In navigation, time can mean a specific hour of the day, or a time interval. After Einstein, the state of motion and location of the clock used to measure time became an important part of its measurement (see *Satellites*).

Days and nights are of equal length on the Spring and Autumn *Equinoxes*, March 21 and September 23 (Equinox means *Equal Night*), because the spin axis is vertical to the Earth's orbit. The Equinoxes are the times year when the relationship between the length of day and night, as well as the rate of change of declination of the sun, are changing at the greatest rate. They are also the points where the Sun rises and sets due East and West, respectively.

Note: The claim that night and day are symmetric is based on the definition that the day starts or ends when the middle of the disk of the Sun touches the horizon, ignoring the effects of the atmosphere.

Trivia: The Moon rises and sets at the same points as the Sun, but at opposite solstices. For example, it rises at midwinter at the same place the Sun does at midsummer. The Earth and Moon also rotate round each other, round some pivotal point, as they proceed on their way around the Sun. Even more strange is that the Moon fits exactly over the Sun when superimposed on it.

The beginning of the day at any location is when the Mean Sun is in transit with its anti-meridian, on the opposite side of the Earth to the point in question. This would be midnight, or 0000 hours *Local Mean Time* (LMT). Similarly, when the Sun is in transit with the meridian concerned, it will be Noon, or 12:00 hours. The angle between a meridian over which a heavenly body is located and where you are is the *Local Hour Angle*, or LHA.

In fact, the Hour Angle is measured Westwards (from the meridian to the celestial body), based on three datums:

- Greenwich
- Local
- Sidereal

The *Prime Meridian* is the standard to which all local mean times are referred - it is currently in the UK. Local Mean Time used to be called *Greenwich Mean Time* (GMT), but is now referred to as *Universal Coordinated Time*, or UTC, which is more accurately calculated, but can be regarded as the same for our purposes (GMT itself only came about because of the railways - previously, every part of Britain ran its own time scheme). The Greenwich day starts when the mean Sun transits the anti-meridian (180° away), and transits the Easterly ones before it reaches Greenwich. The local mean time in those places will therefore be *ahead* of UTC, and that of those West will be *behind*. When calculating, revert everything to UTC first, and don't forget the date!

THE INTERNATIONAL DATE LINE

This is where a change of date is officially made, mainly the 180° meridian which bends to accommodate certain islands in the South Sea and parts of Siberia. As you cross it, you can gain or lose a day, depending on which way you are going. When solving time problems, however, calculating in UTC usually sorts things out automatically.

Since we take (more or less) 24 hours to go round the Sun, in one hour we move through 15°, or we take 4 minutes to go through 1°. Similarly, in 1 minute we transit 15 minutes, or take 4 seconds to go through 1 minute (just to remind you, a degree is split up into minutes, which in turn are split into seconds).

STANDARD TIMES

To save you adjusting your watch constantly as you move round the Earth, some countries adopt standard times, that is to say, legal authorities allocate a standard amount of time East or West of Greenwich, based on State borders. For example, Canadian time zones are:

Zone	Convert (UTC-)
Newfoundland	3.5
Atlantic	4
Eastern	5
Central	6
Mountain	7
Pacific	8

They don't necessarily coincide with the correct longitude lines, but are actually aligned with province boundaries, for convenience (some towns in Northern BC actually keep Alberta time). In theory, standard time is based on the LMT 7.5° either side of a regular meridian, divisible by 15°. Below are the various time zones across the USA:

DAYLIGHT SAVING (DST)

This was originally set up in UK during the First World War (actually 1916) in an attempt to keep people out of pubs during working hours, or to save fuel in munitions factories (depends on which book you read) and to get people up earlier so they could use the daylight.

Essentially, clocks go forward one hour for the summer - in *Spring* they go *forward*, in *Fall*, they *fall back* (Windows will tell you automatically!)

INTERNATIONAL ATOMIC TIME

Since 1 January 1972, UTC has been linked to IAT, which is based on an atomic clock, and which has shown that the length of the average day is increasing by about 2 milliseconds per century, due to tides, winds and other types of friction. That is, atomic seconds are all the same, whereas astronomical seconds are inconsistent because of the Earth's wobble. To compensate for all this, a leap second is inserted or omitted on a day decided by the International Time Bureau. It last happened in 1989.

Remember:

- The length of a day varies because the Earth's orbit is not symmetrical

- The Mean Solar Day is an average of the variations

- The Equation Of Time is the difference between the Mean and Solar days

- At 66.6° (N or S), there is no sunrise in Winter

- At 64.5° latitude (N or S), there is no sunset in Summer

- At 60.5° latitude (N or S), there is continuous twilight as the centre of the Sun does not reach 6° below the horizon

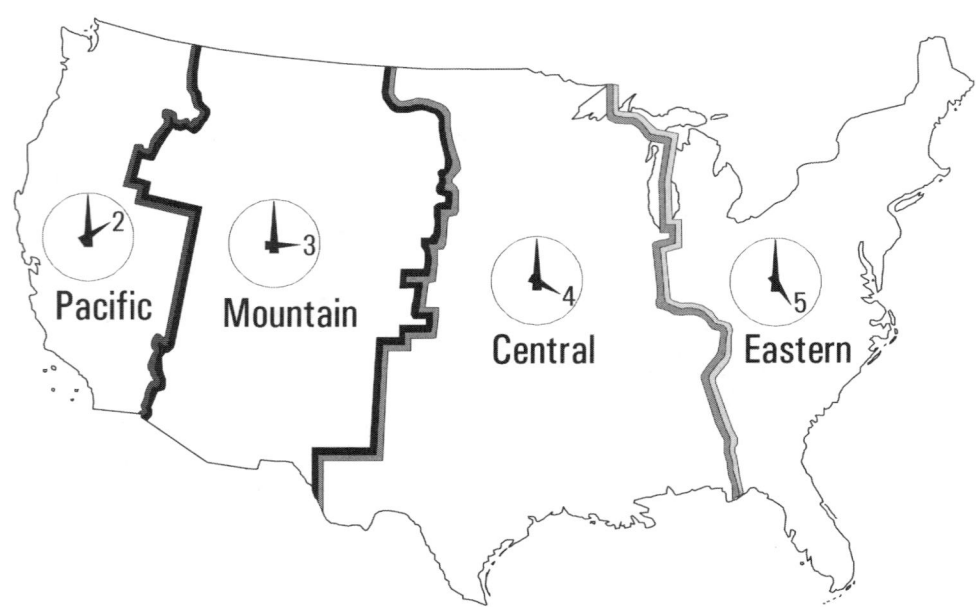

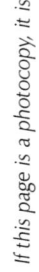

The Air Almanac

Standard times around the world are in three lists on pages A20-A23, *Fast on GMT*, *Slow on GMT*, and *Keeping GMT*.

List I - PLACES FAST ON G.M.T. (mainly those EAST OF GREENWICH)

The times given below should be } *added* to G.M.T. to give Standard Time. *subtracted* from Standard Time to give G.M.T.

			h	m				h	m
Admiralty Islands		...	10		Estonia		...	03	
Afghanistan	...	...	04	30	Ethiopia	...	...	03	
Albania*	...	...	01		Finland	...	...	02	
Algeria*	...	...	01		France*	...	...	01	
Bangladesh	...	...	06		Iran‡	...	...	04	

*Summer time may be kept in these countries
‡ The legal time may differ from that given here

Check the footnotes!

List III - PLACES SLOW ON G.M.T. (WEST OF GREENWICH)

The times given below should be } *subtracted* from G.M.T. to give Standard Time. *added* to Standard Time to give G.M.T.

			h	m				h	m
Argentina		...	03		Chile‡	...	...	03	
Azores	...	...	01		Colombia	...	...	05	
Bermuda*	...	...	04		Cuba*	...	...	05	
Canada	...	...			Ecuador	...	...	05	
Alberta*	...	...	07		Grenada	...	...	04	

SUNRISE, SUNSET

There are also tables for specific days and latitudes in LMT that tell you when the Sun rises and sets, varying with date and latitude (between 60°S to 72°N). There are no calculations involved - the tables have been made up from observations over hundreds of years. Sunrise or Sunset occurs when the Sun's upper edge is on the viewer's horizon, which will be affected by atmospheric refraction - when you see the Sun for the first time, it is still half a degree below the horizon, but this will not affect the figures as they are based on visible phenomena.

At the Equator, Sunrise is always 0600 and Sunset at 1800. Except in high latitudes, the times of Sunrise and Sunset vary only a little each day, so they may be taken as the same for all latitudes. Notice that the Sun rises later and sets earlier as latitude increases in Winter, but it rises earlier and sets later in Summer. However, outside the latitudes above, the Sun will not set in Summer, or rise in Winter. An open square box at the top of a column means the Sun is visible, and a filled in box means it isn't. 4 hash marks (////) means continuous civil twilight. This is part of a Sunset table from the Air Almanac:

Lat	July							
	1	4	7	10	13	16	19	22
°	h m	h m	h m	h m	h m	h m	h m	h m
N 72	■	■	■	■	■	■	■	■
70	□	□	□	□	□	□	□	□
68	□	□	□	□	□	□	////	////
66	////	////	////	////	////	////	////	////
64	////	////	////	////	////	////	////	////
62	////	////	////	////	00 19	00 51	01 11	01 27
N 60	01 01	01 09	01 17	01 26	01 36	01 45	01 55	02 05
58	01 47	01 52	01 57	02 03	02 09	02 16	02 24	02 31
56	02 16	02 19	02 24	02 28	02 33	02 39	02 45	02 51
54	02 38	02 41	02 44	02 48	02 52	02 57	03 02	03 08
52	02 55	02 58	03 01	03 04	03 08	03 12	03 17	03 22
N 50	03 10	03 12	03 15	03 18	03 22	03 25	03 29	03 34
45	03 39	03 41	03 43	03 46	03 49	03 52	03 55	03 58
40	04 02	04 03	04 05	04 07	04 09	04 12	04 14	04 17
35	04 20	04 21	04 23	04 24	04 26	04 28	04 31	04 33
30	04 35	04 36	04 37	04 39	04 40	04 42	04 44	04 46

The Almanac also has tables for Sunrise and Twilight, but the process is the same. It deals with the real Sun, but the times are in LMT.

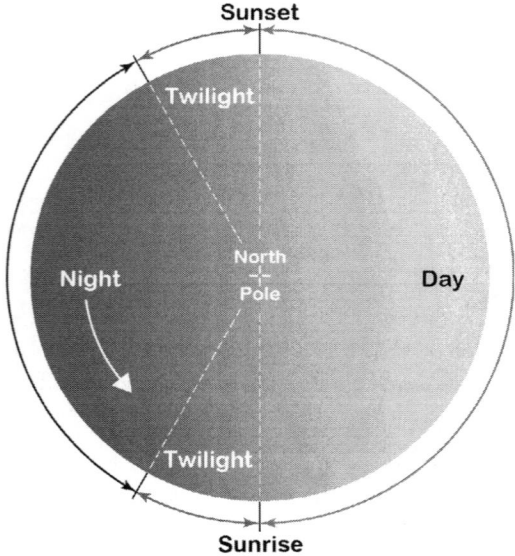

In fact, it is refraction that accounts for twilight. *Civil twilight* exists when the centre of the Sun is within 6° of the horizon, during which you still have a distinct horizon. *Nautical twilight* exists when the Sun's centre is between 6-12° below the horizon (which cannot be distinguished). Between 12-18° below, you get *astronomical twilight*, and *legal twilight* happens 30 minutes before sunrise and 30 minutes after sunset. Remember that the figures are tabulated according to *local mean time*, which is based on the mean Sun, which doesn't exist. You will also have to interpolate, since not every day is shown, or every latitude.

Note: You have to be above 66° 33' N or S before the sun is above or below the horizon for a full 24 hours at some time during the year. However, the atmosphere plays tricks with light. In summer the midnight sun is actually visible at 66°. In winter, you need to go beyond 67° so as not to see the sun on the winter solstice. The onset of darkness is more sudden at the equator because the Sun sets perpendicular to the horizon, while at higher latitudes, it can set more obliquely, allowing it to remain close to the horizon for longer.

The Sun is also used, with other tables, to get a True Bearing, with which to set your DGI, which is very handy when up North.

You could also use the heading of a known feature, such as a runway, or, in emergency, the compass, and subtract the variation, but that won't be so accurate.

Tip: Another way to determine true heading is to ask your GPS (if it is capable) for the true bearing to an NDB. Then subtract your relative bearing for the true heading.

MAPS & CHARTS

A map is a graphical representation of part of the Earth's surface drawn to a scale, as seen from above. On them, features found on the ground are represented by symbols, which are larger than the items they represent, so that you can see them without a magnifying glass. A map's purpose is to provide information on the existence and location of, and distance between ground features.

In aviation, the words *map* and *chart* are interchangeable, as there is no accepted definition of the difference. In the marine world, a chart refers to the ground features underneath the sea. An aviation chart will show parallels and meridians with minimum topographical features, and be used for plotting (see the example under *Variation*, above), while a map will show greater detail of the Earth's surface, so maps are for looking at, and charts are for working on!

The point about them both is that they are small scale representations of the Earth's surface that are only accurate within a relatively small area, since you are trying to show a 3 dimensional object on a 2 dimensional surface. The further from the *centre of projection* you go, the more the distortion you get but, to all intents and purposes, it can mostly be ignored in its general area. You can see the problem if you try to flatten a globe (left), and the Equator and poles pose special problems because their meridians are parallel and converging, respectively.

Distortion can be minimised, but not eliminated, and there are many ways of adjusting for it, each suiting a different purpose, so lines drawn on maps based on different projections will not necessarily cross through the same places (watch those danger areas!)

Projections

The term *projection* means that an imaginary light is placed inside a model of the Earth and the shapes of the land masses are projected onto a piece of paper, which could be *conical* (Lambert), *cylindrical* (Mercator) or *flat*. All projections require sophisticated mathematical techniques to be effective.

The quality of *orthomorphism*, or *conformality*, which is the more modern term, that all charts should strive for, means the scale is correct in all directions, or at least within a very small area if the scale varies, and bearings are correctly represented. That is, the scale at any point is independent of azimuth, meaning

CAPT

that, for a short distance in any direction, it will be equal, so the outlines of the areas to be portrayed must conform. In addition, parallels must always cross meridians at right angles. Otherwise, no chart is perfect, as you will find when you try to fold them!

Lambert's Conformal

Imagine the Earth with a light shining at its centre, then place a cone on top. If it could shine through the crust, an image of the Earth will be projected onto the cone. Where the cone meets the earth, the shadows of the land formations will be accurate, but will be out of shape the further North and South you go. This is the *conic projection*, the basis of the Lambert Conformal, and what most of today's aeronautical charts are based on, as the meridians will be straight, even if they converge towards the North. On a Lambert, Great Circles are assumed to be straight lines (actually they are very shallow curves), and rhumb lines will be curves concave to the nearer pole. Great Circles that are not meridians are curves concave to the Parallel of Origin.

Johannes Lambert overcame the problem of scale expansion in the 18th century by pushing the imaginary cone further into the Earth's surface, to cut it in two places instead of one.

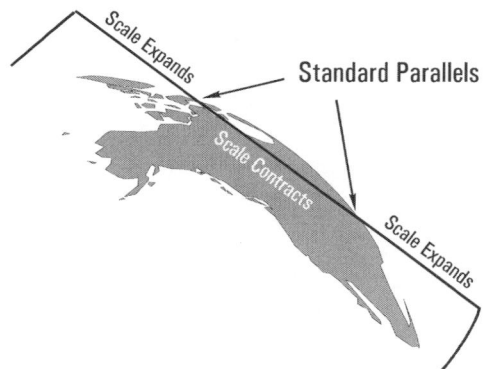

This gives it two *Standard Parallels*, or points where scale is correctly shown (and where the *nominal scale* is). To be sure, there is a slight contraction between them, but this is insignificant (1% or less) if two-thirds of the chart are between the Parallels. The *Parallel of Origin* is midway between them, where the scale will be smallest. Outside the standard parallels, the scale expands, and will be greatest at the top and bottom of the chart. Thus, the Lambert is not technically a constant scale chart, but is regarded as such because, with careful positioning of standard parallels, the errors are reduced to less than 1%.

Here is a good example of a Lambert Projection. Note the converging meridians, and the curved parallels of latitude, which are *arcs of concentric circles*. Lamberts are used between 20°-70° of latitude.

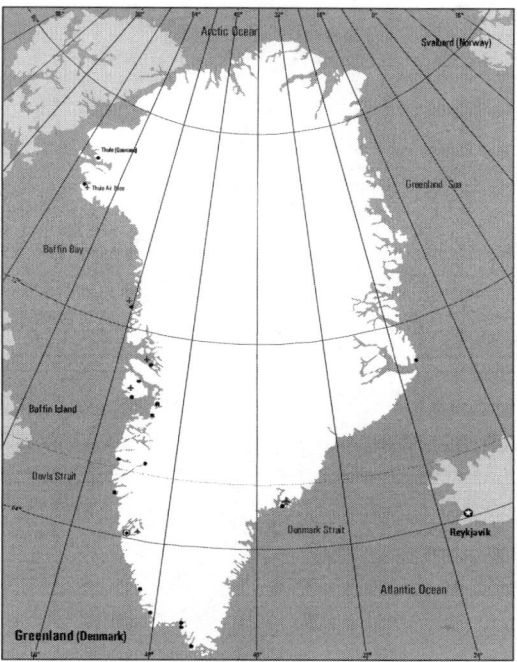

Remember:

- There are 2 standard parallels at which the *scale* is correct

- There is one parallel of origin where *convergency* is correct

- The scale is constant within 1% between 80° N/S

- The maximum spread of latitudes is 24°

- Great Circles and Rhumb Lines are both nearly straight, but Great Circles are concave to the parallel of origin, and Rhumb Lines are concave to the Pole

Scale

Because a map is a representation of the Earth's surface, you need to know to what proportion it has been drawn to gauge distances accurately.

Assuming a constant scale, the ratio between distances on a map and the Earth's surface is expressed as a scale based on the map's size. For a scale of 1:500,000 (commonly referred to as a half-mil), one inch on the map is equal to 500,000 inches on the Earth:

CAA 1:500,000 map (small scale)

There are 63,360 inches to the mile, so an inch on a half-mil map is 7.89 statute miles.

CAA 1:250,000 map (larger scale)

You can tell which chart has a larger scale by looking at the *representative fractions*, obtained by dividing chart distance by Earth distance. Thus, a chart distance of one inch divided by its Earth equivalent of 13.7 nm would be a 1:1000000 map, and of a smaller scale than a 1:500000 (the bigger the number after the colon, or under the dividing line, the smaller the scale is). The representative fraction is always written with the map distance (as the numerator, on top) as 1, regardless of the measurement units.

You find the ground distance between any two points by multiplying the map distance by the denominator so, taking the 1:500,000 scale above, 5 units on the map would be 2,500,000 units of ground distance.

Relief

Information about high ground is given in various ways. *Contours* are lines on a map joining points of equal height (or elevation) above sea level, so they are similar to isobars (the closer they are together, the steeper the slope they represent).

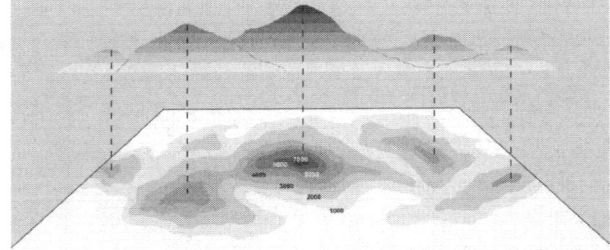

Spot Heights (commonly used on approach plates) show the elevation of prominent peaks with small dots, with the actual height shown next to them. The highest one will be distinguished in some way, possibly surrounded by a square, or printed in bold. Otherwise, on a map, expect water to be blue, woods to be green, and railways and power lines to be black.

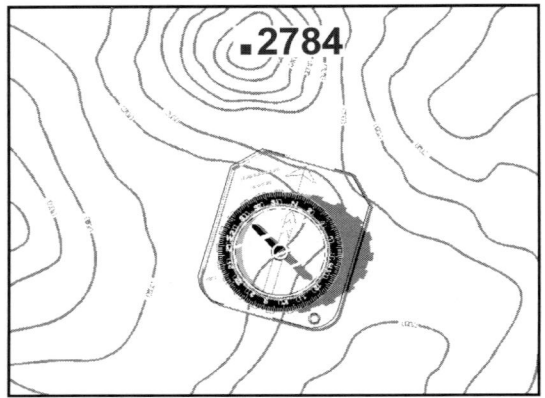

Some maps may give different colours or shading to various layers to make things more obvious, known as *Layer Tinting*.

CAPT

THE TRIANGLE OF VELOCITIES

An aircraft in flight is affected by the wind along its axis and from the side, or a head/tail or beam component.

In flying between point A and point B, you will only get there by just pointing the nose in the right direction if there is no wind, or if it is exactly on the nose or tail. This is very rarely the case, so your aircraft would *drift* off course, according to the wind's direction, if you did nothing to correct it. In other words, you would end up a certain distance left or right of the original target if the wind were blowing across your track from the relevant direction (in the early days of the North Sea, when navaids weren't around, pilots would build in a slight error to their calculations, so that they would know which side of the rig they were just in case it all went wrong).

The smart thing to do would be to make a heading correction towards the wind's direction to maintain a straight track. This, unfortunately, inclines the body of the aircraft more sideways to the track over the ground, which reduces groundspeed, because some of the energy from the engine is used to keep it there. Thus, the speed of the aircraft through the air will not necessarily be the same as its speed over ground - if you are flying into wind, you will go slower relative to the surface, and faster if the wind is behind you:

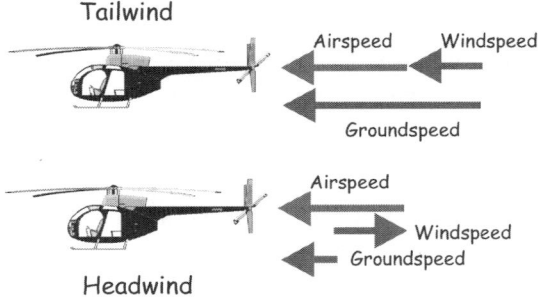

You work out the wind's effect on your trip by getting the forecast winds from the flight planning office, and working out a combination of three sides of a *triangle of velocities*, because a velocity expresses a combination of speed and direction, and we are concerned with those of your aircraft, the wind and the difference between them.

First of all, though, a few definitions:

- *Track*. The path the aircraft intends to follow over the ground, represented by the line on a map from one point to another (*Track Made Good* is the actual path - the difference between them is *Track Error*)

- *Heading*. The direction the aircraft is pointed in, according to its compass

- *Wind Velocity*. The speed and direction of the wind. The faster your aircraft, the less its effect. Forecast winds are given as True

- *True Air Speed* (TAS). The speed relative to the atmosphere, not necessarily the same as that indicated on your ASI, and not necessarily the same as.....

- *Ground Speed*, or the speed of the aircraft over the ground, because of wind

- *Drift*. The difference between heading and track due to wind, measured *from* heading *to* track

- *Air Position*. The position the aircraft would have reached without wind

- *DR Position*. The calculated position of the aircraft

- *ETA*. Estimated Time of Arrival

- *Fix*. Definite confirmation of position by ground observation, radio aids or astro nav

The velocity of an aircraft in flight (i.e. through the air) will therefore consist of its heading and airspeed. In the diagram below, the heading is 270°(T) - the single arrow is the symbol for the heading vector, pointing the right way, of course.

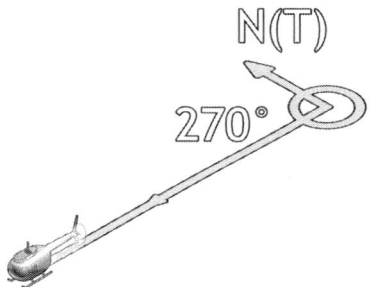

When plotting, a scale is used, so if the heading vector were 3 inches long, at 50 kts to an inch it would equal an airspeed of 150 kts, or the air position after one hour of flight. If we added the wind speed and direction, the resultant between them would represent track and groundspeed, also to scale.

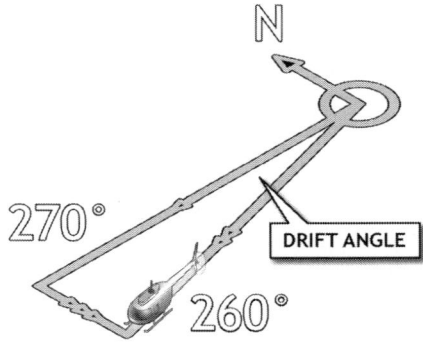

In this case, the wind vector is half an inch long, meaning 25 kts, coming from the North. Joining the ends would therefore show your ground position after one hour, and your track and groundspeed, after measurement (you will have deduced already that two arrows are used for the track and three for the wind - the track arrows always go in the opposite direction to the other two). The *drift angle* is measured *from* the heading *to* the track, in this case about 10°, so the track is 260°.

The diagram shows what would happen if you simply pointed the aircraft nose towards the West - you would drift to Port for the amount indicated. If you wanted to arrive over the intended destination, you would actually have to point the nose to the right (i.e. Starboard) enough to counteract the drift to the left.

All you need to do now is draw the same wind vector on the *opposite* side of the line, and measure its length and angle to find out what heading to steer (280°). The difference between heading and track is now the *Wind Correction Angle*. Don't forget to work out the variation and deviation so that the compass heading is correct.

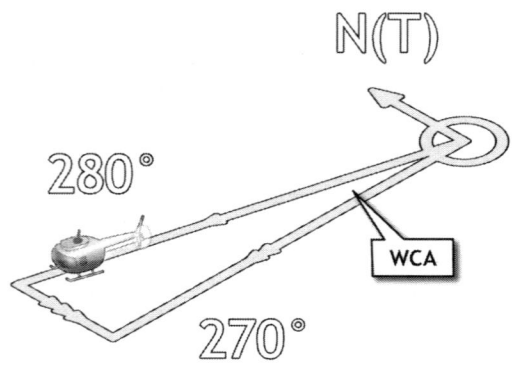

Dead Reckoning

As a navigator you need to know your present position, and how to get to some other one, but the only information you have after some time in flight is your air position, based on the airspeed and heading(s) you used since you started. In theory, if you then add the wind velocity for the relevant period, you should get a ground position, which is called a *Dead Reckoning* (DR) position, because it has been deduced, or calculated, rather than being positively identified. To do this properly, you must keep an account (reckoning) of the course and distance run, and update things by using information from other sources, such as visual reference to landmarks (pilotage) or radio aids. Indeed, once the information chain has been broken, the other sources are required to re-establish your position - any errors with DR are cumulative, so the further you travel without an accurate position fix, the more the likelihood that errors will creep in.

Because you don't have room for a navigation table in your cockpit, various rules of thumb can be used in the form of *Mental Dead Reckoning*, successful use of which requires thorough flight planning and accurate flying (the 1 in 60 Rule is a good example).

DR involves the calculation of your best known position without navaids or visual fixes. In essence, it involves drawing the equivalent triangles of velocity you would create on your Dalton computer (see below) on a map, although it is important to grasp that the triangle's purpose is more to do with finding directions and speeds rather than a position. With no wind, your air position would be the same as your ground position. Dead Reckoning attempts to reconcile the two, having taken into account whatever the wind has gotten up to.

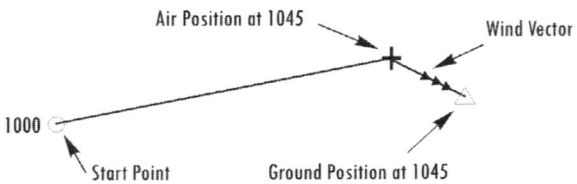

Errors in DR are typically around 2-5%, usually from measurements of heading and speed. In fact any accuracy with Dead Reckoning depends on:

- The flight time since your last fix (the longer it is the less accuracy there will be)

- The accuracy of the forecast wind

- How accurately you maintain speed & heading

An air plot should be maintained constantly - every time the heading is changed, it should be recorded.

Note: There is usually a change of drift or grounsdpeed with a change of heading, which is ignored in mental DR.

FIXES

If you happen to fly over an object that can be identified from a map, you have a *position fix*, which can be used to find what the real wind is, and your actual groundspeed. On the map, simply connect a line from your air position to the fix, and measure the resulting line between them (the wind vector). The line between your start point and the fix would be the *Track Made Good*, which could be used to solve the above problem on the flight computer. The length of the wind vector is proportional to the length of time the plot has been running. Otherwise, the unit of measurement is the local nautical mile, conveniently obtained from the side of the chart in use (for most purposes, use the mean latitude. Similarly, where meridians are converging, use the mid-longitude).

When obtaining a fix, VORs are more accurate than NDBs, and a 90° cut is best, always being aware of coastal effect, or coastal refraction, as described under *ADF*.

Nowadays, since fixes are readily available, the *track plot* is the favoured method, that is, the wind direction is found from the known parts of the other two sides of the triangle, using the Dalton Computer, as discussed below.

The traditional way for a navigator to do the job without a computer would be to draw the required track on the map, and an hour's worth of wind velocity from the start of that line, to scale. Then, with a pair of compasses opened out to the TAS, an arc would be described on the proposed track (the other point would be placed on the end of the W/V line). Joining the two points would produce the heading to steer to make good the track, and its length would tell you the groundspeed. The angle between heading and groundspeed is the *drift*, which could be assumed to be constant for long enough to draw a predictive series of lines for 6 minutes ahead.

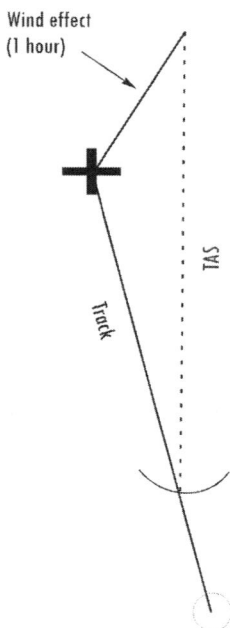

Wind effect (1 hour)

TAS

Track

As mentioned above, the lines you draw will be to scale, so one 3" long at 50 miles to the inch would represent 150 kts. When climbing and descending, take the mean TAS for the leg, and mean wind velocity.

Remember that these velocities go together: *Heading & Airspeed, Track & Groundspeed, Wind Direction & Speed.* Also remember that you have to find mixed pairs, such as heading and groundspeed, rather than the combinations mentioned above, because you start with a mix in the first place (you usually know the airspeed and track already). Given any four, you can work out the others by measurement, but you can do this mechanically with the *flight computer*, described below. On the left is the triangle of velocities on the Dalton Flight Computer.

LOST PROCEDURE

Assuming you have flown as accurately as possible, and the wind velocity was accurately forecast, and you made no mistakes in your flight planning, you should find yourself pretty much on track throughout the flight. However, life is not always like that, and once in a while you may find yourself unsure of your position, the technical term for being lost. The *circle of uncertainty* is a way of trying to remedy this by allowing a percentage of error and drawing a circle of appropriate size centred on your destination. In theory, you should be somewhere inside it. The diameter will very rarely be more than 10% of distance flown.

THE FLIGHT COMPUTER

The E-6B was developed in the United States by Naval Lt. Philip Dalton in the late 1930s. The name comes from its original part number for the US Army Air Corps in World War II. It is a device with a sliding scale, marked with drift angles and TAS arcs, with a frosted circular screen on which you can draw the business end of the triangle of velocities.

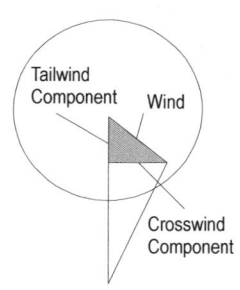

Tailwind Component   Wind

Crosswind Component

There is a dot in the centre of the screen, around which is a compass rose that can be rotated to bring your heading or track under the lubber line at the top, labelled *Index* in the picture overleaf. All you need to do is draw in the wind vector to see how they all relate to each other.

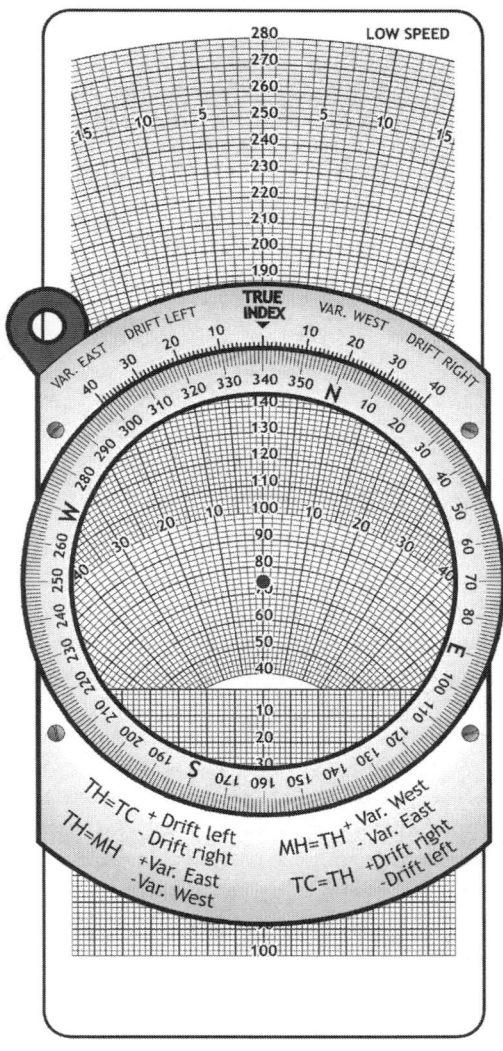

CAPT

Note: There will be an instruction book with your computer, so the details here will necessarily be brief.

The main traps to watch out for are:

- Not checking the calculations mentally (and getting the decimal point in the wrong place)

- Misreading scales (one space may represent 1, or 2)

- Forgetting to apply compressibility to speeds above 300 kts, or applying it the wrong way

- Not matching the 2 drifts, that is, the difference between heading and track on the compass rose against that from the drift lines

Move the sliding scale so the TAS appears underneath the dot in the centre of the frosted screen (say 100 kts). Then rotate the screen so the wind direction (270°) lines up under the index line at the top. Draw in a line vertically downwards from the centre dot equal to the wind speed in knots (30). This is called the wind down method*.

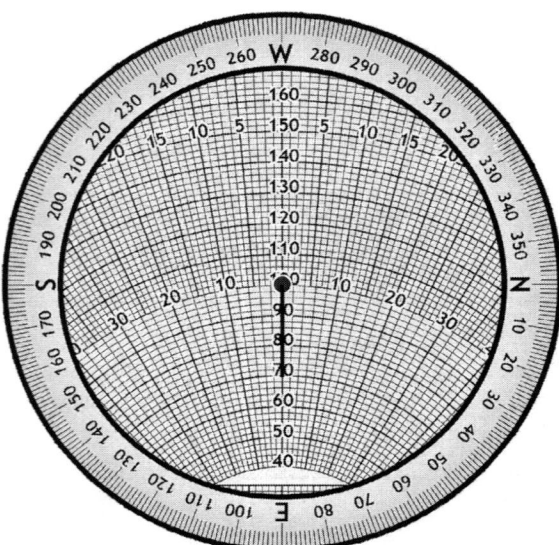

*Wind up is initially slightly simpler if you only want to find the heading you need to fly to maintain a proposed track, but the heading marker will indicate your track and the wind point will be on the TAS, with the groundspeed under the centre dot. When you need to find track from heading and want to find the wind, it is not so easy. For example, in the picture overleaf, you can see immediately that your groundspeed is lower than your airspeed, and that the track is on the right by however many degrees. If you had marked the wind upwards, you would have had to make an extra calculation or at least put the TAS line under the wind dot.

Rotate the screen again until the true track (say 340°) is under the Index. The end of the wind line will point to a drift figure (18° Starboard) and groundspeed of 94 kts, so the headwind is 6 kts.

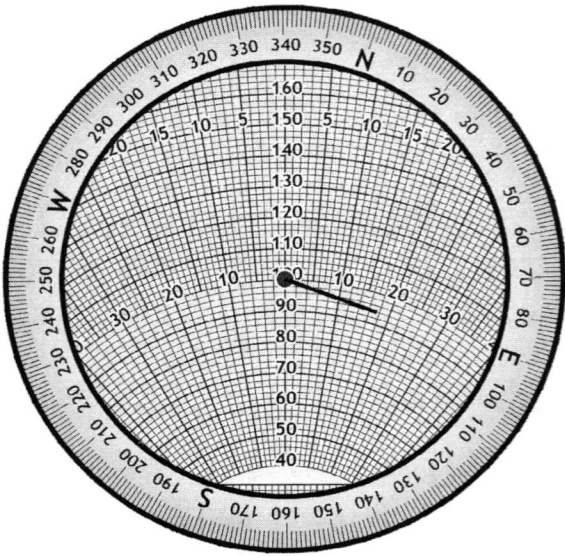

Rotate the plotting disc to the right by 18°, so that 358° is under the index. This time the drift figure is 17°.

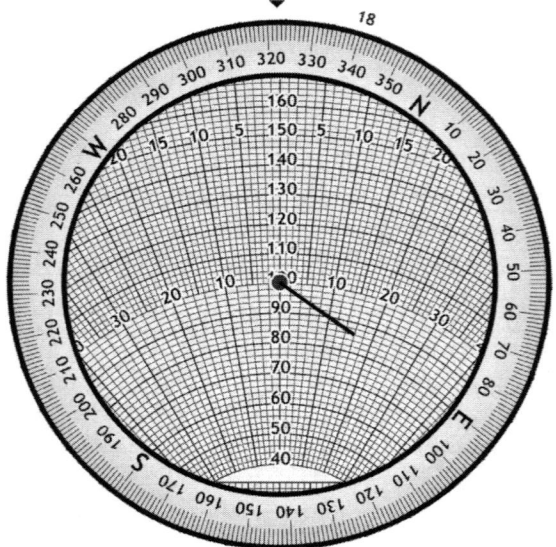

Move the plotting disc again until the drift angle at the index is equal to the drift angle on the slide, in this case with 357° under the index. The new groundspeed is at the end of the wind line (103 kts). Then apply magnetic variation and compass deviation for the heading to fly.

CAPT

The Slide Rule

On the reverse side of all computers is a circular slide rule, with the 60 point on the inner scale conveniently marked to make speed and time calculations easier.

It can be positioned against fuel quantity or distance on the outer scale to read time on the inner scale (the outer, stationary, scale is called the *miles scale*, and the inner one, which rotates, is the *minute scale*, so distance and time are always opposite each other).

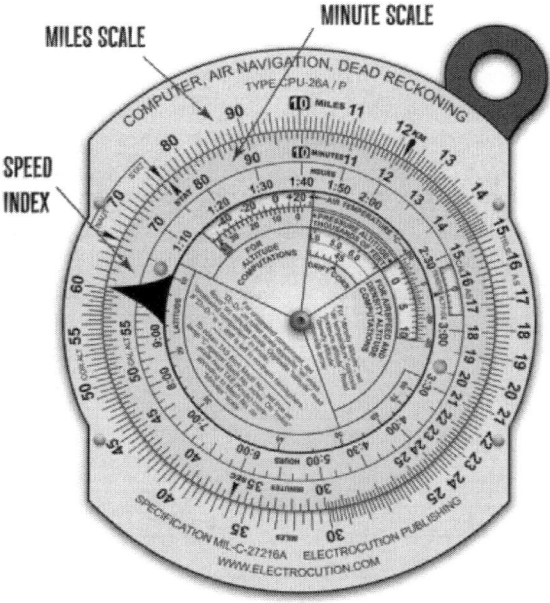

As with any slide rule, you need the approximate answer first, as a gross error check, and to give you an idea where to put the decimal point (if you were wondering how it works, you are adding *indices*, which is also where logarithms come from, but that is outside the scope of these notes).

There are auxiliary scales in the centre for calculations concerning pressure and density altitudes.

The 60 point in the inner scale is variously called the *time index*, or the *mph* or *gph index*. It is used for any calculations involving time*, and will always appear opposite the groundspeed or fuel consumption. In the picture, it is next to 30, which could mean 3, 30 or 300 kts/mph/kilometres per hour, depending on the problem, so you could travel 4, 40 or 400 miles in 80 minutes, respectively. Alternatively, it could mean you travelled 3 miles in one minute, which is 180 mph.

*The number 36 is used to solve rate, time & distance problems when you need the answer in minutes and seconds rather than hours and minutes. It is especially useful in instrument flight when you are dealing with small distances, such as between the outer marker and the threshold on a non-precision approach.

TIME, FUEL CONSUMPTION & DISTANCE

These are the most common problems. Just move the inner scale until the 60 point is opposite the TAS or fuel consumption you have. Read the time on the inner scale against distance on the outer scale, or fuel if you are checking how much is being used.

In the picture below, the speed triangle (60) is opposite 120 (knots or gallons) on the outer scale, which means it will take 6 minutes to go 12 nautical miles, or 6.5 to use 13 gallons, and so on. It will also take 7 minutes to travel 140 miles, so the slide can be used to solve proportion problems as well. Reduce hours (and proportions) to minutes for simplicity. To multiply normally, place 10 on the inner scale against one number on the outer scale, and read the answer on the outer scale against the other, on the inner scale.

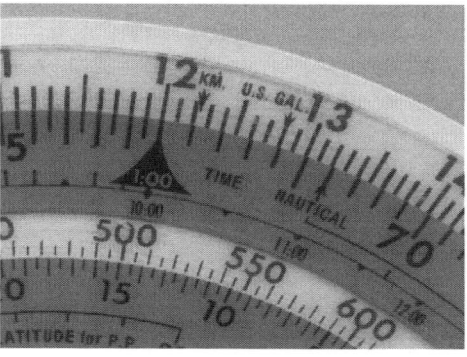

SQUARE ROOTS

These can be found easily, too (useful for VHF ranges). Find the number you want the square root of on the outer scale, then rotate the inner one until the number opposite 10 is the same as the one against your original number. For example, 400 will have 2 opposite, as well as against 10.

TRUE AIR SPEED & ALTITUDE

To find TAS, line up the temperature against the pressure altitude in a window in the rotating slide rule (it may be labelled True Air Speed), then read the TAS on the outer scale against the RAS. Don't forget to allow for compressibility at speeds over 300 kts.

On the previous page, the temperature is -21°C at 10 100 feet (follow the red line). The indicated airspeed is 177 kts, and the TAS is 200.

Notice also that the Density Altitude is 8100 feet.

True altitude is done in the same way, using the Altitude window - lining up the same figures for PA and temperature would give you a true altitude of 18 800 ft against an indicated altitude of 20 000.

CONVERSIONS

These are done by lining up arrows on both scales representing the commodities concerned. For fuel weights, you will need the specific gravity, which is 1 for water, and used as a common denominator. It will vary from place to place, but that in the Flight Manual is the one to use. For example, if the s.g. of fuel is taken as 0.8, how much does 1 gallon weigh? The answer is 8 lbs (water would weigh 10). Alternatively, how many litres do you need from the fuel guy if you can carry 2600 kg and the s.g. is 8.2? Try 3170.

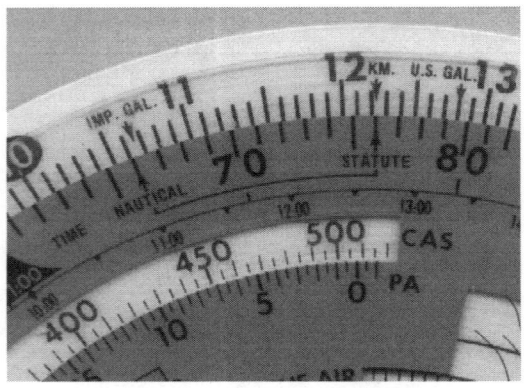

In the picture above, the arrow labelled *km* on the outer scale is opposite the one marked *statute* (miles) on the inner scale. All you do is read off the direct equivalent on each scale - here, 112.5 km is equal to 70 statute miles.

RATIO & PROPORTION

The ratio of any two numbers the result of dividing one by the other, which may be expressed as a fraction. In this case, the number on the outer scale is the numerator and the one on the inner scale is the denominator.

A proportion is the expression of equality of two or more ratios - for example, 6:8 is the same as 3:4. If you set one ration on the computer, you can find any other easily. For example, if asked to find what number 45 has the same ratio with as 6 does to 8, you just line up 6 on the outer scale with 8 on the inner and read off 60 on the inner scale opposite 45. If you climb 6000 feet in 8 minutes, you will climb 9000 feet in 12.

EXAMPLES (SLIDE RULE)

How long will you take to fly 60 nm at 90 kts? Less than hour, so place the 60 index under 90 on the outer scale, move around to 60 and read 40 mins on the inner scale.

How far will you fly in 90 minutes at 105 kts? A quick estimate suggests it will be around 150 nm - place the index against 105 on the outer scale and read off 157.5 on the outer scale against the 9 on the inner scale.

If you travel 47 nm in 24 minutes, what is your groundspeed? Place 24 on the inner scale against 47 on the outer scale and read 117.5 kts against the index.

If you used 40 US gallons over 3 hrs 20 minutes of flight, what is your fuel consumption? 12 US gals/hr.

Picture: 1 in 60 Rule. Track Error + Closing Angle is equal to the Heading Alteration

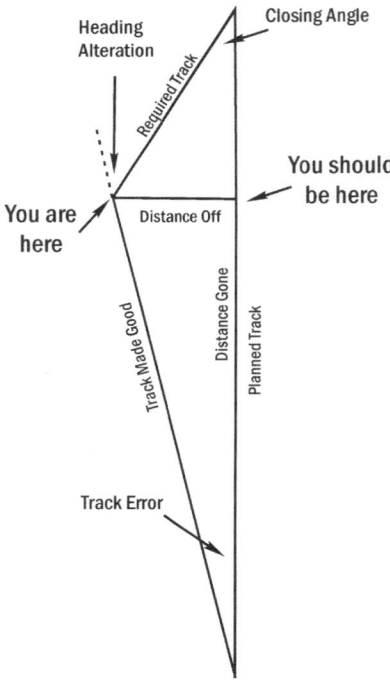

MISCELLANEOUS

The 1 in 60 Rule

This is a common rule that can solve many problems in aviation. It means that, for every 1 degree left or right of track, you will be 1 nm off track for every 60 travelled (or, in other words, with a hypotenuse of 60, the length of the opposite side equals the value of the angle in degrees). This is the formula:

$$\text{Error} = \frac{\text{Distance Off} \times 60}{\text{Distance Gone}}$$

So if, after 40 nm, you are 8 nm off track, your track error angle would be:

$$\text{Error} = \frac{8 \times 60}{40}$$

or 12°, as indicated against the time index on the flight computer when you line up 40 nm under 8:

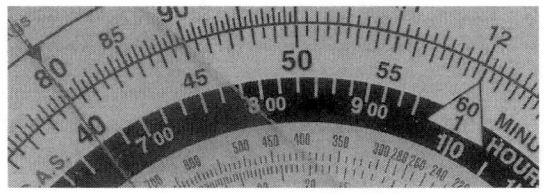

Set the distance off on the outer scale against the distance gone on the inner scale and read the degrees required opposite the 60 index.

Of course, when you are off track, there is the potential for getting lost, so the first thing to do is parallel the original track. Now, at least, you shouldn't get any further off track while you work out how to get to the destination.

- To **parallel your original track**, alter course by the track error in the appropriate direction

- To **get back on the original track** (provided you haven't gone more than halfway), alter course by double the track error. Then apply the correction as a single figure to keep you there

- To **track directly to the original destination**, you would need an extra bit, called a *closing angle*, which you can find by altering the formula above:

$$\text{CA} = \frac{\text{Distance Off} \times 60}{\text{Distance To Go}}$$

Add the combination of closing angle and track error to the heading the appropriate way.

For example, if you are 10 nm off track, having travelled 150 nm, you require to correct by 4° to parallel the original course. If you want to go directly to the destination from your temporarily uncertain position, use the distance instead (say 80 nm) and add the result, which is 7.5° + 4°.

Notes: The time to regain track may be more than that used to create the error in the first place. Also, these rules are approximate, because altering heading changes the relationship of the wind to your machine. 1 in 60 is used convenience - if the exact figures for π are used it should be 1 in 57. The Tan may be used up to 25°, and the Sine is accurate up to 40° (within 10% up to 70°).

Tip: If you have travelled ¼ way along your track, the heading alteration is 4 times closing angle.

You can use the 1 in 60 rule to see if you are still inside an airway. If the centreline was 045°, and you were on the 040° radial, you would be off track by 5°. If the DME says you are 45 nm away, it's a simple calculation:

$$\text{Dist Off} = \frac{\text{TE} \times \text{Dist Gone}}{60}$$

The answer is 3.75 nm, so you are OK. It works for glideslopes, too:

$$\text{Height} = \frac{\text{GP Angle} \times \text{Range}}{60}$$

EXAMPLES

Find the angles to parallel your track, the closing angle and the total, from the miles off, out and left to go:

No	Off	Out	Left	Par	CA	Tot
1	8R	100	150			
2	10R	125	175			
3	12L	60	100			
4	15L	75	50			
5	6R	96	66			

ANSWERS

No	Off	Out	Left	Par	CA	Tot
1	8R	100	150	4.8L	3.2L	8L
2	10R	125	175	4.8L	3.4L	8.2L
3	12L	60	100	12R	7.2R	19.2R
4	15L	75	50	12R	18R	30R
5	6R	96	66	2.75	5.45L	9.2L

En Route

Check your DI against the compass every 15 minutes or so. Also, check your fuel state against progress, noting large reductions in particular, as they may indicate that you have left the fuel cap undone (gauges may read higher), or you have a leak. Pre-plan known events for your first leg, such as a noticeable town, a railway and road crossing, disused airfield, etc. Work out when they should turn up with your pre-planned groundspeed, and you can see if you are running early or late.

GROUND SPEED REVISION

Once you start navigating, you need to ensure that the ground speed you planned for is the one that you are getting. For example, you may have been instructed to reach a waypoint at a specific time.

To calculate your groundspeed, you need two fixes, preferably 10 nm apart. Start the stopwatch on the first one, and see how long it takes to get to the second. If it takes 6 minutes, you are doing 100 kts.

Whatever distance you cover in 6 minutes multiplied by 10 is your groundspeed.

ESTIMATED TIME OF ARRIVAL (ETA)

Constant revision of groundspeed is important - not only do you need a check on the wind, but ATC also need to know your arrival time (within three minutes) so they can slot you in. Noting your timing between pre-marked points on your map is one method, but a useful mental check is to multiply the distance flown in 6 minutes by 10, so, if you fly 20 miles in 12 minutes, you are doing 100 kts. The definition of ETA refers to arrival at the *destination*.

Map Reading

The first thing to appreciate before you use a map is that they contain a lot of information around the sides that is useful before you use it. The most important item is the date - you don't want to be using an out-of-date chart! Also take note of the name and revision - you don't want to be using the wrong one either! You will find a list of what maps are current and their revision state in the AIP.

We already covered scale before, but other information could include what maps are next in series either side.

Get used to recognising ground features from the map and angles and distances between them (when identifying a fix, you need at least three ways of confirmation). The photo below is what you would see if you flew East from Southampton in the map underneath it:

Also get used to not necessarily needing to know exactly which field you are over at all times - a common fault is too much accuracy when you start flying - in higher latitudes there are fewer landmarks, so the charts are less detailed anyway. On top of that, what landmarks there are may well be covered by snow (or sand, in the desert) and whiteout or brownout will make distances and altitudes harder to estimate. Knowing you are so many miles in a particular direction from somewhere is good enough.

If you are operating inside a particular area, choose a prominent landmark and rotate round it, that is, keep an eye on your position in relation to it (when the fog is down in Dubai, all the nannies get lost because they can't see the Burj hotel, the biggest landmark for miles around!) *Check Features* are prominent landmarks selected in the planning stage to look for during the flight.

Tip: The span of your hand is about nine inches, very useful for measuring distance. From the middle of your thumb to the tip is about an inch.

GRID REFERENCES

The UK is divided up into 100 km squares which are given two letters. Then numbers are added to the letters to denote a specific point within the square.

Ordnance survey grid references can consist of either 4 or 6 figures. These in turn will consist of two groups of two or three numbers together. The first group of Eastings is read horizontally, and the second (Northings) is read vertically (along the corridor and up the stairs). In each group, the first two numbers can be found along the side of the map, and the third, in a 6-figure grid, is interpolated inside the relevant grid square.

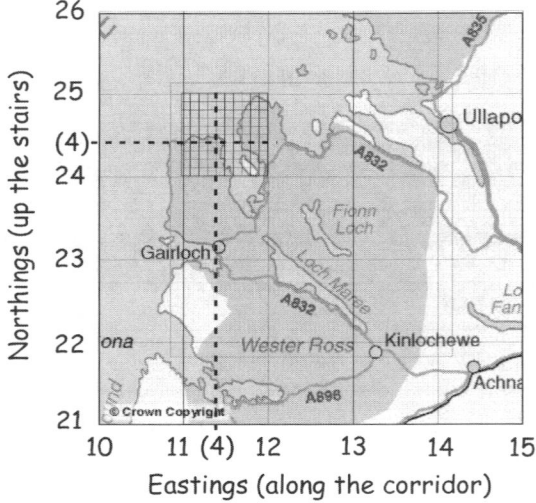

In the example above, the grid reference is 114244, made up of the four-figure grid (1124) which gives you the grid square, and the remaining ones are interpolated from an imaginary grid in that square.

Relative Velocity

You often have to adjust speed to arrive where you're going at particular times. If the speeds of two aircraft are known, subtract one from the other if they are going the same way, or add them if they are travelling head on. Having found their relative velocities, and if you know the distance, the time until they pass can be calculated from:

$$\text{Speed} = \frac{\text{Distance}}{\text{Time}}$$

To find out when to change speed, first sort out what would have happened with no change in speed, then how much time is needed at the lower speed.

RADIO NAVIGATION
•••

The other relevance of AC as used in aircraft is that it is the basis of radio waves, which we use to convey information. The sound of a rotor blade slap from 1100 feet away will take one second to reach your ears, but air travelling at that speed would be ten times more powerful than a hurricane, so the sound you hear is not *in* the air - the sound changes the characteristics of the air instead.

The effect is like the example of electrons moving down a cable given previously. One pushed in at one end affects the others in line until one falls out at the other, so it is easier to imagine a wave of compression pushing air particles in front of it before it affects your eardrums. If this is done too slowly, though, the air particles have a chance to get out of the way, so the effect is not noticeable below a certain rate of vibration, or *frequency*.

A sound wave will only travel so far by itself, which is why it needs help, in the shape of a *carrier wave*, to move over longer distances (if you could transmit a sound wave, it would be so long that huge aerials and large coils and capacitors would be needed). The carrier wave is created at radio frequency (the RF carrier), and a sound wave (the AF signal) is added to it, so that an electronic copy of the original signal is made. The process of frequency shifting is called modulation, described overleaf.

Trivia: Although Marconi transmitted the first CW signal, a Canadian, Reginald Fessenden, transmitted the first *voice* signal from Massachusetts to ships along the Eastern Seaboard. However, Nikola Tesla was ahead of them both - Marconi used 17 of Tesla's patents.

The Transmitter

Radio transmitters are based around high frequency oscillators, but applying lots of power directly to an oscillator (above about 100 MHz) reduces its stability, so a relatively weak signal is used, then amplified for the later stages. The audio signal is treated the same way. A *modulator's* job is to combine the signals from the radio and audio amplifiers by superimposing the amplified speech signal on the RF carrier with a transformer.

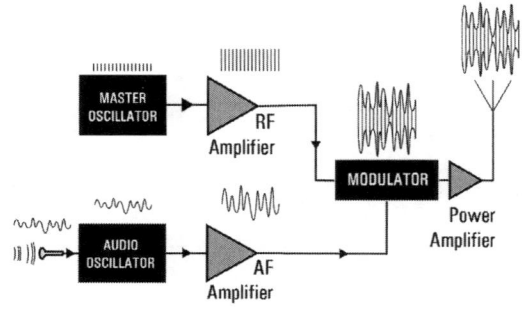

MODULATION

The information to be sent *modulates*, or varies, the carrier wave, although an unmodulated signal travels further than a modulated one for the same power.

The *Depth Of Modulation* is the extent to which a carrier wave is modulated by another frequency, as expressed by a percentage. Modulation is actually done at just below 100% because there is a danger of over-modulation that will cause distortion.

AMPLITUDE MODULATION (A3)

With AM, the amplitude (or power) of a carrier wave is varied according to the strength of an audio (or video) signal applied to it. Its shape changes as the AF signal distorts it.

AMPLITUDE MODULATION

The top part of the picture above shows an RF carrier with alternating cycles above and below the line of nil current flow. The middle part shows a fluctuating DC waveform representing speech from a microphone (it is positive because it is all above the nil current line). When the two are merged together (in the bottom part) the RF carrier takes on the shape of the distorting AF signal.

AM suffers from two practical defects, one being noise, and the other lack of quality. Almost all natural and man-made electrical disturbances, such as atmospheric static, or electrical equipment, radiate energy with amplitude disturbances. The air gets more positively charged as you climb higher*, especially when it is wet. This may cause sudden leaks or discharges that produce electromagnetic waves called *precipitation static*, that interfere with radio transmissions, which is a factor when you want reliability in bad weather. A quick look at a rainfall map of the world will tell you where it is worst, namely the tropics. The lowest frequency where freedom from static interference can be guaranteed is 30 MHz.

*This ionisation of the air creates a layer around the Earth called the ionosphere which has less resistance to the flow of electricity. It is useful for getting longer ranges with certain frequencies (HF) and is discussed later on.

AM transmissions can therefore be noisy because the receiver cannot distinguish between the signals you want to hear and the ones you don't. This has led to the use of systems such as SELCAL (*Selective Calling*), so you don't have to listen to the background noise all the time.

Also, for a quality signal, you need to transmit all the audio frequencies in the range of human hearing. AM channels are not wide enough to do that, for historical reasons.

FREQUENCY MODULATION

Here, the frequency is changed instead of the amplitude, so FM does not suffer from man-made interference. As well, because the signal to noise ratio for FM is lower than it needs to be for AM, you don't need as much power for the same quality of reception (it is also more steady), although FM is more complex to produce.

The whole audio range is covered because they were able to allocate a wider bandwidth to FM transmissions.

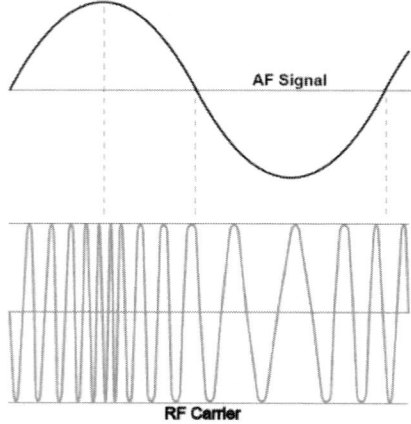

FREQUENCY MODULATION

When the amplitude is positive, the frequency increases above the mean carrier frequency, and *vice versa*. The amount of change is called the *deviation*. The maximum limit is typically ±5 KHz for speech.

PULSE MODULATION

This is used for radar and is described in that section.

FREQUENCY SHIFT KEYING

For data, as used with satellites, where the carrier frequency is shifted above and below the mean (as 1 and 0) to represent bits of information.

Wavebands

The range of electromagnetic waves is quite large, but radio waves only occupy a small part of it, actually between about 3 KHz to 3,000 GHz. This area is split up by International agreement between the people who wish to use it, and consists of frequency ranges, or bands, that share similar characteristics:

Band	Frequency	Wavelength
VLF	3-30 KHz	10-100 km
LF	30-300 KHz	1-10 km
MF	300-3,000 KHz	100-1000 m
HF	3-30 MHz	10-100 m
VHF	30-300 MHz	1-10 m
UHF	300-3,000 MHz	10-100 cm
SHF	3-30 GHz	1-10 cm
EHF	30-300 GHz	1-10 mm

Propagation

If you recall, in the tank circuit, the energy is alternately stored in the electric field of the capacitor and the magnetic field of the coil. An antenna connected to the circuit would therefore alternately radiate electric and magnetic fields. In fact, they surround the antenna at all times, as there is a crossover as each field builds up and dies down.

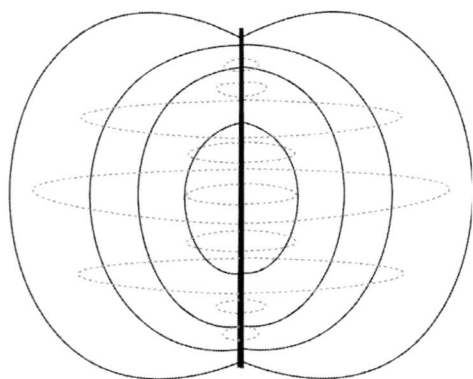

POLARISATION

Electromagnetic radiation is comprised of the E and H fields, which stand for electric and magnetic, respectively. The electric field arises from voltage, and the magnetic one from current. The two act at rightangles to each other.

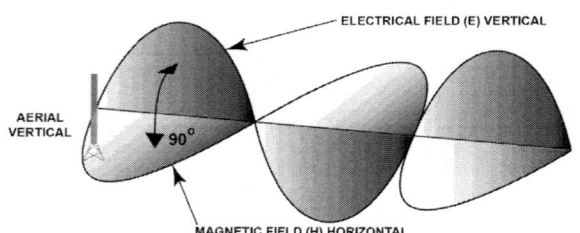

© *Phil Croucher, 2012*

A wave's *polarisation* is noted with reference to the *electrical* field, so a *vertically polarised* wave has a *vertical* electric field, which will come from a vertical aerial (for efficiency, the receiver must have the same orientation). For example, NDBs (and weather-based static) are vertically polarised, whilst VORs and ILS Localisers are horizontally polarised.

ATTENUATION

Although the transmitted power remains constant, some energy is absorbed by the Earth and the ionosphere. The rate of absorption *increases* with frequency (in the ionosphere, it *decreases* as frequency increases).

The remaining energy has to spread itself over a wider area, so the signal gets weaker (attenuates) with distance away from the transmitter (plus coastal refraction and diffraction). The circumference of the wave front increases as the wave spreads, reducing the amount of energy per unit of length. The power of the transmitted signal fades in an inverse square relationship, meaning that a signal 2 nm from its source will have a quarter of the strength of one only 1 nm away. Put another way, you need 4 times the power to double the range of transmission.

Radio waves generally take the scenic Great Circle route, which means that they travel pretty much in a straight line (see *Navigation*) but they may have their direction changed through:

- **Refraction**, which is the *bending* of a wave, typically inside the ionosphere (discussed under *Sky Waves*)

- **Reflection**, from a flat surface such as the Earth or the ionosphere, like light off a mirror, but after reflection, a phase shift will occur, which will depend on the angle at which the surface was struck, and the wave polarisation, discussed below

- **Diffraction**, around corners or following the curvature of the Earth, which can extend ranges beyond the horizon

GROUND (SURFACE) WAVES

Ground waves are associated with LF/MF waves, and may go directly to their destination (if it is close enough), or curve to follow the Earth's surface, depending on the frequency, although contact with the surface and the widening circumference of the wave will eventually weaken their power, cause them to curve downwards and eventually be absorbed by the ground.

The rate of attenuation of a surface wave is around 3 times greater over land than it is over the sea. Typical figures for maximum range are 100 and 300 nm respectively, with high power transmitters. Ground waves are sometimes called *Surface Waves*. The lower the frequency, the better the reception over long distances. Below 500 kHz, you can obtain over 1000 miles just with a ground wave.

DIRECT WAVES

These are contained within the troposphere, and are otherwise known as *tropospheric, or space wave*s. Being direct, they are known as *line-of-sight*, meaning that anything in the way, like hills or buildings, will affect the transmission (direct waves will not bounce like HF waves do).

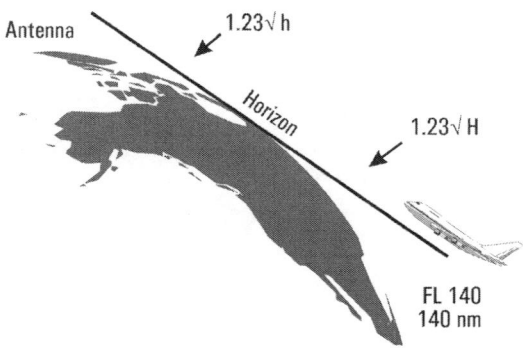

VHF/SHF/UHF reception is line-of-sight and will not curve to follow the Earth's surface, so you have to be high enough to receive your selected station at a particular distance. As an example, when crossing the Irish Sea, you must be above 3000 feet to hear either Shannon or London Information. However, if using the VOR at high altitudes, you might get station overlap and erroneous readings, so don't use VOR bearing information beyond the published protection range (see the AIP).

In General

Radio navigation instruments can give you position information in four ways:

- As a relative bearing *to* a radio station relative to the longitudinal axis of the aircraft (ADF, VOR)

- As a radial *from* a station (VOR)

- As a distance from a station (DME)

- As an actual position (GPS, RNAV, INS)

For the first three, you need a chart with which to compute your position.

Equipment not directly required for navigation should be tuned to ground stations to check accuracy or ground speed, so errors can be detected and the equipment be available in an emergency. Also, don't rely on a beacon until it has been identified and confirmed!

VOR

Very High Frequency Omnidirectional Range is a ground-based short range navigational aid that broadcasts two signals on VHF, using the *phase difference* between them to signify your direction from the transmitting station as one of 360 radials *from* it. The usable frequency range is between 108-117.95 MHz, which is just below aviation voice channels.

Low-powered VORs (as used near terminals) and ILS localisers occupy the space between 108-112, with 50 Hz spacing. Higher powered VORs, which are needed for aircraft at higher altitudes, operate between 112-118 (112-117.95) on odd and even tenths, for another 120 channels. They can be received up to 100 nm away.

136
Voice
720 Channels
118
117.95
Hi Pwr VOR
120 Channels
112
Lo Pwr VOR
ILS
80 Channels
108 MHz

VORs represented on maps have a compass rose round them, aligned with Magnetic North. They are a pain to shut down and realign, which is why a VOR's variation will often be different from its aerodrome.

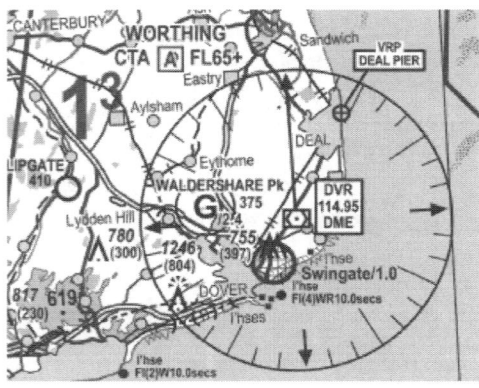

VORs are not sensitive to heading, as is the ADF (below), because they show *track*, although most pilots set the OBS to the heading anyway for neatness so that the left/right needle reads correctly. Neither do they suffer from many of the other problems associated with the ADF, especially night effect.

The *Station Identifier* is transmitted in Morse every 15 seconds (4 times a minute), and you must confirm the frequency and ID before using a VOR for navigation. If there is no ID, but behaviour is otherwise normal, the system is on maintenance (you may sometimes hear a Morse test code of ▬ ••• ▬).

Theory Of Operation

The equipment electronically measures an angle, having transmitted a signal with ~~two~~ three components. There is a 30 Hz FM omniphase signal, received by all stations at a constant phase, and a variable phase (variphase) signal whose phase changes according to its bearing from North. The variphase signal is a 30 Hz tone that modulates the amplitude of the carrier, and its sidebands are used to make the phase angle of the modulation equal to the azimuth angle.

To make separation easier (or to detect which signal is which), the reference signal frequency-modulates a sub-carrier (at 9960 Hz), because the carrier is already modulated by the variphase signal. The result is that an apparently AM signal (rotating at 30 Hz) is eventually seen by the aircraft in terms of varying *power* (amplitude) levels. After demodulation, the signals have their phases compared to derive a bearing.

There is also a voice/ID channel that can carry 1020 Hz Morse and voice signals.

So, both signals are in phase when the "rotating" signal passes Magnetic North, but they get more out of phase by the amount of degrees you go round the circle so, if the phase difference is 30° at your receiver, you are on the 030° radial from the VOR. Your receiver picks up the reference signal first and the maximum point of the variphase signal a little bit later. The time difference is indicated in degrees as your magnetic bearing from the VOR (which is actually called a *radial*).

All this produces a polar diagram called a *limacon*, which has been inherited from an earlier navigation system, and is similar in shape to the cardioid used by the ADF (later), but without an absolute null point, rotating electrically at 30 times/second.

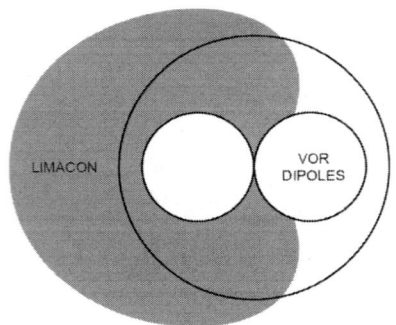

There is no null point because transmission is momentarily interrupted when the maximum point of the limacon passes through North. If it were otherwise, you would get a false North indication.

Because the signal is frequency and amplitude modulated, it is classed as an A9W signal (Doppler VOR, mentioned later, has its modulations the other way round).

In your aircraft, the signals are received by a horizontally polarised V-dipole antenna, then mixed, converted into an intermediate frequency, amplified, detected and demodulated. Then the audio part of the signal is fed into a low-pass filter which allows the reference signal to enter one part of the circuit and the rotating one to enter another, through a 10 KHz bandpass filter, eventually to become 30 MHz AC.

The rotating signal is also fed into a calibrated phase shifter which is controlled by the OBS on the front of the instrument in the cockpit. It is turned until the two signals are in phase and the Course Deviation Indicator (CDI) is in the centre.

The TO-FROM indicator is driven by another phase shifter and phase detector operating in parallel. Because of the nature of VOR transmissions and the way they are used for direction finding, there is a 180° ambiguity, so the CDI is equally sensitive to signals coming from either of two opposite directions (i.e. two radials, 180° apart, from the same VOR). To resolve this an additional circuit indicates TO or FROM with a flag. The reference signal is shifted by another 90° and compared again to the rotating one, to tell whether it is leading or lagging the rotating signal, to make the indicator show the relevant direction.

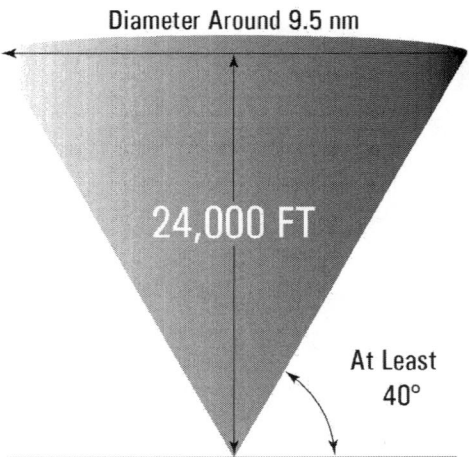

Diameter Around 9.5 nm

24,000 FT

At Least 40°

Over the beacon, you will be in a *cone of confusion,* the same as you would be with any antenna - this is an area where no signal is received, so the TO/FROM flags disappear and the alarm flag comes up. The ICAO limit for the cone is 100° across, and the width can be worked out by finding the tangent of the angle and multiplying it by your height, to get the answer in feet (FL 360 = 6 nm). During this *station passage,* just ignore the signal or use something else.

There are also ambiguities *abeam* the beacon - 90° either side of the selected radial there is a *zone of ambiguity* up to 10° across where the flag will not show at all, and the indications should therefore not be relied upon.

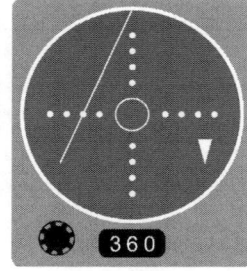

In the bowels of the aircraft will be a large black box, connected to a *remote indicator* in the cockpit, that might also double as an ILS display.

This one is a 5-dot display, using 4 dots plus a circle, so each one is 2°, for an overall width of 10°. For 3 dots plus a circle, each is 2.5°.

Once you select a radial by turning the *Omni Bearing Selector* (the small knob just under the dial), the *Course Deviation Indicator* (CDI) needle will be in the centre (if you are exactly on the selected radial), or either side of it, up to 10° away, so each dot left or right represents 2°, if there are 5 on your display (2½° with 3).

When the needle is in the middle, you will be on the selected radial, which traditionally is *from* the station when on the same side, shown by TO/FROM Flag, which, on later instruments, will be a small white triangle pointing in the relevant direction*. If the indicator shows *TO*, you are on the *reciprocal*, or on the other side. In the example of the display above, the radial selected is N, or 360°, because the *From* flag is showing (as the needle is three dots left, you are on the 006° radial). Thus, when holding *inbound* on the 240 radial, your heading should be 060°. This is a common trap in exam questions (and check rides) - if you are tracking inbound on a radial, set the reciprocal at the top of the display, as radials go *from* a station.

*The changeover sector is within 10° either side of the abeam position. The TO/FROM indicator is independent of the heading. On the side of the radial you have selected, FROM is displayed. On the other side, you get TO.

All you have to do then is watch the needle - if you are going away from a station on a radial, and the needle is pointing left, then you fly left until it centres.

If you are going to the station, then you fly right. The thing to remember is that the needle always points to *where the radial is*, which has *nothing to do with the heading of the aircraft* (remember this for exams).

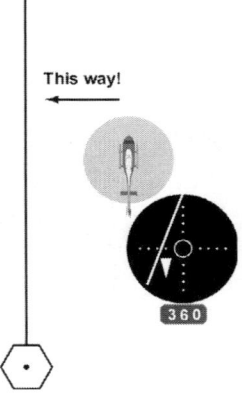

This way!

All you do is follow the needle - the radial is where the needle is*, and you do not necessarily turn that way to get to it - sometimes, having the needle on the left means turn right! *Only if your heading is the same direction as the OBS will it be on the correct side.*

*On the RMI, the tail of the needle shows the radial.

As an example, here is a comparison of the HSI against the OBI - you are heading 320°, and both have a setting of 120° *inbound*. Notice how the HSI presents the information clearly, but the OBI says something quite different - if you had no heading information, you might not realise you were going the wrong way!

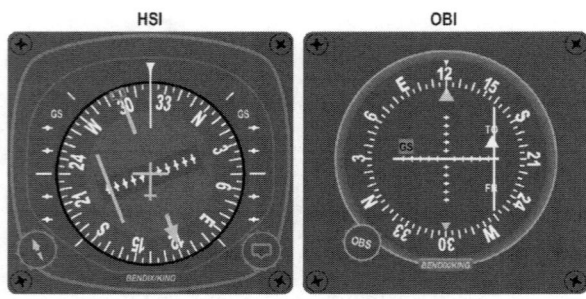

Thus, to get the best results, the heading should approximately follow the OBS setting.

The situation shown above is typically found during a procedure turn - it's not a normal tracking scenario.

For any radial, there are boundaries formed by the CDI and the TO/FROM indicator, creating quadrants around the station (that is, four distinct areas). You will be in one of them. For example, in the picture below, which displays would the pilot see, and in what order, for a helicopter moving from A to B?

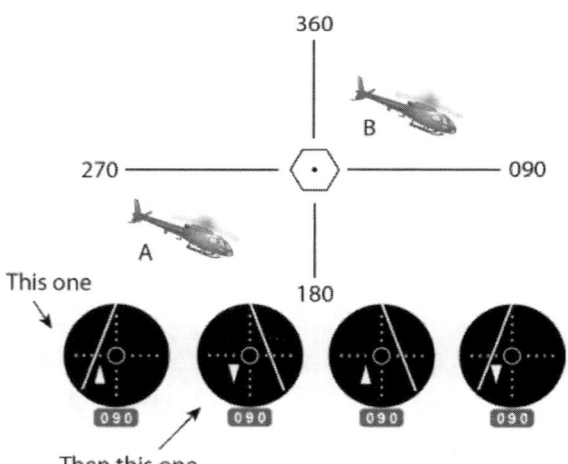

To intercept a radial inbound, tune and identify the VOR station, then select the reciprocal of the desired radial by turning the OBS until you get a TO reading. Fly to whichever side the needle is displaced, turning the shortest way to a heading 90° away from it, until the needle starts to move, at which point reduce the intercept angle to 45° (rather like 2-3 above). As the needle centres, reduce the intercept angle again and maintain the track with suitable adjustments for drift. Do the same outbound, except look

for a FROM reading. A good rule (inbound and outbound) is to subtract the intercept angle if the needle goes left, and add if it goes right to find the heading to steer. For example, 280°-90°=190°.

Here are the needle movements and responses of an aircraft drifting off to the left and coming back on course:

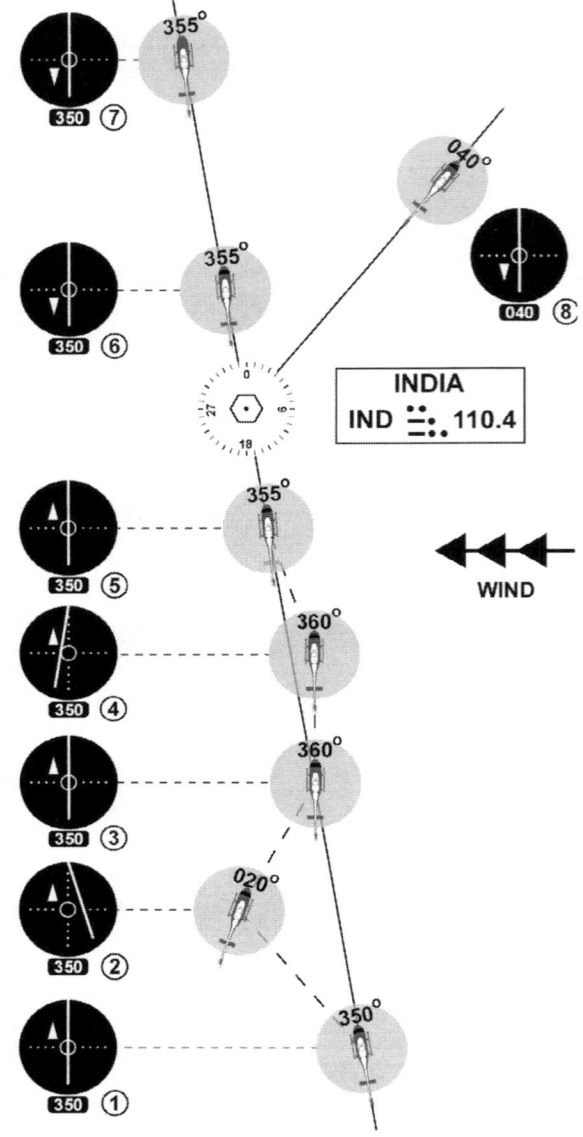

To bracket for drift, turn onto a zero wind heading and see what the drift actually is. Make a large correction the opposite way and see what happens. Then half the original correction. Keep going until the correct heading is found.

When tracking along an airway, tune and identify the station you are going from, track the selected radial until near the mid-point, then tune and identify the next station. The TO/FROM flag should change over. If you have to use another VOR for a fix as a reporting point along the

airway, select the required radial, and when the needle is centred you are over the fix:

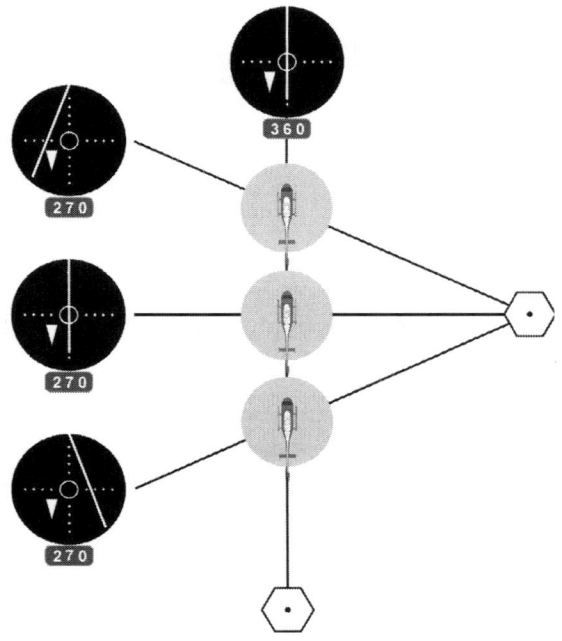

Range

As for standard VHF.

Problems

Although the VOR is less subject to static and interference than an NDB, and it is more accurate, the transmissions depend on line of sight, and there are suspect areas at 90° to a radial (zones of ambiguity), and overhead (cone of confusion), as mentioned above. In addition, certain rotor or propeller RPM settings can cause fluctuations up to ±6° (change them slightly before saying the instrument is not working!)

Transmissions may be adversely affected by uneven propagation over irregular ground surfaces (scalloping), and if bearing information is used beyond published ranges, you may get interference from other transmitters.

The monitor will remove the ID once the measured bearing changes by more than 1°.

ADF/NDB

An *Automatic Direction Finder* (ADF), also known as a *radio compass*, is a device in an aircraft that picks up signals broadcast on the Medium wave band by *Non Directional Beacons* (NDBs), so called because they radiate in all directions, using *surface waves*. The approved ICAO range for aeronautical NDBs is between 200-1750 KHz, but that part of the radio spectrum also includes commercial radio stations, whose use in IFR work is not allowed because of the problems involved with identification, and there are no guarantees of consistency of service, but they are useful to listen to on long journeys (and yes, the needle still points to the station - Capital Radio is very useful for finding Elstree!) If there is no ID, but the system otherwise appears to behave normally, it is undergoing calibration or maintenance.

Transmissions are not dependent on line of sight, but utilise ground waves, so the system is good over long distances, although there are a few problems, mentioned below. It is possible to get 1,000 nm range over sea and 300 nm over land if the power is high enough, but since better systems have come along, NDBs are now only used as enroute navaids on airways, homing beacons for instrument approaches and markers for the *Instrument Landing System* (ILS), with a typical range of about 35 nm.

The primary function of the ADF receiver is to determine the bearing of an *incoming NDB signal*, which is *vertically polarised*. To do this, it uses a *loop aerial*.

When the loop is square (across the bearing) to the beacon, the signal reaches both sides of the loop at the same time and there is no signal detected.

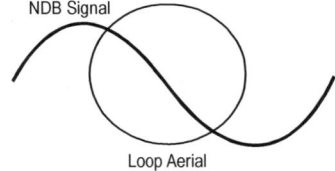

When the loop is sideways-on, however, the signal reaches one part of the loop first. The second part will be out of phase, so a current will be generated, which drives an electric motor to continually seek the null position. It is phase sensitive, so it can always turn the shortest way. Various stages of magnification inside the receiver help this along, but they need not concern us here. The point is that the detected signal is not what is actually used to determine the bearing, but the *null signal point*, since the current flow is slow to build up and break down, and is a bit on the woolly side anyway. The null point is much sharper and easier to find.

Because the current flows in the opposite direction depending on the position of the loop, you also need some way of determining which end is what, otherwise you could be 180° out. A single vertical aerial called a *sense antenna* helps here - the signals are combined algebraically and the magnitude and polarity of the sense aerial arranged to be identical to the loop. The result is a polar diagram called a *cardioid*, with only one null point:

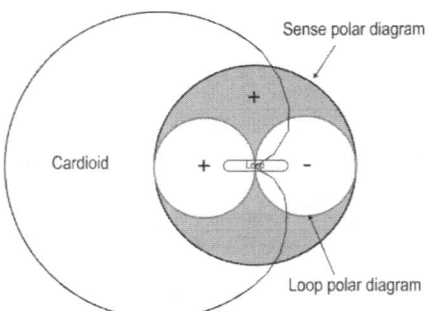

On one side of the loop, the polar diagrams are positive and combine, but on the other, one is positive and the other negative. Thus, they cancel out, hence the null point on one side. The modern (and more stylish) equivalent of the loop antenna is a small housing with two coils at right angles to each other, wound on ferrite cores. They are connected to the stator coils of a *goniometer* which points the needle.

LIMITATIONS*

Limitations of the system include:

- **static**, including local thunderstorm activity, which is likely to cause the greatest inaccuracy and make the needle point towards a storm.

- **night effect,** where the needle swings erratically, at its strongest just after sunset and before sunrise. The loop is designed to receive surface waves - any sky waves will be out of phase and distorted, because they energise the horizontal parts of the loop (waves change their polarisation when reflecting off the ionosphere). If the ionosphere is not parallel with the Earth's surface, they will also arrive from different directions. Low power beacons are virtually unaffected by this as they can only produce a ground wave. Check for an unsteady needle and a fading audio signal.

- **station overlap**, when NDBs have the same frequency. Because this is more pronounced at night, it can easily be confused with *night effect*, below (promulgated ranges are not valid at night for this reason). This will have the greatest effect on ADF accuracy, particularly at night.

- **mountain effect**, or variations caused by reflections from high ground, where two signals might be received at once from different paths.

- **quadrantal error**, or variations from the aircraft itself, in the same way as it might affect a compass. The signal is reradiated by the airframe and the receiver gets an additional (much weaker) signal to contend with. The greatest error lies at 45° to the fore and aft axis, hence the term *quadrantal*. Modern systems have corrector boxes for this.

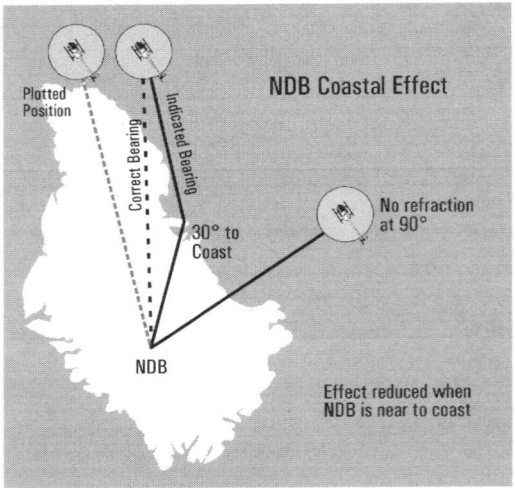

- **coastal refraction**, from radio waves in transit from land to sea, because they travel slightly faster over water, which makes you aircraft appear closer to the shore. This effect is most noticeable at less than 30° to the coastline (i.e. an acute angle), and at lower frequencies, so expect errors if you are using an NDB inland directly in front of or behind you. With two NDBs, one 20 nm, and the other 50 nm inland from the coast, and if the coastal error is the same for both, the error seen by an aircraft will be greater from the beacon that is further away.

- **Identification**. As there is no flag indication of failure, as there is with the VOR, you should continuously monitor the station ID when relying on the instrument. Aside from that, the only way of knowing about problems is seeing the needle rotate to the right if the signal is not received.

USE

The ADF is normally tuned with the function switch in the ANT position (it stands for *antenna*). This removes the needle from the loop and saves wear and tear as it tries to point at every station you tune through - here, the sense antenna is used by itself to obtain the ID. Once there, return the switch to the ADF position (or COMP, on some sets).

As always, check - in this case, ensure that the needle points vaguely where you expect it to.

The fixed card display (*goniometer*) has a compass rose with 0° representing the nose of the aircraft at the top of the instrument, and a needle that points to where the signal is coming *from*, in this case 070° (including thunderstorms if they are stronger than what you are tuned into).

Thus, if a station is ahead, the needle will point to 0°, or 180° if it is behind. However, if you made no allowance for wind, and just pointed the nose of the aircraft at the station (*homing*, as opposed to *tracking*), you would actually follow a curved path towards it.

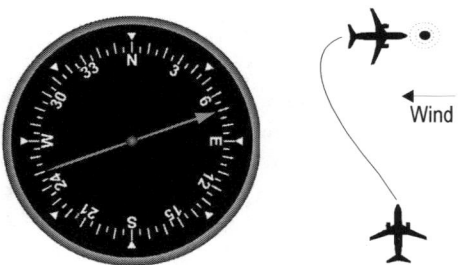

Allowing for drift lets you keep a straight track. If you are heading to a beacon maintaining a relative bearing of zero, and the magnetic heading decreases, you have some right drift, and *vice versa*. Unfortunately, working with fixed cards involves some maths. First, though, some definitions:

- *Magnetic Heading* - angle between longitudinal axis and magnetic North

- *Relative Bearing* - the angle between the aircraft's longitudinal axis and the NDB, which is what you read directly from a fixed card ADF

- *Magnetic Track* or *Bearing* - the angle between aircraft position and the NDB, either to or from

Take note of this formula (you will need it in the exam):

$$MH + RB = BTS \ (MB)$$

In other words, the magnetic heading plus the relative bearing gives you the bearing to the station:

$$MB = MH + RB$$

My **B**uddy
Must **H**ave
Red **B**lood

See *Navigation* for an explanation of Magnetic Heading

Taking the example above, the formula would read:

$$324 + 46 = 010$$

You can get the relative bearing like this:

$$BTS - MH = RB$$

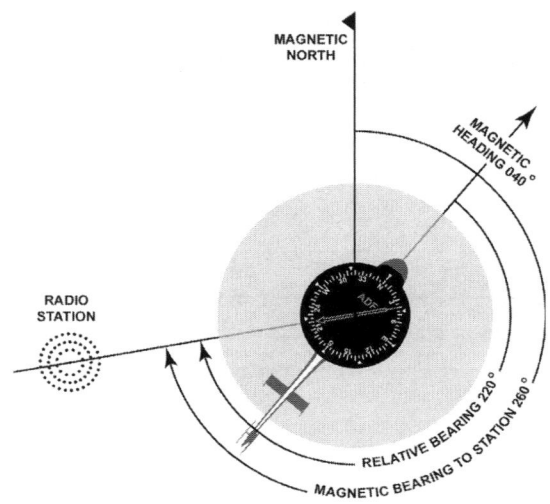

If you split the display into two halves, on a line between 0° and 180°, and call the right half plus, and the left minus, you can use the needle's position to find the track to a station. For example, if the needle is in the right half (the + segment), add the heading to the relative bearing to get the track. If it is in the left, take it away (work the needle back from zero). Whilst turning right, the aircraft heading will increase while the relative bearing decreases, and *vice versa*. If you remain on the same bearing, the heading change will always equal the change of ADF indication.

RMI

The *Radio Magnetic Indicator* is a combination of ADF indicator and slaved compass that replaces the fixed card with one that moves, so the top of the instrument represents the aircraft's compass heading (which includes deviation) and the needle points to the QDM (or QDR, if you look at the other end), which saves you doing the calculations above in your head.

In other words, it always displays the present heading and bearing, and does some of the work required by a fixed display. There may also be a repeater needle from the VORs giving you the same information relative to the stations they are tuned to. In the example below, the heading is 139°, and the ADF QDM is 077°. The VOR needle is pointing to a QDM of 210°.

The RMI does not need a TO/FROM flag, as there is no 180-degree ambiguity. With the VOR, the tail of the needle on the RMI indicates the bearing received *at the aircraft*. In other words, the signal left the VOR on whatever bearing it shows. Change it to True using the variation at the VOR.

As a point of interest, the VOR needle on an RMI will always read correctly if any deviation occurs, but headings and ADF readings will be in error by the deviation. This is because the ADF needle will naturally point towards the transmitting station, regardless of what the compass rose does. The VOR QDM, on the other hand, is created *within the instrument* by subtracting the aircraft heading from the QDM and applying the difference clockwise round the dial from the lubber line. Deviations are automatically applied because the number cruncher ensures that the VOR needle moves in the same direction for the same amount as the compass rose. For either needle, however, if it is off to the left, you fly left, and *vice versa*.

TRACKING

When drifting, the needle will always point to the side of the aircraft the wind is coming from, so corrections inbound should always be made that way, ensuring that the needle goes to the *other* side of the lubber line once a corrected heading is established.

For example, if you want to track 090°, and the wind is coming from the right, to be on track you want to end up in a situation where the heading is an equal amount of degrees the other side of the lubber line as the needle is, such as a heading of 110° (*plus* 20 of the lubber line), looking for a 340° relative bearing (*minus* 20 of the lubber line). Or, for a track of 090°, your heading might be 070° while the ADF needle points to 110° (heading - 20°, looking for + 20° from the needle). If you are going the same way as your track, the needle will tell you which way to go. If it is on the left, your track will be on the left, and *vice versa*. Just turn whichever way until the needle reads the desired intercept on the opposite side. A good ploy is to allow the drift to happen until you get a positive reading, say 10° port, double it the other way (go 20° starboard), and when you are back on track, reduce it by half (10° in

this case) to hold it. This is *bracketing*, and the process may have to be repeated several times in smaller amounts until you get it right. *Do not chase the needle* - hold it steady so you can see the effects of adjustments.

1. If Needle Moves Right →

← 2. Aircraft Is Drifting Left

3. Go this way! Bring needle left of lubber line and allow for wind →

When tracking *outbound*, you want to end up with the needle on the same side as the wind, so, although you are still looking for the plus 20, minus 20 equation, the needle would be pointing at 160° RB (when you make your initial turn, the needle looks like it's going the wrong way, but you get used to it). In short, if the pointy end moves to the right of a line between 0° and 180°, fly right, as drift is to the left, and *vice versa*. If you want to decrease the bearing to or from a beacon, make the needle's reading decrease - for example, if the track is 270° and you want to approach or depart on 260° (decreased), change your heading so the needle reads less by suitable amount for a cut and then wait until the heading is less by the same amount the needle is more.

If you split the display into two halves, on a line between 0° and 180°, and call the right half plus, and the left minus, you can use the needle's position to find the track to a station. For example, if the needle is in the right half (the + segment), add the heading to the relative bearing to get the track. If it is in the left, take it away (work the needle back from zero). Whilst turning right, the aircraft heading will increase while the relative bearing decreases, and *vice versa*. If you remain on the same bearing, the heading change will always equal the change of ADF indication.

To find an intercept heading, just add or subtract the intercept angle to the track you wish to establish, as with an airway. It's common to use 90° inbound and 45° outbound, but use whatever ATC and circumstances (or exam questions) dictate (30° is nice). Note the track, and add or subtract your heading, as appropriate, to get the expected relative bearing when on track, which you will be when the needle of a fixed card points to it.

CAPT

DME

Distance Measuring Equipment is secondary radar (see *Radar*, below), but in reverse. It measures the time difference between *paired pulses* being sent from an aircraft, and received back (on different frequencies). Then the distance is calculated.

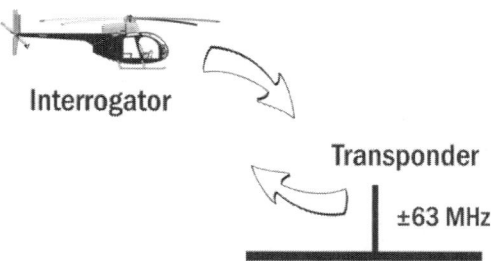

Interrogator

Transponder

±63 MHz

In other words, the aircraft is the first to transmit on UHF, then the DME transponder on the ground returns the signal (with the same pulse spacing), ±63 MHz, after a 50 microsecond delay which is subtracted during the number-crunching. The delay reduces the chances of uncoordinated activity when the interrogating aircraft is near the station. The pulses are 3.5 milliseconds long.

Two frequencies are used because, otherwise, the first pulse received would be the ground return from below (with normal radar, targets are relatively free from other objects. They are more difficult to distinguish the other way round). Similarly, the ground station could self-trigger from other sources, such as those being bounced off a building. *Jittering* is used to identify pulses. That is, only signals with the same jittering pattern are replied to, because they are unique to each aircraft. *Aircraft DME receivers do not lock on to their own transmissions reflected from the ground as they are not on the receiver frequency - the interrogation and reply frequencies differ.*

Thus, signal discrimination depends on *frequency separation* and *pulse spacing.*

DME is UHF-based, between 962 and 1213 MHz, so a typical frequency is 1000 MHz. Its purpose is to continuously display your distance from the station to which it is tuned.

DME is rarely set up by itself, so it is not normally tuned directly - you usually select a VOR frequency and the DME reading will come up automatically, since the frequencies are usually paired. In other words, you select a VHF frequency to receive a UHF signal. The ident, however, is higher pitched than that of a VOR, so you can identify it between VOR idents on the same frequency (it is transmitted only once to the VOR's four).

Instruments in the cockpit will not only show your distance to a station, but will calculate the rate of movement and display the groundspeed (just multiply the distance flown in 6 minutes by 10 if yours doesn't). The

reason it's not completely accurate is because the distance measured is the *slant range* from the station, and not from your equivalent position on the ground, although at long distances and lower altitudes, this will be minimised. In practical terms, the difference is insignificant when more than 10 miles from the station, and the *maximum error occurs overhead* - at 12,000 ft, the instrument would read 2 nm, and 4 nm at 24,000 ft, and so on.

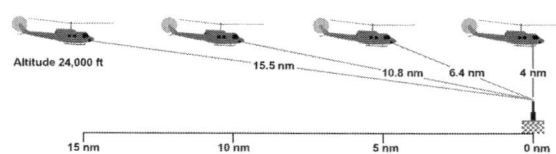

Simple Pythagoras will give you the real distance:

$$D = \sqrt{(S^2 - A^2)}$$

D is the ground distance, *S* is the readout (slant range) and *A* is your altitude in *nautical miles* (above the DME source).

Examples: If the time taken for an interrogation pulse to travel to the ground transponder and back is 2000 micro-seconds, the slant range will be 165 nm. An aircraft at FL 370, 15 nm from a DME station 1000 feet AMSL, will have a DME reading of 16 nm.

The ground station can only respond to a certain number of interrogations in a given period of time - generally, it can handle only up to 100 interrogations before *beacon saturation* occurs. If too many aircraft are interrogating it, the receiver will automatically be desensitized so it can hear and reply only to the strongest. Busy airspace can result in shorter-than-normal DME reception range, particularly with lower-powered DME units. Display counters rotating aimlessly throughout their range indicate that the airborne receiver is conducting a *range* search.

ERRORS

ICAO specifies that range errors should not exceed ± 0.25 nm plus 1.25% of the distance measured so, at 100 nm, the maximum should not exceed ± 1.5 nm.

GPS

The original satellite systems were based partly on hyperbolic navigation aids such as Decca Navigator or LORAN, and Doppler. By measuring the distortions from Sputnik in 1957, it was realised that the satellite's position could be established with some accuracy. It wasn't too hard to reverse the situation.

062 06

There are two systems currently available, with another one coming. The USA one is **NAVSTAR/GPS**, and the Russian system is **GLONASS**, which is only partially operational.

These days, satellite signals are not only used for navigation, but also for specialised clock systems in various earthbound systems, such as cell phone networks and TV stations, since the satellites all have atomic clocks on board. ATC use it for this purpose as well (GPS is a legal source of accurate time).

A satellite system can calculate distance, track and speed from your changing position. It can also give your altitude, but such 3D readouts require 4 satellites. In any case, the datum for altitude information when under IFR or conducting approaches is **barometric altitude**, because the Earth is not a true sphere and there may be wide differences between its actual shape and the WGS 84 model inside the GPS receiver.

GPS reliability approaches 100%, within 100 m of the true horizontal position for 95% of the time and 300 m for 99%. However, it can be affected by atmospheric interference, satellite positioning and tuning inaccuracies.

GALILEO

Although the American GPS system is still usable, it is old technology and originally designed for military use, so for modern purposes, continual workarounds have to be made, which often turn out to be more expensive than starting from scratch. *Galileo* is a European system whose first satellite was launched on the 28th December 2005. Its military capability has prompted China to take a 20% share, and has excited interest from Russia and Israel. It will start with five types of signal - one being available to everyone, like the GPS C/A code, a more precise commercial signal, a *safety of life* service for critical applications, a *public regulated service* (PRS) for government use, and one combined with a distress signal, for rescues.

Galileo should use 30 satellites, with 9 plus a spare in each of 3 planes in a near circular orbit at 23 222 km inclined at 56° to the Equator. Each orbit will take 14 hours. The signals will be transmitted on two bands, 1164-1215 MHz and 1559-1591 MHz. The overlap with GPS will use *spread spectrum technology* to unscramble the mess.

NAVSTAR/GPS

The *Global Positioning System* was originally set up by the US military in 1977 to help submarines get lost more accurately, based on Doppler Shift, as one of six satellites passed overhead. Now the system is managed by an executive board that ensures that all users' needs, including civilians, are considered. This was after the Korean Airlines flight KAL 007 was shot down inside Russian airspace. It is supposed to use 24 satellites, in 6 groups of 4 (60° apart), with at least 21 operational at any time, although there have been over 30 on line, to allow for orbital manoeuvres and maintenance. The original satellites are now used to monitor the atmosphere. The essential idea is that the transmissions from as many satellites as possible, but at least 4 for best results, are received by a device that is permanently tuned to a frequency of 1575.42 MHz, although there is another one used by the military. The satellites' transmissions include atomic time in their signals so the receiver can calculate its distance from them.

The phrase *Full Operational Capability* means that all 24 satellites are working. *All In View* means that a receiver is tracking all the satellites it can find (because it cannot find the ones that it wants), and can instantly replace a lost signal with another already being monitored. *Search The Sky* is a procedure that starts after switching on a receiver to check that no stored satellite data is available. It typically occurs after you move the GPS some distance since its last use, and no stored data is available.

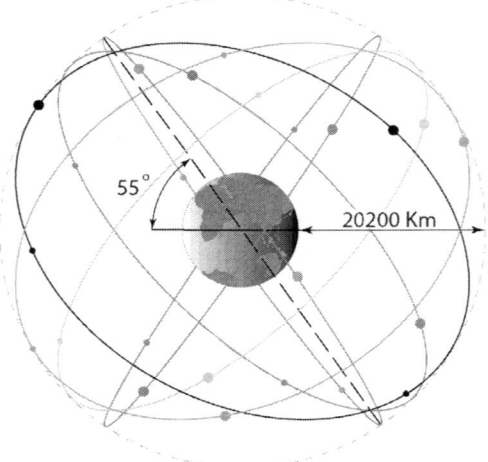

The satellites fly high enough to avoid the problems encountered by other navigation systems. They operate between **6 circular planes, 20 200 km above the Earth, with 4 in each plane**, optimised for wide coverage. Each one should have a 28° view of the Earth, and at least 5 should be line of sight from any point on Earth, provided they are more than 7.5° above the horizon (satellites are *in view* when they are more than 5° above the horizon). The

CAPT

most satellites are visible round the Equator, although a satellite's visibility varies, depending on the time and the observer's location.

Their orbits cross the equator at a **55° angle** (or, rather, the inclination* of the satellite's orbit to the equatorial plane is 55°), so you won't see a satellite directly overhead when North of 55° N or South of 55° S, although this does not affect polar service, because, at high latitudes, receivers can see satellites over the other side of the Pole, so more can actually be visible at high latitudes than elsewhere (they never go right over the Poles). Where the satellite goes South to North it is in the *ascending node*, and in the *descending node* when it goes the other way. The *mask angle* is the lowest angle above the horizon from where a satellite can be used, because of possible range errors.

*The inclination is the angle between the orbital and equatorial planes.

Satellites move once around the Earth, from W-E, every 11 hours 58 minutes (that is, twice a day, getting 4 minutes earlier each day). The height gives the best coverage with the least number of satellites, though you could get a problem flying through the odd ravine, especially as their transmitting power is only around 50 watts, or rather less than the average light bulb, which allows you to use smaller antennae. The signals themselves have less strength than a Christmas tree light.

Although it is guaranteed to be kept running for the foreseeable future, in (US) National Emergencies NAVSTAR may be unavailable, which is why it is still only acceptable as a backup to certificated radio-based navigation aids, at least under EASA. In addition, the satellites are not always in an optimal position, and interference can affect their signals, including jamming, which can be done with minimal equipment. If a position fix from GPS differs from conventional systems by an unacceptable amount, the flight may be continued, but using the conventional systems, so prescribed IFR equipment must still be installed and operational.

The system consists of three basic elements:

- The **Space Segment**, which contains the satellites, transmitting signals that are used by the receivers.

- The **Control Segment** has the ground stations and systems that track the satellites and monitor their status. It includes a Master Control Station in Colorado, and 4 others around the world. The main tasks of the control segment are to:

    - manage performance

    - upload navigation data

    - monitor satellites

- The **User Segment** includes the receivers that select satellites automatically, track their signals and calculate the time taken for them to reach the receiver. *Single channel* receivers move from one satellite to the next in sequence. Although this can be very quick, it is not fast enough for navigation. *Multi-channel* receivers (most suitable for aircraft) continuously monitor position data whilst locking on to the next satellites. *Continuous receivers*, with up to 12 channels, can eliminate GDOP problems by watching more than four satellites. GPS receiver antennae are semi-omnidirectional, and the active element is a quarter wavelength of 1.6 GHz, or approximately 2.5 cm.

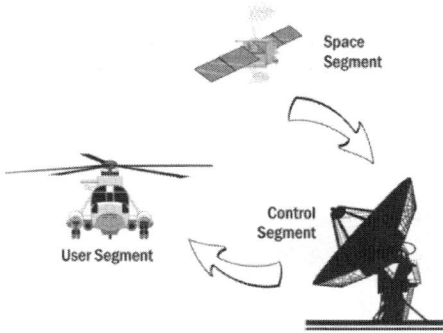

The signals are line-of-sight, and will not pass through water, buildings or solid objects in general, although they do pass through clouds, glass and plastic (regardless of that, though, the best conditions for reception are in clear areas with open skies).

The system depends very much on precision timing between satellites and receivers. It works loosely like DME, except that is it passive - the time it takes for a signal to travel from a satellite to your receiver is multiplied by the speed of light to obtain a distance measurement, which gives you a *Line Of Position* (LOP). One, of course, is no good by itself, and you actually need 4 LOPs to be able to determine your position in terms of latitude, longitude and altitude.

The job can actually be done with three satellites - the fourth is there to correct for timing errors.

For example, you must be somewhere on the surface of a sphere centred on Satellite A, and similarly for Satellite B.

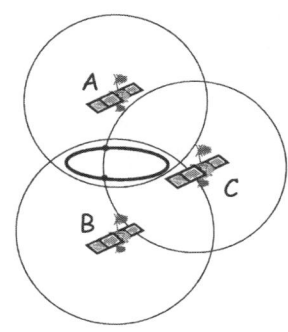

In fact, you must actually be somewhere on the circle formed where they intersect. If you then bring in Satellite C, the three spheres intersect at only

CAPT

two points, and you must logically be at one of them (there are techniques for deciding which one, using "bad mathematics" according to Garmin. Mostly the wrong one will be discarded because it places you somewhere completely wrong, like 100 miles above the Earth). Although satellites and receivers generate time-coded signals together, the satellite signals will lag behind because of their distance. If they are out by 0.6 seconds, the satellite will be 11 160 miles away. 0.7 seconds will be 13 020 miles, and so on.

The system tracks satellite positions to within about 1 m, from 20 200 km up, at 7 500 mph. Then your distances from them are calculated from the time it takes for their signals to get to the receiver. If you are off by even 1 millisecond, your position would be in error by over 300 km, so, for 1 m accuracy, time measurement must be accurate to within 3 nanoseconds. Satellites therefore use atomic clocks for high precision, and continuously transmit their positions, plus a code number in a set code, at exactly the same time. The signal is modulated with a pseudo-random code that allows the time of the transmission to be recovered by the receiver, even though the satellites are all using the same frequency.

The timing accuracy is actually down to one billionth of a second, and the pseudorandom code is repeated every millisecond. The General Theory of Relativity predicts that time runs slower with more gravity, and the atomic clocks in satellites indeed run slightly faster than they would on the surface, so corrections have to be made continually. However, even atomic clocks drift off, so they are kept in line by the Master Station.

In essence, satellites transmit a **Coarse Acquisition** (C/A) code, with a **navigation data message** encoded in it. The C/A code is the ranging code used by the receiver to measure the distance (also called *Standard Positioning Service*, or SPS). It is a 1023-bit pseudorandom number (PRN*) that is transmitted at 1.023 Mbits/second, so it is repeated every millisecond. The navigation message is transmitted at 50 bits per second, or every 30 seconds. It is superimposed on the L1 frequency in subframes.

*The PRN (pulse train) is unique to each satellite, and the *pseudorange* is called that because it is wrong by a local clock error that is caused by the receiver not being in synchronisation with GPS time - the satellite has an atomic clock, and the receiver uses a quartz one*.

*The signals from the fourth satellite required for a 3D fix are used to calibrate the receiver's clock. Time measurement consists of:

- The transit time of the signal

- The offset (time bias) between the transmitter and receiver

Normally, when two PRNs are multiplied together, they give a value of near zero. A satellite's PRN is multiplied by the L1 carrier (described below) at different time shift intervals, until it finds a lock-on, when a particular time shift results in a high multiplication value. Thus, all the other satellites are filtered out and the time-shift required for the lock-on is used to calculate the satellite's range and extract the navigation message from the C/A code.

By decoding the navigation message, the receiver gets the data it needs to correct the pseudo range. When the two code patterns match, the satellite and receiver can be synchronised, which is the first step in finding an LOP (*initial acquisition*).

The receiver in your aircraft can generate the same pseudo random code as the satellite because it has its own code book. The code sequence is started when the local clock says the satellite should have started transmitting its PRN.

The x, y, z position from the centre of the Earth is translated into latitude and longitude using the WGS 84 model, and GPS time is translated into UTC. Your velocity is calculated with a combination of your rate of change of position and Doppler shift from the L1 frequencies of different satellites, compared to the receiver's L1 oscillation frequency.

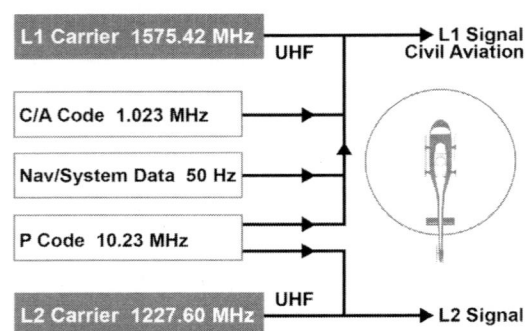

In fact, two UHF frequencies are used, L1 and L2*. The (higher) L1 frequency is 1575.42 MHz and L2 is 1227.60 MHz. Both are multiples of a base frequency of 10.23 MHz (L1 is 10.23 x 154) which is generated by a crystal controlled by an atomic clock. All satellites transmit on both frequencies, but their outputs are multiplexed so they can share the same carrier.

*L2C was added later so that the cheaper receivers could use proper signals instead of having to make do with the carrier, because they couldn't decrypt the military code.

The (digital) information is superimposed on the carriers, using BPSK modulation (*Binary Phase Key Shifting*), where the phase of the carrier wave is modulated. Being digital, the data consists of strings of 1s and 0s, which are simpler to transmit, more reliable, and less prone to jamming because error redundancy checking can be used.

The P (Precise) code is transmitted on L1 and L2. As it is 10.23 MHz, it is ten times more accurate than C/A. It can be encrypted and is therefore almost impossible to jam.

Comparing the L1 and L2 frequencies at the receiver can compensate for ionospheric propagation errors. In other words, differences between the frequencies tell you what the ionosphere is doing - radio waves slow down as they pass through it. As the delay is inversely proportional to frequency, it can be calculated and virtually eliminated.

The basic elements transmitted from a satellite are:

- clock offset from UTC
- ephemeris data (see below)
- almanac data (see below)
- ionospheric delays
- satellite health data
- satellite clock corrections

Actual satellite locations must be measured periodically. The four unmanned monitoring stations send location information to the Master Station in Colorado where a master list is maintained. As the data is needed by all users, it is periodically uplinked to individual satellites, in two parts called the *almanac* and the *ephemeris*.

Almanac data describes approximate orbital data over extended periods of time (many months). As each satellite contains almanac data for the entire constellation, a GPS receiver only needs to download it from one satellite to figure out the approximate location of them all. Almanac information is transmitted every 12.5 minutes and takes **12.5 minutes to download** (30 seconds per data frame), so it will take at least that time before accurate fixes can be determined. This data becomes stale over time or if you move the receiver to another location more than several hundred kilometers away (the initial setup is known as a *cold start*). **Ephemeris information** (stored in the receiver as an almanac) contains precise location information of individual satellites and the parameters needed to predict their positions for the near future. Unlike almanac data, each satellite transmits only its own ephemeris data, so the receiver must gather it from each one in view. Ephemeris data is transmitted every 30 seconds, and takes 12 seconds to download. It is considered valid for up to 4-6 hours.

Note: Receivers calculate the elevation and azimuth data of a satellite relative to the antenna from the Almanac data transmitted by the satellites. Almanac data in the receiver is for fast identification of signals from visible satellites.

SIGNAL AUGMENTATION
AIRCRAFT BASED

Although the ground stations monitor satellites and detect faults, it can take up to two hours for an error to be corrected. **Receiver Autonomous Integrity Monitoring** (RAIM) is a bit quicker than that. It is achieved within the receiver which monitors satellites and verifies their signals, so an extra satellite is needed to detect corrupt information. For the bad signal to be isolated as well, you need one more. Without RAIM, accuracy is not assured*, and you still need 4 satellites for a 3D fix. Thus, RAIM needs 5 satellites in order to work, and 6 to continue working after a failure is detected. FDE (*Fault Detection & Exclusion*) can tell which satellite is faulty and exclude it from the calculations. For it to work, you need at least six satellites with good positioning.

Note: RAIM is the equivalent of an OFF flag. It does not improve position accuracy.

*If RAIM is available, the integrity limits are 4 nm for oceanic, 2 nm for enroute, 1 nm for terminal work and 0.3 nm for GPS approaches. If RAIM is not available, the GPS must be integrated with other systems, such as DME/DME fixing, with traditional equipment (VOR, etc.) as backup. If the GPS is the only equipment meeting the B-RNAV standards, RAIM availability must be confirmed before flight.

RAIM can be assisted with *baroaiding* (barometric aiding), which uses barometric information from the aircraft's altitude encoder in order to use the Earth's surface as a satellite, so you can reduce the number of real satellites required by one. Barometric altitude is the datum for altitude information such as MDA.

SATELLITE BASED

Here, ground-based reference stations monitor satellite signals and relay data to master stations, which assess signal validity and compute error corrections, using a datalink on GPS frequencies. An example is EGNOS, described below. SBAS regionally augments GPS and GLONASS by making them suitable for safety critical applications such as landing aircraft.

The FAA's **Wide Area Augmentation System** (WAAS) allows GPS to be used throughout a flight, including a Cat I precision approach (LPV, or *Localiser Performance with Vertical Guidance*). Satellite signals are received by precisely surveyed ground stations, which detect errors and send them to a Master Station (WMS), which in turn adds correction information based on geographical area (which is fairly constant) and uplinks a correction message to **geostationary satellites** (around the Equator and way above the other satellites) for rebroadcast. This improves the 95% signal accuracy from 100m to 7m, but it can be better than 2 m. The term LPV stands for Lateral Precision Vertical guidance, with lateral accuracy as good

as ILS, with vertical capability. Unlike BARO VNAV, SBAS vertical guidance is not subject to altimeter setting errors, or non-standard temperatures or lapse rates.

When SBAS integrity messages are used, the additional satellites that would be required for RAIM are not needed, because the messages are available wherever the satellite signal can be received. WAAS currently uses two satellites over the Atlantic and Pacific Oceans.

EGNOS, or the *European Geostationary Navigation Overlay Service* is the European equivalent to WAAS. It has three geostationary INMARSAT satellites broadcasting GPS look-alike signals, so the coverage is limited to between 80N and 80S. It is designed to improve accuracy to 1-2 m horizontally and **3-5 m vertically**. Integrity and safety are improved by alerting users within 6 seconds of a malfunction, as opposed to the normal 3 hours.

GROUND BASED

Ground Based Augmentation Systems have corrections sent directly to aircraft receivers (on a VOR frequency) from ground stations at airports, typically within about 20-30 nm. There is a monitoring function in the ground station to assure the integrity of the broadcast. GBAS + GPS is also called *Local Area Augmentation System* (LAAS).

Differential GPS was a workaround (by the US Coastguard) for the intentional errors that were introduced in the C/A code for unauthorised users of the GPS system. It uses a fifth signal from a precisely surveyed ground based transmitter whose position can be compared against that of the receiver. The difference is the intentional error. The nearer the receiver is to a DGPS ground station, the more accurate is the fix. Note that SBAS and GBAS include integrity monitoring and allow approached to be performed.

ERRORS

The effects of the errors below are smallest when the satellites are directly overhead and greatest when they are near the horizon, as the signal is affected for a longer time. Having said that, the most accurate fix comes from 3 satellites with a low elevation above the horizon, 120° from each other and a fourth directly overhead.

- **Clock Bias**. As the receiver's clock is not as precise as the atomic clocks in the satellites, there can be a considerable difference in the measurements, which can introduce a ranging error. When a receiver starts up, its own code will be inaccurate by an unknown error called clock bias, or clock offset, against GPS reference time. The receiver corrects by running a series of simultaneous equations. It must be aware of the satellite's position, which is where the ephemeris comes in. In addition, the size of the atomic clocks in satellites are necessarily smaller than ground-

based ones would be, so there will be some inaccuracies compared with Master system time. Signals are monitored by control segment ground stations and the corrections sent to the Master station, which makes the necessary corrections then relays them to the satellites.

- Satellite **clock drift**. Although the orbital paths of GPS satellites could theoretically be predicted under Kepler's laws of planetary motion, the assumption that the Earth is a perfect sphere of uniform density is not correct, and gravity from other heavenly bodies (e.g. the Moon and the Sun) have their own effects on top of Earth gravity. There is also very slight atmospheric drag, because satellites are not travelling in a perfect vacuum, plus the impact of photons of light emitted by the sun both directly and reflected off the Earth and Moon. This solar radiation pressure is a function of a satellite's size and orientation, distance from the sun, etc., but the end result is that satellites headed towards the Sun are slowed down, and accelerated when headed away. This *clock drift* is virtually impossible to estimate accurately, and is the largest unmeasurable source of error.

- **Ephemeris** (position) **error**. *Ephemeris* is the ability to determine the location of a celestial body (i. e. a satellite) at regular intervals, so this error is caused by the satellite not being where the receiver thinks it is. In other words, there are errors in the satellite's calculation of its own position caused by gravitational effects of the sun, moon and other planets. Ground monitoring stations check satellite positions every 12 hours, so the maximum error is 2.5 metres. The computers at the master control station can predict the satellite's future position at a specific time, which is compared with its actual position from the monitor stations. Updated information on future positions is then uploaded.

- **Ionospheric Propagation**. The ionosphere's effect on radio waves is proportional to their frequency. By noting the time delay between the L1 and L2 signals, much of the effect caused by atmospheric propagation can be removed internally by the receiver. This is proportional to the inverse of the carrier frequency, squared. As the ionosphere changes, the corrections are imperfect (although they are slow and can be averaged over time). The model of the ionosphere is corrected by the ground stations every 12 hours, so the maximum position error is 5 metres.

- **Receiver noise**. Internal noise within receiver circuits can causes position errors of up to 0.3 m.

- **Signal noise**. Similar to Receiver noise.

CAPT

- **Tropospheric**. Water vapour in the atmosphere affects refraction. The maximum error from tropospheric propagation is between 0.3 - 0.5 m.

- **Multi-path reflection.** Antennae should be fitted on the upper fuselage near the Centre of Gravity, as shadowing by parts of an aircraft (like a wing) may stop signals from being received or cause them to come from different directions. Some frequencies, such as 109.5 MHz, have been known to cause the GPS not to work if the antenna is not sited properly. The maximum position error caused by these effects is 0.6 m.

- **C/A Selective Availability**. Now discontinued, but it used to be done by dithering satellite clocks.

- **Manoeuvring Errors**. Caused by aircraft attitudes and similar to Multi-path reflection.

- **GDOP/PDOP.** When satellites are too close to each other, vertical and horizontal position accuracy is degraded, because the lines of constant range do not cut cleanly (the optimum is 60°) resulting in *Geometric (Position) Dilution of Precision*, where you end up anywhere inside a range of positions rather than just one. ICAO requires a PDOP/GDOP of less than 6 for en-route navigation, and 3 or less for non-precision approaches (4 is considered to be good). The normal accuracy of 100 m for 95% of the time assumes a PDOP of 3 and a range error of 33.3 m (range errors are multiplied by PDOP to obtain stated accuracies).

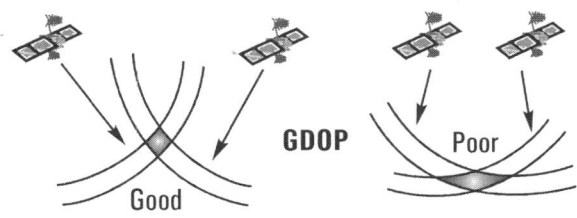

OPERATION

Although it is tempting to use GPS all the time, remember that it is electrical, and therefore reserves the right to go offline at any moment, without warning. The antenna in a GPS is live as well, and equally liable to stop working. A GPS may also have a database of airspace and frequencies inside - although not so important for VFR use, it is still the mark of a professional to keep it up to date.

For GPS approaches, you use a CDI in the same way as you would for an ILS, except that the needle deflection is measured in terms of distance rather than degrees off course. This means that the instrument's sensitivity is fixed all the way down through the approach, and is not so sensitive in the final stages.

However, the sensitivity does vary according to the age of your receiver. For a non-WAAS capable one, you have three levels. In *en-route mode* (more than 30 miles from the destination or departure point), one dot is equal to 1 nautical mile. Inside those figures, it reduces to *terminal mode*, which is one fifth, so *full deflection* is now 1 nm. In *approach mode* (within 2 nm of the FAF), full deflection is 0.3 nm left or right of the centreline. At the MAP, the sensitivity returns to the terminal level.

WAAS capable receivers have a CDI sensitivity of only 2 nm in en route mode. The terminal level remains the same, but approach mode reduces to the *lesser* of 0.2 nm or 2°. The sensitivity of an LPV approach is 350 either side of the centreline at the threshold, or 70 feet per dot!

VDF

The purpose of *VHF Direction Finding* is to provide directional assistance in times of difficulty, rather than for general navigation, so a typical frequency it might be used on is 121.5 MHz. One or more ATC stations can

get a bearing for you to steer (QDM) to get to their location from your transmissions, so *the minimum equipment is a VHF radio*. On its own, a direction-finding station can only find your position in relation to itself - to get an exact position, you need two or even three more, who will all report to a Master Station. On top of that, *you must work out the headings required from the information given*.

The full range of services available could include:

- Emergency Cloudbreak
- Emergency No-compass Homing
- Homing
- Fix
- Track-out Assistance
- Time & Distance Estimates

However, the ICAO recommended practice recognizes only homing, with no compensation for wind drift, which is actually the only element that most pilots are aware of, receive training on, or use.

Being based on VHF, VDF is subject to the usual limitations (line of sight, multipath, etc.), so the higher you are, the better the results you will get. You must transmit for a few seconds for a bright line to spread from the centre of a screen to the outside which is marked with compass bearings. The following services are available, assuming no wind:

- **QDM** - magnetic bearing *to* (i.e to be steered, with no wind)

- **QDR** - magnetic bearing *from*

- **QUJ** - true bearing *to*, with no wind)

- **QTE** - true bearing *from*

When a position is given in relation to another point, or in lat & long, it is a **QTF**. When positions are given by heading or bearing & distance from a known point that is not the station making the report, the known point shall be from the centre of an aerodrome, a prominent town or geographic feature, in that order.

Older equipment uses a cathode ray tube on which the line appears (like a radar sweep) pointing to where your transmission is coming from. More modern digital equipment uses a circle of LEDs at 10° intervals, which will show the same information, with a digital readout in the centre. The controller can store the last transmission, if busy with something else at the time.

Accuracy comes in these classes, in relation to bearing or position, and will be included in the transmission:

Class	Bearing	Position
A	±2°	5 nm
B	±5°	20 nm
C	±10°	50 nm
D	<C	<C

Radar

The use of radar improves aircraft spacing and safety - the word stands for *Radio Direction and Ranging*, but the system was called RDF (*Radio Direction Finding*) until 1943, when the name was changed to harmonise with the Americans (in those days it just about got the distance right). It works on the basis that microwave pulses can be reflected (or echoed) off suitable objects, and the time between transmission and reflection can be used to calculate the distance (the reflection of signals is called scattering - reflections in the exact opposite direction are called *backscatter*). The "blips" representing the objects are displayed on a Cathode Ray Tube and a controller can see the relative positions of aircraft reflecting any pulses.

The radar beam is rather like that from a lighthouse, as the antenna focusses the pulses in one direction with the most energy concentrated in the centre. VHF does not provide the bandwidth required for the short pulses that allow good target definition, so SHF bands are currently used. Thus, radar is limited to line of sight.

The word *pulses*, mentioned above, means that short bursts of electromagnetic energy are mixed with relatively long periods of silence (*relatively long*, in electronic terms, means less than a thousandth of a second). *Continuous Wave radar* is used in radio altimeters and the Doppler system.

Pulses were used originally because early radar sets used thermionic valves as opposed to the transistors of today.

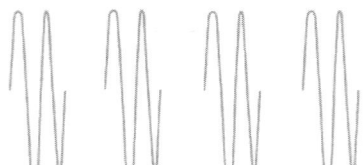

The range of a target is determined by measuring the time taken for a pulse of energy to travel there and back. This is known as *primary radar*, and it has a few limitations. Although technology has improved matters, radar is still quite a crude instrument which requires an understanding of how it works in order to understand its information correctly, especially when you consider the speed of the waves against the ranges involved. Very short intervals of time in the order of millionths of a second have to be measured with accuracy for the best results.

The VHF portion of the electromagnetic spectrum does not allow the bandwidth required for the short pulses that allow good target definition, so SHF bands are currently used. Thus, radar is limited to line of sight.

Secondary Surveillance Radar

This is a development of a system introduced during the Second World War called *Identification Friend or Foe* (IFF), which was supposed to distinguish between friendly and enemy aircraft (friendly aircraft had a small transmitter that gave a distinctive periodic elongation to the blip on the screen, so anything with a primary blip was an enemy). It was codenamed Parrot (or Canary) by the British, which probably has something to do with the current use of the word *Squawk* to mean *transmit the relevant codes*, which you dial up on the transponder and which will appear next to your blip with your height readout, depending on the type of transponder you have.

SSR improves on primary radar by using double-pulse secondary equipment to provide more information, hence the name. Participating aircraft carry a *transponder* (for *transmitter/responder*) that receives the interrogation pulse from the transmitter (1030 MHz ±0.2 Mhz), superimposes information on it and sends it right back on another paired frequency (1090 MHz). This means, first of all, that the range of operation can be doubled immediately, and, secondly, that the blip on the screen can be made much smaller, together with information that makes it more easily identifiable to ATC, because the pulses can be coded. As well, there is no storm clutter, as the principle of echo return is not used. Computer trickery can provide predicted tracks and collision warnings, amongst other things.

The following can be presented on the radar screen:

CAPT

- Pressure Altitude

- Flight Level

- Flight Number or Registration

- Groundspeed

There are standard numbers to squawk, when not otherwise instructed, which are:

- 2000 - from non-SSR area

- 7000 - conspicuity code

In emergency, squawk:

- 7500 - Hijack*

- 7600 - Comms failure

- 7700 - Emergency

You cannot set the number 8! Watch for this in questions that ask you to choose between valid codes

Note: When making routine code changes, you should avoid inadvertent selection of 7500, 7600 or 7700. For example, when switching from 2700 to 7200, switch first to 2200 then to 7200, not to 7700 and then 7200. This applies to 7500 and all discrete codes in the 7600 and 7700 series (i.e. 7600-7677, 7700-7777) which will trigger special indicators in automated facilities.

You will be given details of other traffic according to the clock system, such as "fast mover at 6 o'clock", based on the track seen on the radar. When fitted, *transponders should be used at all times*. When changing squawks as instructed, take care not to dial up the emergency ones by mistake, and *do not switch the transponder to standby* during the change to avoid it, as senior pilots often do, because this will

remove your display from ATC's screen and cause all sorts of alarms to happen.

Modes are used to ask questions, such as "Who are you?" (Mode A) or "How high are you?" (Mode C). The answer comes in the form of a code from the aircraft, of which there are **4096**.

MODE A/B

Mode A is the regular variety, based on the original IFF, which just displays the code you select in the aircraft - you get this just by turning the switch to ON. In other words, it is for basic identification (Mode B is occasionally used in place of Mode A in some countries).

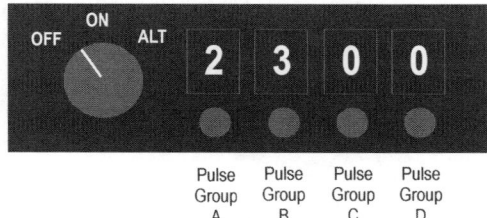

MODE C

This will transmit altitude information alternately with the code information - a Mode C transponder is directly attached to an encoding altimeter (or, more precisely, an altitude digitiser, which selects a different code to that selected in the window), but only Pressure Altitude (or FL) information based on 1013.25 (or 29.92) information is sent from the aircraft (in 100-foot increments) - the conversion to local pressure, if required, is done inside the ATC computer. ATC will not be able to see changes when you move the altimeter subscale. Mode C is selected by

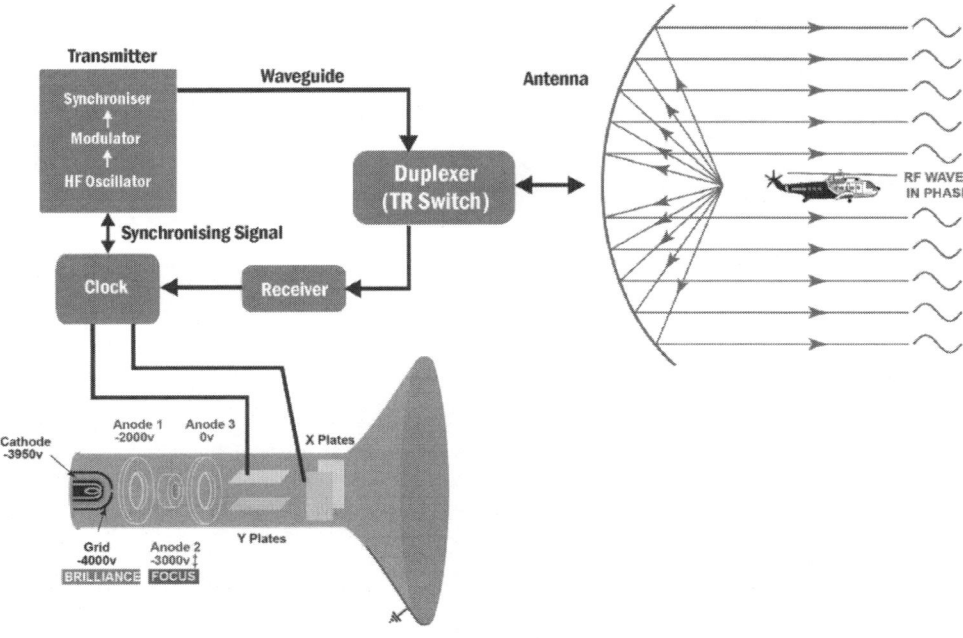

switching to ALT, after switching on for Mode A. The pulses are 21 microseconds apart. You should always use Mode C unless directed otherwise.

hold them and are qualified, having provided suitable evidence. They are not valid without the signature of the holder in ink.

A JAR licence is considered valid for ANO purposes. A non-JAR foreign licence does not allow you to be paid for public transport or aerial work, fly IFR, or give instruction. A JAR licence may be transferred to another state if you are employed there or have established normal residence, which means you live there for at least 185 days in the year, with enough personal or occupational ties to confirm it.

JAR licences are valid for up to 5 years.

You can't hold a licence just by itself - there must be some sort of type rating on it. Licences must bear a valid certificate of revalidation for the rating under Section 2 of Part C of Schedule 8.

If you fail a test required for articles 23, 24, or 25, you cannot use the privileges of the relevant rating, even if there is time left on the original.

Recency

To carry passengers, you must do least 3 take-offs and landings (with circuits) in a helicopter of the same type or class, or approved simulator, in the previous 90 days. Without an IR, one of those landings must have been at night, if you want to fly at night. Helicopter pilots must do at least 2 hours on each type each year.

Recording of Flight Times

Normally, flight time to be credited towards a licence must be flown in the same category of aircraft as the licence (or rating) sought. All solo, dual or PIC flight counts in full towards a higher licence. 50% of P2 (co-pilot) time is counted, but JAR FCL counts it in full on machines which require more than one pilot (must be countersigned by the PIC). SPIC time must be countersigned by the instructor. Instructors and examiners may log instructional and examining time as PIC. *Flight time* is the total time from when an aircraft first moves under its own power with the intention of taking off until it comes to rest after the flight, so it includes taxi time (for helicopters, the flight time stops when the rotors do). This is what goes in your log book and on customer invoices. *Air time*, on the other hand, is between wheels or skids off and when they touch the Earth again. This is what goes in the Tech Log.

A number of flights on the same day, returning to the same departure point, with intervals between flights of less than 30 minutes may be counted as one flight. otherwise, they must be listed separately.

Ratings

A *rating* is an entry in a licence stating special conditions, privileges or limitations pertaining to it. Although all the nonsense concerning the *issue* of your licence must have been done in one JAA state, you can obtain a rating in any JAA state.

CLASS RATINGS

Class Ratings cover *groups* of aircraft, such as single-engined, multi-engined, land, water, etc. They mostly apply to aeroplanes, where your licence can be issued, for example, for *single-pilot, single-engined aeroplanes*. Such ratings are valid for two years.

TYPE RATINGS

Type ratings apply to any aircraft needing 2 pilots, and *any considered necessary*. To obtain one, you must pass a *skill test*.

Your licence will be issued with one type on it. Subsequent type ratings will theoretically need 5 hours each, but JAR FCL allows this to be reduced to 3 hours by the training organisations, if it considers you to have enough time on a similar enough type, *and* if this discretion is in their training manual. A first turbine type will need 5 hours.

Type ratings and multi-engined class ratings are valid for 1 year *from the date of issue*.

NIGHT QUALIFICATION

For aeroplanes, you need 5 hours overall night training (3 dual, and 1 hour dual navigation) and 5 takeoffs and landings as PIC at night. The course is 5 hours ground instruction and 10 hours by sole reference to instruments, on top of any beforehand, plus 5 at night (3 dual and 5 solo circuits), all inside 6 months.

INSTRUMENT RATING

An instrument rating is required for flight in controlled airspace. You must hold at least a PPL with night rating, or a CPL, and a radio licence. You also need 50 hours cross country, with 10 in the appropriate class. For multi-engined machines, you must have 55 hours instruction, 10 of which must be in multi-engined machines. 20 or 30 may be done in FNPT 1 and FNPT 2 simulators, respectively.

The IR is valid for 12 months. The helicopter ground test is valid for 36 months from the date of final pass.

Without an Instrument or Night Rating, you may only fly at night under the instruction of an authorised flight instructor, and no passengers may be carried.

Student Pilot

You must be over 16 to be a student pilot, and you must hold at least a Class 1 or Class 2 medical certificate before flying solo - and you can only fly solo when authorised by a flying instructor.

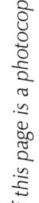

Private Pilot Licence

You must be over 17 to hold a PPL, although you can act as PIC from 16 years of age, under an instructor, in UK airspace. Dual instruction before 14 does not count. There is no maximum validity for UK PPLs.

PRIVILEGES

You can fly as PIC or P2 of a helicopter or gyroplane of any type within a rating in the licence, but not for public transport or aerial work, except instructing, if you are an instructor, or testing, which must be in a machine owned, or operated under a flying club where you and the victim (sorry, student) are members. Towing gliders and dropping parachutists may also be done. No pay may be received, except by instructors in microlights or self-launching motor gliders, under the conditions above.

Note: Some flights can remain as private flights if the costs are shared equally by the up to 4 occupants, including the pilot. A child of any age is a person.

Note: To exercise your privileges, your licence must contain a valid medical certificate and **Certificate of Experience**, if you have flown enough hours in the past 13 months, or a **Certificate of Test** if you haven't. Both are valid for 13 months from the date of signature.

Unless you have an IR or IMC rating, you may not be PIC outside controlled airspace when the vis is below 3 km, under Special VFR in a control zone below 10 km, except on an approved route, or out of sight of the surface. You may not be PIC or P2 IFR in Class D or E airspace, and you need an IR for PIC in IFR in Class A, B or C airspace.

A night rating or qualification is required to be PIC at night.

MEDICAL

You need either a Class 1 or 2 medical certificate, *which is only valid if you meet the initial issuing requirements.* You should inform the authorities in writing of any injury involving your capacity to act as flight crew, or illness that lasts for more than 20 days (on the 21st day), or pregnancy.

RECENCY

You must maintain competency under JAR-FCL 3.025 p1-A-5. To carry passengers, you must do, in the previous 90 days, 3 takeoffs and landings (included in 3 circuits for helicopters) as sole manipulator in the same type or class. With no IR, at least 1 takeoff and landing must be at night. For gyroplanes, you need at least 5 take offs and landings when the centre of the sun was at least 12° below the horizon in the last 13 months, or 5 5-minute flights in free balloons, for balloons.

Helicopter pilots must do at least 2 hours on each type each year, plus a proficiency check (AIC 68/1995 (Pink 114) refers).

EXPERIENCE

At least 45 hours, to include 25 hours dual and 10 hours supervised solo (in the State that is going to issue the licence), with at least 5 hours solo cross country with a flight of at least 270 km (150 nm) having two full stop landings at different airfields. For helicopters, the 25 hours dual must include 5 hours' instruments, and the cross-country flight must be at least 185 km (100 nm).

Flight Radio Telephony Operator Licence

You must be at least 16, although, in theory, you can operate a radio under the supervision of an FI below that. The maximum validity is 10 years, if standalone, otherwise use the validity of an associated licence. It is normally issued for VHF only, unless you pass a separate HF exam, or hold a CPL/ATPL (H), where you have passed the radio nav exams and are exempt. An exemption is also in place to operate without an FRTO licence for aircrew under training.

PRIVILEGES

You can use the radios in any aircraft with automatic frequency control, using external switching devices.

Foreign Licences

Licences from Contracting States (i.e. ICAO) are valid for private purposes on G-registered aircraft automatically, as long as the original licence remains valid and the pilot does not get paid, except for instrument or instructor ratings.

Otherwise, the CAA can validate foreign non-JAR licences at any time, including those under the law of an EEA state (see also Annex 1 to the Chicago Convention). Such licences must be based on equivalent licences under the ANO22. The Commission must be asked for an opinion on licence equivalency within three weeks of receipt by the CAA of all necessary information, or inform you of extra requirements within three months, if it doesn't actually grant the validation.

However, it must, within three months of receipt of the necessary information for the application, either issue the certificate of validation or inform you of any additional requirements or tests.

Night Rating

This allows a PPL or BCPL holder to be PIC at night. There is a special one for gyroplane PPLs.

Without one, your flights must be completed 30 minutes after sunset, unless you are under the instruction of an authorised flight instructor, and no passengers are carried.

CAPT

Flight Instructor

You may not instruct any one learning to fly for a licence or rating unless you are qualified as PIC on the aircraft concerned, and have an instructor rating.

Initially, the licence is restricted until you have done at least 100 hours flight instruction and supervised at least 25 solo flights, and have been recommended. That is, you can do (under supervision) instruction for PPLs, excluding approval of first solo flights and cross country flights, and night flying instruction.

You can do up to 5 hours in an approved simulator.

Medicals

Flight Crew Licences, other than radio licences, are *not valid without a medical certificate*, which is renewed from time to time, as described in JAR FCL 3 and below. *Currency begins on the date the medical assessment is issued.*

You may not act as flight crew if you know or suspect that your physical or mental condition renders you unfit to do so. In other words, you may not exercise licence privileges once you are aware of a decrease in your medical fitness that makes you unable to exercise them safely. *Medicals are only valid if you meet the initial issuing requirements.* A Board of Inquiry or insurance company may interpret the words "medically fit" a little differently than you think if you fly with a cold or under the influence of alcohol or drugs. In any case, you should talk to a medical examiner as soon as possible in the case of:

- admission to a hospital or clinic for over 12 hours
- surgery or other invasive procedures
- regular use of medication
- regular use of correcting lenses

In addition, you should inform the authorities in writing of significant personal injuries involving your capacity to act as a member of a flight crew, or illness that lasts for more than 21 days (after the 21st day), or pregnancy. In these cases, your medical is suspended, but it can be reinstated after an examination, or if you are exempt from one. It can be given back directly after pregnancy.

JAR medicals are only issued for professional and private pilot licences for aeroplanes and helicopters. Flight Engineers have different arrangements.

Class 1

Although intended for professional licences, a PPL holder may hold one at any time. The initial issue must be done at the CAA Medical Centre at Gatport Airwick.

Class 2

Required for the PPL. The initial issue can be done by any aviation medical examiner. If your national licence does not meet Class 2 standards, you can still exercise the privileges of that licence.

Personal Logs

These must be maintained by every member of the Flight Crew of a UK registered aircraft and, regardless of registration, those qualifying for licence purposes. They may be computerised for commercial flights.

Aside from your name and address, log books should also have the date of the flight, name of PIC, type of aircraft, registration, crew position, places and times of departure and arrival, flight times, operational conditions, such as night or IFR, and details of any tests taken.

Flight time is the total time from when an aircraft first moves under its own power with the intention of taking off until it comes to rest after the flight, so it includes taxi time (for helicopters, the flight time stops when the rotors do). This is what goes in your log book. Air time, on the other hand, is between wheels or skids off and when they touch the Earth again. This is what goes in the Tech Log.

A logbook is your personal and private property, not having been issued to you under the ANO.

If you lose it, you will need to provide a Sworn Affidavit that details your flying hours to the best of your knowledge, if you intend to rely on them to get further licences and ratings.

Flight time records must be produced without undue delay upon a request from an Authorised Person. Student pilots must carry them on solo cross-country flights because they contain records of instructor authorisations.

RULES OF THE AIR (ANNEX 2)

Aircraft bearing the nationality and registration marks of a Contracting (ICAO) State must obey these Rules of The Air (Annex 2), wherever they may be, but local state rules take precedence. However, over the high seas, the Rules apply without exception, except where a State has supplied "an appropriate ATS authority", in which case the ICAO rules become subordinate to it.

Compliance & Authority

In flight or on aerodromes, you must comply with:

- The *General Rules*

plus, when in flight:

- The *Visual Flight Rules* (VFR), or
- The *Instrument Flight Rules* (IFR)

according to the flight conditions. It is the responsibility of the PIC to comply with them, whether at the controls or not, but the Rules may be departed from *when absolutely necessary* in the interests of safety. Before starting a flight, the PIC must become familiar with *all appropriate*

information. This should include (when not near an aerodrome, and when IFR), current weather reports and forecasts, allowing for fuel requirements and alternative courses of action.

The PIC has final authority as to the disposition of an aircraft *while in command* - for aeroplanes, this is between when the doors are first closed and opened again at the end of a flight. There seems to be no equivalent definition for helicopters.

Intoxicating Liquor, Narcotics or Drugs

You may not act as pilot or flight crew while under the influence of intoxicating liquor, or any narcotic or drug, by which your capacity to act as such is impaired.

PSYCHOACTIVE SUBSTANCES

People whose functions are critical to safety (e.g. safety-sensitive personnel) must not act as such while under the influence of psychoactive substances that impair human performance.

Trivia: Coffee and tobacco are excluded from the Annex 1 definition of psychoactive substances, but Coca Cola, Pepsi, Tea, and others containing caffeine, are not.

Protection Of Persons & Property

NEGLIGENT OR RECKLESS OPERATION

Aircraft shall not be operated in a reckless or negligent manner that may endanger life or the property of others.

MINIMUM HEIGHTS

You may not fly over any congested area of a city, town or settlement, or over open-air assemblies of people, below a height that allows you to safely make an emergency landing (that is, without undue hazard to persons or property on the surface), except when taking off or landing, or with permission. IFR and VFR restrictions have their own headings, below.

LOW FLYING - RULE 5

The UK Rule 5 is in two parts - the prohibitions, then the exemptions, although here, they are combined. If you are affected by more than one prohibition, you must fly at the greatest height allowed by them all. The prohibitions do not apply to captive balloons or kites, or aircraft taking off or landing, practising approaches or checking navaids at Government or licensed aerodromes, all in accordance with normal aviation practice.

You must have permission in writing from the CAA for variations.

Failure of Power Unit

You must be able, if an engine fails, to make an emergency landing without causing danger to people or property on the surface.

500 Foot Rule

You may not fly closer than 500 feet to any person, vessel, vehicle or structure, unless you are:

- operating under a police AOC
- landing or taking off under normal aviation practice
- hill soaring with a glider
- working under an aerial application certificate (Article 58)
- flying under Article 56(3)(f) (dropping of articles for public health)
- manoeuvring a helicopter inside a Government or licensed aerodrome (or at other sites with permission), under normal aviation practice, not closer than 60 metres to any person, vessel, vehicle or structure outside
- at a flying display, air ace or contest, within 1000 m horizontally of people witnessing the event
- picking up or dropping tow ropes, banners or similar articles at an aerodrome

1000 Foot Rule

Over any congested area of a city, town or settlement, you must be at least 1000 feet above the highest fixed object within 600 metres horizontally, unless you are working under a police AOC, landing a balloon because it is becalmed, or in a CTZ under a Special VFR clearance issued by ATC or on a notified route (such as the London helicopter lanes), in which case you can only land at licensed or Government aerodromes, unless you have CAA permission.

Land Clear Rule

Except in a helicopter, you must be able to land clear when flying over any congested area of a city, town or settlement, if an engine fails. This still applies to police aeroplanes.

OPEN AIR ASSEMBLIES
FLYING OVER

Unless you are a police aircraft, you may not fly over an open air assembly of more than 1000 people below 1000 feet or a height that allows you to land clear if an engine fails, whichever is higher.

LANDING AND TAKING OFF NEAR

Unless you are a police aircraft, you may only take off or land within 1000 metres of an organised open air assembly of more than 1000 people under procedures notified by the CAA, which are: You can only land and take off with

permission of the whoever is in charge of the **aerodrome**, who must ensure that aircraft and members of the public are separated when on the ground. You may not fly overhead below 1000 feet AGL or a height that allows you to land clear if an engine fails, whichever is higher.

If the assembly is not at an aerodrome (a **temporary helicopter landing site**), you need written permission from the organiser beforehand. The organiser should provide written details of the site and procedures, and the local police should be told at least 24 hours in advance. Aircraft and members of the public are separated when on the ground. In addition, landing and taking off may only take place in daylight, with a cloudbase above 600 feet AGL and 3 km flight visibility, in an area set aside for the purpose, at least 30 m away from people outside. Helicopters may not fly overhead below 1000 feet AGL or a height that allows it to land clear if an engine fails, whichever is higher. Approach and departure must be over clear areas, for a safe forced landing if an engine fails.

At a **temporary aerodrome**, follow CAP 428. In addition, written permission from the organiser is required beforehand, and written details shall be provided.

Aircraft Restrictions

DROPPING OR SPRAYING
This must be done under conditions prescribed by the appropriate authorities and clearances supplied by the relevant ATC.

TOWING
This must be done under conditions prescribed by the appropriate authorities and clearances supplied by the relevant ATC.

PARACHUTE DESCENTS
Aside from emergency descents, these must be done under conditions prescribed by the appropriate authorities and clearances supplied by the relevant ATC.

ACROBATIC FLIGHT
This must be done under conditions prescribed by the appropriate authorities and clearances supplied by the relevant ATC.

Formation Flight
This must be done by *pre-arrangement with the PICs concerned*. In controlled airspace, it must also be done under conditions prescribed by ATC, which shall include:

- operating as a single aircraft for navigation and position reporting

- separation between aircraft is the responsibility of the flight leader and the PICs, including when they are joining up and breaking away

- aircraft must be at least 1 km horizontally and 30 m vertically from the flight leader

Unmanned Free Balloons
Their operation must minimise hazards to persons, property or other aircraft, under conditions in Annex 4.

Prohibited, Restricted and Danger Areas
Identification includes the nationality letters (such as EG for UK) of the State which has established the airspace, plus the letters *P, R* or *D* for *Prohibited*, *Restricted* or *Danger*, area, respectively, followed by a number. Numbers must not be re-used for at least a year after the area concerned is cancelled. Aircraft must not fly in any such areas that have had their particulars published, except under conditions applied by or with permission of the relevant State (over whose territory the areas are established).

Avoidance Of Collisions (ANO Rule 17)
There are rules about how aircraft should be flown around other traffic, e.g. *not in such proximity to other aircraft as to create a collision hazard*. Even when you have right of way, you must take any necessary action to avoid collision (in other words, even with clearance, commanders are responsible for not hitting other machines). Another aircraft with an emergency gains priority over you. If you must give way, you must not pass over or under, or cross ahead of, the other aircraft unless you are far enough away not to create a risk of collision, taking due note of wake turbulence. Aircraft with right of way should maintain course and speed.

A glider and whatever is towing it are *one aircraft* under the towing PIC.

APPROACHING HEAD-ON
If there is a danger of collision, each must alter course to the right.

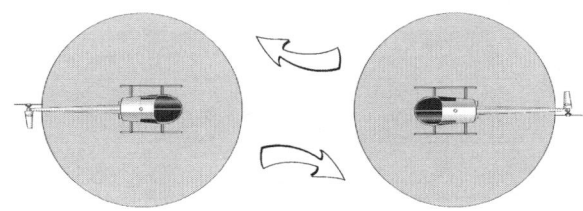

OVERTAKING

You are overtaking when you are approaching another aircraft from behind *at less than 70° from the longitudinal axis*, which means that, at night, you should not be able to see its port or starboard navigation lights. Aircraft being overtaken have right of way, and the overtaking aircraft, whether climbing, descending or in level flight, must keep out of the way by altering course to the right (*well clear* on the ground) until well past and clear, even if their relative positions change. Gliders in UK may go right or left.

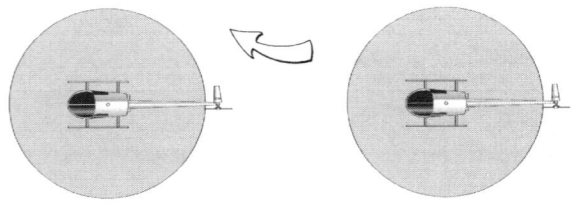

CONVERGENCE

If a steady relative bearing is kept between two aircraft at the same altitude, they will eventually collide. When two aircraft are converging in this way, the one coming from the right has the right-of-way, except that:

- power-driven, heavier-than-air aircraft (flying machines) give way to airships, gliders and balloons

- airships give way to gliders and balloons

- gliders give way to balloons

- power-driven aircraft give way to aircraft that are towing or carrying loads

When two balloons converge at different altitudes, the higher one must give way.

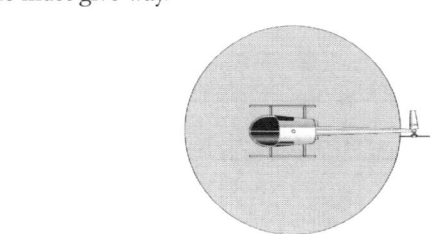

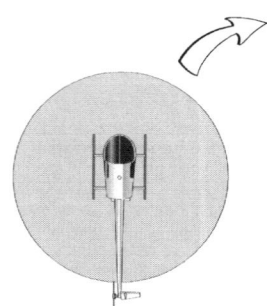

LANDING

Except where ATC dictate otherwise, or in emergency, aircraft landing or on finals have right of way over others in flight or on the ground or water. Where several are involved in landing, *the lowest has right of way,* as long as it does not cut in front of another on finals, or overtake it. However, power driven heavier-than-air aircraft must give way to gliders. *An aircraft whose pilot is aware that another is compelled to land shall give way to it.*

TAKING OFF

Aircraft taxying on the manoeuvring area must give way to those taking off or about to take off.

SURFACE MOVEMENT

If there is a danger of collision between two aircraft taxying on a manoeuvring area:

- when approaching head on, or approximately so, each shall stop or, where practicable, alter course to the right to keep well clear

- when converging, the one with the other on its right shall give way

- aircraft being overtaken shall have right of way, and overtaking aircraft shall keep well clear

Aircraft taxying on manoeuvring areas must stop and hold at all runway holding positions unless authorised by the Tower. They must also stop and hold at all lighted stop bars, and may proceed further when the lights are switched off.

Emergency vehicles must be given priority over aircraft landing and taking off.

Position markings and signs are covered in Annex 14.

Lights & Signals (ANO Rule 8)

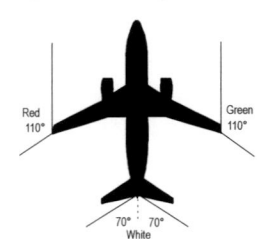

If more than one light is needed to comply with the Rules of the Air, only one should be visible at a time. Where a light must show through specified angles horizontally, the light should be visible from 90° above and below. Lights showing in all directions must be visible horizontally and vertically. You may switch off or reduce the intensity of flashing lights if they *adversely affect the performance of your duties,* or *subject outside observers to harmful dazzle.*

Anti-collision lights are intended to attract attention to your aircraft, and navigation lights are intended to show your relative path to an observer. Navigation lights are set up so that only one can be seen by another aircraft at any time. Anticollision lights are seen from all directions.

CAPT

Other lights may be displayed if they cannot be mistaken for them.

Between sunset and sunrise, you must show anti-collision and navigation lights. On the manoeuvring area, in addition, aircraft must display lights that show extremities of the structure (unless it is stationary and otherwise lit up adequately), and engine running lights (a red one must be displayed when the engine is running in any case).

Simulated Instrument Flight

Fully functioning dual controls must be installed and a fully qualified pilot must occupy the other seat (presumably trained to fly from there) with suitable vision forwards and sideways. If not, an additional observer in full communication with the safety pilot must be carried to fill in the gaps.

Operations Near Aerodromes

Aircraft on or near an aerodrome must, whether or not in an ATZ, observe other traffic to avoid collisions, conform with or avoid the traffic pattern, make all turns to the left on approach or takeoff, unless otherwise instructed, and land and take off into wind, unless the runway configuration or ATC dictate otherwise.

Water Operations

Aircraft or vessels coming *from the right* have the right-of-way. If you are approaching another aircraft or vessel head-on, you must alter heading to the right to keep well clear. Aircraft or vessels being overtaken have the right of way, and overtakers must alter heading enough to keep well clear. Aircraft landing on or taking off from the water shall, as far as practicable, keep well clear of all obstacles and avoid impeding their navigation.

At night, lights conforming to the *International Regulations For Preventing Collisions At Sea* (Revised 1972) must be shown, unless it is impractical, in which case lights conforming as closely as possible must be shown.

Flight Plans

There are many reasons for filing flight plans - first of all, they help get you slotted into the system, even if it isn't quite the route you asked for. Next, they help with radio failures, as, once you're in the pipe, so to speak, everyone knows where you're supposed to be (more or less) and can act accordingly. Then there are forced landings, where an educated guess may be made as to your position, followed by statistics, and, finally, because the law says you must, under certain circumstances (International flights, for example, *always* require a flight plan, as does IFR flight in controlled airspace).

Tip: You can file a flight plan at any time - this also ensures that your destination is notified of your timings.

Officially, you *must* file a flight plan before any flight:

- within controlled airspace under IFR

- in advisory airspace when you need advisory service. Advisory routes must be crossed at 90° at the appropriate IFR level

- in designated areas or along routes where ATC provide flight information, alerting and SAR services, and where they liaise with military units and ATC from other States to avoid interception for identification

- across international borders

- under Special VFR if you wish the destination aerodrome to be notified

- over 40 km when the max takeoff mass exceeds 5700 kg

They are also *recommended* for flights over water more than 10 nm from the coast and/or flight over sparsely populated or remote terrain. You should always file a plan as far in advance as possible, but at least 60 minutes is preferable, with the ATSU at the departure aerodrome, but if there isn't one, you can do it by telephone or radio (in that order) to the unit designated to serve the aerodrome. If there is a delay of more than 30 minutes for a controlled flight, or an hour for an uncontrolled flight, you should either amend the flight plan, or cancel it and submit a new one. If you land at an aerodrome other than the one in the flight plan, you must tell ATC within 30 minutes of the ETA at the planned destination. If, during a flight, you wish to change the profile of a cleared flight plan, you must do nothing until the change is cleared by ATC. In flight, the plan must be received at least 10 minutes before the service is required.

Note: You can file a flight plan up to 5 days in advance, but if you do not notify the date in Box 18, the takeoff time you specify is assumed to be the next time it occurs.

You must stick to the flight plan unless a request has been made for a variation and a *clearance obtained*. In an emergency, of course, you can do what you need and sort it out afterwards. For inadvertent changes:

- **Deviation from track** - regain track as soon as practicable

- **TAS variations** - you must inform ATC if the average variation of your TAS is expected to be more than ±5% from that given in the flight plan

- **ETA changes** - if the ETA for the next applicable reporting point, FIR boundary or destination aerodrome (in that order) is going to change by more than **3 minutes**, you should inform ATC

In controlled airspace, you must report to ATC the time, your position and level at whatever reporting points or

intervals of time as may be established, or as directed. The *standard position report* contains the aircraft identification, position, time, flight level/altitude, next position and time over, ensuing significant point, in that order.

Below are the details for each slot in the flight plan form (see overleaf). The boxes with hyphens in front of them have sub-boxes.

AIRCRAFT ID

The call sign. Without a company callsign, use the registration. Hyphens are not used.

FLIGHT RULES & TYPE OF FLIGHT

The former goes in the first part of Box 8. V=VFR, I=IFR, Y=IFR/VFR, Z=VFR/IFR (the changeover point goes in the route section). Next is the *type* of flight. G=General Aviation, S=Scheduled, N=Non-scheduled, M=Military, X=Other. A Bell 206 would use G.

NO & TYPE OF AIRCRAFT, WAKE TURBULENCE CATEGORY

Box 9 is also in two parts. The first is the number of aircraft, and the second the ICAO code for the type (e.g. BH06 for Bell 206, but the full list is in ICAO Doc 8643). You would only fill in the first part if there are more than one aircraft, so the minimum number to be inserted would be 02. For the Wake Turbulence Category, H=Heavy (above 300,000 lbs), M = Medium (15500-300000 lbs) and L = Light.

EQUIPMENT

Box 10, for comms, nav and transponder, in that order (COM, NAV, SSR). N=None or U/S. S=Standard, that is, VHF, ADF, VOR and ILS. C=LORAN, D=DME, F=ADF, G=GPS, H=HF RTF, I=INS, J=Data Link, K=MLS, L=ILS, M=OMEGA, O=VOR, R=RNP certified, T=TACAN, U=UHF, V=VHF, W=RVSM certified, X=MNPS certified, Y=CMNPS certified, Z=other.

For SSR, N=Nil, A=Mode A, C=Mode C, X=Mode S without ident and PA, P=Mode S with PA & no ident, I=Mode S with ident & no PA, S=Mode S with ident & PA. For example, SD/C is commonly used for standard equipment with DMA and Mode C transponder.

DEPARTURE AERODROME

In Box 13, use the ICAO code or ZZZZ with an entry in Box 18 (Other Information) if there isn't one.

DEPARTURE TIME

Anticipated time in hours and minutes UTC, preferably over 30 minutes ahead. Any delays more than that to your *Off Block Time* must be notified to ATC.

CRUISE SPEED, ALTITUDE, ROUTE

Box 15 is for the flight planned TAS. N=Knots, M=Mach Number. Changes in speed of more than 5% of TAS or M0.01 must be indicated.

For cruising level, A=*Altitude* in hundreds of feet ASL (e.g. A050). F is for *Flight Level*. Under *Route*, include speed and altitude changes, airway numbers and waypoints on the route. DCT (*Direct*) is assumed unless they are included. IFR routes should be used when available, as per IFR charts. You are at the correct level within ±300 feet of the assigned level.

DESTINATION, EET, SAR, ALTERNATE

In Box 16, use the ICAO code. For a VFR flight the EET is from takeoff until overhead the destination. Use your own SAR time, up to 24 hours after ETA. A takeoff alternate is required when the weather at the departure aerodrome is at or below landing minima, or you cannot return to it for other reasons. If you need one that doesn't have an ICAO ID, use ZZZZ, with the details in Box 18 after /ALTN.

OTHER INFORMATION

Use 0 if there is nothing else to add. RMK/ means *Remarks*.

SUPPLEMENTAL INFORMATION

Fuel endurance (to dry tanks) in hours and minutes goes in Box 19. Place an X through the U and V if you don't have the VHF and UHF emergency frequencies (243 & 121.5 MHz). Cross out the survival equipment you don't have, and add with whom the arrival report will be filed. Finally, include your name and licence number, and the person to be notified if SAR is initiated.

CHANGES

Changes must be notified as soon as practicable. If there is a delay of 30 minutes over the estimated off-block time (for a controlled flight) or 1 hour (uncontrolled), you should either make an amendment or cancel the old plan and issue a new one. A significant change includes fuel endurance and number of persons on board.

CLOSING A FLIGHT PLAN

An arrival report for a flight plan that covers the whole route, or the remainder of a flight, should be made in person as soon as possible after landing. Where a flight plan is only in force for a portion of a flight (other than the remainder), you can report to the appropriate ATC. If there is no ATC at the arrival aerodrome, the report should be made to the nearest one as quickly as practicable after landing. If the facilities at the arrival aerodrome are known to be inadequate, you can transmit the equivalent of an arrival report to ATC just before landing.

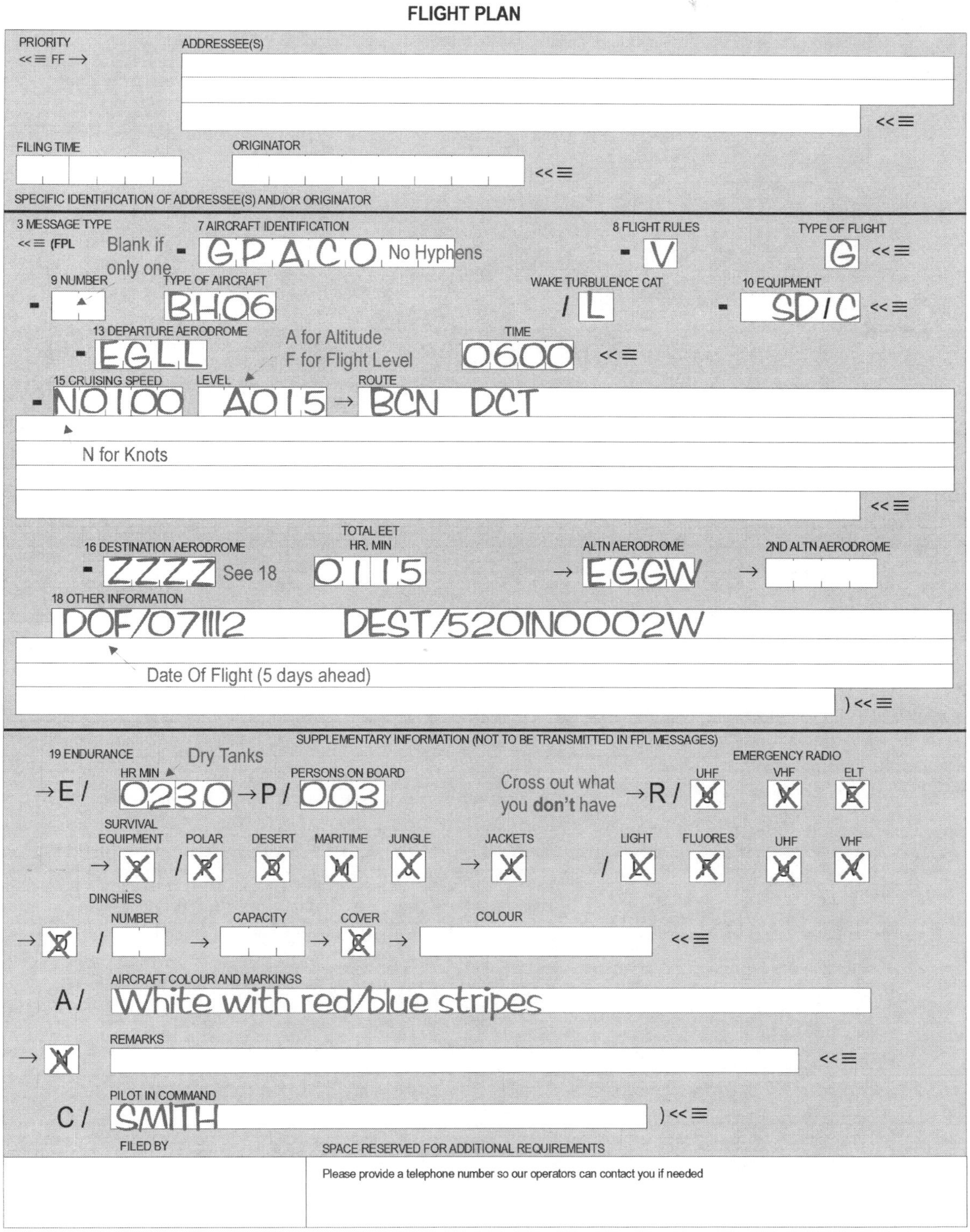

FLIGHT PLAN

PRIORITY	ADDRESSEE(S)
<< ≡ FF →	

FILING TIME	ORIGINATOR
	<< ≡

SPECIFIC IDENTIFICATION OF ADDRESSEE(S) AND/OR ORIGINATOR

3 MESSAGE TYPE << ≡ (FPL Blank if only one

7 AIRCRAFT IDENTIFICATION - G P A C O No Hyphens

8 FLIGHT RULES - V

TYPE OF FLIGHT G << ≡

9 NUMBER - ▲

TYPE OF AIRCRAFT BH06

WAKE TURBULENCE CAT / L

10 EQUIPMENT - SDIC << ≡

13 DEPARTURE AERODROME - EGLL   A for Altitude F for Flight Level

TIME 0600 << ≡

15 CRUISING SPEED - N0100

LEVEL ▲ A015 →

ROUTE BCN DCT

N for Knots

<< ≡

16 DESTINATION AERODROME - ZZZZ See 18

TOTAL EET HR. MIN 0115

ALTN AERODROME → EGGW

2ND ALTN AERODROME →

18 OTHER INFORMATION DOF/07112   DEST/5201N0002W

Date Of Flight (5 days ahead)

) << ≡

SUPPLEMENTARY INFORMATION (NOT TO BE TRANSMITTED IN FPL MESSAGES)

19 ENDURANCE Dry Tanks

HR MIN ▲ → E / 0230

PERSONS ON BOARD → P / 003

Cross out what you **don't** have

EMERGENCY RADIO → R / UHF X VHF X ELT X

SURVIVAL EQUIPMENT → X POLAR / X DESERT X MARITIME X JUNGLE X → JACKETS X / LIGHT X FLUORES X UHF X VHF X

DINGHIES → X / NUMBER → CAPACITY → COVER X → COLOUR << ≡

AIRCRAFT COLOUR AND MARKINGS A / White with red/blue stripes

REMARKS → X << ≡

PILOT IN COMMAND C / SMITH) << ≡

FILED BY

SPACE RESERVED FOR ADDITIONAL REQUIREMENTS

Please provide a telephone number so our operators can contact you if needed

An arrival report should consist of:

- Aircraft ID
- Departure aerodrome
- Destination aerodrome (for diversionary landings)
- Arrival aerodrome
- Time of arrival

If you are going to an aerodrome with no connection to ATC, before departure, you must inform a responsible person at the destination of your ETA so that they can report your non-arrival within 30 minutes to ATC.

Signals

INTERCEPTION

Under Article 9 of the Chicago Convention, contracting states reserve the right to stop aircraft from other states flying over of its territory. As a result, aircraft may need to be led away from an area or be required to land at a particular aerodrome. A copy of the interception procedures must be carried on international flights.

If an aircraft assumes a position slightly above and ahead of you (normally on the left), rocks its wings, then turns slowly to the left in a level turn, you have officially been intercepted. Your response should be to rock your own wings and follow (the intercepter will normally be faster than you, so expect it to fly a racetrack pattern and rock its wings each time it passes). After interception, try to inform ATC and make contact with the intercepting aircraft on 121.5 or 243 MHz. You should also squawk 7700 with Mode C, unless otherwise instructed.

If the aircraft performs an abrupt breakaway manoeuvre, such as a climbing turn of 90° or more without interfering with your line of flight, you have been released.

If it lowers its landing gear and descends to a runway (or a helipad), you are expected to land there (the accepted phrase is *Descend*). However, you can make an approach to check the area, then proceed to land. Lowering your gear or showing a steady landing light means you acknowledge the instruction. Flashing the landing light means the area is unsuitable, as does overflight with the gear up somewhere between 1000-2000 feet.

At night, the substitute for rocking wings is irregular flashing of navigation lights.

Here are some pertinent phrases:

Phrase	Meaning
Callsign	My callsign is....
Cannot	Sorry, can't do that.....
Am Lost	Where the hell am I?
Wilco	Your instructions will be complied with
Mayday	Help!
Hijack	Have been hijacked
Land	I would like to land at....
Descend	I require descent
Repeat	Say that again
Callsign	What is your callsign?
Recleared	Ignore last clearance and receive a new one
Descend	Descend for landing
You land	Land here
Proceed	You may proceed

Lights & Pyrotechnic Signals

Sent from the Tower to an aircraft. Acknowledge by rocking the wings or flashing the landing lights once.

Signal	To Air	To Ground
Steady Red	Give way to others, keep circling	Stop
Red Flashes	Airport unsafe, do not land	Clear landing area
Green Flashes	Return for landing	Cleared to taxi
Steady Green	You may land	Cleared to take off
White Flashes	Land after continuous green. After green flashes, go to apron	Return to start point
Bursting Red/ Green Stars	You are in or near a danger area; push off	
Blinking Runway Lights		Ground staff clear areas

Visual Ground Signals

Refer to *CAP 637 - Visual Aids Handbook* for full details.

Marshalling Signals

Refer to *CAP 637 - Visual Aids Handbook* for full details.

Visual Flight Rules (VFR)

Although the airspace you fly in comes in several varieties (see below), it is, essentially, controlled or uncontrolled, although it's fair to say that, in Europe, once you are above 3000 feet, most airspace is controlled in one form or another. As the names imply, in the first you do as you're told (by ATC), and, in the second, you, as pilot, are responsible for the safe conduct of the flight, which means avoiding obstacles and other aircraft, which you can only do if you can see them. The official definition of a flight under VFR is "one conducted under Visual Flight Rules", conveniently leaving out what the Rules are.

The Visual Flight Rules govern flight in *Visual Meteorological Conditions* (VMC). A flight may only be conducted under VFR if the conditions exist all the way along the route. When the weather gets so bad that you can't see where you are going, *Instrument Meteorological Conditions* (IMC) apply, and you must fly under *Instrument Flight Rules* (IFR), described briefly below, although you can fly IFR at any time, even in VMC (you just have to obey tighter rules for obstacle clearance, etc., since you're not supposed to be looking out of the window). The definition of IMC is actually a negative one, being "weather precluding flight in compliance with Visual Flight Rules", and where this happens could depend on the type of airspace, as well as the weather. For example, even on a clear day, if you are in Class A airspace, you must observe Instrument Flight Rules.

Normally, it's the pilot's responsibility to determine visibility and judge whether to accept a clearance but, when taking off from or approaching to land at aerodromes within Class B, C or D airspace, the visibility reported by the relevant ATC is the visibility for the time being. In other words, ATC do not usually declare airspace under their control as IMC or not.

A VFR flight must be operated at a level appropriate to the track, as per the Tables of Cruising Levels when above 3000 ft MSL (see *Quadrantal Rules*, below).

There two sets of criteria to be observed in relation to this:

- whether or not you are above 3000 feet

- whether or not you are above 140 kts

Conditions for PPL holders are higher than normal, but especially when passengers are carried. So, in Class G airspace (see overleaf), you must be clear of cloud, in sight of the surface, with a flight visibility of 1500 m, or 3000 m if you are carrying passengers.

OVERWATER

Flight shall not be conducted overwater out of sight of land when the flight visibility is less than that for the appropriate airspace, and in any case when visibility is less than 1500 m. The minimum cloudbase shall be 600 feet.

CLASS A AIRSPACE

This is the most restrictive, requiring the most experienced pilots. Except for gliders, all flights are IFR - you may not convert to VFR.

CLASS B AIRSPACE

You must be clear of cloud, with visibility at least 8 km above 10,000' AMSL (5 km below). There is no Class B airspace in UK.

CLASS C, D OR E AIRSPACE

You must be at least 1500 m horizontally and 1000 feet vertically from cloud in visibility at least 8 km (5 km below 10,000' AMSL). Class C does not as yet exist in UK

CLASS F & G AIRSPACE

Above 3,000 ft AMSL, or 1,000 AGL, whichever is higher, you must be at least 1500 m horizontally and 1000 feet vertically from cloud in visibility at least 8 km (5 km below 10,000' AMSL*).

Airspace	A	B	CDE	FG	
				Above 3000 ft AMSL or 1000 ft above terrain whichever is higher	At & below 3000 ft AMSL or 1000 ft above terrain whichever is higher
Distance From Cloud	No VFR	Clear of Cloud		1500 m horizontally 1000 ft vertically	Clear of cloud Surface in sight
Flight Visibility		8 km at and above 10,000 ft AMSL* 5 km below			5 km, but 1500 m by day**

**Helicopters may operate down to 1500m by day, if ATC allows the use of visibility below 5 km, and the probability of encounters with other traffic is low, at 140 kts or less.

Advisory speeds are:

Visibility (m)	Speed (Kts)
800	50
1500	100
2000	120

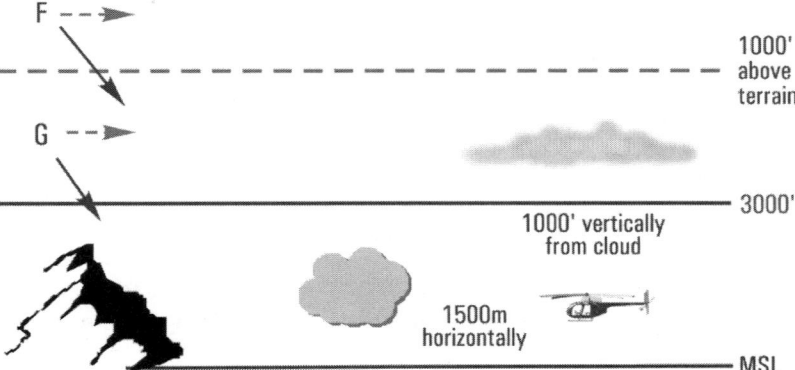

VFR FLIGHT PLAN AND ATC CLEARANCE

Except for gliders, and unless otherwise authorised by ATC, before entering Class B, C or D airspace during notified hours of watch, you must file a flight plan and get clearance beforehand. During the time in there, you must keep a continuous listening watch on the appropriate frequencies and comply with any instructions.

Gliders flying by day in such controlled airspace must remain at least 1500 m horizontally and 1000 feet vertically from cloud in visibility of at least 8 km. The same applies for mechanically driven aircraft without radios, but the visibility becomes 5 km, and with previous permission.

SPECIAL VFR

Except when clearance is obtained from ATC, a VFR flight cannot enter or leave a CTZ when the ceiling is less than 1500 feet, or the visibility is less than 5 km.

Special VFR is used when you want to enter a Class A CTZ or any other type of CTZ at night or in IMC or when the weather isn't good enough for VFR (there is no VFR at night, except Special VFR in a control zone). It's a legal technicality, to allow VFR aircraft to go where the law says only IFR-equipped aircraft may fly, or when certain conditions exist.

You must be clear of cloud and in sight of the surface*, and get clearance from ATC, which means you need radios (except in Class E airspace, but there must still be a way of informing ATC of flight termination). You are therefore absolved from the 1500-foot rule, but not being able to glide clear of a built-up area in emergency (or land safely in a helicopter). Helicopters should fly slowly enough to avoid collisions with other traffic or obstacles. If your radios stop working before entering the zone, remain clear of controlled airspace.

*A PPL holder without either an IMC or Instrument Rating must have an in-flight visibility of at least 10 km.

LOW FLYING

Except when taking off or landing, or with permission, you may not fly over congested areas of cities, towns or settlements, or open-air assemblies of people below 1,000 feet above the highest obstacle within 600 m (2,000 feet). Otherwise, not less than 500 feet above ground or water.

Instrument Flight Rules (IFR)

Generally, all flights in IMC must be conducted under IFR, although you can actually fly IFR at any time, even if the weather is clear - for example, you must obey IFR rules at night. The essential difference between IFR and VFR is that tighter margins are applied for avoiding obstacles and choosing your altitude according to your direction (the *Quadrantal Rule*).

QUADRANTAL RULES

Above 3000 ft amsl, or above the appropriate transition altitude, whichever is higher, you must fly at a level appropriate to your magnetic track (see table below), using 1013.2 mb or 29.92, unless otherwise instructed by ATC or in an established traffic pattern.

Below 24 500 Feet (UK)

Magnetic Track	Cruising Level (ft)
000-089°	Odd thousands
90° - 179°	Odd thousands + 500
180° - 269°	Even thousands
270° - 359°	Even thousands + 500

REGISTRATION MARKS (ANX 7)

Registration marks are assigned by the state of registry or a *common mark registering authority*. The common mark is selected from the series of symbols in the radio call signs allocated to ICAO by the ITCU.

The *nationality mark* is the one that tells you what country the aircraft belongs to, as assigned by ICAO (e.g. G for UK, N for USA), and registration marks are *combinations of letters or numbers* assigned by the State of Registry, which should not be confusable with the five-letter combinations used in the *International Code of Signals,* or other common groupings used in aviation, so any containing the word PAN or the letters XXX or TTT should not be used. The nationality and registration marks are separated by a hyphen. Otherwise, marks must be in Roman characters and be displayed to their best advantage, according to features of the aircraft, and be clean and visible. They must also be on a fireproof metal plate in a prominent position on the fuselage, wing (microlight), or basket or envelope (balloon).

The Certificate of Registration should be kept on the aircraft (Chicago Convention Article 29).

Position and Size of Marks

On heavier than air aircraft (including kites), the first choice for marks is on the lower surface of the port wing, unless they stretch across both, if possible equidistant from the leading and trailing edges, with the tops towards the leading edge. They must be at least at least 50 cm, or as large as possible. They can also be either on the outboard sides, between the wings and tail, or on the vertical tail surface, at least 30 cm tall, or as large as possible, with a margin of at least 5 cm along each side. If there's a choice, use the largest area for the 30 cm letters. On helicopters, with no room on the side, they can be underneath, central, with the tops towards the nose, at least 50 cm tall, or as large as possible.

On airships, try for each side, horizontally near the maximum cross-section or on the lower vertical stabiliser. On free balloons, in two places on diametrically opposite sides. Both must be at least 50 cm tall, and freely visible.

Width, spacing and thickness

The width of standard letters (e.g. other than *I*, *M* and *W*), and the length of the hyphen must be two thirds of the height. *M* and *W* must be somewhere between two thirds and the height itself. *I* must be one sixth of the height. The lines making up letters and hyphens must be one sixth of the height of the letters. Spaces must be equal to a quarter or half the width of a standard letter, all being equal.

AIRWORTHINESS (ANNEX 8)
••••••••••••••••••••••••••••••••••••••

Annex 8 prescribes the minimum standards for aircraft that overfly or land in State territory (the *international* carriage of passengers and cargo). Related to this is Annex 6, Part 1, Chapter 5 (*Performance*), and JAR 145. Standards apply to the complete aircraft, including power units, systems and equipment*. Airworthiness operation limitations must include all limiting mass, C of G position, mass distribution and floor loading information.

*You can find the equipment legally required to be carried on an aircraft in Schedules 4 and 5 of the ANO.

The State of *Registry* determines continued airworthiness. When an aircraft is no longer airworthy, permission can be obtained from it to fly it without fare-paying passengers to where it can be restored to an airworthy condition.

The certificate of airworthiness is required by Article 31 of the Chicago Convention, issued (or rendered valid) by the State of Registry, whose responsibility it is to develop and adopt requirements to ensure continued airworthiness. An aircraft is "airworthy" when it complies with the flight manual, any placards, and the ICAO Airworthiness Technical Manual. The captain is responsible for ensuring airworthiness before flight (engineers sign for their *work*, not the aircraft).

As far as maintenance goes, it can be *Scheduled* or *Unscheduled*, which basically speak for themselves. Both are meant to ensure that an aircraft is kept at an acceptable standard of airworthiness. Depending on the performance category and its maximum authorised weight, there will be different schemes covering this, but the nature of General Aviation means that aircraft are very often not seen by an engineer from one check to the next (but the owner/pilot can do some elementary tasks, as described below).

Types of check include 50-hour and 100-hour, which can be extended by 5 or 10%, respectively, for scheduling, but this should not be used as part of normal operations (lack of planning on your part doesn't justify an emergency on

an engineer's part). In between, there will be times when components need to be changed, either on a planned or emergency basis.

The *Maintenance Schedule* contains the name and address of the owner or operator and the type of aircraft and equipment fitted. It lays down the periods when every part will be inspected, together with the type and degree of the inspection, including periods of cleaning, lubricating and adjustment. They are written for each aircraft, and are subject to CAA approval before moving to a new one.

After work is done, an *Aircraft Maintenance Engineer* (AME) signs a *Certificate of Maintenance Review*, which means that the work done meets applicable standards and the aircraft is released back into service. However, you are still responsible for ensuring that the aircraft is airworthy. Not being an engineer, the only way you can find this out (aside from a thorough preflight) is to check the Technical Log before flight, in which you should find an alert card which shows when the next servicing is due. Simply subtract the current aircraft hours from that figure to see how many hours' flying you can do before the next check.

After an abnormal occurrence (such as a lightning strike or a heavy landing), the aircraft must be inspected (and not flown until it has been done). If nothing has to be taken apart, the inspection can be done by the PIC, but I would suggest you need some technical qualifications to know that you don't need to take anything apart in the first place.

Duplicate Inspections

A duplicate inspection is first made and certified by one qualified person and subsequently made and certified by another. One is required when stuff like engine or primary flight controls have been modified, repaired, replaced or disassembled. Away from base, this may be carried out by a pilot qualified on type.

Elementary Work

This is technically maintenance, but some tasks are not subject to Maintenance Review, which means you don't need an AME to do them (not with public transport). A licensed pilot, who also owns or operates an aircraft, may do elementary work on it, normally limited to those under 2730 kg with a **Private** or **Special Category** C of A. This might include changing spark plugs or tyres, batteries, or bulbs, etc. (the key is that no special tools are required, or that the structure is not affected).

Details of the work, as listed in the ANO, must be entered into an appropriate log, and certified. As stated above, elementary work needs no maintenance release.

AIR TRAFFIC SERVICES (ANX 11)

Whether you need ATC or not depends on the *type of traffic* and its *density*, with due allowance being made for the weather and "other factors". Once that has been sorted out, the airspace is carved up and designated according to the services provided (see *Airspace Structure*).

ATC's mission in life is to *prevent collisions* (between aircraft and obstructions) and *expedite traffic*. They also help with rescues and provide advice and information, which is disseminated through various offices, including area control centres, terminal control units, control towers, etc.

ATC units use UTC, in 24-hour clock format. Clocks must be accurate within ±30 seconds, or 1 second for data links.

An ATSU (*Air Traffic Services Unit*) consists of a combined radar unit and tower.

Services Provided

AIR TRAFFIC CONTROL SERVICE

- *Aerodrome Control Service*, from towers to aircraft and vehicles. The callsign is *Tower* or *Ground*, as appropriate. In a control zone, the Tower provides separation between Special VFR and IFR flights (exam question). In low visibility, ground movements are kept to the minimum, with protection for ILS/MLS sensitive areas. Emergency vehicles get priority

- *Area Control Service*, from *Area Control Centres* (ACCs) for flights in control areas. Their callsign is *Control*, and they are supposed to achieve separation between controlled flights

- *Approach Control Service*, for arriving and departing flights. Their callsign is *Approach*. It might also be *Radar*, or *Talkdown* for PAR

AIR TRAFFIC ADVISORY SERVICE

The idea behind this is to provide a service that is more effective with regard to collision hazard avoidance than a mere Flight Information Service (below). For example, it may be used by aircraft on advisory routes (Class F airspace). Because it is not a *control* service, and therefore does not have the same traffic information to hand, it does not offer the same degree of safety, hence the use of phrases like *advise* and *suggest*. IFR flights using this service should behave the same as controlled flights, except that flight plans (and changes) are not subject to clearance.

ALERTING SERVICE

This must be provided for aircraft using ATC, on a flight plan or otherwise, or which are the subject of unlawful interference (officially, the service notifies appropriate organisations about aircraft needing SAR, and to assist as

required - usually done by a *Rescue Coordination Centre*, or RCC). Alerting is done by the ATS unit responsible for the aircraft at the time, and the decision to initiate it is the responsibility of the flight information or control organisations (another). Alerting Service and FIS are often provided by the same unit (yet another). The states of emergencies are divided into three phases, which are:

- *Uncertainty* (INCERFA), which exists after 30 minutes with no communication, or appearance after ETA, whichever is later

- *Alert* (ALERFA) exists if apprehension exists about the safety of an aircraft or its occupants after failed attempts to get in touch, it fails to land within 5 minutes of ETA or a clearance, it is believed to be subject to unlawful interference, or other data implies trouble short of a forced landing

- The *Distress phase* (DETRESFA) exists where there is reasonable certainty that an aircraft and its occupants are threatened by grave and imminent danger or require immediate assistance - e.g. fuel exhaustion or forced landings

FLIGHT INFORMATION SERVICE

To supply pilots in *C-G airspace* with information about such things as *navaid unserviceability* or *hazardous conditions*, such as volcanic ash, etc., especially that which might not have been available on takeoff or might have developed since then. Their callsign is *Information*.

An *Aerodrome Flight Information Service* (AFIS) provides information in plain language for flights in an ATZ, but instructions or advice cannot be given.

BROADCASTS

ATIS (*Automatic Terminal Information Service*) is broadcast on available VHF frequencies, VOR and NDB (not ILS) at major aerodromes (you can use it as an ID on instrument rides), to reduce congestion on VHF frequencies, although it may have its own channel. You should listen to it and take down the details before you contact ATC, inbound or outbound. ATIS broadcasts should be updated whenever a significant change occurs, and should not last over 30 seconds. The information given need not be repeated, except for the altimeter setting.

Radar Services

Radar allows the best use of airspace by *reducing separation between aircraft*, and the *provision of information*, such as traffic and weather. If SSR is available without primary radar, it will not be possible to detect all aircraft. If SSR is not available, identification is achieved by instructing aircraft to make heading changes of at least 30°, but a backup method is required. Other methods include correlation of position (particularly within 2 km of departure), transfer from another controller, or VDF bearing.

CAPT

Note: Squawking Ident is the only stand-alone method of identification.

Thus, ATC know which aircraft they are talking to with *position reports*, *identifying turns* or *transponders*. You will be told of any change in the identification status. With no SSR, the radar identity of a departing aircraft is established *within 1 nm of the end of the runway*. Before providing ATC service based on radar information, a controller must radar-identify the aircraft *and inform the pilot*.

Note: Radar identification does not stop you being responsible for the disposition of your aircraft, including collision avoidance and obstacle clearance, although ATC accept responsibility for the latter when *vectoring* IFR flights enroute and on approach until within the final approach area.

Normally, turns requested by a controller should be executed as *standard rate turns*.

TERMINAL CONTROL SERVICE

This is from IFR units (ACCs) or *Terminal Control Units* (TCUs) for IFR & VFR flights in specified control areas.

TERMINAL RADAR SERVICE

An extra from IFR units to VFR aircraft in Class C airspace.

RADAR ADVISORY SERVICE

See also *Air Traffic Advisory Service*, above.

This can be requested at any time, but is usually used in IMC, so you should not accept vectors if they take you there and you are not qualified. This can be time wasting, especially if it's a clear day and you're continually given vectors downwind that take ages to catch up on; although you are not obliged to accept the advice, you must inform the controllers, as you must if you change heading or altitude. Once advice is refused, you become responsible for traffic separation, although you are always responsible for obstacle avoidance and obtaining clearances. This can also be expensive, as you become subject to Eurocharges, 100% in UK (but only 25% in France). If you choose not to receive advisory service, you should still submit a flight plan and notify ATS of any changes.

RADAR INFORMATION SERVICE

For informing pilots of the bearing, distance and level of conflicting traffic. Controllers do not offer avoiding action, and updates are only done at pilot request if there is a definite hazard. The responsibility for separation is that of the pilot. RIS is normally only available within 30 nm of an Approach radar head.

RADAR VECTORING

This is achieved by giving you *specific headings* to maintain desired tracks. It may be used when separation is necessary, for noise abatement, when requested or if an operational advantage would be gained. You should be vectored along routes or tracks that you can easily monitor (just in case the radar fails), but you will be told where you are being vectored to, and when it stops (although this can be assumed if you are bound for a final approach or traffic circuit and are given clearance). Otherwise, it continues until you leave the coverage area, go into controlled airspace or are transferred to a unit that doesn't have radar. You should not be vectored into uncontrolled airspace, unless in emergency or you are dodging weather.

VISUAL CLIMB AND DESCENT

If you are being vectored and can see where you are going (that is, you can avoid obstacles yourself and maintain visual reference), you can request permission to climb or descend visually, which may allow you a more direct track. Of course, this means that the responsibility for clearing them is transferred to you, although the proper separation intervals will be maintained.

Airspace Structure

Airspace can be restricted in certain ways, according to its density of traffic, the nature of the operations, the level of safety required and the National interest.

Note: To fly under IFR in controlled airspace, you need an Instrument Rating.

FLIGHT INFORMATION REGION (FIR)

This is a (generally large) area, within which flight information and alerting services are provided. It goes up to, but not including, FL 245 in UK, which has the *Upper FIR* above it. Examples are *London* and *Scottish*, which cover the Southern and Northern halves of the UK, respectively). The procedures in an *Upper Flight Information Region* (UIR) need not be the same as in the underlying FIR, not that that's relevant to helicopters. The bottom limit of a UIR must be the same as the upper limit of the FIR, and it must coincide with a VFR cruising level.

The minimum ATS service inside a FIR is a Flight Information Service and Alerting Service.

ALTIMETER SETTING REGIONS

In a *Military Aerodrome Traffic Zone* (MATZ), you must set the MATZ QFE.

PROHIBITED, RESTRICTED AND DANGER AREAS

Identification includes the nationality letters (such as EG for UK) of the State which has established the airspace, plus the letters *P*, *R* or *D* for *Prohibited*, *Restricted* or *Danger*, area, respectively, followed by a number. Numbers must

not be re-used for at least a year after the area concerned is cancelled.

An *airspace of defined dimensions within which activities dangerous to flight may exist at specified times* is a Danger Area.

Note: If you enter a such an area (by mistake, naturally!), you must, unless otherwise instructed, leave the area as quickly as possible *without descending.*

CONTROLLED AERODROME

This is one where it is deemed that ATC service should be provided to aerodrome traffic. A dead giveaway is that a Tower is involved. When departing a controlled aerodrome in IMC, you contact Departure Control *when advised by the Tower.*

AERODROME TRAFFIC ZONE

The vertical extent of an ATZ is 2000 feet from the surface. Its diameter is determined by the length of the longest runway. If it is longer than 1850 metres, the ATZ will be a circle 5 nm in diameter. Otherwise it will be 4 nm.

When transiting an ATZ, the pilot of an aircraft with a two-way VHF radio must maintain a continuous watch on the appropriate ATZ radio frequency during its notified hours of watch. You must also report your position and height on entering and before leaving an ATZ.

CONTROL AREA

The lowest level of a CTA (*Control Area*) is at least 700 feet (200 m) above the surface. Aerodromes underneath a CTA use the same QNH.

CONTROL ZONE

A CTZ is airspace round busy areas in which IFR traffic is controlled (VFR traffic may or may not be, depending on the airspace notification). It starts at the surface and goes up to the lower levels of controlled airspace above, or the height on the map (or in the AIP). Lateral limits extend to at least 5 nm (9.3 km) from the centre of the aerodrome(s) from where approaches are made.

A CTZ may be Class A (IFR only) or B, C or D if aircraft become involved.

In a CTZ, ATC provides separation between Special VFR and VFR flights.

TCA

A *Terminal Control Area* exists where airways or other routes join near major aerodromes. Aerodromes under a TCA use the same QNH.

ICAO AIRSPACE CLASSIFICATIONS

Controlled airspace is classified into Class A, B, C, D, E, F Special Use Restricted or F Special Use Advisory.

CLASS A

This means most airways, and main control zones and control areas. Separation is provided for IFR aircraft only (VFR is not allowed), from 18,000 ft to FL 600. Since clearance to enter is required, you need continuous two-way radio communication.

CLASS B

Separation is provided between all aircraft, IFR or VFR, from 12,500 feet (or MEA, whichever is higher) to 17,999 feet. It may contain a control zone and TCA. Clearance is required from VFR aircraft before entering, and position reporting is required, so you need a minimum level of radio/nav equipment for continuous two-way radio communication. Unless you can get Special VFR, you must leave when conditions demand IFR. In UK, Class B airspace only exists above FL 245 (Upper Airspace).

Visibility must be 8 km above 10,000 feet and 5 km below that, *clear of cloud.*

CLASS C

Separation is between IFR aircraft, with VFR separated from IFR. VFR aircraft have to look out for themselves and require clearance to enter, so they also need a 2-way radio. They may get traffic information and conflict resolution. If there is no ATC, Class C airspace reverts to Class E. There are no speed restrictions when IFR, but the VFR limit is 250 KIAS, below 10,000 feet. Does not yet exist in UK.

Visibility must be 8 km above 10,000 feet and 5 km below that, 1500 m horizontally and 300 m vertically from cloud.

CLASS D

Control zones and areas of lesser importance, so IFR and VFR traffic is allowed, but separation is provided only between IFR aircraft. However, they are informed about VFR flights (VFR traffic details are also given to VFR flights). The maximum speed is 250 kts IAS for IFR and VFR up to 10,000 feet. For VFR flights, visibility must be 8 km above 10,000 feet and 5 km below that, 1500 m horizontally and 300 m vertically from cloud.

Two-way radio communication is required, as is clearance to enter, so the *minimum radio equipment*, when asked, is *VHF comms.*

CLASS E

Anything that is still controlled airspace, but not meeting the requirements above, like low level airways, control area extensions, transition areas or control zones without a control tower. IFR and VFR flights are permitted, but separation is only between IFR aircraft. All flights receive traffic information as far as is practical.

The maximum speed is 250 kts IAS for IFR and VFR up to 10, 000 feet.

For VFR flights, visibility must be 8 km above 10,000 feet and 5 km below that, 1500 m horizontally and 300 m vertically from cloud.

Two-way radio communication is required for IFR flights, as is clearance to enter.

CLASS F

Advisory Routes, where some limitations are imposed. Separation is between IFR aircraft as far as practicable (with advisory service) and all flights get flight information on request. Clearance is not needed to enter., but IFR flights need two-way radio equipment. ATC advisory service is provided to all *participating* IFR traffic, and Flight Information Service to other flights.

For VFR, visibility must be 8 km above 10,000 feet and 5 km below that, 1500 m horizontally and 300 m vertically from cloud. At and below 900 m, or 300 m above terrain, whichever is higher, 5 km vis, clear of cloud, in sight of land or water.

CLASS G

Anything not designated as A, B, C, D, E or F, where ATC has no authority, so it's free airspace. There's no separation service, but Flight Information Service is provided.

For VFR, visibility must be 8 km above 10,000 feet and 5 km below that, 1500 m horizontally and 300 m vertically from cloud. At and below 900 m, or 300 m above terrain, whichever is higher, 5 km vis, clear of cloud, in sight of land or water.

SEARCH & RESCUE (ANNEX 12)

SAR facilities must be provided on a 24-hour basis, with no overlap on coverage areas. Each SAR region must have a *Rescue Coordination Centre* (RCC). SAR assistance is given regardless of nationality. SAR information, although not normally in an Ops Manual, is nevertheless required by it to be on board.

Procedures

AT THE SCENE OF AN ACCIDENT

The PIC should:

- keep any craft in distress in sight until no longer required

- determine his own position

- be able to report as many details as possible to the RCC, including:

  - type of craft in distress, identification and condition

  - position, time in hours and minutes UTC

  - number of people observed, and if they have abandoned the craft

  - number of persons observed afloat

  - apparent physical condition of survivors

- act as instructed by the RCC

The first aircraft on the scene should take control, until the first SAR one arrives. If it cannot communicate with the RCC, it should hand over to an aircraft that can.

INTERCEPTING DISTRESS TRANSMISSIONS

Distress transmissions are normally given out on the frequency in use at the time, but when over the high seas, say when flying offshore, you will typically be guarding one of the distress frequencies, either *121.5 MHz, 243 MHz* or *2182 KHz* for merchant shipping. ELTs operate on 121.5 MHz and 406 MHz.

If you hear a distress transmission, you must:

- Record the position of the craft in distress

- Inform the appropriate ATS unit or RCC

- At your discretion, whilst awaiting further instructions, proceed to the position given

If you need to direct another craft to the scene, circle it at least once, fly low just in front and rock the fuselage, then fly off in the direction you want them to go. You can use the same signals when they are finished with, but fly behind instead. In theory, they should hoist the *Code Pennant*, which is a flag with vertical red and white stripes, close up, or flash a series of *T*s in Morse Code with a lamp.

On the other hand, they could just turn in the direction requested. A blue and white chequered flag means *Much Regret, Unable* (i.e. *NO*), as does a series of *Ns* in Morse.

GROUND-AIR VISUAL SIGNALS

Survivors can communicate with SAR aircraft visually by making signals on the ground. They should be at least 8 feet high (or as large as possible) with as large a contrast as possible between the materials used and the background.

Need Assistance	V
Need Medical Help	X
No	N
Yes	Y
Going This Way	←

Rescue units can use these (mostly double symbols):

Operation Complete	LLL
Found all personnel	LL
Found some personnel	++
Cannot continue - going home	XX
Split into different groups in directions indicated	← →
Aircraft in this direction	→ →
Nothing found but continuing	NN

AIR-GROUND VISUAL SIGNALS

Indicate your understanding of the ground signals above by rocking your wings in daylight or flashing your landing lights twice at night (or nav lights if you haven't any landing lights).

ACCIDENTS & INCIDENTS (13)

An *Aviation Occurrence* is any accident or incident associated with the operation of aircraft, or a situation that could lead to one. After any occurrence, in UK, the AAIB (01252 512299) must be told as soon as possible, by the commander or the operator, in that order. You can make reports in confidence under the *Confidential Aviation Safety Reporting Program* (CASRP). Under ICAO, however, investigation of accidents or incidents is instituted by the State of *Occurrence*, who must forward notification of accidents or serious incidents by the quickest and most suitable means to the States of *Registry*, the *Operator*, of *Design*, of *Manufacture*, and ICAO when the aircraft weighs more than 2250 kg. However, when the State of Occurrence is not aware of a serious incident, the States of Registry or the Operator must forward the information to the others.

Aircraft Accident

A reportable one occurs when:

- anyone is killed or injured from contact with the aircraft (or any bits falling off), including jet blast or rotor downwash

- the aircraft sustains damage or structural failure

- The aircraft is missing or inaccessible

between the time any person boards it with the intention of flight, and all persons have disembarked (ICAO definition). This does not include injuries from natural causes, which are self-inflicted or inflicted by other people, or to stowaways hiding in places not normally accessible to passengers and crew. *Significant* or *Substantial Damage* in this context essentially means anything that may involve an insurance claim, but officially is damage or failure affecting structure or performance, normally meaning major repairs.

Under ICAO, a *fatal injury* involves death within 30 days. A *serious injury* involves:

- more than 48 hours in hospital within 7 days

- more than simple fractures of fingers, toes and nose

- lacerations causing nerve or muscle damage or severe haemorrhage

- injury to any internal organ

- 2nd or 3rd degree burns or any over 5% of the body

- exposure to infectious substances or radiation

In UK, the *Aircraft Accident Investigation Branch* (AAIB) started as part of the Royal Flying Corps way back when, and is now part of the Department of Transport,

completely separate from any other authority - the Chief Inspector of Air Accidents is directly responsible to the Secretary of State for Transport. As its name suggests, it investigates aircraft accidents, and has teams of investigators on 24-hour standby to go worldwide. The authority to do so derives from the *Civil Aviation Act*, but ICAO also imposes the obligation not to apportion blame, and to investigate accidents impartially, to ensure that they *don't happen again*. Occurrences must be reported to the AAIB and the local police as soon as possible, after which the police must decide if there is enough evidence to justify criminal proceedings.

POST ACCIDENT PROCEDURES

The legal responsibility for notification of an accident (or incident) lies with the pilot, then the operator if the pilot cannot do so. If it happens near an aerodrome, the aerodrome authority must also report it. However, in practice, the AAIB usually get told by the police, since they must also be informed by the people mentioned above. Normally, accidents to gliders, hang gliders, paragliders and parachutists are investigated by the relevant Associations, who have their own safety organisations, which are supervised by the AAIB, who will not attend unless the circumstances are weird enough. As for microlights, balloons or airships, the AAIB will only investigate if there is a fatality.

SITE SECURITY

Only an authorised person (AAIB, a constable or Customs) may normally have access to an involved aircraft, and the aircraft and contents *may not be moved* except under the authority of the Secretary of State. If you do move anything (say for survival purposes, or to provide a marker in a remote area), make sure you note *exactly* where it was before. The police are responsible for guarding the site.

Incident

Any happening other than an accident which hazards or, if not corrected, would hazard any aircraft, its occupants or anyone else, not resulting in substantial damage to the aircraft or third parties, crew or pax. Examples include precautionary or forced landings, due to engine or tail rotor control failure, an external part of the aircraft becoming detached in flight, contaminated fuel, forced, unscheduled, changes of flight plans from by the failure of aircraft instruments, navigation aids or other technical failure, obstructions on rig landing platforms or other landing sites, loss of an external load, with no third party claim, bird strikes, Airprox, in-flight icing, crew incapacitation. The ICAO bird strike information system is *IBIS* (exam question).

SERIOUS INCIDENTS

These are nearly accidents, or have serious potential technical or operational implications, or may result in disciplinary action against aircrew or engineers. A near-collision needing an avoidance manoeuvre is a serious incident, as is fire or smoke in a passenger compartment.

AIRPROX (AIR MISS)

Aircraft **Prox**imity incidents (near misses). The class of risk depends on the basis of *risk of collision, safety not assured, no risk of collision,* or *risk not determined.*

If you are involved in one, you should make the initial report on the frequency in use at the time. If this is not possible, the report should be done after landing, preferably to an ATCC, but any ATS unit will do. All this must be confirmed within 7 days on CA Form 1094.

AERODROMES & AIRPORTS (ANNEX 14)
••

An aerodrome is generally any place for landing aircraft that fits the official definition, which is, broadly, being set apart for the purpose, including any necessary buildings. An aerodrome or airport listed in the AIP that does not need previous permission for use is for public use. Where permission is required, you either need to get it first, or just provide prior notice, so they can get the sheep off the runway. *Aerodrome Traffic* is all traffic on the manoeuvring area of an aerodrome, and flying in its vicinity. The *aerodrome reference temperature* should be the monthly mean of the daily maximums for the hottest months averaged over many years.

A civil aircraft can only land at an aerodrome that is not listed in the UK Air Pilot in an emergency or with prior permission from the operator.

In fact, you need prior permission for three types of aerodrome:

- Those licensed for use only by the licensee with an ordinary aerodrome licence

- Unlicensed aerodromes, which are usually privately owned strips

- Government aerodromes, including military ones

Operations Nearby

There must be no likelihood of collision with other aircraft or vehicles, and the aerodrome must be suitable. This means observing other traffic and conforming to or avoiding the circuit.

Standard Traffic Circuit

The circuit (round a runway) is *part of* an aerodrome traffic pattern, and not *the* traffic pattern (which actually starts when you enter a control zone and ends in the downwind leg). The ICAO definition of a circuit is: *the specified paths to be flown by aircraft operating in the vicinity of an aerodrome*.

Such paths include the *crosswind leg*, which is at right angles to the runway, and is turned onto after takeoff. The *downwind leg* is parallel to the runway, and goes the opposite way to the runway in use - you make the "downwind" call just after turning on to it. The *base leg* is also at right angles, but in the opposite way and at the opposite end to the crosswind leg, from which you turn onto *final approach* (more than 4 nm away, it is a *long final*. Final is reported at the 4 nm point from the runway threshold).

In the UK, you normally make all turns to the left, arriving **overhead** the landing point at 2000' AGL and at 90° to it, in a position to make a descending 180° turn over the dead side to arrive at circuit height over the other end of the runway, going the other way, tight crosswind. Then you join the downwind leg in the normal way, all the while looking for other traffic. You can also join at 45° to the downwind leg, at the height published in the AIP (all circuit details will be in there, too). Only join directly downwind if there is no conflict.

Helicopters

Hover taxying is movement in ground effect at speeds up to about 20 kts, but more likely the normal walking pace, below 25 feet (the height may vary because of external loads, but the pace will be relatively slow). *Air Taxi* is almost like flight, but below 100 feet, often used when ATC would like you to expedite your movement to help with traffic flow. If you've got wheels, it is usual to taxi on the ground, following taxiways and other routes.

Note: *Air taxi* is used for everything!

DO NOT TRY TO TURN BACK TO THE FIELD IF THE ENGINE FAILS ON TAKEOFF - LAND STRAIGHT AHEAD.

READ THAT AGAIN.

AND AGAIN.

Runways

Runway details are declared by the Airport Authority and published in the AIP, although they can be found in many other publications. This declared distance is either the *Take-off Run Available* (TORA) or *Landing Distance Available* (LDA), as appropriate.

Any areas at the ends unsuitable to run on, but still clear of obstacles, are called *Clearways* - the *Take Off Distance Available* (TODA) is TORA + Clearway. The length of the clearway should not exceed half the length of the TORA, and its width should extend at least 75 m either side of the extended centreline.

Part of the Clearway that can support an aircraft while stopping, although not under take-off conditions, is declared as *Stopway* which may be added to the TORA to form the *Emergency Distance Available* (EDA), and marked with yellow chevrons. This is the ground run distance available for an aircraft to abort a takeoff and come to rest safely - the essential point is that Stopway is ground-based and clearways are not, so they can be included in performance calculations. Stopways are the same width as the runway.

The combination of the paved area of the runway and the stopway is called the *runway strip*. The end of a runway is called the *threshold*.

Runways are named after the direction they are facing in, without the last number. For example, one facing West, or 270°, would be called Runway 27. In fact, the naming is to the nearest tenth degree, so one facing 067° is actually Runway 07. A T after the number (as in 07T) would be a *True* direction. Clearances to enter, land on, take off from, cross and back track on runways *must be read back*.

Parallel runways will also be known as *Left* or *Right*, but if there were 3, they would be designated *Left*, *Centre* or *Right*, for example 22L, 22C, 22R. Where no runways are available, takeoff and landing areas will be marked with pyramidal or conical markers, painted orange and white for airports, or just orange for aerodromes.

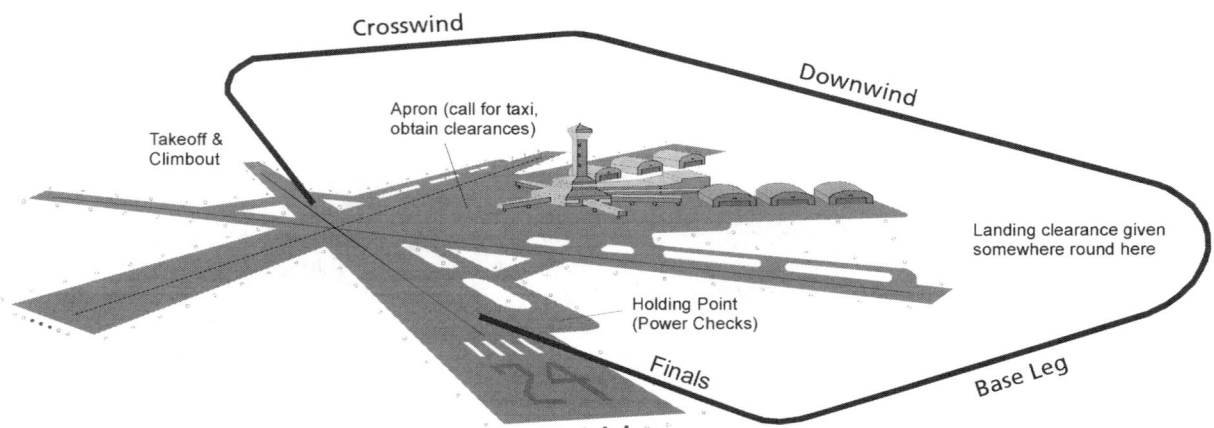

Crosswind

Downwind

Takeoff & Climbout

Apron (call for taxi, obtain clearances)

Landing clearance given somewhere round here

Holding Point (Power Checks)

Finals

Base Leg

CAPT

Refer to the CAA's *Visual Aids Handbook* for full details of signs and signals you might see at an airfield.

The reason that touchdown is made well into the runway or helipad, by the way, is that, if you sink, at least you are likely to hit a suitable surface.

Obstacles interfering with the glideslope may need the threshold to be displaced, but the area behind it can still be used for taxying and takeoff runs, even if it cannot be for landing.

Displacement is marked by large yellow arrows pointing towards the new threshold - a white painted transverse stripe drawn across a runway indicates a temporarily or permanently displaced one (see left). The threshold will be relocated if part of the runway is closed, and crosses will be used instead of arrows.

Markings & Signals

Runway markings must be white. Taxiway and aircraft stand markings must be yellow. Apron safety lines need

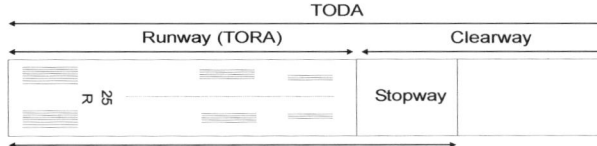

only be conspicuous.

For a 2500 m landing distance, the distance from the threshold to the aiming point is 400m, with 6 pairs of touchdown markings. The distance from the threshold to the fixed distance marking when the runway is 2000 m long is 300 m. A white line across a runway indicates a displaced threshold. Only paved runways require centreline markings. There should be 12 stripes in the threshold markings of a 45 m wide runway.

Two or more white crosses (with arms at 45° to the centre line) along a section or at both ends of a runway or taxiway mean the section between them is unfit for aircraft movement.

APRONS

Those used must be a contrasting colour to those on taxiways.

HOLDING POINTS

A non-instrument runway will have a yellow single solid and a single dashed line across the taxiway (the dashed line is on the runway side). An instrument runway has a double set of each (an *A Pattern*) going to the runway (on the way back, they tell you when you are clear, when *all parts* of the aircraft have crossed the line).

A *B Pattern* looks like a ladder (left), and is used to protect ILS/MLS signals, so it is not so much a holding point, but

a boundary line. An *intermediate* holding position marking is a single broken line.

There may also be a red marker board either side of the taxiway:

When a runway is 2000 m long, and taxi holding positions have not been established, aircraft shall not be held closer to the runway in use than 50 m.

Parking Bays

Those used for aircraft subject to unlawful interference must be at least 100 m from other bays.

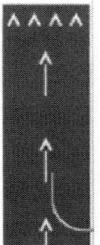

Lighting

Approach lights (and their supports) must be frangible for the last 300 m before the threshold. Any beyond that over 12 m high must be frangible for the top 12 m. Supporting structures surrounded by non-frangible objects only need the bit above them to be frangible.

Aeronautical ground lights must be operated:

- continuously during darkness after the end of evening civil twilight until the beginning of morning civil twilight
- when required for the control of air traffic
- at any time when their use, based on weather, is considered desirable for the safety of air traffic

Lights on and near aerodromes that are not intended for en-route navigation may be turned off if no likelihood of regular or emergency operation exists, as long as they can be turned on again at least *one hour before an expected arrival.*

Tip: One trick for remembering what lights do is to remember that *omnidirectional lights* are intended for use when circling. Runway end lights should therefore be unidirectional, for example, as they must be seen down the runway.

RUNWAYS

Runway *end* lights should show *unidirectional red* (at least 6) in the direction of the runway. Runway *threshold* lights should show *unidirectional green* in the approach direction. Centre line lights for the last 300 m should be red.

Runway edge lights are fixed and (variable) white, except for those between the end and a displaced threshold, which are red (because you can't use the area for landing).

TODA

Runway (TORA)		Clearway
25 R		Stopway

Emergency Distance

However, the remote end (the least of the final 600 m or one-third) of an instrument runway may show yellow, and

 be omnidirectional for circling. Approach lights may be used for centreline guidance when the whole of a runway is used for takeoff when it has a displaced threshold (however, they shouldn't dazzle pilots). Centreline lights on rapid exit taxiways are alternating green/yellow.

Runway lead-in lighting should consist of a group of at least 3 white lights flashing in sequence towards the runway.

TAXIWAYS

Taxiway edge lights are fixed omnidirectional blue, although some may be shielded to prevent confusion.

Paved taxiways should have green centre line markings, for continuous guidance between runways and aircraft stands, but alternating yellow/green ones indicate an ILS sensitive or critical area (the nearest to the perimeter is yellow).

A stopbar across a taxiway shows red lights 3 m apart. Stopbars are used when RVR is less than 350 m, and must be controllable by ATC. If the RVR is less than 550 m, and there are no stop bars, runway guard lights should be used.

IDENTIFICATION BEACONS

A beacon is required if aircraft navigate mostly visually, or reduced visibility is frequent, or it is hard to see the aerodrome. They are green for civil aerodromes, and yellow for those on water. Military aerodromes have a flashing red one. All show a two-letter Morse group.

Aerodrome *location* beacons are for smaller aerodromes, and are white, or white & green (yellow for water).

OBSTACLES

Those less than 45 m high should have *low intensity steady red* lights. Between 45-150 m, *medium red, flashing simultaneously.* Over 150 m, *high intensity white flashing lights* (Type A) by day and night, flashing simultaneously. For towers or pylons supporting cables, etc., high intensity white flashing (Type B).

Signs

15-33 A *mandatory instruction* sign has white text on a red background, found at holding positions, etc. *Information* signs have black text on a yellow background (the other way round for a location sign, and a yellow border if it is stand-alone). A *runway vacated* sign would be at the end of the ILS/MLS sensitive area.

Visual Aids For Navigation

Refer to *CAP 637 - Visual Aids Handbook* for full details.

An aerodrome must have at least one wind direction indicator (*windsock*), which must be visible from aircraft in flight or on the movement area, and free from the effects of air disturbances from nearby objects.

A *landing direction indicator* (which should be in the form of a letter T) must be in a conspicuous position, typically in the signals area (see below). It should be white or orange, depending on which provides the best contrast, and be lit at night. A white T with a disc above (for airborne machines) and a single black ball suspended from a mast (for those on the ground), mean that the directions for takeoff and landing are not necessarily the same.

A white dumb-bell means land and taxi on runways and taxiways only. A black bar across each circular part of the dumbbell perpendicular to the shaft means that you must still take off and land on runways, but other manoeuvres need not be confined to runways and taxiways.

There must be a *signalling lamp* in the control tower, capable of producing red, green and white signals which can be aimed at the target. It should be able to transmit Morse signals at up to four words per minute.

SIGNALS AREA

This is used to provide basic information about an aerodrome to aircraft in flight without the need of a radio. It is a small square surrounded in white that contains relevant symbols, situated next to the control tower.

The principal requirement of a signals area is that it must be visible from the air (obvious, really - it should actually be visible from above 10° above the horizontal from 300 feet). It should be on an even horizontal surface and be at least 9m square. Its colour should contrast with those of the panels used, and it should be surrounded by a white border at least 0.3 m wide.

AERONAUTICAL INFO (ANX 15)

The process of Aviation needs a huge flow of information in order to run smoothly - technically for its *safety, regularity* and *efficiency*, since wrong information can be dangerous. Many accidents have happened because crews have input wrong information, intentionally or otherwise. As with all computers, if you put garbage in, you get garbage out. The role of such support services became more important with the advent of *RNAV* (Area Navigation), *RNP* (Required Navigation Performance), *Computer-based navigation systems* (INS/IRS)

All the above systems require accurate information for their operation, which is obtained from the publications issued by Aeronautical Information Services, such as NOTAMS, etc. To ensure uniformity and consistency, States are urged to *avoid Standards and Procedures other than those established for international use.*

States are required to either provide such services themselves, or in conjunction with another, or through non-government agencies which meet the standards. The responsibility, however, still lies with the State, and information published on its behalf must show where the authority comes from, as well as being accurate, timely and of the quality expected by ICAO. States must share information, in English, with place names spelt as per local usage, and any translations in the Latin alphabet. Published coordinates must conform to WGS-84.

If a 24-hour service is not provided, services must be available from two hours before and after a flight in the area of responsibility, or at other times by request.

Aeronautical Information Publication

The AIP is a summary of the rules and regulations that affect aviation (similar documents are issued by all countries) or, in other words, a publication containing aeronautical information of a *lasting character essential to air navigation.* As such, it is not the final authority for the rules you have to obey, but the law that backs it up is. A clue as to what is or isn't supported by law is given by the word "shall". The AIP should be easy to use in flight, and it is split into three parts:

PART 1 - GENERAL (GEN)

- **GEN 1** - *National Regulations & Requirements.* Entry, transit and departure of aircraft and cargo, Aircraft instruments, Summary of national regulations and differences from ICAO SARPS

- **GEN 2** - *Tables & Codes.* Measurements, Aircraft markings, Holidays, Abbreviations, Chart symbols, List of navaids, Conversions, Sunrise & sunset tables

- **GEN 3** - Services. AIS, Charts, ATC, Met, SAR

PART 2 - EN-ROUTE (ENR)

- **ENR 1** - General Rules & Procedures. VFR, IFR, Airspace Classes, Procedures, radar services, Flight Planning ATC flow management, Interception, Unlawful interference, ATC incidents

- **ENR 2** - *ATS Airspace.* FIR, UIR, TMA, etc.

- **ENR 3** - *ATS Routes*

- **ENR 4** - *Radio Navigation Aids & Systems.*

- **ENR 5** - *Navigation Warnings.* Danger areas, Military stuff, Obstacles, Bird migration, Sporting activities

- **ENR 6** - *En-Route Charts*

PART 3 - AERODROMES (AD)

- **AD 1** - *Aerodromes/Heliports.* Index, Availability, Services

- **AD 2** - *Aerodromes.* Location indicators, Names, Hours, Facilities, Markings, Obstacles, Runways and distances, Communications, Noise abatement

- **AD 3** - *Heliports.* As above.

The above sections should be the same from country to country (but, it would seem, not Canada) so you can find the information easier. When airspace is *notified*, its details are published in the AIP so you can take notice of them.

Permanent changes are issued as *AIP Amendments.* Temporary changes of long duration (3 months) and those of short duration containing extensive text or graphics are issued as *AIP Supplements.* Supplement pages are coloured, so they stand out, preferably in yellow.

AIRAC

The AIP is amended regularly, and you should always make sure yours is up to date. Operationally significant changes are published through the AIRAC system, in Parts 1 and 2, which is aimed at *advanced notification based on common effective dates of circumstances that necessitate significant changes in operational practices.* So there. In fact, AIRAC information must be distributed at least 42 days ahead, so that *common effective days* of 28 days are reached on time.

The initials stand for *Aeronautical Information Regulation And Control.*

NOTAM

A *NOTice to AirMen* is a warning or notice about anything that might affect a flight that is either temporary or happened too late to be in charts, etc., such as changes to frequencies or serviceability of navaids, or hazards. They are in the list of items to be checked before flight and can be obtained by telephone, from ATC or over the Internet.

NOTAMs do not amend the AIP, but they may affect the information it contains - for example, a permanent danger area will have its hours of operation published in the AIP, and variations published by NOTAM. A temporary danger area, on the other hand, may be *activated* by NOTAM (where a permanent danger area has two upper limits, the higher one is raised by Notam). In fact, a NOTAM is generated and issued whenever its information is:

- *Temporary* and of *short duration*, or of *long duration* made at *short notice*, except when it contains *extensive text and/or graphics* (information of short duration with extensive text and/or graphics is published as an *AIP Supplement)*

- Permanent, but operationally significant

Operationally significant means the establishment, closure or significant changes in the operation of aerodromes or runways, or the operation of aeronautical services, electronics, aids to navigation (frequencies, ID, etc), visual aids, fuel, SAR facilities, firefighting, hazards to air navigation (obstacles), and the like.

These items are *not* covered by Notam:

- routine maintenance work on aprons and taxiways which does not affect the safe movement of aircraft

- runway marking, when operations can safely be conducted on other available runways, or the equipment can be removed when necessary

- temporary obstructions near aerodromes that do not affect the safe operation of aircraft

- partial failure of lighting where it does not directly affect aircraft operations

- partial temporary failure of air-ground communications when suitable alternative frequencies are known to be available and are working

- the lack of apron marshalling services and road traffic control

- the unserviceability of location, destination or other instruction signs on the aerodrome movement area

- parachuting in uncontrolled airspace under VFR, when controlled, at promulgated sites or within danger or prohibited areas

- other information of a similar temporary nature

DISTRIBUTION

NOTAMs are issued in three categories to addressees for whom the information has direct operational significance, if they would not otherwise have 7 days prior notification (exam question). The categories are:

- *NOTAMN* - one with new information

- *NOTAMR* - one replacing a previous NOTAM

- *NOTAMC* - one cancelling a previous NOTAM

Temporary NOTAMS must include an expiry date, which may be estimated (with an EST suffix).

A checklist of valid NOTAMs is distributed over the AFTN at regular intervals of up to a month, to the same distribution list as the NOTAMs themselves.

SNOTAM (SNOWTAM)

Tam

A small white Scottish terrier (see left). Seriously, a NOTAM about *snow, ice and standing water on aerodrome pavements*, valid for up to 24 hours, but reissued if there is a significant change in conditions, including the coefficient of friction or the type or depth of deposit, available width of runway or conspicuity of lighting.

The relevant form has *17 sections*. If the cleared length of runway is less than the published length, it would be displayed in Box D, with the cleared length in metres.

ALTIMETER SETTING PROCEDURES
••

Cruising levels are expressed in terms of *flight levels*, when above the Transition Altitude, and *altitudes*, when *at or below* Transition Altitude. The change in reference is made, when climbing, at the Transition Altitude, and, when descending, at the Transition Level. The *Transition Altitude* is the altitude at, or below which, any reference your vertical position is based on altitude (based on QNH). Any higher, you have to use *Flight Levels*. A transition altitude is normally specified for an aerodrome *by the State in which it is located*. It is as low as possible, but normally at least 3000 feet, rounded up to the nearest 1000.

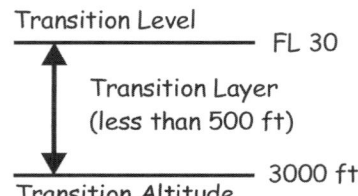

© Phil Croucher, 2012

CAPT

If this page is a photocopy, it is not authorised!

The *Transition Level* is the lowest available flight level available above the Transition Altitude when the altimeter is set to 1013.2 mb, so it would normally be FL 30 in UK, including when the QNH is more than standard. However, if the QNH is less than standard, the transition level will be higher than that. The Transition Level is determined *by the ATS unit concerned*, since it varies with pressure from day to day, and it is always *higher* than the Transition Altitude. The difference between transition altitude and transition level is the *Transition Layer*, which will be *more than zero and less than 500 feet*.

When passing through the transition layer, report flight levels when going up and altitudes when going down - the Transition Level is the latest point at which you change from standard setting to QNH. In other words, when descending to go below Transition Level, if you are cleared to a Flight Level, you must keep 1013.2 set on your altimeter. If you are cleared to an altitude, and no more FL reports are needed, set the QNH as soon as you start descending and report altitudes. Flight level zero is at the atmospheric pressure level of 1013.25 hPa. Consecutive Flight Levels are separated by intervals of at least 500 feet.

Within 20 nm of ground over 2000 ft amsl, increase your safety altitude by these amounts, against windspeed:

Elev (ft)	0-30 Kt	31-50 Kt	51-70 Kt	+ 70 Kt
2-8000	+ 500'	+1000'	+1500'	+2000'
+ 8000	+1000'	+1500'	+2000'	+2500'

This is because the venturi effect over a ridge makes the altimeter misread, on top of causing turbulence and standing waves. All this, plus temperature errors (see below), can make one over-read *by as much as 3000'*.

When the surface temperature is well below ISA (below -15°C), correct MSAs by:

Surface Temp (ISA)	Correction
-16°C to -30°C	+ 10%
-31°C to -50°C	+ 20%
-51°C or below	+ 25%

PRE-FLIGHT CHECKS

Rotating the knob through ±10 hPa must produce a corresponding height difference of about ±300 ft in relevant directions. At a known elevation on the aerodrome, vibrate the instrument by tapping, unless mechanical means is available:

- Set the scale to the current QNH. The altimeter should indicate the elevation, plus the height of the altimeter above it, within ± 20 m or 60 ft for altimeters with a test range of 0-9 000 m (0-30 000 ft) and ± 25 m or 80 ft for altimeters with a test range of 0-15 000 m (0-50 000 ft).

- Set the scale to the current QFE. The altimeter should indicate the height of the altimeter in relation to the QFE reference point, within the same tolerances as above.

- Both should be set to the aerodrome QFE and should indicate within ±60' of zero, within 60' of each other. Thus, they can misread by up to 120 feet between them and still be "serviceable"

- With No 1 on QFE and No 2 on aerodrome QNH, the difference should equal the aerodrome altitude AMSL, to within 60 feet.

- With both on aerodrome QNH, indications should be within ±80 feet of aerodrome elevation, and 60 feet of each other.

Note: No 1 is the handling pilot's primary instrument and No 2 the secondary.

According to JAR 25 the tolerance for an altimeter at MSL is ±30' per 100 kts CAS.

TAKEOFF & LANDING

At least one altimeter must be set to aerodrome QNH before takeoff.

APPROACH & LANDING

Before descending below Transition Level, you must obtain the latest aerodrome QNH.

Transponder Operation

Normally, unless you have an emergency, a communications failure, or are subject to unlawful interference, you must operate the transponder in Mode A as directed by ATC or prescribed by air navigation agreements. In the absence of both, squawk 2000.

Other standard numbers to squawk, when not otherwise instructed, are:

- 0000 - malfunction
- 0030 - lost
- 0033 - parachute dropping
- 0036 - powerline survey
- 2000 - from non-SSR area
- 7000 - conspicuity code
- 7004 - aerobatics
- 7007 - open skies

In emergency, squawk:

- 7500 - Hijack*
- 7600 - Communications failure
- 7700 - Emergency

*Absence of a reply is confirmation that the selection is not accidental.

Note: *You cannot set the number 8* - watch for this in questions that ask you to choose between valid codes.

Mode C must be operated continuously, unless otherwise directed by ATC. The tolerance level for Mode C level information is within ±300 feet of the level (you must report it within ±100 feet, when Mode C is operated).

When asked to *squawk ident*, your return becomes temporarily brighter, so you can be positively identified. Do this only when requested (exam question). If the ident doesn't work, a controller can ask you to switch to standby to avoid a turn for identification. The term *recycle* means *reselect the assigned code*. Modes and codes must be read back.

If a transponder fails during flight in a mandatory area (i.e. *after departure*), you may go to the next planned destination, then complete an itinerary or go to a repair base, as permitted by ATC. It is possible to enter controlled airspace without the required equipment, but ATC must be asked first. Permission is always subject to traffic. If your transponder is unserviceable before departure and you can't fix it, you can take off for a place where repairs can be done. Again, ATC must be informed, preferably before the flight plan is submitted (put an *N* in Section 10 of the flight plan form, or whatever character represents partial serviceability).

CAPT

MTOM to find the Disposable Load. For example:

```
3150  (MTOM)
2060  (BEM of 1875 + Crew)
1090  (Disposable Load)
```

You must fit the fuel and passengers in the Disposable Load, so subtract the fuel required for the trip to find the Traffic Load, or *payload*. If the Traffic Load available is not enough, you must either reduce it, or the fuel, which means you must stop en route to pick up some more.

Note: The Zero Fuel Mass should still be within C of G limits.

DISTRIBUTION & LOADING

There are two aspects to loading a helicopter, the weights themselves and their distribution, and you sometimes get some nasty surprises - unusually shaped fuel tanks mean that you won't get a straight line variation; every fuel load will have a different moment arm, principally because the fuel tanks have a C of G system all of their own, running separately from the aircraft (even in small ones, like the Bell 206 or 407). In this case, it's not enough just to subtract the closing fuel moment from the starting one - for example, say 1,000 lbs has a moment of 1843 and 300 lbs has 558. The result for 700 lbs of fuel may not be 1843-558 (1285), but the actual figure of 1294, which is enough of a difference to cause an insurance company to have qualms about paying up after an accident.

The Centre of Gravity of any object is a point inside it where its weight (or gravitational attraction) passes through, or where its mass is concentrated. It could be described as the average location of its weight force, or better described as its point of balance. The location of the C of G depends on the object's shape, density and the external gravitational field. If a vertical line through the C of G lies outside the base on which the object relies for support, it will overturn, unless you do something to counterbalance the force:

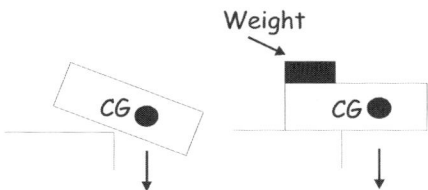

Note that a lighter weight than the one shown above, but further away from the C of G (if there were room) will have the same restraining effect. In the diagrams below, the beam is balanced even though different weights are suspended from it - the difference is compensated for by

each one's distance from the fulcrum:

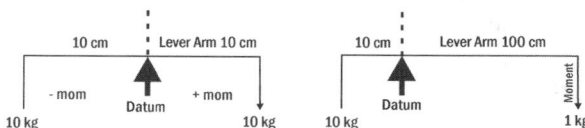

Loads in helicopters work the same way - a 20 lb weight placed in a tailboom will have more effect on fuselage attitude than if it were in the cabin.

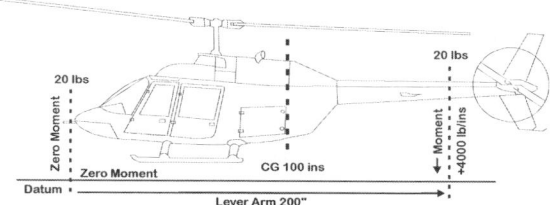

In the picture above, the 20 lbs weight in the tail has an influence of 4000 ft/lbs (20 x 200 inches from the datum). The 20 lb weight at the nose has a zero moment. The C of G comes from the total moment divided by the total weight, or 4000 divided by 40.

The Centre of Gravity, therefore, of an aircraft, is the imaginary point around which its weight forces are said to act, and the point around which the autopilot controls the aircraft. It is normally referenced to the longitudinal axis, and the details are in the Flight Manual. The range in which the C of G works, or, rather, its limits, is determined by aircraft stability and manoeuvrability - when it is outside the design range, control movement is affected.

The *reference datum* is an imaginary point placed in a convenient location by the manufacturer from which all measurements and calculations start and where some C of G ranges are expressed (for example, *106 inches aft of datum*). Mostly, the datum is forward of the nose, so that all moments become positive, but it can be at the rotor mast (depends on the manufacturer). In the Bell 206, for example, the datum is one inch forward of the battery compartment at the front, actually at the bolts holding the pitot tube in place.

The influence (*turning moment*) of an object on the aircraft is found by multiplying its weight by its distance from the datum in Imperial or Metric units, and you must use the same ones throughout.

The formula is:

$$arm = \frac{moment}{force}$$

A station is a location (on the fuselage) identified by a number designating its distance from the datum.

To get the C of G of an aircraft, you multiply the weight of each item in it by the arm of the location it occupies to get the *moment*, or the amount of leverage that item contributes. Then you add the moments and divide that total by the total weight.

The aircraft will have an arm and a moment from when it was last weighed, which is where you start. You can find it in the *weight and balance schedule*, and it may be varied if you add or take off various items, such as the hook or hoist. If anything major is added or taken away, the machine may have to be reweighed before its 4-year limit.

Because a helicopter's fuel tanks are often behind the C of G, you have to calculate the *Zero Fuel* C of G as well, to ensure you have the correct range of flight control movement. For example, you may exceed the forward limits if you don't have much fuel on board, because fuel in the tanks will bring the nose up.

Note: The effect of the C of G on power and range are mostly due to the resulting angle of the fuselage, with some contribution from horizontal stabiliser download. Any range data in the flight manual is usually conservatively placed at worst C of G.

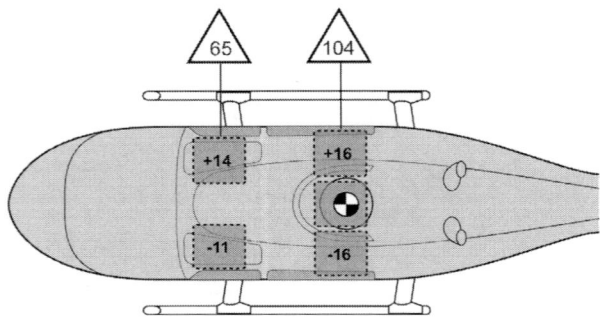

Here is a simplified typical calculation for a Bell 206 (the principles are exactly the same for larger or smaller machines, there are just more or less seats):

Item	Wt	Arm	Moment
Aircraft	1881	116.5	219137
Front pax	185	65	13000
Rear Pax	185	104	19240
Baggage	50	147.50	7375
Zero Fuel CG	2301	112.45	258756
Fuel	310	110.7	34273
Total	**2611**	**112.22**	**293025**

The total C of G for takeoff is 112.22, obtained by dividing the total moment figure (293025) by the total weight, or mass (2611), so it is an average.

You will notice above that both the takeoff C of G and Zero Fuel C of G are computed - this is to ensure that the C of G remains within limits at *all fuel loads*, in case of controllability problems. A recent R44 accident illustrates this very well - it was overweight, with its C of G beyond the forward limit when it struck a ridge in NW Australia. Sadly, all aboard were killed, after an autorotation in which the pilot was not able to flare properly (he broadcast that he was going in hard). To be fair to the pilot, he was known to be conscientious, but even careful pilots can be caught out!

Note: *If a helicopter is loaded for flight and the centre of gravity is within limits for takeoff, the C of G must be calculated for landing.*

The procedure, then, is to multiply the weights by the arms to get the moments, and divide the total moments by the total weights to get the C of G. Next, refer to the flight manual to see if the figure fits into the authorised range on a graph like the one below.

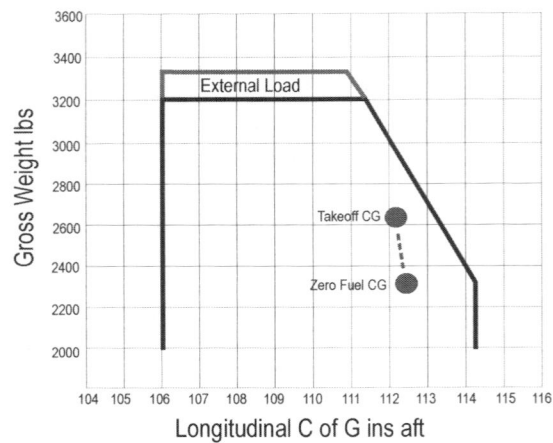

Simply take the all-up weight and the final C of G, and line them up horizontally and vertically. If they are inside the envelope, you are OK, but don't forget you have to land again! Your C of G may well be fine for takeoff, but check again after the fuel has been used!

Figures on the outside of some diagrams are the longitudinal moments. Below is one for the Hughes 300.

Item	Wt	Arm	Mom
Aircraft			
Pilot		83.2	
Pax C		80	
Pax R		83.2	
Zero Fuel			
Fuel		108.5	
Total			

CAPT

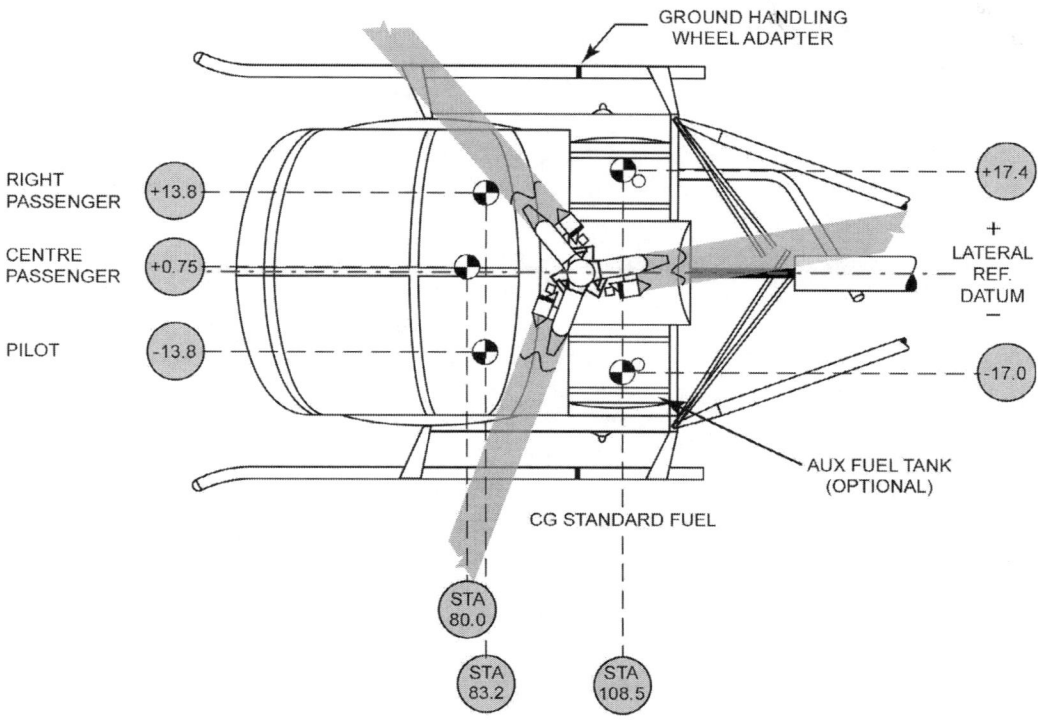

GROUND HANDLING
WHEEL ADAPTER

RIGHT PASSENGER +13.8

CENTRE PASSENGER +0.75

PILOT -13.8

+17.4

+
LATERAL
REF.
DATUM
−

-17.0

AUX FUEL TANK
(OPTIONAL)

CG STANDARD FUEL

STA
80.0

STA
83.2

STA
108.5

PERFORMANCE

• •

The regulations require your aircraft to have adequate performance for any flight, meaning its ability to get off the ground in the first place, to maintain certain rates of climb against distance, and land, so you can avoid hard objects (obstacles), particularly when you can't see them.

Many accidents are performance-related, especially those that happen during taking off and landing, when the helicopter is heavy, and operating in hot and thin air. Since you are trying to get a large, heavy object into or out of a relatively small place at some speed, the whole point of performance calculations is to ensure that the space *required* for taking off and landing is not more than the space *available*, taking due account of an engine failure right when you don't want it, and that you have enough engine power to cope with the situation. The idea is to keep the helicopter's mass within limits during all phases of a flight, because the less the weight of the machine, the better it can fly when less power is available. Unfortunately, the charts in flight manuals tend to be optimistic, and they are based on new machines and skilled pilots in the first place, so, although the graphs will give you a maximum weight for the conditions, you would be wise to give yourself a margin, as the maximum weight is a *limit* and not a *target*.

It is your responsibility to decide whether or not a safe takeoff (and landing) can be made under the prevailing conditions. Performance requirements will be worked out before a C of A is issued, over a wide range of conditions,

and they are subsequently incorporated in the Flight Manual, which forms part of the C of A.

You must not be heavier than the Performance regulations you choose to work under say you are allowed to be. The conditions under which you operate determine how heavy your aircraft can be and, as a result, your payload. Over a whole trip, the weight could be dictated by:

- Maximum weight
- WAT limits (see below)
- Space available
- Obstacles
- The route
- Hovering OGE

PERFORMANCE CLASSES

• •

The Performance Class determines the outcome after an engine fails. Single-engined helicopters automatically come under Class 3.

Class 3

Multi-engined types operated in this class *may* have to make a forced landing, while single-engined types *will*. If you are flying over water in a twin-engined helicopter and you don't have enough power to get back to shore if an engine fails, you must observe Class 3 limitations and conditions. Class 3 is not allowed in IMC or at night.

PERFORMANCE CHARTS

Graphs you can expect to meet in the average flight manual include Rate Of Climb, or Takeoff Distance to clear a 50-foot obstacle (something like this):

Gross (lbs)	PA (ft)	25°C	-5°C	15°C	35°C
2150	SL	373	401	430	458
	2000	400	434	461	491
	4000	428	462	494	527
	6000	461	510	585	677
	8000	567	674	779	896
2500	SL	531	569	613	652
	2000	568	614	660	701
	4000	611	660	709	759
	6000	654	727	848	986
	8000	811	975	1144	1355
2850	SL	743	806	864	929
	2000	770	876	929	1011
	4000	861	940	1017	1102
	6000	939	1064	1255	1538
	8000	1201	1527	-	-

On a standard day at Sea Level, it will take 864 feet to climb to 50 feet at 2850 lbs. If you add equipment that takes up engine power, you should also look in the *Supplements* at the back of the Flight Manual. Below is a HIGE chart for a Schweizer 300. To hover IGE on a 4°C day, MAUW should be less than 1790 lbs.

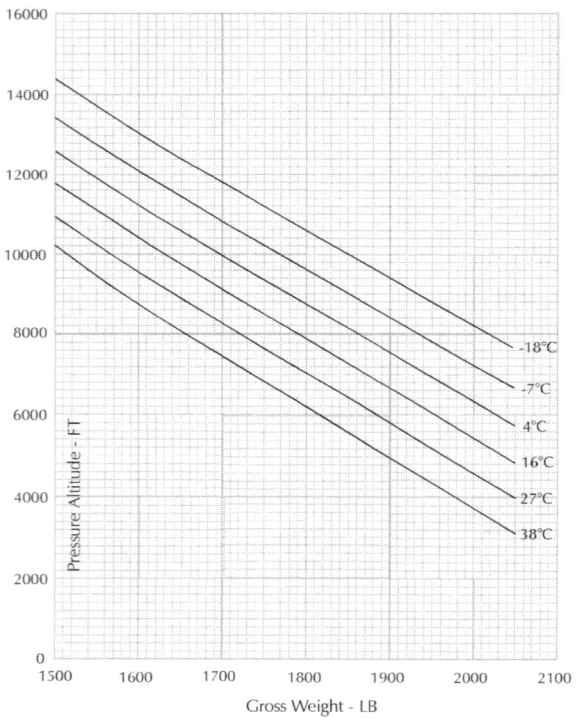

HOW NOT TO DO IT

It is a common misconception that if you can get the helicopter off the ground within its power limitations, it is automatically within its weight limitations. The two reconstructed charts below, which relate to Robinson R22 performance, show just how wrong you can be (this was a real accident).

The pilot thought he was at a low density altitude, and that, because the gauges were reading low, he was within the maximum weight limits. In fact, the weight of the machine *at the time of the accident* was calculated to be 1400 lbs, and that was still over the maximum all up weight! You can see from the graphs that a hover OGE is impossible in the prevailing conditions, and IGE, the machine could just manage a 2-foot hover. The plots are completely off the graph!

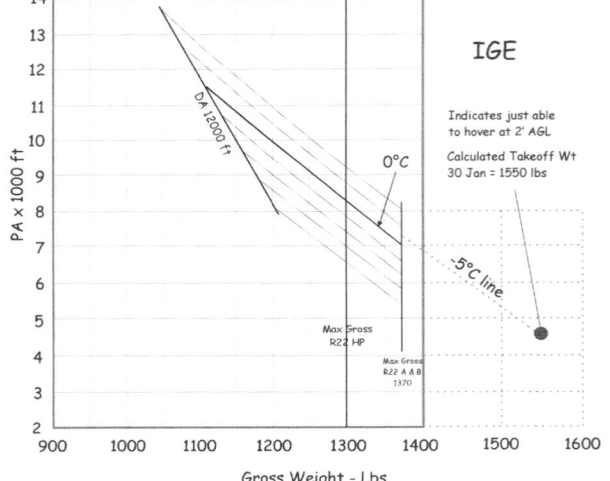

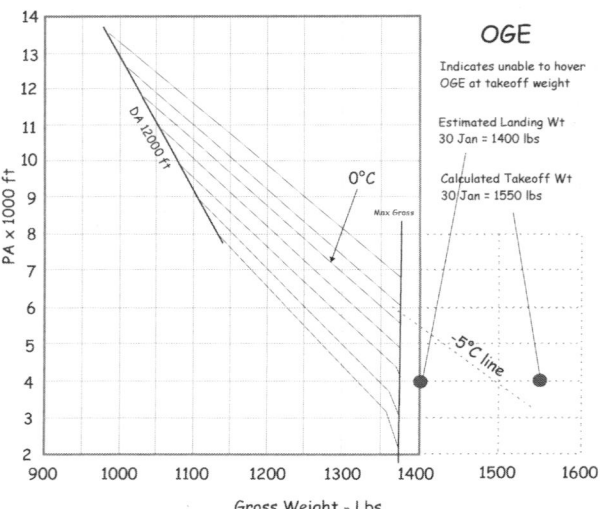

CAPT

FACTORS AFFECTING PERFORMANCE

Pressure Altitude

If the sea level pressure is less than standard, the air is less compressed, and your engine (and rotor blades) think they are at a higher altitude and will not perform so well. Thus, when the sea level pressure is *less* than it should be, you are at a *higher* pressure altitude, or the equivalent of being at a greater height. A high pressure altitude means a higher *altitude* rather than higher *pressure*.

So, to use performance charts effectively, you must find the Pressure Altitude you are really at (for how, see *Pressure Altitude* in *Meteorology*), then modify it for temperature by finding............

Density Altitude

This is the altitude where the air in question matches the ISA density, or where the actual density equals what it would be in the standard atmosphere. In other words, it is your real altitude resulting from the effects of non-standard temperature, but also including height, pressure and humidity, all of which can make the air thinner and which are mentioned below. In standard conditions, the Density Altitude is the same as the Pressure Altitude - as temperature increases above the standard, so will Density Altitude, which can be defined as *Pressure Altitude corrected for temperature*, so once you have found your PA above, you then have to modify it. The details will be in the Flight Manual, although humidity is usually ignored in the average performance chart, because high air density and humidity do not often go hand in hand. However, if there is moisture around, say after a good shower, you would be wise to be careful.

Note: Pressure Altitude has more to do with engine power, and Density Altitude affects aerodynamic efficiency.

Anyhow, the idea is that the more the density of the air decreases, the higher your aircraft thinks it is, and the less efficiently your engine and rotors will perform. In the lift formula, you will see that the lift from an aerofoil is directly dependent on air density, as is drag. The effects are as valid at sea level as they are in mountains when temperatures are high - for example, 90° (F) at sea level is really 1900' as far as your machine is concerned. In extreme circumstances, you may have to restrict your flying operations to early morning or late afternoon.

Here is a handy chart:

°F/C	60/15.6	70/21.1	80/26.7
1000	1300	2000	2700
2000'	2350	3100	3800
3000'	3600	4300	5000
4000'	4650	5600	6300
5000'	6350	6900	7600
6000'	7400	8100	8800
7000'	8600	9300	1000
8000'	9700	10400	11100
9000'	11000	11600	12400
10000'	12250	13000	13600

It shows that, at 6,000 feet and 21°C, for example, you should think in terms of 8,100 feet. If you want to work it out for yourself, add 120' to the Pressure Altitude for every degree above ISA at a particular altitude (it's accurate enough for Government work). For every degree below ISA, subtract 120'. Thus:

$$DA = PA \pm (120 \times ISA\ Dev)$$

ALTITUDE

Air density drops off by 0.002 lbs per cubic foot (2½%) for every 1000 feet in the lower layers of the atmosphere. The rate of climb is negatively affected by high temperature and pressure altitude, and *dirty rotor blades*.

HUMIDITY

Adding water vapour to air makes it less dense because the molecular weight is lower (dry air is 29 - water vapour is 18). On cold days, humidity is less of a problem simply because cold air holds less vapour. A relative humidity of 90% at 70°F means twice as much than at 50°F.

The change in DA due to humidity is very low, at only 400 feet from between 0 to 100%, so the effect on the rotors is not much. In other words, the range of humidity between 0-100% makes a difference of only 400 feet in DA, so when not limited by engine output, that would be a difference of about 20-25 kg off your MAUW.

TEMPERATURE

As heat expands air, it becomes thinner. Thinner air is less dense (*Boyles Law*). On the surface, an increase in temperature will decrease density and increase volume, with pressure remaining constant. At altitude, however, pressure reduces more than temperature does, and produces an apparent contradiction, where temperature will decrease from the expansion. Rising temperature will lower the performance-related takeoff mass.

PRESSURE

Air density reduces with atmospheric pressure (*Charles Law*). When you compress air, its density increases.

Runway Length

Helicopters don't need runways, but they do need space within which to take off, also called *reject areas*. The heavier you are, the more space you need.

TODR will increase by 10% for each 1,000-foot increase in aerodrome altitude and 10% per 10°C increase in temperature (factor by 1.1). LDR increases by 5% for each 1,000-foot increase in PA and 10°C increase in temperature (factor by 1.05).

DR (*Distance Required*) is the horizontal distance from the end of the TODA. LDR (*Landing Distance Required*) is the distance from a specified point on the approach until the helicopter comes to rest.

Aircraft Weight

Greater mass means slower acceleration or deceleration and longer distances.

Runway Slope (Gradient)

Again, helicopters don't need runways, but they may still have to take off over sloping ground without hitting anything. If the slope is unknown it can be calculated by taking the altimeter setting at each end of the runway and finding the height difference.

Tip: Compare the Touch Down Zone Elevation with the airfield elevation from the approach plate.

When landing on a runway that is usable in either direction, regard it as a 0° slope.

Surface Winds

Headwinds reduce the distances required and improve the flight path after take-off. Tailwinds have reverse effects.

Obstacles (The Climb)

Takeoff requirements also need to consider obstacles along the takeoff path which cannot be avoided visually.

V-SPEEDS

In other words, significant operating speeds.

Speed	Explanation
V_{NE}	Never Exceed speed. A red line on the ASI of a helicopter is the V_{NE} for power on, and a blue line is that for power off. It may not be exceeded under any circumstances because it concerns aerodynamic and structural limitations.
V_{NO}	Normal Operations. 10% less than V_{NE}.
V_Y	Best rate of climb, or the most height in the shortest time. It occurs with the greatest difference between power available and power required. Also minimum power airspeed (minimum required for level flight).

FLIGHT PLANNING

This may appear tedious in the early stages, but planning is actually around ¾ of a trip - you're not just getting paid for the flying! The more planning you do, the more answers you will have to hand when things go wrong and the better the trip will be, as any plan you have spent time over is better than one cooked up on the spur of the moment. If you get into a little routine, the process will become speedier as time goes by.

In general, you need to know:

- How to use charts and other aids to find out bearings and distances

- How to calculate the fuel required, and how to use it efficiently

- How much payload your machine can carry as a result, and how it might affect your takeoff and landing weights, and techniques, although this is more to do with performance

However, for the general planning required for a trip, points to remember (in more or less this order) are:

- Airspace you will fly through (controlled or uncontrolled). There might be several factors that affect your choice of route:

  - Routes inbound and outbound (ATC sometimes have preferences)

  - Restricted areas

- Radio frequencies required

- Maps and preparation, according to the route chosen

- NOTAMs/AIP

- Weather (destination and alternates, including takeoff), including enroute forecasts, weather and winds, etc. TAFs & METARs

- Minimum safe altitudes, and performance. There is no VFR flight over congested areas of cities below 1000 feet above the highest obstacle within 600 m

- Best level for performance and comfort (Quadrantal Rule)

- Best level for winds aloft

- Fuel required

- Weight & Balance/Performance

- Documents required to be carried

- Flight plans (see *Air Law*)

- Aircraft serviceability

THE PLOG (NAV/FLIGHT LOG)

The letters are short for *Progress Log*, or a sheet of paper which tabulates the details of a particular flight, used for flight planning and checking progress on the actual trip. It's otherwise called a *Nav Log*, or *Flight Log* (I'm told that a navigation log used to be just that - the progress of a ship was carved on a lump of wood). Once you've drawn your proposed track on the map, you put its details in the appropriate boxes on the plog, work out the wind, obtain your intended heading and groundspeed, apply the magnetic variation, calculate the fuel required, fill 'er up and you're ready to go.

Overleaf is a sample form, partly filled in with details of a trip from Glasgow (GOW) to Inverness (INS). Notice that the Flight Level (or altitude, in this case) is higher than the Safety Altitude, which is the higher of the highest ground within 5 nm of track, plus 1299 feet, or the highest structure, plus 1000 feet (in this case, I've taken the biggest blue figure in the lat/long boxes en route, off the half-mil map).

Otherwise, there's not much else you can usefully put in at this stage, so get out your whizzwheel and see if you can fill in the rest, given that the wind is 180/15. If you want to cheat, the picture below it will show you what it should look like.

Here is what the track looks like on the map:

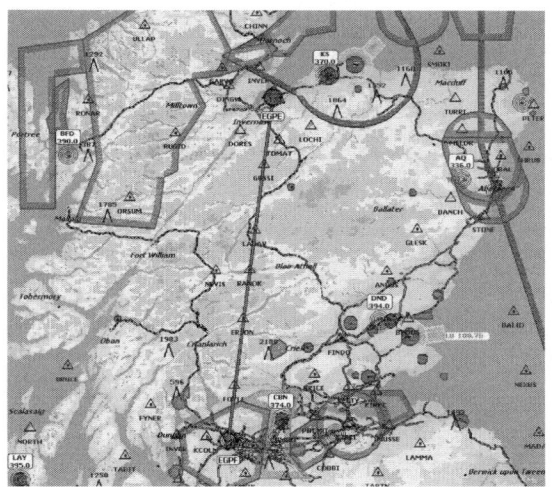

The figures for an alternate have been left out for clarity, but you should always choose one and work out the figures for it in the same way, before you go - by definition, an alternate is for when you *really* need one, and there's never enough time to do things on the run. When planning a trip with a lot of legs, if there's room, leave a line between each one, in case you have to change things, or you note any differences, such as wind velocity, and have to work out a new groundspeed.

The Douglas Protractor

The line on the map above can naturally be drawn with any straight edge, but using it to determine the track you need to fly is done with a Douglas protractor, or similar:

You can either place the line in the middle (with the arrow on) along a longitude line and read off the track on the outside figures, or place the line along the track and read it off on the inside figures (the ones that are reading backward). It also has its uses as a parallel rule.

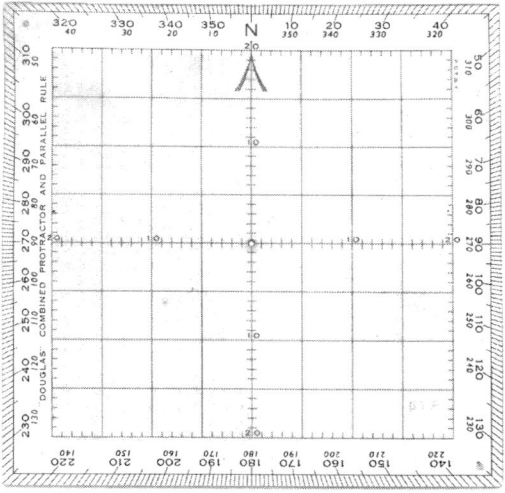

FUEL

Very few aircraft will actually take a full load of passengers and fuel, so you need to know how long it will take between two points, find out how much fuel it will take, *then* fit the passengers in. *Do not put the passengers in first and fit the fuel in afterwards!* Not unless you plan to stop en route, at least. Of all the things there is absolutely no excuse for in Aviation, running out of fuel in flight is one of them! If you have to take less fuel, then you will have to stop and pick up some more on the way, or leave someone behind. If you take the same fuel anyway, you will be overweight, with not enough power in the engines to get you out of trouble, and *invalid insurance.*

Fuel and oil consumption rates and weights should be in the Flight Manual. It's usual to keep a check on the fuel contents to see if things are going according to plan, keeping track of fuel consumption.

Fuel Management

Minimum fuel figures are calculated for *level* aircraft. Odd attitudes may cause a fuel boost pump to become uncovered and give you a nasty surprise just when you don't want it. On a Bell 206, the unusable fuel after a boost pump failure can be up to 10 US gals, which is uncomfortably close to the minimums.

Fuel management means you should check and record the contents regularly in flight, to ensure that:

- Actual consumption compares with planned consumption

- The remaining fuel is enough to complete the flight

- Check the expected fuel remaining on arrival at the destination.

For piston-engined helicopters, where the engine RPM and internal temperatures are more or less constant, the Specific Fuel Consumption won't change much.

The TAS for using the least amount of power is found at the bottom of the power required curve (see left), but, in practice, a little more speed is used to take the edge off the rotor drag. Best endurance speed is the same for best rate of climb and minimum rate of descent.

You must be able to fly for 20 minutes at normal cruising speed *after* reaching your destination.

Here are some suggestions for pre-flight calculation of usable fuel:

- **Taxy Fuel**, at least what you expect to use before takeoff, including start, taxi and run-up

- **Trip Fuel.** That required for the trip as planned

- **Reserve Fuel**, which must be on board at takeoff, but not necessarily used. It might consist of:

  - **Alternate Fuel**, if a destination alternate is required

  - **Final Reserve Fuel.** For Day VFR navigating visually, 20 minutes at best range speed

- **Extra Fuel** as required (it might be more expensive where you are going)

Time	From	To	FL/ Alt	Safety Alt	TAS	W/V	Track T	Drift	Hdg T	Var	Hdg M	G/S	Dist	Time	ETA
1200	GOW	INS	4500	4300	90	180/15	007			+5.5			104		
Alternate											Totals →				

Time	From	To	FL/ Alt	Safety Alt	TAS	W/V	Track T	Drift	Hdg T	Var	Hdg M	G/S	Dist	Time	ETA
1200	GOW	INS	4500	4300	90	180/15	007	+1	008	+5.5	013	105	104	60	1300
Alternate											Totals →				

THE GREENHOUSE EFFECT

The Earth is about 33° warmer than it would be without its atmosphere. The difference is the *Greenhouse Effect*, and the gases that help the process along are the *Greenhouse Gases*. The primary heat-trapping gas is water vapour, with CO_2, methane and sodium dioxide amongst the secondaries. CO_2 takes up only 0.038% of the atmosphere.

The wavelength of radiated energy is inversely proportional to the temperature of whatever is emitting it. As the Sun is very hot, its radiations are of shorter wavelength than those from the Earth, which has a much lower temperature (in fact, around 99% of the Sun's energy is emitted in the shorter wavelengths). This is a similar (but not identical) effect to that produced by the glass in a greenhouse, that lets short wave radiation (light) in, and is less transparent to the longer infrared radiation going out. Essentially, long wave energy radiated from the surface of the Earth is absorbed by the greenhouse gases that act as a thermal blanket around the Earth, and is reradiated back towards it.

Between the Equator and 35°N & S, more energy is absorbed than is radiated, so there is a surplus. Similarly, there is a deficit between 35°N & S and the relevant Pole.

The Seasons

We get seasons (and varying day lengths) because the Earth is not vertical in space - it is inclined at an average angle of 23½°, so that different areas are pointed towards the Sun in their turn, and receive sunlight for longer periods each day, hence Summer.

At the Summer Solstice in June, the Sun is above the Tropic of Cancer at 23.5°N. In Winter, in December, it is over the Tropic of Capricorn at 23.5°S. It is above the Equator at the March and September Equinoxes.

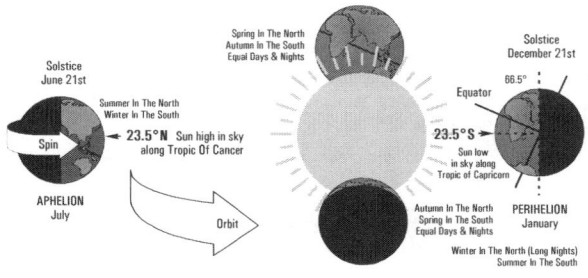

The paradox is that, in the Northern Hemisphere's Winter (on the right, above), the Earth is at its *closest* point to the Sun (after Kepler's Laws), where you would expect it to be warmer, proving that the Earth's heat is self-created.

The reason for the paradox is that the Sun's rays are distributed differently. In Winter, they are spread over a wider area and are less effective.

They have also travelled further and have had a longer path through the clouds.

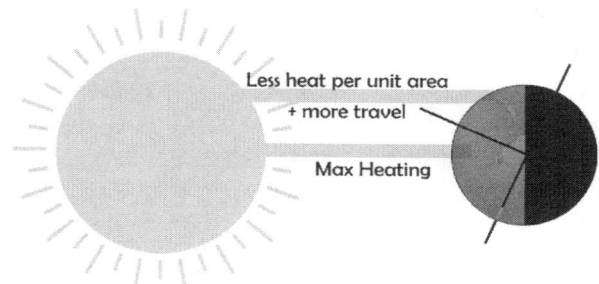

The distance of the Earth from the Sun can vary by as much as 3 million miles, as explained in *Navigation*.

THE ATMOSPHERE

This has already mostly been mentioned in *Human Factors*, but there are a few points relating to meteorology that need to be made.

Almost all weather happens in the troposphere, because it contains more than 75% of the mass of the atmosphere, which is drawn to the Earth by gravity. About half of that mass is below 18 000 feet.

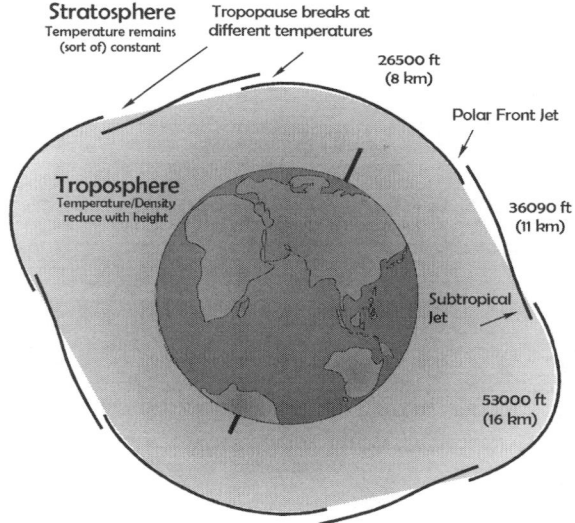

The tropopause is the boundary between the troposphere and the stratosphere. It normally represents the maximum limit for winds and clouds, because that's where the temperature abruptly stops decreasing so much with altitude. Temperature *decreases* with height in the troposphere, officially until the rate is less than 2°C per 1000 feet. This is because, as pressure decreases, so does the temperature, resulting in *adiabatic cooling**.

Adiabatic means that the air gets hot, or cold, all by itself, according to whether it is being compressed or expanded - no energy is added or taken away, or exchanged with the outside world. In other words, as air expands, the molecules have more room to move around in, so they slow down, which has the effect of reducing the temperature. Similarly in reverse. Thus, as a parcel of air rises (into a region of lower pressure, which makes it expand), it cools adiabatically, through its own expansion, in the short term. Conduction between different sources of air takes quite a long time.

Over the Equator, the tropopause lies at around 16-18 km, higher than it is at the Poles (8 km), because the air is warmer and has expanded, taking the tropopause with it.

North of 60°N in Winter, the tropopause will be found at about 29 000 ft. At 50°N, at around 36 090 feet (average 11 km). However, the height of the tropopause can be locally affected by the movement of various airmasses, so there can be sudden variations.

At 40°N, 55°N and between 60-70°N, it changes height quite abruptly, and can fold over, or even break, which is an instrumental factor in the formation of jetstreams which can affect the weather at lower levels.

So, the average temperature of the troposphere determines the height of the tropopause, although the temperature of the tropopause itself is determined by its height. The *lowest* tropopause temperature is around -75°C at its *highest* point at 16 km around the Equator, otherwise it will be more like -56.5°C and -45°C at the Poles. The heights will vary by a couple of thousand feet between January-July.

Although oxygen may be important to pilots and engines, the proportion of gases making up the atmosphere has no relevance to meteorology, except that it holds water as:

- a gas (water vapour)

- a liquid (clouds or rain)

- a solid (ice)

Water vapour is important because it is invisible, and affects the humidity ratio of the air. Because it weighs five-eighths of an equivalent amount of dry air, water vapour will also reduce the density of the air and your engine's punch, but that's the subject of the *Performance* chapter. The water vapour content on average is around 1%, but can get as high as 4%. The troposphere (the lower part of the atmosphere) contains more than 90% of all water vapour, but the correction is small and generally negligible. The presence of water is expressed as relative humidity, described later, and its importance lies in the energy that is released and consumed as it changes from gas to liquid to ice and back.

Otherwise, dry air may be regarded as a uniform gas that obeys the General Gas Laws that connect temperature, pressure and density in this way:

$$p = RT\rho$$

ρ is the density, T the absolute temperature and p the pressure. R is a constant that depends on the gas.

The molecules in a gas are in constant, random motion, which produces a uniform pressure on any boundary surface. The amount of pressure depends on the number and mass of the molecules (density), and how fast they are moving (depends on temperature).

The constant doesn't change, of course, and if temperature stays the same, pressure is proportional to density - because you are increasing pressure by cramming more molecules into a smaller space, density automatically increases. If pressure stays the same, an increase in temperature reduces the density. So you can calculate density if you know the pressure and temperature.

TEMPERATURE
•••

The temperature of the atmosphere (and its variation) is the basis of all weather, and is intimately linked with pressure, and therefore wind.

The quantity of heat in a substance is a measure of the kinetic energy of its molecules, after the temperature, mass and nature of the material. For example, a bucketful of warm water will melt more ice than a cupful of boiling water because it contains more heat.

Temperature is therefore a measure of the *quality* of heat (or the rate at which molecules are moving), which means it cannot strictly be measured, but only compared against other temperatures. As you heat an item, its molecules need more room in which to oscillate, so it expands. As the distance between the molecules grows, the molecular force that keeps them together gets weaker.

As mentioned, most, if not all, of the Earth's heat comes from the Earth itself, that is, from below. The Sun's rays do not produce heat (or light) until they hit something (which is why it's cold and dark in space), so the air will get warmed by *conduction* from the ground which has been heated up by them, known as *insolation*. In other words, *terrestrial radiation* and *conduction* are primarily responsible for heating the lower atmosphere, followed by convection.

Rising parcels of warm air are called *thermals*, or *convection currents*, which is what keeps gliders up in the air.

CAPT

Along with surface characteristics, the latitude of a place will have an effect on local temperature. The standard for comparison is that applied to water, which has a specific heat value of 1. Smaller quantities increase temperature more rapidly.

Since the Earth does not get hotter and hotter as the Sun shines on it, it follows that heat must be radiated away somewhere. This explains the difference in temperatures between day and night, known as *diurnal variation*. The temperature begins to rise shortly after sunrise (after an initial dip) because the Sun's radiation exceeds that of the Earth, and starts to fall mid-afternoon, when it falls below, carrying on through the night until the process starts again. This is less marked over water, which reacts more slowly. In fact, changes over the sea will not be much more than 1°C. The maximum variation would happen inland with clear skies over a dry area, such as the desert.

Clouds will also absorb and reflect energy from the Sun during the day, and act as a blanket overnight to stop heat being radiated away, further reducing diurnal differences. Clouds can reduce the normal 50% insolation the Earth might receive on a sunny day right down to 15% (the remainder is reflected back by clouds and the atmosphere). Windspeed and relative humidity will also have an effect.

There are two ways of measuring temperature (or rather the average kinetic energy of molecules), called *Fahrenheit* or *Celsius*, and it's a real pain to convert between the two. The quick and easy way is to use a flight computer:

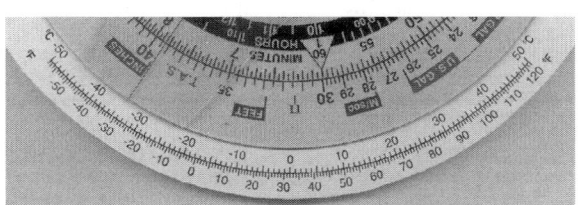

But here are the calculations if you want to show off:

F - C $Tc = (5/9)*(Tf-32)$

C - F $Tf = (9/5)*(Tc+32)$

16°C is equal to 61°F, 20°C is 68°F and 30°C is 86°F, for gross error checks and quick conversions - however, given the standard of performance charts in the average flight manual, doubling the Celsius amount and adding 30 to get Fahrenheit, or subtracting 30 from Fahrenheit and dividing the remainder in half to get Celsius is probably good enough!

The Fahrenheit scale assumes that water freezes at 32°, and boils at 212°. Celsius starts at 0° and finishes at 100°, which is more logical, but the scale is coarser. The *freezing level* (in flight) is where the temperature is 0°C.

For each °C of cooling, a gas will reduce its volume by 1/273. -273°C is equal to 0 K (*Kelvin*), or *Absolute*, which is the point at which all molecular motion is supposed to have stopped, and therefore has the least kinetic energy. At this point, the will be zero pressure, which is why absolute temperature is in the gas equation, above.

Alternatively, you could say that 0°C is equal to 273 K (or A), from which you can deduce that the 1° steps in both scales are the same (*Rankin* is an absolute scale with the same divisions as Fahrenheit - add 459.69 to Fahrenheit totals. Kelvins are base units rather than a scale, so they don't carry a degree sign).

Thermometers are covered in the *Instruments* chapter.

Air temperature at the earth's surface is defined as the shade temperature measured in a louvred screen about four feet off the ground. A *Stevenson Screen* is a louvred cabinet that allows air conditions to be monitored without being directly exposed to sunlight. Inside it, you will find a selection of thermometers, amongst other things, such as hygrometers.

The louvres provide shade as well as free air flow and the white exterior increases reflection of solar radiation. The doors open toward the Poles to reduce the risk of sunlight falling on the thermometers inside when they are opened. The cabinet is positioned over grass to reduce insolation.

LAPSE RATES

The standard reduction of temperature with height is 1.98°C per thousand feet.

Graph: Standard Temperature Distribution

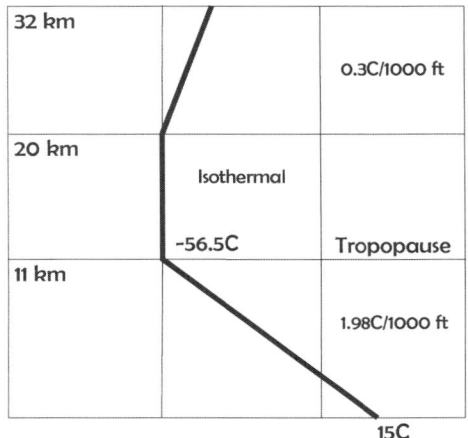

32 km		0.3C/1000 ft
20 km	Isothermal	
	-56.5C	Tropopause
11 km		1.98C/1000 ft
		15C

INVERSIONS

Where it remains constant, there is an *isothermal layer*. Where it *increases* (typical in anticyclonic conditions), you have an *inversion*. The end result is that cold air is underneath warmer air, which can happen during the passage of a cold front, or a cooler onshore breeze might be flowing over warm sea water. Cool air that is rising will lose its buoyancy and be stopped from rising further upon reaching its equilibrium level. In a thunderstorm, this happens just above the tropopause, where the cloud material settles into a layer that causes the anvil shape. Thus, conditions in an inversion are stable, because lifted air is always cooler than the environment.

However, aircraft performance is affected by variations in temperature, and inversions will do so adversely. Large ones encountered shortly after takeoff can seriously degrade your climb performance, particularly when you're heavy. Even a small one in the upper levels can prevent you reaching a preferred cruising altitude. At lower levels, expect deteriorating visibility, as an inversion can prevent fog clearance for prolonged periods until it is blown away by horizontal movement of air. Below a low level inversion, visibility is often moderate or poor because there is no vertical exchange to carry pollutants and haze into the free atmosphere (industrial pollutants, especially incinerated pesticides during the stubble burning season, collect at the base of an inversion).

When flight planning, you can find the top of an inversion (assuming the air below it is well mixed, as it would be in the presence of insolation) by allowing 400 feet for every degree of difference (in Celsius) between the temperature and dewpoint.

Inversions can be caused by:

- *Overnight radiation cooling* of air at the surface, which is strongest at sunrise and a few hundred feet thick

- *Katabatic winds* in mountains that settle in valleys

- A *subsidence inversion* is a stable layer at some height (4-6 000 ft in mid latitudes) in the low troposphere of an older high in the mid-latitudes which can be responsible for trapping thick haze and smoke in the lower levels. More permanent inversions are associated with large high-pressure systems, where descending currents of air near the centre cause the air to warm up by compression, so the air at middle altitudes becomes warmer than that at the surface. In other words, the top layer subsides more than, and therefore warms more rapidly than, the bottom layer, so when the top layer reaches a higher temperature, you get an inversion

Frontal or *sea breeze* inversions form when a wedge of cooler air forms under warmer air

THE INTERNATIONAL STANDARD ATMOSPHERE

To make sure that everyone works on the same page, a couple of typical scientists went to a typical place on the South coast of England many years ago and measured the temperature and pressure, which turned out to be 1013.25 millibars (29.92" of mercury) and 15.5° Centigrade. This was adopted as the International Standard Atmosphere, and now everyone who makes altimeters, or whatever, calibrates them with it so that everything is standard. The pressure actually works out to be around 14.7 lbs per square inch, which equates to 20 tons on the average person. In short, ISA is a standard that provides universal values of temperature, pressure, density and lapse rate, by which others can be compared.

In the standard atmosphere, ½ sea level pressure is obtained at 18 000', one third at 27 500' and ¼ at 33 700'. Thus, pressure decreases with height, but not linearly (a layer 1 millibar deep is about equal to 27 feet at sea level - at 3 000 feet, it's 30 feet, or around 90 feet at the heights jets fly at, i.e. 35 000 feet). The sea level pressure on which the standard atmosphere is based relates 1" of mercury to 1,000 feet of altitude, so you would expect to see an altimeter read 1 000 feet less if you set it to 28.92 instead of 29.92 inches. Some countries use hectopascals, or hPas, instead of millibars, which contain 1000 Pascals. Many people also use them interchangeably.

ISA CONVERSIONS

The ambient temperature is almost never standard, so we often have to compare it against what it should be under ISA conditions. Although the reduction is technically 1.98°C per 1000', 2° is often used for convenience, as is done with the *jet standard atmosphere*, which is used by engine manufacturers and which doesn't have a tropopause - a point to watch above 36,000 feet.

Because ISA is a standard atmosphere, and aircraft specifications are based on it, actual atmospheric conditions are given in terms of *ISA Deviation*. For example, you might be asked what the temperature deviation is at FL 290 with an OAT of -47°C? First of all, find out what the temperature difference from sea level *should* be, so, using 2°C per thousand feet, we find it should be 58° lower (29 x 2). Given that the temperature at sea level is always 15°C in ISA, subtract one from the other to get -43°C (-58+15). As the OAT is -47°C, the temperature deviation is ISA - 4°C (that is, 4° colder than it should be). In short, find ISA by multiplying the altitude in thousands of feet by -2 and adding 15, then apply deviation. Height changes by 4% for every 10° deviation.

The other way round, you could have to find temperature, given a deviation at a flight level. If it's ISA -7°C at FL 250, +15 (ISA) - 50 (25 x 2) gets us -35°C, normal ISA temperature. Applying the deviation, which is colder, we get -42°C.

CAPT

Tip: To find what the standard temperature should be at any level, line up the two tens on the inner and outer wheels of your flight computer and take a look in the altitude window against the height you require:

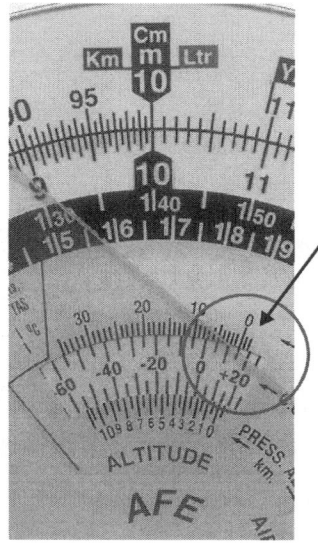

15°at Sea level or -5° at 10,000 ft

Pressure

For meteorological purposes, atmospheric pressure is the total effect of the air molecules in random motion. At a given height, the only thing that stops the air above you falling to the ground is the pressure of the air below you acting upwards, so the total pressure acting on your aircraft is equal to the weight of the air above you.

The weight of a column of air is commonly measured in terms of *millibars* (or *hectopascals*) or *inches of mercury*. Variations in atmospheric pressure can be traced directly to variations in air density, which in turn are often caused by temperature differences (there is a twice daily variation around the Earth).

The distribution of pressure at the surface has a major impact on the type of weather we get. Pressure differentials, for example, provide the forces for the generation of wind and changes in weather.

PRESSURE SYSTEMS

During the day, the pressure is measured at many hundreds of weather stations, converted to sea level pressure (using ISA) and marked on a map, with the points that have equal pressure being connected up. The lines that join the dots are called *isobars* (*iso* is Greek for *same*), and will be 4 hectopascals apart, counting up and down from 1000. The closer they are together, the more the millibars drop per mile and the more severe the pressure gradient will be, for stronger winds (air moves from high to low pressure).

Isobars are like contours, and make common patterns, two of which are the *low* or *high*, other names for *cyclone* and *anti-cyclone*, respectively (nothing to do with the cyclones that seem to damage trailer parks). Another name for a low is a *depression*. The exact position of a system will be marked by an X.

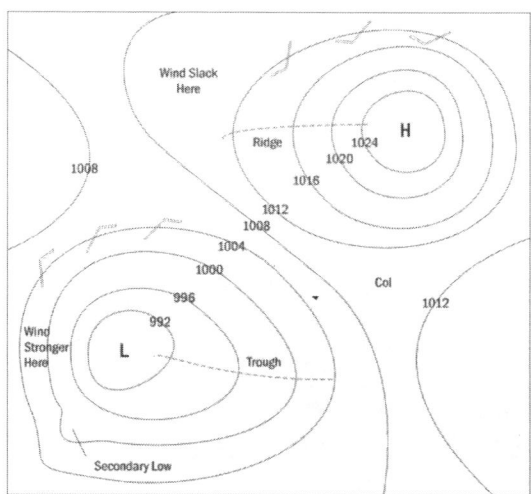

In the diagram above, the air is going into the High at the top, twisting to the right, and coming out of the low at the bottom, twisting left (air moves clockwise round a high, and anticlockwise round a low). Thus, if you were flying from East to West, it would be best going South of a High and North of a Low, in the Northern Hemisphere.

Note: Isobars are based on readings corrected to a certain level, usually sea level. Contours, discussed more fully in *Upper Winds*, are illustrations of how the height of a pressure varies and would look like a series of hills and valleys if you could see them in 3D.

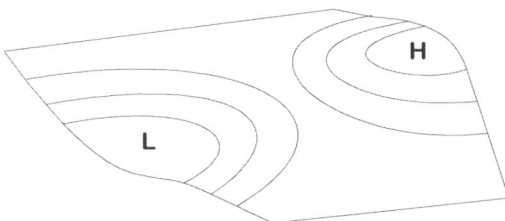

In tropical regions, especially nearer the Equator, isobars do not give an accurate indication of the wind, so they are replaced by *streamlines*, which resemble spirals, unlike isobars, which never meet.

ANTICYCLONES

An anticyclone is an area of high pressure (on the Earth's surface) between around 1020-45 hPa (even up to 1060 hPa). Above every surface high pressure, there is a low pressure at altitude.

The isobars around the centre are more or less concentric and are widely spaced, so winds are usually light and variable, although they usually blow clockwise and outwards (in the Northern Hemisphere), faster towards the outside of the system. As a result, weather conditions are usually quiet, dry and settled, but just because cloud is mostly absent in a high, don't expect clear skies, as the descending air might trap haze or smoke, leading to a phenomenon called *anticyclonic gloom* near industrial areas. As an example, this picture shows what the Persian Gulf looks like on a hot VFR day:

As air descends in a high, it gets warmed by adiabatic compression. This also leads to low relative humidities, and the absence of cloud. However, the descending air might not get to ground level, because of convection and turbulence, leaving a cooler moist layer around 500-1500 m deep immediately above the surface. The boundary between this cooler air and the subsided air aloft is characterized by a subsidence inversion which limits the upward movement of convection currents, preventing extensive air cooling and cloud formation. Unfortunately, if the air is moist below the temperature inversion, a dreary formless layer of cloud can form which becomes difficult to disperse because of the light winds. Such debilitating weather is common in winter when the Sun's radiation is too weak to burn off the cloud layer.

In Winter, a short cloudless day can mean a long night with more radiation cooling than the Sun can cope with the next day, due to its low angle. The second night of cooling therefore starts with a lower air temperature than the first. This can mean successive nights of frost, which become progressively harder. When the air is particularly moist, cooling at night soon results in fog. Britain in particular can experience episodes of anticyclonic fog between September and May.

Anticyclones may be either warm or cold. Warm highs result from convergence in the upper troposphere and subsidence beneath, producing relatively warm air throughout the troposphere above the subsidence inversion (the Azores High is a good example).

Note: "The Azores High" is really a succession of highs that are stagnating in that position. It gets smaller in Winter, which moves the fronts that normally progress between Scotland and Iceland further South over the UK.

Warm highs also form in temperate latitudes from convergence just ahead of a ridge in the upper westerlies. They are either extensions of subtropical highs, linked to them by a strong ridge of high pressure, or as persistent blocks that disrupt the more normal westerly flow and prevent depressions from following their usual routes.

As an example of the influence a high pressure area can have, a strong one commonly sits over Eastern Canada in late Spring because most of the Hudson Bay is still frozen. It is very good at stopping the movement of other systems and weather. There are permanent ones over the Poles, as well, not to mention the Siberian high with an elongated section that stretches back into NW Europe in April. When this happens, the clockwise flow brings in warm moist Mediterranean air over Italy, up the Alps and into the upper atmosphere. This air takes longer to slow and cool down, so over NW Europe there is a high tropopause height in April with a cold temperature. With such blocking highs, the normal Easterly movement of depressions and fronts becomes more South-North, or meriodonal (in line with meridians), a good illustration of which is the Bermuda High which is a semipermanent feature in that general area. It can be responsible for thunderstorms, high density altitudes and low visibility in haze - the clockwise circulation sends warm, damp ocean air up the Eastern half of the United States, which destabilises in the warmth of afternoon heating, to cause thunderstorms.

Cold anticyclones are shallow, often no more than 3000 m deep, which form over cold surfaces due to convergence aloft caused by the contraction of the cold low level air. They may be found over Antarctica and the Arctic Ocean at any time in the year, also over northern Eurasia, Greenland, and North America during the winter.

Air mass subsidence concerns the descent of larger masses of air over wide areas, typically found in the Earth's circulation at subtropical latitudes, where the deserts are.

A ridge of high pressure is a wedge-shaped extension of an anticyclone or belt of high pressure, with similar weather characteristics to an anticyclone. In temperate latitudes as in the British Isles, ridges of high pressure often occur between two depressions and move with them. They give rise to intervals of fair weather between the cloud and rain of the low-pressure systems.

CAPT

NON-FRONTAL DEPRESSIONS

High level divergence produces areas of low pressure at ground level. Lows are generally found meandering around the Equator and in temperate latitudes, where they tend to dominate the scene with clouds and rain. On the other hand, a dry, sunny region can get very warm from intense surface heating, and create a *thermal low,* typically over land in Summer. Lows are often classed as *deep* or *intense, shallow* or *weak,* but these are relative to each other.

A secondary low can be a smaller one inside a larger system that forms at the tip of the warm sector, in which the weather is more intense as it feeds on its bigger brother. A secondary low can also form in the cold air advection behind a cyclone, or at the triple point of an occlusion, or when air moves across barriers and is lifted. In any case, it will move around the primary Low cyclonically (anticlockwise in the Northern Hemisphere).

An orographic or Lee Trough (Low) exists in the lee of a range of hills after the air has gone over and round the range, where it gets compressed before and after being forced round. The air going over the ridge reduces in height and spreads out horizontally, to resemble a high pressure, so the Coriolis effect is reduced, and the process is reversed further down the lee slope, to resemble a low.

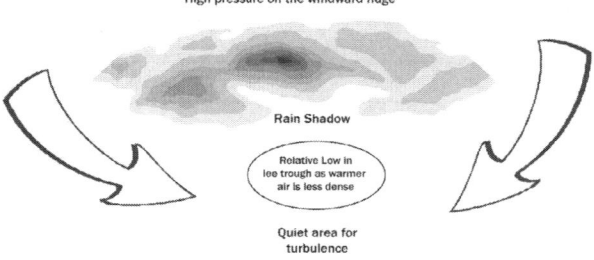

High pressure on the windward ridge

Rain Shadow

Relative Low in lee trough as warmer air is less dense

Quiet area for turbulence

Also, as the air behind the barrier has not been compressed, it is at a relatively lower pressure anyway. A difference of 2 or 3 mb can mean that your altimeter misreads by nearly 100 feet.

Winds that are deflected around large single mountain peaks or through the valleys of mountain ranges can increase their speed, which results in a local decrease in pressure (Bernoulli's Principle). A pressure altimeter would be subject to increased errors in its indications, which will be present until the airflow returns to normal speed some distance away from the range.

A *trough* is an elongated region of relatively low atmospheric pressure, often associated with fronts and identified as an extension of isobars away from a low pressure center, with similar weather characteristics. However, the region between two high pressure centers may also assume the character of a trough when there is a detectable wind shift at the surface.

WIND

Because the Earth is heated unevenly, air at the Equator becomes warmer than it does at the Poles, so it expands upwards around the middle of the Earth and contracts down to the surface higher up the latitude scale.

This general trend gives rise to regular patterns of air movement, in the shape of winds that were well known to navigators on the high seas, such as the *trade winds.*

Wind is the *horizontal* movement of air from high to low pressure, just like the air from a pricked balloon - the larger the pressure difference, the faster the wind will flow. Wind is expressed as a velocity, so it needs direction and speed to fit the definition. The wind always comes *from* somewhere, expressed as a *true bearing* in weather reports (*magnetic* from the Tower), so a *Southerly* wind is *from* 180°. The speed is mostly in knots, or nautical miles per hour, as if you didn't know already. Wind direction is measured with a *wind vane,* while speed is measured with an *anemometer,* which should be placed on a mast 6-10 m above the runway and calibrated after *Saint Venant* (to allow for compressibility) for best results. 10 m is used to make sure that the wind is not affected by small local obstacles. A *pressure tube anemometer* works in the same way as a pitot tube. A more common type has three cups on stalks that are driven round by the wind, and the speed of rotation gives the wind speed.

Obstacles interfere with the wind in different ways. A forest is like large brush, slowing the air down and mixing it up. It will also tend to build up before an obstacle and create turbulent eddies behind it. This is one effect that will result in *gusts* and *lulls* as the speed varies. *Gusts* are rapid changes of speed and direction that don't last long, whilst *squalls* do. A gale has a minimum wind speed of 34 kts, or is gusting at 43 kts or more.

Veering is a clockwise change in wind direction with height or time - backing is the reverse.

Geostrophic (Coriolis) Force (Effect)

Under normal circumstances, air would just move from high to low pressure, *across* the isobars, due to the *Pressure Gradient Force,* or PGF, which makes it move from high to low pressure. The size of the PGF depends on the spacing of the isobars and inversely on air density (the denser the air is, the more force you need to move it).

Outside the Equator, in the Northern Hemisphere, air moves clockwise round a high pressure area and anticlockwise round a low, because the Earth is spinning, and deflects normal air movement, until eventually the wind blows *along* the isobars (instead of across) at around 2,000 feet. Thus, an imaginary force *appears* to cause a moving body to follow a curved path.

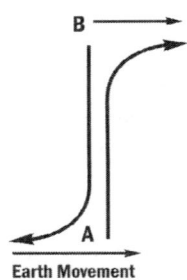

Earth Movement

The Earth moves faster at the equator than it does at the Poles (based on a cosine relationship), so, if you fire an artillery shell from the North Pole to the Equator (B to A, on the left), progressively more of the Earth's surface would pass under its track, giving the illusion of the object curving to the right (or West of A) as it lags behind - the Earth is moving slower towards the North. If you threw whatever it was the other way, it would "move" to the East of B, because you are adding the Earth's movement at both latitudes. That is, B will be moving slower relative to A. In other words, a bullet might fly in a straight line, but its target will move to the right.

In the Southern hemisphere, air is deflected to the left.

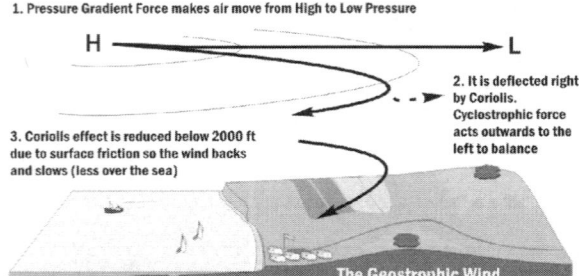

1. Pressure Gradient Force makes air move from High to Low Pressure

2. It is deflected right by Coriolis. Cyclostrophic force acts outwards to the left to balance

3. Coriolis effect is reduced below 2000 ft due to surface friction so the wind backs and slows (less over the sea)

The Geostrophic Wind

This apparent movement (East or West) is often called the *Coriolis Effect*, after a Frenchman who noticed that a billiard ball tends to veer to the right in the Northern hemisphere, and to the left in the Southern hemisphere. It is actually *Geostrophic Force* when it refers to air movement, although no "force" is involved, hence the use of the word "effect". As the wind moves towards low pressure, its speed progressively increases, and so does the deflection due to Coriolis, which is directly proportional to wind speed and the sine of the latitude.

However, there is another force involved, called *cyclostrophic force*, which operates outward (like centrifugal force), at 90° to the instantaneous motion, to the left in the Northern Hemisphere and the right in the Southern Hemisphere. This combination of geostrophic and cyclostrophic effects is called the *gradient wind*. In lower latitudes, the sine value of the latitude is small, so the cyclostrophic effect will predominate. At higher latitudes, it will only do this at higher windspeeds.

In high pressure areas, the combination of descending air and cyclostrophic force makes the winds blow outwards, but this is offset by the pressure gradient in a low being much steeper, creating stronger winds anyway. This is known as the *isallobaric effect*, since lines joining places with an equal *rate of change* of pressure are *isallobars*. Thus,

cyclostrophic (centrifugal) force helps a high to decay by removing mass from it. In low latitudes, highs will dissipate rapidly and winds will be slight.

In low pressure areas, the cyclostrophic force acts inwards, and is often large enough by itself to keep a swirl going once it starts, leading to revolving storms in the tropics.

As you descend, friction with trees, rocks, etc. will slow the wind down, which lessens the geostrophic effect and gives you an effective change of wind direction to the left. As this is enough to reduce the wind speed enough to stop it deflecting, it will tend to blow towards the low pressure, i.e. inwards, to contribute towards the lifting effect, since it is forced up, to cause adiabatic cooling, and precipitation.

In any case, wind in a *low* would be *lower* than the equivalent geostrophic wind, and *higher* round a *high*.

Over the sea, the geostrophic effect will be less, giving about 10° difference in direction, as opposed to the 30° you can expect over land (the speed reduces to about 70% over water, and 50% over land).

As always, there is a mathematical solution:

$$GF = 2w\rho V \sin\theta$$

where w = the Earth's rotational velocity, ρ is density, V is the wind speed and θ is the latitude. You can see that, as latitude increases, so will the geostrophic force, or that the wind speed will decrease. To get windspeed, at 2,000 feet, the wind is parallel to the isobars (*when they are straight and parallel*), meaning that the PGF must be balanced by another force, which we shall call GF, as displayed in the diagram above. Now all you need to do is swap GF for PGF and play with the formula:

$$V = \frac{PGF}{2w\rho\sin\theta}$$

It also shows that the windspeed increases with height as density reduces, but it all breaks down within about 15° of the Equator, or you would have an infinite windspeed. Given the same pressure gradient at 40°N, 50°N and 60°N, the geostrophic wind speed will be greatest at 40°N.

According to Professor *Buys Ballot's Law* (a Dutch meteorologist who lived in Utrecht in 1857), if you stand with your back to the wind in the Northern hemisphere, the low pressure is on your left (on the right in the Southern hemisphere), so if you fly towards lower pressure, you will drift to starboard as the wind is coming from the left. It's the opposite way round in an anticyclone. Buys Ballot's Law, by the way, had already been deduced by US meteorologists William Ferrel and James Coffin, but they didn't get to be famous. Note that it does not always apply to winds that are deflected by local terrain, or local winds such as sea breezes or those that flow down mountains.

CAPT

Mountain Winds

Understanding how air moves around terrain is one of the keys to good mountain flying. Winds can increase your operational ceiling, payload, rate of climb, range and cruise speed. They can also do the opposite, and be very difficult to predict, with formidable up- and downdraughts associated with them. When cruising downwind, along a lee slope or not, sudden wind reversals could make you exceed V_{NE} or even take away your airspeed.

The area of lift from high ground is greatest where the air is made to move sharply in a different direction, and, in line with Bernoulli, the greatest windspeed is found at the top of the crest, where it has to move a greater distance in the same time:

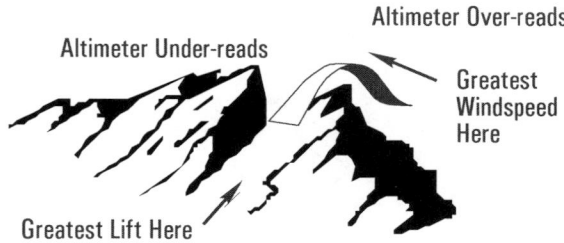

Altimeter Over-reads

Altimeter Under-reads

Greatest Windspeed Here

Greatest Lift Here

There can also be a drop in pressure. This will cause the altimeter to over read, and because the greatest windspeed is over the highest point of the mountains that is where the greatest over-reading occurs. Therefore you are lower than expected just when you need height to clear the mountain, so safety altitudes must be suitably adjusted.

There are several types of wind, which can be loosely be grouped into:

- **Prevailing winds**, which are steady and fairly reliable, and starts to affect you from about 6,000 feet AGL upwards. Indeed, upper winds can come in many directions at different levels, and are usually the opposite of lower winds. Where mountains are concerned, they also acquire a vertical element.

- **Local Winds**, on the other hand, have effects in more limited areas. They can be subdivided into other types, such as *valley, anabatic, katabatic,* etc., and which are infinitely variable.

  - **Valley winds** can be felt up to 2,500 feet above the valley floor, and reach peak strength around mid-afternoon. Inside mountains, the same venturi effect that causes a wing to fly or pulls fuel vapour into the throat of a carburettor will cause the wind to speed up as it passes through narrower channels or along valleys (the *Mistral* is a good example).

- Cool air that is generated overnight with radiation cooling will flow down a slope, because it is more dense, and therefore more subject to gravity, causing a **katabatic** wind. It's the same effect as in a closed room on a cold day, where there is a draught near a window even when nothing is open - the air next to the window is cooled, and flows downwards. The katabatic effect usually happens around sunset and overnight (when the heating effect of the Sun is lost), and its significance is not just that you might get some wind from somewhere you don't expect (and downdraughts from severe slopes), but also that it slips underneath the air not in contact with the slope - if there is a river at the bottom of the valley, the extra moisture could also cause fog, so be careful when flying to valley airfields in the evening. Katabatic winds tend to stay within 500 feet of the surface, and can arise quite suddenly, even up to gale force. Glaciers have permanent katabatic winds.

An **anabatic** wind flows *up* a hill, due to ground heating and air expansion during the day. It is not a regular thermal movement, that is, the whole layer does not move vertically away from the slope, but is rather a *slide* of the layer up the hill, so, to get any lift benefit, you have to fly close to the surface. Anabatic winds are quick to decline with cloud cover.

THE DEMARCATION LINE

The demarcation line is the point at which smooth air is separated from turbulent air around a peak, rather similar to that over an aerofoil. In the picture below, the snow follows the demarcation line. Above or to the windward side (on the left), air is relatively smooth and upflowing - below, or to the right, in the lee, it is downflowing and turbulent. The demarcation line steepens as wind velocity increases (and the severity of the slope), as does the area of downflow, and moves toward the top of the hill.

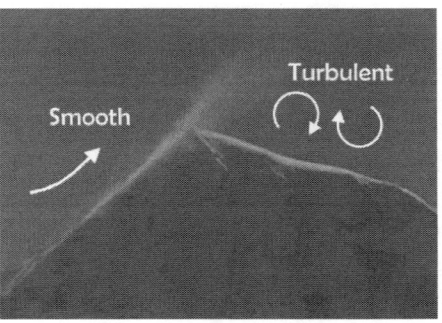

Turbulent

Smooth

So, in general, air moving up is smooth (left of the line above), and that moving down is turbulent (to the right). You can visualise the difference if you think of a waterfall,

An aircraft affected by mountain waves can expect severe turbulence below any rotors, downdraughts that may be stronger than the rate of climb and greater than normal icing in associated clouds

and the state of the water before and after dropping over the edge. As a guide to wind speed, the snow in the picture is light and powdery, so it might be around 10-15 kts.

MOUNTAIN WAVES

Waves generated downwind from mountains play an important role in the transport of energy and momentum around the atmosphere. When there is a sharp vertical change in stability or wind direction, the wave energy might be ducted horizontally downstream to generate stationary lee waves that become trapped between the ground and a layer of more stable air, or possibly an inversion. Under the wave crests, there may be horizontal vortices (rotors) that pose a severe threat to aircraft.

The trapped lee waves are associated with marked adverse pressure gradients as they go up and down, sometimes associated with pressure drops of over 5 hPa over just a few kilometres. There could also be large vertical increases of temperature (inversions) in the order of 10°C over 200 metres. When a mountain range has an airflow at the 10,000 foot level greater than about 20 knots (depends on the size of the range), blowing broadside on (within about 30°) and over it in stable conditions*, standing waves can exist downwind, noticeable by turbulence and strong persistent up and downdraughts. At that speed and angle they seem to hit a resonant spot.

*The "stable conditions" are a layer of stable air about 2-3,000 feet above the peaks, acting as a lid on convection, sandwiched between less stable layers above and below

Note: The wind speed and direction should be more or less constant up to about 18,000 feet, although it doesn't have to be particularly fast over the peaks. However, it must increase with height.

Downdraughts can be particularly dangerous when flying towards a range into a headwind, as the airflow follows the general shape of the surface, so you will experience a strong downdraught just before the ridge:

When into wind, height variations are out of phase with the waves. They are usually in phase when downwind.

Note: This does not just apply to light aircraft! 747s have lost complete engines in mountain wave downdraughts, but the most common problems are severe reductions in rates of climb and excessive rates of sink. As well, **the combination of mountain waves and non-standard**

temperature may result in your altimeter over-reading by as much as 3 000 feet!

If you are flying parallel to a mountain ridge on the downwind side in a smooth downdraught, as a result of the local drop in pressure associated with the wave, the rate of climb indicator and the altimeter will not indicate a descent until you descend through a layer equal to the error caused by the mountain wave (they may indicate a climb for a short while), so you may not recognise the fact that you are in a downdraught until after passing through the original pressure level which, in the downdraft, is closer to the ground than before you entered the wave.

The wind needs to be fairly straight in direction, so warm sector winds and jetstreams can be very conducive to the formation of waves. The waves will be more dangerous in Winter simply because the wind speeds are stronger, and there will be a longer wavelength. There can be several miles between their peaks and troughs, which can extend between 10,000-20,000 feet above the range and up to 200 or 300 miles downwind:

Rotors are always in circular motion, constantly forming and dissipating as water vapour is added and taken away. They are dangerous, and the most turbulence will be found in them, or between them and the ground. Rotor clouds are formed in the same way as lenticular clouds, that is, from air forced upwards and condensing, then dissipating as they proceed downwards in the wave.

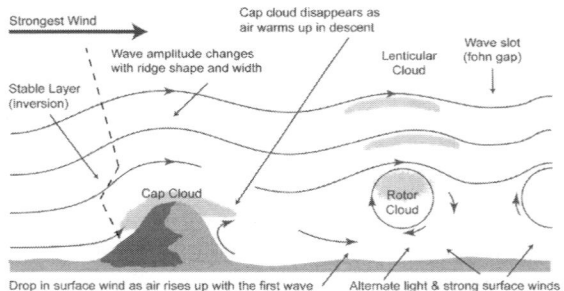

Rotor streaming is a phenomenon that occurs when air flowing across a mountain is enough to create waves, but decreases in effect with altitude above the mountain - that is, they are only strong in the lower levels. The air downstream of the mountain still breaks up and becomes turbulent, similar to a rotor, but there are no lee waves, so the rotors travel downwind rather than stay in one place as they normally would. Watch for ragged cumuliform cloud.

If the rotor forms in an inversion, warm air from above is rotated downward and heated further as it is compressed. On the other way up, cold air is expanding to cool further. Thus, very cold air ends up lying over warm air and conditions are extremely unstable.

As a clue to the existence of waves, you will see a *cap cloud* over the top of the range, creeping down the *lee side* (downwind), as a result of the downdraught.

It disappears as air descends and warms adiabatically.

At the crest of each wave, there will be a *lenticular cloud*, with a *rotor cloud* downwind from each one (the lowest in the system). This is a lenticular cloud viewed from above:

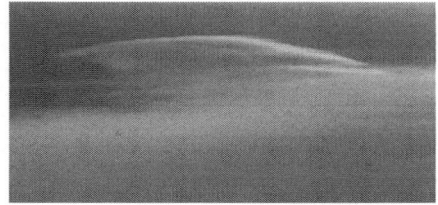

Lenticular clouds are a form of altocumulus that remain stationary with reference to the ground, and will produce airframe icing. They are formed by orographic uplift in stable air over mountain tops.

Note: The fact that lenticular clouds stay in the same place does *not* mean that the wind speed is nil!

Watch for long-term variations in speed and pitch attitude in level cruise (the variations may be large). Near the ground in a mountain wave area, severe turbulence and windshear may be encountered, especially at the bottom of a rotor where you may get a performance decreasing shear if you are going in the same direction as the wind.

Windshear

This is the name for sudden airspeed changes over about 10 kts resulting from sudden horizontal or vertical changes in wind velocity - more severe examples will change not only airspeed, but vertical speed and aircraft attitude as well. Officially, it becomes dangerous when variations cause enough displacement from your flight path for substantial corrective action to be taken; *severe* windshear causes airspeed changes greater than 15 kts, or vertical speed changes over 500 feet per minute. Expect it to occur mostly inside 1,000 feet AGL, where it is most critical, because you can't quickly build up airspeed. You can often tell the presence of windshear by clouds moving in different directions or plumes of smoke rising then going off at extreme angles.

Although mostly associated with thunderstorms, where you have the unpredictability of microbursts to contend with, it's also present with wake vortices, temperature inversions, mountain waves and the passage of fronts, not forgetting obstructions near the runway, and can occur over any size of area. You can even get it where rain is falling from a cumulus cloud, as the air is getting dense from the cooling, and will therefore fall quicker. Helicopters, especially, can suffer from windshear above and below tree top level in forest clearings, when a backlash effect can convert any headwind to tailwind.

All fronts are zones of windshear - the greater the temperature difference across them (over 10°C), the greater the changes will be. The surface wind speeds associated with a front, particularly over rough ground, can influence windshear production (friction + windspeed + instability = mechanical turbulence). Warm fronts tend to have less shear than cold ones, but as they're slower moving, you catch it for longer. In general, the faster the front moves (say, over 30 kts), the more vigorous the weather associated with it; if it goes slower, the visibility will be worse, but you can still get windshear even then and for up to an hour after its passage.

Warm air moving horizontally above cold air can produce turbulence at the point where they join, as would be typical with an inversion, at around 2,000-4,000 feet with a windspeed of 25 kts or more (low level windshear is likely to be greatest at the top of a marked surface-based inversion). In a valley, in particular, when the moving warm air hits a mountainside, it will be forced downwards, but unable to penetrate the cold air, so it is forced to move over the top of that in the valley bottom, so watch out on those cold, clear mornings.

The most significant effect of windshear is, of course, loss of airspeed at a critical moment, similar to an effect in mountain flying, where a wind reversal could result in none at all! You would typically get this with a downburst from a convective type cloud, where, initially, you get an increase in airspeed from the extra headwind, but if you don't anticipate the reverse to happen as you get to the other side, you will not be in a position to cope with the resulting loss. This has led to the windshear classifications of *performance increasing* or *performance decreasing (Microbursts)*.

Windshear is *occasional* if it exists for about a third of the time, *intermittent* between then and two thirds, and *continuous* over that. The alert is given when the mean surface wind is over 20 kts, and the difference between it and the gradient wind is over 40 kts. There also needs to be a temperature difference of 10° between the surface and 1,000 feet and CBs or heavy showers within 5 nm.

Vertical windshear is expressed in kts/100 ft.

MICROBURSTS

These are small, intense downdraughts that spread out in all directions when they reach the surface, commonly associated with thunderstorms in the mature stage. You are most likely to encounter them within 1,000' of the ground, that is, right on the approach. They are most dangerous where the vertical push converts to the horizontal, between the base of the microburst and the ground - you could get a vertical speed of over 6000 feet per minute and a horizontal one over 45 kts, with a 90-knot shear across the microburst. The diameter of any damage will be up to 4 km, and the duration from 1-5 minutes from first striking the ground, or more, though the maximum intensity is in the first 2-4 minutes. The vertical windshear is expressed in kts/100 feet.

A transit through a microburst involves a performance-increasing shear to start with, followed by a performance-decreasing one, because the downflow divides at the surface (although the burst might be "only" 45 kts, the complete shear will be double that). With the former, you get more airspeed and lift from either increased headwind or decreased tailwind, taking you above the glidepath - recovery involves reducing power and lowering the nose, and using a higher power setting than before when re-established, or the aircraft will sink. The latter is the opposite, of course - you lose airspeed, the nose pitches down and altitude decreases. Recover by increasing power and setting it to less than the original when established.

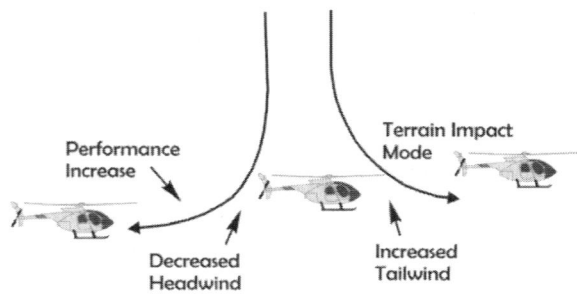

The helicopter on the left in the picture above gets an increased headwind, so power is reduced to compensate. This takes effect just as the downburst is encountered, and the headwind becomes a tailwind, so IAS decreases.

Being so close to the ground, you are likely to be taking off or landing, and therefore more vulnerable. The angle of attack reduces inside a downburst, because induced flow increases, so collective should be increased on entry, and reduced (quickly) on exit. Where the air is dry, the microburst will become more vigorous, because the dry air absorbs any moisture, cooling the air and making it more dense, so it falls faster. For more on Wake Turbulence, refer to the *Operations* chapter.

SQUALLS

A squall is a sudden increase of at least 16 kts in average wind speed to a sustained speed of 22 kts or more for at least one minute.

Diurnal Effects

The pressure around the Earth varies up and down by about 2 mb twice a day, at 10 and 4, am and pm. It is more detectable in the tropics because it is masked elsewhere by more extreme weather. In low latitudes (i.e. nearer the Equator), interruptions to this schedule may mean an impending tropical storm. As a result, the surface wind increases speed and veers during the day in the Northern Hemisphere, and *vice versa* by night. In the Southern Hemisphere, it increases and backs by day, decreasing and veering by night. Because of this effect, many local winds can be predicted with clock-like regularity.

Note: The *diurnal variation* actually refers to temperature differences, which is what is ultimately responsible for winds in the first place, although there are diurnal pressure variations, too. The variations are greatest in calm conditions, with no cloud, over land. In desert regions, the difference between day and night temperatures can be as much as 25°C, while over the sea, usually less than 1°C.

The lowest temperatures occur 30 minutes after sunrise.

LAND & SEA BREEZES

These arise out of a temperature difference between land and sea areas. Air over land warms up and cools down faster than that over the sea, because land has a lower specific heat than water does and needs less heat to warm it up. Thus, temperature changes over land will occur a lot more frequently than they do over the sea.

When the land is warmer than the sea, the air over it becomes less dense and the space left by the rising air is filled with an extra component coming from over the water to produce a *sea breeze* which is added to any existing wind (in fact, a relatively high pressure is created at about 1000 feet over land, to produce a pressure gradient aloft).

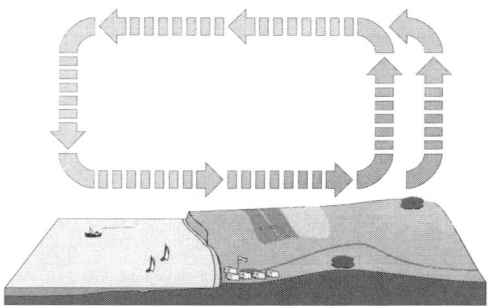

With lower pressure at the same height over the water, there will be air movement towards the sea, at the upper levels (because the column of warm air is taller, and the relative pressure is higher), which will subside to come back towards the land. At night, the process is reversed to get a land breeze. However, land areas are poor conductors of heat and will only be affected through a shallow layer. As a result, land breezes are weaker because the temperature differences are smaller and so is the local pressure gradient.

A prevailing wind can oppose a sea-breeze and delay its development, or go with it and increase its speed, although, at latitudes greater than about 20°, Coriolis can change the direction of a sea breeze by itself.

If a convergence is created, sea breezes can be strong enough to create their own cold fronts, well inland*, and even trigger thunderstorms, as the colder sea air undercuts the land air. Overleaf are possible examples for the UK.

*In Australia, for example, sea breezes have been encountered 400 km away from the sea.

Knowing this is useful when you're going to a destination near the sea, and the wind (and landing direction) could be different than what you might expect, or you might be offshore and know that a tailwind will be around to help bring you home. Fishing fleets time their movements in and out of port around these winds.

Note: Although land and sea breezes arise from temperature differences, they are not thermal winds in the true sense because the geostrophic force does not achieve an eventual balance with the pressure gradient that make the wind flow parallel to the local isobars.

The sea breeze has some effect on temperature and precipitation in the tropics.

THE BAROMETER

This is an instrument that measures atmospheric pressure, using mercury or an evacuated capsule, hence the *aneroid* (no fluid) barometer (*baros* is Greek for *weight*). The mercury barometer is quite simple - a long test tube with a vacuum inside is inverted and its end placed into a quantity of mercury. Air pressure makes the level rise or fall, and the height of its column in the tube is measured.

You could actually use any liquid, but mercury is very dense, which means you can have a shorter tube.

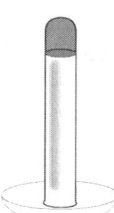

Aneroid barometers are smaller and used in confined spaces, particularly instrument panels, but they are calibrated against mercury barometers. A device that measures pressure changes over time (with a moving pen over a moving paper drum) is called a *barograph*.

ALTIMETRY

The altimeter is simply an aneroid barometer calibrated in feet rather than millibars or inches of mercury (its inner workings are described fully in Instruments). It measures the pressure difference between a selected pressure surface and that at the level of an aircraft.

Although altimeters are calibrated to ISA, the actual sea level pressure varies from hour to hour, and place to place. You would be very lucky to hit the standard atmosphere more than, say, 25% of the time, so you need a means of adjusting any instruments based on it to cope with the differences. To allow you to set the zero reference correctly, an altimeter has a *setting window* in which you can adjust the figures of a *subscale* for the correct pressure on the ground by turning a knob on the front.

This is actually part of an important preflight check, where you make sure that if you turn the knob to the right, the height readings increase, and *vice versa*.

If the subscale is set wrongly, the zero reference will be displaced by an amount proportional to 1 inch per 1000 feet. This means that your relative height to obstacles, such as mountains, etc. will not be maintained.

For example, if the proper altimeter setting is 29.92 inches, but you have 30.12 inches set in the subscale, the altimeter will be over-reading by 1000 feet. When flying from high to low pressure, your altimeter will also over-read (from HIGH to LOW, it is HIGH), so you would be lower than planned and liable for a nasty surprise. It's therefore much safer to be going the other way (that is, from LOW to HIGH, where your instrument is LOW).

An *increase* in pressure equals a *decrease* in altitude, so if you start with 29.92, then go to where it is 30.92, the altimeter reading would be 1,000 feet less, even though the figures themselves increase.

Also, in a pre-flight operational test, the tolerance for the QNH setting for an altimeter is ±80'. If you have two altimeters, they should be within ± 60 or 80 feet of each other (that is, they can misread by nearly 120 or 160 feet and still be useable).

To convert from inches to millibars, if you have an old altimeter, start at 29.92 and find the difference between it and the current pressure. Divide the difference by 0.03" inches and apply the result to 1013. In other words, 1 Mb (hPa) is about equal to 0.03". For example, if the current pressure is 30.02, that is, 0.1" above 29.92" (or 3 x 0.03), add 3 Mb and set 1016.

A more formal way is to use this formula:

$$\frac{millibars}{1013.25} = \frac{ins}{29.92}$$

The standard atmosphere has a temperature element that also affects the altimeter. Remembering that air density decreases as it gets warmer, a point in your imaginary column of air above a station would be higher on a warm day than otherwise. If, therefore, as is typical near the Rockies in Winter, the air is *very much* colder than standard (actually below about -16°C), you will be lower than you should be (actually, the phrase above is still valid, in that going from HIGH *temperature* to LOW, your instruments will be HIGH). A *cold low* will lower True Altitude to a point where it is dangerous to fly in mountains.

This is serious stuff because, in low temperatures, combined with other effects caused by movement of wind over ridges, you could be *as much as 3000 feet below your projected altitude*, which could really spoil your day (although when coming down the ILS, you are relying more on a radio signal than the altimeter). More practically, you could have a 150-foot difference on a published minimum of 500 feet and be too close to the ground.

Another factor that arises from the diagram below is the creation of a wind purely from the temperature difference.

The cooler column has a lower pressure at a given altitude, and the warmer one has a higher pressure, causing air to move, from left to right, in this case, so, applying Buys Ballot's law, low temperature is on the left in the Northern Hemisphere if you stand with your back to the wind. The vertical distance between two pressure levels is less in cold air, as pressure decreases at a greater rate. Pressure in the upper levels depends on the mean temperature of the column of air beneath the point concerned.

In simple terms, when the surface temperature is well *below* ISA (starting at -16°C), correct your altitudes by:

Surface Temp (ISA)	Correction
-16°C to -30°C	+ 10%
-31°C to -50°C	+ 20%
-51°C or below	+ 25%

Altimeter Settings

The *altimeter setting* (QNH) is the *station pressure* reduced to mean sea level under *ISA temperatures* and *standard lapse rates*, that is, taking the elevation of the aerodrome into account, expressed in inches of mercury (Hg) in North America, or hectopascals in Europe. It is what your altimeter must be set to when flying near aerodromes or other places that may issue it, because otherwise it will only tell you your height above the point you started from.

Its other importance is its use on weather maps to create isobars. To adjust station pressure for sea level, take the elevation and get its equivalent in inches. 500 feet would therefore be 0.5", which is *added* to whatever the reading is, because the sea is *lower* and would give lower figures anyway. MSL pressure is station pressure corrected to sea level using the average temperature over the last 12 hours.

Note: The word *height* refers to distance above a ground-based datum. The word *altitude* is used for distance above *sea level*, so the helicopter on the right has a height of 1000 feet (above the aerodrome, or QFE) and an altitude of 1500 feet (above the sea, or QNH). The difference is the *elevation* of the aerodrome. When using the *standard setting* of 1013 hPa or 29.92 inches (QNE), above the *transition level*, your vertical displacement is expressed in Flight Levels, which are the altimeter readings with a digit knocked off the end - FL 30 means 3000 feet when set to standard.

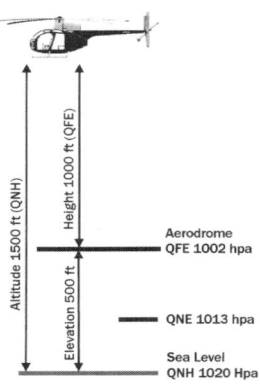

The barometric pressure is constantly changing and varies from one place to another. What would happen if you departed the spot in the diagram above and returned several hours later to find the 1020 QNH above had reduced to 995 Mb? The altimeter would be over-reading by 675 feet and you would only be 325 feet off the ground (1020 - 995 x 27 = 675, 1500 - 675 = 825 AMSL = 325 AGL). The altimeter needs constant updating as you fly.

Three settings are used throughout a flight:

- **QFE** is used near an airfield, particularly in the circuit, and is the pressure read directly from an altimeter that is set to zero when on the ground - officially at the highest usable point on an aerodrome. A lower QFE reading means a higher elevation for the airfield

- **QNH** is used for general transit elsewhere, below the transition altitude. It is the QFE converted to a pressure that would theoretically exist at sea level at that point under ISA conditions - this is done because reporting stations are not all at the same level. You add the pressure change for elevation above sea level on a standard day. It is forecast for one or two hours ahead over large areas

   Note: Regional QNH is a UK setting that is the *Lowest Forecast Pressure* for a complete Altimeter Setting Region, which changes on the hour, is valid for an hour and is available for an hour before that anyway, so don't expect accuracy!

- **QNE** is the altimeter reading at the runway threshold with 1013.25 set on the subscale

True Altitude

This is your (geometric) elevation above mean sea level. It would be the distance you could normally find with a tape measure, but this is impractical, so we have to use instruments such as the altimeter instead, which shows you an indicated altitude.

The only time an altimeter will indicate true altitude is in ISA conditions. As such conditions are rare, indications are almost always in error due to temperature.

The difference between true and standard (ISA) altitude is 4 feet per thousand feet per degree of deviation from ISA. That is, true altitude changes by 4% for every 10°C deviation from ISA conditions, or 2% for every 5.5°C*.

*4% is correct for the stratosphere, but more like 3.5% for lower altitudes. 4% for every 11°C is more accurate.

One source of error can occur when the temperature at a level might be close to ISA, when the lapse rate is not.

Note: All calculations should be rounded to the nearest lower hPa. The barometric lapse rate near mean sea level is 27 ft (8m) per hPa. Also, the airport elevation must be taken into account - that is, *only use the layer between the ground and the position of the aircraft.*

In practice, true altitude is obtained from knowing the outside air temperature (OAT) at whatever level you are flying at, and use of a computer. This will be reasonably accurate when the actual lapse rate is, or is near, that of the Standard Atmosphere, i.e., 2°C per 1 000 feet, but if it's very hot, or very cold, you need further adjustments.

Pressure Altitude

Pressure altitude is the height in the standard atmosphere that you may find a given pressure, usually 29.92" or 1013 Mb, but actually whatever you set on the altimeter - if you set 1013 on the subscale and the needles read 6,000 feet, the PA *for that setting* is 6,000 feet. PA is a starting point for any calculations for performance, TAS, etc., and is the altimeter setting used above the transition altitude, where all altimeters must be set to 1013 hPa so that everybody is using the same standard (every country has a different transition altitude). Below the transition altitude, local altimeter settings are used.

If an altimeter is set to 1013, it is measuring Pressure Altitude with respect to Mean Sea Level. In ISA conditions, Pressure Altitude is the same as True Altitude.

If the sea level pressure is different from 1013, obstacle clearance heights and airfield elevations, etc. must be converted before using them. To do this, get the local altimeter setting, find the difference between it and 29.92 (or 1013), convert it to feet (1"=1,000 or 1 mb=27 feet at sea level), then apply it the *opposite* side of 29.92. You could also get PA from the altimeter, by placing 29.92 or 1013 in the setting window, and reading the figures directly.

The significance of this concerns performance - if the pressure on the surface is less than standard, you are effectively at a higher altitude, and your machine will not fly so well. You often need to calculate the pressure altitude of a location so you know your performance.

For example, for a helipad on the side of a mountain at 400 feet above sea level, with an altimeter setting of 29.72, your PA at that location would actually be 600 feet, since the difference between 29.92 and 29.72 is 0.2, or 200 feet *added*, and where you would enter your performance charts, since they are calibrated for standard atmosphere (the altimeter setting is *below* the standard pressure, so your answer should be *above*). Again, you are *adding* because the sea is *lower*, and the figures ought to be higher. In the exam, write down 29.92 first, then subtract the altimeter setting and multiply by 1,000. If the answer is negative, take it away from the elevation. If it's positive, then add. The same principles apply if you are using millibars and 1013, where 1 Mb = 27 feet in the lower levels.

Pressure levels with altitude are:

Height	Pressure Level
Surface	1013
10 000	700
18 000	500
24 000	400
30 000	300
34 000	250
38 000	200
58 000	100

Density Altitude

This is the altitude in the Standard Atmosphere at which the prevailing density occurs, meaning your real altitude from the effects of height, temperature and humidity, and is used to establish performance, as it is a figure that expresses where your machine thinks it is, as opposed to where it actually is - see *Performance*. For now, it is *pressure altitude corrected for non-standard temperature,* or the true air temperature at a given level. Thus, density altitude has the same value as pressure altitude at standard temperature.

To find DA on the flight computer, set the aerodrome elevation or Pressure Altitude against the temperature in the *airspeed* window.

In the picture, the temperature is -21°C at 10 100 feet (follow the red line about midway). The indicated airspeed is 177 kts, and the TAS is 200. The Density Altitude (bottom right) is 8100 feet - that's quite a difference!

If you want a formula:

        PA ± (118.8 x ISA Dev)

(Multiplying the ISA Dev by 120 is usually good enough).

Note: If you use a flight computer for Density Altitude questions, check the answers with the above formula!

Indicated Altitude

The altimeter setting is the pressure that would have been measured by the ground station if it was at MSL. Indicated and Pressure Altitudes are the same in ISA conditions.

Calibrated Altitude

Corrections need to be made for airspeed, altitude, imperfect static pressure lines, etc. The Indicated Altitude thus corrected becomes the Calibrated Altitude.

Absolute Altitude

The geometric height above terrain - what would be measured by a radar altimeter.

Calculations

Tip: Always draw a diagram and place the numbers in order, with the large ones at the bottom.

Q: What minimum flight level will clear high ground rising to 1800 m AMSL by at least 1500 ft on a track of 225°(M), if the Regional QNH is 990 hPa? How much is the clearance at that level? (1 hPa=27 hPa)

A: 1800 m is equal to 5910 ft. The difference between the QNH and QNE (1013 - 990) is 23 hPa, or 621 feet. Your minimum height is 621 + 5910 + 1500, or 8031 feet. The next applicable even flight level is FL 100, and the high ground is cleared by 3469 feet (10000 - 621 - 5910).

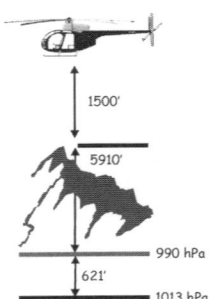

Q: A helicopter is flying at 2500 feet AGL near an airfield which is at 350 ft AMSL. The QFE is 995 hPa. If another aircraft flies over at FL 40, what is the approximate vertical separation between them? (1 hPa = 27 feet)

A: 1015 feet. 350 feet divided by 27 is 13 mb, so the QNH is 1008 (995 + 13). The difference between the QNH and QNE is 5 mb, so the distance from sea level to the datum is 135 feet, making the airfield elevation 485 feet from the standard pressure level. Add 2500 feet to that to get 2985 and subtract that from 4000.

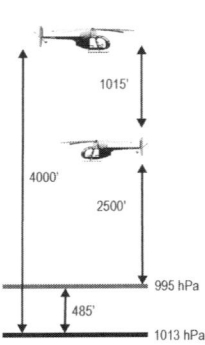

TRUE ALTITUDE

To use the flight computer, you must start with the pressure altitude. Simply set 1013 or 29.92 on the subscale and take the reading, or calculate it as shown above. Place the temperature against the pressure altitude in the Altitude window. For example, 6 120 feet, against an OAT of -20°C. Opposite your indicated altitude on the inner scale read your true altitude on the outer scale.

MOISTURE

A given parcel of air can hold a certain amount of moisture at a certain temperature. This ability is increased as the air gets warmer, and decreased as it gets colder. The source of such water vapour is mainly evaporation from oceans, lakes, vegetation, etc. As particles of exposed water break off into the air, the *average* rate of motion of those left behind decreases, which is detected as cooling, thus, heat energy is used up as molecules break away, and is regarded as being hidden within the vapour as *latent heat*.

Latent Heat

In the solid and liquid states, water molecules are bound strongly together, but as a gas, the bond is weak. Rather a lot of energy is required in the form of heat to make it weak - 600 times more, in fact, than is required to raise the temperature of water by 1°C*. The heat energy that is used to break the bonds is absorbed by the water vapour, from which position it is used to keep the molecules apart, which is required for the water vapour to remain as a gas. Because this energy is stored with the water molecules, it is known as latent heat, and it accounts for how water vapour is able to transport large amounts of heat, albeit hidden, around the globe. The heat is released again when it condenses, warming the surrounding air. As it is now less dense, the warmed air will rise further.

In short, latent heat is that added to a substance when it changes its state, without its temperature changing. Sensible heat is that which can be seen or felt.

*The energy required to raise the temperature of 1 gram of water (or ice) by 1°C is 1 calorie. The latent heat of fusion (melting) of water is 80 calories per gram, but the water (or ice) remains at 0°C because the calories are being used to change its state. The latent heat of vaporisation, on the other hand, is 600 calories per gram at 0°C.

- **Condensation** occurs when moist air become saturated

- **Evaporation** is the process of liquid water turning into vapour

- **Deposition** occurs when water vapour goes directly to the solid state (i.e. ice) without a liquid stage, but it can be referred to as sublimation.

- **Sublimation** occurs when ice is converted directly to water vapour

- **Freezing** is the process of turning water into a solid. Zero degrees is actually when water becomes capable of freezing. A Supercooled Water Droplet is one below freezing, but not frozen. It gets away with this from the absence of hygroscopic nuclei* to bind on to.

- **Melting** (or fusion) is the change of state of water from a solid to a liquid state.

Dewpoint

This is the temperature at which cooling results in 100% saturation, or the point at which water vapour *begins* the process of condensation (at constant pressure*) into visible droplets. Condensation actually occurs below the dewpoint. Without hygroscopic nuclei for water particles to bind on to, condensation may not actually occur, even when air cools below its dewpoint (*supersaturation*).

If the temperature and dewpoint at an airfield are the same, it will take very little incentive for clouds to form - the further apart they are, the less likely you are to get cloud, and therefore icing if the temperature is low enough (however, the warmer the wet air is, the more likely you are to meet bad weather).

*Pressure changes when air is lifted, so the dewpoint can change with altitude.

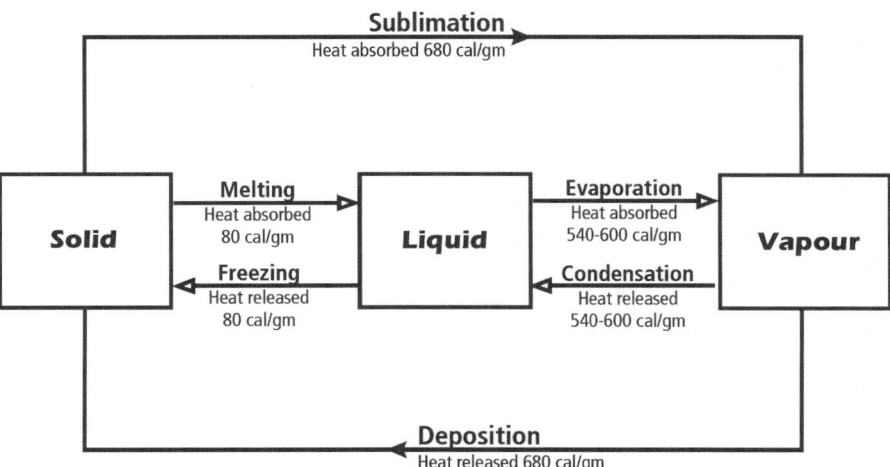

Humidity

The *absolute humidity* is the actual mass of water vapour in a given volume of moist air, expressed in grams per cubic metre (i.e. as a volume). Over the sea, it is usually at its minimum at dawn, and at its maximum shortly after noon, because of the temperature (opposite to relative humidity).

RELATIVE HUMIDITY

For a particular temperature, relative humidity can tell you how close the air is to being saturated. It is a measure of how much moisture an air parcel is holding against the maximum possible at that temperature (and pressure) or, in other words, the *percentage saturation*, which will *decrease* if the air gets warmer, as when subsiding in a high pressure area, because temperature is raised by compression, and it can absorb more moisture. Thus, the amount of water vapour that air can hold is determined by the temperature:

Temp	Vapour
30°C	27 gms/kg
15°C	11 gms/kg
0°C	4 gms/kg

Relative Humidity is officially defined as the vapour pressure (or mixing ratio) divided by the saturation vapour pressure (or saturation mixing ratio), multiplied by 100. It is *not* the dewpoint divided by the temperature!

Humidity is also known as *vapour pressure*, because water vapour exerts its own partial pressure. At saturation point, this will be maximum. As air rises, it expands, and reduces its pressure, and hence the partial pressure, which ultimately reduces the dewpoint. This is because there is only one dewpoint for a particular vapour pressure.

Relative humidity could change as a result of the air absorbing more moisture, say when moving over the sea, but it is more likely to change quickly through temperature changes (including diurnally with the Earth's atmosphere), at least for our purposes. On a typical day, relative humidity is high in the morning (as it is cooler) and lower in the late afternoon (when it gets warmer).

Relative humidity can also indicate the drying power of the air, since evaporation is most intense at high temperatures and low humidities, and *vice versa*. Water added to air makes it moister, and less dense, and more likely to rise.

MEASUREMENT

The *hygrometer* is an instrument that measures how wet the air is. A piece of human (or horse) hair, which gets longer as it gets moister, is laid out against a calibrated scale of known humidities (its length increases by about 2.5% between 0-100% relative humidity). A "suitable linkage" transmits its movements to show relative humidity.

Another method is to use two thermometers inside a Stevenson's screen. One measures the temperature of the ambient air, and the other has its bulb surrounded with wet muslin, using distilled water. If the air is dry, the water in the muslin will evaporate and absorb latent heat, so the wet-bulb thermometer will indicate a lower temperature. Thus, the drier the air is, the greater will be the difference between the readings. Relative humidity is then deduced with the use of tables, or a tephigram.

The *dewpoint depression* is the difference between the temperature and the dewpoint, while the *wetbulb depression* is the difference between the wet and dry bulb temperatures. When the air is saturated, the wet and dry bulb temperatures will be the same, not because the wet bulb is evaporating, but because the dry bulb is covered with moisture and both become wet bulbs, and there is no evaporation. In unsaturated air, the dewpoint is always lower than the wet bulb temperature.

Wet bulb temperature is always between the dewpoint and dry bulb temperatures, except at 100% RH (saturation point) where they are all the same.

Mostly, air is made to reach its saturation point by force, such as being moved up the sides of mountains or over large areas of slower moving air (*large scale ascent*) and, if the conditions are right, cloud will form. In fact, the ways of cooling air are many, including:

- Turbulence (not with thunderstorms)
- Convection
- Orographic
- Frontal
- Convergence (as with low pressure)

Lapse Rates

A lapse rate is a change of temperature values with height, usually a decrease, which is regarded as positive - a negative lapse rate is a temperature increase, otherwise known as an inversion. A layer of air which does not change with height is known as isothermal.

ENVIRONMENTAL LAPSE RATE

This is the actual measured change, which is about 6.5°C per 1000 m (1.98°C per 1000 feet). However, it does vary, depending on local air conditions. Several factors may influence this:

- *Height*. Lapse rates depend on ground temperature, and are normally very high near the ground in the presence of strong insolation

- *Time of Year*. Lapse rates are lower in winter or during a rainy season

- *Surface*. Lapse rates are lower over land than they are over the sea

- *Air Masses*. Different air masses have different lapse rates

ADIABATIC LAPSE RATE

The rate of change of temperature with height of air which is changing its temperature adiabatically is called an adiabatic lapse rate, and there are two variations:

DRY ADIABATIC LAPSE RATE

The DALR is the (constant, fixed) *decrease in temperature of unsaturated air with height* at around 3°C per 1,000 feet* or 9.8°C (10°C) per 1,000 m (*Dry* in these circumstances just means a relative humidity of less than 100%).

*In practice, there is an excess of around 1° near the ground, so the first 1 000 feet should really decrease at the rate of 4°C per 1,000 feet. This is called *super-adiabatic*, and it is not a factor for the exams, I'm just being picky.

The dewpoint temperature of unsaturated air decreases at around 0.5°C per 1 000 ft.

SATURATED ADIABATIC LAPSE RATE

The SALR allows for *latent heat*, or the energy that is released when water condenses. Converting water from one state to the other (without a rise in temperature) requires energy, which is stored with the vapour, as the water molecules must be kept apart with that energy. Condensed water molecules are strongly attracted to each other, and are balanced by equally strong repulsive forces. The energy that goes with the vapour is the *latent heat of vapourisation*. When vapour condenses back into a liquid the latent heat is released into the surrounding air as *sensible heat* and affects the SALR.

The presence of latent heat means that the air will cool more slowly. In fact, there can be so much heat released that flight in normally stable layer cloud can be quite bumpy, from internal eddying. Latent heat leads to the *Chinook*, which is a dry, warm, downslope wind in the lee of the Rockies, commonly found from Calgary southward all the way through to Colorado, that can raise the air temperature to over 20°C in Winter.

This is an example of the figures involved:

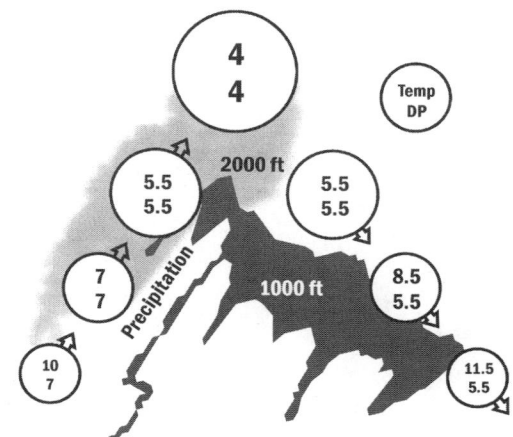

It can be seen that the temperature on the lee side of the mountain is warmer, which is why you can grow grapes in the Okanagan Valley in the middle of the Rockies.

The SALR can range from 4°C to as high as 9°C per 1000 m, but the average (for lower levels anyway) is 6°C per 1000 m, or 1.8°C per 1000 feet, for Europe. The reason for the variation is simply that warm air can hold more moisture - and there is more latent heat with which to warm the air as condensation takes place. This also explains why high clouds are thinner - there is less moisture to condense out because the air is cooler.

Knowledge of the cloudbase is important for many reasons, particularly when descending on approach.

Knowledge of the cloudbase is important for many reasons, particularly when descending on approach.

To find it, you need the wet and dry bulb temperatures. Take the difference between the two, and subtract it from the wet bulb temperature to get the dew point, where vapour will condense. Now take the difference between the dewpoint and the dry bulb temperature and multiply it by 352 (220 in Fahrenheit) for the probable height of the condensation.

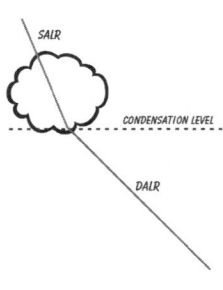

If the temperature and windspeed increase, so does the cloudbase. If the humidity increases, cloudbase decreases.

THE BRADBURY RULE

The rate of closure of the HMR against the DALR is around 2.5°C per 1000 feet, or 1°C per 400*, so, when

CAPT

© *Phil Croucher, 2012*

finding out a freezing level, find the cloud base, then switch to the SALR (the dew-point lapse rate is 0.6°C per 1000 feet). To find the cloudbase, just multiply the difference between the surface temperature and dewpoint (T_{dry}-T_{dew}) by 400 to get an approximate height.

*This rule of thumb is named after the glider pilot/meteorologist Tom Bradbury. It is a better method for predicting the base of cumulus cloud TAFs, which usually give the lowest base during the forecast period.

Note: This only works if cumulus actually forms.

For example, if the ground temperature is 10°C, and the dewpoint 7°C, the cloudbase should be at 1,200 feet (3 x 400). Then divide whatever the dewpoint temperature is by 1.8 and add the converted number in thousands of feet to the cloudbase to get the freezing level. Divide 7 by 1.8 to get 3.8889, which becomes 3889 feet, so the freezing level is at 5089 feet.

A more formal way is to divide the difference between the temperature and dewpoint by 2.5 to obtain the cloudbase in thousands of feet. The result is the same.

Stability

Remembering the previous mention of convection currents, you can see that air has vertical movement as well as horizontal, and it is often associated with turbulence and/or the formation of clouds. The less vertical movement there is, the more stable the air is, and the less bumpy, because it tends to resist vertical motion - a parcel of air in stable conditions will tend to return to its original level after rising or sinking. On the other hand, a parcel in unstable air will rise or sink more quickly - that is, it will continue accelerating.

Thus, the amount of vertical motion in the air *is largely determined by the stability of the atmosphere,* and what happens to a parcel of air after it is lifted.

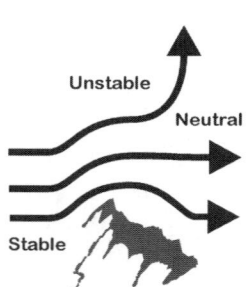

A cold air mass moving over a warmer surface will be unstable because the lower layers will pick up moisture and temperature, which will be warmer than the surrounding air. This heating from below causes the lapse rate to steepen, and the moisture makes the air less dense. This will carry on into the night over the sea, as the water will keep its heat better than land will. On the other hand, a warm air mass over a cold one will have its lower layers reduced in temperature, possibly as far as an inversion, which is about as stable as you can get.

Instability arises when air is upset by small disturbances, such as when air warmer than that surrounding it begins to rise, as it is bound to do, because it is less dense.

Air may have been lifted in the first place by:

- convection
- convergence
- mechanical turbulence
- orographic means (i.e. over geographic barriers, like a mountain range)
- frontal means

The warmer it is when it starts, the more energy a given bubble of air has to keep going. As it rises, the air expands, and cools adiabatically, matching the air around it, until it eventually cools off quicker than the surrounding air, and stops, when it reaches a level of the same density. Once it becomes saturated, though (and cloud forms), cooling slows down and allows the ascent to continue further, because the condensation releases heat and gives the (now less dense) parcel of air a boost (so if the air is already hot and moist before it hits relatively cooler air, say from the Caribbean, thunderstorms are highly likely). In addition, the air containing water vapour is less dense.

If the environmental lapse rate lies to the left of the DALR (being steeper), air is *absolutely unstable,* which is quite a rare condition. If the lapse rate is between the DALR and SALR (that is, between 1.8 and 3°C per 1000 feet), it is *conditionally unstable,* meaning stable when dry, but unstable if saturated. When the air is dry, continued vertical motion can only occur under forced conditions - when the trigger is removed, an unsaturated air parcel is always colder than its surroundings. When saturated, once the trigger is removed, the air will always be warmer than its environment (ideal for thunderstorms).

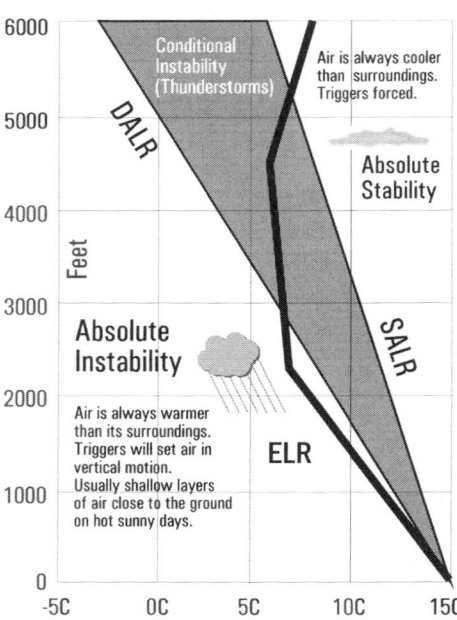

Note: The relative humidity of conditionally unstable air is unknown, otherwise it would be stable or unstable.

To the right of the SALR, limited convection is possible, and to the right of the isothermal (i.e. vertical), you get total stability from an inversion. Thus, in flight, you can estimate stability by the *rate of change* of temperature with height - the more rapid the change, the more instability there is. You can infer stability from a low rate of change or even an inversion. If the lapse rate above the condensation level is greater than the SALR, the rising air gets warmer than that around it, which will give intense ascents and be instrumental in forming thunderstorms. Then all you need is a *trigger action* to cause condensation.

CLOUDS

Clouds are symptoms of the weather - in theory, if you know what clouds belong to what weather systems, you can deduce what weather is coming, and when, based on the known movement characteristics of those systems. For example, if you see wisps of cirrus cloud approaching from the West, like this:

You know that in around 15-20 hours it will be raining continuously from low, grey cloud, and you might encounter freezing rain, because that's what happens with a warm front, and they move at around 15-20 knots, assuming they are not blocked by something like a high pressure system. If you notice that the wind has picked up and the altimeter setting has dropped a bit, you would know it is quite close. Similarly, if you see Cu or Cb clouds, you know the air is unstable.

The amount of cloud in the sky is reported in *Oktas*, or eighths of the sky area. *Opacity* is a function of cloud depth and droplet distribution. The *cloud base* is the height of the first available cloud above the official aerodrome elevation, although this may differ between countries (in the USA, for example, it is the height of the base of a cloud layer, of which there can be many). It can be measured by releasing a balloon which ascends at a known rate and timing its disappearance into cloud. At night, beams of a searchlight can be reflected, and the angles calculated with an *alidade*. In a *cloud base recorder*, a narrow

beam of light continually swings from near the horizontal to the vertical. Inside, a photo-electric cell only receives light from the vertical, and for any cloud base, there will be only one angle that provides this. However, these are now largely obsolete, and the *laser beam ceilometer* is now in widespread use.

Cloud names were coined by an amateur meteorologist, Luke Howard, in 1803, who based them on the Latin words for *hair, heap, layer* and *rain-bearing* (*cirrus, cumulus, stratus* and *nimbus*) not to mention *middle* and *broken* (*alto* and *fracto*). Others, as modifications, were added by Kaemtz and Renou, whose work was followed by scientists at Upsala University - Hildebransson used height in a classification.

Clouds form in the first place because air contains water vapour, and because the air is cooled, causing the vapour to condense out at the saturation point (it binds on to *hygroscopic nuclei*, the official name for dirt, which can include pollen and pollutant particles). Air holds more vapour when it is warm, and a given amount can become saturated in two ways - you can either add more water vapour to it, or reduce its temperature. The excess vapour changes from gas to liquid, with the droplets *coalescing* into clouds as they collide. When they get heavy, they fall under gravity. The *Bergeron-Findeisen* theory says that some water droplets turn to ice and grow after sublimation of water vapour and collision with supercooled water droplets (see *Icing*). However, I have seen snow materialise out of the sky in Northern Canada (e.g. formating on nothing at all), and favour the coalescence theory, since Bergeron-Findeisen doesn't explain clouds in Summer that have no freezing level. However, coalescence does tend to occur in warmer and deeper clouds.

Cooling occurs when air expands as it is forced upwards in various ways:

- **Uplift** over a land or air mass, or a depression (orographic or frontal lifting). The exact type depends on the stability (or otherwise) of the air

- **Convection currents**, where air that is warmer than its environment become buoyant and rises (such as thermals rising from a heated surface). If the rising air is warmer than its surroundings and condensation occurs, you get cumuliform cloud. If it remains cooler than its surroundings, you get stratiform cloud

- **Eddying** (at the surface, or at the boundaries of two layers of air)

- **Waves** in the lee of mountains

Clouds affect surface heating by shielding the Earth and absorbing the Sun's Rays, or acting like a blanket to keep the heat in at night. Those above the freezing level are largely ice crystals. Otherwise, there are two main types, *layer*, or *heap*, associated with stable and unstable conditions (below), which might also be called *stratiform* or *cumuliform*, meaning horizontally or vertically developed, respectively. Stratiform clouds tend to form when an entire layer of air rises, not just a small convective cell.

There are a further three classifications based on the height of the cloud base, namely:

Low (Strato)

From sea level to about 6500 feet, mainly water:

- *Stratus* (St), thin, uniform, low, boring, associated with relatively stable air. Not much precipitation. At ground level, is called fog or mist. Caused by large areas cooling, rather than individual pockets of air, as with cumulus

- *Stratocumulus* (Sc). Like stratus, but cumulus-like, with small globules popping up here and there, and well-defined bases. Often formed in eddy currents which cause stratus to clump up, because the stratus tops will be cool from reflecting the Sun's rays and the bases warm from absorbing the Earth's infrared radiation. Can also form from cumulus joining up under an inversion. Sc can produce light rain or snow - any heavy showers will come from embedded cumulus

- *Nimbostratus* (Ns). Thick, dark, low rain cloud, typical in warm fronts, which may be found through all layers, but at least starts in the *alto* range. Moderate to heavy continual rain or snow

Middle (Alto)

Between 6 500-23 000 feet, made of water, ice, or supercooled water droplets, depending on temperature:

- *Altocumulus* (Ac) is similar to Sc (above), but higher. Size of cloudlets is between one and three finger-widths, with noticeable shading (not dark and gloomy, like stratus)

- *Altostratus* (As), similar to stratus, but higher, medium sheet greyish or bluish cloud, any thickness up to 10-12,000'. No ground shadow

High (Cirro)

Between 16 500-45 000 feet, made of ice crystals, so they have some transparency:

- *Cirrocumulus* (Cc) is high sheet cloud, made of small cloudlets (for want of a better word) which do not cast shadows, looking like a mackerel sky

- *Cirrostratus* (Cs) translucent high cloud, very delicate, made up of ice crystals. When in front of the Sun, you may see a halo round it

- *Cirrus* (Ci) is a high and fibrous filament indicating that a warm front is around 200 nm away. Otherwise known as *Horse tails*, or *Mares' tails*, they are precipitating clouds but the precipitate evaporates well before reaching ground level - the falling ice streaks form the distinctive filaments

Other

- *Heap clouds* (i.e. vertically developed):

  - *Cumulus* (Cu), are small amounts of heap cloud at low and medium levels, looking a bit like small balls of cotton wool (see below) with flat bases. It's actually *convection cloud*, which gives you a clue as to how it is made, and glider pilots seek out the thermals underneath them for the lift they provide (when a cumulus cloud is removed from its thermal, it can still grow from the latent heat that is released inside it making it warmer than its surroundings to cause it to float upwards). In strong winds, you might see them in long lines (called *cloud streets*, or *radiatus*), and you will get showers from larger ones. So-called "fair weather cumulus", typically seen on a nice Summer's day, normally forms directly as such, but (less commonly) can develop from stratus or strato-cu that has broken up with morning heating (they can also spread out into strato-cu or alto-cu in the presence of an inversion). Characteristics of cumuliform cloud include large water droplets, instability, turbulence, showers, and mainly clear ice. *Cumulus Congestus* is cumulus with a large vertical extent. *Mediocris* are as tall as they are wide, and *Humilis* are the smallest, being wider than they are tall. They are known as fair weather clouds because they do not produce any precipitation. *Cumulus Fractus* clouds are decaying, and appear ragged and woolly - otherwise, their outlines are sharper in Winter than in Summer

CAPT

Cloud streets in Manitoba, Canada

Characteristics of cumuliform cloud include large water droplets, instability, turbulence, showers, and mainly clear ice. *Cumulus Congestus* is cumulus with a large vertical extent. *Mediocris* are as tall as they are wide, and *Humilis* are the smallest, being wider than they are tall. They are known as fair weather clouds because they do not produce any precipitation. *Cumulus Fractus* clouds are decaying, and appear ragged and woolly - otherwise, their outlines are sharper in Winter than in Summer. Identical clouds, well isolated, dense, with well defined contours, developing vertically in a cauliflower shape, with the sides lit by the sun being bright white and their essentially horizontal bases, relatively dark, are *towering cumulus*, which are typically found between FL 30 and FL 150. A *cumulus congestus* is cumulus of great vertical extent

Fair Weather Cumulus

Over land, fair weather cu usually forms in the morning and reaches its maximum in terms of number and size by mid afternoon. They dissipate rapidly in the evening once the ground cools and convection currents die out. Over the sea, this is less marked and tends to be the reverse because the sea temperature stays the same while the air aloft cools

- **Cumulonimbus** is towering storm cloud. "Towering" means up to as much as 60,000 feet, and the anvil shape at the top is due to it meeting the tropopause, where temperature starts to remain constant, stopping the cloud's ascent. CBs are mostly found around late afternoon, and can project into the stratosphere. They are cumulus congestus until the upper regions turn into ice crystals. See also *Thunderstorms*

- **Lenticular**, found at the crest of standing waves formed in the lee of mountain waves

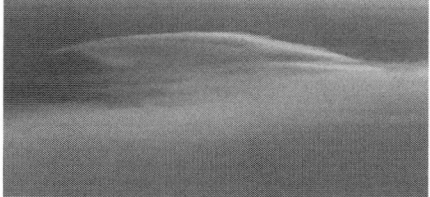

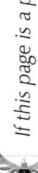

Classification Table

Genus	Species	Notes
Cumulus 2 000-3 000 ft	Humilis	Wider
	Mediocris	As wide as tall
	Congestus	Taller
	Fractus	Decaying - ragged, broken up
Cumulonimbus 2 000-60 000 ft	Calvus	Indistinct top
	Capillatus	Anvil shaped top
Stratus 0-6 500 ft	Nebulosus	Grey, generally featureless
	Fractus	Separate, ragged shreds
Stratocumulus 2 000-6 500 ft	Stratiformis	Clumps over a large area
	Lenticularis	Smooth lens shape
	Castellanus	Crenellated tops
Altocumulus 6 500-18 000 ft	Stratiformis	Form over a large area
	Lenticularis	Smooth lens shape
	Castellanus	Crenellated tops
	Floccus	Cumulus-like tufts
Altostratus 6 500-23 000 ft		Corona round Sun or Moon
Nimbostratus 2 000-18 000 ft		Thick, grey, featureless, lots of rain & drizzle
Cirrus 16 000-45 000 ft	Fibratus	Straight or curved filaments
	Uncinus	Hooks or commas
	Spissatus	Grey patches
	Castellanus	Small clumps with crenellated tops
	Floccus	Independent small round tufts
Cirrocumulus 16 500-45 000 ft	Stratiformis	Extensive layer
	Lenticularis	Smooth lens shape
	Castellanus	Crenellated tops
	Floccus	Cumulus-like tufts
Cirrostratus 16 500-30 000 ft	Fibratus	Fibrous or striated appearance
	Nebulosus	No variation in tone

Precipitation

This is the collective term for all the moisture that condenses into the atmosphere, but most people use it as a general term for rain or snow.

It comes from anything with *nimbo* in its name and is the end result of a chain of events that starts with the cooling through ascent of a parcel of dirty moist air ("dirty" meaning that it contains microscopic particles that water can bind on to). Once the saturation point is reached, condensation occurs and droplets coalesce to fall out as rain, snow, or whatever, according to temperature.

If the precipitation is very fine, and appears to float down, it is called drizzle. *Virga* is like a fine mist that evaporates before reaching the ground, which looks like streamers just below the cloud base. It should be avoided because it is turbulent*, and may be coming from a microburst.

*As rain changes from liquid to vapour, it removes heat from the air. The colder air can descend rapidly, creating a dry microburst.

Otherwise it is rain, if it is not frozen to form snow**. It is interesting to note that a drop of rain typically takes about forty minutes to reach the Earth's surface, whereas snowflakes may take as much as an hour and a half.

**Anything larger than 0.5mm droplet size is freezing precipitation - and must be avoided, even if your aircraft is cleared for flight in icing conditions (a dot from a pencil on a piece of paper is the largest size that would have been tested for an icing clearance).

A good rule of thumb is that if the moisture in the air is descending (as opposed to drifting around), the droplet size is larger than 0.5mm.

CAPT

Continuity

Showers are local outbreaks of precipitation from detached heap clouds, however long its duration.

Otherwise, precipitation falls from an extensive layer of cloud over a larger area, reported as:

- **Intermittent**, lasting less than an hour

- **Continuous**, or prolonged, lasting an hour or more

Hail & Sleet

Hail forms from large water droplets forced above the freezing level, although there is also an accretion and growth process as well. Raindrops can turn into small pieces of ice which may collide with supercooled water droplets and get larger, until they get so large that they fallout of the sky at some speed and cause damage to people or property. Hail is typically found coming out of thunderstorms.

Early studies said that hailstones were recycled through the cloud depth, but others indicate that they can grow while suspended in a strong updraught before falling out. Snowflakes are combined ice crystals which come from the freezing of water vapour without going through a liquid stage. Sleet is half-melted snow (i.e. mixed rain and snow), that begins to unfreeze during descent below freezing level when it is quite high above the surface (in the US, the word refers to ice pellets).

TURBULENCE

This is found in cloud and clear air (that is, *Clear Air Turbulence*, or CAT), and usually comes from friction when air currents mix, from various sources, such as *convective*, *orographic*, *windshear* and *mechanical*, and is reported as:

- *Light*, with small changes in height or attitude, near stratocumulus

- *Moderate*, more severe, but you are still in control. Good indicators are Cumulus-type clouds, which may also warn you about....

- *Severe*, with abrupt changes, and being temporarily out of control, indicated by Cumulonimbus and lenticular clouds, if there are many stacked on top of each other. Expect the latter when winds across mountain ranges are more than 40 kts

- *Extreme*, impossible to control

If turbulence is likely, use the turbulence speed in the flight manual, which will be rather less than normal. Advise the passengers to ensure their seat belts/harnesses are securely fastened. Catering and other loose equipment should be stowed and secured until the risk has passed.

THUNDERSTORMS

The Earth has a surplus of electrons, and the ionosphere doesn't - if you take the air between them as a dielectric, you have a very large capacitor (see *Electricity* in *ACK*) with a potential difference between its "plates" in the order of 360,000 volts, reducing with height at about 100 volts per metre (the body's resistance is high, so you don't notice the 200 volts between your feet and your head). However, capacitors leak, and they break down when one plate gets overcharged and the dielectric becomes a conductor (it gets ionised). The thunderstorm replenishes the Earth's negative charge through this mechanism, and it is estimated that, at any time over the planet, there are over 40,000 active thunderstorms (the highest frequency is in tropical areas). The power contained in a thunderstorm is more than 4 nuclear bombs put together (some say 10), which is a very good reason to avoid flying through them. Lightning itself is a discharge of around a million volts with an associated current of between 10,000-40,000 amps, heating the air up to 30,000°C. This can fuse sand or start a fire.

The hazards associated with thunderstorms include:

- **Electrical and Magnetic**. Lightning, obviously, plus damage to compasses and radios. Lightning could explode a fuel tank. The temperature band for lightning is between +10° to -10°C

- Severe **turbulence** from strong up- and downdraughts, which can be encountered up to 20 miles away and 5 000-10 000 ft above. Even over baby ones near to larger storms, you will need at least 5000 feet clearance - *sprites* have been known to go up 75 miles into space (for the exam, clear the top of a severe thunderstorm by 1,000 feet for each 10 kts of wind). The currents inside a thunderstorm will easily be enough to suck in the average light aircraft, or spit it out

- Severe **icing**

- Heavy **precipitation**, e.g. hail over ¾" across

- Strong, variable **winds** (squalls and microbursts)

- Rapid **pressure changes.** Pressure usually falls rapidly as a thunderstorm approaches, then rises rapidly with the first gust. It returns to normal after it passes

There are two main types of thunderstorm:

- **Air Mass** (non-frontal), triggered by convection (surface heating), so they are very common by day, over land, in Summer, forming in late afternoon and dissipating by the evening. They are often isolated and can usually be avoided. Look for them

CAPT

© *Phil Croucher, 2012*

in cols and weak lows where there has been enough time to heat the air by surface contact. Air mass thunderstorms can also be triggered by orographic uplift (i.e. after hitting the side of a mountain), so they can be found by night and day, and have more icing and turbulence, because the added updraughts can support more (and larger) water drops.

- **Mass Ascent**, or frontal, thunderstorms are found at air mass boundaries under cold front (and occlusion) conditions, that is, where cold air undercuts warm air, in a line along or just ahead of a cold front* (in the warm sector), to form line squalls. These are more frequent in Winter, simply because there are more fronts, and can therefore form by night and day, over land and sea. They are difficult to avoid because they cover larger areas. The frontal conditions can also produce other types of cloud, so mass ascent thunderstorms can be embedded and not easily detected. Frontal thunderstorms move the fastest.

*They can also develop on a warm front if the warm air is conditionally unstable. These would be embedded thunderstorms, which may look like something like this in the early stages:

The airflow is greatly disturbed anywhere near a thunderstorm, usually noticeable by strong up- and downdraughts, together with heavy rain and lightning, or even tornadoes, mentioned later. Because of the inflow of warm air and the outflow of cold, the *gust front* can extend up to 15-20 miles ahead of a moving storm (a gust front is formed from the cold air outflow from a thunderstorm). Avoid them even at the cost of diversion or an intermediate landing, but should this be impossible, there are certain things you can do, mentioned later.

In the picture below, there is a positive charge in the anvil. There is a negative charge in the freezing layers, and a positive charge below. Once the charge becomes high enough, the natural resistance of the air is breached and you get a lightning discharge (there are negative cloud base to positive ground strikes, and highly positive anvil cloud to positive ground strikes). Once a contact is made, say with a flagpole, air molecules will heat up enough to

reduce the air's resistance even further, to allow more charge to flow.

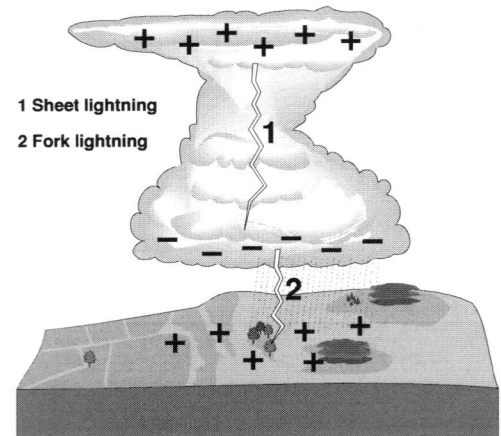

1 Sheet lightning
2 Fork lightning

To start a thunderstorm, you need:

- *moisture* (high relative humidity), particularly in the lower levels and preferably throughout a deep layer

- cloud tops above the 0° isotherm, preferably up to the tropopause

- a *steep* (conditionally unstable) *lapse rate*. A deep layer of instability can occur when a land surface is warmed up during the day at the same time as air is cooled above

- a *lifting*, or *trigger*, *agent*, which could be orographic, convective (thermal), frontal or nocturnal, as occurs in the midwest plains after night-time radiation from the cloud tops, which would increase lapse rates (of course, you could get two trigger actions, as when a front hits the Rockies). Turbulence is not a thunderstorm trigger because it is only instrumental in forming layer type clouds.

The instability and moisture content determine the severity of any storm, and a high temperature and dewpoint close together are a good early warning as the air is hot, and contains lots of water vapour. Convective activity over land in mid-latitudes is greatest in the Summer, in the afternoons, so you can expect local isolated thunderstorms arising from thermal triggering mostly in the mid-afternoon, from warm updraughts (thermal triggering depends on relatively light winds that allow high surface temperatures to develop). Isolated thunderstorms of a local nature are generally caused by *unstable air, high humidity and a lifting force.*

Structure

Although the clouds associated with a thunderstorm may extend for some distance, a thunderstorm is actually a collection of several cloud cells in varying stages of development, with varying diameters, typically a few hundred feet across. The different cells may be developing, maturing or dissipating at rates of their own, which could form their own trigger actions and make the storm self-perpetuating.

DEVELOPMENT STAGE

During the development, or cumulus stage, which takes around 15-20 minutes, several cumulus clouds will begin to merge, where the system consists mainly of updrafts, and will grow to around 4 miles wide at the base and 20,000 feet in height. That is, warm, moist unstable air is forced to rise because of the trigger agents mentioned above. Water droplets are merging as well, to form larger raindrops, which get to be a hazard once they get above the freezing level and become supercooled (see *Icing*, below). When they are big enough, they will fall, and pull cold air down with them (and drier air in from above), which is where the downdrafts come from. The drier air causes some evaporation, which absorbs latent heat and makes the air even colder, to fall faster. So, rain at the surface is a good indication of the transition to ....

THE MATURE STAGE

This is distinguished by rainfall (or precipitation), but mostly by downdraughts and updraughts over about 15-20 minutes. In the mature stage, rain falls through or immediately beside the updraught, inducing frictional drag to retard it and turn it into a downdraught. This will reduce the cell's lifecycle to somewhere between 20 minutes and 2½ hours. In a Steady State thunderstorm, this will be several hours because the precipitation falls outside the downdraught. Tornadoes often form with steady-state thunderstorms associated with cold fronts or squall lines.

Whilst some heating takes place in a downdraught, there is also a lot of evaporation which will cancel it out and increase cooling, so cool air ends up near the surface below the cloud, on top of turbulence in the shape of microbursts. This means that there will often be a roll of stratocumulus ahead of the storm caused by mixing of the descending cool air with a warm moist updraught.

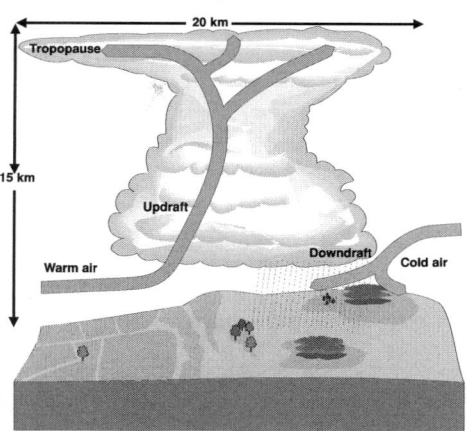

The storm will move under the influence of the upper winds, with the average movement following the 700 Mb (10 000 ft) wind. It can produce lightning at this stage from large static discharges, with the most severe being within 5 000 feet of the freezing level.

THE DISSIPATION STAGE

The third stage, which starts after the updraughts cease. It is distinguished by the presence of an anvil, formed as the clouds at the top of the storm meet the tropopause, and therefore an inversion, where they spread out in the wind. Characteristics are downdraughts and disappearing cloud.

Windshear

When wet-bulb cooling occurs in the middle and upper levels of a thunderstorm, the cooling of the air causes it to become negatively buoyant (i.e it sinks), and accelerate toward the earth's surface causing a derecho, a macroburst or a microburst. In other words, cold air from high altitudes is forced down to balance the powerful updraughts caused by the warm air rising inside the cells. The cold air spreads out when it hits the ground to form a cushion, or *cold dome*, ahead of which are more, called *downbursts*, which may themselves contain *microbursts*, which, technically, are concentrated inside a 4 km radius. Expect lightning as well at this stage, which comes from the friction between up- and downdraughts and between water and air molecules.

Thus, a well-developed line of thunderstorms pushes a mass of cold air in front of it, which forces warm air up, to form more storm cells. The leading edge of cold air becomes the windshift line, only sometimes marked by roll cloud. As the top of the cloud reaches the tropopause, inversion conditions stop the ascent and strong upper winds produce the distinctive anvil shape.

Cumulonimbus Mamma clouds often occur with violent thunderstorms and tornadoes.

Takeoff and Landing

Not if thunderstorms are overhead or within 5 nm, due to the risk of lightning strikes. The same goes for refuelling!

Squall Lines

A *squall line* is a line of intensive thunderstorms, which can be hundreds of miles long and which Murphy's Law dictates will be right across your flight path (they will be too wide for a detour and too severe to penetrate). Severe squall lines will prompt a SIGMET to be issued.

Squall lines occur under the same conditions as thunderstorms and can appear anywhere that air is moist and unstable, but often ahead of cold fronts in late afternoon or early evening, or before a "dew point front", which separates air masses that only have different moisture levels. They are the product of severe cold frontal conditions, where a cold front nudges under the warm sector (watch for an acute bend in isobars at the front, or low roll cloud across the advance). They can move so fast that they can get embedded into the warm frontal cloud. However, the normal propagation method comes from a line of updraughts along an outflow boundary from a thunderstorm, spreading out as they hit the ground and nudging air upwards to its dewpoint. Precipitation falls behind the system, and a classic squall line has the updraught along the front and the downdraught on the back.

These clues will help you detect squall lines before flight:

- A well defined warm sector, with high dewpoints, especially ahead of and parallel to the cold front (hot moist air has a lot of energy)

- Cold air aloft, where any warm air rising into it gets a buoyancy boost (watch for a trough aloft). Jetstreams can give air a similar boost as it gets sucked up from lower levels

- Strong Southerly winds just ahead of the cold front

ICING

Ice on your airframe is dangerous because it makes the machine heavier, displaces the Centre Of Gravity, and distorts the lift-producing surfaces, to produce less lift and more drag. In addition, it can jam the controls, block instruments, vision, and cause interference with radios as it covers the antennae. In particular, with helicopter rotor blades, or with propellers, it may cause an imbalance which leads to severe vibration.

Ice will form on an airframe if there is water in a liquid state combined with either the air or the airframe temperature below 0°.

Zero degrees is actually when water becomes *capable* of freezing, from which you can infer that it doesn't necessarily do so. A *Supercooled Water Droplet* is one below freezing, but not frozen. It gets away with this from the absence of hygroscopic nuclei to bind on to.

When such a droplet strikes an airframe, however, just below 0°, some of it will freeze on impact, releasing latent heat and warming the remainder, which then flows back, turning into *clear ice* when the freezing is slow, which can gather without noticeable vibration. The time taken for this to happen depends on the temperature of the aircraft surface (lower temperature, quicker freezing), the initial temperature of the water drop (lower temperature, quicker freezing), and the size of the water drop (large drops, slower freezing).

In other words, the airframe will act as one giant ice nucleus, and the freezing is *behind* the point of impact, and therefore behind the influence of deicing equipment, where it can pile up and distort the lift-producing surfaces. 1/80th part of a SWD will freeze on impact for each degree below zero, assuming a large droplet - small ones will form *rime ice* - see below. The worst place to penetrate cumuliform cloud is between 0 to -10°C, where most SWDs are - you are most likely to find large ones in the lower levels of cloud that has formed in unstable air (cumulus), in temperatures only a few degrees below freezing, and you can expect clear icing from them.

Ice is reported as:

- *Trace*, meaning slight, non-hazardous, perceptible

- *Light*, with occasional use of deicing equipment. Flights over 1 hour might be inadvisable, but *No change of course and altitude necessary,* from ICAO

- *Moderate*, where use of above equipment is necessary. Time to consider diversion. The ICAO phrase is *Change of course and/or altitude desirable*

- *Severe*, where the equipment is useless and you must divert. ICAO: *Change course and/or altitude immediately*

CAPT

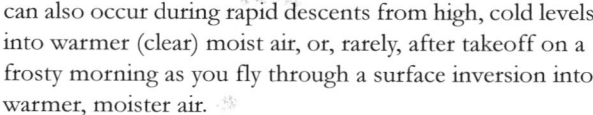

If you are getting light-moderate icing and you start seeing ice crystals, you can expect the icing intensity to decrease. Altocumulus and Altostratus are the most likely clouds to produce light to moderate icing, when not subject to orographic lifting. Moderate to severe icing is most likely to occur in Nimbostratus. You can virtually rule out icing in Cirrus cloud.

Types Of Icing

RIME ICE

This comes from *smaller* SWDs well below 0° (actually from -10° to -20°C), when freezing is fast. It is opaque and granular and moves forward as it builds up on sharp surfaces like antennae. On a helicopter rotor blade, it is more likely to occur on the top rather than the leading edge. Below -40°C, you will likely only encounter ice crystals, which will not stick to the aircraft, or *very small* SWDs. However, ice accumulation is too unpredictable to assume anything - you can get severe icing in towering cumulus down to -25°C. It is worst at the top of CBs.

CLEAR (GLAZE) ICE

Clear ice is transparent, with no trapped air, so it is very hard to get rid of. It is found most often in cumulus clouds and unstable conditions between 0 and -10°C, where large supercooled water droplets are found. It is a problem because it is very heavy and can affect controls and surfaces, aside from being difficult to remove. It is the most dangerous form of aircraft icing The most serious risk is on the front surfaces of the aircraft, but because it can run back behind the effect of deicing equipment, it is dangerous to the rear as well.

MIXED ICE

A mixture of the above two types. It is often called cloudy ice, and it can be formed from large or small SWDs between 0°C and -20°C in layer and heap type clouds.

RAIN ICE

This can be found when clear of cloud, above the freezing level, commonly just ahead of a warm front, where there is a freezing level above you and rain is falling from the overhanging cloud. It builds up quickly and immediate action is required. The best option is to climb or fly faster - do not descend unless you know where you are and that the freezing level is above the surface. Turning takes time and increases the chances of losing control.

HOAR FROST

This is a light crystalline deposit which forms away from clouds and precipitation. It is the only type of icing that occurs in clear air, typically forming after a clear night when the airframe has been allowed to creep below 0°C and the surrounding air gets cooled below its dewpoint. It

can also occur during rapid descents from high, cold levels into warmer (clear) moist air, or, rarely, after takeoff on a frosty morning as you fly through a surface inversion into warmer, moister air.

Although it is technically light icing, it has the same effect as a bad paint job and can increase drag markedly. It increases the stalling speed, reduces visibility and impairs communication.

ENGINE ICING

Icing in piston engines can occur in temperatures as high as 30°C, but the maximum for jet engines is around 5°C.

Note: Both values are **above** 0°C - airframe icing only occurs at sub-zero temperatures (with the possible exception of hoar frost).

In both types, fuel can freeze, which may be prevented with additives.

PISTON ENGINES

In piston engines, impact icing restricts the flow of air into the engine by blocking the intakes. Induction icing occurs inside the venturi from evaporation and expansion of the fuel, between -10°C and +30°C, with a relative humidity of 30% or more and a reduced power setting (i.e. warm weather, high humidity and low power settings).

Avoiding Icing

Pitot head, static vent and fuel vent heaters should be on whenever you encounter icing, together with anything else you feel is appropriate. Otherwise, you need warmer air to get rid of ice effectively - just flying around in clear air can take hours to shift it, but you could at least say you won't get any more. Aerodynamic heating comes from air friction, which may get rid of ice, but only at high speeds, so will not likely benefit helicopters, except for rotor blades, which may be warmer by 1° or so, from their speed. Climbing out is often not possible, due to lack of performance or ATC considerations, and descending has problems, too - if you're getting clear ice, it's a fair bet the air is warmer above you, since it may be freezing rain, from an inversion, probably within 1,000 feet or so, as you might get before a warm front, or after a cold one. The most dangerous position to be in is in rain - it is quite common to fly above a freezing level (always being aware that there may be two!) if there is no moisture around.

In this position, landing on your first attempt becomes more important as you are unlikely to survive a go-around without picking up more. You basically have three choices, go up, down or back the way you came. Going up is a good first choice if you know the tops are nearby, if only because you won't have a chance to do so later, but you present more of the airframe to icing risk, which is why there is often a minimum speed for climbing in icing conditions, slightly more than normal. To keep out of

trouble, before going, check that the freezing level is well above any minimum altitudes, which will help get rid of ice in the descent. Try to make sure the cloud tops are within reach as well, or that you have plenty of holes.

Deicing

De-icing is the process of removing ice from an airframe after it has formed. *Anti-icing* is the process of stopping it from forming in the first place. A one-step procedure does both at the same time using a combination fluid. The two step procedure involves de-icing, then anti-icing (de-icing fluid is hot, and anti-icing fluid is cold, because it increases its thickness and effective working time. Although heating a fluid increases its *deicing* properties, unheated fluids are more effective for *anti-icing*).

The operator must establish procedures for its removal (including inspections), and a commander is not allowed to take off the external surfaces of the aircraft are clear of any deposit that would affect performance or control of an aircraft, other than that in the Flight Manual. In addition, a commander may not take off into known or expected icing conditions unless the aircraft is certificated and equipped to cope.

When an aircraft is contaminated by ice on the ground, approved de-icing methods include:

- applying de-icing fluids (but see below)

- warming the airframe with hot air blowers

- placing the aircraft in a warm hangar

- sweeping surfaces which have frost and light ice on them

Sitting behind a running jet engine is not approved!

DEICING FLUIDS

These are not generally used on helicopters.

AIR MASSES

A large body of air will have the characteristics of its origin (the *source region*), particularly with regard to moisture and temperature, in that, a mass of air can originate from Tropical or Polar regions (i.e. be warm or cold) or be Maritime or Polar (wet or dry). The effects might be spread throughout the air mass by conduction, convection or turbulence.

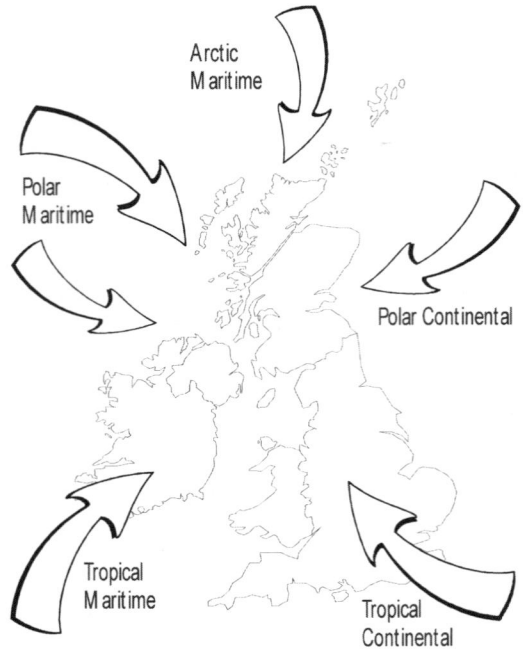

To acquire the characteristics to meet the classification, a mass of air has to stay in one more or less uniform place for several days, so one definition of an air mass could be *a huge body of air with uniform properties of temperature and moisture*. For the necessary stagnation for air to acquire such characteristics, light winds are needed, so a source region is likely to be subject to high pressure. Air masses are basically *Arctic* or *Polar*, *Tropical* or *Equatorial*, *Maritime* (sea-based) or *Continental* (land-based). Arctic and Polar only really differ at the upper levels, otherwise they are much the same, especially at the surface.

Thus, air masses vary as to moisture content and temperature. It's what happens when one moves away from its source region that is important, as well as what happens when it mixes with others - refer to *Tornadoes* to see the effects that occur when N Westerly airflow meets S Easterly airflow over the USA. Air masses of the same type mix well, but others don't, and will produce problems at the transition point (the process in an air mass that leads to widespread NS and AS cloud is *lifting*). Air from the Azores would be warmer and more humid than North Russian air. Europe in Summer is affected by Tropical Continental air from the South Balkans and the Near East, but the main air masses that affect the UK are:

CAPT

- **Polar Continental**, which is dry and cold because it comes from polar land regions, such as Siberia. It has little energy and is only significant in Winter. On its way to the UK it passes over the North Sea. If it has a short sea track, from Belgium or the Netherlands to the SE coast it remains dry, and produces cloudless skies. However with a long sea track it picks up moisture, and is also warmed more in the lower levels (in Winter the sea is warmer than the land). It comes to resemble a Polar Maritime airmass, and give cumuliform cloud and showers on the East coast. Cloud disperses inland. In Summer, the North Sea cools the air, and it becomes more stable and can form low cloud and sea advection fog on the East coast

- **Tropical Continental**, dry and warm, during Summer. The source is North Africa (the Azores), and it is warm and dry, but cooled from below as it tracks North, so it stays stable, and will tend to poor visibility, despite cloudless skies. It stays dry because its journey is mostly over land

- **Polar Maritime**, which is cold, moist and stable at its origin (the Arctic), becomes warmer and more unstable as it comes South East across the North Atlantic, typically from East of Greenland (surface heating from the sea increases the temperature). It is moist because of surface evaporation, leading to convective cumuliform cloud. Any instability is increased during the day in Summer. In showers, visibility will be poor, but will improve as the air mass moves inland as moisture is lost.

  Returning Polar Maritime sweeps out wide into the Atlantic before turning round and going back towards the Pole. After the initial warming over the Atlantic, the unstable elements are cooled in their lowest layers as the air goes North again. Over the British Isles, this will produce dull, overcast weather, sometimes with drizzle, albeit still with showers and even thunderstorms

- **Tropical Maritime**, moist and warm, from tropical oceans. It picks up moisture on its travels, so relative humidity increases and the air mass becomes cooler and more stable as it moves North. In Winter, you can expect stratiform cloud and drizzle, with poor visibility after cloud has been heated away by the warmer land mass. In Spring and early Summer, you will get advection fog in Western areas, particularly Cornwall and Devon, and advection fog in the English Channel

There are also *Arctic Continental*, *Arctic Maritime* (as for Polar, but colder), which only affect the UK in Winter. Also, *Equatorial Maritime*, plus *Returning Polar Maritime*, which has travelled well South of the British Isles and is

coming back from the South West with Tropical Maritime properties at low level. There is no *Equatorial Continental* because there is no land mass in the region large enough to produce the required effects.

Prevailing Westerly winds mean that the UK is most commonly affected by maritime air masses.

Identification

First, determine the air mass's stability by asking whether it is warm air passing over a cold surface, tending to stability, or the other way round, which tends to instability.

The *stability* of an air mass is affected by its *origin* and *how it got to where it is*, in terms of track and time. Apply Buys Ballot's law and follow the isobars back.

Next, determine the likely moisture content. Air coming from over the sea is likely to be clean. From a continent, it is likely to be polluted, with poor visibility.

FRONTOLOGY
••

A front is a line of discontinuity, or a narrow transition zone between air masses where they are forced to mix, even though they don't want to. Otherwise, the boundary between two air masses might occupy several kilometres.

The process starts in mid-high latitudes when low pressure systems form along the boundary between cold polar air and warmer air from temperate zones. Some parts of the boundary being faster than others causes them to catch up and the end result is that warmer air is forced upwards. The weather associated with fronts depends on the air masses concerned and the way in which they interact - if the warm air that is forced upwards is dry and stable, for example, you won't necessarily see any clouds.

This is a plan view of a frontal system:

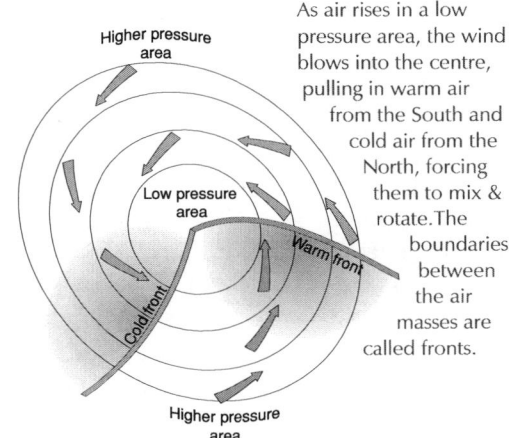

Higher pressure area

Low pressure area

Cold front

Warm front

Higher pressure area

As air rises in a low pressure area, the wind blows into the centre, pulling in warm air from the South and cold air from the North, forcing them to mix & rotate. The boundaries between the air masses are called fronts.

The narrow part (depicted by the red or blue line) is actually the ground position, as the effects of a front with height are felt for some distance either side. The difference is usually in temperature (which can actually be very small), but may be purely due to moisture content. Fronts are always associated with depressions, which are sometimes referred to as *frontal waves*. A series of fronts or depressions, one after the other, is referred to as a *Westerly Wave* (an *Easterly Wave* is a wave in a trade wind belt from E-W with severe convective activity in the rear of its trough). Depressions usually form on cold or stationary fronts, and will rotate *anticlockwise* around a low.

Warm tropical air could be forced over colder arctic air, for example, because it is less dense and, if moist, will form a typical cloud structure that we can use to tell when a front is coming. The name of a front, that is, *warm*, or *cold*, comes from whichever air mass is overtaking the other, whereas the type of weather you get is determined by the stability and moisture content of the *warm air mass*. The actual temperature is less important than its relationship to that of the surface it is passing over.

The *Polar Front* is where South- and North-Westerly airstreams meet to form long series of depressions, starting off the Atlantic Coast of North America, generally lying between 40-70°N in the temperate latitudes, and similarly in the Southern Hemisphere. It is the boundary between polar and tropical air (Polar Front depressions move along it toward the East, being most Southerly during Winter). In Summer, you can generally expect to see the Polar Front range from *Newfoundland* to the *North of Scotland*, and, in Winter, further South from *Florida* to *South-West England*. It lies in a trough of low pressure with highs on each side - interaction between them cause a bend, or wave, in the Polar front, and so the whole process starts. A *dew point front*, or *dry line*, forms when two similar air masses with only a moisture difference between them meet. Other than that, there is little contrast across it.

Frontogenesis means the forming of a front, and *frontolysis* means its dissipation. The cold air mass does not move at a *stationary front* (where surface winds tend to flow parallel to the frontal zone), and you get an *upper front* with any temperature gradient aloft. To try and find where a front might be on the surface (looking at a weather map in the exam), look at the temperature, pressure, dew point and wind velocity as depicted in station circles. On the ground, watch for the wind picking up a bit, and the altimeter dropping slightly. In fact, knowing the signs given out by an approaching front can be very useful when operating in remoter places. You need to watch these items:

- *Wind speed and direction*. Winds veer as a front approaches and back as it passes. For a cold front, they will start from the South and end up Westerly or North Westerly - with a warm front, look for winds to start from the East (ish) and end up in the South (ish). Any farmer will tell you that the wind will reverse direction as a thunderstorm approaches. With a stationary front, surface winds will tend to flow parallel to the frontal zone

- *Temperature*. The greater the temperature, the more active the front will be, with more violent weather. It gets colder as a cold front passes, and warmer as a warm front goes by. The greater the temperature *difference*, the more violent the passage will be

- *Humidity*. Humidity will be high, and the temperature and dew points will be close together with a cold front passage. If the temperatures are both high, there will more of a likelihood of thunderstorms, due to the energy in the air. The temperature and dewpoint spread will widen once the front has gone through, and humidity will decrease. This will not be so noticeable with a warm front passage, since the slope is shallower

- *Clouds*. Cold fronts and warm fronts bring cumuliform and stratiform clouds, respectively

- *Pressure trends*. Pressure always falls as a front approaches, because massive amounts of air are being lifted. The faster the rate of change, the more severe the weather is likely to be, and it may include thunderstorms and heavy rain. Pressure will rise again after the front passes by

Knowing where fronts (and lows) are is important, as that is where the weather tends to be worst, according to the strength of the system.

It's best to fly toward fronts, to get the best weather to find your way home in should things deteriorate, as they tend to do. Also, make frequent updates to your altimeter settings, or use the *Regional QNH*, which is a *prediction* of the lowest sea level pressure over the next hour.

CAPT

The Warm Front

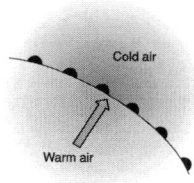

This exists where warm air overtakes a colder air mass and is forced upwards over it, meaning clouds. Its symbol on a weather map, resembling beads of sweat, is shown on the left. The frontal slope has a gradient of somewhere between 1:150 and 1:200, although the clouds themselves will be about 5 miles high, starting with Nimbostratus at more or less ground level, through alto-stratus to cirrostratus. When flying towards it, you would see the clouds the other way round, of course, so once you start seeing cirrus clouds, you know that a warm front is somewhere ahead, anywhere between 300-600 miles away, or nearly 24 hours at a typical speed of about 25 kts, so have an overnight kit if you have to wait it out (rain will typically be 200 miles ahead). You can use the typical slope figure to work out the cloud base in front of the system. At 100 miles, it will be 2,640 feet, which comes from 1/200*100, making half a mile, multiplied by 5280 (feet).

Clouds will therefore appear in this order as you fly towards a warm front - cirrus, cirrostratus, altostratus, stratus and nimbostratus. The extensive cloud layers are caused by unstable warm air overrunning retreating cold air, with a high moisture content. Thus, the precipitation will change from steady rain to heavy showers.

The shallow slope ensures that whatever is coming will last some time, and you can expect the pressure to fall, the cloud to get lower, the wind to back and increase in speed, rising humidity, bad visibility, drizzle and rain, though not necessarily in that order. The freezing level will be lower in front than behind, and the slope means that freezing rain will be falling on anything underneath (see diagram below), so if you are flying towards a warm front, or towards the rear of a cold front, in between their freezing levels and that in the warm sector, watch out!

Picture: Cross Section Of A Frontal System

Supercooled water droplets from above will freeze onto your cold airframe. Once you see ice pellets, expect freezing rain next. If you are thinking of trying to descend out of it, remember that the cloud base lowers in precipitation.

As the front passes, you will experience *frontal fog* in front (from the added water), followed by advection fog afterwards. The rain will stop, then become drizzle under an overcast sky, and the wind will veer. As humidity rises to saturation point, visibility could be poor. You will then be in the warm sector, where conditions will be more settled for a few hours (the pressure will rise abruptly), with broken or overcast stratus, just a few hundred feet thick. The further you are away from the low centre, the more the cloud is likely to break up, but don't be fooled - high ground upwind could be holding the cloud back, giving a false impression that the system has passed on. The warm sector is called that because it has the warmest air of the whole system, stuck as it is between the warm and cold fronts.

When asked to predict the future position of a warm front (and the type of weather), use the direction of the isobars in the warm sector, since the front moves parallel to them.

As warm air finds it hard to displace cold air, a warm front will move at about half the speed of a cold front in the same conditions.

After the warm sector comes......

The Cold Front

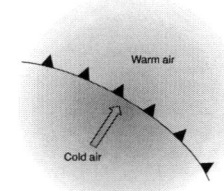

The cold front occurs when cold dense air moves towards the Equator (from the Poles) and undercuts warm air to force it aloft. A cold front has a much steeper slope (1:50) than a warm front, and brisker activity, with more of a likelihood of thunderstorms, because the convergence is

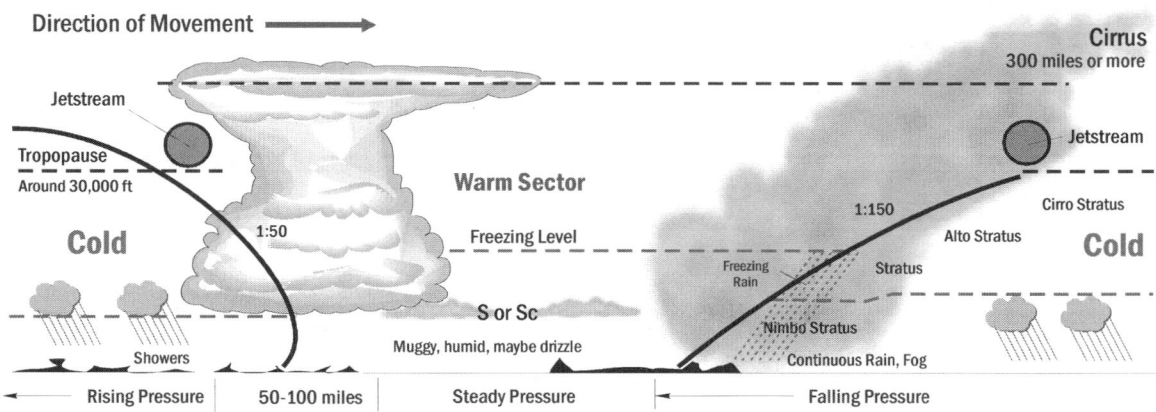

typically stronger, providing a greater forcing mechanism. The rain becomes more showery and the wind veers more, to the West or Northwest. Pressure gets higher, and temperature and humidity decrease. In temperate climates, large amounts of Cu-nim are unusual at this point, but they are not over continental land areas. The rain belt is relatively small compared to the warm front, and visibility will improve markedly.

A cold front moves at about the speed of the wind perpendicular to it just above the friction level (about 2,000 feet, for 15-25 kts), but they are faster in Winter because the air is colder and exerts greater pressure. However, friction with the ground will slow the lower levels, so there is a bulge effect along the leading edge. The friction, coupled with strong heating from below as the cold air crosses warmer ground, often creates gusty wind conditions. The weather is generally colder after its passage, and with less cloud, because pressure is greater to the West and less to the East, limiting the inflow of air.

Expect questions on weather at a cold front, and after its passage (pressure rising, wind veering, fair weather cumulus and good visibility, because the turbulence has removed the pollution from the lower layers). The associated weather is actually determined by the stability and moisture content of the warm air mass, the speed of the front, and steepness of the frontal surface. Wind shifts will be usually more pronounced (in fact, it will veer about 30° and increase in speed).

Typical Frontal Cloud Distribution

The Occlusion

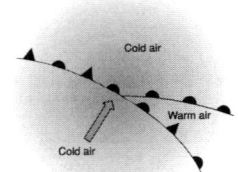

Cold fronts move faster than warm fronts. When a cold front catches up with a warm front, the warm sector is lifted from the ground (shut off), leaving only one front on the surface, with another on top, although some scientists say that frontal occlusions occur when storms redevelop farther back into the cold air. In most cases, storms start to weaken after a frontal occlusion occurs. Whatever the reason, the essential point with an occluded front is that warm air is isolated as it is forced aloft to condense and form clouds. The greatest danger is thunderstorms masked by stratiform cloud

The point where occluding starts is the *triple point,* because there are three air masses involved: that ahead of the occlusion, the warm air aloft, and the air behind the occlusion, or where the cold, warm and occluded fronts meet. It is the nearest location of warm air to the centre, and therefore the point of most lifting, so it is often a focus for a secondary low. It lies at the rear edge of the cloud band associated with the occluded front, within a sharp trough, but the air mass behind the boundary can be either warm or cold.

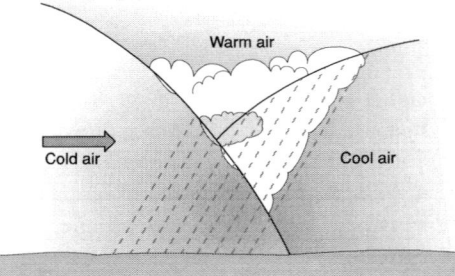

If the air behind the occluded front is the coldest, it will plough under both air masses to produce a cold front occlusion (see above). The weather is initially like a warm front, but during the passage, showery weather similar to that of a cold front occurs. This kind of occlusion is common in Summer. A cold occlusion is more or less the same as Trough of Warm Air Aloft, again from a cold front catching up with a warm one. Trowals are parts of systems in their decaying state. They are found on constant pressure charts above 700 mb (around 10,000 ft), and can affect surface weather severely.

If the air is warmer than the air ahead, which is typical of Britain in Winter, it will ride over the colder air mass, because it is lighter, for a warm front occlusion, even though the air masses are cold. The weather is like a warm front, mostly occurring in Winter, and less common.

In fact, a wide variety of weather can be found along an occluded front. As they are associated with mature systems, it can be very unsettled with rain and/or snow likely and possibly thunderstorms, potentially over a prolonged period. However, you do get more rain with a warm occlusion, plus a quicker transition from warm to cold front weather.

These pictures show how a cold front can catch up to a warm front and produce an occlusion:

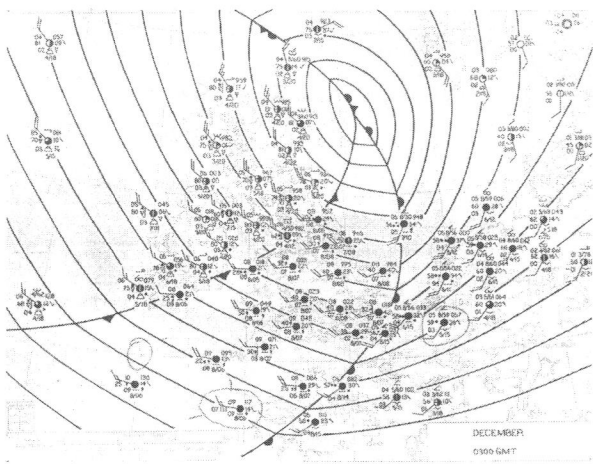

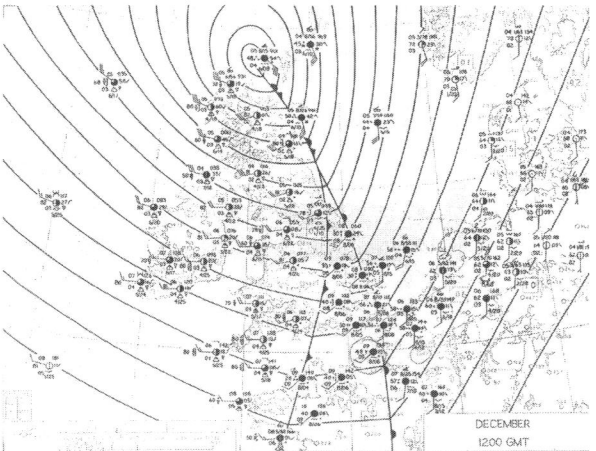

VISIBILITY

Defined as the greatest horizontal distance a dark object (of known dimensions) can be seen and recognised against a light background, usually prominent objects from the tower, or a measure of the opacity of the atmosphere in a particular direction. The *prevailing visibility* is the greatest met or exceeded through at least half the visible horizon. This, of course poses a problem at night, so *night visibility* really refers to how far you would be able to see in daylight. Visibility may be reduced by fog, mist, cloud, precipitation, sea spray, smoke, sand, dust and industrial haze, etc. Here is a reminder of how bad it can be:

The best visibility in haze is obtained when down-sun and up-moon.

Measuring Visibility

If possible, the Mk 1 eyeball is used, but machinery is often used in remote places or where constant information is required.

METEOROLOGICAL VISIBILITY

Met vis is defined as *the greatest horizontal distance at which known objects can be seen and recognised by an observer on the ground with normal eyesight under conditions of normal daylight illumination*. Put another way, it gives information on the transparency of the atmosphere to a stationary ground observer, who will measure the distance in a number of directions and report the least one as the met vis.

Various other factors will determine whether the same object can actually be seen by aircrew.

Visibility is quoted in metres up to and including 5000 m (5 km) and in kilometres thereafter. It is generally greater than RVR.

RUNWAY VISUAL RANGE

RVR is the maximum distance that a pilot 15 feet above the runway (in the touchdown area) can see marker boards by day and lights by night, when looking towards the touchdown or landing area. It is reported when normal visibility is 1500 m or less, or when shallow fog is reported or forecast. The readings are valid *for the time being*, which means every 30 minutes when traffic is continuous, or within 15 minutes if traffic is light. RVR is *never* forecast (probably the basis of a trick question).

RVR is measured with a *transmissometer*, which is a device that uses a photoelectric cell to produce an equivalent to daytime visibility (the strength of current in the cell depends on the clarity of air between the transmitter and receiver). Because only a small portion of the atmosphere can be sampled, three are used - one at each end of the runway, and the middle, so you will get figures from ATC for the *touchdown zone*, *mid-point* and *stop end*. If you only get two figures, the first will be for the touchdown zone, and the other will be specified. However, mid-point or stop end values are suppressed when they are equal to or above that of the touchdown zone, and are above 400 m, or if the values are 800 m or greater.

Fog

Fog is essentially cloud at ground level, which exists when you cannot see more than 1,000 metres (not inclusive) due to water droplets in the air (i.e. a relative humidity of 100%). It is not really cloud, because you cannot see anything at all in clouds, but the process of formation is the same, with the other difference being that fog forms downwards and clouds form upwards - therefore you cannot fly under fog. With *freezing fog*, the water droplets are supercooled. When only freezing fog occurs, there will be just about as much freezing of the fog droplets onto surfaces as there will be sublimation from the surface, so there is not much (rime) ice accumulation. There may also be freezing drizzle, in which case a film of ice will coat surfaces. *Ice fog* is composed of tiny ice crystals, where the temperature is becoming too cold for supercooling. Ice fog will only be seen in cold Arctic/Polar air.

- *Radiation fog* forms over land, preferably low-lying, when temperatures approach the dewpoint with very slight winds (2-8 kts), with moisture present. It doesn't form over the sea, because the diurnal temperature variation is less. It is often found in the early morning after a clear night, since it likes high relative humidity, light winds and clear skies. Its vertical extent is typically 500 feet, and it usually clears quickly, once the Sun's heat gets to work, often getting worse before it gets better. If the winds are just enough to stir things up, fog will form. If there is no wind, you will get dew on the ground, and if the wind is too strong you will get low level stratus. Radiation fog disperses with wind, heat, or a drier air mass. You can expect the densest type the night after an afternoon of heavy rains, in low lying areas, which, naturally, is where you will find most airfields

Radiation Fog In The Rockies

- *Valley Fog* is radiation fog found in valleys.

- *Advection fog* arises from warm air flowing over a cold surface, and it can be encountered immediately after the passage of a cold front. Advection simply means the sideways movement of air in bulk - warm advection means warm air replacing colder air, and *vice versa*, as you would find with fronts. It is not the same as radiation fog because air movement is involved, and the coolness does not arise from diurnal variations, but longer periods, as with the sea, where this type of fog is commonly found. In the Atlantic provinces of Canada, it occurs when moist air passes over the cold Labrador Current. It is also the type of fog that rolls in to cover the San Francisco bridge. Winds over 15 kts will lift advection fog into a layer of low stratus or stratocumulus.

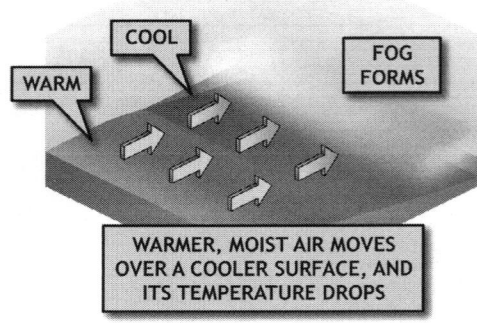

If this page is a photocopy, it is not authorised!

CAPT

- *Orographic (Hill) Fog* is low cloud covering high ground, which may or may not have helped with its formation - if moist air is forced up the side of a hill, it will condense. An observer on the ground sees low cloud - a person on the hill is in fog.

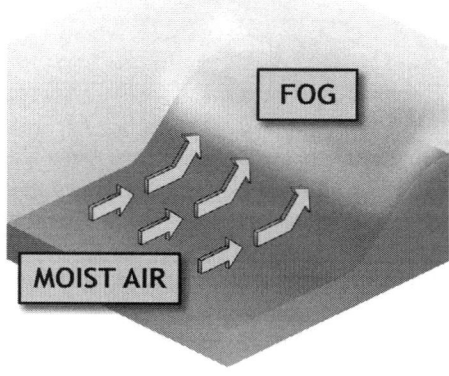

- *Upslope fog* is a larger scale type of hill fog that forms from adiabatic cooling of moist, stable air as it moves up slopes, typically over the Canadian prairies when air is moving from East to West (Winnipeg is about 800 feet ASL, Regina to the West is about 1900, and Calgary, in the foothills of the Rockies, is about 3500 feet ASL)

- *Frontal fog* may simply be low cloud touching high ground, or come from rain falling through unsaturated air beneath:

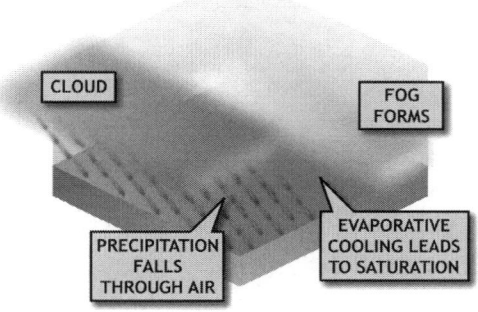

- *Steam Fog,* or Arctic Smoke, comes from cold air moving over warm water.

In the process, heat and moisture are transferred from the warm water to the cooler, drier air in a shallow layer near the lake surface. You now have an unstable situation with warm, saturated air at the lake's surface below cooler air which rises to form steam fog.

- In *shallow fog*, you may be able to see the whole of the approach and/or runway lights from a considerable distance, even though reports indicate fog. On descending into the fog layer, however, your visual reference is likely to drop rapidly, in extreme cases from the full length of the runway and approach lights to a very small segment, but typically about half. This may give the impression that you're pitching nose up, making you more likely to hit the ground when you try to correct it. *You should be prepared for a missed approach whenever you have the slightest doubt about forward visibility.* The minimum RVR to land from a visual circuit is 800m.

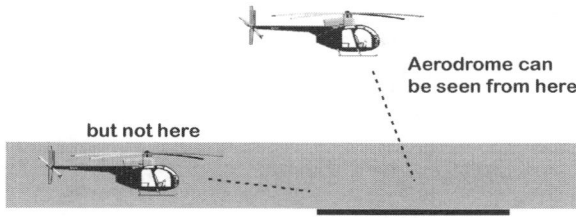

The types of fog just in front of and just after the passage of a warm front are *frontal* and *advection* fog.

Mist

This is essentially, thin fog, except that the visibility is between 1,000 - 5000 m, inclusive.

Whiteout

This is defined by the American Meteorological Society as:

"An atmospheric optical phenomenon of the polar regions in which the observer appears to be engulfed in a uniformly white glow".

You can see only dark nearby objects - no shadows, horizon or clouds, and you lose depth perception:

In other words, you cannot distinguish between the ground and the sky - the snow-covered surface cannot be detected by the naked eye because of the lack of normal colour contrast. Whiteout typically occurs over unbroken snow cover beneath a uniformly overcast sky, when the light from both is about the same. Blowing snow doesn't help, and it's particularly a problem if the ground is rising. In fact, there are several versions of whiteout:

- *Overcast Whiteout*, which comes from complete cloud cover with light being reflected between a snow surface and the cloud base. Perspective is limited to within a few feet, but the horizontal visibility of dark objects is not materially reduced

- *Water Fog*. Thin clouds of supercooled water droplets contacting a cold snow surface. Horizontal and vertical visibility is affected by the size and distribution of the water droplets

- *Blowing Snow*. Winds over 20 kts picking up fine snow from the surface, diffusing sunlight and reducing visibility

- *Precipitation*. Small wind-driven snow crystals from low clouds with the Sun above. Light is refracted and objects obscured caused by multiple reflection of light between the snow covered surface and the cloud base. Spectral reflection from the snow flakes and obscuration of landmarks by the falling snow are further complications.

Once you suspect whiteout, *immediately* climb or level off towards an area where you can see things properly. Better yet, put the machine on the ground before you get anywhere near whiteout.

Note: If you are at maximum weight, you may not have the power to pull up out of a snow or dust cloud!

Flat light is a similar phenomenon, but comes from different causes, where light is diffused through water droplets suspended in the air, particularly when clouds are low. *Brownout* comes from blowing sand or dust.

MET SERVICES & INFORMATION
••••••••••••••••••••••••••••••••••••••

The meteorological service operates a vast intelligence system that gathers information every half an hour and transmits it to a central point for analysis. Even ships at sea contribute information. The reports are combined with the findings of a low-orbit satellite that flies round the world every 107 minutes. It measures wave-heights, amongst other things, whilst others might look at conditions in the troposphere and stratosphere. A Cray computer crunches the results and the information is used to try to forecast the weather.

ATIS (*Automatic Terminal Information Service*) is broadcast on available VHF frequencies, VOR and NDB (not ILS) at major aerodromes, to reduce congestion on VHF frequencies, although it may have its own channel. You should listen to it and take down the details before you contact ATC, inbound or outbound. ATIS broadcasts should be updated whenever a significant change occurs, and should not last over 30 seconds. The contents of an ATIS broadcast are mentioned in the *Air Law* section.

TAFs

Terminal Aerodrome Forecasts describe forecast conditions at an aerodrome for between 9 and 24 hours. The validity periods of many longer ones may not start for up to 8 hours after the time of origin, and the details only cover the last 18 hours. 9-hour TAFs are updated and re-issued every 3 hours, and 12- and 24-hour TAFs, every 6 hours, with amendments issued as and when necessary. They are not available for offshore operations, and are only issued after 2 consecutive METARS (which will look suspiciously similar - in fact, many groups in METARs are found in TAFs, but differences are noted below). A TAF may be sub-divided into 2 or more self-contained parts by the abbreviation 'FM' (from) followed by the time UTC to the nearest hour, expressed as 2 figures.

Note: On Nov 5th 2008, the format for TAFs changed slightly, although this will not affect exam questions until CQB 15 is introduced. Essentially, some larger airfields will have a 30-hour validity, there will be a day of the month added to some time fields, and a FM (from) prefix which will provide a full time figure. AIC 47/2008 refers.

MESSAGE TYPE

TAF or TAF AMD, for *amended*. The acronym AMD will be inserted between TAF and the aerodrome identifier, and will cover the remainder of the validity period of the original forecast.

STATION IDENTIFIER

4-letter ICAO indicator for aerodrome.

DATE AND TIME OF ISSUE

A 6-digit code, with the date as the first two, then the time in UTC.

VALIDITY PERIOD

A METAR reports conditions at a specific time, but the TAF has the date and time of origin, followed by the start and finish times of its validity period in whole hours UTC, e.g. TAF EGLL 130600Z (date and time of issue) 0716 (validity 0700 to 1600 hours UTC), normally 9 hours.

WINDS

To the nearest 10°, in knots, True. 000000KT is calm, VRB means variable, less than 3 kts. Gusts are in 2 digits. WS means windshear, when significant, with speed and direction at a height.

HORIZONTAL VISIBILITY

Minimum visibility. RVR is not included because it is *never* forecast.

WEATHER

If no significant weather is expected, this is omitted. After a change group, however, if the weather ceases to be significant, 'NSW' (no significant weather) will be inserted.

A minus (-) means light, no sign is moderate, and + means heavy. It is described in 7 ways, such as SH for showers, DR for drifting, FZ for freezing, MI for shallow, BL for blowing and BC for batches.

FC=Funnel Cloud (Tornado), TS=Thunderstorm, DZ=Drizzle, FG=Fog (< 1 km), BR=Mist (> 1 km), GS=Small Hail, FU=Smoke, SS=Sandstorm, VA=Volcanic Ash, PO=Dust/Sand, RA=Rain, SG=Snow Grains, PL=Ice Pellets, IC=Ice Crystals, SA=Sand, SN=Snow, HZ=Haze, GR=Hail, DU=Dust, SQ=Squall, DS=Duststorm.

CLOUD

Up to 4 cloud groups, in ascending order of bases, and cumulative, based on the amount of the sky covered, in eighths, or oktas. The cloud ceiling is the height of the first layer that is broken or overcast. The first group is the lowest individual layer; the second the next of more than 2 oktas and the third the next higher of more than 4 oktas. A group has 3 letters for the amount (FEW = 1 to 2 oktas,

SCT, or scattered = 3 to 4 oktas; BKN, or broken, = 5 to 7 oktas, and OVC, or overcast = 8 oktas) and 3 for the height of the cloud base in hundreds of feet above ground level. For clear sky, expect SKC. VV means vertical visibility in hundreds of feet which, if you get it at all, means an obscured ceiling. CB means thunderstorms and is added as necessary. Clouds may cover the sky, but not conceal it if transparent, hence the term opacity.

SIGNIFICANT CHANGES

In addition to 'FM' and the time (see above) significant changes may be indicated by 'BECMG' (becoming) or 'TEMPO' (temporarily). 'BECMG' is followed by a four-figure group indicating the beginning and ending of the period when the change is expected. The change is expected to be permanent, and to occur at an unspecified time within it. 'TEMPO' will similarly be followed by a 4-figure time group, indicating temporary fluctuations. 'TEMPO' conditions are expected to last less than 1 hour each time, and collectively, less than half the period indicated.

PROBABILITY

Probability of a significant change, either 30 or 40%. The abbreviation 'PROB' will precede the percentage, followed by a time group, or a change and time group, e.g.:

```
PROB 30 0507 0800FG BKN004
```

or

```
PROB40 TEMPO 1416 TSRA BKN010CB
```

EXAMPLE

```
EGHH 0615 VRB06KT 9999 SCT 030
```

was issued at Heathrow for 0600-1500, with variable wind at 6 kts, visibility more than 10 km and 3-4 oktas of cloud at 3000 above the airfield elevation.

METARs

Meteorological Aerodrome Reports are compiled half-hourly or hourly while the office is open, about 15 minutes after observations are made. The elements of a report are separated with space, except temperature and dewpoint which use a /. Missing information has the preceding space and that element omitted.

METARS are reports, not forecasts, but you may see an outlook tagged on the end after the word TREND. They represent a 2-hour period from the time of the observation. NOSIG means no significant changes expected in the next 2 hours.

Countries may modify the code - for example, the USA reports temperature and dewpoint in °C and uses current units for the remainder of the report.

MESSAGE TYPE

METAR means a routine actual weather report. SPECI means a significant change off the hour (i.e between normal reporting times), normally because the weather has changed significantly since the last report. The METAR format is used.

STATION IDENTIFIER

4-letter ICAO indicator for aerodrome, plus time of observation in UTC.

WINDS

The first three numbers are the direction to the nearest 10° (T) and the next two the speed in knots. G + Gusts. 000000KT is calm, VRB means variable, less than 3 kts.

HORIZONTAL VISIBILITY

The minimum is in metres, followed by one of the eight points of the compass if there is a difference in visibility by direction, as with 4000 NE. If the minimum visibility is between 1500-5000 m in another direction, minimum and maximum values, and directions will be given, e.g. 1400SW 6000N. 9999 means 10 km or more, while 0000 means less than 50 m.

```
EGZZ 231020Z 02006KT 4000 0900NE
R27/0600U R32/0150D PRFG OVC007
12/11 Q1028
```

In the example above, 4000 is the prevailing visibility, which is the best figure that can be applied to at least 50% of the horizon (contiguously or otherwise), so if the visibility varies from 8 km down to 4000 m for at least half of the visible horizon, the prevailing visibility is 4000 m.

If the visibility in a particular direction is less than 1500 m or is less than half of the prevailing figure, the lowest visibility observed (900 m above) is reported, with the direction (NE - NDV means *No Directional Variation* of visibility sensors). If the lowest value applies in several directions, the most operationally significant one is given. If the visibility is fluctuating wildly (such as with a rapid shower transition), only the lowest visibility is reported.

With an automated system, NCD is inserted in place of the cloud code when no cloud has been detected and the absence of CB or TCU cannot be detected. On the other hand, NSC means that the system is capable of detecting their absence

RUNWAY VISUAL RANGE (RVR)

RVR figures are assessed when the visibility gets below 1500m. If the touchdown visibility is less than 400m, all three parts of the runway are reported. Between 400-800m, the mid- and end-points are only given if they are less than the touchdown zone. Above 800m you only get them if they are lower than 800m.

An RVR group has the prefix R followed by the runway designator, then an oblique stroke followed by the touch-down RVR in metres. If RVR is assessed simultaneously on two or more runways, it will be repeated; parallel runways are distinguished by L, C or R, for Left, Central or Right parallel respectively, e.g. R24L/1100 R24R/1150. When the RVR is more than 1500m or the maximum that can be assessed, the group will be preceded by P, followed by the lesser value, e.g. R24/P1500. When less than the minimum, the RVR will be reported as M followed by the minimum value, e.g. R24/M0050.

PRESENT WEATHER

Any precipitation. A minus (-) means light, no sign is moderate, and + means heavy. It is described in 7 ways, such as SH for showers, DR for drifting, FZ for freezing, MI for shallow, BL for blowing and BC for batches. See under TAFs for other codes.

The abbreviation UP indicates when it has not been possible to identify precipitation using automatic observation. REUP should be used to indicate that the automatic system has been unable to identify a recent precipitation.

CLOUD

Up to 4 cloud groups may be included, in ascending order of bases. A group has 3 letters for the amount (FEW = 1 to 2 oktas, SCT, or scattered = 3 to 4 oktas; BKN, or broken, = 5 to 7 oktas, and OVC, or overcast = 8 oktas) and 3 for the height of the cloud base in hundreds of feet above ground level.

Apart from significant convective clouds (CB) cloud types are ignored. Cloud layers or masses are reported so the first group represents the lowest individual layer; the second is the next individual layer of more than 2 oktas; the third is the next higher layer of more than 4 oktas, and the additional group, if any, represents significant convective cloud, if not already reported, e.g.:

```
SCT010 SCT015 SCT018CB BKN025
```

The symbol /// denotes that the automated station cannot detect the type of cloud group at this level. ////// is used in front of CB (or TCU) where the automatic system has detected a CB (or TCU) and where the coverage (or height) of these clouds has not been measured

CAVOK AND SKC

CAVOK will replace visibility, RVR, weather and cloud groups when visibility is 10 km or more, there is no cloud below 5000' or the highest MSA, whichever is greater, and no cumulo-nimbus; and there is no precipitation, thunderstorm, shallow fog or low, drifting snow.

© *Phil Croucher, 2012*

Otherwise, the cloud group is replaced by 'SKC' (sky clear) if there is no cloud report.

Note: This term is not used in Canadian TAFs.

AIR TEMPERATURE AND DEWPOINT

Shown in °C, separated by /. A negative value is indicated by an 'M' in front of the appropriate digits, e.g. M10/03 or '01/MO1

PRESSURE SETTING

QNH is rounded down to the next whole millibar and reported as a 4-figure group preceded by 'Q'. If less than 1000 Mb, the first digit will be '0', e.g. 'Q0993'.

QNH is the QFE reduced to MSL under ISA. Although the met office would correct for temperature and pressure, for our purposes, only pressure is used, at 27 feet per mb (hPa) at sea level through to 50 feet at 18,500 feet (if you want to include temperature, use the average below the aircraft). QFF is similar, but using long term monthly mean temperature and humidity, and is closer to reality.

RECENT WEATHER

Significant weather seen since the previous observation, but not currently relevant, will be reported with the standard present weather code preceded by the indicator 'RE', e.g. 'RETS'.

WINDSHEAR

Included if windshear is reported in the lowest 1600 feet, beginning with 'WS': 'WS TKOF RWY20".

RUNWAY STATE

For snow or other contamination, an 8-figure group may be added at the end.

TREND

For when significant changes are forecast during the next 2 hours. The codes 'BECMG' (becoming) or 'TEMPO' (temporarily) may be followed by a time group (in hours and minutes UTC) preceded by one of 'FM' (from), 'TL' (until) or 'AT' (at). These are followed by the expected change using the standard codes, e.g. 'BECMG FM 1100 250/35G50KT' or 'TEMPO FM 0630 TL0830 3000 SHRA'. Where no such significant changes are expected, the trend group will be replaced by the word 'NOSIG'.

DENEB

Fog dispersal is in progress.

Area Forecast

This covers several hundred square miles. Cloud bases are reported above sea level.

SIGMETs

Warning of serious weather, covering 60 minutes flying time ahead of the aircraft.

AIREPs

Reports by pilots, commencing with *UA*. *UUA* is *urgent*. AIREPs are similar to position reports in content, except that they also have met information at the end, like temperature, wind, turbulence, icing and other relevant information.

CHARTS

Weather information is issued in many ways, including the charts mentioned below. Those showing *expected* patterns are *prognosis* charts, but you can bet they won't be anything like what you see when you get there.

Note: As the weather map tries to be a simple representation of weather that pilots can understand, it will not show all of the weather that might affect your flight, particularly any local variations - for example, you will have to guesstimate many surface winds based on isobar spacing and the application of friction effects. For best results, they should be used in conjunction with TAFs and/or METARs.

Note: According to Met Form 216, reported cloud bases are within 500 feet and fronts can be up to 95 nm away from their reported position.

All charts show expected conditions anyway!

FORM 214

This is a *spot wind chart* issued by the Met Office that shows you the winds you can expect at selected heights, *for a particular time*, so you will need to correlate its information with that on Form 215 (overleaf) to see how movement of pressure systems might change the winds for when you want to fly. Boxes are placed on certain intersections of latitude and longitude, with details of wind direction, speed and temperature between 1000-24000'. Below is a simplified version.

The location of each wind box is shown at the top. The column on the left is the altitude in thousands of feet, the second the wind direction in °T, then the wind speed in knots, followed by the temperature in °C, which can give you important information as to atmospheric stability and other conditions. If the temperatures are dropping rapidly, for example, you can expect good visibility, as long as

57N 0230E		
24 320 60	-35
18 310 45	-21
10 310 25	-08
05 310 20	+01
02 310 20	+07
01 300 20	+09

there are no fronts around, which is characteristic of an unstable atmosphere and a steep lapse rate (see *Stability*).

The less steep the lapse rate, the poorer the visibility. Thus, if you get an increase in temperature with altitude at lower levels, followed by a steep decrease, you can expect any early morning mist or fog to clear relatively quickly. Check the wind vectors to see how high the inversion might be, since wind direction usually changes significantly above them. Flight above that point will be in clearer weather.

To get the answers to exam questions, you have to interpolate between the boxes and the figures in them, as you can guarantee that the level given will not coincide with any in it! For real world flight planning, as a gross error check, take the present wind, add 30°, double the speed and subtract 10% to see how the results compare against the 2000 ft wind. If they are wildly different, don't trust the chart!

FORM 215

The *Significant Weather Chart* (see below) is a low level forecast for the next 6 hours, graphically represented

The freezing level is given in the right hand column.

Significant weather is shown in scalloped lines, in Zones that are identified with a letter in a square.

Note: Scalloped lines do *not* represent cloud!

Some temperature rises with altitude can lead to two freezing levels that cannot be detected with this form, since it only shows one freezing level, and the higher one at that, although more information may be found in the text description.

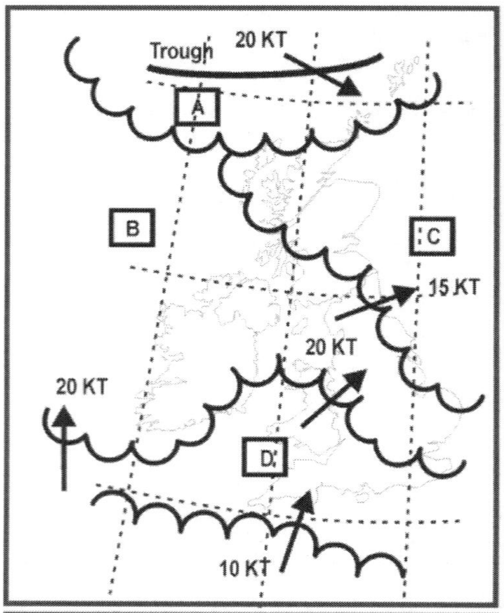

All heights in 100s of feet above mean sea level
XXX means above chart upper limit

Cloud amount (Oktas) FEW: 1-2 SCT:3-4 BKN: 5-7 OVC: 8
MOD/SEV ICE
MOD/SEV TURB
TS/CB implies GR/
Speed of movement in KT
Temperatures in DEG C
Hill FG implies VIS <200M

This forecast may be amended at any time
Issued by Met Office Anytown at 040945 Z
Forecaster: Duty Forecaster
Contact telephone 0870 800 1000
© Crown Copyright 2006

Forecast Weather Below 10000 FT

Met Office

Valid 041400 to 042300Z APR 31st. Fronts/Zones valid at 041800Z

AREA	SURFACE VIS AND WX	CLOUD	0 C
A	30 KM NIL OCNL 8 KM SHRA ISOL 4000 M SHRASN/SHGS ISOL 1200 M +TSGS ISOL 500 M +TSSN MON OCNL (ISOL NE) E OF 02 E ISOL HILL FG	SCT/BKN (LOC OVC) CU SC 020-030 ISOL CB 020/XXX ISOL BKN ST 010-030	010 N 025 S
B	40 KM NIL OCNL ISOL HILL FG	SCT CU SC 030-050	020-030
C	15 KM NIL/-RA OCNL ISOL 7 KM RA	BKN/OVC SC/AC 025 OCNL BKN SC 015/025	040

Outlook Until: 050600 Z
Showers dying out LAN Zone A

To request a True Bearing, the correct phraseology is:

True Bearing, True Bearing, Callsign, Request True Bearing, Callsign

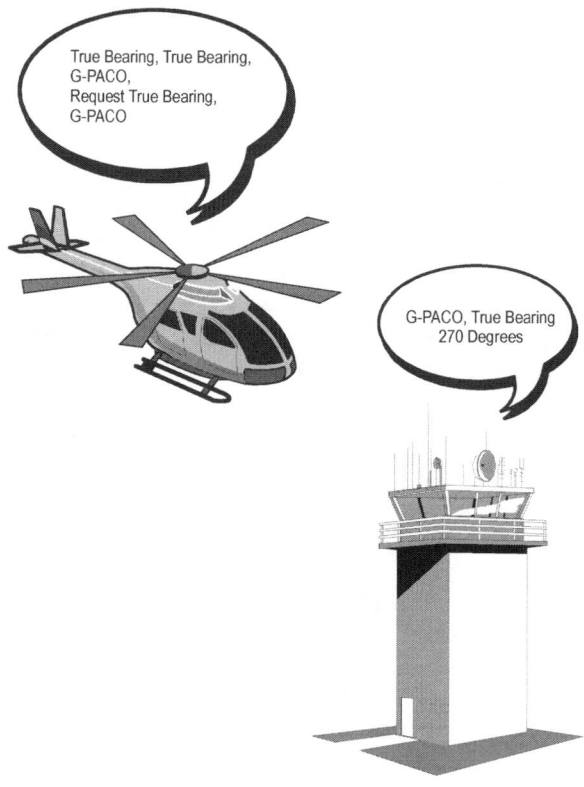

CATEGORIES OF MESSAGE

Messages must be dealt with in this order:

- Distress
- Urgency
- Direction Finding
- Flight Safety (ATC messages, avoiding weather)
- Meteorological
- Flight Regularity (parts and materials)
- UN Charter
- Government messages
- Service communications
- All others

OPERATING PROCEDURES

A message consists of four parts: The *Callup*, The *Reply*, The *Message* and The *Acknowledgement*.

Phonetic Alphabet

LETTERS

To make transmissions clearer, letters are pronounced in certain ways, as shown in the table below. Speak all words plainly and clearly, with none of them running together and no accentuation. Do not shout, or speak too quickly. Although the phraseology can be a bit longwinded (*day-si-mal* for decimal, for example), and you may feel a bit stupid pronouncing some of the words, remember they are that way to reduce ambiguity, which would have been handy in Tenerife when two 747s collided with each other because the clearances got confused (see *Human Factors*). The word *decimal*, by the way, is an ICAO word, replaced with *point* in the USA).

Letter	Word	Speech	Morse
A	Alfa	**ALF**AH	·–
B	Bravo	**BRAH**VOH	–···
C	Charlie	**CHAR**LEE	–·–·
D	Delta	**DELL**TAH	–··
E	Echo	**ECKOH**	·
F	Foxtrot	**FOCK**STROT	··–·
G	Golf	**GOLF**	––·
H	Hotel	HO**TELL**	····
I	India	**IND**EAH	··
J	Juliet	**JEW**LEEETT	·–––
K	Kilo	**KEYL**OH	–·–
L	Lima	**LEE**MAH	·–··
M	Mike	**MIKE**	––
N	November	NO**VEM**BER	–·
O	Oscar	**OSS**CAH	–––
P	Papa	PAH**PAH**	·––·
Q	Quebec	KEH**BECK**	––·–
R	Romeo	**ROW**MEOH	·–·
S	Sierra	SEE**AIR**RAH	···
T	Tango	**TANG**GO	–
U	Uniform	**YOU**NEEFORM	··–
V	Victor	**VIK**TAH	···–
W	Whiskey	**WISS**KEY	·––
X	X-ray	**ECKS**RAY	–··–
Y	Yankee	**YANG**KEY	–·––
Z	Zulu	**ZOO**LOO	––··

NUMBERS

Number	Speech
0	**ZER**O
1	WUN
2	TOO
3	TREE
4	**FOW**ER
5	FIFE
6	SICKS
7	**SEV**EN
8	AIT
9	**NIN**ER

*The reason you might say *Two Thousand Four Hundred* rather than *Two Four Zero Zero* is that it can be construed as *To Four Zero Zero*, as in *Cleared To Four Zero Zero*

Numbers (as used for altitude, cloud height, visibility and RVR information) should generally be spoken individually, except for whole thousands (or hundreds) where they occur as round figures. 65 is therefore *six-five*, while 2000 is *two thousand*. Eleven thousand is *One One Thousand*. In other words, combinations of thousands and whole hundreds must be transmitted by pronouncing each digit in the number of thousands, followed by the word *Thousand*, followed by the number of hundreds, followed by the word *Hundred*. For example:

- Altitude 800 (Eight Hundred)
- 1,500 (One Thousand Five Hundred)
- 6,715 (Six Seven One Five)
- 12,000 (One Two Thousand)
- 200 (Two Hundred)

Use the word *decimal (daysimal)* when you need a decimal point - *one one six decimal two* means 116.2. Altitude above sea level is expressed in thousands of feet, plus hundreds, but flight levels use separate digits, thus 2500 is said as two thousand five hundred, but FL 100 is *flight level one zero zero*. You express a heading separately, e.g. *two five zero* for 250°.

Note: The word *To* is not used with flight levels: *Climb Flight Level 100*

Morse Code

Although the codes are printed on maps, etc., it's still a good idea to learn them. It stops you peering at your map in the murk and moving your head around too much. Amateur radio clubs are a good source of inexpensive training materials. Starting off at a high speed is best, with the simplest letters. E, for example, is one dot (*dit*). Listen to a stream of Morse, picking out that letter only, then add another, such as T, which is a dash (*dah*), then I (2 dots), M (2 dashes) and so on. In a few days you could be up to a speed of 20 wpm.

Time

Time is expressed in terms of the 24-hour clock, based on UTC (*Universal Co-ordinated Time*), or what used to be called Greenwich Mean Time. The letter Z (for *Zulu*, meaning GMT - sorry, UTC) is used as shorthand in things like flight plans, etc. The first two figures of a 24-hour time represent the hour past midnight, and the second two the minutes past the hour, so 2345 means 45 minutes past eleven in the evening (take away 12), or a quarter to midnight. If you see a timegroup:

220345Z

It means a quarter to four GMT on the 22nd of the month. Usually, you only transmit the numbers for minutes ("arriving at 45"), but this only relates to the *current* hour, and if there will be no misunderstanding. If there is any possibility of confusion, or you mean another hour, include the other figures. Time is normally given to the nearest minute, except that control towers may state the time to the nearest half minute when issuing a taxi clearance to a departing aircraft.

You can *Request a Time Check* from ATC at any time.

Transmission Technique

Assuming you are within the performance range of your equipment, and after listening out first, to make sure you don't interfere with another transmission, call ATC, using their name, and normal conversational tones (no need to shout!), followed by their function, as in *London Tower*. Then use the words *This Is*, followed by your own identifier (you should use the full callsign on initial contact with ATC, but you can subsequently use any abbreviations they make. See *Callsigns*, below). Normally, your callsign is the same as your aircraft's markings, unless you have applied to ICAO for permission to use a company name or a flight number. Include the frequency you are on, in case they are listening to several, so they know which button to push, then the word *Over*, as an invitation for them to respond:

> *"London Approach, this is Golf Papa Alpha Charlie Oscar on one one eight decimal two, over."*

You should maintain an even rate of speech, not above 100 words per minute, with a constant volume, avoiding hesitation.

ATC will reply with your full callsign, but may well shorten it afterwards, to the country letter followed by the last two of your registration, as in *Golf-Charlie Oscar*, if there will be no confusion with another aircraft. You can use it from then on. Don't be concerned if there is a short delay - the controller might be writing down your details first, or may even have to put down the coffee (in Canada, you may be on a remote link). If you receive no reply, wait ten seconds before trying again.

CAPT

If the field has an ATIS (continual weather broadcasts, changed every half hour), obtain the information and include the code letter with your initial call:

"with information Delta."

The format is the same if ATC call you first, but you can omit the word *over* if the reply is obvious and there will be no misunderstanding.

Standard Words & Phrases

If you need to make a correction, say the word "Correction" followed by the last correct word or phrase before continuing. If you need to get something repeated, use the words *say again* (if you say *repeat*, you might well get an artillery barrage, because that's what the gunners use!) You can specify parts of a message by saying *say again all after*, or *all before*....

A message from ATC to all stations listening out on a frequency would be a *general call*, and be preceded with the words *All Stations*. A message to multiple stations can be done in any convenient sequence, but the replies must be in the order given.

Confirm Squawk means "What code is set on your transponder?"

Phrase	Meaning
Acknowledge	Confirm that you have received this message
Affirm	Agreement
Approved	Permission granted for proposed action
Break	Separation between parts of a message
Break Break	Separation between parts of a message when busy
Cancel	Annul previously transmitted message
Changing to	Going to another frequency
Check	Examine a system
Cleared	Proceed under the conditions specified
Confirm	Did I get that right?
Contact	Get in touch with....
Correct	That is correct
Correction	Oops - made a mistake
Disregard	Ignore my last
Go Ahead	Proceed with message
How Do You Read?	What is my readability?
I say again	I repeat
Monitor	Listen out on (frequency)
Negative	No, or not correct
Out	This conversation is over - no reply is expected
Over	I have finished speaking and I expect a response
Read Back	Repeat the message back exactly as received
Recleared	Ignore your last clearance and receive a new one
Report	Pass me the following information (as in Report altitude).
Request	I would like......
Roger	The last messages has been received (if not understood!)
Say again	Repeat what you just said
Speak Slower	Reduce your rate of speech
Standby	Wait to be called
Verify	Check and confirm
Wilco	Your instructions will be complied with (Will Comply)
Words Twice	Send every word twice

HELICOPTERS

Helicopters are different! There is some standard phraseology that is unique to their operation. Firstly, the manufacturer's name or model as a prefix in the callsign may be replaced with the term *helicopter*. In addition, these terms have specific meanings:

Phrase	Meaning
Lift	A manoeuvre where the helicopter gets airborne and enters the hover
Hover	A manoeuvre where the helicopter holds position whilst airborne in ground effect, waiting to proceed. Spot turns, etc. are allowed
Air Taxi	Proceeding at a slow speed above the surface, normally below 20 kts in ground effect
Ground Taxi	Movement in contact with the ground, under a helicopter's own power (for wheeled helicopters, to reduce downwash)
Taxi	Ground or Air Taxi, according to preference
Hold	Come to a standstill - either hovering or on the ground (on the ground if ground taxiing)
Touchdown	Come into contact with the surface

Callsigns

You should use your full callsign until it is abbreviated by ATC, then you can use the shortened version. For example, XY-ABC can become X-BC. *Cherokee* XY-ABC would become *Cherokee BC*. A6-GLC becomes A-LC. *Norjet 123* cannot be abbreviated (in general, you can shorten callsigns that contain registration marks).

Once satisfactory communication has been established, and there will be no confusion, you are allowed to abbreviate a ground station's callsign.

Position Reports

This is the order of information contained in a position report:

- Callsign
- Position
- Time at position
- Level or altitude
- Next position
- ETA at next position

Talking to Air Traffic Control

You should comply with ATC instructions as soon as they are issued, but sometimes a climb or descent is left to your discretion, in which case the words *When Ready* will be used. You should report *leaving* your present level once you

have departed from it and are maintaining a positive rate of climb or descent.

Control is based on *known traffic only*, so you are still responsible for safe procedures and good judgement - clearances are not an authority to violate the rules! Information about flight conditions is meant as assistance or reminders.

ATS units are identified by the name of the location, then the service available:

- *Centre*: En route area control (as in *Area Control Centre*, or ACC), including RAS and FIS
- *Approach*: Approach control (as separate function)
- *Departures*: Departure control (separate function)
- *Final/Director*: Radar control providing vectors onto final approach
- *Tower*: Aerodrome control or aerodrome and approach control when provided from an aerodrome control tower
- *Ground*: Surface movement control

The name of the location or the service may be omitted once satisfactory communication has been established.

On a typical flight, you might talk to several ATC departments, loosely in the following order (some may be combined at smaller airfields). In general, the procedure for outbound aircraft is:

- Obtain the ATIS or current weather
- Request startup clearance, stating the ATIS version you have, but....*
- Obtain taxi instructions (up to a limiting point - normally the holding point of the runway in use)
- *Obtain departure clearance or instructions while taxying, which is difficult in the hover, so maybe get it beforehand.
- Change to Tower for takeoff clearance, also difficult in the hover, so you will often taxi on the Tower frequency

On the way back in:

- Obtain the ATIS or current weather
- Request joining instructions, stating the ATIS version you have
- Report position in the circuit, such as downwind, finals, etc (the *finals* call is made within 7 km. *Long finals* is at 15 km)
- If ATC require you to *Go Around*, they will say so, at which point you climb away and start the circuit again. You can initiate a Go Around at any time by saying *Going Around*

GROUND CONTROL

The Ground Controller handles all movements on the manoeuvring area, including aircraft and vehicles, and possibly start clearances (departure clearances given by Ground are *not* clearances to takeoff!) Typically, you would be talking to Ground up to the holding point, and afterwards when landing - this helps ATC with planning and keep the tower frequency clear (but a helicopter may taxi on the Tower frequency, as your hands are full in the hover). It also reduces fuel waste from delays. It often helps if you say where you are, and include the current ATIS:

"G-PACO on Helipad 1 with Bravo, request start"

Bravo is the latest ATIS. You will get an acknowledgement, with the current QNH.

TOWER

For traffic close to the aerodrome, including the circuit. After takeoff, you may be asked to change to Approach (below), but, more typically, you will stay with the Tower until clear of the area. Taxi instructions will contain a clearance limit, meaning a point beyond which you must not go without further permission. This will normally be the holding point of the runway in use (you are automatically cleared across those on the way, *holding short* when you get there), but may be elsewhere if they are busy. On a large airfield, taxiways to be used will be included:

"Taxi to the hold for 19, via taxiway Alpha, then Bravo."

When landing, if told to *continue*, because of traffic on the runway, that is *not* a clearance to land - you still need permission. If the runway is long enough, in daylight, you may be allowed to *land after* whatever is on it already. The words "go around" mean "initiate a missed approach".

However, helicopter operations are a lot more informal at smaller airfields.

APPROACH

Sometimes known as *Radar*, these controllers sit in a darkened room in front of radar screens, so have no visual contact with the traffic they are dealing with (don't worry, they are fed frequently). Approach controllers guide the aircraft during its approach or departure to or from the airport. Mostly, arrivals and departures are handled by a single approach unit but, at busier airfields they may be separate, with different controllers, callsigns and frequencies.

Under IFR in controlled airspace, you will be given descent clearance to whatever limit is used by ACC before handover to Approach. Outside controlled airspace, do not enter until cleared to do so.

The phrase *Under RADAR Control* is only used when a radar control service is being provided, meaning that you must do what you are told. ATC will assume responsibility for separation and terrain avoidance.

A *Radar Advisory Service* is only provided under IFR, regardless of the weather. You will be given the bearing, distance and height of known conflicting traffic, plus *advisory* avoiding action, which should nevertheless not be ignored. If you do, you must advise ATC. You remain responsible for terrain avoidance.

You can get A *Radar Information Service* (RIS) under IFR or VFR. You still get information on conflicting traffic, but without avoiding action. You are responsible for separation from other aircraft and terrain avoidance.

A *Flight Information Service* is *not* a radar service. It is merely someone to talk to.

RADAR IDENTIFICATION

You can be identified by information from yourself (position reporting, or in relation to a prominent object), by making turns that can be seen on radar, or by identing with SSR. You should be advised if radar identification is lost, or about to be lost, and appropriate instructions should be given.

Heading information and instructions are in degrees magnetic.

RADAR VECTORING

You may be given specific vectors for lateral separation purposes, and left to resume your own navigation when it is completed (they may be nice and tell you where you are). *Orbits* (complete turns) may be used for delaying purposes or for increasing separation.

AREA

Area controllers are not necessarily based at an airport, and control aircraft that are passing through the airspace without landing.

Clearances and Readbacks

You should start a transmission with the callsign of the service provider followed by the aircraft callsign. When a readback of an ATC message is required, you should terminate the read back transmission with the aircraft's radio callsign.

You must comply with any clearances received and acknowledged. If you don't like them, you should say so at the time, since an acknowledgement without further comment is taken as such. Clearances are valid only in controlled airspace, and there will be some form of the

word "clear" in the text to identify them. Clearances must always be read back (although you don't need to read back the wind velocity). You must also comply with instructions in the same way, unless safety is a factor. An instruction will be identifiable, but the word "instruct" may not be included. All clearances should be read back, to ensure that they have been received and transmitted properly in the first place, to the right aircraft.

If a clearance or an instruction is not suitable, you may request and, if practicable, obtain an amended one. Use the words *Unable To Comply* if you have a problem with a clearance. Clearances are supposed to be passed slowly and clearly, since you will need to write them down, and preferably before startup, since you will not want to be bothered while taxying, hovering or when lining up for takeoff. They will contain the aircraft identification (as per the flight plan), the clearance limit (usually the destination) and the route, levels, changes and any other instructions, especially about departure manoeuvres.

These clearances should be read back in full:

- Taxy instructions
- Clearances to enter, land on, take off from, cross, backtrack and hold short of the runway in use
- Heading, speed and level instructions
- Altimeter settings
- Transponder codes
- Airways or route clearances
- VDF information
- Frequency changes
- Type of radar service

Route clearances must be read back completely. Others (including conditional clearances) need only contain key elements and include sufficient detail to clearly indicate that they will be complied with.

Note: The word *Takeoff* is only used by a pilot when actually cleared for takeoff - up till then, the word *Departure* is used.

CONDITIONAL CLEARANCES

A conditional clearance depends on the actions of another aircraft, such as when being given clearance to cross a runway after a taxying aircraft has passed. Correct identification of the aircraft involved is essential. Conditional clearances must be given in this order:

- Identification
- The condition (specify)
- The clearance

For example: "G-PACO - Behind the A 340 on short final, Line up". You: "Behind the A 340, Line Up, G-PACO".

Note: This implies the need for you to identify the aircraft or vehicle causing the conditional clearance.

Readability Scale

To check a radio, call up another station (if they're not busy) and ask how they read you (don't take more than about ten seconds). They will reply with a readability grading on the following scale:

- 1 - unreadable
- 2 - readable now and then
- 3 - readable with difficulty
- 4 - readable
- 5 - perfectly readable

"Reading you Strength Three", for example.

Transfer Of Communication

When ATC want to hand you off to another ATS unit, they will say something like:

Contact Ground (or whatever) on (frequency)

Contact London on 118.75

WEATHER INFORMATION
••

ATC will happily provide weather information if required, but it helps to keep the airways clear if you use the following automated services (including Datalink). Refer to *Meteorology* for details about TAFs and METARs.

ATIS

This is routine information for departing and arriving aircraft supplied by a continuous and repetitive broadcast on discrete VHF frequencies and/or VOR, and possibly NDB (but not ILS) at major aerodromes. The *Automatic Terminal Information Service* reduces congestion on VHF frequencies, because it saves ATC saying the same stuff over and over, although they will still give you the QNH anyway. You should listen to it and take down the details before you contact ATC, inbound or outbound. On first contact with ATC, you should state the version you have received, such as "Information Golf", or whatever. ATIS broadcasts should be updated whenever a significant change occurs, and should not last over 30 seconds.

These are the items transmitted in the correct order:

- ATIS ID
- Time (24 hour clock)
- Wind Velocity (Degrees/Knots)

- Visibility (Metres)

- Low Cloud (oktas/feet)

- Medium Cloud (oktas/feet)

- High Cloud (oktas/feet)

- Temp/Dew Point (Degrees)

- Altimeter (hPA/Inches)

- Runway in use

- Anything else useful, such as runway missing, lights out, etc.

Scattered, with reference to cloud cover, means that half, or less than half, of the sky is covered (3-4 oktas). *Broken* means 5-7 oktas, and *overcast* means 8 oktas (100%). CAVOK means more than 10 km visibility and no cloud below 5000 feet. Visibility less than 5 km is reported in metres, and in km above that.

RADIO FAILURE

Try another frequency, or talk to other aircraft first. You will at least then know that your radio is OK. Make sure also that the facility is not closed, that you are not out of range, you have selected the right frequency, and that the volume is set! In case the set is transmitting, you can transmit your message twice, preceded by the words *Transmitting Blind*.

If all that fails, essentially, you must comply with the last clearance, which hopefully included permission to land or clear the area. If you don't need to enter controlled airspace, carry on, maintaining VFR as necessary; don't enter it even if you've been previously cleared. If you must do so, divert and telephone for permission first. If you're already in controlled airspace, where clearance has been obtained to the boundary on leaving, or the field on entering, proceed as planned. If in doubt, clear the zone the most direct way as quickly as possible, avoiding airfields, and making blind transmissions, in case the transmitter is working. If you are in a circuit, and your radio fails, repeatedly switch the landing lights on and off.

In the open FIR, with unlimited visibility and no cloud, land at the nearest suitable aerodrome and inform the ATS unit.

Squawk 7600 for communications failure. If you can hear ATC they will likely ask you to push the ident button if you cannot transmit.

Receiver Failure

Make reports at scheduled times or positions (i.e. advise the time of your next transmission), preceded by the phrase "Transmitting Blind due to receiver failure".

DISTRESS & URGENCY PROCEDURES

An emergency exists the moment you become doubtful about position, fuel, weather, or anything else that could affect the safety of your flight. The first transmission should be on the frequency in use at the time, then the international one of 121.5 MHz, followed by others.

The first station receiving a Distress or Urgency call (see below) should *acknowledge it* and take immediate action to ensure that the necessary information is made available to ATC and the operating agency, and take control of communications if necessary, including imposing radio silence by saying *Stop Transmitting - MAYDAY*, after which everyone should shut the heck up (this may also be done by the aircraft in distress). If and when the threat is over, the Distress call must be cancelled by notification on ALL frequencies on which the original message was sent.

INTERCEPTING DISTRESS TRANSMISSIONS

Distress transmissions are normally given out on the frequency in use at the time, but when over the high seas, say when flying offshore, you will typically be guarding one of the distress frequencies, either *121.5 MHz, 243 MHz* or *2182 KHz* for merchant shipping. ELTs operate on 121.5 MHz and 406 MHz.

If you hear a distress transmission, you must:

- Record the position of the craft in distress (take a bearing)

- Inform the appropriate ATS unit or RCC

- At your discretion, whilst awaiting further instructions, proceed to the position given

Once there, if a rescue is in progress, do not interfere without checking with whoever is in charge.

If you need to direct another craft to the scene, circle it at least once, fly low just in front and rock the fuselage, then fly off in the direction you want them to go.

You can use the same signals when they are finished with, but fly behind instead. In theory, they should hoist the *Code Pennant*, which is a flag with vertical red and white stripes, close up, or flash a series of *T*s in Morse Code with a lamp. On the other hand, they could just turn in the direction requested. A blue and white chequered flag means *Much Regret, Unable* (i.e. *NO*), as does a series of *N*s in Morse.

Distress

The Distress call (MAYDAY) is used when threatened by *grave and imminent danger* and in *most urgent need* of *immediate assistance*. You can use the letters SOS in Morse Code (··· --- ···), or the spoken words MAYDAY, repeated 3 times, followed by relevant details, like your position, and what is happening:

> *MAYDAY MAYDAY MAYDAY*
> *Callsign (e.g. G-JLBI)*
> *Type (e.g. Helicopter)*
> *Nature of emergency (e.g. Total Engine Failure)*
> *Intentions of PIC*
> *Position (e.g. 20 Miles E of London VOR)*

Repeat as necessary. You can also fire rockets or red lights at short intervals, and parachute flares. Control of distress traffic is the responsibility of the aircraft in distress. To cancel a MAYDAY:

- State MAYDAY once
- Say ALL STATIONS three times
- Aircraft ID
- Station called
- Time
- Name of station in distress
- DISTRESS TRAFFIC ENDED
- Station called
- OUT

Distress frequencies are:

- 121.5 MHz - VHF Aeronautical Emergency Frequency
- 243 MHz - UHF Military Emergency Frequency
- 500 KHz - MF International Distress Frequency
- 2182 KHz - MF International Distress Frequency (this is officially in the MF band, but most HF radios can deal with it)

The squawk code for an emergency is 7700.

Tip: If you don't have time to change the squawk, keep pressing the Ident.

Urgency

The Urgency call (or "PAN") spoken three times, indicates a very urgent message concerning the safety of a ship, aircraft or other vehicle, or of some person on board or in sight, but immediate assistance is not required. It has priority over all other messages except Distress (above). If you just wish to mention you are compelled to land, but don't need help right away, switch the landing lights and/or navigation lights on and off in an irregular pattern.

Include as much information as you can, but the format follows that of Distress:

> *PAN PAN PAN*
> *Callsign*
> *Type*
> *Nature of problem*
> *Intentions of PIC*
> *Position*

The phrase *PAN PAN MEDICAL* means that the following message concerns a protected medical transport using aircraft assigned exclusively to medical transportation., as defined in the *Geneva Convention of 1949*, which also mentions something about conflicts.

Simulations

You can simulate emergency incidents (but not the state of distress) on 121.5 MHz. Use the word PRACTICE in front of the keyword, such as PRACTICE MAYDAY or PRACTICE PAN.

Speechless Code

If speech is difficult, you may use the Press To Transmit switch for limited communication:

Code	Meaning
One short	Yes, or acknowledge
2 short	No
3 short	Say again
4 short	(H in Morse) Request Homing
One long (2 secs)	Manoeuvre complete
One long, 2 short, one long	(X in Morse) Got another emergency

CAPT

INDEX

· ·